ORGAN LITERATURE:

A Comprehensive Survey

by

CORLISS RICHARD ARNOLD

The Scarecrow Press, Inc.
Metuchen, N.J.   1973

Library of Congress Cataloging in Publication Data

Arnold, Corliss Richard.
    Organ literature.

    Bibliography: p.
    1. Organ music--History and criticism. I. Title.
ML600.A76   785'.09   72-8824
ISBN 0-8108-0559-6

To Betty

PRELUDE

The inspiration and need for an organized, comprehensive introduction to the vast literature for the organ and its development (a field which has often been ignored by general music historians) grew from a course on organ literature taught at Michigan State University. The purpose of this book is to provide such an introduction.

The text discusses organ composition styles and their development in a general, non-detailed fashion according to various geographical areas and periods. Charts give a view of the entire school of composers and show how important relationships (such as those of teacher, student, and contemporaries) occurred during the same period. The historical background pages provide a few key items to establish an historical setting for each chapter. Several maps help to clarify geographical relationships within schools. The bibliographies (to each chapter as well as a general one at the end of the book) and the Appendix devoted to Bach should prove helpful in guiding serious organists, students, teachers, and performers to sources for more detailed study.

In the Biographical Catalog of Organ Literature the reader will be able to find a brief biographical sketch and ready references to published organ music under the composer's name.

I have written this book in the sincere hope that it will become a valuable handbook for my organist-colleagues.

February 1972   Corliss R. Arnold
                                  Sac. Mus. Doc., F. A. G. O.
                                  Assoc. Prof. of Music
                                  Michigan State University
                                  East Lansing, Michigan

ACKNOWLEDGMENTS

It would have been impossible to complete the task of writing so large a book as this without the assistance of many friends and acquaintances. Colleagues at Michigan State University, who helped in a number of different ways, were Dr. Paul A. Varg, former Dean of the College of Arts and Letters, Dr. Hans Nathan, Dr. William Hughes, Dr. Theodore Johnson, and Dr. John Curry. Dr. C. William Young of Wayne State University read the manuscript and offered many helpful suggestions.

Friends in Europe who helped in my research were Mr. John B. Ferguson, M. B. E., F. L. A., Director, Books Department, British Council, London; Mrs. Christine England, A. L. A., Librarian at the British Council Library, Paris; Mr. Jack Dove, F. L. A., F. R. C. O., A. R. C. M., F. R. S. A., Borough Librarian and Curator, Hove Central Library, Hove, England, and the Music Librarian at Hove, Mr. Phil Green; Mr. L. Fenton of British and Continental Music Agencies Ltd., London; Mr. Julian Mitchell-Dawson of J. & W. Chester Ltd., London; M. Jean Bonfils, organist, musicologist, teacher, prominent music editor, Paris; M. E. Ploix and M. Jean Leguy of the firm E. Ploix, Paris; and Professor Grethe Kroghe of the Royal Conservatory of Music, Copenhagen.

Last, and certainly not least, I am grateful to my family whose patience over a long period of time permitted me to finish this arduous effort.

C. R. A.

TABLE OF CONTENTS

Part I

HISTORICAL SURVEY

1. TABLATURES, MANUSCRIPTS, AND EARLIEST PUBLISHED ORGAN MUSIC IN WESTERN EUROPE: 1300-1600

The history of music for the organ is inextricably associated with the development of the organ in its many stages. Before considering music written for the organ, therefore, it might be wise to review a few of the milestones in the history of this, the oldest of keyboard instruments.

All knowledge about the organ up until the fourteenth century is based upon written descriptions, pictures, carvings, and preserved fragments of the instruments themselves. A Greek named Ktesibios, who lived in Alexandria, built an organ called a hydraulis about 250 B. C. Pressure was provided hydraulically by water, which was pumped by hand. This instrument became popular in Rome where it was used for entertainment at feasts and gladitorial combats. Two widely separated historical facts illustrate that organ building during the first millenium after Christ took place mainly in the Byzantine Empire. The obelisk of Theodosius, which was erected during the A. D. 300's, depicts an organ with bellows. In 757 Copronymos, a Byzantine emperor, sent Pippin, the father of Charlemagne, an organ as a gift. In England Bishop Aldhelm (ca. 640-709) described the powerful sound of the organ in his writings. Over 200 years later Wulstan described a harsh sounding and loud organ, which was built in Winchester, England, about 980. This instrument required 70 men to keep the 26 bellows filled with wind.

Until the thirteenth century several ranks (complete sets of pipes of the same type and quality) formed a large mixture, and there had been no provision for separating the individual ranks by the means of stops. In addition, all of the pipes in one rank had the same width, which resulted in a somewhat rough sound in the lower, longer pipes and progressed gradually to a milder sound in the upper, shorter pipes. The familiar Ghent altar piece by Jan van

Eyck shows an angel playing a positive organ of this description.   During the thirteenth century keys controlling
pallets under the pipes replaced slides, and the range of
pitches encompassed three octaves.

The organ developed rapidly after 1300 when instruments grew in size and gained refinement in both sound
and control.   Solo stops and softer stops were added to the
medieval organ, which had contained only principals and
mixtures.   The pedalboard was rather universally adopted
in the Netherlands and Germany long before it became a
standard part of the organs in other countries.   The organ
in Halberstadt, Germany, built in 1361, had three manuals
and an early form of the pedal clavier.   As an example of
one of the larger instruments of that time, the organ in the
Cathedral of Amiens contained 2500 pipes. During this period
two kinds of smaller organs were developed: the portative, a
portable organ which was used in processions, and the positive,
an organ of moderate size which was stationary.   Francesco
Landini (1325-1397) was an expert performer on the organetto,
as the portative organ was called in Italy.

The use of stops to render some ranks silent while
others could be played probably began in Italy between 1400
and 1450.   An organ built in 1470 in the church of St.
Petronio, Bologna, is the oldest organ which exists today
to have stops.   By the end of the fifteenth century the
organ in Germany had become an instrument similar to that
of today in that it contained tonal resources for full chorus
sounds, and solo registers of strongly contrasting timbres,
all controlled from different keyboards.   Arnolt Schlick
(before 1460-ca. 1521) described in detail the type of organ
which existed early in the sixteenth century in his Spiegel
der Orgelmacher und Organisten (1511).   The specification
for a two manual and pedal organ found in Schlick's book is
given below.   This specification indicated that independent
voices were available on manuals and in the pedal, thus
permitting polyphonic composition.

Werk (F-a^2)

Principaln 8'	Gemser hörner 4'	Rauss pfeiffen
(two ranks,	Gemser hörner 2'	or a
wide and	Hultze glechter	Schallmey
narrow)	Schweigeln	Zinck
Octaff 4'		Regal or
Doppelloctaff 2'		Super regall
Zymmell		
Hintersatz		

Positiff zü Ruck (F-a^2)

Principaln 4'   Gemsslein
Zymmelein
Hindersetzlein

Pedal (F-c^1)

Principaln 16'   Trommetten or
Principaln 8'   Bassaun
Octaff 4'
Hindersatz

    The organs in England and Italy of this same period, however, contained stops having less variety of color and no pedal. The compositions written for this type of organ were homophonic in character. Another type of organ was the regal, a sixteenth-century Italian organ which utilized only reeds.

    The beginnings of written keyboard music took place within about a century before the period known as the Renaissance. Renaissance is a French term which signifies "rebirth" and refers to the great interest in the arts and culture, especially of ancient Greece and Rome, for the pleasure and benefit of man. This general interest in the arts arose and flowered roughly between 1450 and 1600. During this period there was much interest in discovery and colonization of the New World by such powers as England, Spain, France, and Portugal. Two other historical events occurred during the Renaissance which had great significance to organ music: the invention of printing and the division of the Christian church into Roman Catholic and Protestant branches. Gutenberg's invention made it possible to obtain many copies of printed material of uniform quality, moderately priced, which could be disseminated over a wide area. After the break from the Roman Catholic Church, Martin Luther was interested in using music as a very important element of his form of congregational worship, and the rise of the Lutheran choral led to its utilization in various types of organ and choral music. The Roman Catholic Church continued to use the organ as a solo instrument and as an accompaniment for the choir.

    During the Renaissance the musician's profession became raised to a higher level of importance from that of the Middle Ages (from the fall of the Roman Empire to the Renaissance). Both the church and courts, according to their wealth and musical inclinations, were the chief patrons

HISTORICAL BACKGROUND

ca. 1300-ca. 1370	French Ars nova
1305	Papacy moved to Avignon
1307	Dante The Divine Comedy
1337-1453	Hundred Years' War
1353	Boccaccio Decameron
1360	Machaut Messe de Notre Dame
1386	Chaucer The Canterbury Tales
1415	Battle of Agincourt
1426	van Eycks began Ghent altarpieces
1431	Jeanne d'Arc burned at the stake
1434-1494	Medici family held great authority in Italy
1454	Gutenberg invented printing from movable type
1455-1485	War of the Roses
1478	Botticelli La Primavera
1485-1603	Tudor dynasty ruled in England
1492	Columbus discovered America
1495	da Vinci The Last Supper
1498	Savonarola executed in Florence
1503	da Vinci Mona Lisa
1504	Michelangelo David
1511	Erasmus The Praise of Folly
1516	Raphael Sistine Madonna
1517	Luther posted theses at Wittenberg
1519	Magellan sailed around the world
1519-1556	Charles V ruled the Holy Roman Empire
1534	Parliament declared Henry VIII the head of the Catholic Church in England
1540	Society of Jesus founded
1545	Council of Trent convened; concluded 1563
1555	Peace of Augsburg
1558-1603	Reign of Elizabeth I in England
1562	Genevan Psalter
1588	War between England and Spain
1594	Shakespeare Romeo and Juliet
1597	Morley A Plaine and Easie Introduction to Practicall Music

of musicians.   More and more individual musicians gained
fame for their musical prowess.

It is important that some general characteristics of
Renaissance musical style should be kept in mind, even
though many medieval practices continued, and others, which
became much more highly developed during the Renaissance,
had been anticipated years earlier.   During the later Middle
Ages musical texture had often been that of three lines of
quite different qualities of sound, and often each part entered separately.   Renaissance compositions, however, often
began with all parts simultaneously, and the preferred tone
color was homogeneous.   Harmonies of the Renaissance
generally employed triads and chords of the first inversion.
Tendencies toward the major-minor system had also begun.
Keyboard music was either systematically imitative or improvisatory in style.   Sometimes chords alternated with
free melodies in conjunct motion, and sometimes rhythmic
patterns were employed.   Instrumental forms no longer de-
pended upon texts to prove their worth, and new instrumental forms emerged which were complete and satisfying
in themselves.   An international musical language was common to all countries until national musical idioms began to
make themselves known about the middle of the sixteenth
century.

During the Middle Ages solo voices sang polyphonic
music, and the clergy, cathedral chapters, or monastic
choruses sang plainchant in unison.   About 1450 choruses
began to sing polyphonic sacred music.   Sometimes instruments doubled the voice parts or substituted for voices to
an extent which is not known today.   Instrumental arrangements of compositions which were originally vocal were
often performed with embellishments added by the performer,
but instrumental music was still closely related to vocal
music at the beginning of the sixteenth century.

The lack of any written keyboard music from pre-
Christian times and the first 1300 years of the Christian
era prevents our knowing much about such music.   Before
1450 little instrumental music was permanently recorded
since most of the instrumental music performed was ap-
parently either improvised or played by memory.   Prior
to 1600 keyboard notation in England, France, and Italy
was similar to the notation of today--notes written upon a
staff.   The keyboard notation in Germany and Spain, however, was in tablature form.   Tablature is the general

name applied to systems of instrumental notation to indicate tones by means of letters, numbers, or other symbols, sometimes in combination with a staff.

Most of the earliest keyboard music recorded in the Middle Ages was written to be performed upon all keyboard instruments, organs, clavichords, or harpsichords, not upon only one type of keyboard instrument, because stylistic traits for individual keyboard instruments had not been clearly defined.   Many sources of keyboard music from the fourteenth, fifteenth, sixteenth, and early seventeenth centuries contained material which could be appropriately performed on the organ.   Four different types of literature were found in these documents: intabulations (direct transcriptions of polyphonic choral music such as motets and ballades), [1] cantus firmus compositions (works based upon pre-existing sacred or secular melodies), preambles (free preludes not based on pre-existing melodies), and dances. [2]

The first document of keyboard music extant is the Robertsbridge Codex, dated ca. 1325. [3]   Although this manuscript is in the British Museum, certain notational practices suggest that the codex might be French[4] or Italian[5] in origin. Notes for the upper part are written on a staff of five lines; pitches for the lower parts are indicated by letters written under the notes.   Three of the six compositions found in the Robertsbridge Codex are intabulations.   The three remaining compositions belong to a kind of medieval instrumental composition known as the estampie.   The estampie, which probably was a dance in origin, was the most important instrumental form of the thirteenth and fourteenth centuries.   It consisted of repeated sections called puncti. Each punctus had two different endings, the first called ouvert and the second, clos.   The estampies from the Robertsbridge Codex are written in two voices for the most part: the lower part moves slowly, and the upper voice is written in quicker time values.   The archaic character of these estampies, suggested by the use of parallel intervals of fifths and octaves, is similar to polyphonic music of the ninth century. [6]

The Reina manuscript[7] might be of Italian origin, also.   Two keyboard pieces are found among the French and Italian secular compositions for polyphonic ensembles. One of the pieces has been identified as an arrangement of a ballata by Landini.   The Faenza manuscript, [8] dated before 1520, is a significant source of keyboard music in

MAJOR ORGAN TABLATURES, MANUSCRIPTS, AND EARLIEST PRINTED ORGAN MUSIC

1300　　　1400　　　1500　　　1600

ca. 1325, Robertsbridge Codex
late fourteenth century, Reina Manuscript
before 1420, Faenza Manuscript
1448, Ileborgh tablature
1452, Paumann Fundamentum organisandi
ca. 1470, Buxheimer Orgelbuch
1511, Schlick Spiegel der Orgelmacher und Organisten
1512, Schlick Tabulaturen etlicher Lobgesang
ca. 1510–1524, tablatures by Buchner, Kotter, Sicher, Kleber
sixteenth century, Johannes de Lublin tablature
1531, Attaingnant tablatures
1571, 1575, 1583, Ammerbach tablatures
1577, B. Schmid the elder Zwey Bücher
1607, B. Schmid the younger Tabulatur Buch
1617, Johann Woltz Nova musices

Italy before 1500. This collection contains organ Mass sections and instrumental transcriptions of many Italian and
French secular vocal compositions from the fourteenth and
early fifteenth centuries. The upper part is decorated in a
variety of ways, and the tenor of the original composition is
given to the lower voice. Both parts are notated on staves
of six lines each These pieces can be performed on
stringed keyboard instruments as well as on the organ. The
Mass sections of the Faenza manuscript assign the plainsong
in long notes to the lower part. Only parts of the plainsong
are used, which suggests that the pieces were planned for
alternation between voices and organ in the Mass. These
manuscripts, which contain Italian relationships, emphasize
the major role Italy played in the early development of keyboard music.

The practice of alternation between liturgical organ
music and Gregorian plainsong sung by a unison chorus
developed as an outgrowth of at least two practices, respon-
sorial singing of Psalmody (between soloists and choir) and
alternation of polyphony and plainsong (between two choral
bodies). Only two examples of this second procedure, which
was performed in the period from the twelfth through the
sixteenth centuries, are the organa of the Notre Dame school
and Tallis's Audivi vocem. Organ music in the alternation
practice substituted for the polyphonic choir. Alternation
between organ and plainsong sung in unison by the clergy or
monastic bodies was practiced in performance of alternate
verses of the Psalms, the Te Deum, and the Magnificat in
one of the eight psalm tones, in alternate verses of Latin
hymns such as the Salve Regina, and in the various sections
of the Ordinary of the Mass (Kyrie, Gloria, Credo, Sanctus,
and Agnus Dei).

The psalm tones were different melodic formulas
which were used for the chanting of the complete book of
the Psalms during the Roman Catholic Office. The basic
melody of the first psalm tone is given in Example 1. This
example shows the binary structure and the inflected mono-
tone to which many of the syllables are sung.

     Example 1. Basic melody of the first
            psalm tone.

Example 2 shows how the psalm tone is applied to the first
verse of the first Psalm.

Example 2.   First psalm tone applied to
the first verse of Psalm 1.

Example 3 shows how the same psalm tone is applied
to the first two verses of the Magnificat, the canticle of
Mary. [9]   The organ settings were composed for either the
odd verses or the even verses, and the alternate verses
were sung.

Example 3.   First psalm tone applied to the
first two verses of the Magnificat.

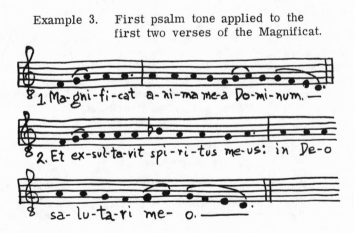

The most common alternation arrangement of a Mass Kyrie was: Kyrie (organ), Kyrie (plainsong sung by singers in unison), Kyrie (organ), Christe (plainsong), Christe (organ), Christe (plainsong), Kyrie (organ), Kyrie (plainsong), and Kyrie (organ).

Four smaller German sources of organ music are the Sagan Gloria fragment[10] (1433), two fragments from the Dominican monastery at Breslau[11] (1430 and ca. 1450), and another by Ludolf Wilkin of Winsem (Windesheim)[12] (1432). Most of the pieces found in these manuscripts are based on plainsong or are Mass movements. The Sagan fragment pieces are intended for alternation between singers and the organ. In all four of these manuscripts the lower part sustains long notes under an active upper part. Sometimes melodic and rhythmic patterns are treated sequentially in the upper part, and the melodic intervals generally move in a stepwise fashion. A few single notes are added from time to time to fill out the harmony.

The tablature of Adam Ileborgh[13] dated 1448 contains five short preambles (preludes), which were the first compositions written specifically for keyboard use. They are not based on pre-existing melodies. When there are two lower parts, they move in intervals of fifths and thirds and support the running upper part. The upper part covers a range which extends from a twelfth to two octaves. There are also a few chromatic alterations in the upper part, which usually progresses in conjunct intervals.[14]

The Fundamentum organisandi[15] (1452) by Conrad Paumann (ca. 1410-1473) is bound in a manuscript with the Lochamer Liederbuch. It was written primarily with the purpose of teaching how to write counterpoint for instruments.[16] Paumann's treatment of popular German songs as the basis of his composition is especially noteworthy. In Mit ganczem Willen much freedom is immediately noticed in that the melody is not always treated in long, equal notes in the lowest part. The melody enters at irregular intervals, sometimes on short note values, with other notes interpolated in the same voice. The number of voices also varies from two to five. The most common harmonic intervals between the two lower parts are fifths and thirds, although the texture is in two parts for about half the time. The uppermost voice contains much rhythmic variety but also utilizes rhythmic patterns.

From the Carthusian monastery at Buxheim in southern Germany comes the very important Buxheimer Orgelbuch (ca. 1470).[17] This collection of compositions by many different composers is in the "old" German tablature: the highest part on a staff and the lower part(s) in letters beneath. Although two-part and four-part writing is represented, the majority of the writing is in three parts. Over 250 different compositions of various types, such as secular songs, German and Latin organ hymns,[18] Mass movements, and other arranged vocal works, are found in this collection, with titles in four different languages. Twenty-seven pieces were written for organ. Paumann's name and a version of his Fundamentum are found in the manuscript; other composers whose composition characteristics identify them have familiar names, such as Binchois, Dufay, and Dunstable. The intabulare and organisare techniques are used: the intabulare technique takes an entire song and applies keyboard writing techniques to all parts, especially the highest one; the organisare technique employs the melody of the original song as cantus firmus, and adds an instrumental part to accompany it. The Buxheim collection also contains settings of Mass movements using the alternation practice. A Kyrie in four voice parts in chordal style is found in the book. The Gloria[19] is an extensive movement having nine parts in which, most of the time, the chant stands out in the lower part in notes of equal value. The free keyboard preambles (preludes), which have no basis on pre-existing vocal compositions, are quite short. Sometimes they have a free, scalewise melody in the upper part without any harmonic support; this type of writing alternates with chordal sections. Independence can also be observed in the lowest part, no longer limited to equal length note values.

Paul Hofhaimer (1459-1537) was better known as a performer and teacher than as a composer, but a few of his compositions have survived through his pupils' efforts. These works demand considerable technical proficiency. They contain the use of imitation, suspensions, and much florid decoration. Excessive embellishment and the addition of cadenzas, passing tones, and runs has caused the name "colorists" to be applied to the group of composers who utilized this technique. The group of pupils and composers who were strongly influenced by Paul Hofhaimer were called "Paulomimes." This group included Buchner, Kotter, Sicher, and Kleber. These composers' works include both sacred and secular compositions. Sometimes keyboard decorations were added or left to the performer to improvise, but both customs were common in the period.

Most of the 120 compositions which Hans Buchner
(1483-1540) wrote for his Fundamentum[20] (ca. 1525) were
composed in three or four parts.   These pieces were Mass
movements, introits, sequences, hymns, and responses, all
based on sacred melodies.   Some of the characteristics of
Buchner's writing are a preference for duple rather than
triple rhythm, imitation used freely, an altered cantus firmus, restriction to regular meter, and rather dense ornamentation in the upper voices at times.

Hans Kotter (1485-1541) used harmony in his tablature to establish form.   He also fitted the melody and his
musical ideas into a regular rhythmic unit.   This differen-
tiated his work from that of the Buxheimer Orgelbuch and
the Ileborgh tablature.   In chordal sections the sense of
harmonic root movement by fifths is clearly shown;   the
melodic efforts are very short and are rigidly kept within
the harmony.   Diatonic lines flow at the interval of a tenth
between the two lower parts and are balanced with the third
voice, all within a clear sense of harmonic progression.
The first application of the term fantasia to a keyboard composition and the earliest known dances in German tablatures
are found in the Kotter book, four of which are settings of
the Spagna[21] melody.   The style of writing suggests that the
settings might not be written for the organ but perhaps for
some stringed keyboard instrument. [22]

Fridolin Sicher (1490-1546), a pupil of Hans Buchner,
collected a large number of organ works in tablature,[23]
most of which are intabulations, along with a few preludes
and arrangements of cantus firmus vocal works.   Long notes
are often repeated, a fact which does not suggest an organ
arrangement since there would be no difficulty in sustaining
tones at the organ.

The tablature of Leonhard Kleber (1490-1556)[24] dated
1524 contains 112 numbers which show the strong influence
of the Hofhaimer school, even though Kleber was not one of
Hofhaimer's pupils.   Most of these highly decorated pieces
are transcriptions of vocal works.   The influence of the
Buxheimer Orgelbuch is noticeable in Kleber's 18 short preludes, which alternate chordal sections with improvisatory
scale passages. [25]

Two Polish tablatures were written under German

influence. Johannes de Lublin assembled a very large collection[26] which contains a treatise on counterpoint and a
wide variety of intabulations of both sacred and secular works
by German, French, Italian, and Polish composers. The
brief preludes included in the tablature usually begin with
block chords, contain a contrapuntal section, and close with
a flourish. The second Polish tablature[27] (called the Cracow
tablature) is similar to the Lublin tablature. It contains a
wide variety of pieces such as preludes, Mass movements,
motets, Protestant hymns, canons, and secular songs from
several countries. [28]

    In 1531 the printer Pierre Attaingnant issued the first
keyboard works published in France, which consisted of seven
books, four for secular purposes and three for use in the
church. The first of the three books for the church contained versets for the Cunctipotens and Fons bonitatis Kyries.
The versets were to be played in alternation with plainsong.
The second book contains two preludes, versets on the
Magnificat in eight tones, followed by versets on the Te
Deum. The third book consists of 13 motets by various
composers and one prelude arranged for organ. Attaingnant
probably wished to publish a collection for the organ which
would include works of divergent styles and conceptions. [29]
Even though Attaingnant called his works "tabulatures," he
used two staves of five lines each. Homophonic writing
(music in which one voice is predominant melodically; the
predominant voice is supported in an accompanimental way
by the other voices) prevails in the dances and in the chanson
settings, with decoration appearing most frequently in the
outer parts. In the motet arrangements the parts are elaborately decorated. The embellishment changes the melodic
lines into fantasies based on the original harmonies of the
vocal works. Three-part writing predominates in the organ
Mass movements.

    A few collections introduced the French organ school.
The first collection to appear after Attaingnant's publications
was the Premier Livre de Tablature d'Espinette (1560), which
came from the printshop of Simon Gorlier. Charles Guillet
of Bruges issued Vingt-Quatre Fantasies à Quatre Parties,
Disposées Selon l'Ordre des Douze Modes in 1610 written as
much for strings as for the organ (tant pour les violes que
pour l'orgue). In this book there are many similarities to
Sweelinck's writing. [30] François Eustache Du Caurroy (1549-
1609) composed 42 contrapuntal Fantaisies in from three to
six voices. He often approached the variation form in these

works.   Claudin Le Jeune (ca. 1530-1600), Valerien Gonet, and Guillaume Costeley (ca. 1531-1606) all wrote fantasies. Costeley's composition has the title of Fantazie sus Orgue ou Espinette.

Elias Nicolaus Ammerbach (1530-1597) wrote the first published German organ tablature (1571).   Two other tablatures by him appeared in 1575 and 1583.   The "new" German organ tablature in the first book uses only letters (no staves) with rhythmic signs.   Both sacred and secular works are included in all three of Ammerbach's tablatures.   Dances fill one section of the first tablature.   Ammerbach's intabulations draw from famous choral composers such as Isaac, Senfl, Lassus, Clemens non Papa, and Josquin des Pres. The amount of coloration of the intabulations ranges from very little to extremely florid writing in every part.   The number of parts extends from four to six, and there is a gradual widening of the vocal ranges.

In 1577 Bernhard Schmid the elder (1520-1590) published a keyboard tablature for musical amateurs, Zwey Bücher einer neuen künstlichen Tabulatur auff Orgeln und Instrumenten (Strassbourg: B. Jobin, 1577).   Schmid pleaded for instrumental music in the church.   The musical selections included in the book were Italian, French, and German secular songs, and a number of intabulated motets and dances.   Most of the pieces are in five parts.

A volume for organists' use for all Sundays and festivals of the liturgical year was collected by Johann Rühling (1550-1615) and printed in 1583.   Most of the 86 pieces (without the usual decorative instrumental writing) came from the Latin motets of Lassus and Clemens non Papa.

Jacob Paix (1556-after 1623) assembled two tablatures. The first, Ein Schön Nutz unnd Gebreulich Orgel Tabulaturbuch (1583), contains intabulated motets (principally by Palestrina and Lassus), fantasias, songs from France, Germany, and Italy, dances, and some of his own compositions. All were highly ornamented, especially the vocal works. Paix employed the thumb, and used parallel fifths and octaves, imitation, and spaces between measures to stand for bar lines.   The second tablature, Thesaurus Motetarum (1589), contains 22 intabulated motets with no added coloration. [31]

The Dresden court organist August Nörminger (ca.

1560-1613) collected a large number of simple settings of
Protestant chorales, intabulated songs, and rather short
dances (pavans, galliards, passamezzi) with the coloration
at its most florid in the songs.   The compilation was entitled Tabulaturbuch auff den Instrumente[32] (1598).

A significant change in taste is shown in the younger
Bernhard Schmid's (1547-1625) preference for Italian works
in his published keyboard tablature, Tabulatur Buch ... auff
Orgeln und Instrumenten zu gebrauchen (1607).   He included
ornamented motets, canzoni alla francese, Italian organ toccatas, intonations by Gabrieli, and dances.

In Johann Woltz's Nova Musices Organicae Tabulatura
(1617) the Italian influence is even greater.   This book is a
large collection which contains 85 Latin motets, 53 sacred
German compositions, 50 canzoni alla francese, 20 fugae by
Simon Lohet, and seven miscellaneous compositions.   The
coloration was to be added by the performer.

National schools or organ composition began to rise
about the middle of the sixteenth century.   The earlier
stages of evolution of these different schools of organ composition will be studied in the next three chapters.

Notes

1.   Sometimes original voice parts are omitted or are
      placed in a different range for ease of performance
      by the hands.   Keyboard decoration and figuration are
      frequently added.   Sometimes single notes or a new
      accompanying part is inserted for additional sonority.
2.   The reader will find publication references to printed
      music, facsimiles, and some tablature transcriptions
      under the name of the composer or under the title
      of the more important manuscripts in Part II, the
      Biographical Catalog.
3.   British Museum, Add. 28550.
4.   Willi Apel, Geschichte der Orgel- und Klaviermusik
      bis 1700, Kassel, Germany: Bärenreiter Verlag, 1967;
      p. 21.
5.   Archibald T. Davison and Willi Apel, Historical Anthol-
      ogy of Music, Cambridge, Mass.: Harvard University
      Press, 1946, 1949; p. 221-222.
6.   Constant reference has been made to the definitive arti-
      cle by Clyde William Young, "Keyboard Music to 1600,"

Musica Disciplina, XVI (1962) and XVII (1963). This
excellent article also gives references to sources,
additional transcriptions, facsimiles, and the like.
Dr. Young has graciously given the author permission
to use material from this article, which makes further reference under individual topics unnecessary.

7. Bibliothèque Nationale, fr. nouv. acq. 6771.
8. Faenza, Biblioteca Communale 117.
9. The text of the Magnificat in Latin (Luke 1:46-55) fol-
    lows: 1. Magnificat anima mea Dominum. 2. Et
    exultavit spiritus meus: in Deo salutari meo.
    3. Quia respexit humilitatem ancillae suae, ecce enim
    ex hoc beatam dicent omnes generationes. 4. Quia
    fecit mihi magna qui potens est: et sanctum nomen
    ejus. 5. Et misericordia progenie in progenies
    timentibus eum. 6. Fecit potentiam in brachio suo
    dispersit superbos mente cordis sui. 7. Deposuit
    potentes de sede, et exaltavit humiles. 8. Esurientes
    implevit bonis, et divites dimisit inanes. 9. Sus-
    cepit Israel puerum suum: recordatus misericordiae
    suae. 10. Sicut locutus est ad patres nostros,
    Abraham et semini ejus in secula. GLORIA PATRI:
    Gloria Patri, Filio, et Spiritui Sancto! Sicut erat in
    principio, et nunc, et semper et in secula seculorum.
    Amen.
10. Breslau [Wrocław], University Library, I. Qu 438.
11. Breslau [Wrocław], University Library, I. Qu 42 and
    I. F. 687.
12. Berlin, Deutsche Staatsbibliothek, Theol. Lat. Quart.
    290.
13. Curtis Institute of Music, Philadelphia.
14. Young suggests that the first indication of the use of
    pedal might be in the Breslau manuscript, I. Qu 42
    [note 11]. ("Keyboard Music to 1600," Musica Dis-
    ciplina, XVI (1962), p. 119-120). Sumner suggests
    that the first real evidences of the use of pedal are
    found in the Ileborgh preludes (William Leslie Sumner,
    The Organ 2nd ed. , 1955, p. 71).
15. Berlin, Deutsche Staatsbibliothek, 40613.
16. The word fundamentum was the title chosen by several
    composers for books which were designed to give in-
    struction in writing counterpoint. Four of these books
    were Conrad Paumann's Fundamentum organisandi, the
    Buxheimer Orgelbuch, Buchner's Fundamentum, and
    Johannes de Lublin's organ tablature.
17. Munich, Bayerische Staatsbibliothek, Cim. 352b, (olim
    Mus. 3725).

18. The earliest organ settings of Latin hymns are found in Paumann's Fundamentum and in the Buxheimer Orgelbuch.
19. Folios 81v-82.
20. Zürich, Stadtbibliothek, Codex 284.
21. The Spagna (abbreviation of Il Re di Spagna) tune is a famous basse danse melody which was frequently used as the cantus firmus for polyphonic compositions during the fifteenth and sixteenth centuries. The basse danse was a dance which probably began with low [Fr., bas, low] gliding foot movements.
22. A manuscript similar to the Kotter tablature (Basle, Universitäts Bibliothek, F. IX. 58) contains two dances by Johann (or Hans) Weck, two Spagna settings, and five intabulations.
23. St. Gall, Stiftsbibliothek, 530.
24. Berlin, Deutsche Staatsbibliothek, 40026 (olim, Z 96).
25. An anonymous tablature from Trent (Biblioteca Civica, 1947) also shows influences from the Hofhaimer school.
26. Cracow, Academy of Sciences, Ms. 1716.
27. Warsaw, State Archives.
28. The small Munich Manuscript (Bayerische Staatsbibliothek, Ms. 2987) contains nine French chansons. The music is primarily chordal in character, and the coloration (decoration) does not interfere with the harmonic structure.
29. M. Alfred Bichsel, "The Attaingnant Organ Books," The Musical Heritage of the Lutheran Church, St. Louis: Concordia Pub. House, 1959; vol. V; p. 156-165.
30. Gotthold Frotscher, Geschichte des Orgelspiels und der Orgelkomposition, Berlin: Merseberger Verlag, 1959; vol. II; p. 667.
31. A number of other similar sources include the manuscript tablature (1585) of Christoph Löffelholtz (1572-1619) (Berlin, Deutsche Staatsbibliothek, Mus. Ms. 40 034), the Tabulatur-Buch Auff dem Instrument Hertzogk zu Sachsen (Dresden, Sächsische Landesbibliothek), a manuscript tablature (Berlin, Deutsche Staatsbibliothek, Mus. Ms. 40 115), the Künstlich Tabulatur-Buch (1594-1596) by Johann Fischer (sixteenth/seventeenth century) (Thorn, Ratsbibliothek), and a manuscript tablature ascribed to Cajus Schmidtlein (Danzig [Gdansk], Staatsarchiv).
32. Berlin, Deutsche Staatsbibliothek, Mus. Ms. 40 089.

Bibliography

Andersen, Poul-Gerhard. Organ Building and Design, translated into English by Joanne Curnutt. New York: Oxford University Press, 1969; p. 140-142.

Apel, Willi. "Early German Keyboard Music," Musical
Quarterly, vol. XXIII (1937), p. 210-237.

_____. "Die Tabulatur des Adam Ileborgh," Zeitschrift
für Musikwissenschaft, vol. XVI (1934), p. 193-212.

_____. "Du Nouveau sur la Musique Française pour
Orgue au XVIe Siècle," Revue Musicale, vol. XVIII
(1937), p. 96-108.

_____. Geschichte der Orgel- und Klaviermusik bis 1700.
Kassel, Germany: Bärenreiter Verlag, 1967; p. 100-
104.

Bedbrook, Gerald Stares, "The Buxheim Keyboard Manuscript," Music Review, vol. XIV (1953), p. 288-295.

Benedictines of Solesmes, eds., Liber Usualis. Tournai,
Belgium: Desclée et Cie., 1950.

Bichsel, M. Alfred. "The Attaingnant Organ Books," The
Musical Heritage of the Lutheran Church. St. Louis:
Concordia Pub. House, 1959; vol. V, p. 156.

Bowles, Edmund A. "A Performance History of the Organ
in the Middle Ages," Diapason (January 1970), p. 13-
14.

Carapetyan, Armen. "The Codex Faenza, Biblioteca Communale, 117," Musica Disciplina, vol. XIII (1959);
vol. XIV (1960); and vol. XV (1961).

Dart, Thurston. "A New Source of English Organ Music,"
Music and Letters, vol. XXXV (1954), p. 201-205.

Davison, Archibald, and Willi Apel. Historical Anthology
of Music. Cambridge, Mass.: Harvard University
Press, 1964; vol. I.

Frotscher, Gotthold. Geschichte des Orgelspiels und der
Orgelkomposition. Berlin: Merseberger Verlag, 1959;
vol. I: p. 1-175, 186, 221; vol. II: p. 717, 936.

Howell, Almonte C. "The French Organ Mass in the Sixteenth and Seventeenth Centuries." Unpublished dissertation, University of North Carolina, 1953.

Jeppesen, Knud. Die italienische Orgelmusik am Anfang des
Cinquecento, 2 vols. Copenhagen: Munksgaard, 1943
(2nd ed., 1960).

Kendall, Raymond. "Notes on Arnold Schlick," Acta
Musicologia, vol. XI (1939), p. 136-143.

Kinkeldey, Otto. Orgel und Klavier in der Musik des 16.

Jahrhunderts. Leipzig: Breitkopf und Härtel, 1910.

Kinsky, Georg. "Kurze Oktaven auf besaitenen tasteninstrumente," Zeitschrift für Musikwissenschaft, vol.
II (1919-1920), p. 65-82.

Lunelli, Renato. L'arte organaria del rinascimento in Roma
e gli organi di S. Pietro in Vaticano dalle origini a
tutto il periodo Frescobaldiana. Vol. X of Historiae
musicae cultores biblioteca, Florence: 1958.

_____. Der Orgelbau in Italien in seinen Meisterwerken
vom 14. Jahrhundert bis zur Gegenwart. Mainz,
Germany: Rheingold, 1956.

Lowinsky, Edward E. "English Organ Music of the Renaissance," Musical Quarterly, vol. XXXIX (1953), p. 373-
395, 528-553.

Marrocco, W. Thomas, and Robert Huestis, "Some Speculations Concerning the Instrumental Music of the Faenza
Codex 117," Diapason (May, 1972), p. 3.

Perrot, Jean. L'Orgue de Ses Origines Hellénistiques à
la Fin du XIIIe Siècle. Paris: Editions A. et J.
Picard et Cie., 1965 (English ed., The Organ from
Its Invention to the End of the Thirteenth Century,
translated by Norma Deane, New York: Oxford University Press, 1971).

Raugel, Félix. "The Ancient French Organ School," Musical
Quarterly, vol. XI (1925), p. 560-571.

Rokseth, Yvonne. La Musique d'Orgue au XVe Siècle et au
Début du XVIe. Paris: Librairie E. Droz, 1930.

Schering, Arnold. "Zur Alternatim-Orgelmesse," Zeitschrift
für Musikwissenschaft, vol. XVII (1935), p. 19-32.

Schlick, Arnolt. Tabulaturen etlicher Lobgesang und Lidlein
uff die Orgeln und Lauten. Klecken, [West] Germany:
Gottlieb Harms, 1924.

Schnoor, Hans. "Das Buxheimer Orgelbuch," Zeitschrift
für Musikwissenschaft, vol. IV (1921-1922), p. 1-10.

Schrade, Leo. "The Organ in the Mass of the 15th Century,"
Musical Quarterly, vol. XXVIII (1942), p. 329-336,
467-487.

Siebert, Frederick Mark. "Mass Sections in the Buxheim
Organ Book: A Few Points," Musical Quarterly, vol.
L (1964), p. 353-366.

_____. "Performance Problems in Fifteenth-Century
Organ Music," Organ Institute Quarterly, vol. X, No.
2 (1963), p. 5.

Stevens, Denis W. "Organ Mass," Grove's Dictionary of
Music and Musicians, Eric Blom, ed. New York: St.
Martin's Press, 1954; Vol. VI, p. 339-344.

Sumner, William Leslie. "The French Organ School," Sixth

Music Book.   London: Hinrichsen Edition Ltd. , 1950;
p. 281-294.

_____.   The Organ: Its Evolution, Principles of Con-
struction, and Use.   London: Macdonald and Co. ,
1952 (3rd ed. , 1962).

White, John R.   "The Tablature of Johannes de Lublin,"
Musica Disciplina, vol. XVI (1963), p. 137-162.

Williams, Peter.   The European Organ 1450-1850.   London:
Batsford, 1966.

Young, Clyde William.   "Keyboard Music to 1600," Musica
Disciplina, vol. XVI (1962), p. 115-150, and vol. XVII
(1963), p. 163-193.

_____.   "The Keyboard Tablatures of Bernhard Schmid,
Father and Son."   Unpublished dissertation, University
of Illinois, 1957.

2.   ITALY: 1350-1650

The organ in Italy was used for both secular and
sacred purposes during the fifteenth, sixteenth, and seventeenth centuries.   Varieties of organs for secular use included chamber organs, small reed organs called regals,
portable organs, and outdoor organs.   Organs were used in
connection with opera, the "new" musical entertainment established by the Florentines, and with oratorio, another new
seventeenth-century musical form.   In churches organs were
used with orchestral groups, and at Mass to accompany
choirs or as a solo instrument at various prescribed places
during the services.   Costanzo Antegnati (ca. 1549-1624),
who belonged to a famous family of organ builders, organ
composers, theorists, and organists, wrote in his L'Arte
Organica (Brescia, 1608) that the organ should be used only
"to praise and magnify the Lord and not for other profane
uses."   The magnificent Cathedral of San Marco in Venice
contained two organs and held difficult examinations for
organists who wished to fill the coveted positions of first
or second organist.

Two authors who wrote about matters related to the
organ were Adriano Banchieri (1567-1634), whose Conclusioni
nel suono dell'organo and Organo suonarino progressed
through several editions, and Girolamo Diruta (1561-?),
who wrote the first Italian organ method.   Diruta's book,
entitled Il Transilvano, was issued in two parts and was
written in question and answer form.   In addition to instruction in registration Diruta included organ pieces composed
by himself and other composers.   Luzzaschi, A. and G.
Gabrieli, Merulo, and Diruta had works in Part I.   Diruta,
Luzzaschi, Fatorini, G. Gabrieli, Mortaro, and Banchieri
were represented in Part II.

Before the sixteenth century, music composed for
keyboard instruments consisted of dances, arrangements of
vocal music, music for liturgical functions, and free preludes.   A number of new keyboard forms developed in Italy
during the sixteenth century.   The close relationship of

HISTORICAL BACKGROUND

1492	Columbus' first voyage to America
1495	da Vinci Last Supper
1498	Petrucci received license to print music
1498	Savonarola burned at the stake
1503	da Vinci Mona Lisa
1504	Michelangelo David
1506	Michelangelo Sistine Chapel
1516	Raphael Sistine Madonna
1519	Charles V became Holy Roman Emperor
1527	Rome sacked by mercenaries
1538	Titian Venus of Urbino
1541	Michelangelo Last Judgment
1545	Council of Trent convened; concluded 1570
1576	Tintoretto Ascension of Christ
1582	Pope Gregory's calendar reform
1592	Tintoretto Last Supper
1597	Peri Dafne
1600	Peri Euridice; Caccini Euridice; Cavalieri La Rappresentazione
1602	Galileo discovered the law of gravity
1605	Monteverdi Fifth Book of Madrigals
1608	Frescobaldi became organist at St. Peter's
1615	G. Gabrieli Canzoni e sonate
1631	Galilei Dialogo dei due massimi ...
1642	Monteverdi L'Incoronazione di Poppea
1650	Carissimi Jephtha

---

instrumental music to vocal music is evident in two new forms which grew from vocal prototypes, the canzona and the ricercar. Italian organ music designed for use in the church were Mass movements, versets, and hymns. Free forms (completely original compositions, i. e. , compositions not based on preexisting material) such as toccatas, fantasias, and intonations probably emerged from improvisation, which was widely practiced during the Renaissance. Musical distinctions cannot always be made, however, between various titles such as canzonas, ricercars, and fantasias, in order to identify the form. Some characteristics which can be listed as primary identifying factors in determining nomenclature can be found in several different types of

ITALIAN ORGAN COMPOSITION: 1350-1650

1350	1400	1450	1500	1550	1600	1650

Reina Manuscript, late fourteenth century
Faenza Manuscript, before 1420
1468 Fogliano, Jacopo---1548
1470/1480 Antico, Andrea (publisher) ?
before 1490 Cavazzoni, M.   after 1559
1498 Segni, G. ------ 1561
1505 Buus, J. ------1564
1510/1520 Gabrieli, A. -----1586
1525 Cavazzoni, G.   ?
1525/1526 Palestrina, G. 1594
? Valente, Antonio ?
1527 Annibale Padovano 1575
? Bell'Haver, V. ------ 1587
1530/1540 Rodio, Rocco------1615
1533 Merulo, Claudio-----1604
1530/1540 Guami, Giuseppe-----1611
ca.1540 Maschera, F. 1584
1545 Luzzaschi, Luzzasco 1607
1547 Malvezzi, C. 1597
ca.1549 Antegnati, Costanzo 1624
? Soderini, Agostino ?
ca.1550 de Macque, J. 1614
ca.1555 Gabrieli, G. 1612
? Mayone, Ascanio 1627
? Pellegrini, Vincenzo 1631
? Cima, Andrea ?
1561 Diruta, Girolamo ?
1567 Banchieri, Adriano 1634
ca.1575 Trabaci, G. M. -----1647
1583 Frescobaldi, G. 1643
? Carradini, Nicolò ?

compositions. Loose terminology of the period does not permit
limiting these forms to some exclusive features. As only
one example, fantasia was sometimes used interchangeably
with ricercar. Even though embellishment was frequently
improvised in performance, the Italians often wrote out the
ornamentation they wished. Northern Europeans used ornamentation symbols to indicate the embellishment they desired.

The first keyboard music printed in Italy was entitled
Frottole intabulate da sonare organi, which was published by
Andrea Antico in Rome (1517). Frottole were simple, secular songs for three or four parts which were primarily
chordal in style; the melody in the upper part was predominant. This type of song flourished in northern Italian
city-courts during the early part of the sixteenth century.
Most of the pieces in the book published by Antico were
four-part arrangements of frottole by Trombocino and Cara
and were printed on two staves of five lines each. The unknown arranger changed the upper parts into flowing lines,
but the lowest part was only slightly altered.

The canzona is important as one of the major keyboard forms which developed in Italy during the sixteenth
century and the first half of the seventeenth century. Canzona is the Italian word for chanson, a short, strophic,
vocal composition of the 1400 and 1500's of Franco-Flemish
origin. [1] The text of the chanson was usually amorous.
Many arrangements of the chanson for lute and keyboard
were made during the sixteenth century in France, Spain,
Germany, and Italy. Characteristics of the chanson were
a lively tempo, themes of distinctive rhythmic character,
sectional construction, with each section beginning with imitative counterpoint, and writing in both imitative and homophonic styles. The imitative counterpoint grew from the
harmony. Although most of the sections were written in
duple meter, some sections were composed in triple meter
for variety. Many canzonas can be identified by the rhythm
of the initial notes:

$$\text{♩♩♩|♩} \qquad \text{♩♫♩.}$$

The first organ canzonas, which were probably keyboard transcriptions, were found in Recerchari motetti canzoni, Libro I (1523), by Marco Antonio Cavazzoni (fl. 1490-
1559). The canzonas of Andrea Gabrieli (ca. 1515-1586) are

(cont. on p. 28)

ITALIAN ORGAN BOOKS: 1517-1616*

Pub. Date	Composer/Author	Title
1517	A. Antico (pub.)	Frottole intabulate da sonare organi
1523	M. A. Cavazzoni	Recerchari motetti canzoni, Libro I
1542	G. Cavazzoni	Intavolatura cioè ricercari, canzoni, himni, Magnificati
1543	G. Cavazzoni	Intabulatura d'Organo cioè Misse, Himni, Magnificat
1543	J. Buus	Il primo libro di Canzoni francese
1547/1549	J. Buus	Recercari ... da cantare et sonare d'organo et altri stromenti (two books)
1549	J. Buus	Intabolatura d'Organo di Recercari
1567	C. Merulo	Ricercari d'intavolatura d'organo
1568	C. Merulo	Messe d'intavolatura d'organo
1576/1580	A. Valente	Intavolatura de cimbalo; Secundo libro di Versi Spirituali
1584	F. Maschera	Primo libro di canzoni alla francese
1592	C. Merulo	Canzoni d'intavolatura d'organo
1593	G. Diruta	Il Transilvano, Part I (editions 1597, 1612, 1625)
1593	A. Gabrieli	Intonationi d'organo ... et Giovanni suo nepote
1595	A. Gabrieli	Ricercari ... composti & tabulati per ogni sorte di stromenti da tasti

1596	A. Gabrieli	Terzo libro de Ricercari
1598/1604	C. Merulo	Toccate d'Intavolatura d'organo (two books)
1599	V. Pellegrini	Primo libro delle Canzoni de intavolatura d'organo...
1603/1609	A. Mayone	Diversi capricci (two books)
1603	G. M. Trabaci	Ricercate, Canzone francese, Capricci...
1604	Annibale Padovano	Primo libro di Toccate ed Ricercari d'organo
1605	A. Banchieri	L'organo suonarino (other editions 1611, 1628, 1638)
1605	A. Gabrieli	Canzoni alla francese... (two books)
1606	C. Merulo	Canzoni d'intavolatura d'organo
1607/1608	C. Merulo	Ricercari d'intavolatura d'organo (books 2 and 3)
1608	A. Soderini	Libro delle canzoni
1608	C. Antegnati	Intavolatura de Ricercari d'organo
1609	G. Diruta	Il Transilvano, Part II (second edition: 1622)
1609	A. Banchieri	Conclusioni del suono dell' organo (later edition: 1626)
1611	C. Merulo	Canzoni d'intavolatura d'organo
1615	G. M. Trabaci	Il secundo libro de Ricercate...
1616	G. M. Trabaci	Ricercari per l'organo

*A similar table of the published compositions of Frescobaldi is provided later in this chapter.

also mostly arrangements of vocal chansons. The first effort to write original canzonas instead of arrangements of
chansons was taken by Girolamo Cavazzoni (1525-?), the son
of Marco Antonio. Girolamo used thematic material from
the chanson Il est bel et bon in one canzona and Josquin's
chanson Faulte d'argent in his Canzone sopra Falt d'argent,
but he altered the elaboration of the themes. The canzonas
written "in the French style" were called canzoni alla francese.

The canzonas of Claudio Merulo (1533-1604) were
published in three books (1592, 1606, 1611). Five of
Merulo's 23 canzonas were arrangements; the 18 remaining canzonas were original, but they might have been intended for instrumental performance. A large number of
Italian composers wrote original organ canzonas toward the
end of the sixteenth century and deep into the seventeenth
century. Important composers of the canzona form during
this period were Vincenzo Pellegrini (?-1631), Ascanio
Mayone (fl. late 1500's to early 1600's), Andrea Cima
(second half, 1500's), Giovanni Maria Trabaci (ca. 1575-
1647), Agostino Soderini (second half, 1500's), and Girolamo
Frescobaldi (1583-1643). Canzonas of Trabaci were the
earliest canzonas which are known to have followed the practice of using rhythmic and melodic variants of the same
theme as themes for the various sections of the canzona.
This type of canzona has been called the variation canzona.
Frescobaldi used the variation principle in many of his canzonas; several of Frescobaldi's compositions in canzona
form used phrases from popular songs which he adopted for
development and imitative treatment.

The keyboard canzona contributed its lively character
and the marked rhythmic nature of its themes to the fugue;
the contrasting sections of the instrumental canzona led to
the seventeenth-century sonata.

The ricercar was another prominent form in Italian
organ literature of the sixteenth and seventeenth centuries.
The word ricercar comes from an Italian verb which means
"to look for," "to serach," or "to attempt."[2] The first use
of the term ricercar was applied to lute music in which the
pieces resembled preludes. The development of the organ
ricercar began with two ricercars found in Marco Antonio
Cavazzoni's Recerchari motetti canzoni (1523). The ricercars in Cavazzoni's book precede two motets in the same
keys and might have been intended to function as preludes

to the motets.   These long ricercars are similar to preludes, because the ricercars are continuous and improvisational, and they contain alternations of chordal and scale
passages.   The ricercars of Jacopo Fogliano (1468-1548)
contain a greater use of imitation than those of Cavazzoni
and thus point to the imitative ricercar.

The earliest ricercars in a more contrapuntal style
were four ricercars composed by Girolamo Cavazzoni (1525-
?) in his Intavolatura per organo cioè recercari canzoni
himni magnificati (1542).   In the younger Cavazzoni's ricercars the number of themes is smaller, and the themes are
usually slow and lack rhythmic or melodic individuality.
These ricercars contain from five to nine rather lengthy
sections, and each section has its individual theme method-
ically treated in imitation.   Free, non-imitative passages
are sometimes found between sections.

Andrea Gabrieli wrote at least 17 imitative ricercars
in which he tightened the form by reducing the number of
sections and themes.   About one-third of Gabrieli's ricercars
are monothematic (i. e. , employ only one theme);   several
have only two or three themes.   The countersubject of the
fugue was foreshadowed by Gabrieli's use of the same melodic material each time a new entry of the principal theme
occurred.   Gabrieli also incorporated into his ricercars the
contrapuntal devices of diminution, augmentation, inversion,
and stretto.

Ricercars were also composed by the italianized
Netherlander Jacques (Giaches) Buus (1505-1564) and Annibale Padovano (1527-1575).   Both of these composers wrote
instrumental ensemble ricercars and keyboard ricercars.
Claudio Merulo's (1533-1604) ricercars contain many sections
and themes, although at least one ricercar is monothematic.
Other Italian composers who contributed to ricercar literature were Ascanio Mayone, Costanzo Antegnati, and Trabaci. [3]

The word toccata comes from the Italian infinitive
toccare (to touch).   The toccata in the hands of early Italian
keyboard composers was an improvisatory, free form which
employed full chords and running scale passages.   The toccatas of Andrea Gabrieli were written in this style.   Claudio
Merulo, a major contributor to the form, enlarged and varied
the materials used in the toccata by alternating sections of
chordal and imitative writing and by balancing the activity
between the different voice parts.   Later the larger toccatas

of Frescobaldi were written in short sections and in different moods. Frescobaldi also wrote short pieces which are now called liturgical toccatas in a slow, dignified style. These stately toccatas were rather chromatic and were performed at designated places in the Mass such as before the Mass (Toccata avanti la Messa delli Apostoli) and for the elevation (Toccata per l'elevatione). Trabaci and Mayone preceded Frescobaldi in writing this type of toccata.

Capriccios were imitative contrapuntal works written for organ by such composers as Mayone, de Macque, Trabaci, and Frescobaldi. As the word caprice suggests, a capriccio was a free, lighthearted composition written with a variety of musical material in no standardized form or order, and often connected with one special musical feature, such as the cuckoo motif, dance melodies, or a tune constructed from tones of the hexachord. [4]

The sixteenth-century organ prelude in Italy was called an intonatione (intonazione). Andrea Gabrieli and his nephew Giovanni wrote intonationi for their publication Intonationi d'organo di Andrea Gabrieli, et di Gio. suo nepote (1593). These rather short intonations, which were written for liturgical use, were composed in the church modes and were similar to the earliest toccatas in which full chords were interlaced by running scale passages.

Organ Masses of the sixteenth-century Italian school often included all five parts of the Mass Ordinary (Kyrie, Gloria, Credo, Sanctus, and Agnus Dei) and were written to be performed at the organ in alternation with Gregorian chant portions which were sung. Sometimes the Credo was omitted as an organ composition. Mass movements composed by Buus have been found in a manuscript from Castell' Arquato dated ca. 1540. Three plainsong Masses composed according to the alternation principle were written by both Girolamo Cavazzoni and Claudio Merulo. The organ Masses by these two composers were named Missa Domenicalis, Missa Apostolorum, and Missa Beata Virgine. Frescobaldi also wrote three organ Masses by similar titles in his Fiori Musicali (1635). Frescobaldi provided organ pieces, however, for only the Kyrie of the Ordinary of the Mass. The remainder of his Mass compositions were free compositions intended for other places in the Mass, such as before the Mass (Toccata avanti la Messa), after the epistle (Canzona dopo l'Epistola), after the Credo (Ricercare dopo il Credo), for the elevation (Toccata per l'elevatione), and after the post-communion prayer (Canzona dopo il Post Comune).

Organ settings of Latin hymn melodies also appeared
in sixteenth-century Italian organ literature. Girolamo
Cavazzoni included 12 organ hymns in his Intavolatura cioè
ricercari canzoni himni magnificati (1542). Cavazzoni wrote
the plainsong melody in notes of uniform value. Two of the
plainsong hymn melodies most frequently arranged by Italian
composers of this period for organ were Pange lingua and
Veni creator spiritus.

Girolamo Frescobaldi was Italy's most important
organ composer. He was an outstanding performer and
teacher, and his influence was great. For this reason it
is appropriate to study his works in detail.

It is difficult to differentiate between Frescobaldi's
imitative contrapuntal forms such as the canzonas, ricercari,
fantasias, and capriccios.[5] Since Frescobaldi did not allow
established ideas to inhibit his great creative powers, there
are always exceptions to general statements about his treatment of forms. The ricercari are not based on pre-existing
tunes. They are dignified, monothematic, and are composed
in a more strictly contrapuntal, academic fashion than the
other three imitative forms. The ricercari are consistent
in character and never change from the common meter with
which they begin. The other three forms are more sectional.
They are light and cheerful in character and employ contrasting materials of harmony, figurations, and other free,
virtuoso elements. Four ricercari and three capriccios are
based on themes built from tones representing hexachord
syllables.

The canzoni alla francese of Frescobaldi were based
on popular secular melodies from which melodic fragments
were treated contrapuntally. The canzoni alla francese
utilized variation techniques in which the initial theme received both rhythmic and melodic alteration; this practice
is called thematic metamorphosis. The canzonas (not canzoni alla francese) also used the distinctive identifying rhythm
at the beginning in each voice but were not based upon pre-
existing melodies. Both the canzonas and the canzoni alla
francese have at least three sections, of which one section
(usually a middle one) is in triple meter.[6]

The fantasias printed in 1608 usually fall into three
sections which are indicated by the meter changes. Of 12

ORGAN PUBLICATIONS OF FRESCOBALDI 1608-1645

Type of works	Date	Title (and vol. no. in Pidoux ed.)	Publisher (and place)
•12 fantasies	1608	Il Primo Libro Delle Fantasie... (I)	Tini and Lomazzo (Milan)
•10 ricercari	1615		Zannetti (Rome)
{ 5 canzonas and	1624	Il Primo Libro di Capricci..et Arie...	Soldi (Rome)
11 capriccios, arias	1626	Il Primo Libro di Capricci, Canzon Francese e Recercari..et Arie (II) (pub. without Capriccio sopra l'aria: Or che noi rimena; added Capriccio sopra un soggetto. Both are included in Pidoux ed.)	Vincenti (Venice)
•combined into:	1642	repub. without change	
• toccatas, kyries, canzonas, ricercari	1635	Fiori Musicali (V)	Vincenti (Venice)
• 12 toccatas, variations on dances, arias	1637	Toccate d'Intavolatora... Partite di Diversi Arie et Corrente, Balletti, Ciaccone, Passachagli... Libro Primo (III)	Borbone (Rome)
• 11 toccatas, 6 canzonas, 3 hymns, 3 Magnificat verses, variations on dances	1637	Il Secondo Libro di Toccate, Canzone, Verse d'Hinni, Magnificat, Gagliarde, Correnti et Altre Partite d'Intavolatura ... (IV)	Borbone (Rome)
• 11 canzonas (published posthumously)	1645	Canzoni alla Francese in Partitura ... (I)	Vincenti (Venice)

fantasias, three each are based on one subject (sopra un soggetto), two subjects, three, and four subjects. The full texture is four-part. The imitative entries often change the melodic intervals while maintaining the same rhythm of the initial subject.

Frescobaldi used a number of different sources for his capriccio themes: melodies constructed from the hexachord, popular tunes, aria melodies, musical materials such as durezze (dissonances) and ligature (suspensions), martial or trumpet motifs, and pastoral themes. The theme occurs against many different kinds of counterpoint and in different meters. One capriccio (Capriccio di obligo di cantare, 1626) has an unusual technique, that of using a solo voice without text in combination with the organ; the voice part is an integral part of the composition. Frescobaldi followed this same technique in the ricercar before the elevation toccata in the third Mass of the Fiori Musicali, the Messa della Madonna.

In general, the toccatas are florid. They maintain the same meter and virtuoso character throughout, with partly imitative, partly figurative components. Frescobaldi's liturgical toccatas in Fiori Musicali, however, are brief, simple, slow, and meditative compositions. Brief melodic imitation between the parts is found, but there is no change from four-part texture. There are two toccatas "alla levatione" found in the Secondo Libro, (1637) which are much longer. Chromaticism is used in the slower toccatas for color. Less interesting works are the variations (partite) on popular tunes and dances.

Frescobaldi's attitude toward his compositions, their performance, and their use as didactic works is revealed in the prefaces to his publications. [7]

The compositions of Frescobaldi have a number of striking characteristics, some of which are listed here: frequent changes of meter, chord root movement of seconds and thirds, shifting harmonies, unusual resolutions of dissonances, chord functions in unusual relationships, and rhythmic and melodic alterations of themes.

The sound of Italian organs of the Renaissance was vocal, sweet, silvery, light, quick, and sensitive. Although Italian organs of the sixteenth century usually had only one manual, the richness of principal and flute sonorities avail-

FIORI MUSICALI (1635)

Forms	Messa della Domenica (Orbis factor)	Messa delli Apostoli (Cunctipotens genitor Deus)	Messa della Madonna (Cum jubilo)
liturg. toccata	Toccata	Toccata	Toccata
cantus firmus settings of the sections of plain-song Kyries	Kyries: (Orbis factor) Kyrie: 2 Kyries; 4 Christes; 6 Kyries	Kyrie: 3 Kyries; 2 Christes; 3 Kyries	Kyrie: 2 Kyries; 2 Christes; 2 Kyries
canzonas	Epistle: Canzon dopo la Pistola (Canzona after the Epistle)	Epistle: Canzon dopo la Pistola	Epistle: Canzon dopo la Pistola
ricercari	Credo: Recercar dopo il Credo (Ricercar after the Credo)	Credo: Toccata avanti il Recercar (Toccata before the ricercar); Recercar Cromaticho post il Credo (Chromatic ricercar after the Credo); Altro recercar (another ricercar)	Credo: Recercar dopo il Credo; Toccata avanti il Ricercar; Ricercar con obligo di cantare la quinta parte senza toccarla (Ricercar with the fifth part sung and not played)
liturgical toccatas	Elevation: Toccata Cromaticha per le levatione (Chromatic toccata for the Elevation)	Elevation: Toccata per le levatione Recercar con obligo del Basso come appare (Ricercar with obligatory bass, as is evident)	Elevation: Toccata per le levatione
canzonas	Communion: Canzon post il Comune (Canzona after the Communion)	Communion: Canzon Quarti Toni dopo il Post-Comune (Canzona in the fourth mode after the Post-Communion [Prayer])	Bergamasca; Capriccio sopra la Girolmeta

able provided a wide variety of possibilities for the music of the period. The tonal design of these organs was based upon the ensemble concept and had become somewhat standardized by 1500. Italian organ builders were faithful to this concept for three and a half centuries. The ripieno (organum plenum) was constructed of individual ranks of flutes and principals at various pitches (16', 8', 4', 2 2/3', 2', 1 1/3', 1', 2/3', 1/2', 1/3', 1/4').[8]

Pedals of early Italian organs have been called "pull downs," because the pedals were attached to the lower keys of the manual and, when played by the toes, pulled down the key desired. The pedal compass was no more than two octaves, and the lower octave was what is called a short octave;[9] the upper octave was chromatically complete. One of the earliest Italian organs which had pedals was one built by Fra Domenico di Lorenzo in 1379 for the Annunziata church in Florence; the organ in this church had 12 pedals of a primitive type.

The specification given below is found in Costanzo Antegnati's book as an example of a model organ specification. An organ of this specification was built by a member of the Antegnati family in Brescia.

Brescia, Italy: Old Cathedral, built by
G. G. Antegnati in 1536

50 notes

Principale	16
Principale	16
Ottava	8
Decimaquinta	4
Decimanona	2 2/3
Vigesimaseconda	2
Vigesimasesta	1 1/3
Vigesimanona	1
Trigesima terza	2/3
Flauto in ottava	8
Flauto in decimaquinta	4
Vigesima seconda	2

Pedal: C-c
Lower octave of the second
    Principale 16

The books of Antegnati, Banchieri, and Diruta gave
instruction about registrations which should be used for different types of music, different modes, and for different parts
of the Mass.[10] In general, Italian registration practices for
some of the different forms are as follows: ricercars should
use principals of only unison pitches (8', 4', 2'); toccatas
and intonations use the full sound of the ripieno; canzonas
employ flutes or lighter combinations of flutes and principals;
soft toccatas for the elevation should utilize the delicate sound
of the Voce Umana. The Voce Umana (sometimes called
Fiffaro), however, is not the same as the German Vox Humana or the French Voix Humaine, both of which are regals,
but a principal stop found only in the upper part of the manual. The Voce Umana was usually tuned sharp so that it
would have a gentle undulation when it was combined with
the Principal 8'.

In summary, the Italian imitative forms, especially
the canzona and the ricercar, contributed elements such as
marked rhythmic character and learnedness to the development of the fugue, which led to the fugues of J. S. Bach.
Many German organ composers, who were deeply influenced
by Frescobaldi, drew upon his works for inspiration and
developed certain characteristics into larger forms, such as
the capriccios of Froberger. The influence of Frescobaldi
can be observed to a great extent in the South German school
and to a lesser degree in the Middle German school, both of
which will be studied in subsequent chapters.

Notes

1. Josquin, Janequin, Crecquillon, Sermisy, Lassus, and
   Jacob were the principal composers of the French chanson.
2. Apel suggests that "study" might be a general translation of the word ricercar.
3. Italian composers of the second half of the 1600's who
   contributed to ricercar literature were Giovanni Salvatore (early 1600's-ca. 1688), Bernardo Storace (second
   half, 1600's), Fabrizio Fontana (?-1695), and Bernardo
   Pasquini (1637-1710).
4. The hexachord originated from the initial syllables of
   six successive lines of a hymn to St. John the Baptist.
   The syllables were used by Guido d'Arezzo as an aid
   to memorizing pitches. The pitches were arranged in
   the order of ut (do), re, mi, fa, sol, la (c, d, e, f,
   g, a). Composers such as Frescobaldi, Sweelinck, and

English virginalists selected tones represented by syllables from the hexachord to construct simple themes which were used as bases for compositions.

5. Charlene Polivka Dorsey, "The Fantasie and Ricercari of Girolamo Frescobaldi," American Guild of Organists Quarterly, vol. XII, no. 3 (July 1967), p. 101-105, 122.

6. This type of sectional composition in different meters gave rise to the sectional capriccio or canzona of Frescobaldi's pupil Froberger.

7. The reader is encouraged to study the preface to the Fiori Musicali in the Pidoux translation and the other prefaces to books written by Frescobaldi and provided by Pidoux for information on performance practice.

8. The Regal (Cornamusa or Zampogna) reed stop was added later, perhaps in the seventeenth century. Cantus firmus compositions in which the melody stood out in sharp relief from the other voices by means of a reed stop were composed in northern Europe and France but not in Italy during this period.

9. The short octave was so called because it was incomplete and contained fewer keys than a complete chromatic octave. The E key sounded low C, the F-sharp key D, and the G-sharp key E.

10. Peter Williams, The European Organ 1450-1850, London: Batsford, 1966; p. 214. Also Luigi Ferdinando Tagliavini, "The Old Italian Organ and Its Music," Diapason (February 1966), p. 14-16.

Bibliography

Apel, Willi. "The Early Development of the Organ Ricercare," Musica Disciplina, vol. III (1949), p. 139-150.
_____. "Neopolitan Links between Cabezón and Frescobaldi," Musical Quarterly, vol. XXIV (1938), p. 419-437.

Dart, Thurston. "Cavazzoni and Cabezón," Music and Letters, vol. XXXVI (1955), p. 2-6.

Dorsey, Charlene Polivka. "The Fantasie and Ricercari of Girolamo Frescobaldi," American Guild of Organists Quarterly, vol. XII, No. 3 (July 1967), p. 101.

Frotscher, Gotthold. Geschichte des Orgelspiels und der Orgelkomposition. Berlin: Merseberger Verlag, 1959; vol. I, p. 175-243, 360-377.

Jeppesen, Knud. Die italienische Orgelmusik am Anfang des Cinquecento, 2 vols. Copenhagen: Munksgaard, 1943

(2nd ed. , 1960).

Kratzenstein, Marilou. "A Survey of Organ Literature and
    Editions: Italy," Diapason (February 1972), p. 22-24.

Pidoux, Pierre, ed. Girolamo Frescobaldi Orgel- und
    Klavier Werke. Kassel, Germany: Bärenreiter Verlag,
    1959; vol. V, preface.

Redlich, Hans Ferdinand. "Girolamo Frescobaldi," Music
    Review, vol. XIV (1953), p. 262-274.

Schrade, Leo. "Ein Beitrag zur Geschichte der Tokkata,"
    Zeitschrift für Musikwissenschaft, vol. VIII (1925-1926),
    p. 610-635.

Shannon, John R. "A Short Summary of the Free Organ
    Forms in Italy, 1450-1650," American Guild of Organ-
    ists Quarterly, vol. VI, no. 3 (July 1961), p. 75.

Sutherland, Gordon. "The Ricercari of Jacques Buus,"
    Musical Quarterly, vol. XXXI (1945), p. 448-463.

Tagliavini, Luigi F. "The Old Italian Organ and Its Music,"
    Diapason (February 1966), p. 14-16.

Tusler, Robert L. The Organ Music of Jan Pieterzoon
    Sweelinck, 2 vols. No. 1 of Utrechtse Bijdragen tot
    de Muziekwetenschap, Bilthoven, The Netherlands,
    1958.

Vennum, Thomas, Jr. "The Registration of Frescobaldi's
    Organ Music," Organ Institute Quarterly, vol. II,
    No. 2 (Summer 1964).

3. ENGLAND AND THE NETHERLANDS: 1475-1650

England

Early English keyboard music was designed for organs or virginals, a general term applied to all kinds of harpsichords in England toward the end of the sixteenth century. English church musicians were more interested in choral music than instrumental music and therefore very small organs satisfied their needs in the church. Many English organs of the sixteenth century had only one manual, no pedal, and about six stops. An extract from an indenture made on July 29, 1519, shows that "Antony Duddyngton, Citizen of London, Organ-Maker," agreed to build for All Hallows Church, Barking, "an organ of one stop, called Pryncipale except for its bass, called Diapason, having double pipes, inner and outer, with natural keys only. "[1]

From the time of the separation of the English Church from the Roman Catholic Church the organ in churches often symbolized popery. Puritanism gradually increased within the English Church during the sixteenth century to the extent that Royal Visitors were commissioned to inspect churches' worship practices in order to make recommendations and corrections, which would make the services conform to the will of the high church officials. The Royal Visitors also sometimes abolished use of certain types of music or organist positions. Some high officials in the English church, who were influenced by Calvinist thought, wished to abolish singing and organ playing entirely. The general discouragement of using the organ at services led to the complete disposal of the organ Mass in England toward the middle of the sixteenth century. Although there were brief periods of interest in organs and organists during the reign of Mary and of James I, so many organs were neglected or destroyed that the need for liturgical music for organ was greatly reduced. One of the few churches which was able to continue using an organ in worship was the Chapel Royal, where two organists were often appointed to share the duties. The Chapel Royal was exempt from the jurisdiction of a bishop and was under

HISTORICAL BACKGROUND

1485	Tudor dynasty established
1509-1547	Reign of Henry VIII
1516	Sir Thomas More Utopia
1534	Separation of English Church from Roman Catholic Church
1536	Dissolution of the monasteries
1544	Cranmer, Archbishop of Canterbury, translated and arranged the Litany in English
1549	The Book of Common Prayer
1547-1553	Reign of Edward VI
1553-1558	Reign of Mary Tudor
1558-1603	Reign of Elizabeth I
1562	Sternhold and Hopkins One and Fiftie Psalmes
1564-1616	Shakespeare
1577	Sir Francis Drake began voyage around the world
1588	War between Spain and England; English defeat of the Spanish Armada
1588	Marlowe Doctor Faustus
1590	Edmund Spenser The Faerie Queen
1594	Shakespeare Romeo and Juliet
1601	Shakespeare Hamlet
1603-1625	Reign of James I
1609	Henry Hudson explored Hudson River
1611	King James version of The Bible
1620	Pilgrims arrived at Cape Cod
1625-1649	Reign of Charles I
1630	Puritans established Boston
1649	Commonwealth established; concluded 1660

---

the direct supervision of the sovereign.

An unnamed piece, which has been attributed to John Dunstable (ca. 1385-1453), and a Felix namque seem to be the total of all presently known English organ composition of the fifteenth century. The unauthenticated Dunstable piece is usually in three-part texture and contains a considerable amount of rhythmic variety and syncopation, especially in the lively upper part. Open fifths and octaves occur frequently between parts, and there is no use of imitation.

The melody of the plainsong offertory Felix namque was frequently used as a cantus firmus for organ pieces of the sixteenth and seventeenth century in England.

Example 4.   Felix namque es (Offertory)

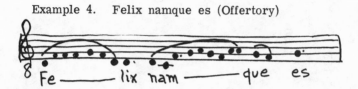

Composers who wrote polyphonic elaborations on this theme included John Redford (ca. 1485-1547), Thomas Tallis (ca. 1505-1585), William Blitheman (ca. 1510-1591), Thomas Preston (ca. 1564-?), and Thomas Tomkins (1572-1656).

Thomas Taverner (ca. 1490-1545) used a plainsong antiphon as the basic melody for his Mass Gloria tibi Trinitas. In the Benedictus of Taverner's Mass this same melody appeared with the text in nomine and subsequently became known as the "in nomine" melody and the inspiration for most of the pieces for organ or viols by that title rather than by its proper title Gloria tibi Trinitas.[2] In nomine and Felix namque compositions were written by English composers only.

Example 5.   Gloria tibi Trinitas (antiphon
                     for Vespers, Trinity)

The one extant example of an English organ setting of the Ordinary of the Mass was written by Philip ap Rhys (sixteenth century). A setting of the Credo is not included in this Mass. The Mass is found in a composite manuscript.[3] Thomas Preston wrote a setting of Mass propers based on Gregorian melodies which follows the alternation principle.

Arrangements of Latin hymns, antiphons, and offer-

ENGLISH ORGAN COMPOSITION: 1475-1650

1300   1400   1500   1600   1650

ca. 1385 Dunstable, J. 1453
ca. 1485 Redford, J. 1547
ca. 1490 Taverner, J. 1545
1497 Tye, Christopher 1572
ca. 1505 Tallis, Thomas 1585
ca. 1510 Blitheman, William 1591
? Thorne, John 1573
? ap Rhys, Philip ?
? Coxsun, Robert ?
ca. 1530 White, R. 1574
ca. 1543 Byrd, William--------1623
ca. 1550 Allwood, Richard ?
ca. 1560 Mulliner Book
1560 Philips, Peter------1628
ca. 1563 Bull, John ----------1628
ca. 1564 Preston, Thomas ?
? Strogers, Nicholas ?
1572 Tomkins, Thomas----------------1656
1583 Gibbons, O.-----1625
Fitzwilliam Virginal Book

tories were common cantus firmus compositions in this period. Some plainsong fantasias were quite long and were actually a series of variations, because the cantus firmus was repeated with different types and styles of accompaniment. The longer fantasias were probably not designed for the liturgical service, but the shorter, easier plainsong fantasias were so designed. One of the earlier English composers, John Redford, used the technique of substituting a melody derived from the original plainsong at the interval of the lower sixth or octave. Redford then used the arranged melody as the cantus firmus for his setting rather than the original plainsong melody. An example of this technique is Redford's O lux on the faburden. At least four of Redford's titles end: "... with a meane" which might refer to the middle part of his three-voice polyphonic composition. The significance of this term is vague, as are the three whole note chords with fermatas at the end of Glorificamus. The middle chord is a discord which seems to have little relation to what has preceded or to what follows. [4] These unusual chords suggest that a keyboard convention might have existed which has not yet been deciphered.

Composers, such as Allwood, Preston, Thorne, and Coxsun, wrote similar compositions based upon Gregorian melodies. Three-part texture seems to have been preferred, and the rhythms frequently change, even as often as from measure to measure, a technique which promotes a restless feeling in the music.

One of the largest sources of sixteenth-century organ literature is called the Mulliner Book (ca. 1560), [5] which was named for its compiler Thomas Mulliner. Redford, Tallis, Allwood, Taverner, and Tye are represented in the collection, of which over half of the pieces are based on sacred melodies. The book contains 120 compositions for organ or virginal (harpsichord) and eleven pieces written in lute tablature. The Mulliner Book also contains dances and two pieces of the prelude type called voluntaries. The voluntary is free and rather improvisatory. In the Mulliner Book the voluntaries are short and written in imitative counterpoint. Some other short pieces which are based on one subject and which are treated imitatively are called points. Voluntaries, points, and verses were appropriate for liturgical use.

The long life of Thomas Tallis spanned the reign of Henry VIII and a major portion of the reign of Elizabeth I.

Most of his keyboard music had a religious character and
was intended for the organ, although it was also playable on
the stringed keyboard instruments.   Most of the pieces by
Tallis are short settings of plainsong melodies and usually
have the melody in the tenor.   The even numbered verses of
Ecce tempus idoneum were written by Tallis as organ settings to be played in alternation with verses one, three, and
five to be sung in unison.   Two compositions by Tallis which
are entitled Felix namque are long pieces; these compositions contain characteristics which denote virginal writing
such as passages of notes of small denomination, scales in
parallel thirds or sixths, and figures built on broken chords.

Late sixteenth- and early seventeenth-century keyboard music in England was centered in virginal books.   Organ music in the early part of the 1500's had been principally of religious character, but later in that century all
keyboard music underwent a gradual secularization.   The
principal virginal collection is the Fitzwilliam Virginal Book,
which contains 297 works by a large number of composers
and exhibits a wide variety of types of compositions.   Although some of these compositions might have been performed on the organ and some show characteristics of organ-
istic writing, the general purpose of the Fitzwilliam Virginal
Book is for performance on stringed keyboard instruments
and not for liturgical use.   Several compositions by Jan
Pieterszoon Sweelinck appear in this collection, a fact which
testifies to the close musical relationship between England
and the Netherlands.

Thomas Tomkins, organist of Worcester Cathedral
from ca. 1596-1646, wrote more than 30 pieces for keyboard
between 1646 and 1654.   About half of these pieces are
dances.   The fancies, voluntaries, or verses are contrapuntal pieces which generally begin with imitative entries,
usually are written in four parts, and are liberally ornamented with dashes (/) and double-dashes (//) which indicate slides and double mordents or trills.   Some of these
pieces are short and others long and sectional.   Many tran-
sient modulations or cadential patterns to near-related keys
are employed.   These pieces show the transition between
vocally written organ works of the sixteenth century and the
compositions which employ rhythmic figures and scale passages for a keyboard instrument and a skillful keyboard
performer. [6]

The disposition of the organ Tomkins played in

Worcester after 1613 is given below (numbers are probable pipe lengths).

Worcester, England, Cathedral. Built Thomas Dallam, 1613.

Great Organ		Chaire Organ[7]	
Two open diapasons	8	Principal	4?
Two principals	4	Diapason	8
Two fifteenths	2	Flute	8
Twelfth	2 2/3	Fifteenth	2
Recorder	8	Two-and-Twentieth	1

Orlando Gibbons (1583-1625) was the outstanding English composer-performer at the turn of the seventeenth century. His works are found in several virginal books of the period and follow the same general style as those of Tomkins. The lines are vocal, usually moving in step-wise motion with few leaps greater than a fourth. [8]

The Netherlands

The Lowlands ("nether lands") covered a wide area in the sixteenth and seventeenth centuries, from what is now northern France, through Belgium and Holland to Denmark. By the marriage of Mary of Brabant to Maximilian the Lowlands became a part of the Holy Roman Empire. In 1555 the Lowlands passed from Emperor Charles V to his son Philip II of Spain, against whom the Netherlands fought for their independence. Toward the latter part of the sixteenth century the Calvinistic northern section of the divided country achieved independence, but the southern part was unable to wrest itself from Spanish rule and stayed within the Catholic fold.

Dutch Protestant clergymen objected to having "popish" organs in the churches, but their objections were to little avail because of the power of the burgomasters, the cities' secular authorities. The city magistrates had the organs built as objects of great municipal pride and in rivalry with other communities, whether church authorities approved or not. Sometimes, in the larger churches, organ recitals were held daily, either before or after the church services. The tradition of organ recitals in Haarlem probably dates from early in the sixteenth century. [9]

HISTORICAL BACKGROUND

After the Norman conquest of England in 1066 the Low Countries were connected ecclesiastically and politically with
France and Germany, economically and culturally with England.

1405	Duchy of Brabant established
1425-1432	University of Louvain founded
	Rise of independent cities; leading merchants formed town councils to govern autonomous cities
1464	Estates-General (representative assemblies) established
1482	Maximilian I, Holy Roman Emperor, became regent of the Netherlands
1511	Erasmus The Praise of Folly
1515-1555	Reign of Charles V, Holy Roman Emperor
1555	Netherlands passed to Philip II of Spain
1566	Brueghel the Elder The Wedding Dance
1567-1573	Duke of Alba, Spanish governor of the Netherlands, sent to enforce the Inquisition and taxation
1568-1648	Eighty Years' War: revolt of Netherlands against Spain organized by William the Silent, founder of the House of Orange
1579	Union of Utrecht joined seven northern provinces
1581	Independence of the Netherlands declared; northern provinces gained independence, southern provinces remained under Spanish rule
1585	Elizabeth of England sent Earl of Leicester to aid the Netherlands
1588	English defeat of the Spanish Armada
1591	Peter Philips' works began to be published in Antwerp
1599-1641	Van Dyck
1602	Dutch East India Company founded
1609-1620	English Pilgrims found refuge in Leiden
1613	John Bull settled in Antwerp
1624	Franz Hals The Laughing Cavalier
1626	Peter Minuit bought Manhattan
1631	Rembrandt The Anatomy Lesson
1632-1675	Jan Vermeer

1642	Rembrandt The Night Watch
1648	Treaty of Westphalia concluded Eighty Years' War with Spain
1664	New Amsterdam became New York
1689	William III of Orange became King of England

The use of the organ in services became more important when singing and chanting were discontinued about the last quarter of the sixteenth century. The organ was used for a new and quite different purpose--accompanying congregational singing on the metrical psalms--by 1649. [10]

The compositions of sixteenth- and seventeenth-century Dutch organ composers included organ hymns, fantasias, fugues, canzonas, ricercars, toccatas, variations on sacred and secular melodies, and dances. The earliest printed Dutch keyboard music was written by Henderick Joostszoon Speuy (ca. 1575-1625). In 1610 Charles Guillet (?-1654) published Vingt Quatre Fantaisies à Quatre Parties Disposées Selon l'Ordre des Douze Modes. The Tabulatur-Boeck by Anthoni van Noordt (?-1675), the organist of the Nieuwe Kerk, Amsterdam, contains fantasies and psalm settings in variations. Abraham van den Kerckhoven (1627-1702) wrote short organ hymns and organ verses in various modes. These short pieces were written in four-part texture, often in imitation.

Jan Pieterszoon Sweelinck (1562-1621) was the most outstanding organist, composer, and teacher in northern Europe during this period. Many organists travelled to Amsterdam to hear him play and to study with him. Since many of his pupils came from Germany, Sweelinck gained the reputation of being a deutscher Organistenmacher, a "maker of German organists." As a composer his works are transitional from the Renaissance to the early Baroque period because he knew the techniques of the sixteenth century and was able to anticipate some of the changes to come in the approaching musical period. His pupils carried on these developments which led to the works of J. S. Bach. His composition style combined figurations and variation techniques of virginal writing with strong contrapuntal writing.

The forms used by Sweelinck were fantasies, toccatas, variations on chorale, secular, and dance melodies, preludes, and ricercars. In his variations the basic melody remains in approximately the same form, but the counterpoint changes from variation to variation or even within the same variation. [11] Rhythmic patterns provide much vitality and interest and often progress

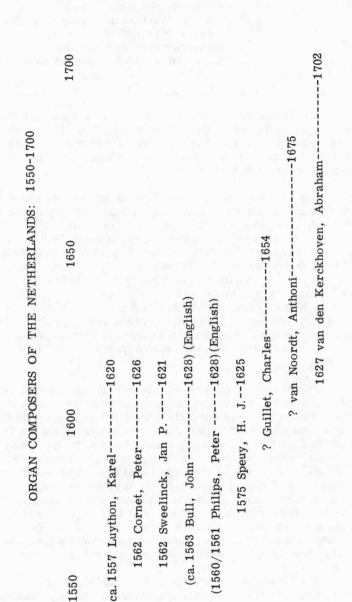

ORGAN COMPOSERS OF THE NETHERLANDS: 1550-1700

1550   1600   1650   1700

ca. 1557 Luython, Karel----------1620

1562 Cornet, Peter----------1626

1562 Sweelinck, Jan P. -----1621

(ca. 1563 Bull, John-----------1628) (English)

(1560/1561 Philips, Peter -----1628)(English)

1575 Speuy, H. J.--1625

? Guillet, Charles----------1654

? van Noordt, Anthoni---------------1675

1627 van den Kerckhoven, Abraham-----------1702

to more active patterns in each successive variation. Sweelinck used chromaticism for added color and maintained a strong tonal center (Ricercar brevis and Fantasia chromatica). He and some of his English contemporaries wrote pieces based upon themes built on various arrangements of the hexachord syllable tones (Fantasia Ut, re, mi, fa, sol, la). Points of imitation are used at the beginning of pieces and at the beginnings of sections. The fantasias and toccatas are Sweelinck's most extended works. In them his writing sometimes resembles works of his English virginalist contemporaries. The echo fantasias utilize dramatic contrasts of volume and quality, which are easily attained at the organ by alternating louder and softer combinations on two manuals. The texture usually encompasses no more than four voices with frequent reduction of the texture to two or three parts. The pedal part of Sweelinck's compositions is never very active because the pedal division of Dutch organs at that time was quite limited.

Sweelinck wrote many variations and allowed the color of various organ stop combinations to add interest to his writing. His variations, like those of Cabezón, do not present the theme in simple form at the beginning, but start immediately with the first variation. The variations on the secular melody Mein junges Leben hat ein' End' are especially interesting.

The specifications are given below of the famous Amsterdam organ which was played by both Sweelinck's father and later by Sweelinck.

Amsterdam, The Netherlands, Oude Kerk.
Built by Hendrik and Herman Niehoff,
and Hans Suys von Köln, 1539-1542

Hoofdwerk (50 notes)	Bovenwerk (41 notes)	Rugwerk (38 notes)
Prestant 16	Prestant 8	Prestant 8
Octaaf 8 (and 4 ?)	Holpijp 8	Octaaf 4
Mixtuur	Openfluit 4	Mixtuur
Scherp	Quintadeen 8(4 ?)	Scherp
	Gemshoorn 2	(Quintadeen 8?)
	Sifflet 1 (1 1/3 ?)	Holpijp 4
	Terscimbel	Kromhoorn 8
	Trompet 8	(Regal 8?)
	Zink	Baarpijp 8
	(Nazard 2 2/3 ?)	Schalmei 4
	Pedaal	(Siffluit ?)

could be coupled to the Hoofdwerk for notes F to d^1.
                    Nachthoorn 2
                    Trompet 8

Couplers: Hoofdwerk to Rugwerk
            Bovenwerk to Rugwerk
Tremulant

        Sweelinck's pupils took home to Germany, Warsaw, and
Danzig their strong impressions of this instrument. In the last
half of the seventeenth century, Dutch organs such as those in
central Holland and in the A-Kerk, Groningen, increased the
size of the pedal division to accommodate new organ music demands. Churches even commissioned new instruments or had
their instruments rebuilt to adapt to the new organ music and
newer uses of the instrument in church services.

        Arp Schnitger was the famous Hamburg builder who
brought the design of the northwest German organ to Holland.
Schnitger's sons built organs of great importance in Zwolle and
Alkmaar. The Pedal and Great divisions of the Alkmaar organ
were built in the German tradition of no duplication of ranks and
full compass of pitches from 32' to 2', in addition to both solo
and chorus stops. [12]

        During Sweelinck's lifetime some English composers
crossed the English Channel for political, religious, or other
reasons. John Bull, one of these English composers, became
a good friend of Sweelinck. Reference has already been made to
the fact that compositions by Sweelinck are found in the Fitzwilliam Virginal Book, which indicates that close musical communication existed between England and the Netherlands. Sweelinck also wrote Pavana Philippi, a set of variations on a pavane
melody by Peter Philips, another English composer who had left
his native land.

        Dr. Bull wrote most of his music for the virginal. His
Prelude and Carol on the Dutch melody Laet ons met herten
reijne contains explicit organ registration markings, probably
the first such exact registration indications, which are found in
red ink in the original manuscript. [13]

                            Notes

1. Margaret Glyn, ed. , Early English Organ Music, Lon-

don: Plainsong and Medieval Music Society, 1939;
preface.

2.   The Allwood In nomine is not based on this melody.
3.   British Museum [B. M.] Add. 29 996.
4.   Taverner also has three whole note chords with fermatas
at the end of an In nomine.
5.   B. M. add. Ms. 30513.
6.   Willi Apel, Geschichte der Orgel- und Klaviermusik bis
1700, Kassel, Germany: Bärenreiter Verlag, 1967;
p. 309-314.
7.   The English term Chaire organ might come from the
fact that this division, which was attached to the gallery rail, furnished a sitting place for the organist
while he played the larger (Great) division.   See John
Fesperman, The Organ as Musical Medium, New York:
Coleman-Ross, 1962; p. 55.   Sumner traces the mean-
ing of the old word chair as a "helper," one who "takes
a turn" and proposes this as one explanation of the
English term Chair Organ, as one which was "turned
to" or one that "took a turn."   See William Leslie
Sumner, The Organ: Its Evolution, Principles of
Construction and Use, 2nd ed. , London: Macdonald,
1955; p. 156.
8.   Willi Apel, Geschichte der Orgel- und Klaviermusik bis
1700, Kassel, Germany: Bärenreiter Verlag, 1967;
p. 314-318.
9.   Peter Williams, The European Organ 1450-1850, London:
Batsford, 1966; p. 27.
10.   Ibid. , p. 37-38.
11.   Research has proved that many of the 24 cycles of
chorale variations which Seiffert included in the 1943
edition of Sweelinck's works were written by composers
other than Sweelinck such as Heinrich Scheidemann,
Henderick Speuy, and possibly Jacob Praetorius.   Although some of the cycles may be incomplete, at least
13 can be considered authentic.   See Sweelinck Opera
Omnia: The Instrumental Works, Amsterdam: Vereniging voor Nederlandse Muziekgeschiedenis, 1968;
vol. I, fasc. II, Introduction.
12.   Peter Williams, The European Organ 1450-1850, London:
Batsford, 1966; p. 41.
13.   John Klein, First Four Centuries of Organ Music, New
York: Assoc. Music Pub. 1948; vol. I, p. 148.

Bibliography

ENGLAND

Apel, Willi. Geschichte der Orgel- und Klaviermusik bis
    1700, Kassel, Germany: Bärenreiter Verlag, 1967;
    p. 21-24, 298-306, 319-337.
_____. Masters of the Keyboard. Cambridge, Mass. :
    Harvard University Press, 1947; p. 56-59.
Benedictines of Solesmes, eds. Liber Usualis. Tournai,
    Belgium: Desclée and Co. , 1950.
Caldwell, John. "Keyboard Plainsong Settings in England,
    1500-1660," Musica Disciplina, vol. XIX (1965), p. 129-53.
_____. "The Pitch of Early Tudor Organ Music," Music
    and Letters, vol. 51, no. 2 (April 1970), p. 156.
Dart, Thurston. "John Bull, 1563-1628," Musical Times,
    no. 1442, vol. 104 (April 1963), p. 252
_____ et al. "Early English Organ Pedals," Musical
    Times, no. 1416, vol. 102 (February 1961), p. 107-9.
Foster, Donald H. "The Organ Music of Thomas Tomkins,"
    Diapason (July 1970), p. 23-25.
Frotscher, Gotthold. Geschichte des Orgelspiels und der
    Orgelkomposition. Berlin: Merseberger Verlag, 1959;
    vol. I, pp. 263-300.
Glyn, Margaret Henrietta. Early English Organ Music.
    London: The Plainsong and Medieval Music Society,
    1939; preface.
le Huray, Peter. Music and the Reformation in England.
    London: Jenkins, 1967.
Lowinsky, Edward E. "English Organ Music of the Renais-
    sance," Musical Quarterly, vol. XXXIX (1953), p. 373-
    395, 528-553.
Marigold, W. G. "An Episode in the Early Development
    of the Organ Pedal," Musical Opinion, no. 1109, vol.
    93 (February 1970), p. 261-263.
Maslen, Benjamin J. "The Earliest English Organ Pedals,"
    Musical Times, no. 1411, vol. 101 (September 1960),
    p. 578.
Mellers, Wilfrid. "John Bull and English Keyboard Music,"
    Musical Quarterly, vol. XL (1954), p. 364-383, 548-71.
Miller, Hugh W. "John Bull's Organ Works," Music and
    Letters, vol. XXVIII (1947), p. 25-35.
_____. "Sixteenth Century English Faburden Compositions
    for Keyboard," Musical Quarterly, vol. XXVI (1940), p. 50.
Pfatteicher, Carl. John Redford, Organist and Almoner of
    St. Paul's Cathedral in the Time of Henry VIII: With
    Especial Reference to His Organ Composition. Leip-
    zig: C. G. Röder, 1934.

Stevens, Denis, ed. <u>Early Tudor Organ Music, II: Music</u>
<u>for the Mass, Early English Church Music</u>, vol. 10.
London: Stainer & Bell, 1969.
_____. "The Keyboard Music of Thomas Tallis," <u>Musical</u>
<u>Times</u>, (July 1952), p. 303-307.
_____. <u>The Mulliner Book: A Commentary</u>. London:
Stainer and Bell, 1952.
_____. "Organists and Organ Music of Tudor Times,"
<u>American Guild of Organists Quarterly</u>, vol. V, no. 2
(April 1960), p. 43-47.
_____. "Pre-Reformation Organ Music in England,"
<u>Proceedings of the Royal Musical Association</u>, vol.
LXXVII (1952), p. 1-10.
_____. "Thomas Preston's Organ Mass," <u>Music and</u>
<u>Letters</u>, vol. XXXIX (1958), p. 29-34.
_____. <u>Thomas Tomkins</u>. New York: St. Martin's
Press, 1957.
_____. <u>Tudor Church Music</u>. New York: Merlin Press,
1955.
_____. "A Unique Tudor Organ Mass," <u>Musica Disciplina</u>,
vol. VI (1952), p. 167-175.
West, John E. "Old English Organ Music," <u>Proceedings of</u>
<u>the Musical Association</u>, vol. XXXVII (1911), p. 1-16.
Young, Clyde William. "Keyboard Music to 1600," <u>Musica</u>
<u>Disciplina</u>, vol. XVII (1963), p. 185-187.
(Also see the following articles in the <u>Harvard Dictionary of</u>
<u>Music</u>: "Felix namque," "In nomine," "Virginal
Book," Organ hymn section in "Organ Chorale," and
"Meane."

THE NETHERLANDS

Curtis, Alan. <u>Sweelinck's Keyboard Music: A Study of</u>
<u>English Elements in Seventeenth-Century Dutch Com-</u>
<u>position</u>. New York: Oxford University Press, 1969.
Tusler, Robert L. <u>The Organ Music of Jan Pieterzoon</u>
<u>Sweelinck</u>, 2 vols. No. I of <u>Utrecht Bijdragen tot de</u>
<u>Muziekwetenschap</u>. Bilthoven, The Netherlands:
Creyghton, 1958.
_____. "Style Differences in the Organ and Clavicembalo
Works of Jan Pieterszoon Sweelinck," <u>Tydschrift voor</u>
<u>Musikwetenshap</u>, vol. XVII (1959), p. 149-166.
Williams, Peter. "Sweelinck and the Dutch School," <u>Musical</u>
<u>Times</u>, no. 1522, vol. 110 (December 1969), p. 1286-
1288.

4. SPAIN AND PORTUGAL: 1500-1600

At the turn of the sixteenth century small positive organs existed in Spain. The disposition of a positive sometimes used in processions is given below.

León, Spain, Cathedral. Positive organ,
ca. 1550?, divided, with no pedal.

Left Hand stops	Right Hand stops
Flautado 8	Flautado 8
Octava 4	Octava 4
Lleno	Lleno
	Corneta

An important sixteenth-century organ was the so-called Emperor's Organ in the Cathedral of Toledo. The instrument was designed along conservative lines which resembled the organs planned according to the Blockwerk principle about 1450 and offered little variety in sound quality. The chorus ranks, moreover, were not separated as in Italian organs, which made the Spanish organ much less versatile. The Toledo organ, which was begun by Gonzalo Hernandéz de Córdoba and finished by Juan Gaytan between 1543 and 1549, had two chests and possibly two manuals. The Main chest supported the Blockwerk (Principal 16', Flautado 8', partial stopped 8' rank, Octave, and eight or nine other ranks) plus another mixture, which contained from eight to 28 ranks. The second chest supported a Principal 8' and a mixture. The pedal consisted of 13 keys which played the lowest chromatic octave of the Principal 16'.[1]

The strong influence of Italian musicians was felt throughout Europe during the sixteenth century. The leading musicians from Germany, the Lowlands, and the Iberian peninsula were willing to endure the hardships of travel to

HISTORICAL BACKGROUND

1491-1556	Ignatius de Loyola
1492	Unification of Spain; Ferdinand and Isabella
1492	First voyage of Columbus to America
1497	Vasco da Gama sailed to India
ca. 1509-1586	Morales
1513	Balboa discovered the Pacific Ocean
1515-1582	St. Teresa
1518	Cortes' conquest of Mexico
1519	Magellan sailed around the world
1519-1555	Charles V ruled as Holy Roman Emperor
1540	Society of Jesus founded by Loyola
ca. 1541-1614	El Greco
1541	de Soto discovered the Mississippi River
1545	Council of Trent convened; concluded 1563
1555-1598	Reign of Philip II
1568	Revolt of the Netherlands began
1571	Naval battle of Lepanto
1588	War between Spain and England
1588	Defeat of the Spanish Armada
1605	Cervantes Don Quixote, Part I
1605	Thomas Luis da Victoria Requiem

gain inspiration and instruction from musicians in Italy. Naples belonged to the Spanish crown from 1503 until 1707, and Spanish musicians traveled in other European countries in the retinue of their royal patrons. It was natural, therefore, that there should be close relationships between Italian and Spanish music of the period.

In addition to dances and intabulations of chansons and motets the musical forms and types used by keyboard composers of the Iberian peninsula were tientos (the Spanish counterpart of the Italian ricercar;   Portuguese, tento), organ hymns, psalm and Magnificat versets, variations, and Mass movements, forms which were employed at the same time by composers in Italy.   Keyboard music was written for both harpsichords and organs.

The Spanish composer F. de la Torre (ca. 1500-?) wrote a basse danse called Alta in which the two lower parts

move slowly under a quickly moving soprano part.   The
tenor is the basic melody part around which the other parts
are built. [2]

Most of our knowledge about Spanish musical practices of the sixteenth century is drawn from texts written by
two theorists, Juan Bermudo (fl. 1500's) and Fray [Brother]
Tomás de Santa [Sancta] Maria (?-1570).   Bermudo's work
is entitled Declaración de instrumentos musicales (Osuna,
1549, 1555).   Musical compositions in the work included
settings of liturgical melodies and hymn arrangements.

Tomás de Santa Maria's work Libro llamado Arte de
taner fantasia assí para tecla como para vihuela (Valladolid,
1565) is similar in theoretical content.   His compositions
are no longer than 40 or 50 measures and illustrate the
technique of writing in two, three, and four parts.   These
pieces employ strict imitation and are simple, direct, and
dignified.   Tomás principally used notes of larger denomination.   The imitative entries always appear after discreet
intervals, and the four parts establish strong cadences.
After cadences thinner textures present more imitation which
grows naturally from the preceding material.

The first of two printed collections of Spanish keyboard music is the Libro de cifra nueva para tecla, harpa
y vihuela (Alcalá de Henares, 1557) compiled by Luys Venegas de Henestrosa.   It contains Spanish pieces, intabulations
of both French and Spanish composers' vocal writings, and
some Italian instrumental music.   The Spanish composers
represented are Francisco Perez Palero, Pedro de Soto,
Pedro [Pere] Vila (1517-1582), and Antonio, who was probably Cabezón (1510-1566).   The Italian composer represented
was Giulio Segni (1498-1561).   Some of the tientos consisted
of polyphonic writing throughout.   Other tientos only begin
with imitative entries and continue without using any particular polyphonic devices.   Latin hymn settings are included
which contain several different styles of writing such as
scale passages, imitative sections, decoration going from
part to part, and the melody part played above an active
lower part or between two other voices.   Mass movements
and versos (psalm or Magnificat versets) were written in
these same ways.   Venegas de Henestrosa rearranged the
music; this is especially noticeable in the transcriptions of
vihuela (stringed instrument) and lute music.   The Christmas
carol from this collection employs double canon as its primary unifying element.

SPANISH AND PORTUGUESE ORGAN COMPOSITION: 1500-1600

1500   1550   1600

SPAIN

ca. 1500 de la Torre, F. ?
1500 Cabezón, Antonio de------------------------1566
ca. 1500 de Soto, Francisco------------------------1563
    ca. 1510 Bermudo, Juan   ?
        1510/1520 Santa María, Tomás de------------------------------1570
        1517 Vila, Pedro Alberto------------------------------------1582
    before 1520 Mudarra, Alonso ------------------------------------1580
                        ? Jimenez ?
                    ca. 1550 Paléro, Francisco Fernandez ?
                    1557 Libro de Cifra Nueva para tecla, harpa y vihuela
                        1560/1570 Aguiléra de Herédia, Sebastián--after 1620
                        1564 Peraza, Francisco------1598

PORTUGAL

    ? Yepes ?
    ca. 1525 Carreira, Antonio------------------------------------1587/1597

The music by Antonio Cabezón is generally somber
and reserved. Twelve years after his death Antonio's son,
Hernando, published Obras de Música para tecla, arpa y
vihuela (Madrid, 1578). This collection contains compositions
principally by Antonio, but there are a few by Hernando and
one selection by Antonio's brother Juan.

In addition to tientos Cabezón wrote variations
(diferencias) on popular secular tunes, harmonized settings
(versillos) of all eight psalm tones, Magnificat settings
in eight tones (fabordone y glosas), some plainsong hymn
settings, and decorated intabulations of pre-existing chansons or motets. In Spain these were called glosas.
Cabezón wrote several sets of variations. Different polyphonic settings on the same theme presented in different
voices provided an opportunity to demonstrate his great
contrapuntal ability. The themes for the variations
were so well known that the composition begins, not
with the theme, but with the first variation. Examples
of this practice are the diferencias on El Canto llano
del Caballero, on La Pavana Italiana, and on Guardáme las
vacas. In the Caballero piece there are five variations:
in variation one the melody is stated simply in the soprano
voice; variation two offers the melody in the soprano part
slightly decorated; variation three has the unembellished
melody in the tenor; variation four has the melody in the
alto; variation five is in three-part texture with the melody
in the lowest part. La Pavana Italiana progresses smoothly
from variation to variation, but keeps the melody in the
uppermost part and sometimes decorated. Another series
of variations following this type with decorated melody remaining in the soprano is Diferencias sobre la Gallarda
Milanesa. Other characteristics of Cabezón's variations
are that they flow continuously from one to the other, they
fluctuate between modal and tonal harmonies, and, although
the writing is always contrapuntal, little imitation is employed.

Cabezón freely glossed such pieces as Josquin des
Pres' motet Ave Maria and Philippe Verdelot's Ultimi mei
suspiri and Ardenti mei suspiri. Here his imagination encouraged him to add much decorative material to the instrumental transcription, extending the length beyond that of
the original.

The liturgical compositions of "the Spanish Bach" fall
into two general categories, hymns and the versos (versillos).

The hymns are short, with some independence of the three
or four parts permitted. Cabezón wrote four settings for
each psalm tone. In each instance he first wrote a setting
with the melody in the soprano. The second setting has the
melody in the alto, the third in the tenor, and the fourth in
the bass. He has similarly arranged the Magnificat verses
with at least six settings on each tone, frequently employing
points of imitation.

Less significant composers used the prevailing forms
for their keyboard works. Alonso Mudarra (1506-1580) was
a contemporary of Cabezón. In one 16-measure tiento by
Mudarra imitation is not used. Its principal interest lies
in the harmony and might have been more appropriately
played on the harp. Pere Alberch Vila (1517-1582) wrote a
tiento which is highly unified. Vila's tiento uses imitative
devices and is in motet style.

A Tiento de sexto tono by Pedro de Soto (fl. 1500's)
alternates between two-part and four-part texture, and the
counterpoint grows from the harmonic background. A similar composition is one by Francisco Fernandez Palera[o]
(fl. 1500's) entitled Versillo de octavo tono. The Medio
registro alto de primer tono by Francisco Peraza (1564-
1598) offers the opportunity to use a different quality of
sound in the right hand solo part from the left hand accompaniment. This was possible on Spanish and Italian instruments in which certain stops were available for the upper
register of one manual, and different stops were available
for the lower register on the same manual. Sebastián
Aguiléra de Herédia (1570-?) is represented by a work of
large dimension and great variety of mood in his Obra de
octavo tono alto.

A work which contains contrasting musical ideas is
the Tiento de cuarto tono por E la mi a modo de Canción
by Francisco Correa de Arauxo (1576?-1663). Three sections begin with imitative entries, but an interlude and the
final section have quite different rhythmic and melodic character from that of the standard tiento.

The Portuguese Yepes (fl. 1500's) glossed one of
Thomas Crequillon's chansons, Je Prens en Gre. Ornamentation is added where long notes are sustained by the voices
in the original.

In addition to versets Jiminez (fl. 1500's) wrote a

Batalla de sexto tono. Battle pieces were popular program pieces of the sixteenth and seventeenth centuries, which suggested the drama of war by imitating the cries of the wounded, the general confusion, trumpet fanfares, drum rolls, and the exchange of gunfire. Repeated notes on one pitch, answering back and forth between voices on extremely simple, primary harmonies, and sections of changing meters were musical characteristics of these battle pieces.

Notes

1. Peter Williams, The European Organ 1450-1850, London: Batsford, 1966; p. 236-237.
2. Archibald T. Davison and Willi Apel, eds., Historical Anthology of Music, Cambridge, Mass.: Harvard University Press, 1946; vol. I, p. 227.

Bibliography

Anderson, Poul-Gerhard. Organ Building and Design, translated into English by Joanne Curnutt. New York: Oxford University Press, 1969; p. 156-159.

Apel, Willi. "Early Spanish Music for Lute and Keyboard Instruments," Musical Quarterly, vol. XX (1934), p. 289-301.

_____. "Spanish Organ Music of the Early 17th Century," Journal of the American Musicological Society, vol. XV (1962), p. 174-181.

Dart, Thurston. "Cavazzoni and Cabezón," Music and Letters, vol. XXXVI (1955), p. 2-6.

Frotscher, Gotthold. Geschichte des Orgelspiels und der Orgelkomposition. Berlin: Merseberger Verlag, 1959; vol. I, p. 243-263.

Howell, Almonte C. "Cabezón: An Essay in Structural Analysis," Musical Quarterly, L (1964), p. 18-30.

Kastner, Santiago. Cravistas Portuguezes, 2 vols. Mainz, Germany: B. Schotts Söhne, 1935-1950.

Kratzenstein, Marilou. "A Survey of Organ Literature and Editions: Spain and Portugal," Diapason (October 1971), p. 22-24.

Sharp, G. B. "Antonio de Cabezón," Musical Times, no. 1485, vol. 107 (November 1966), p. 955; and no. 1486, vol. 107 (December 1966), p. 1053.

Speer, Klaus. "The Organ Verso in Iberian Music up to 1700," Journal of the American Musicological Society, vol. XI (1958), p. 189-199.

Stevenson, Robert Murrell. Juan Bermudo. The Hague:
    Nijhoff, 1960.
Williams, Peter. The European Organ 1450-1850. London:
    B. T. Batsford, 1966; p. 235-244.
Young, Clyde William. "Keyboard Music to 1600," Musica
    Disciplina, vol. XVII (1963), p. 179, 182-189.

5. NORTH GERMAN SCHOOL: 1600-1725

Chorale-Based Works

It is astounding to observe how prolific the German composers of the first half of the seventeenth century were and to discover the high quality of their compositions when one remembers that the bulk of these composers' work was done in the midst of the ravages of the Thirty Years' War (1618-1648). The initiator of the North German School of organ literature was the Dutchman Sweelinck, whose most famous pupils were Jacob Praetorius (1586-1651) and Heinrich Scheidemann (ca. 1596-1663) in Hamburg, Melchior Schildt (1592/93-1667) in Hannover, Paul Siefert (1586-1666) in Danzig, Anders (Andreas) Düben II (ca. 1590-1662), who settled in Stockholm, and the illustrious Samuel Scheidt (1587-1654) of Halle. Two other students of Sweelinck were Peter Hasse the Elder (ca. 1585-1640) and Gottfried Scheidt (1593-1661). Most of these composers wrote with simplicity of style and seriousness of purpose.

Chorale literature is the body of German hymnody of the Lutheran Church. Sources of chorale melodies were plainsong, secular songs, pre-Reformation sacred songs, and newly composed melodies. Authors of texts for chorales include Martin Luther (1483-1546), Leonhard Lechner (ca. 1550-1606), composer-poet Philipp Nicolai (1556-1608), Martin Rinkart (1586-1649), Paul Gerhardt (1607-1676), Johann Rist (1607-1667), and Joachim Neander (1650-1680).

The congregation of Lutheran churches first sang the chorale in unison and unaccompanied. Toward the end of the sixteenth century the choir led the congregation in the singing of the chorales. About 1650 the organ began to accompany the congregational singing. When choir, congregation, and organ combined forces on the chorales, the alternation between organ and congregation on different stanzas of the chorale fell into disuse, although the alternation practice is encouraged in some churches today. [1]

HISTORICAL BACKGROUND

1546	Death of Martin Luther
ca. 1550-1606	Leonhard Lechner
1556-1608	Philipp Nicolai, chorale composer-author
1585-1672	Heinrich Schütz
1586-1649	Martin Rinkart, author of chorale texts
1605	M. Praetorius Musae Sionae
1607-1676	Paul Gerhardt, author of chorale texts
1607-1667	Johann Rist, author of chorale texts
1617	Schein Banchetto musicale
1618-1677	Johann Franck
1618-1648	Thirty Years' War, Catholics vs. Protestants
1619	Praetorius Syntagma musicum
1623	Schütz Historia der ... Auferstehung
1624	Scheidt Tabulatura Nova
1629	Schütz Symphoniae Sacrae I
1637-1657	Reign of Ferdinand III, Holy Roman Emperor
1640	Frederick William became Elector of Brandenburg
1645	Hammerschmidt Dialogues; Schütz Seven Last Words
1646-1716	Gottfried Leibnitz, philosopher
1647	Johann Crüger Praxis pietatis melica
1650-1680	Joachim Neander, hymnwriter
1650	Scheidt Görlitzer Tabulatur-Buch
1664	Schütz Christmas Oratorio
1685-1750	Bach
1685-1759	Handel
1689	Kuhnau Clavier sonatas
1700-1746	Reign of Philip V of Spain
1701	Frederick I of Prussia crowned
1704	Telemann founded Collegium musicum(Leipzig)
1711-1740	Reign of Charles VI, Holy Roman Emperor
1722	Zinzendorf reestablished Moravian Brotherhood
1724-1804	Immanuel Kant
1725	Fux Gradus ad Parnassum
1731	Treaty of Vienna
1740-1786	Reign of Frederick the Great of Prussia
1742-1745	Reign of Charles VII, Holy Roman Emperor
1745	Stamitz went to Mannheim
1748	War of Austrian Succession ended
1749-1832	Goethe
1750	Quantz Flute concertos
1755	Graun Der Tod Jesu
1759-1805	Schiller
1759	Haydn First Symphony
1770-1827	Beethoven
1791	Mozart Requiem
1798	Haydn Creation

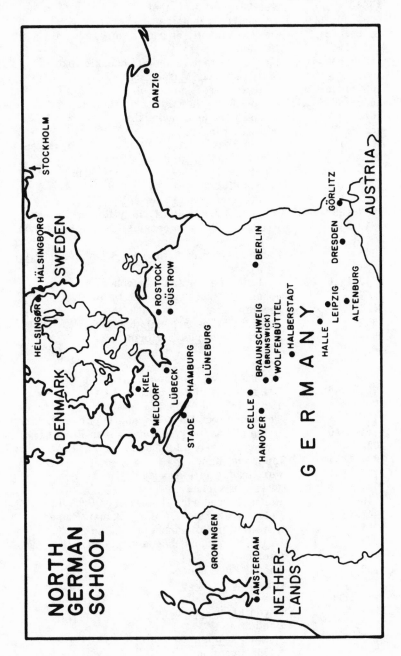

The use of chorale melodies as cantus firmi of organ
compositions developed into three general types of chorale
settings: a series of variations (chorale partita), an extended treatment of each phrase of the chorale melody continuously in a variety of ways (chorale fantasia), and shorter
pieces with the melody of one stanza of the chorale rather
clearly emphasized (chorale prelude or organ chorale).   The
chorale prelude was played as an introduction to the congregational singing of the chorale, but later all organ arrangements based upon chorale melodies were called chorale preludes, whether they were played before the congregation sang
the chorale or in some other function.

Most of Sweelinck's chorale-based works were variations on chorale melodies and usually included several of the
following types of treatment in various combinations: a simple four-part setting of the tune, with the melody in the soprano part; a two-part setting with the chorale melody as
one of the parts (bicinium) or trio setting (hands on two
manuals, with or without pedal), which employed rhythmic
figures, both eighth-note and 16th-note scale passages, and
repeated rhythmic patterns outlining the harmony; use of
parallel thirds, sixths, or tenths, which were often varied
by being changed into stereotyped, virginalistic figures of
broken thirds, which were carried into numerous and sometimes monotonous sequences; and free contrapuntal treatment
of the voices with the melody in any voice.

Sweelinck's most famous pupil was Samuel Scheidt,
and many of Scheidt's compositional techniques can be traced
directly to Sweelinck's influence.   Scheidt spent most of his
life in the small university town and cultural center of Halle
where, although his principal responsibility was to the ducal
court, he served churches as well.   The works of Scheidt
display great clarity, even though they are not oversimplified,
and include use of imitation, chromatic alteration, and, in
chorale or Latin hymn settings, the cantus firmus is always
clear and distinct from the other parts.   Unlike many litur-
gically oriented organ books the chorale and hymn settings of
Scheidt are not arranged in order according to the church
year.

Scheidt's very important Tabulatura nova appeared in
1624 in three parts.   In this work he employed the Italian
method of writing for the keyboard, called partitura, which
placed each voice line on a separate staff.   At the end of
the third part of Tabulatura nova a number of interesting

NORTH GERMAN SCHOOL OF ORGAN COMPOSITION: 1600-1725

1550	1600	1650	1700	1750	1800

(1562 Sweelinck--1621)
ca. 1585 Hasse, P. the elder 1640
1586 Siefert, Paul------------1666
1586 Praetorius, Jacob-----1651
1587 Scheidt, Samuel-------1654
ca. 1590 Düben, Anders II----1662
1592/93 Schildt, M. ------1667
1593 Scheidt, Gottfried ----1661
ca. 1596 Scheidemann, H. -----1663
1596 Decker, Johann ------1668
? Abel, David 1639
? Meyer, D. ?
1601 Strungk, Delphin--------1694
? Olter, Marcus ?
1613/14 Karges, Wilhelm 1699
1614 Tunder, Franz 1667
1621 Weckmann, M. 1674
1623 Reincken, Johann Adam---------1722
1626 Flor, Christian 1697
1629 Capricornus (Bockshorn), S. 1665
1637 Buxtehude, Dietrich 1707
1649 Kneller, Andreas---------1724
Middle seventeenth century Lüneburg Tablatures
? Hasse, Peter, the younger ?
1654 Lübeck, Vincent--------------1740
1661 Böhm, Georg------------1733
1664 Leyding, G. 1710
1665 Bruhns, N. 1697
1665 Hanff, Johann 1711/12
ca. 1670 Brunckhorst, A. --1720
1681 Telemann, Georg P.--------------1767

instructions on registration and playing are given for the
organist. Scheidt stated that these pieces were written for
an organ with two manuals and pedal, and he emphasized
that the melody must be brought out on a strong stop in
order to be understood clearly [". . . auff den Rückposetif mit
einer scharffen Stimme (den Choral desto deutlicher zu
vernehmen) spielen . . . den Bass mit dem Pedal"], the bass
part played in the pedal. He indicated different methods of
playing the pieces, what to avoid when assigning both the
tenor and bass to the feet, and registration suggestions.

Scheidt's Instructions
from Tabulatura nova,

Part III

To the Organists.

    These Magnificats and hymns as well as several
Psalms to be found in the first and second parts of my
Tabulatura nova can be played on any organ with two
manuals and pedal, the melody being in the soprano or
tenor particularly on the Rückpositiv with a sharp stop
so that one hears the chorale melody even more clearly.
If it is a bicinium and if the chorale melody is in the
soprano, one plays the melody with the right hand on
the upper manual or the Great manual and the second
part with the left hand on the Rückpositiv. If the melody is in the highest of four parts, one plays the melody on the Rückpositiv with the right hand, the alto and
tenor on the upper manual or on the Great with the left
hand, and the bass with the pedal. If the melody is in
the tenor, one plays it on the Rückpositiv with the left
hand and the other parts on the upper manual or on the
Great with the right hand, and the bass in the pedal.
    Within four parts the alto can also be played on
the Rückpositiv but one should take the soprano on the
upper manual with the right hand, and play the tenor
and bass on the pedal, the two voices simultaneously.
But in addition it must be arranged that the tenor is
not higher than c^1 because one seldom finds the d^1 on
the pedal and the two voices cannot be set too far apart
for the octave, fifth or third, otherwise they cannot be
reached with the feet.

N. B.

However, the most beautiful and easiest arrangement is to play the alto in the pedal; there is also an
advantage for the hands as far as the stops of the organ are concerned because one can distinguish between
4' and 8' tone. The 8' tone must always be on the
Positiv and 4' tone in the pedal ... Various registrations or stop combinations to pull if one wishes to play
a chorale on two manuals in a manner so that it can
be heard distinctly:
On the Great: Grob Gedact 8', Klein Gedact 4',
these two together, or Principal 8' alone, and other
stops or combinations according to one's taste.
On the Positiv: a sharp stop to bring out the
chorale clearly. Quinta dehn or Gedact 8', Klein Gedact or Principal 4', Mixtur or Zimmel or Superoctaf,
these stops together or other combinations according
to one's taste.
In the Pedal to bring out the chorale distinctly:
Untersatz 16', Posaunen Bass 8' or 16', Dulcian Bass
8' or 16', Schalmei, Trommete, Bauer Flöte, Cornet
and other stops which are often found in small and
large organs. All this I have put down for the sake
of those who do not yet know such a way of performance and yet want to make use of it, also for the
sake of other noble and knowledgeable organists who,
however, may make use of it at their discretion.
Vale.

Luther's associate Justus Jonas might have prepared
the Kirchenordnung (Church-Ordinance) for Halle, of which
only a fragment exists today. The instructions given in the
Kirchenordnung apply more to the singing of the choir than
to the singing of the congregation. The use of Latin in
Lutheran churches was quite common for more than a century after Luther's death, although the practice was gradually
being discarded. Choirs often sang Latin hymns which had
no German translations at that time. German was used much
more after the end of the Thirty Years' War, but the Halle
city council did not completely discard the use of Latin in
Lutheran services until 1702. [2] Thus, the Magnificat was
sung in Latin, as were a number of other portions of the
service. Since St. Moritz, the church in which Scheidt was
organist, was the youngest and least favored place of worship in the city when special music was called for at festivals,

Samuel Scheidt: Tabulatura Nova (1624)

PART I

4 variation cycles on chorale melodies (Nos. 1, 3, 5, 12)
3 fantasias: continuous pieces but sectional according to changing rhythms (Nos. 2, 4, 13)
3 dances: variations on a passamezzo (No. 6); two courantes (Nos. 8, 9)
3 variation cycles on secular melodies (Nos. 7, 10, 11)
12 canons on chorale melodies, a hexachord melody, psalm tones, Latin hymn melodies (No. 14)

PART II

2 fugues (Nos. 1, 3)
2 echo pieces (No. 2)
3 variation cycles on chorale melodies (Nos. 4, 5, 9)
2 fantasias (one listed as a toccata) (Nos. 6, 12)
1 variation cycle on a secular melody (No. 8)
2 variation cycles on dances: allemands (Nos. 10, 11)
1 variation cycle on a Latin hymn melody (No. 7)

PART III

1 set of alternation verses on Kyrie and Gloria (No. 1)
9 sets of six versets on reciting tones of Magnificat; the ninth is on the Tonus peregrinus (Nos. 2-10)
6 variation cycles on Latin hymn melodies (Nos. 11-16)
1 setting of the Credo (Wir glauben) with the melody in only the bass part (No. 17)
1 variation cycle on a chorale melody (No. 18)
2 pieces for full organ (organo pleno) (Nos. 19, 20)
Instructions on how to play and how to register the organ pieces

the organ often had to substitute for a less musically
able choir.   This might explain why there were a number of
Scheidt settings of the Magnificat.

        Toward the end of Scheidt's life the publishing of his
Tabulatur-Buch was subsidized by the town council of Görlitz
in 1650.   This volume contains the harmonizations of 100
chorales, which Scheidt believed to be the most widely used
in Germany at that time.   Scheidt's Tabulatur-Buch was similar to many cantionals published about this time by such
composers as Raselius, Calvisius, Hassler, and Eccard.
In cantionals the chorale melody was placed in the uppermost
voice part and was harmonized in simple, homophonic settings.   The Tabulatur-Buch can hardly have served as a
Choralbuch, since a congregation would find it difficult to
sing to these harmonizations,[3] and it differs a great deal
from other chorale books of the time.   However, it contains
four-part organ settings of chorale melodies which could well
have been used in alternation with congregational singing,
with the organ playing every other stanza.   The Mecklenburg
Kirchenordnung (1650) says: "Where organs are available,
there should the organist play every other stanza."   The organ solo verses were played in a variety of styles: iso-
metric or rhythmic, highly decorated or plain, or in different harmonizations.[4]

        Other North German pupils of Sweelinck such as
Düben, Scheidemann, and J. Praetorius incorporated imitative entries developed from the initial chorale phrase melody
in the lower three parts.   When the final voice enters (usually the fourth voice), the melody is very simply stated in
notes of long value or occasionally, as in some of Praetorius' writing, the melody becomes highly ornamented.   In
some of Heinrich Scheidemann's chorale settings the melody
is frequently presented in long notes in the pedal.   Scheidemann also sometimes indicated manual changes for echo effects, one of Sweelinck's most characteristic idioms.   Andreas Kneller (1649-1724) and Vincent Lübeck (1654-1740)
also wrote chorale works in a series of variations similar
to examples of the Sweelinck school.   Nikolaus Bruhns
(1665-1697) contributed a long, sectional chorale fantasia on
Nun komm der Heiden Heiland ("Now Comes the Gentiles'
Saviour") which contains a wealth of musical ideas.

        Franz Tunder (1614-1667), organist of the Marien-
kirche, Lübeck, showed how the florid, virtuoso writing of
the North German School was incorporated into chorale-

based works.   Some of his musical characteristics are
flourishes of rapid 16th-notes at the beginning of his chorale
settings (a technique also found in compositions of his son-
in-law, Dietrich Buxtehude), use of double pedal, echo passages, brief imitative sections drawn from inner phrases of
the chorale melody, and a wide variety of compositional devices applied to the chorale phrases throughout the piece.
Tunder contributed considerably to the development of the
chorale fantasia;   an excellent example is his lengthy work
on Komm, Heiliger Geist, Herre Gott ("Come,   Holy Ghost,
Lord God").

      Dietrich Buxtehude (1637-1707) wrote most of his
chorale settings for two manuals and pedal.   The format is
usually limited to a short, concentrated setting of only one
stanza (the shortest one is only 21 measures long).   Three
present the melody with little or no decoration.   Coloratura
(highly embellished) treatments are the most frequent, in
which ornaments, pauses, and rests in the middle of phrases
heighten the interest and make Buxtehude's style personal.
Tiny interludes separate the various phrases.   With the
melody in the right hand the accompanying parts make use
of Vorimitation[5] and develop simple and naturally the accompanying style already begun.   The chorale settings by Buxtehude are subjective, warmly expressive, and full of flights
of imagination inspired by the melody itself and a word or
phrase of the chorale text.   His sound-painting employs
chromaticism to depict words such as "pain," "death," or
"sin. "

      Buxtehude's chorale variations sometimes have the
melody clearly delineated, sometimes decorated.   The variations on Auf meinen lieben Gott ("In My Beloved God") form
a small suite, with the melody treated in different dance
styles (sarabande, courante, and gigue).   The chorale fantasias were probably used to conclude the church services.
One extended fantasia presents the melody in richly varied
forms and styles including sections in imitative counterpoint,
florid 16th-note scale passages, flowing or broken thirds,
sixths or tenths, independent pedal parts, triplet or gigue
sections,[6] echo effects, and sections which change meter or
were like ricercars.

      The specifications of the Lübeck organ, which both
Tunder and Buxtehude played, are given on the following
page.

Lübeck, Germany, Marienkirche "Totentanz"
sacristy Chapel organ.

Brustwerk	Hauptwerk
built by Henning Kröger, 1621-1622	partially built by J. Stephani, 1475-1477

Brustwerk	Hauptwerk
Gedackt 8'	Quintadena 16'
Quintadena 4'	Prinzipal 8'
Hohlflöte 2'	Oktave 4'
Quint 1 1/3'	Mixture VIII-X
Scharff IV	Quintade 16'
Krummhorn 8'	Spitzflöte 8'
Schalmey 4'	Nasat 2 2/3'
	Rauschpfeife II
	Trompete 8'

Rückpositiv	Pedal
built by Jacob Scherer, 1557-1558	1475-1477, 1621-1622

Rückpositiv	Pedal
Prinzipal 8'	Principal 16'
Oktave 4'	Oktave 8'
Scharff VI-VIII	Oktave 4'
Quintatön 8'	Oktave 2'
Rohrflöte 8'	Mixture IV
Rohrflöte 4'	Zimbel II
Sesquialtera II	Subbass 16'
Sifflöte 1 1/3'	Gedackt 8'
Dulzian 16'	Quintaton 4'
Trechterregal 8'	(Nachthorn 1' ?)
	Posaune 16'
Coupler: Rückpositiv/Hauptwerk	(Dulzian 16' ?)
Tremulant	Trompet 8'
	Schalmey 4'
	Kornett 2'

The strong influence of Buxtehude is suggested in the
chorale compositions of Johann Nicolaus Hanff (1665-1711/12)
by the coloratura settings of only one stanza, imitative entries on the melodies of successive chorale phrases, and
other characteristics, such as the florid codetta at the end
of Wär Gott nicht mit uns diese Zeit ("If God Be for Us").

Nine out of 14 chorale-based works by Georg Böhm (1661-1733) are in the form of variations. Each variation is called a partita, a versus, or a variatio. Some of the variations suggest performance on stringed keyboard instruments rather than on organs, for they can be performed without pedal (manualiter, i. e. , on manuals alone) and resemble Böhm's suites for stringed keyboard instruments.

The final important North German composer of the organ chorale considered here is the Hamburg organist Georg Philipp Telemann (1681-1767). His collection of chorale settings is entitled 24 fugierende und veränderte Choräle[7] and contains both a bicinium and a three-part arrangement of 23 different chorale melodies plus one additional bicinium and three-part treatment (i. e. , four in all on one melody) of Herr Jesu Christ, dich zu uns wend ("Lord Jesus Christ, Turn Thou to Us"), all of which make 48 different settings. The style is extremely simple and occasionally includes ostinato (continuously repeated) figures. Most of the arrangements have the melody in the upper voice, which could be taken by a 4' stop in the pedal. These settings could have been used between stanzas sung by the congregation.

Free Organ Works

Free compositions of the North German School were usually cast in the forms of a präambulum (prelude), toccata, fantasia, a rare capriccio, and later, fugue, even though no clearly defined structure had been established for these types of compositions by the middle of the seventeenth century. Two streams of musical influence upon composers of the North German School came from Sweelinck and Frescobaldi. Composers such as Marcus Olter (fl. 1600's), Wilhelm Karges (1613/14-1699), and Tunder show the influence of Frescobaldi. Karges also wrote in the slow, harmonic style of North German contemporaries such as David Abel (?-1639) and Peter Hasse the elder (ca. 1585-1640).

In addition to works whose composers can be readily identified, the Lüneburg organ tablatures are a collection of free compositions, chorale variations, chorale preludes, and dances dating from seventeenth century which are of uncertain provenance. Some works have been identified as compositions by Sweelinck, Weckmann, Scheidemann, Schildt, and Capricornus, but the remaining pieces in these tablatures are anonymous. The large majority of the free works are preludes of from six to 128 measures in length, with the titles

in the singular form spelled in a number of different ways
(praeambulum, praeludium, praelude, preludium, praeam).
Most of the preludes are basically homophonic and have
rhythmic imitation as well as melodic imitation at times.
Their harmonic rhythm is rather slow with an exchange of
notes between parts in the prevailing harmony over a sustained pedal part. Some of the shorter preludes closely
resemble intonations. Other free works include fantasias,
fugues, toccatas, and one cantzoem. [8]

Preludes had been single, short pieces such as those
found in the fifteenth- and early sixteenth-century präambeln
in Kleber's tablature (1524), those by Melchior Schildt, and
those found in the Lüneburg tablatures. Some of Schildt's
preludes have less than ten measures. During the second
quarter of the seventeenth century the prelude evolved into
a piece in two sections, the first slow and harmonic, the
second more contrapuntal and lively in character, developing
material in a fugal style. Works of this type were written
by Jacob Praetorius, Decker, and Tunder. As composers
enlarged their contrapuntal material, the second section began to stand alone as a longer piece, and this practice
eventually led to the distinctly separated larger preludes
and fugues of J. S. Bach.

The first section of the early seventeenth-century
präludium contained chords which moved slowly in root position and in first inversions. The harmonies were decorated
in simple ways, perhaps with no more than passing tones or
a few decorated resolutions of suspensions. The piece never
strayed far from the original key, usually only enough to
suggest another closely related key. There was little, if
any, ornamentation indicated. Perhaps Jacob Praetorius
showed real daring by putting a flourish of 16th-notes or
32d-notes at the end of the sections in his preludes. Two
preludes of Christian Flor (1626-1697) are more florid and
active than most earlier seventeenth-century preludes.

The works of Franz Tunder in the prelude genre exhibit more inventive writing than the free works of his contemporaries. Tunder's preludes were divided into two parts,
a slower part followed by a fugal one; there is no complete
break between the two sections. The fugal section actually
sounds the entry of the first voice while the final chord of
the slower section is being held.

The style of Matthias Weckmann (1621-1674) strongly

strongly suggests the influence of the Frescobaldi school by
metamorphosis of the same melodic subject (Fantasia in D
Minor).   Weckmann's fugal subjects frequently employ a repeated note at their beginnings.   Weckmann's canzonas and
toccatas were designed to be played on manuals alone.

The sectional structure of Frescobaldi's canzonas
might have had an effect upon Johann Adam Reincken (1623-
1722), whose Toccata in G is divided into five contrasting
sections.   The form of Reincken's toccata is similar to the
toccatas of Froberger and Muffat of the South German School.

The large number of imaginative free organ works of
Dietrich Buxtehude (1637-1707) can be divided into preludes,
toccatas, fugues, canzonas, canzonettas, and the variation
forms of chaconne and passacaglia.

The preludes (or toccatas) and fugues of Buxtehude
seem to be a group of loosely related sections.   If there
are five, there might be as many as three different fugue
expositions, sometimes ending with or separated by dignified
harmonic interludes or brief, improvisatory sections.   In
the fugues Buxtehude assigned the pedal part as much importance as any other individual voice part.   The rather
loosely woven works entitled "toccata" contain a wide variety
of compositional devices with just a sampling of each.   The
Toccata in F, for example, reveals a fugue as well developed as in the compositions named prelude (or toccata) and
fugue.   Profuse ornamentation was not indicated by Buxtehude.   Trills and a few mordants were the chief ornaments
used.   He sometimes chose to write out the ornamentation
rather than to use embellishment symbols.   Furthermore,
Buxtehude incorporated a wider range of keys than his predecessors and contemporaries did: E major and F-sharp
minor are two examples of keys which were unusual at that
time.   One example of the vigor in Buxtehude's writing is
exhibited by the recurrence of the gigue rhythm.   Repeated
notes, too, occur frequently in his themes of fugue subjects,
as in the D major fugue, which begins with six A's.   One of
the fugues in A minor has a subject which contains four
eighth-note E's followed by four eighth-note D's; the ostinato
of the famous C Major Chaconne begins with four C's in the
pedal.   In summary, Buxtehude's writing has exuberance,
variety, and vitality.   His compositions are fresh and interesting.

Although few in number and not long in duration,

Georg Böhm's free organ compositions exhibit fine craftsmanship in unifying and developing his material. His Prelude and Fugue in C Major contains a stirring pedal cadenza
at the beginning of the prelude, a feature usually connected
with the North German School.

     Vincent Lübeck wrote six preludes and fugues. The
structure of these pieces is similar to that of some compositions by Buxtehude because they generally alternate toccata sections with fugal ones. Active pedal passages, rapid
scale figures for the manuals, voice lines outlining chords,
and series of repeated notes and chords are characteristics
of Lübeck's free organ works.

Notes

1. Albert Schweitzer, J. S. Bach, New York: Macmillan,
   1947 [reprint]; vol. I, p. 31-37.
2. Walter E. Buszin, "The Life and Work of Samuel
   Scheidt," The Musical Heritage of the Lutheran Church,
   St. Louis: Concordia Pub. House, 1959; vol. V,
   p. 55.
3. Ibid., p. 63. Schweitzer wrote that the Scheidt Tabulatur-
   Buch was intended for accompaniment of congregational
   singing. See Albert Schweitzer, op. cit., p. 35.
4. Walter E. Buszin, op. cit., p. 63-64.
5. Vorimitation ("anticipatory imitation") is a contrapuntal
   device often used in settings of chorale melodies for
   organ in which the melody of the chorale phrase (in
   long notes or in a decorated form) is anticipated by
   several voices sounding the same tune, usually in
   diminution, sometimes in inversion. Another similar
   term, Zwischenimitation ("inner imitation"), refers to
   the same anticipatory imitation of inner phrase melodies used as each new chorale phrase is forthcoming.
6. The strong, markedly accented rhythms usually associated with the gigue are either

   or rhythms derived from these basic patterns.
7. Sometimes printed 24 fugirte und verändernde Choräle.
8. John Shannon, ed., Free Organ Compositions from the

Lüneburg Tablatures, 2 vols. , St. Louis: Concordia
Pub. House, 1958; preface.

Bibliography

Bradshaw, Murray C. , "Pre-Bach Organ Toccatas: Form,
    Style, and Registration," Diapason (March, 1972),
    p. 26-28.
Buszin, Walter E. "Buxtehude: On the Tercentenary of His
    Birth," Musical Quarterly, vol. XXIII (1937), p. 465-
    490.
_____. "The Life and Work of Samuel Scheidt," The
    Musical Heritage of the Lutheran Church. St. Louis:
    Concordia Pub. House, 1959; vol. V, p. 43.
Fosse, Richard C. "Nicolaus Bruhns," The Musical Heri-
    tage of the Lutheran Church. St. Louis: Concordia
    Pub. House, 1959; vol. V, p. 92.
Frotscher, Gotthold. Geschichte des Orgelspiels und der
    Orgelkomposition. Berlin: Merseberger Verlag,
    1959; vol. I, p. 377-470.
Hedar, Joseph. Dietrich Buxtehudes Orgelwerke. Stock-
    holm: Wilhelm Hansen, 1951.
Pauly, H. J. Die Fuge in den Orgelwerken Dietrich Buxte-
    hudes. Regensburg, Germany: G. Bosse, 1964.
Powell, Kenneth G. "An Analysis of the North German
    Organ Toccatas," Diapason (April 1971), p. 27-29.
Schuneman, Robert A. "The Organ Chorales of Georg Böhm,"
    Diapason (March 1970), p. 12-14.
Schweitzer, Albert, J. S. Bach, 2 vols. , New York: Mac-
    millan, 1947 [reprint].
Shannon, John, ed. Free Organ Compositions from the
    Lüneburg Tablatures, 2 vols. St. Louis: Concordia
    Pub. House, 1958.
_____. "North-German Organ Music: A Short Study of
    a Style," Music/The A. G. O. -R. C. C. O. Magazine,
    vol. III, no. 9 (September 1969), p. 22.
Sharp, G. B. "Franz Tunder: 1614-1667," Musical Times,
    no. 1497, vol. 108 (November 1967), p. 997.
_____. "Nicolaus Bruhns," Musical Times, no. 1482,
    vol. 107 (August 1966), p. 677.
Spiess, Lincoln B. "Michael Praetorius Creuzburgensis:
    Church Musician and Scholar," The Musical Heritage
    of the Lutheran Church. St. Louis: Concordia Pub.
    House, 1959; vol. V.

6. SOUTH GERMAN SCHOOL: 1600-1775

[The Historical Background chart found at the beginning of
Chapter 5 is also appropriate for this chapter.]

Chorale-Based Works

There were few compositions based on chorale melodies in the South German School because there were few
Protestant composers in southern Germany and Catholic organists in their services had no use for pieces based on
Lutheran melodies. Composers in Catholic cities seemed
to write little for the church but were more interested in
the secular suite and contrapuntal forms. The organ Mass
had virtually vanished. Published organ music was designed
for either liturgical use or for teaching.

The chorale-based works composed by this school of
organ composers were written by Ulrich Steigleder (1593-
1635), Johann Pachelbel (1653-1706) and his son Wilhelm
Hieronymus Pachelbel (1686-1746), Johann Erasmus Kindermann (1616-1655), Johann Kaspar Ferdinand Fischer (ca.
1667-1746), Johann Philipp Förtsch (1652-1732), and Johann
Krieger (1652-1735). W. H. Pachelbel composed a Fantasia
on Meine Seele, lass es gehen, which incorporates broken
chords and other stringed keyboard instrument figures. Johann Philipp Förtsch wrote 32 canons in from two to eight
voices on Christ der du bist der helle Tag ("O Christ, who
art both day and light"). Fischer included four chorale settings and five short ricercars on Ave Maria klare at the end
of his Ariadne Musica Neo-Organoedum (1702, 1710, 1715).

The most productive composer of chorale-based works
was the Nürnberg master Johann Pachelbel. Pachelbel's
compositions are characterized by their simplicity of conception, natural flow, and uncontrived sound. The cantus
firmus is always clearly heard. The principal characteristic
of his chorale-based works is the frequent use of Vorimitation.
Although this technique was adopted by many other composers

SOUTH GERMAN SCHOOL OF ORGAN COMPOSITION: 1600-1775

1550   1600   1650   1700   1750   1800

(1583 Frescobaldi 1643)

1561 Steigleder, Adam 1633
1564 Hassler, H. L. 1612
ca. 1570 Erbach, Chr. 1635
1593 Steigleder, J. 1635
1612 Ebner, W. 1665
1616 Froberger, J. J. 1667
1616 Kindermann, J. 1655
1627 Kerll, Johann Kasper 1693
1631 Scherer, Sebastian Anton 1712
? Poglietti, Allesandro 1683
ca. 1649 Techelmann, Franz 1714
ca. 1649 Richter, F. -----1711
1649 Krieger, J. the elder 1725
1652 Förtsch, Johann P. -------1732
1652 Krieger, J. the younger 1735
1653 Pachelbel, J. 1706
1653 Muffat, Georg 1704
1656 Reutter, Georg, the elder 1738
1663 Murschhauser, F. X. --1738
1664 Speth, Johann 1719
1665/1670 Fischer, Johann K. F. 1746
1682 Rathgeber, Valentin------1750
1686 Pachelbel, Wilhelm ----1746
1690 Muffat, Gottlieb-----------------1770
1703 Kolb, Karlmann------1765
1703 Sorge, Georg Andreas------1778

of chorale settings, it is especially connected with Pachelbel's name. Pachelbel frequently used a combination form which links an introductory prelude on the first phrase melody (sometimes called a prelude-fugue) to a setting of one stanza of the chorale with the cantus firmus in the pedal in long notes. In the latter part the left hand often doubles the cantus, while the soprano and alto parts are written in flowing 16th-notes. The famous Vom Himmel hoch pastorale-trio is followed by this type of setting.

Pachelbel also wrote three-part chorale settings with one of the parts playing the melody in long notes. His chorale variations frequently contain settings which seem to be written for cembalo (harpsichord) and not for organ.

Free Compositions

The Italian forms adopted by the Catholic South German school were the non-liturgical toccata, canzona, ricercar, capriccio, fantasia, and fugue. The pedal division of the organs in that area was much less developed than the pedal divisions in northern Germany. The music written, therefore, required little, if any, pedal work. A toccata primi toni by Adam Steigleder (1561-1633) is found in the Woltz tablature (1617), in which there is simple elaboration (usually 16th-note scale passages) of unsurprising harmonic progressions; this toccata closely resembles an intonation. It was obviously written for the organ and no other medium.

The South German School made several contributions to the development of the fugue. Kindermann placed two different kinds of fugues in his Harmonia organica (1645): some were the type we would now expect to find under the title and the others were based on chorale melodies. Pachelbel's fugue subjects were broken into figurative motifs and developed separately. These various elements from several different composers point to the rise of the fugue form and the decline of the canzona and ricercar.

Hans Leo Hassler (1564-1612) employed the organ forms of his teacher, Andrea Gabrieli: the ricercar, canzona, and toccata. Christian Erbach (ca. 1570-1635) used these same forms and also wrote versets for the alternation practice.

One of the outstanding composers in this school was Johann Jacob Froberger (1616-1667), who was sent by

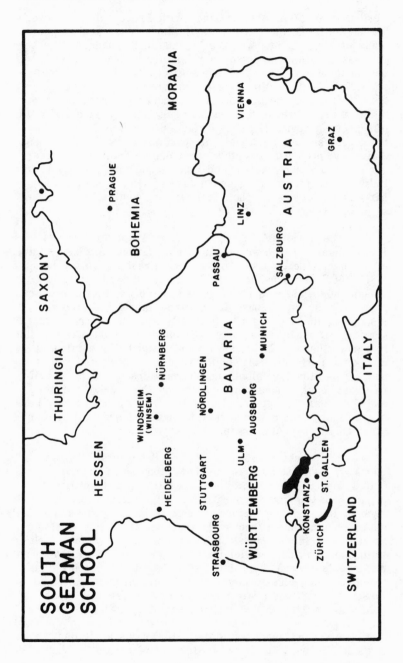

Ferdinand III of Austria to study with Frescobaldi.   Froberger assimilated much from his Italian teacher and adopted
many of his techniques.   The toccata in the hands of Froberger was a composite form, a miniature suite.   The form was
sectional and had meter changes for each section.   Free,
recitative sections often began and closed his toccatas.   A
typical order of the sections in a Froberger toccata is: a
fantasia-recitative section, a short fughetta, a strongly rhythmic section, and a final free, fantasia section.   Even though
his toccatas were sectional, all parts seem to belong to one
entity and progress smoothly from one to another.   Froberger's composition was formed from techniques absorbed from
Italian, German, and French sources.   His influence was
particularly strong on the Viennese and south German group
of composers.

     The Modulatio organica of Johann Kasper Kerll (1627-
1693) contains seven short Magnificat versets for each of the
eight chant tones.   Kerll and Johann Erasmus Kindermann
(1616-1655) continued to write canzonas and ricercars, although their canzonas no longer used the traditional canzona
rhythm at the beginning.   Kerll made use of pedal point
throughout the Toccata per li Pedali.   Kerll's lengthy Passacaglia in D Minor is a virtuoso number built on a descending
four-note theme.   It is easy to understand why a talented
composer-performer of Kerll's reputation attracted pupils
such as Johann Pachelbel and Franz Murschhauser.   Kerll
wrote at least two capriccios, one on the "cuckoo" theme
and the other Der steyrische Hirt.   Both pieces employ keyboard figures which sound better on a stringed keyboard instrument than on the organ.

     The works of Sebastian Anton Scherer are in two
books.   The first book is entitled Intonationes breves per
octo tonos (1664) and the second Partitura in cymbalo et
organo.   In the first book are found four intonations for
each of the eight chant tones.   One pedal note is sustained
during several measures while the manual writing is florid.
Some of the intonations do not use the pedal.   Some employ
imitation, flowing parallel thirds in 16th-notes, and balanced
movement between the parts.   The Partitura contains eight
toccatas which change meter without altering the pace and
lessen the sectionality found in earlier toccatas.   Pedal
points are sustained under much parallel writing.

     Alessandro de Poglietti (?-1683) was an Italian who
lived in Vienna.   He is known for his ricercari.   Franz

Mathias Techelmann (ca. 1649-1714) and Ferdinand Tobias
Richter (ca. 1649-1711) were in the same Viennese circle.
Johann Philipp Krieger the Elder (1649-1725) wrote a simple
Toccata in A Minor. The accompanying fugue exhibits neat
cadences and transitional contrapuntal material, which help
to clarify the form. Johann Philipp's brother, Johann Krieger (1651-1735), composed much more music in the standard
Italian forms, including a very long Ciacona[1] with many variations and a Passacaglia. [1] Most of these pieces use the
pedal sparingly and many do not use the pedal at all.

The chief work for which Georg Muffat (1653-1704) is
known is the Apparatus musico-organisticus (1690), which
contains 12 sectional toccatas, one ciacona, and one passacaglia. Some of the sections are short, but the tempo
changes are striking, as from grave to allegro. The pieces
are improvisatory in nature and are liberally graced with
embellishments. Again, little pedal is needed. The 11th
toccata from the Apparatus suggests a suite because of its
series of related, but contrasting, short pieces. This toccata begins with a slow, homophonic alla breve section followed by a faster, fugal, four-part movement. A lyric,
dignified Adagio in $\frac{3}{2}$ meter then precedes a $\frac{3}{4}$ Allegro. After
a tiny Adagio interlude the toccata concludes with a dancing
$\frac{6}{8}$ movement. Syncopation, some chromaticism, and sequences are tastefully employed.

Johann Pachelbel, Froberger, and J. K. F. Fischer
are the three outstanding composers of the South German
School. Pachelbel spent the last part of his life in southern
Germany. Pachelbel's free works include preludes, toccatas,
fugues, ricercars, and a few chaconnes and fantasies. Pachelbel's writing, while not profound, is direct and interesting.
The voice leading is always clear and flowing within simple
but strong harmonic progressions. Pachelbel used chordal
figurations and sequences to excellent effect. The pedal is
used principally to support the basic harmonies by holding
sustained tones. Additional characteristics are echo effects,
off-beat repeated or separated 16th-notes against a legato
line in the other hand, brilliant passages of scale passages
in 16th-notes, preference for two-part and three-part writing,
and practically no ornamentation. The Pachelbel toccatas
are not broken into obvious sections and are medium length,
unified pieces of from 30 to 50 measures.

Pachelbel chose to write many double fugues: two
subjects developed independently and then combined. This

technique is observed in some of his fugues and ricercars
which were inspired by the Magnificat.   Pachelbel wrote 94
of these fugues for use in the Lutheran vesper service.
These short compositions were used in alternation with the
singing of Magnificat verses or as introductions to the Magnificat, but only a few of these fugues are actually based on
the chant tones.

Pachelbel's free compositions were generally conceived as ensemble works and not for melodies with accompaniment.   Pachelbel spent the last 11 years of his life in
his native Nuremberg as organist of the Sebalduskirche.   The
specifications of the organ there, which are given below, re-
veal that there were few mutations, mixtures, and only one
reed, and that the organ contained a small pedal division.
The simple design of the instrument is closely related to the
unaffected, natural flow of Pachelbel's contrapuntal lines.

Nuremberg, Germany: Sebalduskirche.
Built by Heinrich Traxdorf, 1444;
rebuilt by Sigmund Layser, 1691

Hauptwerk	Pedal
Principal 8	Principal 16
Octava 4	Octav 8
Quinta Cymbel II	Quint 3
Super Octava und Decima	Sub Bass 16
2 and 1 1/2	Violon Bass 8

Rückpositiv

Principal 4
Grob Gedackt 8
Quinta cum Octava 3 and 2
Super Octava 2 and 1
Quintaton 8
Cymbel II
Dulcian 8

Georg Reutter the Elder (1656-1738) wrote in the
forms of toccata, capriccio, fugue, and canzona.   Among
other works a short toccata in G major by one of Johann
Pachelbel's sons, Wilhelm Hieronymus, gives evidence of
a style similar to that of his father.   Another son, Karl
Theodore Pachelbel, became influential in early American
musical circles.

Johann Kaspar Ferdinand Fischer (1665/1670-1746)
wrote 20 short preludes and fugues in 19 different keys with
five short ricercari on chorale melodies which form the
Ariadne Musica. All of these pieces are brief; the shortest
prelude contains only seven measures and the longest, 25.
Ariadne foreshadowed Bach's Wohltemperirte Clavier of 48
preludes and fugues.

In Fischer's Blumen Strauss each of eight preludes
composed in a different church tone is followed by six brief
"fugues" and a finale, which usually is closely related to the
prelude. Franz Xaver Anton Murschhauser (1663-1738), a
pupil of Kerll, wrote the Octi-tonium novum organicum
(1696) along the same pattern as Fischer's Blumen Strauss,
with an extra cycle written for the Quinti toni irregularis.
His other major work was the Prototypen longo-breve organicum (1703, 1707).

The toccatas of Johann Speth (1664-1719), found in
his Ars magna consoni et dissoni (1693) resemble those of
Froberger in length and structure, with a few similar to
Pachelbel's nonsectional toccata. His Magnificats are simpler than those found in Kerll's Modulatio.

In 1743 the Musicalischer Zeit-Vertreib of Valentin
Rathgeber (1682-1750) was published. This work contains
60 two-part and three-part song and dance pieces in the
style galant. [2] The last ten pieces are Christmas pastorales.

Another volume of short works arranged in cycles is
the 72 Versetl samt 12 Toccaten (1726) by Gottlieb Muffat
(1690-1770), the son of Georg Muffat. Twelve short toccatas
are written in 12 keys. Each toccata is followed by six
brief fugues (versetl). None of these miniature pieces uses
the pedal. Another major work by Gottlieb Muffat was the
Componimenti musicali (1739). The Toccata I and Fugue
was composed along the same general lines as those of his
contemporary, Bach--two separate and well-developed pieces.

The Certamen aonium (1733) of Karlmann Kolb (1703-
1765) is similar to the cyclic works of Muffat and Fischer.
A praeludium is followed by three verses and a cadentia for
each one of the eight church modes. These pieces frequently adopt cembalo figures. Georg Andreas Sorge (1703-
1778), who was strongly influenced by Italian music, wrote
a Toccata per ogni Modi.

BOOKS PUBLISHED BY LEADING COMPOSERS IN THE SOUTH GERMAN SCHOOL

Date	Composer-Author	Title
1645	Kindermann	Harmonia Organica
1664	Scherer	Intonationes Breves per octo tones
1664	Scherer	Operum musicorum secundum
1683	Pachelbel, J.	Musicalischen Sterbens-Gedancken
1686	Kerll	Modulatio organica
1690	Muffat, Georg	Apparatus musico-organisticus
1693	Pachelbel, J	Erster Theil etlicher Choräle
1693	Speth	Ars magna consoni et dissoni
1696	Murschhauser	Octi-Tonium novum Organicum
1699	Pachelbel, J.	Hexachordum Apollinis
1702	Fischer	Ariadne Musica Neo-Organoedum
n.d.	Fischer	Blumen Strauss
1703	Murschhauser	Prototypen longo-breve organicum
1726	Muffat, Gottlieb	72 Versetl samt 12 Toccaten
1733	Kolb	Certamen Aonium
1739	Muffat, Gottlieb	Componimente Musicali
1743	Rathgeber	Musicalischer Zeit-Vertreib

Many composers of this school wrote pieces which were conceived for either harpsichord or organ. Instruction books, which included music for these instruments, came under the strong and debilitating influence of operatic, secular, orchestral, concert, and dance music. This weakened the integrity and strong tradition of fine organ music and its influence during the eighteenth and nineteenth centuries.

Notes

1. The chaconne (ciacona) and passacaglia are two closely related, baroque, variation forms. The terms were rather indiscriminately interchanged because, in addition to their being variation forms, both forms are continuous and are usually found in triple meter. In general the passacaglia is based on an ostinato (repeated melody) which usually occurs in the bass, and the chaconne is a continuous series of variations based upon recurring harmonies.
2. Style galant is a term applied to the light, homophonic (accompanied melody) music of the rococo period in the eighteenth century which contrasts with the serious polyphonic music of the baroque period. The emphasis changed from the purposeful to the amusing and encouraged a general deterioration of musical quality.

Bibliography

Buszin, Walter E. "Johann Pachelbel's Contribution to Pre-Bach Organ Literature," The Musical Heritage of the Lutheran Church. St. Louis: Concordia Pub. House, 1959; vol. V, p. 140.

Frotscher, Gotthold. Geschichte des Orgelspiels und der Orgelkomposition. Berlin: Merseberger Verlag, 1959; vol. I, p. 470-559.

Kratzenstein, Marilou, "A Survey of Organ Literature and Editions: South Germany," Diapason (March 1972), p. 18-21.

Nolte, Ewald. "The Magnificat Fugues of Johann Pachelbel: Alternation or Intonation," Journal of the American Musicological Society, vol. IX (1956), p. 19-24.

Sharp, G. B. "J. J. Froberger: 1614-1667, a Link Between the Renaissance and the Baroque," Musical Times, no. 1498, vol. 108 (December 1967), p. 1093.

7. MIDDLE GERMAN SCHOOL: 1600-1750

[The Historical Background chart found at the beginning of Chapter 5 is also appropriate for this chapter.]

Thuringia and Saxony lie in the heartland of Germany. Into this middle section of Germany flowed organ compositional features of style and form from both the North and South German Schools.

Generations of the Bach family lived in and around Thuringia. Religion and music were probably the two most important factors in the lives of this family, and several of the earlier branches of the Bach family tree who contributed to organ literature used the chorale melody as the basis of their compositions.

Both Johann Michael Bach (1648-1694) and Johann Bernhard Bach (1675-1749) wrote variations on chorale melodies. The Choraele, welche bey wärenden Gottes Dienst zum Praeambuliren by Johann Christoph Bach (1642-1703) contains 44 chorale settings. Johann Heinrich Bach (1615-1692) was probably the earliest member of the family whose organ compositions have come down to us. Both Friedrich Wilhelm Zachau (Zachow) (1663-1712), Handel's teacher in Halle, and Johann Gottfried Walther (1684-1748), a cousin of J. S. Bach, composed chorale variation cycles on Jesu, meine Freude ("Jesus, Joy and Treasure").

Organ chorales were frequently written for manuals alone (manualiter) in either two or three parts and had the melody in long notes in the uppermost part or in the pedal. Imitative settings might offer the chorale melodies of each phrase treated as points of imitation (chorale motet), as a chorale fughetta, or more extensively as a chorale fantasia.

One of the leading composers of the Middle German School was Michael Praetorius (1571-1621), a versatile musician whose life was founded in the Reformation movement and also one who was alert to new styles in music. Praetorius

MIDDLE GERMAN SCHOOL: 1600-1750

1600   1650   1700   1750

(1587 Scheidt, Samuel 1654)
1571 Praetorius, M. 1621
   1615 Bach, Johann Heinrich 1692
   1625 Ahle, Johann Rudolf 1673
      1640 Strungk, N. A. ---1700
      1642 Bach, J. Christoph 1703
      1645 Werckmeister, A.   1706
      1645/1650 Ritter, Christian ca. 1725
      1647 Alberti, J. F. ----1710
      1648 Bach, J. M.   1694
        1660 Kuhnau, Johann-----1722
        1663 Zachau, Friedrich 1712
        1666 Buttstett, Johann----1727
        1666 Vetter, Nicolaus-----1734
          1675 Bach, Johann Bernhard----------1749
          1678 Volckmar, Tobias---------------1754
          ? Heuschkel, Johann ?
          1679 Armsdorff, A. 1699
          1679 Kauffmann, G. F. 1735
          1684 Walther, Johann Gottfried 1748
          1685 Bach, Johann Sebastian 1750

is famous for his treatise in three volumes on music, the
Syntagma musicum (1619). Volume One deals with a history
of church music, and Volume Two, De Organographia, is a
significant survey of instruments, with special emphasis on
organ building and information about organs existing at that
time. 1 Volume Three is concerned with the subject of music theory. Praetorius' compositions for organ include nine
organ hymns, one set of variations on Nun lob mein Seel den
Herren ("Now Praise the Lord, my Soul") (1609), and a collection of bicinia and tricinia (1610), which were based on
chorale melodies. The bicinia were written for two singers
or to be played on two manuals. In the tricinia the organist
plays the middle part with the two outer parts which are
sung, an unusual type of sacred music. Six of the organ
hymns are Latin (dating perhaps as early as 1607), and
three are German chorale settings (1609). The chorale fantasias on Ein' feste Burg ("A Mighty Fortress") and Wir
glauben all in einen Gott ("We All Believe in One True God")
treat all the chorale phrases as a point of imitation. It
was the publishing practice of the time of Praetorius to
print each of the voice lines separately in part books for
both choral and organ music. Each individual organist then
had to transcribe and arrange the parts for his own instrument and into the type of notation which suited him best.
The organ hymns of Praetorius were written some 15 years
before Scheidt's Tabulatura nova appeared in 1624. The set
of variations uses mechanical figurations similar to those of
the English virginalists. 2

Several styles of counterpoint were used by different
composers of the Middle German School in setting chorale
melodies. The counterpoint of Johann Friedrich Alberti
(1647-1710) was harmonically oriented. Ach Herr, mich
armen Sünder ("O Lord, My Grievous Sins") by Johann
Kuhnau (1660-1722) is another expressive example of the
same kind of counterpoint. Zachau's treatment of Komm,
heiliger Geist, Herre Gott ("Come, Holy Ghost, Lord God")
returned to the style of a ricercar. Georg Friedrich Kauffmann (1679-1735) introduced the use of solo instruments such
as the oboe, which played the unadorned chorale melody
while decorative and supporting contrapuntal lines (usually
in three parts) were played by the organist. Kauffmann's
large collection is entitled Harmonische Seelenlust (1733).

Johann Gottfried Walther (1684-1748) was the author
of the first musical dictionary, the Musikalisches Lexicon
(1732). He composed at least 290 extant pieces for the

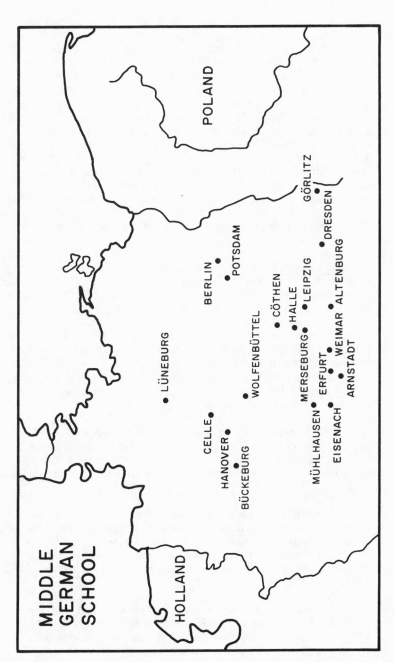

organ.   Of these the large majority are based on chorale
melodies.   The two most common types of chorale settings
by Walther are the manualiter three-part motet style with
the melody in the soprano part and the pedal chorale type
in three-part or four-part texture with the melody in the
pedal.   The next most frequent types of chorale settings by
Walther are the four-part manualiter and canonic treatment
of the melody between the soprano and pedal parts.   Walther
also employed the bicinium technique, <u>pedaliter</u> (an organ
composition which employs the pedal) motet, and a few
coloratura and melody chorale arrangements.   All of these
last mentioned types are usually settings of one stanza of
the chorale.   Most of these settings were intended for alternation with the congregation's singing.   A small portion of
the settings was written to precede the singing of the chorale,
as a means of introducing the chorale to the congregation.

Walther's counterpoint included the use of <u>Vorimitation</u>
and <u>Zwischenimitation</u> devices, and free counterpoint which
outlined the harmony.   He made a generous use of ornamentation and chromaticism for color.   Walther also added notes
to final chords in order to strengthen cadences.

Not all of the 14 Walther chorale partitas were first
planned to be played in a series.   Five were so planned,
however.   One is the famous <u>Jesu, meine Freude</u> ("Jesus,
Joy and Treasure") partita. [3]   One partita, <u>Herr Jesu Christ,
dich zu uns wend</u>, ("Lord Jesus Christ, Turn Thou to Us"),
contains as many as 13 settings of the tune.

The free works of Walther include a few preludes,
fugues, one concerto of five movements, and 14 transcriptions of violin concerti. [4]   J. S. Bach may have received
inspiration for his concerto transcriptions for the organ from
Walther.

There are only a few free works by other composers
of this school which have survived other than those composed by Johann Sebastian Bach.   Nicolaus Adam Strungk
(1640-1700) used the double-fugue form in rather lengthy
works, and the compositions of Andreas Werckmeister (1645-
1706) are canzonas.

Kuhnau's free works include two preludes and fugues
in B-flat major and G major and a lengthy <u>Toccata in A
Major</u>.   The preludes are dignified, and the chords are
filled out irregularly, sometimes with as many as eight

chord tones sounding.   The fugues are plain and uneventful;
they continued the same style which was set forth in the preludes.   The toccata, however, is rich in variety of subject
matter and contains an active pedal part in the north German
manner.   The toccata is composed of many short sections of
widely diversified character marked by strongly contrasting
tempos.   The sections include an opening fantasia, a dotted-
note figure which introduce a repeated chord section, a
short chromatic interlude, a lengthy fugue in triple meter,
and an Adagio recitative-fantasy.   The form of this work
suggests the toccatas of Froberger.

Three free works by Zachau were called fugues.
The first fugue is in two sections; the second part was
constructed from a diminutive form of the same subject.
The second "fugue" contains a Grave chordal section of 15
measures before the fugue actually begins.   The third fugue,
which resembles the sectional works of Frescobaldi, contains themes which evolved from the same subject.

The next chapter covers the works of J. S. Bach,
the giant of organ literature, who is the outstanding organ
composer of the Middle German School.

Notes

1.   Praetorius wrote about performance practices as well.
Other theorists who wrote about registration practices
of the late baroque period were Werckmeister, Mat-
theson, Adlung, and Marpurg.
2.   Lincoln B. Spiess, "Michael Praetorius Creuzburgensis:
Church Musician and Scholar," The Musical Heritage
of the Lutheran Church, St. Louis: Concordia Pub.
House, 1959; vol. V, p. 69-72.
3.   Richard A. Carlson, "Walther's Life; Walther's Works,"
Organ Institute Quarterly, vol. V, no. 4 (Autumn
1955), p. 38.
4.   The composers whose concerti Walther transcribed for
organ were Albinoni, Blamr, Corelli, Torelli, Gregori,
Mangia, Meck, and Telemann.

Bibliography

Carlson, Richard A.   "Walther's Life; Walther's Works,"
Organ Institute Quarterly, vol. V, no. 4 (Autumn 1955),
p. 29-39.

Frotscher, Gotthold. Geschichte des Orgelspiels und der
    Orgelkomposition. Berlin: Merseberger Verlag,
    1959; vol. I, p. 559-661.
Praetorius, Michael. Phantasy on the Chorale A Mighty
    Fortress Is Our God, Heinrich Fleischer, ed. Intro-
    duction. St. Louis: Concordia Pub. House, 1954.
Spiess, Lincoln B. "Michael Praetorius Creuzburgensis:
    Church Musician and Scholar," The Musical Heritage
    of the Lutheran Church. St. Louis: Concordia Pub.
    House, 1959; vol. V, p. 69-71.
Johann Gottfried Walther Orgelchoräle, Hermann Poppen, ed.
    Kassel, Germany: Bärenreiter Verlag, 1956; preface.

8. BACH: 1685-1750

The artistic contributions to organ literature made
by J. S. Bach (1685-1750) are so great that the work of this
musical genius seems to be the vortex of organ study. For
convenience the works of Bach are usually grouped in three
large periods: the earlier years and Weimar period (1695-
1717), 22 years in all, during which a large portion of the
organ works were written; the middle, Cöthen period
(1717-1723), six years principally concerned with orchestral
composition; and the third, Leipzig period of 27 years (1723-
1750) spent in composition of choral works such as the cantatas and the passions, and also the mature organ works.
In order to cover this large body of material easily and
thoroughly the first major period will be divided into three
parts with a brief study of the chorale-based works and the
free compositions in each part. [1]

A brief summary of major contributions to types of
chorale settings before Bach is appropriate at this point.
Many of the technical possibilities and artistic foundations of
the chorale prelude were established by Samuel Scheidt as
early as 1624, for he indicated that the melody of the chorale
could be placed in any voice part and that even double pedaling could be accomplished at the organ. Pachelbel contributed the chorale fugue, fugal treatment of phrases of the
chorale melody. Böhm expressed the chorale melody in
luxuriant coloratura settings. The chorale preludes of Buxtehude treat the chorale melody in both easy and complex
ways: sometimes the melody is stated very simply with
only slight ornamentation, and sometimes he expressed the
chorale melody rhapsodically in fantasias. The mature
Bach, inspired by the texts of the chorales, took the methods
of treatment worked out by earlier masters and infused
greater imagination and color into them, thus raising those
same forms to even greater heights.

LIFE OF BACH

Dates	Chronology	Music Composed	Age
1685	born, March 21, Eisenach		
1694	mother died		
Earlier Years and Weimar Period:			
1695	father died; lived with bro-ther in Ohrdruf 5 years		10
1700-1702	singer, St. Michael's school, Lüneburg	Organ: chorale settings, partitas	15
1703	chamber orchestra musi-cian to Duke Johann Ernst, Weimar, April to August		18
1703-1707	organist, New Church, Arnstadt; trip to hear Buxtehude, Lübeck, Oct. 1705 to Jan. 1706	Organ: chorale settings, small free works	18
1707	married Maria Barbara Bach		22
1707-1708	organist, St. Blasii, Mühlhausen, 1 year		22
1708-1717	court musician, organist for Duke Wilhelm Ernst, Weimar, 10 years	Organ music: lar-ger free works; chorale settings; 6 concerti	23
1717		Orgelbüchlein	
Cöthen Period:			
1717-1723	Kapellmeister to court of Prince Leopold, Cöthen, 6 years	Instrumental music	32
1721	married Anna Magdalena		36
1721	Wülcken		
Leipzig Period:			
1723-1750	Cantor, St. Thomas and St. Nicholas Churches, Leipzig (27 years)	cantatas; passions; organ music: 6 trio sonatas; larger pre-ludes, fugues	38
1739		Clavierübung, Part III pub.	54
1746-1747		Six Chorales (Schübler) pub.	60
1746-1747		Canonic Variations on Vom Himmel hoch pub.	60
1750	died, July 28, Leipzig		65

I. EARLIER YEARS AND WEIMAR PERIOD (1696-1717)

Ohrdruf, Lüneburg, Weimar (1696-1703)

This period of about nine years is represented by chorale-based works with one possible exception, the Pedal exercitum. In addition there are about 22 chorale settings which might have been written in this early period, although their authenticity is doubtful. One of these is the little trio on In dulci jubilo ("In Sweetest Joy") (BWV 751). Most of the chorale partitas were written in this period. Some of the variations might have been composed a few years later, however. The variations are for manuals alone; Keller suggests, therefore, that these were, for the most part, intended for the clavichord or Positiv in the home rather than for performance on a large organ in church. [2]

Arnstadt, Mühlhausen (1703-1708)

Bach composed his first free organ works while he was working in Arnstadt and Mühlhausen. In addition to two sets of chorale variations, there are ten chorale settings, including the A major fantasy on In dulci jubilo (BWV 729) and the trio setting of Nun freut euch ("Lift Up Your Hearts, Ye Christians All") (BWV 734), which assigns the cantus firmus to the pedal part.

The little Prelude and Fugue in C Minor (BWV 549) and Fugue in C Minor (BWV 575) show that they are early works because they contain such a diversity of material and lack unity. The Pastorale (BWV 590) exhibits more coherence in each one of its four sections. The virile "Gigue" Fugue in G Major (BWV 577) resembles the Buxtehude Fugue in C Major and contains similar rhythmic intensity. Three tempo indications in French (très vitement, grave, lentement) mark the three divisions of the Fantasia in G Major (BWV 572). The long alla breve middle section separates two toccata sections. These early free works omit use of the pedal for complete sections, or the pedal sustains long pedal points.

Weimar (1708-1717)

Most of the chorale settings found in the Kirnberger collection[3] suggest that they were written in the earlier part of the Weimar period, as does Bach's one setting of Ein' feste Burg ("A Mighty Fortress"). Five variations from the Sei gegrüsset ("Be Thou Welcome") partita might have been written during this period.

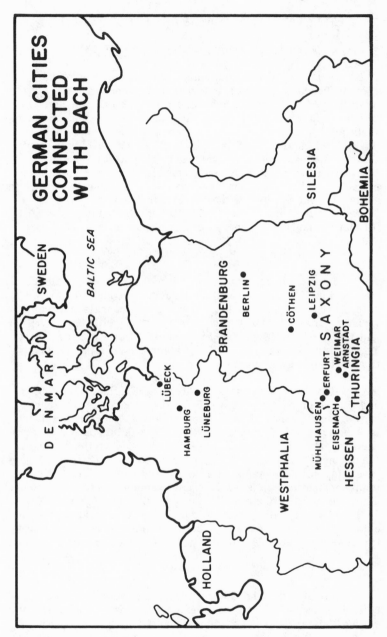

By far the most important chorale treatments at the end
of the Weimar period are those found in the Orgelbüchlein (Little
Organ Book). Bach knew chorales intimately and used them constantly. It is possible that the collection might have been
planned for Wilhelm Friedemann Bach's instruction.

A LITTLE BOOK FOR THE ORGAN
wherein the beginning organist
may learn to perform chorales of every sort
and also acquire facility in the use of the pedal
which, in the chorales found herein, is
handled entirely obbligato.
To the most high God alone be praise,
For what herein is written for man's instruction.
Composed by
Johann Sebast. Bach,
pro tempore Capellmeister
to His Serene Highness the Prince
of Anhalt-Cöthen

Bach planned this book at Weimar. The design had
been to include 164 settings of 161 melodies on 92 sheets of
paper. The task was not completed, however, because he
accepted, against the will of the Duke of Weimar, the court
musician's office for Prince Leopold of Anhalt-Cöthen. It is
quite possible that most of the Little Organ Book was written
while Bach was detained by the Duke of Weimar and perhaps
a few more chorales were added in Cöthen. Since his duties
in Cöthen did not call for this type of music, he never
finished the book. The order of these splendid miniatures
was that found in the hymnbook of the Grand Duchy of Weimar authorized for use in 1713. The contents fall into two
parts: chorales arranged according to the Christian year
and chorales of faith and different aspects of the Christian
life. Part one was to contain 60 settings, of which Bach
finished 36; part two was to have 104 settings of which only
10 were completed. These 46 pieces are examples of the
Orgelchoral, a setting of one stanza of the chorale, without
interludes, incorporating rich harmonizations and colorful
decoration; two settings of the same chorale, Liebster Jesu,
wir sind hier ("Blessed Jesus, We Are Here") are included.
Most of these pieces are of four-part texture with the melody
in the soprano. Three are coloratura settings: Das alte
Jahr ("The Old Year Now Has Passed Away"), O Mensch,
bewein dein Sünde gross ("O Man, Bewail Thy Grievous Sin"),
and Wenn wir in höchsten Nöthen sein ("When We Are Found
in Greatest Need").

Bach repeatedly used certain motives which could be named or associated with different words. The theory of affections was manifested in choice of key, figuration types, textures used, and harmonic progressions. Words such as "joy," "weeping," "arising," and "sorrow" stimulated his imagination. [4] As examples, many Christmas chorales have descending motives symbolizing Christ's coming down from heaven to earth, the incarnation. Herr Christ, der ein'ge Gottes Sohn ("Lord Christ, Thou Only Son of God") (BWV 601) uses a trumpet or fanfare motive, which suggests Christ, the King; in Durch Adams Fall ist ganz verderbt ("Through Adam's Fall Was All Destroyed") (BWV 637) the fall is pictured musically by a jagged, angular leap downward of a diminished seventh. These individual motives were used to unify the composition and to offer one central idea or concept for one particular setting.

At Weimar Bach was able to study many scores by Italian composers such as Legrenzi, Corelli, Vivaldi, and Frescobaldi. It was here in 1714 that he copied Frescobaldi's Fiori musicali, which probably inspired Bach's Canzona in D Minor (BWV 583). The Fugue in C Minor (BWV 574) adopts a theme by Legrenzi, and the Fugue in B Minor (BWV 579) uses a melody by Corelli as a subject. In Weimar Bach also transcribed six concerti for organ: the first and fourth on concertos by Prince Johann Ernst; the second, third, and fifth by Vivaldi; the sixth has long been listed as of doubtful authenticity, and has now been proved to be a concerto by Vivaldi. The stirring first movement of the second concerto in A minor and the beautiful siciliano of the Concerto in D Minor are especially appealing.

The Allabreve in D Major (BWV 589) might also have grown from Italian prototypes. Bach's interest in older composers' works and in established forms rather than in the more commonplace music of his day led some contemporaries to consider him out-of-date. His music was the outgrowth of a fusion of several types of organ writing, Italian, German, French, of forms new and old, derived from many influences, and yet uniquely fashioned.

Keller suggests, with many good reasons, that the Eight Little Preludes and Fugues (BWV 553-560), known to most organ students at an early stage of development, could have been written by Bach's favorite pupil, Johann Ludwig Krebs. [5] This does not suggest that they are not worthy of use as instruction pieces.

Several elements of the dual, combination form of prelude (fantasia or toccata) and fugue can be pointed out which recur to different degrees in the principal periods of Bach's organ composition. One element used frequently in the Weimar period is the virtuoso style drawn from the North German school and expressed in brilliant toccata passages for manuals, in the long, ornate pedal solos, in many different kinds of figuration, massive chords, dramatic pedal points, and in improvisational and recitative sections. Another element of prominence was drawn from Italian instrumental works, the concertato (orchestral) style, in which there is marked contrast between smaller and larger choruses or between solo (or thin) texture and chorus. Many of Bach's themes built on broken chords suggest the Italian violinistic style of Vivaldi and Corelli.

The "Cathedral" Prelude and Fugue in E Minor (BWV 533) is of small dimension but of serious and moving quality. The "Little" Fugue in G Minor (BWV 578), the subject of which is similar to a folksong, is another work of moderate length but one of great beauty and contrapuntal craftsmanship. The careful organization and flowing counterpoint of the fugue make it a delight to perform and to hear.

The Prelude and Fugue in D Major (BWV 532) is a combination of two virtuoso pieces of great vitality. An ascending D major scale in the pedal opens the prelude. After nine measures of fanfare a passage in F-sharp minor continues in French overture style and closes by employing tremolando in both hands. A 32d note flourish up the D major scale ends the first of three sections of the prelude. The Allabreve middle part contains 80 measures, which are composed of many sequences and possibilities for echo effects between manuals. A free-recitative Adagio, which incorporates double pedaling and rich harmonic progressions in five-part texture, closes the prelude. The head of the fugue subject is based on a germ-motive composed of the repetition of three notes, D, E, and F-sharp, in 16th-notes. The fugue concludes with a stunning solo pedal passage built upon the initial motive arranged sequentially.

The combination of a prelude stemming from the earlier part of the Weimar period (ca. 1709) and a fugue from the Leipzig period or reworking of earlier composed works is the Prelude and Fugue in A Minor (BWV 543). A variety of rhapsodic ideas make up the prelude. The fugue, however, is highly unified, with the architecture of the work

easily delineated by the performer if he changes to a lighter
registration for secondary sections unaccompanied by pedal
and then returns to the Great manual for the principal parts
of the fugue. This work closes with a brilliant pedal cadenza
and virtuoso manual display, both characteristics which are
identified with the North German school.

The popular Toccata and Fugue in D Minor (BWV
565) contains a large number of opportunities for echo effects (a prominent characteristic of Baroque organ music)
in both the toccata and the fugue. Pyramids of tone arising
from broken chords and striking tempo changes are some of
the easily noticed factors in the toccata. The violinistic
fugue subject moves in 16th-notes stepwise downward from
A to D and returns upward while repeating the note A between each successive scale step. After a striking deceptive
cadence in D minor, the final section of the fugue contains
a fiery recitative-fantasy which leads to a dignified close in
a short Adagio section.

The great Toccata, Adagio, and Fugue in C Major
(BWV 564) is a magnificent composition of imposing grandeur
and balanced construction. The toccata offers opportunities
for echo effects in both the manual and pedal parts. A long
pedal cadenza follows the brilliant, virtuoso first section on
the manuals. After the introductory section comes a closely
unified section of much rhythmic vitality. One can change
manuals to underline the three figurational thematic ideas,
although this treatment might sound complex and confusing
to the listener; to play the entire section on one manual
lends a sense of unity to the whole. The Adagio in A minor
is a highly embellished aria, which is accompanied by pizzicato pedal and neutral harmonic background. A brief
interlude of rich harmonies and seven-part texture, which
resembles the old Italian toccata di durezze e ligature, mod-
ulates from A minor to C major for the stunning fugue. The
fugue subject is in four segments, which are separated by
rests. The first three segments are constructed from approximately the same terse, rhythmic, violinistic motive,
but the second and third segments are placed on successively
higher tonal levels. The sequence leads to a 16th-note
figure built upon a stepwise melody which rises and falls
from a repeated D. The return to the principal manual for
the closing section brings a sharp and startling finish on a
brief eighth-note chord. The concertato style is especially
noticeable in this Toccata, Adagio and Fugue.

The last of the larger preludes and fugues of the
Weimar period is the Prelude and Fugue in A Major (BWV
536). The prelude is a short, light, sparkling piece, and
the fugue is sober and contains thematic material of a more
pastoral nature than that found in the prelude.

The exuberant toccata and the restrained alla breve
fugue in F major (BWV 540) make a strongly contrasting
combination. Although the canonic writing over a pedal
point might suggest the use of two manuals at the beginning
of the toccata, the addition of a third voice soon afterwards
nullifies that type of treatment. Brilliant pedal cadenzas
follow the two canonic sections. The second pedal solo section ascends to f^1 on the pedal board, a pedal note not found
on many pedal divisions of that era. The balance of the
438-measure long toccata is based on a new theme drawn
from an ascending arpeggiated figure on a triad which is
followed by chords on the second and third beats. Neapolitan
sixth chords bring a surprise element to the harmony several
times. The fugue in ricercar style is dignified, and Bach's
contrapuntal mastery is constantly exhibited in the double
fugue.

Keller places the great C minor Prelude and Fugue
(BWV 546) in the Leipzig period,[6] although for the fugue
Schmieder suggests the late Weimar period and Leipzig for
the prelude.[7] The prelude has a number of different components: the double-chorus, the "sighing motive," triplets
along the scale line, and a regular use of the Neapolitan
sixth chord, all organized into a grand whole. Although the
fugue might seem to suggest that it is a double-fugue, it
does not actually become one.

A theme which was extracted from a suite by Raison
is raised to much greater heights than in its original form
by the artistry of Bach in the Passacaglia in C Minor (BWV
582). The theme is eight measures long and is followed by
20 variations and the Thema fugatum, which has two counter-
subjects. Even though the theme is at times broken into
two voice parts (or even one), and taken from the pedal and
put into other voices, it is always present. Although some
manuscripts indicate that this work was composed for "cembalo ossia organo," the Passacaglia could not possibly reach
such a wonderful variety of expression on a harpsichord as
on the organ. Toward the end of the fugue there is a dramatic use of the Neapolitan sixth chord before the fugue is
closed.

It is interesting to study the stop list of the organ
Bach had at his disposal while he worked in Weimar.

Weimar, Germany, Schlosskirche.
Built by Ludwig Compenius, 1658;
rebuilt by Heinrich Nicolaus Trebs, 1719-1720.

Hauptwerk	Positiv	Pedal
Quintatön 16'	Prinzipal 8'	Gros untersatz 32'
Prinzipal 8'	Viola di gamba 8'	Sub-bass 16'
Gemshorn 8'	Gedackt 8'	Violon bass 16'
Gedackt 8'	Kleingedackt 4'	Prinzipal bass 8'
Octave 4'	Octave 4'	Posaune bass 16'
Quintatön 4'	Waldflöte 2'	Trompeten 8'
Mixtur VI	Sesquialtera II	Cornetten bass 4'
Cymbel III	Trompeta 8'	
Glockenspiel	Tremulant	
Tremulant		

Hauptwerk/Pedal coupler; Positiv/Hauptwerk coupler;
Cymbelstern

Many twentieth-century organs have been built in imitation of the art of Baroque organ builders, which reached
its zenith about the turn of the eighteenth century.   The
Baroque organ is known for its brilliance and clarity, its
homogeneous ensemble, and facilities for emphasizing one
voice and accompanying with less aggressive sounds.   The
two outstanding organ builders of the Baroque period were
Arp Schnitger (1648-1720), working in northern Germany and
the Netherlands, and Gottfried Silbermann (1683-1753), who
built organs in eastern France and central Germany.

II. CÖTHEN (1717-1723)

One of the most celebrated works of Bach, the Fantasia and Fugue in G Minor, is associated with Bach's audi-
tion for the organist's position at St. Jakobi Church in Hamburg.   This instrument, one of Schnitger's finest organs,
was "rediscovered" during the third decade of the twentieth
century and extolled as an example of the ideal of the organ
building art near the turn of the eighteenth century.   The
specifications are given on the next page.

Hamburg, Germany, St. Jakobi Kirche.
Built by Arp Schnitger, 1688-1692

Hauptwerk	Oberwerk
Prinzipal 16'	Prinzipal 8'
Quintatön 16'	Holzflöte 8'
Oktave 8'	Rohrflöte 8'
Spitzflöte 8'	Oktave 4'
Gedackt 8'	Spitzflöte 4'
Oktave 4'	Nasat 3'
Rohrflöte 4'	Oktave 2'
Superoktave 2'	Gemshorn 2'
Flachflöte 2'	Scharff IV-VI
Rauschpfeife III	Cymbel III
Mixtur VI-VIII	Trompete 8'
Trompete 16'	Vox humana 8'
	Trompete 4'

Rückpositiv	Brustwerk
Prinzipal 8'	
Gedackt 8'	Holzprinzipal 8'
Quintatön 8'	Oktave 4'
Oktave 4'	Hohlflöte 4'
Blockflöte 4'	Waldflöte 2'
Nasat 3'	Sesquialter II
Oktave 2'	Scharff IV-VI
Sifflöte 1 1/2'	Dulcian 8'
Sesquialter II	Trechterregal 8'
Scharff IV-VI	
Dulcian 16'	
Bärpfeife 8'	
Schalmei 4'	

Pedal

Prinzipal 32'	Rauschpfeife III
Oktave 16'	Posaune 32'
Subbass 16'	Dulcian 16'
Oktave 8'	Trompete 8'
Oktave 4'	Trompete 4'
Nachthorn 2'	Cornett 2'
Mixtur VI-VIII	

The Fantasia and Fugue in G Minor (BWV 542) is an astounding work of great proportion in its development of

content, beauty of form and order, and contrapuntal craftsmanship. The fantasia twice balances the fugato sections
with improvisational recitatives. The harmonic intensity,
richness, and chromatic growth in the manual parts over the
long descending Phrygian mode in the pedal is especially effective. The fugue is based on a Dutch folksong and follows
closely the general contour of the song. A new motive of
only four eighth-notes receives a large share of development,
which adds more interest and excitement when the new motive
is used with the principal subject.

III.   LEIPZIG (1723-1750)

      When Bach left Weimar and went to Cöthen, he be-
came a court musician, and his principal duties were to provide orchestral music. In 1723 he became the Cantor at the
Thomaskirche in Leipzig, where his chief responsibilities
were to conduct, to compose, and to teach in the school;
an organist played under Bach's supervision, although Bach
probably played from time to time. These facts do not suggest, however, that in the two latter periods of his life Bach
was no longer interested in the instrument, as some of his
greatest organ compositions prove.

      It is interesting to study the Lutheran service in
which Bach functioned. From the material given by Schweitzer the following annotated list of items in the order of services has been established:[8]

The service began at 7 a.m. and lasted from three to four
hours.

          Organ prelude
          Motet
          Introit
          Kyrie, sung once in German: Kyrie, Gott Vater in
              Ewigkeit; sung once in Latin: Kyrie eleison.
          Possible preludizing on the chorale Allein Gott ("To
              God Alone Be Highest Praise")
          Gloria intoned from altar, answered by choir with
              et in terra pax or by congregation with German
              Gloria in chorale form: Allein Gott
          Collect
          Epistle read or sung in old psalmody
          Organist preludized on congregational hymn
          Congregational hymn

Gospel (chanted by priest)
Credo (intoned by priest)
Organist preludized for tuning of instruments
Cantata sung by choir which lasted on the average of
    20 minutes
Hymn--German Credo: <u>Wir glauben all</u> ("We All
    Believe in One True God")
Sermon (lasted exactly one hour, from 8 to 9 a. m.)
Prayer
Blessing
Congregational hymn
Communion celebration during which German hymns
    were sung or preludizing and improvising by the
    organist took place.

Vespers at St. Thomas, Leipzig:[9]
    (Service began at 1:15 p. m.)
    Various prayers and hymns
    Sermon (usually on the Epistle)
    German Magnificat
    Hymn: <u>Nun danket alle Gott</u> ("Now Thank We All
    Our God")

    The stop list below is that of the organ in the Thomas-
kirche at the time of Bach's tenure.

Leipzig, Germany, Thomaskirche.
Built in 1489;
rebuilt by Johann Scheibe, 1721-1722.

Hauptwerk (middle manual)	Rückpositiv (lowest manual)
Prinzipal 16'	Prinzipal 8'
Prinzipal 8'	Gedackt 8'
Quintadena 16'	Quintadena 8'
Octava 4'	Gedackt 4'
Quinta 3' (2 2/3')	Querflöte 4'
Super octava 2'	Violin 2'
Spiel-pfeife 8'	Rauschquinte II
Sesquialtera II	Mixtur IV
Mixtur VII-X	Spitzflöte 4'
	Schallflöte 1'
Brustwerk (uppermost manual)	Krumbhorn 16'
	Trommet 8'

Grossgedackt 8'   Pedal
Prinzipal 4'
Nachthorn 4'   Sub-bass 16'
Nasat 3' (2 2/3')   Posaunenbass 16'
Gemshorn 2'   Trommetenbass 8'
Zimbel II   Schallmeyenbass 4'
Sesquialtera II   Cornet 3'
Regal 8'
Geigend regal 4'

Tremulant; Vogelsang; Cymbelstern

The chorale-based organ works of Bach from the
Leipzig period include the Clavierübung, Part III (Keyboard
Practice), the six "Schübler" chorales, the Great Eighteen
chorales, and the Canonic variations on Vom Himmel hoch
("From Heaven Above to Earth I Come") (BWV 769), which
he wrote in connection with his joining the Mizler Society
for Musical Sciences in 1747.   In the canonic variations
Bach's contrapuntal ability is exhibited by his ingenious inter-
twining of all four lines of the chorale, presenting them simultaneously at the end of the fifth variation.   His unsur-
passed understanding of contrapuntal possibilities is shown
in the Art of the Fugue and the Musical Offering.

Clavierübung, Part III

The Clavierübung, Part III (BWV 669-689), was en-
graved and published in 1739.   The title page reads:

Third Part
of the
KEYBOARD PRACTICE
composed
of
several preludes
on the
Catechism and other hymns
for the organ
for music lovers
and especially for connoisseurs
of such work
composed by
JOHANN SEBASTIAN BACH
Royal Polish and Electoral Saxon
Court Composer, Capellmeister and

Director Chori Musici in Leipzig
Published by the author

This collection is sometimes called the Catechism because of the larger chorale (pedaliter, "with pedal") settings and the smaller (manualiter, "manual alone") settings, which might be likened to the longer and shorter Lutheran Catechisms and because of Bach's choice of chorales representing such subjects as the Ten Commandments, the Creed, Prayer, Baptism, Holy Communion, and Penitence. The Clavierübung, Part III, is sometimes referred to as the organ Mass because of the settings of chorales which correspond to the Lutheran Mass: the three-fold Kyrie, the Lutheran Gloria (Allein Gott in der Höh' sei Ehr--"To God Alone be Highest Praise"), the Ten Commandments (Dies sind die heiligen zehn Gebot--"These Are the Holy Ten Commandments"), and the Lutheran Credo (Wir glauben all' in einen Gott--"We All Believe in One True God"). Bach's grand design for the collection does suggest these conceptions. He also obviously hoped that it would sell well and appeal to keyboard players other than organists. This might be the reason he included the four duettos, which have no liturgical significance and no connection with chorales; the duettos strongly suggest performance on stringed keyboard instruments. The manualiter chorale settings could also be performed on keyboard instruments other than the organ.

The Clavierübung, Part III, offers two settings of ten chorales and three arrangements of Allein Gott, perhaps in honor of the three persons of the Trinity, framed by the pieces in E-flat major, the prelude at the beginning and the fugue at the end of the entire work. Most of the manualiter settings are smaller compositions, which are built on only the initial chorale phrase melody. A manualiter fugue is based on Jesus Christus, unser Heiland ("Jesus Christ, Our Saviour"), and a complete arrangement of one stanza of Vater unser ("Our Father, Who in Heaven Art") is given a beautiful setting for one manual. One admires the intense rhythmic vigor imparted to the shorter setting of Dies sind die heiligen zehn Gebot ("These Are the Holy Ten Commandments") and the fughetta in A major on Allein Gott ("To God Alone be Highest Praise").

In the larger chorale settings the first ones associated with the three persons of the Trinity are indeed profound. Flowing counterpoint makes the large trio on Allein Gott an

absorbing piece, alternating phrases of the chorale melody
between the hands and ending with the final phrase sounded
first by the pedal and then by the right hand.   The large
setting of <u>Dies sind die heiligen zehn Gebot</u> presents the
chorale in canon for the left hand.   The fugue on <u>Wir glauben</u>
<u>all' an einen Gott</u> is called the "Giant" fugue because of the
sturdy strides made by the ascending broken thirds in the
pedal part, which give the work breadth and strength.   The
complex rhythms of the large work based on <u>Vater unser</u>
make it difficult to understand and to perform.

      <u>Aus tiefer Not</u> ("Out of the Depths") is a work in six
voice parts.   Each chorale phrase is introduced imitatively
in most of the voice parts.   The piece was written for double
pedal;   the right foot has the melody of the chorale in augmentation.   The cantus firmus of the Communion hymn <u>Jesus</u>
<u>Christus, unser Heiland</u> ("Jesus Christ, Our Saviour") is in
the pedal part;   the other two parts are played on separate
manuals in intricate and technically demanding counterpoint.
This counterpoint begins with a broken tenth contracting to
a broken octave and then to a broken sixth, all in eighth-
notes;   this same figure is repeated three more times, each
time one step higher.   A 16th-note continuation of the line
enters soon thereafter to become a foil to the bounding
eighth-notes in the other hand.

      The three principal themes of the <u>Prelude in E-flat</u>
might also be considered symbolic of the Trinity, as have
the three subjects of the E-flat fugue.   (The key signature
also contains three flats.)   The structure of the prelude can
be shown by the graph below.   The sections composed of
primary thematic material is indicated by the straight line.
Secondary thematic material is indicated by dotted lines and
tertiary thematic material is shown by x's.   The numbers on
the lines give the exact measure numbers in the prelude, and
the numbers in parenthesis denote the number of measures
in the section. [10]

1--32 33--50 51--70 71--98 99--111 112--129 130--174 175--205

1--32	33--50	51--70	71--98	99--111	112--129	130--174	175--205
_____	. . . . . .	_____	xxxxxx	_____	. . . .	xxxxxxxx	_____
(32)	(18)	(20)	(28)	(13)	(18)	(45)	(31)

By using three different planes of tone quality the performer
can make a distinction between the sections so that the form

can be easily comprehended by the attentive listener.

The three expositions of the <u>Fugue in E-flat Major</u> have been said to be symbolic of the three persons of the Trinity. [11]   The first subject is combined with the second subject in the middle section, and all three themes are combined in the final section.

SIX CHORALES
of several types
to be played
on an
Organ
with two manuals and pedal
composed by
Johann Sebastian Bach
Royal Polish and Electoral Saxon Court Composer
Capellmeister and Director. Chor. Mus. Lips.
Published by Joh. Georg Schübler
at Zella in the Thuringian Forest
to be purchased in Leipzig from the Capellmeister Bach,
from his Sons in Berlin and Halle,
and from the publisher in Zella

The Six Chorales (BWV 645-650), often called the "Schübler" Chorales, were published after 1745 by Georg Schübler of Zella. [12]   Each one of the six is a trio arrangement made by Bach of vocal movements from his own cantatas.   All six pieces are for two manuals and pedal, in which the melodies stand out distinctly from the other parts. <u>Wachet auf, ruft uns die Stimme</u> ("Wake, Awake, a Voice Is Calling") is a transcription of the tenor solo of Cantata 140. In <u>Wo soll ich fliehen hin</u> ("O Whither Shall I Flee") the frantic soul in search of refuge is musically depicted by a nervous contrapuntal motive set against the melody in the alto range played by a 4' pedal;   the cantata from which this movement was taken has been lost.   The third chorale, <u>Wer nur den lieben Gott lässt walten</u> ("If Thou but Suffer God to Guide Thee"), is transcribed from a duet for soprano, alto, and basso continuo from Cantata 93;   the decorative counterpoint was drawn from the initial chorale phrase.   The fourth Schübler chorale is based on the German chorale arrangement of the chant tone to which the Magnificat was often sung (<u>Tonus Peregrinus</u>).   <u>Meine Seele erhebt den Herren</u> ("My Soul Doth Magnify the Lord") is introduced by a pedal solo passage, which is repeated at the end (<u>ritornello</u>).   The com-

position Bach arranged is found in his Cantato 10, where it
was a duet for alto and tenor.   The counterpoint of Ach
bleib bei uns ("Abide with Us") contains large leaps over a
wide range, and sounds least appropriate of all the six chorales to the organ.   Bach's original movement was for soprano, violoncello piccolo, and basso continuo, and came
from Cantata 6.   Kommst du nun ("Praise to the Lord") is
a delightful piece which Bach transcribed from the alto solo
with violin obbligato and basso continuo from Cantata 137.
The cantus firmus is played on a 4' pedal stop with the melody in the alto range.

Eighteen Chorales

In 1878 Wilhelm Rust assigned this title to a group of
larger chorales when he was preparing Volume XXV of the
Bach-Gesellschaft.   He patterned the title after that of the
Six Chorales.   These larger chorales have no relationship
to each other, liturgical or otherwise.   They were probably
sketched in the Weimar period and rewritten in Leipzig;   indeed, Bach worked on them shortly before his death.   Bach
dictated the last three chorale preludes to his son-in-law,
Altnikol.   The final work Bach composed was the final chorale in the collection, Vor deinen Tron tret' ich ("Before Thy
Throne I Now Appear"), because he realized that his life
was rapidly drawing to a close.   The text, which is usually
associated with this melody, is Wenn wir in höchsten Nöten
sein ("When We Are Found in Deepest Need").

The two chorales found at the beginning of the great
Eighteen are settings of Komm, heiliger Geist, Herre Gott
("Come, Holy Ghost, Lord God").   The first setting is a
lengthy fantasia with the cantus firmus in the pedal;   the
second has the embellished melody on a separate manual.
An Wasserflüssen Babylon ("By the Waters of Babylon"), a
poetic arrangement of Psalm 137, gives the tender ornamented melody to the tenor part on a separate manual.   One
of the favorite chorales from this set is the beautiful coloratura setting of Schmücke dich, o liebe Seele ("Deck Thyself,
My Soul, with Gladness").   Trio writing at its purest is
found in Herr Jesu Christ, dich zu uns wend' ("Lord Jesus
Christ, Turn Thou to Us").   Von Gott will ich nicht lassen
("From God I Ne'er Will Turn Me") assigns the melody to a
4' stop in the pedal.   The rhythmic motive used in this piece
is called the "joy" motive, two 32d-notes followed by a 16th-
note.   One of the most exquisite pieces in all organ literature is the coloratura treatment of Nun komm der Heiden

Heiland ("Now Comes the Saviour of the Gentiles"); the ornate soprano melody spins above the moving pedal and sedate-
ly flowing alto and tenor parts. Trio and organo pleno settings of the same melody follow as numbers ten and 11 in the
series. An embellished setting, an arrangement with the
melody in the tenor disguised, and a splendid trio on Allein
Gott ("To God Alone be Highest Praise") are the next three
chorales. Two settings of Jesus Christus, unser Heiland
("Jesus Christ, Our Saviour") are numbers 15 and 16; the
first has the cantus firmus in the pedal, and the second was
written for manuals alone. The 17th chorale is an organo
pleno arrangement of Komm, Gott Schöpfer, heiliger Geist
("Come, Creator-God and Holy Ghost"), the first eight measures of which are exactly the same as the Orgelbüchlein
setting of the chorale. The composition continues in flowing
16ths and discards the off-beat pedal and rhythmic pattern of
the earlier setting.

Leipzig Period: Free Works

Forkel, Bach's first biographer, states that Bach
wrote the six sonatas for two manuals and pedal for his
eldest son, Wilhelm Friedemann. [13] They were probably
conceived for stringed keyboard instruments with pedals.
The chamber music character of the writing seems to support this thesis. The sonatas, nevertheless, are admirably
suited to the organ. In general they follow the Italian violin
concerto or the Italian instrumental trio sonata form: fast,
slow, fast. All of the movements, with the one exception of
the last movement of the first sonata, were given tempo
markings by Bach. Schweitzer has remarked that scarcely
any difficulty of old or modern organ music has not been
met in the sonatas if one has studied them thoroughly. [14] A
wide variety of moods is presented here: restrained, cheery,
graceful, lofty, lyric, vigorous, pastoral, and lustrous.

The Prelude and Fugue in G Major (BWV 541) is a
vivacious and joyous combination of two pieces which are
closely related in quality, consistent in spirit and in technical demand.

Toward the close of the Weimar period and on into
the Leipzig period Bach's preludes and fugues became more
independent of each other. Each part became longer, and
both parts tended to treat the subject material contrapuntally
throughout and concentrated on one or two motives in a consistent manner. A significant number of the later fugues

can be classified in the ricercar type in which the subjects
are composed of notes of longer duration and much less
marked rhythm than the subjects of earlier fugues.   Virtuoso
pedal passages and concertato treatment does recur from time
to time in later preludes and fugues but to a much smaller
degree than that found in the Weimar period.

The so-called "Dorian" Toccata and Fugue in D Minor
(BWV 538) is a brilliant work, one of the few Bach organ
works in which manual changes were indicated by Bach himself.   This composition generates a vitality which continues
throughout the piece.   The subject of the fugue is much more
serious in nature than the thematic material of the toccata.
The subject ascends from D to the D an octave higher and
then descends to its starting point, frequently using syncopation.

The Prelude and Fugue in E Minor (BWV 548) is a
great work in which the harmonic tension produced by suspensions is similar to that found in the Prelude and Fugue
in B Minor.   The fugue subject grows in everwidening broken
intervals to the distance of an octave, a fact which has
caused the fugue to be given the programmatic title of the
"Wedge" fugue.   Bach used the simple sequence and scale
in such a melodic fashion that one is scarcely aware of the
musical materials from which these mature pieces were
fashioned.   One characteristic frequently employed in the
pedal part of these later works is the 16th-note progression
downward with a step back on alternating notes.

The Prelude and Fugue in B Minor (BWV 544) is
ornate, symmetrical, melodic, and majestic.   The performer
must allow the piece to be an expressive organo pleno.
Manual changes can clarify the structure of the prelude as
shown by the graph below.   The sections composed of primary thematic material is indicated by straight lines.   The
numbers in parentheses denote the number of measures in
each section, and the numbers on the lines give the exact
measure numbers. [15]

```
1----16        27-----42        50----72            78------85
        . . . . . .              . . . . . .         . . . . . . . .
_____
        17--26              43--49              73-----78
  (16)    (10)      (16)      (7)      (23)      (5 1/2)   (7 1/2)
```

The fugue has an unassuming subject, but it is beauti-
fully and naturally developed.   When the new theme enters

in measure 59, it is treated with so much prominence that
it might be considered a new countersubject. The architecture of the fugue is easily understood, and the episodes of
secondary subject matter, which do not call for pedal, might
suggest performance on a different manual.

The Prelude and Fugue in C Major (BWV 547) is
dated about 1744. Both the prelude and fugue are lyric in
character. The prelude is written in $\frac{9}{8}$ time and the fugue
in common meter. Each measure of the prelude is directly
related to one of four distinct ideas which are found in the
soprano part of the first four measures. The pedal part of
the fugue enters only 24 measures before the end of the 72-
measure composition, and there are over 50 appearances of
the fugue subject.

Notes

1.   The order followed here corresponds with the chronology
     of works prepared by Wolfgang Schmieder in his The-
     matisch-systematisches Verzeichnis der Werke Joh.
     Seb. Bachs, Leipzig: Breitkopf und Härtel, 1950. The
     abbreviation BWV refers to a rearrangement of words
     in the title of this same index: Bachs Werke Verzeich-
     nis. The abbreviation S. refers to Schmieder and is
     sometimes used instead of BWV.
2.   Hermann Keller, The Organ Works of Bach, translated
     by Helen Hewitt, New York: C. F. Peters Corp. ,
     1967; p. 176.
3.   Johann Philipp Kirnberger's Collection consists of 24
     chorale settings which he copied by J. S. Bach and a
     few other composers such as Walther, J. L. Krebs,
     and Bernhard Bach. Kirnberger (1721-1783) was a
     pupil of Bach in 1749. The collection is listed in the
     Schmieder catalog as numbers 609 through 713.
4.   Albert Schweitzer, J. S. Bach, London: Adam and
     Charles Black, 1923 (reprint, 1947); vol. II, p. 25-
     74.   See also F. E. Kirby, A Short History of Key-
     board Music. New York: Free Press, 1966; p. 116-
     117.
5.   Hermann Keller, The Organ Works of Bach, translated
     by Helen Hewitt, New York: C. F. Peters Corp. ,
     1967; p. 72.
6.   Keller, op. cit. , p. 148.
7.   Schmieder, op. cit. , p. 421.
8.   Albert Schweitzer, op. cit. , vol. I, p. 126-129.

9. Schweitzer, op. cit., vol. I, p. 128.
10. Based on the analysis found in Keller, op. cit., p. 160.
11. The English hymntune St. Anne, first published in 1708,
    has been attributed to William Croft (1678-1727), who
    was organist of St. Anne's Church, Soho, London.
    The first subject of the E-flat Fugue has the same
    melody as the St. Anne hymntune, which is the ex-
    planation of why the E-flat Fugue is often called the
    "St. Anne" fugue. The similarity is merely coinci-
    dental because it is highly unlikely that Bach ever
    saw this particular English hymntune or that Bach
    was familiar with it. This same melody can also be
    found as the subject to Buxtehude's fugue in E major
    and in two different movements of Handel's O Praise
    the Lord with One Consent, a Chandos anthem.
12. Schübler is listed as one of the pupils of Bach in Hans
    Löffler, "Die Schüler Joh. Seb. Bachs," Bach-
    Jahrbuch, Evangelische Verlaganstalt Berlin, vol. 40
    (1953), p. 6, 10.
13. Keller, op. cit., p. 130.
14. Schweitzer is quoted in Keller, op. cit., p. 134.
15. Based on the analysis given in Keller, op. cit., p. 158.

Bibliography

Aldrich, Putnam. "On the Interpretation of Bach's Trills,"
    Musical Quarterly, vol. XLIX (1963), p. 289-310.
_____. Ornamentation in J. S. Bach's Organ Works.
    New York: Coleman-Ross Co., 1950.
Bodky, Erwin. The Interpretation of Bach's Keyboard Works.
    Cambridge, Mass.: Harvard University Press, 1960.
Clough, F. F., and G. F. Cuming. "Bach's Organ Works
    in BWV Numbering," Eighth Music Book. London:
    Hinrichsen Edition Ltd., 1959; p. 193-206.
David, Hans T., and Arthur Mendal. The Bach Reader.
    New York: W. W. Norton and Co., 1945.
Dickinson, A. E. The Art of J. S. Bach. London: Hin-
    richsen Edition Ltd., 1950; p. 67-93.
_____. Bach's Fugal Works. London: Isaac Pitman and
    Sons, 1956.
Donington, Robert. Tempo and Rhythm in Bach's Organ
    Music. London: Hinrichsen Edition Ltd., 1961.
Dufourcq, Norbert. J. S. Bach: Le Maître de l'Orgue.
    Paris: Librairie Floury, 1948.
Emery, Walter. Bach's Ornaments. London: Novello and
    Co., 1953.

_____. "On the Registration of Bach's Organ Preludes and Fugues," Musical Times, No. 1432, vol. 103 (June 1962), p. 396; no. 1433, vol. 103 (July 1962), p. 467.

Frotscher, Gotthold. Geschichte des Orgelspiels und der Orgelkomposition. Berlin: Merseberger Verlag, 1959; vol. II, p. 849-969.

Geiringer, Karl. Johann Sebastian Bach--the Culmination of an Era. New York: Oxford University Press, 1966.

Grace, Harvey. The Organ Works of Bach. London: Novello and Co. , 1922.

Heiller, Anton. "Chorales of the Clavierübung, Part 3," The Diapason (October 1962), p. 8.

Hinrichsen, Max, ed. Eighth Music Book. London: Hinrichsen Edition Ltd. , 1956.

Kasling, Kim R. "Some Editorial, Formal and Symbolic Aspects of J. S. Bach's Canonic Variations on 'Vom Himmel hoch da komm ich her'," Diapason, Pt 1 (May 1971), p. 18; Pt 2 (June 1971), p. 16-17; Pt 3 (July 1971), p. 20-21; and Conclusion (August 1971), p. 20-21.

Keller, Hermann. Die Orgelwerke Bachs: Ein Beitrag zu ihrer Geschichte, Form, Deutung und Wiedergabe. Leipzig: C. F. Peters, 1948 (English ed. , The Organ Works of Bach, translated by Helen Hewitt, New York: C. F. Peters Corp. , 1967).

Klotz, Hans. "Bachs Orgeln und seine Orgelmusik," Die Musikforschung, vol. II (1950), p. 189-203.

Lawry, Eleanor. "Symbolism as Shown in Chorale Preludes of Bach Is Studied," The Diapason (August 1949), p. 6.

Löffler, Hans. "Die Schüler Joh. Seb. Bachs," Bach-Jahrbuch in Auftrage der neuen Bachgesellschaft, Alfred Dürr and Werner Neumann, eds. Berlin: Evangelische Verlaganstalt, 1953; vol. XL, p. 5.

Moeser, James C. "Symbolism in J. S. Bach's Orgelbuchlein," The American Organist, vol. 47, no. 11 (November 1964), p. 14-20; vol. 47, no. 12 (December 1964), p. 14-22; vol. 48 (January 1965), p. 12-16; (February 1965), p. 22-25; (March 1965), p. 16-22; (April 1965), p. 14-21; (May 1965), p. 11-14; (June 1965), p. 12-17; and (July 1965), p. 11-13.

Pirro, André. L'Orgue de J. S. Bach. Paris: Librairie Fischbacher, 1897.

Reinburg, Peggy Kelley. "Affektenlehre of the Baroque Era and Their Application in the Works of Johann Sebastian Bach (Specifically in the Schübler Chorales),"

American Organist (June 1968), p. 15.

Richards, Ruthann. "The Orgelbüchlein--Its History and
Cantus Firmus Treatment," Diapason (October 1969),
p. 24-25.

Riedel, Johannes. The Lutheran Chorale: Its Basic Traditions. Minneapolis: Augsburg Pub. House, 1967.

Schmieder, Wolfgang. Thematisch-systematisches Verzeichnis der musikalischen Werke von Johann Sebastian
Bach. Leipzig: Breitkopf und Härtel, 1950.

Schweitzer, Albert. J. S. Bach, le Musicien-Poète. Leip-
zig: 1905 (English ed. , J. S. Bach, translated by
Ernest Newman, 2 vols. , London: Breitkopf und
Härtel, 1911; reprint, London: Adam and Charles
Black, 1947.

Spitta, Philipp. Johann Sebastian Bach, 2 vols. Leipzig:
1873-1880 (English ed. , Johann Sebastian Bach: His
Work and Influence on the Music of Germany, translated by Clara Bell and John Alexander Fuller-
Maitland, 3 vols. , London: Novello and Co. , 1899;
reprint, New York: Dover Pub. , 1951).

Sumner, Willian Leslie. Bach's Organ-Registration, London:
Hinrichsen Edition Ltd. , 1961.

_____. The Organs of Bach. London: Hinrichsen Edi-
tion Ltd. , 1954.

Taylor, Stainton de B. The Chorale Preludes of J. S.
Bach. London: Oxford University Press, 1942.

Terry, Charles Sanford. Bach: A Biography. London: Oxford University Press, 1928.

_____. Bach's Chorals, 3 vols. Cambridge, England:
University Press, 1915-1921.

_____. The Music of Bach: An Introduction. London:
Oxford University Press, 1933 (reprint, New York:
Dover Pub. , 1963).

Tusler, Robert L. The Style of Bach's Chorale-Preludes.
New York: Da Capo Press, 1968.

Williams, Peter F. "J. S. Bach and English Organ Music,"
Music and Letters, vol. XLIV (1963), p. 140-151.

9. CLASSICAL FRENCH ORGAN SCHOOL: 1600-1800

The founder of the Classical French organ school, Jehan Titelouze (1563-1633), was of English ancestry ("Title-house").[1] The family had emigrated to France by way of the Spanish Netherlands. At the age of 22 Titelouze was appointed organist of the church of St. Jean, Rouen. In 1591 he became the organist of the Rouen Cathedral, where he served until the end of his life. He became a canon there in 1610. Titelouze was a priest, scholar, teacher, performer, composer, theoretician, and expert in building organs. He carried on a lively correspondance with Mersenne, the author of Harmonie universelle and also a prominent musical theoretician.

Titelouze wrote two collections of organ music for the church. The first, Hymnes de l'Eglise pour Toucher sur l'Orgue, avec les Fugues et Recherches sur Leur Plain Chant (Balard, 1623), appeared one year before Scheidt's Tabulatura nova (1624). Titelouze's first book embraces 12 Latin hymns, each containing three or four versets. His second volume, Le Magnificat, ou Cantique de la Vierge pour Toucher sur l'Orgue, Suivant les Huit Tons de l'Eglise, appeared in 1626. This volume contained settings of six versets in all eight tones for the Magnificat: Magnificat, Quia respexit, Et misericordia, Deposuit potentes, Suscepit Israel, and Gloria Patri et Filio. Titelouze always wrote two settings of the Deposuit verse so that when the Benedictus (which needed seven organ versets) was sung to the same tune, there would be enough organ pieces provided.

The music of Titelouze, as Harvey Grace wrote,[2] is music of "austere gravity." He was faithful to the modes when the major-minor system began to take precedence. The lack of modulation, some chromaticism, and diatonic discords, are characteristics of his music. As a general practice Titelouze wrote in four parts in continuous flow, uninterrupted by cadences. Each voice usually begins by imitating the initial motive of the plainchant. The polyphony is vocal in style in the slower movements. The forms employed by

HISTORICAL BACKGROUND

1608	Champlain founded Quebec
1610-1643	Reign of Louis XIII
1612	Louvre begun
1616-1634	Richelieu became member of the Council
1621-1696	LaFontaine
1622-1673	Molière
1623-1662	Pascal
1632-1687	Lully
1635	Académie française established
1636	Mersenne Harmonie universelle
1639-1699	Racine
1643-1715	Reign of Louis XIV
1657-1726	Lalande
1682	LaSalle explored Mississippi River region
1683-1764	Rameau
1684-1721	Watteau
1694-1778	Voltaire
1709	Dispersion of nuns of Port-Royal
1712-1778	Rousseau
1714-1787	Gluck
1715-1774	Reign of Louis XV
1722	Rameau Traité de l'harmonie
1732-1806	Fragonard
1774-1792	Reign of Louis XVI
1789-1794	French Revolution

Titelouze were the plein jeu, the ricercar (he used the term recherche), and choral figuré in which the melody notes are not actually ornamented. The plainsong cantus firmus is written in notes of equal value. [3] The pedal reed often played the cantus firmus in the tenor range. The pedal division of French organs of that time was very small and usually contained only one 8' reed, one 8' Bourdon, and perhaps a 4' flute. There was no 16' sound in the pedal division. The left hand played the part which performed the bass function (the real bass part).

François Roberday (1624-1680) is a little known figure in organ history. He issued a collection, Fugues et Caprices, à Quatre Parties Mises en Partition pour l'Orgue (1660), which contained three pieces by other composers: Frescobaldi, Ebner, and Froberger. His own pieces were composed on themes given him by musical acquaintances such as Couperin, d'Anglebert, and Froberger. These polyphonic pieces incorporate thematic metamorphosis, which

Frescobaldi had so effectively employed. 4

By 1650 French organ composers had accepted the
new musical style which established registration practices
for specific musical types on the organs whose specifications
had become rather standardized throughout France. The didactic counterpoint of Titelouze began to be replaced by more
melodic, less austere music influences principally by Italians
such as Cavalli and Lully. The public preferred the secular,
the music of ballet and the theater, the dance, and solo and
orchestral music. Lute music was especially popular. Ho-
mophony supplanted polyphony: one voice was predominant,
supported by the other voices. The clavecin (harpsichord)
was popular with its many short programmatic pieces and
dances, all elaborately embellished. Since organists were
often clavecinists also, the style of popular music influenced
the "old fashioned" organ music. Organists-clavecinists
Charles Racquet, Jacques Champion de Chambonnières, and
Robert Cambert, who were active in numerous musical pur-
suits, influenced organ music. Other organ composers were
Henri DuMont (1610-1684), Etienne Richard (d. 1669), and
Jacques-Denis Thomelin (ca. 1640-1693), the court organist
for Louis XIV and teacher of François Couperin. 5

The accompanied solo type of instrumental composition
was incorporated into organ literature: basse de trompette
and basse de cromorne. Clever effects such as duos, echos,
and dialogues replaced Gregorian chant. The compositions
of Louis Couperin (1625-1661) responded to the taste of the
day in chacones, sarabandes, and fantasy pieces like Les
Carillons de Paris. The superscription of Les Carillons
tells that it was written "to imitate the carillons of Paris
and which was always played on the organ of St. Gervais between vespers of All Saints' Day and that of the dead. " Another of his compositions is the Chacone in G Minor, the refrain of which could be played on the Grand Orgue; this
same composition was probably intended for harpsichord
originally. French composers of this period used the term
chacone for a rondeau with several couplets and a repeated
refrain.

Jean Henri d'Anglebert (1635-1691) is noted for his
Pièces de clavessin (1689), which included a valuable table
of French ornaments. His contrapuntal ability is shown by
five fugues based on a single subject.

Organ music of the latter half of the seventeenth

CLASSICAL FRENCH ORGAN SCHOOL: 1600-1800

1600	1650	1700	1750

1563/1564 Titelouze, J. 1633
1597 Racquet, Charles------1664
after 1601 Chambonnières, J. ------1670/1672
1610 DuMont, Henry------------1684
ca. 1621 Richard, E. 1669
1624 Roberday, François -----1680
1625 Gigault, Nicolas--------------1707
ca. 1626 Couperin, Louis 1661
1628 d'Anglebert, Jean-Henri------1691
1630 Lebègue, Nicolas--------------1702
1632 Nivers, Guillaume-----------------1714
? Geoffroy, Jean-Nicolas ?
ca. 1653 Jullien, Gilles ------1703
? Raison, André ------1719
ca. 1653 Boyvin, Jacques-----1706
1668 Couperin, François--------1733
1669 Marchand, Louis--------1732
1672 de Grigny, N. 1703
1676 Clérambault, Louis-Nicolas------1749
? Guilain, Jean-Adam-Guillaume ?
ca. 1676 DuMage, Pierre---------1751
1682 Dandrieu, Jean-François 1738
1694 Daquin, L.-C. --1722

CHRONOLOGICAL LIST OF IMPORTANT FRENCH ORGAN
BOOKS BY INDIVIDUAL COMPOSERS
OF THE SEVENTEENTH CENTURY

1623	J. Titelouze	Les Hymnes pour toucher sur l'orgue avec les Fugues.
1626	J. Titelouze	Le Magnificat ou Cantique de la Vierge.
1636-1643	Ch. Racquet	Pièces d'orgue.
1656-1661	L. Couperin	Pièces d'orgue.
1660	Roberday	Fugues et Caprices.
1650-1669	E. Richard	Pièces d'orgue.
1665	G. Nivers	Premier Livre d'orgue.
1667	G. Nivers	Deuxième Livre d'orgue.
1675	G. Nivers	Troisième Livre d'orgue.
1676	N. Lebègue	Premier Livre d'orgue.
1678-1679	N. Lebègue	Troisième Livre d'orgue.
1685	N. Gigault	Livre d'orgue.
1688	A. Raison	Livre d'orgue.
1689	D'Anglebert	Fugues et Quatuor.
1689	Boyvin	Livre d'orgue.
1690	Fr. Couperin	Livre d'orgue.
1690	G. Jullien	Premier Livre d'orgue.
1699	N. de Grigny	Premier Livre d'orgue.

century in France became confined to forms which were used by all French organ composers of that period. Registration indications became titles for pieces. Most of these pieces are rather short because of the brief time allotted for organ playing between various sections of the Mass. [6]

In the Cérémoniale de l'Eglise de Paris (1662) instructions were given about the use of the organ in the Catholic Mass. In short preludes the organ gave the pitch to the choir and alternated with the choir on sections of the Kyrie, Gloria, Sanctus, and Agnus Dei. As a solo instrument the organ was allowed to play at the offertory, [7] at the elevation, and for the postlude. At vespers the organ played more frequently between psalms or in alternation with sung verses of the Magnificat. [8]

Guillaume-Gabriel Nivers (1632-1714) wrote with froideur et la grâce facile, (detachment and flowing elegance)[9] and remained faithful to the ecclesiastical modes. Nivers seemed to prefer the duo type and the reed or cornet solo (récit), which was the only ornamented part. He also

(text continued on page 127)

TITLES OF FRENCH ORGAN COMPOSITIONS OF THE SEVENTEENTH AND EIGHTEENTH CENTURIES AND EXPLANATION OF PERFORMANCE.*

Title	English Translation and Description
Basse de trompette Basse de cromorne	Trumpet (or cromorne) solo in the bass (lower) range of the keyboard. The solo would be accompanied by foundation tone in the upper two parts.
Cornet de cromorne	Cornet solo (with flute accompaniment). The cornet is a compound of five different pitches (8', 4', 2 2/3', 2', 1 3/5'), usually of flute quality, played as a melody.
Cromorne en taille	Cromorne solo in the tenor (range of the keyboard, accompanied by flutes)
Dialogue	Dialogue (of alternating sections between manuals or of alternating solo colors)
Dialogue sur les grands jeux	Literally: "Dialogue on big stops." Dialogue alternating between two choruses or ensembles on different manuals, usually between <u>Grand orgue</u> and <u>Positif</u>.
Duo	Duo (duet). Composition for two voices, usually contrasting, for example, a reed stop with a combined sound of Bourdon 8', Doublette 2' and Larigot 1 1/3' or a similar combination.

Echo
Echo. Composition employing echo effects by using the same musical material on two or more manuals of diminishing volume and perhaps changing colors.

Fonds d'orgue
Organ foundation (tone). The combination of all principals and flutes at 16', 8', and 4' pitches was used for this type.

Fugue
Fugue. Fugues were frequently based on plainsong or Latin hymn melodies. The most frequent characteristic quality of sound used for fugues was that of the reeds.

Jeu (jeux)
Stop (stops); the word jeu (jeux) can also mean a combination of stops.

Musette (Muzète)
Musette. (Bagpipe) Composition written over a drone bass (pedal point).

Offertoire sur les Grands Jeux
Literally: "Offertoire on big stops." Composition which usually falls into several contrasting sections with such inclusions as (1) alternations between manuals, (2) melody on one manual and accompaniment on another, (3) tempo and meter changes between sections, and (4) echo effects. The predominant sound of the grands jeux was a reed sound supported by foundation stops.

Plein jeu
Literally: "Full stop." A bright ensemble, full sound on Grand Orgue and Positif choruses combined with mixtures providing the characteristic color. Plein jeu at one time meant the enormous mixture called Blockwerk elsewhere.

Point d'orgue
Organ point. Composition employing a pedal- or organ-point as its principal characteristic.

Title	English Translation and Description
Tierce	Composition for a melody and accompaniment. The melody stop incorporated the Tierce 1 3/5' stop which provided its characteristic color.
Trio	Trio. Composition written for three voice parts which could be played in one of three ways: (1) all three parts on one manual, (2) two upper parts on one manual and the third part on another manual, and (3) the two upper parts on two different manuals with the third part in the pedal.
Récit - - de Basse de Trompette - de Cromorne - de Nazard - de Tierce en taille - de Voix humaine	Solo. A solo melody of individual color accompanied by flutes or sufficient foundation tone to support the solo. The solo color to be used was indicated by the stop name in the title such as "trompette," "cromorne," and "nazard."
Other French terms: à 2; à 3; à 4; à 5; à 6	The number denotes the number of voices in the composition. A Fugue à 4 would be a fugue written for four voice parts.
Premier/Dernier Kyrie Sanctus Agnus	First/Last (Final). These words were used to indicate which setting of a particular Mass movement would be played by the organ, e.g., the first Kyrie; the last Kyrie.

*For thorough discussion of these types of compositions and their registrations see Fenner Douglass., The Language of the Classical French Organ, Yale University Press, New Haven, 1969, pp. 106-114. The organs of this period are discussed in Peter Williams, The European Organ 1450-1850, B. T. Batsford Ltd., London, 1966, pp. 169-203.

alternated between manual choruses and used echo effects.
His Diminution de la Basse was replaced later by the Tierce
en taille. Nivers wrote three Livres d'orgue (1665, 1667,
1675), and attained a fine synthesis of polyphony and homo-
phony. [10]

Nicolas Gigault (1624-1702) published pieces for liturgical use in his Livre de Musique pour l'Orgue (1685). While
Gigault was not an inspired composer, his works have a degree of interest, they are highly ornamented and make use of
quick manual changes. The pedal supplies soft support or
sounds the plainsong themes in the tenor part. [11]

Three Livres d'Orgue (1676, 1678-1679, 1685?) came
from the pen of Nicolas-Antoine Lebègue (ca. 1630-1702).
Lebègue wrote for the liturgical and concert organ. For the
most part his music is tuneful and charming rather than
learned, profound, or contrapuntally developed. Lebègue
employed the ecclesiastical modes in his organ Mass, which
contains 19 short pieces, and he also referred to the Kyrie
Cunctipotens plainsong melody in this Mass. The Mass conformed strictly to the requirements of the Cérémoniale of
1662. He wrote the second book for those who had only a
moderate ability (qu'une science médiocre). Lebègue is the
first to have systematically exploited the varieties of forms
of the récit, duo, basse de trompette, dialogue, fugue grave,
and solo de cornet. [12] As for the concert organ music,
Lebègue added great impetus to what was to become a widespread interest in imitating orchestral instruments, bells,
and, later, even extra-musical activities. He often used the
various contrasting colors and effects of the organ combined
with dance rhythms and was one of the first to write variations on French carols (noëls). These were written as familiar music, intimate, picturesque, very human, to suggest
Christmas characters such as the shepherds, Joseph, the
Virgin Mary, and the ordinary French citizen's naïve pleasure
at the coming of the Christmas season. [13]

Gilles Jullien (1650-?), the organist of the Chartres
cathedral from 1663-1703, brought out his Premier Livre
d'Orgue the same year that François Couperin issued his two
organ Masses (1690). Jullien used all the forms which were
currently being written and grouped them into suites on each
of the eight ecclesiastical modes. That Jullien was not a
"finished" musician is revealed by a number of parallel octaves, awkward jumps, and monotonous passages. Surpris-
ingly enough he used the récit en taille for Cromhorne or

Tierce only once each. Jullien indicated that his four-part
fugues be performed on two manuals. [14]

André Raison (?-1719) wrote two Livres d'Orgue
(1688, 1714). In his five Masses he used the forms already
in vogue and added some originality by putting the trompette
piece in the tenor range. He employed quick manual changes
and wrote in "frank tunefulness." [15] Raison's Offerte in the
fifth tone is one example of how the secular had entered the
church. The tendency of secularization was to grow much
stronger and practically eliminate the organ's liturgical function in the eighteenth century. The Offerte was written for
the entry of the king to the Hôtel de Ville in Paris on January 30, 1687. Strains of Vive le Roy are incorporated at
the end of the piece. Raison, the teacher of Clérambault,
wrote the Trio en Passacaille (Christe from Messe du
Deuziesme Ton), the theme of which J. S. Bach presumably
borrowed for his monumental Passacaglia in C Minor (BWV
582). [16]

Jacques Boyvin (ca. 1653-1706) also wrote series of
pieces based on the eight church tones, which seems to have
been one of the chief factors common to all French organ
books of the period. His tierces en taille are well developed, and the pedal trompette has a prominent part in the
Grand Prélude in C major. [17]

Louis Marchand (1669-1732) was the organist of a
large number of Parisian churches. He was an ill-tempered
virtuoso and rival of Couperin. It is common knowledge that
Marchand avoided the confrontation with Bach at Dresden during his concert tour in Germany and temporary exile from
France. The better known compositions of Marchand are the
three-voiced Récit de flute, the heroic Dialogue in C major,
and the six-part Plein jeu. [18]

The famous Grand Jeu of Pierre DuMage (ca. 1676-
1751), organist of the Collegiate Church of St. Quentin,
closes DuMage's Livre d'Orgue (1708). The Grand Jeu is
divided into several sections: a solemn introduction, a quick,
dancing, fugal section in triple meter which incorporates
double echos, and a return to the solemnity of the first section.

The two outstanding composers of the Classical French
school at the end of the seventeenth century were François
Couperin (1668-1733) and Nicolas de Grigny (1672-1703).

Couperin was part of the family dynasty which presided at the organ console of St. Gervais in Paris for many years. He wrote two organ Masses, his only publications for organ. The first Mass contains 21 pieces and is designed for the use of parish churches (Messe pour les Paroisses). The Parish Mass frequently employs plainsong melodies. The second Mass (Messe pour les Convents) is easier to play and is designed for convent use. There seems to be no connection with plainchant in any of the 21 pieces in the second Mass. Couperin followed the examples of Titelouze and Lebègue and never decorated the plainsong melody when it was incorporated into his pieces, although there is a wide use of embellishment in his works. Couperin employed much variety in his short works--the Kyrie fugues for reed stops, the Chromhorne and Tierce solos, the dialogues, duos, and plein jeu settings.[19]

The specifications of the organ at St. Gervais, where the Couperin family were organists from 1650 until 1826, are typical of organs of the Classical French period, and the stop list is given below.

Paris, France, St. Gervais.
Built by Pierre Thierry, 1649-1650; rebuilt, 1625.
Maintained by Alexandre Thierry
during the tenure of François Couperin.

First keyboard	Second keyboard
Positiv (49 notes: A, C, D-c^3)	Grand Orgue (49 notes: A, C, D-c^3)
Bourdon 8'	Montre 16'
Montre 4'	Bourdon 16'
Flûte 4'	Montre 8'
Doublette 2'	Bourdon 8'
Fourniture III	Prestant 4'
Cymbale III	Doublette 2'
Nasard 2 2/3'	Fourniture III
Tierce 1 3/5'	Cymbale III
Larigot 1 1/3'	Flûte 4'
Cromorne 8'	Grosse Tierce 3 1/5'
	Nasard 2 2/3'
Third keyboard (37 notes: c-c^3)	Tierce 1 3/5'
	Trompette 8'
	Clairon 4'
Bourdon 8' and Flûte 4'	Voix Humaine 8'
Cymbale III	Cornet V (2 octaves)

Nasard 2 2/3'   Fourth keyboard
Doublette 2' and Tierce 1 3/5'
Cromorne 8'   Récit
                                          (3 octaves: C-c³)
                Pédale
(29 notes: A, C, D, E, to e)   Cornet Séparé V

Flûte 8'
Flûte 4'
Trompette 8'

    Grand Orgue/ Positiv; Grand Orgue/ Pédale; Tremblant
      doux; Tremblant fort
    Changes made in 1714: removed lower octave of Echo;
      removed Flûte 4' from Grand Orgue and put in Trom-
      pette 8'

      Nicolas de Grigny (1672-1703),[20] a student of Lebègue,
was organist of Notre Dame in Rheims. Grigny's Premier
Livre d'Orgue (1699) contained about 50 pieces, which included an organ Mass and five Latin hymn settings. The
famous Récit de Tierce en Taille from the Mass is especially
beautiful. Grigny renewed the tradition of Titelouze in his
five Latin hymn arrangements and, unlike Couperin, retained
the modal character of plainsong when he utilized it as a
cantus firmus. Just as Couperin often used four voices in
many of his compositions, de Grigny frequently utilized five-
part texture. Grigny advanced the fugue development into
more extended compositions and treated the same forms and
styles of the classical school but in a more serious and intellectual way. Grigny accomplished the difficult synthesis
of liturgical and concert organ composition and also coupled
warmth with a strong sense of lyricism.

      The Premier Livre de Pièces d'Orgue by Jean-
François Dandrieu (1682-1738) appeared after his death.
Dandrieu played with great facility and had thoroughly absorbed the characteristics of music of his time. Although
his pleins jeux and fugues are majestic, the larger part
of his music is of a light, playful quality, with markings
such as vivement, tendrement, and légèrement. Duos, such
as one marked en cor de chasse (suggesting the hunting horn
by its gigue rhythm) and musettes are typical of his writing.

      Louis-Nicolas Clérambault (1676-1749) dedicated his
Premier Livre d'Orgue (1710) to Raison. His two suites

contain the usual series of short pieces, each of which shows some Italian influence, which was widely felt in France at that time. The tempo indications gayement, gay, gracieuse-ment are not those of liturgical music. Clérambault's work as a French polyphonist is exhibited by his fugue in the first tone. The familiar Basse et Dessus de Trompette comes from the First Suite and the Caprice sur les Grands Jeux from the second. Each of the four suites in four different modes by Guilain (?1600's-1700's?) contains at least one Petit plein jeu, a Duo, a Trio, a Basse de Trompette or Cromorne, a Dialogue, and a récit of some sort. [21]

Les Noëlistes

In the widespread attempt to please the public, both religious and secular carols were used as themes for varia-tions by French organist-composers about the beginning of the eighteenth century. The tunes were simple, easily assim-ilated, and remembered. Each variation (couplet) had a change in rhythmic treatment, usually progressing from slower to quicker and quicker note values; the early variation or theme might present the melody in quarter notes, and the following variations probably would move to even eighth-notes, to tri-plets, and thence to 16th-notes or a rapid rhythmic figure. The harmony is often limited to dominant and tonic chords, and usually no modulation is employed. These variations relied upon the variety of note-values and color of stops to hold the listener's attention. Cromhorne is answered by cornet; echo effects; plein jeu, oboe, musette, clairon, piccolo, flutes--all these colors and effects and more charmed the audience. As Dufourcq writes, [22] these pieces required little imagination to compose, only spirit and fin-gers. Such are the noëls of Dandrieu, M. Corrette, Dornel, and Daquin. The noëls of Lebègue led to those of Pierre Dandrieu and thence to those of the best of the noël writers, Daquin, the "king of the Noëlists." [23]

Pierre Dandrieu (d. 1733), a priest, issued one organ book containing a variety of types of pieces: Noels, O filii, Chansons de Saint Jacques, Stabat Mater et Carillons, le Tout Revu, Augmenté, Extrêmement Varié et Mis Pour l'Orgue et le Clavecin (1714). The volume contained such carols as Joseph est Bien Marié, Jacob Que Tu Es Habile, and Une Jeune Pucelle. [24]

Louis-Claude Daquin (1694-1722) was an outstanding virtuoso, a court favorite, and a prominent improviser. The citizens of Paris flocked to hear him play his carol variations during the Christmas season at one of the many churches in which he held the position of organist simultaneously. In the Nouveau Livre de Noëls Daquin treated 12 carols in many colorful ways. His work exhibits charm, grace, virtuosity, and warmth.

Michel Corrette (1709-1795), the father and son Beauvarlet-Charpentier, and Claude Balbastre (1727-1799) from Dijon also wrote in this simple form. Balbastre wrote four suites of variations on Burgundian carols. [25]

Decline of the Classical French School

The entire eighteenth century and the first half of the nineteenth century were a secular age in France. This was the Age of Reason, of interest in philosophy, and of the rise of the common man. Music of this period was under the influence of Italian music, the theater, and ballet. Compositions were performed during Mass which had no liturgical significance whatsoever. Dances, songs, marches, imitations, patriotic airs, and picturesque improvisations were often played in this anti-ecclesiastical era. Some improvisations depicted cannon fire and battles. Some compositions by Michel Corrette were entitled April Showers, Enchanted Lovers, Seven-league Boots, Stars, The Taking of Jericho. Chatt wrote Agriculture and The Sovereignty of the People. [26]

The Te Deum offered many opportunities in improvisation for the imaginative organist. Mercier, in his Tableau de Paris wrote about Daquin, "more sublime than ever, played in the Judex crederis which carried impressions into the hearts so vivid that everyone paled."[27] At another time he wrote that the organist "plays during the elevation of the host and of the chalice some ariettas, sarabandes--hunting pieces, minuets, romances, rigaudons."[28] Beauvarlet-Charpentier explained in his Te Deum that his piece ends with "prolonged thunder at the will [of the performer] to depict the upsetting of the Universe."[29] Michel Corrette told how to make a storm and thunder at the organ by putting a board across the last octave of the pedals with the trumpet and bombarde stops drawn which the foot could play at will. At the end, to give an imitation of a clap of thunder, one struck the lowest keys with the elbow. [30]

Such was the degradation of the organ in France for over a century. Not until the middle of the nineteenth

DECLINE OF THE CLASSICAL FRENCH ORGAN SCHOOL: 1710-1850

1650   1700   1750   1800   1850

ca. 1660 Dandrieu, Pierre 1733
1684 Dagincour, François 1758
ca.1685 Dornel, Antoine------1765
? Corrette, Gaspard   ?
1709 Corrette, Michel------------1795
(1709 Bédos de Celles, Dom F. --1779) L'Art du Facteur d'Orgues
1715 Février, Pierre------ca.1780
? Siret, Nicolas 1754
(? Père Pingré ?)
1727 Balbastre, Claude-Bénigne 1799
1734 Beauvarlet-Charpentier, J.-J. 1794
1740 Lasceux, Guillaume-----------1831
1745 Séjan, Nicolas---------1819
1757 Marrigues, Jean-Nicolas ------1834
1766 Beauvarlet-Charpentier, J.-M. 1834
1786 Séjan, Louis-Nicolas   1849

century did the organ regain some of its integrity through the unappreciated efforts of Boëly and later through the compositions of men such as Franck and Saint-Saëns.

Notes

1. Norbert Dufourcq, La Musique d'Orgue Française de Jehan Titelouze à Jehan Alain, Paris: Librairie Floury, 1949; p. 37.
2. Harvey Grace, French Organ Music Past and Present, New York: H. W. Gray Co., 1919; p. 5.
3. For additional study of the works of Titelouze see Willi Apel, Geschichte der Orgel- und Klaviermusik bis 1700, Kassel, Germany: Bärenreiter Verlag, 1967; p. 488-492.
4. Dufourcq, op. cit., p. 51, and Apel, op. cit., p. 703.
5. Dufourcq, op. cit., p. 53-61.
6. Dom Bédos de Celles (1709-1779) wrote about organ construction and registration for a large number of different forms and effects in his monumental L'Art du Facteur d'Orgues (1770).
7. In France the offertoire was a prominent part of the organ Mass; this was not true in organ Masses of other countries.
8. Dufourcq, op. cit., p. 62.
9. Dufourcq, op. cit., p. 61.
10. Dufourcq, op. cit., p. 62-63; Apel, op. cit., p. 706-707.
11. Dufourcq, op. cit., p. 71-73; Apel, op. cit., p. 709-711.
12. Dufourcq, op. cit., p. 66.
13. Dufourcq, op. cit., p. 64-70; Apel, op. cit., p. 707-709.
14. Dufourcq, op. cit., p. 76-77.
15. Grace, op. cit., p. 29.
16. Dufourcq, op. cit., p. 74-75; Apel, op. cit., p. 712-713.
17. Dufourcq, op. cit., p. 77-79; Apel, op. cit., p. 713-715.
18. Dufourcq, op. cit., p. 75-98; Apel, op. cit., p. 723.
19. Apel, op. cit., p. 716-719.
20. Norbert Dufourcq, in the Preface to his edition of the organ works of Nicolas de Grigny, cites a baptismal notice that de Grigny was baptized in Saint-Pierre-le-Vieil Oct. 8, 1672, not 1671, which is the date usually given for his birth.

21.   Apel, op. cit. , p. 724.
22.   Dufourcq, op. cit. , p. 114.
23.   Dufourcq, op. cit. , p. 114.
24.   Dufourcq, op. cit. , p. 115-116;   Apel, op. cit. , p.
      722-723.
25.   Dufourcq, op. cit. , p. 118;   Apel, op. cit. , p. 723-
      724.
26.   Dufourcq, op. cit. , p. 110.
27.   Dufourcq, op. cit. , p. 121.
28.   William Leslie Sumner, "The French Organ School,"
      Hinrichsen Musical Year Book, London: Hinrichsen
      Edition Ltd. , 1949-1950;   vol. 6, p. 284.
29.   Ibid. , p. 284.
30.   Dufourcq, op. cit. , p. 121.

Bibliography

Andersen, Poul-Gerhard. Organ Building and Design. New
      York: Oxford University Press, 1969;   p. 140-156.
Apel, Willi.   Geschichte der Orgel- und Klaviermusik bis
      1700. Kassel, Germany: Bärenreiter Verlag, 1967;
      p. 487-493, 703-728.
Borrel, Eugène. L'Interpretation de la Musique Française
      de Lully à la Révolution. Paris: Librairie Félix
      Alcan, 1934.
Bouvet, Charles. Une Dynastie de Musiciens Français: Les
      Couperin, Organistes de l'Eglise Saint-Gervais. Paris:
      Bossuet, 1919.
Brunold, Paul. François Couperin, translated by J. B. Han-
      son. Monaco: L'Oiseau Lyre, 1949.
Citron, Pierre. Couperin. Bourges, France: Editions du
      Seuil, 1956.
de Wall, Marilou.   "The Tonal Organization of the Seventeenth
      Century French Organ," American Guild of Organists
      Quarterly, vol. VIII, no. 1 (January 1963, p. 12;
      vol. VIII, no. 2, (April 1963), p. 43; vol. VIII, no.
      3 (July 1963), p. 89.
_____.   "Interpretation of French Organ Music of the 17th
      and 18th Centuries," The Diapason (April 1964), p.
      42.
Douglass, Fenner. The Language of the Classical French
      Organ: A Musical Tradition Before 1800. New Haven,
      Conn. : Yale University Press, 1969.
Dufourcq, Norbert. Le Grand Orgue et les Organistes de
      Saint-Merry de Paris. Paris: Librairie Floury,
      1947.

_____. Nicolas LeBègue (1631-1702). Paris: Librairie
    Flowry, 1954.
Fesperman, John. "Rhythmic Alterations in 18th Century
    French Organ Music," Organ Institute Quarterly,
    vol. IX, no. 1 (Spring 1961), p. 4-10; vol. IX, no.
    2 (Summer 1961), p. 13-22.
Gay, Harry W. "Saint Quentin, Its Collegiate Church and
    Pierre du Mage," The Diapason (May 1958), p. 8.
_____. "Notes upon Jean Titelouze (1563-1633)," The
    American Organist, vol. 42, no. 9 (September 1959),
    p. 299-307.
_____. "To Know Nicolas de Grigny, Perform His Many
    Pieces," The Diapason (September 1957), p. 18.
Goodrich, Wallace. The Organ in France, Boston: Boston
    Music Company, 1917.
Grace, Harvey. French Organ Music, Past and Present.
    New York: H. W. Gray Co., 1919.
Grimes, Conrad. "The Noels of Louis-Claude Daquin,"
    The Diapason (December 1968), p. 24.
Hardouin, Pierre. "Le Grand Orgue de Saint-Gervais de
    Paris," L'Orgue, 1949, p. 91.
_____. "François Roberday (1624-1680)," Revue de
    Musicologie, vol. XLV (1960), p. 44-62.
Howell, Almonte C. "French Baroque Organ Music and
    the Eight Church Tones," Journal of the American
    Musicological Society, vol. XI (1952), p. 106-108.
Mellers, Wilfrid. François Couperin and the French Clas-
    sical Tradition. London: Denis Dobson, 1950 (re-
    print, New York: Dover Pub., 1968).
Moeser, James. "French Baroque Registration," The
    American Organist, June 1967, p. 17 and July 1967,
    p. 21.
Raugel, Félix. Les organistes; Paris: H. Laurens, 1923.
Sharp, Geoffrey B. "Louis Marchand, 1669-1732," Musical
    Times, no. 1521, vol. 110 (November 1969), p. 1134.
Shay, Edmund. "French Baroque Organ Registrations," The
    Diapason (November 1969), p. 14.
Stevlingson, Norma. "Performance Styles of French Organ
    Music in the 17th and 18th Centuries," Music/The
    A. G. O. and R. C. C. O. Magazine, vol. III, no.
    2 (February 1969), p. 26.
Sumner, William Leslie. "The French Organ School,"
    Sixth Music Book. London: Hinrichsen Edition Ltd.,
    1950; p. 281-294.
Tessier, André. "Les Messes d'Orgue de Fr. Couperin,"
    Revue Musicale, vol. VI, no. 1.
_____. Couperin. Paris: Librairie Renouard, 1926.

Williams, Peter. The European Organ 1450-1850. London:
    B. T. Batsford, 1966; p. 169-203.

10. ENGLAND: 1650-1800

The seventeenth century in England witnessed many struggles for control of the government. The reign of the house of Stuart, the rise of Puritanism, the establishment of the English Commonwealth, and the restoration of a monarch, the Glorious Revolution of 1688--all were events related to the political unrest of the nation. During this period many organs were destroyed, and most forms of music were abolished or forbidden in worship. This made it necessary that keyboard music, especially organ music, be performed on small instruments (harpsichords, clavichords, organs) in the home rather than in church. The English organs of this period had no pedal board, and a performer did not change registration during the course of a piece.

"Father" Bernard Smith (d. 1708) and Renatus Harris (ca. 1652-1724) were two competitive organ builders who had been trained in their craft on the continent and who began serious organ building in England after the Restoration of Charles II to the throne (1660). The German-born Smith was probably superior in tonal matters, but Harris surpassed Smith in mechanical ones. Smith is given much credit, however, for enlarging and transforming the tonal qualities of the old English organ. Renatus Harris built a four manual instrument (no pedal) at Salisbury Cathedral in 1710 in which he introduced duplexing (borrowing). [1]

John Snetzler (1710-1785) was another foreign-born organ builder who contributed to building pedal divisions and increasing the number of reeds in many instruments during the eighteenth century. The earliest date which can be ascertained for the introduction of pedals to English organs is 1720; the few pedals of the organ at St. Paul's Cathedral, London, were probably pull-downs and playable by the toes only. Another important fact in organ history is that the first Swell (enclosed) organ in England was built by Abraham Jordan at the church of St. Magnus the Martyr in London in 1712.

HISTORICAL BACKGROUND

1603-1625	Reign of James I
1604	Shakespeare <u>Othello</u>
1605	Bacon <u>On the Advancement of Learning</u>
1605	Ben Jonson <u>Volpone</u>
1606	Shakespeare <u>Macbeth</u>
1611	King James version of <u>The Bible</u>
1625-1649	Reign of Charles I
1649-1660	English Commonwealth
1653	Oliver Cromwell dissolved Parliament
1660	Pepys <u>Diary</u>
1660	Restoration of Charles II to throne; ruled until 1685
1665	London plague
1666	London fire
1667	Milton <u>Paradise Lost</u>
1678	Bunyan <u>Pilgrim's Progress</u>
1675	St. Paul's Cathedral begun by Wren
1682	William Penn founded Philadelphia
1685-1688	Reign of James II
1689-1702	Reign of William and Mary
1697	Dryden <u>Alexander's Feast</u>
1702-1714	Reign of Anne
1711	Pope <u>Essay on Criticism</u>
1714-1727	Reign of George I
1719	Defoe <u>Robinson Crusoe</u>
1726	Swift <u>Gulliver's Travels</u>
1727-1760	Reign of George II
1738	Wesley's reform movement begun
1754	Samuel Johnson <u>Dictionary</u>
1760-1820	Reign of George III
1766	Goldsmith <u>The Vicar of Wakefield</u>
1770	Gainsborough <u>The Blue Boy</u>
1775-1781	Revolutionary War in America
1776	American Declaration of Independence
1776	Burney, general history of music
1777	Sheridan <u>School for Scandal</u>
1786	Joshua Reynolds <u>The Duchess of Devonshire</u>

Many of the organ compositions written in England
during the seventeenth and eighteenth centuries were called
voluntaries.   In the seventeenth century the terms fancy,
verse, and voluntary were interchangeable.   Dances, airs,
and marches were composed for either organ or harpsichord.
The early form of the voluntary was that of a through-
composed piece of moderate length.   It contained much imitation between voices, texture in three parts or four parts,
and a great amount of ornamentation.   The voluntary later
developed into a piece divided into two sections (slow, fast),
the first a shorter one written for diapasons, and the second
for a solo and accompaniment, including echo portions. [2]
Benjamin Rogers (1614-1698) and Matthew Locke (ca. 1630-
1677) were two composers of preludes and voluntaries from
the first half of the seventeenth century.   Melothesia: or,
Certain General Rules for Playing upon a Continued-Bass
(1673), which contained seven organ pieces, was Locke's
largest opus.

English fugues of the eighteenth century can usually
be classified in two types.   The first has a lively tempo,
loose construction, parts added whimsically by the composer,
and episodes built upon broken chords.   The second type of
fugue conformed to the stricter rules of fugue construction
such as correct answers to the fugue subject, episodes derived from the subject, and a consistent number of voices.
The alla breve fugue, as the second type is called, was frequently written in minor keys. [3]

Dr. John Blow (1649-1708) was a teacher of Purcell
and the organist of Westminster Abbey and St. Paul's Cathedral.   He composed verses, voluntaries, and preludes.   His
Voluntary for Full Organ uses a rapid 16th-note figuration
which suggests toccata writing.   The 16th-note figuration became a common characteristic of the voluntary in the
eighteenth century.   The Verse in C Major has a number
of places which suggest manual changes for a double-organ
(an organ which had two manuals). [4]

Henry Purcell (1659-1695) was a musical genius in
seventeenth-century England.   He wrote, however, less than
ten works for the organ.   Hugh McLean suggests that the
best-known organ work connected with Purcell's name,
Voluntary on the Old 100th, might have been composed by
either Blow or Purcell, or even composed by Blow and altered by Purcell. [5]   Although this was not the first English
prelude on a hymn-tune, it was one of the earliest. [6]   It is

possible that copyists intended that the piece be played on
divided stops or half-stops[7] because the left-hand accompaniment part never goes above c^1. After an introduction in
which each of the three parts enter on the initial phrase
melody in imitation at the octave and unison, the complete
psalm-tune is presented in the lowest part. Here the registration would make the left-hand part more prominent. Later
the same kind of treatment is given with the entire psalm
melody in the right hand (probably on the Cornet) and with
the accompaniment in the left hand.

Purcell's Voluntary for Double Organ in D Minor is
a lengthy and showy piece for two manuals. This, like the
other Voluntary in D Minor, contains rapid scales and running figurations in 32nd-notes with much rhythmic variety.
The two verses, one in F and the other in the Phrygian
mode, are shorter pieces. All the Purcell works are highly
ornamented. The texture in Purcell's pieces is usually three-
part and, with the exception of two voluntaries, always begins with imitation. These pieces give the impression of
spontaneity and of improvisation.[8] Daniel Purcell (d. 1717),
the son of Henry Purcell, wrote psalm harmonizations with
interludes.

In the hands of Dr. William Croft (1678-1727) the
voluntary usually took the form of a two-section work of
moderate length. The first part was a slow introduction
followed by a fast second part. The second section was
often a fugato based on one subject, which first appeared in
all voices imitatively. The counterpoint grows from the
harmony, with the lower voices usually supporting the principal melody in the highest voice part. The lines are vocal,
there is much stepwise movement, and a frequent use of sequence, with uncomplicated, flowing rhythms. Not all of the
Croft voluntaries were in the two-part form; some are in
the same tempo throughout and are unified by one theme.[9]

George Frideric Handel (German form: Georg Friedrich Händel) (1685-1759) invented the organ concerto and
wrote 21 concertos for organ and orchestra.[10] These concertos were written to provide a change of fare during the
intermissions in his oratorio performances. Two announce-
ments of oratorio performances read:[11]

> "The Messiah" with organ concerto.
> "Esther" with organ concerto.

ENGLAND: 1650-1800

| 1600 | 1650 | 1700 | 1750 | 1800 | 1850 |

1614 Rogers, Benjamin 1698
1615 Gibbons, C. 1676
ca.1630 Locke, M. 1677
1649 Blow, John 1708
1659 Purcell, H. 1695
? Purcell, D. 1717
ca.1670 Clarke, J. 1707
ca.1674 Barrett, J. ca.1735
1677 Reading, John------1764
1678 Croft, Wm. 1727
1685 Handel, George F. 1759
1687 Hine, Wm. 1730
1690 Roseingrave, T. 1766
ca.1695 Greene, M. 1755
? Hart, P. 1749
ca.1703 Travers, J. 1758

```
1710    Avison, C.      1770
1710    Arne, T. A.     1778
1710    Boyce, Wm.      1779
ca.1711 Keeble, John    1786
1713    Stanley, C. J.  1786
1715    Felton, Wm. 1769
1715    Alcock, John----------1806
1715    Nares, James    1783
1725    Walond, Wm. 1770
1726    Burney, Charles---------1814
1726    Jones, William-------1800
1733    Dupuis, T. S. --1796
1734    Cooke, Benj. ---1793
1738    Battishill, J. ------1801
        1752    Marsh, John-------1828
        ?       Kirkman, J. 1792
        1757    Wesley, Charles--------1834
        1765    Attwood, Thomas-------1838
        1766    Wesley, Samuel --------1837
        ?       Guest, George ------1831
```

The concertos reflect tremendous assurance, vitality, fire, and strong secular gaiety, all of which is associated with this renowned musician. Handel synthesized his style from native German, Italian, and English characteristics with the purpose of pleasing English audiences. The concertos are virtuoso pieces, but most of them were written for the typical English organs without pedals. Concerto No. 7 (the first concerto in the second set) is the only concerto which has an independent pedal part. This work could have been written for performance on an organ on the continent which had pedals. The concerto might have been played on one of Handel's several trips away from England. The first movement contains rocking 16th-note figurations in the pedal part on broken intervals in the harmonies and quick scale passages on the manuals. Many of the concertos allow the organ soloist to extemporize cadenzas, and there is much dialogue between the organ and the full orchestra (ripieno). At times the organ plays with a few orchestral instruments (concertino). Strongly contrasting dynamics also help to clarify the form.

The orchestra consisted of strings and two oboes, with cellos, contrabasses, and bassons on the continuo part.[12] The continuo was also played by the left hand on the harpsichord. The Sixth Concerto is an exception to this orchestration because it calls for harp, two flutes, and muted violins, with the violas, cellos, and contrabass all playing pizzicato. The 16th concerto in F major in six movements adds two horns to the basic orchestration already mentioned.

Forms used in the various movements are the French overture, recitative, fugue, variation, march, and modified dance forms (bourée, gigue, menuet). The general division of the concertos into four movements is taken from the Italian church sonatas. The most common arrangement of the movements was slow-fast-slow-fast. Occasionally a short, slow interlude introduces a quick movement. Handel often borrowed themes or whole movements from his own concerti grossi or compositions for other media and included them in his organ concertos. Sometimes he left notes for the organist to improvise a complete movement. William Felton (1715-1769) adopted Handel's concerto form for compositions for organ or harpsichord.

In addition to the concertos Handel wrote fugues and voluntaries. Six Fugues or Voluntaries for the Organ or Harpsichord was published by Walsh in 1735, and another edition was published in 1784 by Harrison.[13] Twelve Volun-

taries and Fugues for the Organ or Harpsichord ... by the
Celebrated Mr. Handel was published by Longman and Bro-
derip.[14] The fugues are characterized by rhythmic vitality
and smooth, flowing counterpoint, although some of the fugue
subjects contain rather wide leaps. The harmonic rhythm
usually changes every beat. Three of the six fugues are
double fugues. The G major fugue subject resembles some
fugues by Buxtehude because of the use of repeated notes on
one pitch.

Handel's voluntaries are divided into two sections in
slow-fast arrangement. The slow sections (Grave, Largo)
were intended to be played on small diapasons. The fast
sections emphasized the use of solo sounds such as the cornet, trumpet, or flute, and short echo passages. The texture is nearly always two-part and three-part. Cadential
trills are the principal ornaments employed. These voluntaries do not incorporate imitation as a unifying feature.

Thomas Roseingrave (1690-1766) was organist at St.
Georges, Hanover Square. He wrote fugues and voluntaries
for the organ. His ability to improvise contrapuntally was
greatly admired, but his part writing was eccentric at
times.[15] His two books were Voluntarys and Fugues Made
on Purpose for the Organ or Harpsichord and Six Double-
fugues for the Organ or Harpsichord.

Dr. Maurice Greene (ca. 1695-1755) was the organist
of St. Paul's Cathedral, London, and a friend of Handel.
His voluntaries, like those of Handel, fall into two sections.
The figural counterpoint is derived from the harmony. There
is little ornamentation except at cadences, and most of the
voice movement is stepwise. Since there are few accidentals
or modulations the music has a bland effect. The solo sounds
indicated in the Allegro sections are cornet or trumpet, and
echo passages are occasionally incorporated. Greene's two
volumes are Ten Voluntaries for Organ or Cembalo (1770)
and Twelve Voluntaries for the Organ or Harpsichord, published by J. Bland, London (1780?).[16]

Dr. William Boyce (1710-1779) was a pupil of Greene
and Dr. John Christopher Pepusch (1667-1752), a highly
respected teacher of many of the organists of that time. Ten
Voluntaries for the Organ or Harpsichord by Boyce was published after his death in 1785. He wrote antiphonally for the
solo Trumpet and echo in a dramatic manner, and his voluntaries resemble their German counterpart, the prelude and

fugue.   The texture of the Boyce voluntaries is three-part,
and the form employed is the slow larghetto followed by a
lively fugue or trumpet and echo piece.   The compositions
of Boyce are more attractive than many of those of his contemporaries because of their fresh and interesting rhythms
and tunes.

Dr. Boyce played at All Hallows-the-Great church
between 1749 and 1769.   The specifications are given below.

London.   All Hallows-the-Great, Thames Street.
Built by Glyn and Parker, 1749.

Great	Swell
Open Diapason 8'	Trumpet 8'(G-d^3)
Stopped Diapason 8'	Cornet III (G-d^3)
Principal 4'	
Twelfth 2 2/3'	Choir
Fifteenth 2'	Open Diapason 8'
Sesquialtera IV	Stopped Diapason 8'
Cornet V (c$\sharp^1$-d^3)	Flute 4'
Trumpet 8'	Twelfth 2 2/3'
	Vox Humana 8'

The Swell and Choir were played from the same manual, and
there were no pedals.

An outstanding composer of voluntaries was the blind
genius Charles John Stanley (1713-1786).   He wrote three
sets of ten voluntaries (Op. 5, 6, and 7), which were published in 1742.[17]   These pieces exhibit a wide variety of interesting harmonic, melodic, and rhythmic features within
the two section voluntary form for three voice lines.   Small
diapason tone, clear and unforced, is used for the opening
slow movements.   The second sections call for flute, trumpet, or cornet solos, and echo passages.   William Walond
(1725-1770) was another successful composer of voluntaries.
The Oxford organist wrote Six Voluntaries for Organ or
Harpsichord, published by J. Johnson (ca. 1760).

The Wesleys were a remarkable musical family.
Charles Wesley (1757-1834) and Samuel Wesley (1766-1837)
were the sons of Charles and nephews of John Wesley, the
two clergymen whose efforts at church reform eventually
produced the Methodist Church.   Charles' music was in-

fluenced by that of Bach, whom he admired a great deal.
Some of Charles' voluntaries contained four movements and
are dated about 1815.   His Six Concertos for the Organ or
Harpsichord ... were written about 1778 and published in
1781.[18]

Twelve Short Pieces for Keyboard (there are actually
13) by Samuel Wesley appeared in 1815. These are little character pieces,[19] which were composed in various forms, such as
through-composed pieces, dances, solos for "hautboy," flute,
cornet, vox humana, fugues, and ensemble pieces for a full
sound.   Probably the best known pieces from this group are the
Air in F major and a gavotte in the same key.   Two other books
of pieces by Samuel Wesley were Six Introductory Movements for
the Organ, Intended for the Use of Organists as Soft Voluntaries,
to be Performed at the Commencement of Services (ca. 1825) and
Six Voluntaries for the Organ (1820-1830).   The meeting of
Samuel Wesley and Felix Mendelssohn was an interesting
historical event.   Wesley composed the Fugue in B minor
for the occasion and was congratulated warmly by Mendelssohn after his performance.[20]

Notes

1. A practice in organ building whereby the organist can
    secure the (same) sound by drawing stops on two dif-
    ferent manuals, although the pipes are actually sound-
    ing in only one division and not two.
2. For a general description of the several types of volun-
    taries see Percy A. Scholes, The Oxford Companion to
    Music, 9th ed. , London: Oxford University Press,
    1959;   p. 1103.
3. Peter F. Williams, ed. , Three Voluntaries of the Later
    18th Century (Tallis to Wesley series, No. 22), Lon-
    don: Hinrichsen Edition Ltd. , 1961;   preface.
4. Willi Apel, Geschichte der Orgel- und Klaviermusik bis
    1700, Kassel, Germany: Bärenreiter Verlag, 1967;
    p. 737-741.
5. Hugh McLean, Henry Purcell: The Organ Works, Novello
    & Company, London, 1957, Preface, iii.
6. McLean mentions the anonymous O Lord Turn Not Away
    in Musica Britannica, vol. I, p. 80;   and The Psalms
    by Dr. Blow Set Full for the Organ or Harpsichord as
    They Are Played in Churches or Chapels, London:
    John Walsh, 1731.
7. Half-stops were used to play the melody above middle C

as a solo in the right hand on such stops as the Cornet or Trumpet and as an accompaniment on softer registration in the left hand below middle C.

8. Apel, op. cit. , p. 741-744.
9. Apel, op. cit. , p. 745.
10. Francis Routh, "Handel's Organ Works," Handel's Four Voluntaries for Organ or Harpsichord (Tallis to Wesley series, No. 19), London: Hinrichsen, 1961.
11. Marcel Dupré, ed. , G. F. Handel: Seize Concertos, vol. I, Paris: Bornemann, 1937; preface, ii.
12. Although only the bass line was written out, the continuo player was expected to fill out the harmonies.
13. Gordon Phillips, ed. , Handel: Six Fugues or Voluntaries, London: Hinrichsen Edition Ltd. , 1960; preface.
14. Francis Routh, "Handel's Organ Works," George Frideric Handel: Four Voluntaries. London: Hinrichsen Edition, Ltd. , 1961.
15. Denis Stevens, ed. , Thomas Roseingrave: Compositions for Organ and Harpsichord, University Park: Pennsylvania State University Press, 1964; editor's note.
16. Several other composers of this school who also wrote fugues, concertos, and voluntaries in groups designed for either organ or harpsichord are Philip Hart (d. 1749), Charles Avison (1710-1770), Dr. Thomas Augustine Arne (1710-1778), John Travers (ca. 1703-1758), and John Keeble (ca. 1711-1786).
17. Republished in a facsimile edition by Oxford University Press in 1957.
18. Gordon Phillips, ed. , The Wesleys (Tallis to Wesley series, No. 5), London: Hinrichsen Edition Ltd. , 1960; preface.
19. Character pieces were short compositions which rose to prominence during the nineteenth century. These pieces are usually composed in ternary form (A B A) and express many different moods and emotions or depict objects or actions. The character piece is typical of the programmatic compositions of the Romantic period in music history.
20. Gordon Phillips, ed. , Samuel Wesley and Dr. Mendelssohn (Tallis to Wesley series, No. 14), London: Hinrichsen Edition Ltd. , 1962; preface.

Bibliography

Anderson, Poul-Gerhard. Organ Building and Design, translated into English by Joanne Curnutt. London: Oxford

University Press, 1969; p. 169-176.

Apel, Willi. Geschichte der Orgel- und Klaviermusik bis
1700. Kassel, Germany: Bärenreiter Verlag, 1967;
p. 309-318, 737-745.

Clutton, Cecil, and Austin Niland. The British Organ.
London: B. T. Batsford, 1963; p. 52-89.

Dawes, Frank. "Philip Hart," Musical Times, no. 1469,
vol. 106 (July 1965), p. 510.

_____. "The Music of Philip Hart (c. 1676-1749)," Pro-
ceedings of the Royal Musical Association, vol. 94
(1967-1968).

Dupré, Marcel, ed. G. F. Haendel: Seize Concertos, vol.
I. Paris: Bornemann, 1937; preface, ii.

Frotscher, Gotthold. Geschichte des Orgelspiels und der
Orgelkomposition. Berlin: Merseberger Verlag,
1959; vol. II, p. 805-848.

Hutchings, Arthur. "The English Concerto with or for
Organ," Musical Quarterly, vol. XLVII (April 1961),
p. 195-206.

McLean, Hugh. Henry Purcell: The Organ Works. London:
Novello and Co., 1957; preface, iii.

Oldman, C. B. "Thomas Attwood, 1765-1838," Musical
Times, no. 1473, vol. 106 (November 1965), p. 844.

Phillips, Gordon, ed. Handel: Six Fugues or Voluntaries.
London: Hinrichsen Edition Ltd., 1960; preface.

_____. "Purcell's Organs and Organ Music," Organ and
Choral Aspects and Prospects (Ninth Music Book).
London: Hinrichsen Edition Ltd., 1958; p. 133-135.

_____. Samuel Wesley and Dr. Mendelssohn (Tallis to
Wesley series, No. 14). London: Hinrichsen Edition
Ltd., 1962; preface.

_____. The Wesleys (Tallis to Wesley series, No. 5).
London: Hinrichsen Edition Ltd., 1960; preface.

Redlich, Hans F. "Samuel Wesley and the Bach Revival in
England," Seventh Year Book. London: Hinrichsen
Edition Ltd., 1952.

Routh, Francis. "Handel's Organ Works," Handel's Four
Voluntaries for Organ or Harpsichord (Tallis to Wesley series, No. 19). London: Hinrichsen Edition Ltd.,
1961.

Scholes, Percy A. "Voluntary," The Oxford Companion to
Music, 9th ed. London: Oxford University Press,
1956; p. 1103.

Stevens, Denis, ed. Thomas Roseingrave: Compositions for
Organ and Harpsichord. University Park: Pennsylvania State University Press, 1964; editor's note.

_____. Thomas Tomkins: Three Hitherto Unpublished

Voluntaries (Francies, Verses) (Tallis to Wesley
series, No. 17). London: Hinrichsen Edition Ltd.,
1959; preface.

West, John Ebenezer. "Old English Organ Music," Proceedings of the Musical Association, vol. XXXVII
(1911), p. 1-16.

Williams, Peter F., ed. Three Voluntaries of the Later
18th Century (Tallis to Wesley series, No. 22). London: Hinrichsen Edition Ltd., 1961; preface.

11. SPAIN, PORTUGAL, AND ITALY: 1600-1800

Spain and Portugal

The two principal forms of Spanish and Portuguese
organ music of the seventeenth and eighteenth centuries were
versets (versos, versillos) and tientos. Versets were composed on the various chant tones for alternation between the
organ and verses sung. The tientos were usually pieces of
short duration, in three of four voice parts, which were frequently introduced by imitation. The tiento had its Italian
counterpart in the ricercar. Tientos were contrapuntal, but
the counterpoint was derived from the simple harmonic background. The use of accidentals and modulation was infre-
quent, and even that resulted only when closely related keys
were introduced.

A Portuguese priest, Father Manoel Rodriguez Coelho
(1583-ca. 1623), composed 24 tentos in his Flores de musica
para o instrumento de tecla e harpa (Lisbon, 1620), the first
instrumental work which was published in Portugal. [1] Pedro
de Araujo (fl. 1600's) wrote a Tento de segundo tom in this
same style.

A composition which presents a number of contrasting
musical ideas is the Tiento de quarto tono por E la mi a
modo de Canción by Francisco Correa de Arauxo (1575/1577-
1663). Three sections begin with imitative entries, but an
interlude and the final section have different rhythmic and
melodic character from that of the standard tiento. Most of
Correa's tientos are more dignified, longer, and more developed than those of Cabezón and other sixteenth-century
Iberian composers. The seventeenth-century tientos are
sectional, sometimes beginning sections with imitative entries
and at other times begin with two or more parts sounding
simultaneously. If there are a number of sections, the
meter usually changes from duple to triple meter (often $\frac{3}{2}$
time) in at least one section and returns to duple meter for
the last portion of the piece. The same material is alternated between higher and lower parts of the keyboard, sug-

HISTORICAL BACKGROUND

1588	War between Spain and England
1588	Defeat of the Spanish Armada
1605	Cervantes Don Quixote, Part I
1605	Thomas Luis da Victoria Requiem
1617-1682	Murillo
1621-1665	Reign of Philip IV of Spain
1635	Velásquez Surrender of Breda
1637-1657	Reign of Ferdinand III, Holy Roman Emperor
1656	Velásquez The Maids of Honor
1665-1700	Reign of Charles II of Spain
1678	Murillo Mystery of the Immaculate Conception
1700-1746	Reign of Philip V of Spain
1702-1714	War of Spanish Succession
1755	Lisbon earthquake
1759-1788	Reign of Charles III of Spain
1756-1763	Seven Years' War between Spain and England
1773	Pope Clement XIV dissolved Jesuit order
1788-1808	Reign of Charles IV
1805	Battle of Trafalgar
1808-1814	War for Spanish independence from France

gesting the echo effect. The texture varies from two to four parts. The little ornamentation used is found at a few principal cadences. The most common dissonances are passing tones and chains of suspensions. Other tiento composers from this period were Diogo de Alvorado (d. 1643) and Pablo (Pau) Bruna.

The versos were tiny pieces, ten to 20 measures in length. Imitation of the chant melody was the principal unifying factor, and sometimes the added voices merely harmonized. Composers such as Agostinho da Cruz (ca. 1590-1633?), Lucas Puxol, Francisco Llusá (Llissa), Cándido Eznarriaga, Gabriel Menalt (d. 1687), and Diego de Torrijos (?-1691) wrote versillos.

Bartolomeo de Olague, probably from the seventeenth-century Catalan school, wrote a composition entitled Xácara de 1º tono, a series of variations of dance-like character built on a short harmonic theme in triple meter which suggests a chaconne.

Juan Cabanilles (1644-1712) was an outstanding Spanish
composer who wrote tientos, passacaglias, gagliardas, battle
pieces, paseos, diferencias, toccatas, pedazo de música,
gaitilla, and xácara. Cabanilles wrote with rhythmic interest
and vitality and freely used 16th-note patterns in sequences.
His tientos, like those of Correa de Arauxo, are developed
at some length, and employ more chromaticism than in those
of his predecessors. Sometimes there is a tiento conceived
as an entity, but most are sectional and adopt melodic metamorphosis when progressing to a different section. The texture never exceeds that of four parts, and the tientos are
not always forced into imitative counterpoint. Some begin
very majestically with slow-moving, full chords. Fray
(Brother) Miguel Lopez (1669-1732) composed a number of
short, direct versillos, always imitative but melodic and
interesting. These pieces contain active eighth-note figures.

About the turn of the eighteenth century some new
forms were used: tocata, fuga, paso, sonatina, and sonata.
These reflect Italian influence, which was very strong in
Spain. José Elías (ca. 1675-ca. 1749) wrote an extended
Tocata de Contras Quinto Tono, which contained long 16th-
note scale passages in a single line or in thirds over pedal
points; the harmonies seldom change.

Joaquin Martinex Oxinagas wrote several florid pieces
under the title Fuga. The texture is principally three part,
with sections in invertible counterpoint and with echo effects
suggested. Sequences supply a large part of the unifying
material. In the same Italianate style were pieces by Juan
Moreno y Polo (d. 1776).

Domenico Scarlatti, the famous Italian harpsichord
sonata composer, spent from 1720 or 1721 until his death
in 1757 in the service of royal patrons in Portugal and Spain.
His influence was powerful and made itself felt in practically
all of the eighteenth-century keyboard music of Spain and
Portugal. Some of the composers who were influenced by
Scarlatti were José Antonio Carlos Seixas (1704-1742),
Freixanet, Manuel de Santo Elias (fl. 1750's-1790's), Padre
Anselm Viola (1730-1798), Joao de Souza Carvalho (1745-
1798), and José Lidon (1752-1827). Lidon composed a stir-
ring two-part Sonata da 1º Tono para clave o para organo
con trompeta real. This sonata is dramatic when played on
strong, fiery reed stops for which Iberian organs are famous.
Many compositions by these composers are in binary form.
They utilize two-voice texture and could be played on all

keyboard instruments. Rhythmic vitality, pleasing melodies
and harmony, with key relationships which clarify the structure are features of music composed under Scarlatti's influence.

Fray Antonio Soler (1720-1783) is famous for Seis
Conciertos para dos Organos. The two instruments sometimes play simultaneously, at other times antiphonally. These
concertos are all written in two movements. The first movement is in duple meter, usually in a slower tempo than the
second movement. The Minue in triple meter is the second
movement, a series of variations. A generous amount of
ornamentation is employed throughout these pieces. The concertos do not use pedal, however.

Spanish organs of the seventeenth and eighteenth centuries are especially interesting. Half-stops had become
popular in Spain by 1620, where they were used for colorful
solo sounds played by the right hand above $c\sharp^1$ and accompanied
by the left hand on the lower part of the same keyboard.

The most striking element of the Spanish organs of
this period was the inclusion of horizontal trumpets called
reeds en chamade, a French term which has no connection
with the reeds' origin or name. There are horizontal reeds
to be found on the organ in Burgos; the date of the building
of the organ might be 1636. Cavaillé-Coll, the famous nineteenth-century organ builder, was deeply impressed by the
brilliant reeds found in Spanish organs. Horizontal reeds
were easy for the tuners to reach, and they gave an even,
strong, penetrating, direct sound, which stood out above the
mild chorus stops and delicate mixtures.

Spanish baroque organ building reached its climax
during the eighteenth century in the large instruments designed for the major cathedrals. It is not uncommon to find
two organs in large Spanish churches, as the specification
schemes of two organs in the Braga Cathedral confirm. [2]
The organs, which were built in 1737-1738, were not connected. The organ on the south side of the choir has one
manual of 45 notes. The manual divided between c^1 and
$c\sharp^1$. The organ has no pedal. Stops are arranged for the
left side and for the right side of the manual and affect only
that corresponding side of the manual. Three horizontal
reeds are found on both sides, and the stop for one additional
reed (Trompeta real 8') is found on the right hand side. The
second organ (on the north side of the choir) has two manuals

SPAIN AND PORTUGAL: 1600-1800

1600   1650   1700   1750   1800   1850

1575/1577 Correa de Arauxo 1663
1583 Coelho, M. R. ca.1623 ?
? de Alvorado, D. 1643
ca.1590 da Cruz, A. 1633 ?
? de Araujo, Pedro ?
? de Torrijos, D. 1691
1644 Cabanilles, J. 1712
? Puxol, Lucas ?
? Menalt, G. 1687
? Bruno, Pablo (Pau) ?
? de Olague, Bartolomeo ?
? Llussá, Francisco ?
? Eznarriaga, Cándido ?
? Ximenes, José ?
1669 Lopez, M. 1732
ca.1675 Elías, J. ca.1749
? Oxinagas, Joaquin Martinez ?
? Moreno y Polo, Juan------1776
1704 de Seixas, J. 1742
(1720-1757 D. Scarlatti in Portugal and Spain)
1729 Soler, Antonio 1783
ca.1730 Freixanet ?
? de Santo Elias, Manuel ?
1739 Viola, Anselm-----1798
1745 Carvalho, Joao----1798
1752 Lidon, José----------1827

and pedal.   The stops are either halved or available on only
the treble or bass side.   Part of the stops for the second
manual form an Echo division inside the case.   The pedal
has only one stop, the Contras 16'.

Italy

Seventeenth-century Italian composers continued to
write ricercars, canzonas, fugues, toccatas, Mass movements, Magnificat versets, and organ hymns.   Two new
forms which were introduced during this period were the
pastorale and sonata.

Michel Angelo Rossi (ca. 1600-ca. 1674) published two
books: Toccate e corrente per organo, o cembalo (1657)
and Toccate e corrente d'intavolatura d'organo e cimbalo.
Among his compositions is a Partite sopra La Romanesca,
a series of four variations on a famous secular tune.   Rossi
continued the toccata tradition of his predecessors but cast
his toccatas in the form of three sections.   Each section is
introduced by sustained chords before beginning the running
sixteenth-note figures and fugato passages.   If the pedal is
used, long, sustained notes are held as pedal-points to support the active manual voices.   Rossi also composed versetti.

Vagueness of terminology still existed.   There was a
close relationship between the sectional canzona and the sonata
in which sections are written in different meters, but the
sections are based on related thematic material.   A sonata
of this type is the Sonata chromatica by Tarquinio Merula
(ca. 1590-after 1652).   Ambiguity also appears again in the
works of Carlo Francesco Pollaroli (1653-1722), whose capriccio and sonata exhibit no stylistic differences.   Pollaroli's
Fuga is an extended work constructed on one subject.

Annuale, Che contiene tutto quello che deve fare un
organista per risponder al choro tutto l'anno by Giovanni
Battista Fasolo (early seventeenth century) appeared in Venice
in 1645.   This book provided organ pieces to play in response
to the sung portions of the Te Deum, Masses, the Magnificat,
and organ hymns.   All of these pieces are necessarily short
and in four parts.   The parts sometimes enter imitatively or
as simple, harmonizing voices.

Bernardo Pasquini (1637-1710) wrote sectional toccatas
which change meter at the different sections and frequently

HISTORICAL BACKGROUND

1503-1707	Naples belonged to Spain
1600	Galileo law of falling bodies
1621-1623	Reign of Pope Gregory XV
1637	First public opera house, Venice
1642	Monteverdi L'Incoronazione di Poppea
1643	Death of Frescobaldi
1650	Carissimi Jephtha
1662	Cavalli Ercole amante
1681	Corelli trio sonatas
1698	Torelli violin concertos, Op. 5
1707	A. Scarlatti Mitridate eupatore
1733	Pergolesi La Serva padrona
1735-1759	Reign of Charles, King of Naples
1760	Villa d'Este erected in Tivoli
1763	Excavations begun at Pompeii and Herculaneum
1769	Mozart travelled in Italy
1778	La Scala opened in Milan
1792	Cimarosa Il Matrimonio segreto
1796	Napoleon's battles in Italy

---

have 16th-note activity occurring in one part. Pasquini's Introduzione e pastorale is long and contains an introduction which is in the rocking, dotted rhythm associated with the siciliano. Some of Pasquini's sonatas appeared in Sonate da organo di vari autori, edited by Aresti around 1687.

Giovanni Maria Casini (1670?-1714) composed Pensieri per l'organo in partitura (1714). The eighth pensiero from Book Two is in three separate sections, but all three parts are based on the same melodic material. The third section is a lively gigue. Much of the voice movement is stepwise, and there are many parallel thirds and sixths and much chromaticism. Sonatas and toccatas by Azzolino Bernadino della Ciaja (1671-1744) appeared in his Sonate per cembalo ... e grave stile ecclesiastico, per grandi organi (1727).

The opera composer Nicolo Antonio Porpora (1686-1766) and Giuseppe Bencini (fl. early 1700's) contributed fugues. Porpora's fugue writing, however, suggests composition for strings rather than for organ.

Domenico Zipoli (1688-1726), the organist of the Jesuit church in Rome and a missionary to Argentina, wrote a two-part work called Sonate d'intavolatura per organo, o

ITALY: 1600-1800

1600   1650   1700   1750   1800   1850

? Rossi, Michel Angelo ?
? Salvatore, Giovanni ---1688 ?
? Merula, T. 1652
? Fasolo, G. B. ?
1637 Pasquini, Bernardo 1710
? Fontana, Fabrizio 1695
? Aresti, Giulio Cesare ?
? Storace, Bernardo ?
1653 Pollaroli, C. F. 1722
ca.1657 Bassani, G. B. 1716
1670 ? Casini, G. M. 1714
1671 della Ciaja, A. B. 1744
ca.1673 Aldrovandini, G. 1708
1684 Durante, Francesco----1755
(1685 Scarlatti, Domenico --1757)
1686 Porpora, Nicolo Antonio 1766
1686 Marcello, B. 1739
1688 Zipoli, D. 1726
? Santini, Giuseppe Maria ?
? Marzola, Pietro ?
? Palafuti ?
? Bencini, Giuseppe ?
ca.1704 Pescetti, Giovanni B. 1766
1706 Martini, Giovanni Battista 1784
1762 Santucci, Marco 1843

<u>cimbalo</u> (1716). Part One contained seven types of organ composition: verset, toccata, canzona, elevation, post-communion, offertory, and pastorale. Part Two contained only two types, suites and variations. Zipoli's writing is easy and direct. The phrases are evenly matched, and simple harmonies change at regular intervals. The <u>versetti</u> are a bit more extended than others had been before Zipoli's time; the canzona is in two forms, through-composed and sectional. The <u>Pastorale</u>, probably Zipoli's best-known composition, is in three sections. The slow first and last sections are written in $1\frac{2}{8}$ time, and the middle section contrasts by being quick and in a dotted rhythm.

Benedetto Marcello (1686-1739) wrote vocal settings for one to four voices with basso continuo for Giustiniani's paraphrases of the first 50 Psalms. [3]

The outstanding eighteenth-century Italian organ composer was Padre Giovanni Battista (Giambattista) Martini (1706-1784), a Franciscan with whom Mozart studied. Martini had two volumes published, <u>Sonate d'intavolatura per l'organo, e'l cembalo</u> (1742), and a collection, <u>Sonate per l'organo e il cembalo</u> (1747). Most of his compositions suggest writing for the cembalo rather than for the organ.

Several books of <u>versetti</u> were written during the eighteenth century: <u>Libro di Sonate d'organo d'intavolatura ... fatto per comodo da sonare alle Messe, Vespri, compiete, ed altro</u> (1720) by Giuseppe Maria Santini (1778-1862); <u>Versetti in tutti li tuoni Coralli</u> by Pietro Marzola (fl. 1700's); and <u>112 Versetti per organo per rispondere al coro in tutti i tuoni del canto fermo</u> by Marco Santucci (1762-1843). An unusual composition is the <u>Sonata a 3 organi col basso</u> by Carlo Zenolini (Zanolini) (fl. 1700's).

Notes

1. M. S. Kastner, ed. , <u>Cravistas Portuguezes</u>, vol. I, Mainz, Germany: B. Schott's Söhne, 1935; preface. Also see Willi Apel, <u>Geschichte der Orgel- und Klaviermusik bis 1700</u>, Kassel, Germany: Bärenreiter Verlag, 1967; p. 507-613.
2. Peter Williams, <u>The European Organ 1450-1850</u>, London: Batsford, 1966; p. 245-260.
3. Organ transcriptions of Psalms 19 and 20 have been made by such editors as Guilmant and Biggs.

Bibliography

SPAIN AND PORTUGAL

Andersen, Poul-Gerhard. Organ Building and Design, trans-
    lated into English by Joanne Curnutt. New York: Ox-
    ford University Press, 1969; p. 159-169.
Apel, Willi. Geschichte der Orgel- und Klaviermusik bis
    1700. Kassel, Germany: Bärenreiter Verlag, 1967;
    p. 507-537, 751-754.
Williams, Peter. The European Organ 1450-1850. London:
    B. T. Batsford Ltd. , 1966; p. 243-261.
Wyly, James. "The Pre-Romantic Spanish Organ: Its
    Structure, Literature, and Use in Performance. " Un-
    published Ph. D. dissertation, University of Missouri,
    1964.

ITALY

Andersen, Poul-Gerhard. Organ Building and Design, trans-
    lated into English by Joanne Curnutt. New York: Ox-
    ford University Press, 1969; p. 115-121.
Apel, Willi. Geschichte der Orgel- und Klaviermusik bis
    1700. Kassel, Germany: Bärenreiter Verlag, 1967;
    p. 473-747, 476-479, 677-682.
Williams, Peter. The European Organ 1450-1850. London:
    Batsford, 1966; p. 212-230.

12. GERMANY AFTER BACH: 1725-1800

Although Bach exerted a strong influence upon his pupils, the taste of the music-loving public was rapidly changing. Polyphonic elements and forms were incorporated, but other styles of music such as the style galant took precedence. The importance of chorale settings and polyphonic forms, which had reached their zenith in the works of Bach, was greatly diminished. Chorale settings were written by few composers; the few settings were not convincing and lacked the strength and energy of pure contrapuntal works because of the secular style in which they were written.[1]

Johann Ludwig Krebs (1713-1780) was the outstanding pupil of Bach.[2] Krebs' artistic compositions owe much to his famous teacher and show that he probably was an able performer, if we can judge by the active and demanding pedal solos and the carefully wrought, technically challenging writing for manuals in his works. Krebs also composed for solo instruments and organ. He assigned the chorale melody to the oboe or trumpet, and a contrapuntal trio of interweaving voices was written for the organ. Krebs' Fantasie for oboe and organ is a beautiful free work in ternary form.

Bach's sons made few contributions to organ literature. Wilhelm Friedemann Bach's chief musical ability was improvisation. Carl Philipp Emanuel Bach (1714-1788) wrote Preludio e sei Sonate per Organo (1790) for house organ. Other sons who wrote organ compositions were Johann Christoph Friedrich Bach (1732-1795) and Johann Christian Bach (1735-1782).

Johann Christian Kittel (1732-1809), one of the last pupils of Bach, became an influential teacher. Among his writings are a three-part organ method Der angehende praktische Organist, Vierstimmige Choräle mit Vorspielen (1803), Vierundzwanzig kurze Choralvorspiele, and Grosse Präludien.[3]

Even though Wolfgang Amadeus Mozart (1756-1791) wrote that he was very fond of the organ, he left few organ

1725	Fux Gradus ad Parnassum
1740-1786	Reign of Frederick the Great of Prussia
1742	C. P. E. Bach Prussian Sonatas
1742-1745	Reign of Charles VII, Holy Roman Emperor
1745	Stamitz went to Mannheim
1748	War of Austrian Succession ended
1750	Quantz flute concertos
1752	First German Singspiele
1753	C. P. E. Bach Versuch über die wahre Art
1755	Graun Der Tod Jesu
1755	Haydn first quartets
1764	Winckelmann Geschichte der Kunst der Altertums
1769	Mozart travelled in Italy
1781	Kant Critique of Pure Reason
1782	Mozart Die Entführung
1782	Schiller Die Räuber
1786-1797	Reign of Frederick Wilhelm II of Prussia
1786	Mozart Le nozze di Figaro
1787	Goethe Iphigenia
1789-1794	French Revolution and rise of Napoleon
1791	Mozart Requiem
1792	Beethoven went to Vienna
1800	Haydn Seasons

compositions. His sonatas for several combinations of small instrumental ensembles and organ contain elements of the church trios and other keyboard forms. The organ, however, supplies little more than a figured bass with a few solo passages. These sonatas were written to be used as interludes between the Epistle and Gospel at High Mass when Mozart was serving at the Salzburg Cathedral. He called them "sonata all'epistola." The archbishop had ruled that the service should last no longer than 45 minutes, thus limiting the length of time available for music to a few minutes.

Mozart's two Fantasias in F Minor (K. 608 and K. 594) were written during the last two years of his life for a mechanical flute organ in a large clock. The naïve Andante in F Major was also written for a musical clock. The two fantasias are technically quite difficult, especially since some adapting must be done in order that they can be performed on the modern organ. The fantasias were commissioned by Count von Deym for his museum-art gallery in Vienna. The

larger fantasia (K. 608) is in three sections. Massive chords
separated by flourishes, which suggest the French overture,
introduce the first and third sections. The Andante section in
the middle is a series of variations in A-flat major. Stirring
fugal parts are found in the center of the two outer sections and
draw the whole fantasia to a brilliant close. The other, less frequently played but quite beautiful, Fantasia in F Minor(K. 594)
is also in large ternary form. The first theme of the opening
and closing parts is played by the pedal, which outlines the harmonies sustained on the manuals. The middle division of the
fantasia is in the parallel major key and contrasts a strong rhythmic and chordal motive with quick-flowing streams of parallel
thirds, sixths, and tenths in 16th-notes.

Franz Joseph Haydn(1732-1809) wrote 32 tiny pieces for
a mechanical flute organ in a clock (Spieluhrstücke). He also
wrote three concertos in C major about 1760. The concertos
are written for organ (or cembalo), two oboes, and string orchestra. There is no organ pedal part, nor are the oboes used
in the slow movements. The three movements are arranged in
fast-slow-fast order.

Johann Christoph Oley (1738-1789), a pupil of J. S. Bach,[4]
composed chorale preludes in the stolid, learned style. [5]

Justin Heinrich Knecht (1752-1817) gave his pieces
dramatic titles and subjective markings such as Sehnsuchts-
voll (full of yearning) and Etwas feurig und doch angenehm
(rather fiery and yet pleasing), and musical characteristics
of broken chords, colorful, romantic chromaticism, and
orchestral effects. One of his compositions was entitled
Die Auferstehung Jesu ("The Resurrection of Jesus") with
subtitles such as schauervolle Stille des Graves (dreadful
stillness of the grave), das Zurückstürzen der römischen
Schaar (the falling backwards of the Roman troops) and
Triumphgesang der Engle (angels' song of triumph). Knecht
is also known for his Orgelschule des Choral (1795-1798).

Abbé Georg Joseph Vogler (1749-1814) was a man of
many talents: writer, acoustician, inventor, teacher, composer, virtuoso organist, and priest. His conceptions of
organ building were not successful, although many of them
were cordially received. At his recitals his improvisations
included fantastic effects like Seeschlacht mit Trommelrühren
(sea battle with drum rolls), Geschrei der Verwundeten (cries
of the wounded), Jauchzen der Sieger (shouts of the victor),
and Das Wetter in April (April Weather). His performance

GERMANY AFTER BACH: 1725-1800

1700	1750	1800	1850

(1685 Bach, Johann Sebastian 1750)
1690 Krebs, Johann Tobias 1762
1696 Vogler, Johann Caspar 1763
ca.1700 Kniller, Anton ?
1702 Eberlin, Johann E. 1762
1702 Schneider, Johann-------------------1788
1705 Kellner, Johann Peter--------1772
1710 Bach, Wilhelm Friedemann--------1784
1713 Krebs, Johann Ludwig--------1780
1714 Homilius, Gottfried ----------1785
1714 Bach, Carl Philipp Emanuel ------1788
1715 Doles, Johann Friedrich--------------1797
1716 Seger, Joseph Ferdinand ------------1782 (Bohemian composer)
1718 Marpurg, Friedrich Wilhelm------1795
1721 Kirnberger, Johann Philipp-------1783
1732 Bach, J. C. F.------------1795
1732 Kittel, Johann Christian ------------1809
1732 Haydn, Franz Joseph-----------1809
1735 Bach, Johann Christian ------1782
1736 Albrechtsberger, Johann Georg ------1809
1738? Oley, Johann Christoph ------1789
1749 Vogler, Georg Joseph----------1814
1752 Knecht, Justin Heinrich------1817
1756 Mozart, W. A. ------1791
1770 Beethoven, Ludwig van 1827

of H. H. Knecht's Pastoral Festival Interrupted by a Storm stirred the imagination of the sensation-seeking public. The great array of combinations and color possibilities of the organ (which often fascinate laymen) were exploited by both Knecht and Vogler and anticipated and contributed to the decadent organ style and the decline of the influence of the organ which marked a major portion of the nineteenth century. [6]

Ludwig van Beethoven (1770-1827) wrote very few organ works. They consist of Zwei Praeludien durch alle Durtonen für Orgel (auch für Klavier), Op. 39 (1789), Zweistimmige Fuge für Orgel (D major) (1783), and three short pieces which can be played as a group: Adagio, Scherzo, and Allegro (1799). The last three pieces were composed for a mechanical organ in a clock at the request of Count von Deym, the same man who commissioned Mozart's fantasias. [7] A principal theme is the unifying item in each of the two preludes which progress through all major keys. The short Fugue in D Major is in two voices, with additional voices added for the last 15 measures to strengthen the final cadence. This piece was composed when Beethoven was only 13 years of age.

The Bohemian (Czech) school of organ composers is a small one, which is related to the stronger schools in Germany and Italy. Bohuslav Czernohorský (1684-1742), a Minorite friar, was the first important composer and teacher in the school. He was followed by Jan (Johann) Zach (1699-1773), Joseph Seger (Seeger) (1716-1782), František Xaver Brixi (1732-1771), Jan Křtitel Vanhal (1739-1813), and Jan Křtitel Kuchař (1756-1829). Anton Rejcha (Reicha) (1770-1836) was a Bohemian teacher whose pupils such as Liszt, Gounod, Franck, and Berlioz became far better known than he. Light-hearted organ music of the Czech school was written in forms such as the fugue, toccata, prelude, and pastorale. [8]

Notes

1. Composer-pupils of J. S. Bach who wrote a few chorale settings are Johann Kaspar Vogler (1693-1763), Johann Schneider (1702-1788), Johann Tobias Krebs (1690-1762), the father of Johann Ludwig Krebs, Heinrich Nicolaus Gerber (1702-1755), Johann Peter Kellner (1705-1722), Johann Trier (1716-1789/1790), Johann Friedrich Agricola (1720-1774), Johann Philipp Kirnberger (1721-1783), Gottfried August Homilius (1714-1785), Johann Friedrich Doles (1715-1797), and Johann Gottfried Müthel (1728-1788).

2. Bach himself said, in making a pun on their names, that
    his pupil was the best crab (Krebs) in the brook (Bach).
3. Some less significant composers: Johann Scheibe (1708-
    1776), Johann Eberlin (1702-1762), and Johann Albrechts-
    berger (1736-1809), one of Beethoven's teachers. Eber-
    lin, under the influence of Bach's Wohltemperirte Clavier,
    issued IX Toccate e fughe per l'organo (1747).
4. Hans Löffler, "Die Schüler Joh. Seb. Bachs," Bach-
    Jahrbuch im Auftrage der Neuen Bachgesellschaft, Al-
    fred Dürr and Werner Neumann, eds., Berlin: Evangel-
    ische Verlaganstalt, Vol. XL (1953), p. 6, 26.
5. For an interesting comment on the music of this period
    see the General Preface to J. G. Oley, Four Chorale
    Preludes, London: Novello and Co., 1958.
6. William Leslie Sumner, The Organ: Its Evolution, Prin-
    ciples of Construction, and Use, London: Macdonald
    and Co., 1952 (2nd ed., 1955); p. 206.
7. Ludwig Altman, ed., Beethoven Organ Works, London:
    Hinrichsen Edition Ltd., 1962; preface.
8. A Century of Czech Music, 2 vols., Karel Paukert, ed.,
    Chicago: H. T. FitzSimons Co., 1965.

Bibliography

Altman, Ludwig, ed. Beethoven Organ Works. London:
    Hinrichsen Edition Ltd., 1962; preface.
Biba, Otto. "The Unknown Organ Music of Austria,"
    Diapason (January 1971), p. 10.
Emery, Walter, ed. J. G. Oley Four Chorale Preludes.
    London: Novello and Co., 1958; general preface.
Frotscher, Gotthold. Geschichte des Orgelspiels und der
    Orgelkomposition. Berlin: Merseberger Verlag, 1959;
    vol. II, p. 1048-1122.
Harmon, Thomas. "The Performance of Mozart's Church
    Sonatas," Music & Letters, vol. 51, no. 1 (January
    1970), p. 51.
Löffler, Hans. "Die Schüler Joh. Seb. Bachs," Bach-Jahr-
    buch im Auftrage der Neuen Bachgesellschaft, Alfred
    Dürr and Werner Neumann, eds. Berlin: Evangelische
    Verlaganstalt, Vol. XL (1953), p. 6, 26.
Mansfield, Orlando A. "Mozart's Organ Sonatas," Musical
    Quarterly, vol. VII (1922), p. 566-594.
Mulbury, David. "Bach's Favorite Pupil: Johann Ludwig
    Krebs," Music/the A. G. O. Magazine, vol. II, no. 2
    (February 1968), p. 24.
Paukert, Karel, ed. A Century of Czech Music, 2 vols.

Chicago: H. T. FitzSimons Co. , 1964.

Sumner, William Leslie. "Beethoven and the Organ," Musical Opinion, no. 1110, vol. 93 (March 1970), p. 323-325.

_____. The Organ: Its Evolution, Principles of Construction, and Use.   London: Macdonald and Co. , 1952 (2nd. ed. , 1955); p. 205-208.

Tangeman, Robert. "Mozart's Seventeen Epistle Sonatas," Musical Quarterly, vol. XXXII (October 1946), p. 588-601.

13.   GERMANY AND ENGLAND: 1800-1900

Germany

The two most prominent organ building firms in Germany during the nineteenth century were the Schulze and Walcker companies.   J. A. Schulze and his son J. F. Schulze did not break with tradition, but the theories of Abt Vogler and Knecht did influence them somewhat.   Eight-foot stops predominated on the manuals;   mutations and mixtures were used less and less because they were not well made and sometimes contained a tierce which did not blend well with the ensemble.   Schulze also employed free reeds, increased the wind-pressure, and developed a solo manual. [1]

The Walcker firm began building organs in the eighteenth century.   In 1820 E. F. Walcker moved the firm to Ludwigsburg where he built many organs, some of the largest in the world, along dark, somber tonal schemes.   One unusual characteristic of some of Walcker's organs was the inclusion of two pedal boards.   One of the most important nineteenth-century instruments built by this firm was erected in Paulskirche, Frankfurt. [2]   The specifications are given below.

Frankfurt, Germany, Paulskirche.
Built by E. F. Walcker, 1827-1833.

Hauptwerk (I)	Oberwerk (II)	Manual (III) (enclosed)
Untersatz 32'	Bourdon 16'	Quintatön 16'
Prinzipal 16'	Prinzipal 8'	Prinzipal 8'
Viola da Gamba 16'	Salizional 8'	Harmonica 8'
Tibia major 16'	Dolce 8'	Bifra 8'
Oktave 8'	Gedackt 8'	Hohlflöte 8'
Viola da Gamba 8'	Quintatön 8'	Lieblich Gedackt 8'
Jubalflöte 8'	Quinteflöte 5 1/3'	Dolcissimo 8'
Gemshorn 8'	Oktave 4'	Spitzflöte 4'
Quinte 5 1/3'	Flauto traverso 4'	Lieblich Gedackt 4'
Oktave 4'	Rohrflöte 4'	Flûte d'amour 4'

HISTORICAL BACKGROUND

1797-1828	Schubert
1797-1856	Heine
1801	Haydn Seasons
1804	Schiller William Tell
1804	Beethoven "Eroica" Symphony
1806	Holy Roman Empire dissolved
1806	Goethe Faust
1808	Beethoven "Pastoral" Symphony
1813-1883	Wagner
1814	Beethoven Fidelio
1815-1866	German Confederation
1822	Schubert "Unfinished" Symphony
1823	Beethoven Ninth Symphony
1844-1900	Nietszche
1845	Wagner Tannhäuser
1847	Communist Manifesto
1854	Hanslick On the Beautiful in Music
1858	Brahms Ein deutsches Requiem
1859	Wagner Tristan und Isolde
1862	Bismarck became chancellor of Prussia
1867-1916	Reign of Franz Joseph I of Austria-Hungary
1871	Bismarck became chancellor of Germany
1888-1918	Reign of Kaiser Wilhelm II
1888	Hugo Wolf Mörike Lieder
1895	R. Strauss Till Eulenspiegel

Hohlpfeife 4'
Fugara 4'
Tierce 3 1/5'
Quinte 2 2/3'
Oktave II
Waldflöte 2'
Tierce 1 3/5'
Oktave 1'
Mixtur V
Scharff IV
Cornet V
Tuba 16'
Trompete 8'

Quinte 2 2/3'
Oktave 2'
Mixtur V
Posaune 8'
Vox humana 8'

Nasard 2 2/3'
Flautino 2'
Hautboy 8'
Physharmonika 8'

Pedal II (upper)

Violon 16'
Subbass 16'
Prinzipal 8'
Flöte 8'
Flöte 4'
Waldflöte 2'
Fagott 16'

Pedal I (lower)

Couplers

Subbass 32'
Contrabass 32'

Tierce 6 2/5'
Quinte 5 1/3'

Oberwerk to Hauptwerk
Manual to Hauptwerk

Prinzipal 16'   Oktave 4'   Manual to Oberwerk
Oktave 16'   Posaune 16'   Pedal I to Pedal II
Violon 16'   Trompete 8'   Hauptwerk to Pedal I
Quinte 10 2/3'   Clarine 4'   Oberwerk to Pedal II
Oktave 8'   Clarinetto 2'
Violoncello 8'

Slider chests; mechanical action

One of the major expressions of Romanticism in German
organ music is found in the organ compositions of Felix Mendelssohn (1809-1847), which include Three Preludes and Fugues,
Op. 37 (C minor, G major, D minor), and Six Sonatas. The
preludes and fugues were dedicated to Thomas Attwood, the
London organist, and were composed between 1835 and 1837.
Mendelssohn's interest in earlier music, especially the music
of Bach, suggested the prelude and fugue form. He employed
harmonically determined counterpoint in these pieces.

The English publishers Coventry and Hollier commissioned Mendelssohn to write three voluntaries for the organ.
Since Mendelssohn was not familiar with the voluntary form,
he chose to name his compositions sonatas, even though no
movement is in sonata-allegro form. [3] Sonata No. 3 in A
major was composed in August, 1844, and the other five
(No. 1 in F minor, No. 2 in C minor, No. 4 in B-flat major, No. 4 in D major, No. 6 in D minor) were all composed
within two months, December, 1844, and January, 1845.
Most of the slow movements were cast in simple binary form;
several movements approached a rondo form.   The Allegretto
(Sonata No. 4) resembles many of Mendelssohn's songs without words.   The first movement of the Sixth Sonata is a
series of variations on the chorale Vater unser im Himmel-
reich ("Our Father, Who in Heaven Art").   Musical inspiration seems to have guided the form of these pieces rather
than any predetermined mold.   Another chorale, Aus tiefer
Not ("Out of the Depths"), appears in the first movement of
the third sonata.   The use of chorales suggests that Mendelssohn intended these sonatas for church performance. [4]   He
also decided to close the third and sixth sonatas with slow,
soft movements, an unusual procedure.

Remarkable features of the sonatas include: close
imitation between parts; use of pedal points and sequences;
fugues of loose construction; crossing parts; combination of
themes; filling out of harmonies with added voices and un-

resolved discords at the ends of phrases; melodies built on
arpeggio or scale figures; phrases sometimes repeated an octave above or below; phrased pedal part, sometimes using
staccato articulation for a complete section, with a number of
pedal scales; and manual technique calling for a toccata touch.
Mendelssohn's other organ compositions include a Fugue in F
Minor (1830), Praeludium in C Minor (1841) and Two Pieces:
Andante con variazione in D Major [and] Allegro in B-flat
Major (1844).

Mendelssohn's enthusiasm for the music of Bach encouraged him to perform the following recital of Bach organ
works in St. Thomas' Church, Leipzig, on August 6, 1840:

> Fugue in E-flat Major
> Schmücke dich
> Prelude and Fugue in A Minor
> Passacaglia and Fugue in C Minor
> Pastorale
> Toccata in F Major

The most prominent pupil of Johann Christian Kittel
(a pupil of Bach) was Johann Christian Heinrich Rinck (1770-
1846). Rinck's organ music, which is designed for concert
use, is melodious and charming and contains many figurations
on harmony and sequences. Adolphe Hesse (1809-1863) admired Bach's organ works and encouraged many pupils to
study them. Hesse's own compositions contain elements of
imitation, but are homophonic in character.

Robert Alexander Schumann (1810-1856) composed
three sets of pieces in 1845 which can easily be played on
the organ, although he wrote them for the pedal-piano (Pedal-
flügel). These compositions include the Studies (Etudes),
Op. 56, Sketches, Op. 58, and Six Fugues on the Name of
BACH, Op. 60. [5] The six studies (C major, A minor, E
major, A-flat major, B minor, and B major) are written in
the form of canons. Some of the studies resemble such
divergent works as those of Bach or Mendelssohn's Songs
without Words.

The four Sketches (C minor, C major, F minor, and
D-flat major) are pianistic in nature. Schumann's six fugues
(B-flat major, B-flat major, G minor, B-flat major, F
major, and B-flat major), the subjects of which spell Bach's
name musically, were inspired by the counterpoint of Bach.

GERMANY: 1800-1900

1800	1850	1900	1950

1770 Rinck, J. C. ----1846

1809 Mendelssohn, F. 1847

1809 Hesse, Adolphe------1863

1810 Schumann, R. ---1856

1811 Liszt, Franz (Hungarian)------1886

1824 Bruckner, Anton------------1896

1827 Merkel, Gustav Adolph----1885

1833 Brahms, Johannes ------1897

1834 Reubke, J. 1858

1839 Rheinberger, Joseph-------1901

1863 Kaun, Hugo-----------1932

1873 Reger, Max--1916

1877 Karg-Elert, Sigfrid ----1933

1874 Schmidt, Franz --------1939 (Austrian)

Franz Liszt (1811-1886), the famous Hungarian virtuoso pianist, composed three large works for organ, a few
short pieces, and an organ Mass (1879). Liszt's interest in
the organ is indicated by his purchase of a pedalboard in
1854, his visit with Franck at Ste. Clotilde in 1866, and his
examination of the newly installed Cavaillé-Coll organ at the
Trocadéro in Paris in 1878. His interest in orchestral music and his own dazzling keyboard technique gave the predominant character and form to the three larger organ works.
The Fantasy and Fugue on Ad nos, ad salutarem undam
(1850), the theme of which was taken from the choral of the
three Anabaptists in Meyerbeer's opera Le Prophète, is a
long, rhapsodic work, full of pianistic arpeggios, pedal trills,
key changes, double-pedaling, virtuoso cadenzas, and many
tempo changes. Alexander Winterberger (1834-1914), a pupil
of Liszt, played the first performance at Merseburg in 1855. [6]

The Prelude and Fugue on B-A-C-H was composed in
1855. The piece was intended for the organ inauguration at
the Merseburg Cathedral, but it was not completed in time
for the celebration. A second version appeared in 1870.
Although the Prelude and Fugue is similar to the "Ad nos"
fantasy, it is much shorter.

Liszt's third large composition is the Variations on
Weinen, Klagen, Sorgen, Zagen, based on the basso ostinato
of the first chorus of Bach's cantata for the third Sunday
after Easter and the basso ostinato of the Crucifixus from
Bach's Mass in B Minor. The variations were composed in
1863.

Liszt's Messe für die Orgel zum gottesdienstlichen
Gebrauch contains the following pieces to be played during
Mass but not for alternation with a choir: Kyrie, Gloria,
Graduale, Credo, Offertorium, Sanctus, Benedictus, and
Agnus Die. Liszt also wrote an organ Requiem zum gottes-
dienstlichen Gebrauch containing an Adagio; Dies irae; Re-
cordare, pie Jesu; Sanctus; Benedictus; Agnus Dei; and Post-
ludium.

Julius Reubke (1834-1858), the son of an organ
builder and a pupil of Liszt, lived only 24 years, but he
left one of the finest Romantic works for organ, a large
fantasy, The Ninety-Fourth Psalm (Sonata). This one composition is in three movements based on one theme (idée
fixe) in two segments, the first a rhythmic idea, and the
second, a chromatically descending theme. The sonata is

a virtuoso work which closes with a brilliant fugue. The
"program" for the sonata is a selection of nine verses from
Psalm 94. The brooding grave introduction and larghetto is
based on the text verses beginning, "O God, to whom ven-
geance belongeth, show thyself ..." and "... how long shall
the wicked triumph?" A supple manual technique is required
to execute the broken chords (the diminished seventh chord
is used often), scale passages in 16th-notes, the variety of
articulations, and rhythms, all of which are balanced by an
active pedal part, wherein the sonata motive frequently appears. A short grave section returns to the mood of the
opening section and diminishes in sound and animation in order to introduce the soft adagio movement. Restless chromaticism and modulations constitute the treatment of the
sonata motive in the slow movement, which is based on the
text verse beginning, "In the multitude of my cares within
me thy comforts delight my soul."

The (Allegro) fugue in C minor employs the sonata
motive as the subject and the answer, which is real (i. e. ,
an exact transposition of the fugue subject into the dominant
key). The excitement rises and subsides frequently in order
to interpret, "But the Lord is my defence.... And he ...
shall cut them off in their own wickedness...." Jagged,
dotted rhythms and a change to a quicker triplet rhythm in
the piu mosso section further heighten the fierce climax
which closes the final movement with a thrilling, virtuoso
pedal part under brisk, manual chords.

Josef Anton Bruckner (1824-1896), the famous Austrian
symphonist, was best known in the organ field as an improviser. Bruckner organ compositions include two preludes in
E-flat written about 1836 and 1837, two Orgelstücke in D
minor (ca. 1846), a Prelude and Fugue in C Minor (ca. 1847),
and a Fugue in D Minor (1861/62).

Gustav Adolph Merkel (1827-1885) was a Dresden
organist who wrote some 60 volumes of organ works in a
combination of Baroque and Romantic styles. [7] His pieces
include naïve, easy, melodic pastorales, chorale preludes
which suggest concert performance, songs without words,
and organ forms especially connected with the Baroque period
such as passacaglias, fugues, and canons. The nine organ
sonatas by Merkel were all composed in three movements
and in minor keys. The Sixth Sonata contains two chorale
melodies, Aus tiefer Not ("Out of the Depths") and Wie schön
leuchtet der Morgenstern ("How Brightly Shines the Morning
Star").

A great composer of symphonic and piano works who wrote organ compositions was Johannes Brahms (1833-1897). Brahms' earlier compositions for the organ were written in Düsseldorf and were primarily contrapuntal in character. These include the Chorale Prelude and Fugue on O Traurigkeit, O Herzeleid (early 1856), two preludes and fugues in A minor and G minor (1856/1857), and the Fugue in A-flat Minor (April 1856). The G minor prelude contains many different elements and suggests a fantasy. The A-flat minor fugue employs rich harmonies and a moderate use of chromaticism. The cross-rhythms of the chorale prelude on O Traurigkeit anticipated this same characteristic used in some of the chorale settings Brahms wrote 40 years later.

The Eleven Chorale Preludes, Op. 122, were Brahms' final compositions. These pieces were written during his last summer (1896) at Ischl in Upper Austria (and perhaps at Carlsbad) when he was in a somber frame of mind, ill, tired, and bereaved at the loss of several close friends. (He had written the Vier ernste Gesänge upon Clara Schumann's death.) These chorale preludes are personal and are written about life in retrospect and life after death.

Some of the preludes suggest Brahms' interest in Bach by their contrapuntal nature: Schmücke dich ("Deck Thyself, My Soul, with Gladness") and Mein Jesu der du mich ("My Jesus Calls to Me"). Herzlich thut mich erfreuen ("My Faithful Heart Rejoices") is quite pianistic. Rich harmonies abound in Es ist ein Ros' entsprungen ("Lo, How a Rose E'er Blooming"), the two settings of Herzlich thut mich verlangen ("O Sacred Head, Now Wounded"), and two of O Welt, ich muss dich lassen ("O World, I Now Must Leave Thee"). These miniatures contain much rhythmic and melodic imitation: Herzliebster Jesu ("Ah, Blessed Jesus") and Herzlich thut mich verlangen [I] ("O Sacred Head, Now Wounded"); echo passages: O Welt, ich muss dich lassen [II] ("O World, I Now Must Leave Thee") and Herzlich thut mich erfreuen ("My Faithful Heart Rejoices"); and the use of unifying elements such as the diminished fifth interval in melodic form, often inverted, in Herzliebster Jesu ("Ah, Blessed Jesus"). O wie selig ("O How Blessed Are Ye Faithful Souls") is a chorale which expresses exaltation of life beyond death.

Joseph Gabriel Rheinberger (1839-1901) was a prolific composer who wrote 20 organ sonatas in as many keys and a large number of meditations, character pieces, monologues,

fughettas, trios, two organ concertos (Op. 137 in F and Op.
177 in G minor), some suites for organ, violin and cello,
Op. 149, and two suites for violin and organ, Op. 150 and
Op. 166. Seventeen of the sonatas contain fugues. Rheinberger was able to write original and expressive music in
such strict contrapuntal forms as canon, fugue, and ground
bass. 8   Perhaps Rheinberger's best compositions are the
Sonata in F-sharp Major, Op. 111, Sonata in D-flat Major,
Op. 154 (1888), the first movement of the C Major Sonata,
Op. 165, Fantasie-Sonata in B Major, Op. 181, and Cantilena
from Sonata 11 in D Minor, Op. 148, the Twelve Monologues,
Op. 162, and the Ten Trios, Op. 189. Rheinberger's organ
works were conceived in the classic trandition and for a
classic organ, although his compositions have sometimes
been considered of mediocre quality, sentimental, and un-
imaginative. Rheinberger's organ had no swell division;
changes of dynamics could be observed only by adding or
taking off stops. The dynamic indications in his music must
not be taken too literally but in a relative manner, according
to the music's demands. Rheinberger disliked ostentation and
avoided dramatic writing; there is only one toccata in nearly
200 pieces.

German Romanticism in organ music reached a high
point in the works of Max Reger (1873-1916). Reger's music
is popular in Germany, and most organ recitals there contain
at least one of his compositions. He employed traditional
forms such as toccata, trio, passacaglia, chorale-fantasia,
and especially fugue. Reger frequently used contrapuntal devices such as imitation, sequence, and canon. The texture,
however, tends to become thick, the harmonic rhythm rapid,
and the use of chromaticism extreme. A highly developed
keyboard technique is necessary in order to perform the complex chords, which frequently involve octaves and constantly
changing rhythms.

There are 29 opus numbers (at least 220 compositions)
of organ works, a quantity of unnumbered ones, and at least
20 arrangements of Bach works for the organ. At least eight
opus numbers are collections of both character pieces and
compositions written in old forms. The Benedictus, Op. 59,
No. 9, is probably Reger's best known organ composition in
America. The Introduction and Passacaglia in D Minor, Op.
59, No. 5, are also well known. Reger's Opus 59 contains
three pieces inspired by texts from Mass Ordinary sections:
Kyrie eleison (No. 7), Gloria in excelsis (No. 8), and
Benedictus (No. 9). These pieces incorporate fragments of

plainsong melodies associated with the Latin texts.

An extraordinary ability to develop thematic material is exhibited in the larger, virtuoso works, which are rather orchestral in character (Variations and Fugue on an Original Theme in F-sharp Minor, Op. 73; the chorale fantasias Ein' feste Burg, Op. 27, Freu dich sehr, Op. 30, Wie schön leuchtet and Straf mich nicht, Op. 40, Alle Menschen, Wachet auf, and Hallelujah! Gott zu loben, Op. 52). Reger's smaller and easier cantus firmus compositions on chorale melodies treat single stanzas in reharmonization, as solo melody with accompaniment, echo phrases, and melody in canon (Leicht ausführbare Vorspiele, Op. 67, Kleine Choralvorspiele, Op. 135a).

Although Franz Schmidt and Sigfrid Karg-Elert lived well into the twentieth century, their music is late Romantic in style. Franz Schmidt (1874-1939), a famous Austrian teacher and composer, wrote in an appealing style similar to that of Brahms and Reger. Schmidt wrote eight long works, six chorale settings, and a group of four short preludes and fugues. The most frequent organ forms he used include toccata, prelude, chaconne, variation, fugue, and chorale prelude. A tonal center is often established without chromaticism; as the piece progresses, chromaticism is gradually added. A bravura style characterizes the fourth (D major) of the Vier kleine Praeludien und Fugen and the much longer Toccata in C major (1924). The four short chorale preludes are consistent in style, and the chorale melodies are treated in conventional ways.

Sigfrid Karg-Elert (1877-1933) was encouraged by Reger to write for the organ. He approached composition for the organ through an understanding of wind instruments, as a pianist of brilliant technical ability, and as a student and admirer of Bach.[9] Many times Karg-Elert's compositions seem to be sentimental and contain bizarre registration indications, which denote an imperfect understanding of the tonal possibilities of the organ.[10]

Karg-Elert's 13 opus numbers contain works for the harmonium, for which instrument both French and German composers have written a considerable amount of material of delicate or intimate nature. Many of these short compositions are character pieces such as the Aquarelles, miniatures, monologues, Intarsien (inlaid work), consolations, portraits, impressions, and romanesque pieces. Karg-Elert's organ

works are original and include a wide variety of forms such
as cantus firmus settings of both chorale and plainsong melodies, character pieces, passacaglias, chaconnes, fugues,
canzonas, and partitas. Karg-Elert's works may be grouped
into five musical categories: simple harmonic, contrapuntal
(historical), mixed styles, tone paintings (with involved harmonic structures), and final phase.

Many organists are familiar with only one or two of
the chorale-improvisations, the large chorale-improvisation
on In dulci jubilio ("In Sweetest Joy"), and perhaps one of
the selections from Cathedral Windows or one of the Pastels
from Lake Constance. The chorale-improvisations and pieces
from Cathedral Windows lend themselves to use in the church
service because of the basic chorale and plainsong melodies.
Op. 65 and Op. 78 contain 66 and 20 chorale settings, re-
spectively, for different seasons of the church year.   Probably Karg-Elert's most familiar piece is the Marche Triomphale on Now Thank We All Our God, Op. 65, No. 59.
Canons, trios, echo phrases, extremely chromatic writing,
pianistic passages, tender and slow treatments which contrast with strong and rugged settings, siciliennes, and solo
airs are utilized by Karg-Elert in Op. 65. His seven Pastels from Lake Constance, Op. 96 (1919) are German Impressionism at an advanced stage. The altered chords arranged in rapid harmonic rhythm make a strong impression,
and the score calls for kaleidoscopic registration changes.

England

Some of the first organ compositions published in
England in the nineteenth century were Charles Wesley's
voluntaries (ca. 1815) and Samuel Wesley's Twelve Short
Pieces (1815), Six Introductory Movements (ca. 1825), and
the Six Voluntaries (1820/1830). Samuel Wesley showed
remarkable musical ability at an early age and was examined
by experts who were interested in exceptionally talented youth
such as Mozart and Crotch, who were also prodigies. [11]
Samuel admired Bach intensely and worked to introduce
Bach's music to the English people. In 1810 Wesley and
C. F. Horn published Bach's Well-Tempered Clavier in the
first English edition. These two men also published the
Bach trio sonatas in a piano duet version. [12]

Samuel Sebastian Wesley (1810-1876) was a brilliant
performer. He became the organist of a succession of

HISTORICAL BACKGROUND

1788-1824	Byron
1791	Boswell Life of Johnson
1794	Haydn visited London for the second time
1792-1822	Shelley
1795-1881	Carlyle
1800-1859	Thomas Macaulay
1805	Battle of Trafalgar
1810	Scott The Lady of the Lake
1812	Bryon Childe Harold
1813	Philharmonic Society of London founded
1812-1815	War of 1812
1813	Jane Austen Pride and Prejudice
1815	Battle of Waterloo
1821	Constable The Hay Wain
1833	Oxford movement began in Church of England
1836	Dickens Pickwick Papers
1837-1901	Reign of Victoria
1843	Dickens Christmas Carol
1848	Thackeray Vanity Fair
1853	Crimean War began
1859	Tennyson Idylls of the King
1859	Darwin Origin of the Species
1864	Lewis Carroll Alice in Wonderland
1868	Browning The Ring and the Book
1883	Stevenson Treasure Island
1885	Gilbert and Sullivan The Mikado
1891	Doyle Adventures of Sherlock Holmes
1893	Oscar Wilde Salomé
1894	Kipling Jungle Book
1898	Boer War

---

several cathedrals and had high musical standards, which he would not compromise. His compositions contain frequent use of chromaticism, altered and seventh chords, and feminine cadences. Most of his music falls into neat, four-measure phrases. His best known organ composition is probably the Choral Song and Fugue from the First Set of Three Pieces for Chamber Organ. A Second Set of Three Pieces, for a Chamber Organ was issued by Sacred Music Warehouse Novello, Ewer and Co. , between 1867 and 1876. [13]

Thomas Attwood Walmisley (1814-1856) was the organist of Trinity and St. John's Colleges at Cambridge University. His compositions are melodic, flowing, and employ a small amount of chromaticism. The Prelude and Fugue in

E Minor is a solid, well-designed piece and is written in
rhythmic simplicity, which is characteristic of much English
organ music of the nineteenth and twentieth centuries.

In 1829 Mendelssohn made his first trip to England.
He performed Bach's organ works and later his own, both of
which needed an adequate pedal board and pedal division.
Mendelssohn's playing and interest in organ music helped to
establish a new conception of the organ and its music in
England.

Between 1830 and 1850 the organ building firm of
William Hill and Dr. Henry John Gauntlett attempted to extend the ability of the English organ to reach the capabilities
of continental instruments. One of their major contributions
was an adequate, independent pedal organ and enlarged Swell
division which could perform the function of accompanying,
serve as a German Positiv, or as a solo division. It is indeed regrettable that the improvements and superior design
of instruments such as the one at George Street Chapel,
Liverpool, which was built by Hill and Gauntlett, were not
appreciated and not accepted as examples to be followed
after 1850. [14]

The Great Exhibition of 1851 introduced organs which
were built by the Swiss-German Edmund Schulze, by Aristide
Cavaillé-Coll, and by Henry Willis. Probably the outstanding
contribution which Schulze made to English organ building was
large diapason tone, which seems to have appealed enor-
mously to English taste, a proclivity which has survived for
at least 100 years. As a result of his instrument shown at
the 1851 Exhibition Willis was commissioned to build the
100-stop organ for St. George's Hall, Liverpool. This instrument had complete diapason and reed choruses, a modern
console, and a heavy-pressure wind supply, which was provided by a steam engine. Toward the end of his life "Father"
Willis included fewer and more subdued mixtures in his designs and used a standard wind pressure of 3 1/2", 7", and
15" for his reeds. [15]

During the nineteenth century many organs were built
in cathedrals and town halls such as St. George's Hall,
Liverpool, where William Thomas Best (1826-1897) served
as organist from 1855 to 1894 and played weekly recitals.
These programs were very well attended, and Best, the
leading English concert organist of the nineteenth century,
frequently performed his transcriptions of orchestral works

which introduced fine orchestral music to Liverpool audiences.
The listeners would not have been able to hear such music
otherwise due to the lack of orchestras in many cities of that
period.   Although Best did not compose much organ music,
his Christmas Fantasy on Old English Carols contains some
pedal passages which demand more from the performer than
had been required before from either English organists or
organs by English composers.

Best was also the organist of a parish church.   A
brief analysis of the specifications of the organ, which are
given below, reveals that there was only one mutation on the
entire organ, one mixture on both manuals, nine of the 26
stops on the organ were reeds, and that there were only four
pedal stops (two of them reeds).

Wallasey, England, Parish church.
Built by Henry Willis, 1861. [16]

Great	Swell	Pedal
Double diapason 16'	Open diapason 8'	Open diapason 16'
Open diapason 8'	Stopped diapason 8'	Bourdon 16'
Flute 8'	Principal 4'	Trombone 16'
Gamba 8'	Harmonic Flute 4'	Bassoon 8'
Dulciana 8'	Mixture III	
Principal 4'	Contra fagotto 16'	
Harmonic flute 4'	Trumpet 8'	
Twelfth 2 2/3'	Oboe 8'	
Fifteenth 2'	Vox humana 8'	
Mixture IV		
Trumpet 8'		
Clarion 4'		
Clarinet 8'		

Toward the end of the nineteenth century Robert Hope
Jones, an electrical engineer, made many changes in the
mechanical and tonal features of organs in both England and
America, which, unfortunately, effectively altered (ruined?)
the taste of many organists, organ builders, and organ audiences for perhaps more than one generation.   His alterations
included an electric action, developed high pressure reeds to
an excessive degree, took out all brightness of diapason tone
by covering the upper lips of the pipes with leather, invented
large-scale clarabellas (which he called tibias), completely
suppressed reed tone in the pedal, and allowed no stop above

ENGLAND: 1800-1900

1750	1800	1850	1900	1950

ca. 1770 Webbe, Samuel--------1843

1775 Crotch, William--------1847

1777 Russell, W. 1813

1785 Adams, Thomas---------1858

1810 Wesley, Samuel Sebastian 1876

1814 Walmisley, T. A. 1856

1826 Best, William Thomas--------1897

1848 Parry, Charles H. H. 1918

1852 Stanford, Charles V. 1924

1857 Elgar, Edward--------1934

1859 Harwood, Basil-------------1949

1865 Wolstenholme, W. 1931

1866 Wood, Charles 1926

a two-foot piccolo in his design. [17]

One of England's most distinguished composers of the late nineteenth century was Sir Edward Elgar (1857-1934). His <u>Sonata in G Major</u>, Op. 28, was composed in 1895 and dedicated to Dr. C. Swinnerton Heap. The influence of Romantic orchestral composers combined with his own individual taste and ability is expressed in frequent key and meter changes, a great sense of tone-color and harmony, and a wide variety of rhythmic patterns. This was one of the few English organ works of the nineteenth century of larger dimension.

The organ works of Basil Harwood (1859-1949) were influenced by German Romanticism and contain the type of chromaticism and tunefulness which is associated with Mendelssohn and Rheinberger. In larger forms Harwood composed two organ sonatas and an organ concerto.

Three composers closely connected with the Anglican church are Sir Charles Villiers Stanford (1852-1924), Sir C. Hubert H. Parry (1848-1918), and Charles Wood (1866-1926). Stanford is famous for his choral music for the church; perhaps his best known organ composition is the <u>Prelude and Fugue in E Minor</u>. Parry exhibited much more color and imagination in his hymn-tune settings than does Charles Wood. Wood's arrangements have a monotonous quality because his rhythms seem to be limited to quarter-note and eighth-note movement, and his harmonies stay within simple diatonic triads and seventh chords. Wood also chose to use manual and pedal parallel octaves a great deal. Parry, however, displayed rhythmic, tempo, and harmonic variety, changes in manual and pedal articulations, interesting registration possibilities and appropriate writing based on the hymn texts. At the beginning of each prelude Parry listed the specific lines of the hymn which inspired his writing.

Notes

1. Peter Williams, <u>The European Organ 1450-1850</u>, London: B. T. Batsford, 1966; p. 165-167.
2. <u>Ibid.</u>, p. 94-95.
3. In brief, sonata-allegro (sonata) form consists of three sections: exposition, development, and recapitulation. The first theme, usually dramatic, is connected to the second, often lyric, theme by a modulatory bridge.

Many types of treatment such as melodic fragmentation
and rhythmic alteration are given to the themes in the
freely composed development section before a restate-
ment of both themes of the exposition recur in the
tonic key.   A coda often sums up the thematic material and closes the movement.

4.   Orlando A. Mansfield, "Some Characteristics and Pecu-
liarities of Mendelssohn's Organ Sonatas," Musical
Quarterly, vol. III (1917), p. 526-576.
5.   The name of Bach can be spelled musically in German
musical notation because B signifies the English B-flat
and the German H indicates the English B-natural.
As a melody the name would be arranged thus: B-
flat, A, C, B-natural.
6.   Marcel Dupré, ed. , Trois Oeuvres pour Orgue de Franz
Liszt, Paris: S. Bornemann, 1941; preface.
7.   Gotthold Frotscher, Geschichte des Orgelspiels und der
Orgelkomposition, Berlin: Merseberger Verlag, 1959;
vol. II, p. 1173.
8.   Harvey Grace, The Organ Works of Rheinberger, London: Novello and Co. , 1925;   p. 120.
9.   Godfrey Sceats, The Organ Works of Karg-Elert, London: Hinrichsen Edition, 1940; p. 5. (rev. ed. ,1950.)
10.   Ibid. , p. 8.
11.   Thomas Armstrong, "The Wesleys, Evangelists and
Musicians," Organ and Choral Aspects and Prospects,
London: Hinrichsen Edition Ltd. , 1958;   p. 99.
12.   Ibid. , p. 100.
13.   Peter F. Williams, ed. , The Wesleys, Set Two, London: Hinrichsen Edition Ltd. , 1961;   preface.
14.   Cecil Clutton and Austin Niland, The British Organ,
London: B. T. Batsford Ltd. , 1963;   p. 91-94.
15.   Ibid. , p. 100.
16.   Clutton and Niland, op. cit. , p. 103.
17.   Clutton and Niland, op. cit. , p. 106-107.

Bibliography

GERMANY

Bacon, Allan.   "The Chorale Preludes of Max Reger," The
Diapason (February 1962), p. 30-31.
Bakken, Howard, "Liszt and the Organ," The Diapason (May
1969), p. 27-29.
Barker, John Wesley, "Reger's Organ Music," Musical
Times, no. 1496, vol. 108 (October 1967), p. 939;

no. 1498, vol. 108 (December 1967), p. 1142; no. 1500, vol. 109 (February 1968), p. 170.

Dupré, Marcel, ed. Trois Oeuvres pour Orgue de Franz Liszt. Paris: S. Bornemann, 1941; preface.

Frotscher, Gotthold. Geschichte des Orgelspiels und der Orgelkomposition. Berlin: Merseberger Verlag, 1959; vol. II, p. 1122-1195.

Gay, Harry W. "Study of Brahms' Works Expanded by Vivid Detail," The Diapason (March 1959), p. 38.

Gibson, David. "Franz Liszt's Christmas Tree," The Diapason (December 1970), p. 28.

Gotwals, Vernon. "Brahms and the Organ," Music/The A. G. O. and R. C. C. O. Magazine (April 1970), p. 38-55.

Grace, Harvey. The Organ Works of Rheinberger. London: Novello and Co., 1925.

Hathaway, J. W. G. Analysis of Mendelssohn's Organ Works: A Study of the Structural Features. London: Reeves, 1898.

Klotz, Hans. "Gedanken zur Orgelmusik Max Regers," Mitteilungen des Max-Reger-Instituts, vol. VII (1958).

Mansfield, Orlando A. "Some Characteristics of Mendelssohn's Organ Sonatas," Musical Quarterly, vol. III (1917), p. 562-576.

Sceats, Godfrey. The Organ Works of Karg-Elert, London: Orphington, 1940 (rev. ed., London: Hinrichsen Edition Ltd., 1950).

Trevor, C. H. "The Organ Music of Max Reger and Its Performance," Organ and Choral Aspects and Prospects. London: Hinrichsen Edition Ltd., 1958; p. 78.

Walsh, Stephen. "Schumann and the Organ," Musical Times, no. 1529, vol. 111 (July 1970), p. 741-743.

Williams, Peter F. The European Organ 1450-1850. London: B. T. Batsford, 1966; p. 94-95.

ENGLAND

Armstrong, Thomas. "The Wesleys, Evangelists and Musicians," Organ and Choral Aspects and Prospects. London: Hinrichsen Edition Ltd., 1958; p. 99.

Clutton, Cecil, and Austin Niland. The British Organ. London: B. T. Batsford Ltd., 1963; p. 89-107.

Williams, Peter F., ed. The Wesleys, Set Two. London: Hinrichsen Edition Ltd., 1961; preface.

14.   FRANCE: 1800-1900

From the degradation to which organ composition in France had sunk for nearly a century and a half only one man appeared who made an earnest attempt to improve the situation, Alexandre Pierre François Boëly (1785-1858). Boëly's admiration for the organ music of Bach and classic masters is evident in his compositions in which he combined contrapuntal techniques and forms with harmonic materials of his own time.   The works of Boëly have been divided into four books.   The first book contains his youthful works in the forms of preludes, fugues, canons, and free pieces.   The contents of the second book include preludes, versets based on plainsong, offertories, and pieces published after Boëly's death.   Preludes, hymn versets, and noëls from the period 1828-1854 are found in the third book, and, in the fourth, various pieces for the harmonium,[1] organ, or pedal piano. Probably the best known composition by Boëly is the Fantaisie et Fugue in B-flat major.   Boëly's compositions in this combination form probably gave rise to similar works by his pupil Camille Saint-Saëns and later Gigout.   Boëly deserves much credit for bringing back to French organ music the seriousness of purpose and dignity which it had lost after the death of Grigny.[2]

A few music editors such as Niedermeyer, d'Ortigue, Boëly, Miné, and Fessy exhibited interest in better music of the polyphonic school.   It was the Belgian Jacques-Nicolas Lemmens (1823-1881), however, who encouraged more study of classic masters.   Lemmens' deep interest in Bach and his own scholarly approach made his teaching at the Brussels Conservatoire influential in both Belgium and in France through pupils such as Guilmant and Widor.   Another pupil, Clément Loret, was an effective teacher in the Niedermeyer school in Paris.[3]

The music of Louis James Alfred Lefébure-Wély (1817-1869) and Antoine Edouard Batiste (1820-1876) was published in many nineteenth- and early twentieth-century collections in France, England, and America.   Even though

HISTORICAL BACKGROUND

1796-1875	Corot
1703	Purchase of Louisiana from France
1804	Napoleon became emperor
1810-1849	Chopin
1811-1886	Liszt
1814	Napoleon exiled to Elba
1815-1824	Reign of Louis XVIII
1815	Napoleon defeated at Waterloo
1818-1893	Gounod
1824-1830	Reign of Charles X
1829	Balzac La Comédie Humaine
1830-1848	Reign of Louis-Philippe
1831	Victor Hugo Notre Dame de Paris
1834-1917	Degas
1837	Berlioz Requiem
1838	Daguerre took first photographs
1839-1906	Cézanne
1840-1917	Rodin
1841-1919	Renoir
1841	Saxophone invented
1844	Dumas Three Musketeers
1844-1924	Anatole France
1851-1931	Vincent d'Indy
1852-1870	Napoleon III and Second Empire
1857	Flaubert Madame Bovary
1857	Baudelaire Les Fleurs du Mal
1859	Gounod Faust
1861	Paris Opéra built
1862	Hugo Les Misérables
1863	Manet Olympia
1870-1871	Franco-Prussian War
1871	National Society for French Music founded
1873	Degas Place de la Concorde
1875	Bizet Carmen
1878	Renoir Madame Charpentier et Ses Enfants
1879	Pasteur vaccines
1880	Rodin The Thinker
1880	Zola Nana
1884-1920	Modigliani
1885	de Maupassant Contes et Nouvelles
1889	Eiffel Tower finished
1890	Valéry Narcissus
1892	Debussy Afternoon of a Faun (1st ed.)
1892	Toulouse-Lautrec Au Moulin-Rouge
1894	Schola Cantorum founded
1896	Gaugin Maternité
1899	Ravel Pavane pour une infante défunte

the quality of this music might be questioned today, perhaps
these men were part of the effort to improve organ music of
that period.

The works of Camille Saint-Saëns (1835-1921) are conceived in classical forms, balanced, logically developed, and
often pianistic in nature. His Fantaisie in E-flat major is
probably his best known piece.

The "symphonic" school of nineteenth-century French
organ composition was encouraged by the orchestral organs
of Aristide Cavaillé-Coll (1811-1899). The Cavaillé-Coll
company built organs from about 1840 until about 1900 and
exerted much influence upon the organ writing of such composers as Franck, Widor, Guilmant, Gigout, Dubois, Boëllmann, and Vierne, and less significant composers such as
Samuel Rousseau (1853-1904) and Théodore César Salomé
(1834-1896). The manual divisions of Cavaillé-Coll organs
are dominated by brilliant, high-pressure reeds. Other characteristics are harmonic flutes, orchestral reeds, and strings.
Cavaillé-Coll generally suppressed the inclusion of mutations
and mixtures, a practice which transformed the basic character of the organ from a polyphonic instrument to a homophonic, orchestral one. C. S. Barker patented his pneumatic
lever in France in 1839; Cavaillé-Coll used the Barker lever
extensively in his organs. The use of ventils made groups
of stops in the various divisions usually reeds, available as
a body, to be added or discarded according to the will of the
performer. The practice of adding the reeds from the Swell
(Récit), Great (Grand Orgue), or Positif division(s) to the
foundation stops already drawn is still common in twentieth-
century French organ music. Gradual crescendos and di-
minuendos became much more easily manipulated by the use
of coupling devices.

One of the most significant changes made in the design of organs by Cavaillé-Coll was in the pedal division.
In the Classical French organ there were rarely more than
three pedal stops, an eight-foot reed, an eight-foot flute, and
perhaps a four-foot flute. The pedal part often sounded the
plainsong melody in long notes on the trumpet or played a
soft part in trios. The only way a 16-foot sound could appear in the pedal was through the Great to pedal coupler
(tirasse). The left hand part performed the real bass function on the manuals most of the time. The nineteenth-
century change, however, increased the size of the pedal
division considerably and moved the voice which performed

the bass function into the pedal, where the bass had been played in German and Dutch organs for 200 years. [4] Cavaillé-Coll built a number of organs in England and made his influence felt there as well as in France.

One of Cavaillé-Coll's best known instruments is the organ found at the Church of Ste. Clotilde, Paris, where Franck played for 31 years. The specifications are given below.

Paris, Ste. Clotilde.
Built by Aristide Cavaillé-Coll, 1859.

Récit (upper manual)

Bourdon 8'	Basson-Hautbois 8'
Flûte harmonique 8'	Voix humaine 8'
Viole de gambe 8'	Trompette 8'
Voix celeste 8'	Clairon 4'
Flûte octaviante 4'	
Octavin 2'	

Positif (middle manual)

Montre 8'	Bourdon 16'	Clarinette 8'
Prestant 4'	Gambe 8'	Trompette 8'
Quinte 2 2/3'	Flûte harmonique 8'	Clairon 4'
Doublette 2'	Bourdon 8'	
	Salicional 8'	
	Flûte octaviante 4'	

Grand Orgue (lower manual)

Montre 16'	Bourdon 16'	Bombarde 16'
Montre 8'	Gambe 8'	Trompette 8'
Prestant 4'	Flûte harmonique 8'	Clairon 4'
Octave 4'	Bourdon 8'	
Quinte 2 2/3'		
Doublette 2'		
Plein-jeu V		

Pédale

Sub-bass 32'	Flûte 8'	Basson 16'
Contrebasse 16'		Bombarde 16'
Octave 4'		Trompette 8'
		Clairon 4'

FRANCE: 1800-1900

1800	1850	1900	1950

1785 Boëly, Alexandre--1858
1817 Lefébure-Wély, Louis 1869
1820 Batiste, Antoine----1876
1822 Franck, César Auguste--------1890
1833 Loret, Clément---------------1909
1834 Salomé, Théodore--------1896
1835 Saint-Saëns, Charles-Camille------1921
1837 Chauvet, Charles-Alexis 1871
1837 Dubois, François-Clément-Théodore --1924
1837 Guilmant, Félix Alesandre--------1911
1844 Widor, Charles-Marie------------1937
1844 Gigout, Eugène----------------1925
1846 Périlhou, Albert --------------------1936
1849 Dallier, Henri---------------------1934
1851 d'Indy, Vincent-----------------1931
1852 Hillemacher, Paul--------------1933
1853 Rousseau, Samuel 1904
1858 Erb, Marie-Joseph----------------1944
1861 de Bréville, Pierre---------1949
1862 Boëllmann, Léon 1897
1863 Pierné, Gabriel-----------1937
1864 Ropartz, Joseph-Guy-Marie------------------1955
1865 Marty, Adolphe ------------1942
1867 Koechlin, Charles------------------------1950

Pédales de combinaison

Tirasse Grand Orgue	Octaves graves Récit
Tirasse Positif	Anches Pédale
Tirasse Récit	Anches Grand Orgue
Grand Orgue sur machine	Anches Positif
Copula Positif sur Grand Orgue	Anches Récit
Copula Récit sur Positif	Tremblant du Récit
Octaves graves Grand Orgue	Expression du Récit
Octaves graves Positif	

The greatest organ composer of the French school in
the nineteenth century was César Auguste Franck (1822-1890).
A Belgian by birth, but French by education and adoption,
this modest man exerted a profound effect upon his pupils and
the development of organ music.   The organ compositions of
"Père Franck" were composed with the Cavaillé-Coll organ
at Ste. Clotilde in mind.   Franck was organist there from
1859 until his death.   As the organ professor at the Paris
Conservatoire, Franck emphasized the study of composition
in his organ teaching.   An early and perhaps trite work, the
Andantino in G minor, was composed in 1858 but was not
published until 1889.   Six Pièces (1862), compositions of
somewhat uneven quality, appeared when the composer was
40 years old.

The first of the Six Pièces, the Fantaisie, Op. 16,
in C major, contains four sections.   The melodic line of the
opening section is primarily drawn from the tonic chord;   the
second theme enters as a canon.   The final section of the
Fantaisie is a serene Adagio, which is based (like the first
section) both harmonically and melodically to a great degree
on the C major chord.

The Grande Pièce Symphonique, Op. 17, the precursor
of all later organ "symphonies,"[5] is a major work in three
large movements.   After a lengthy introduction, a pedal solo
presents the principal theme followed by a dignified, legato
second theme.   The movement closes softly after a passage
which functions as a bridge to the lyric second movement.
The Andante movement is in three sections.   The first and
third parts in B major have a stately melody which, in the
first section, is frequently treated in short echo phrases.
The middle section in B minor is the caprice or scherzo
section of the "symphony" in which Franck used one of his
most frequent unifying devices, a canon, between outer voice
parts.   In the final section of the movement there is a re-

turn to the thematic material of the beginning section with the addition of a double pedal part. An extended interlude after the second movement incorporates four different themes from the preceding two movements to introduce the final movement. The last movement utilizes the principal theme of the first movement in its parallel major key (F-sharp major) over an active pedal part in eighth-notes. A fugue closes the entire work.

The Prélude, Fugue et Variation, Op. 18, is one of Franck's loveliest compositions. The cantabile melody of the prelude in B minor is presented over a simple accompaniment. A short interlude of nine measures' length anticipates the fugue subject and returns the tonality to B minor. In the latter part of the fugue, the primary musical accent seems to fall on the second beat of several successive bars. After the climactic end of the fugue, the serene melody of the prelude returns over a flowing 16th-note middle voice part.

Franck dedicated the Pastorale, Op. 19, in E major, to his friend Aristide Cavaillé-Coll, the organ builder. The tripartite composition opens with a melodic four-measure theme which is followed by a chordal theme. Crisp, staccato chords against a legato melody and a fughetta are the principal material found in the quicker middle section. In the final section the two themes of the first section are sounded simultaneously, and the piece closes in the same style with which it began.

The Prière, Op. 20, is a reserved and noble composition in which the opening section states harmonies in a somewhat choral fashion without employing the pedal. In the second section melodic phrases are exchanged between the pedal and uppermost voice of the manual parts, a technique Franck also used in the Grande Pièce Symphonique.

The Final, Op. 21, one of Franck's less inspired works, introduces long pedal solo passages and several bravura sections for the manuals alone.

The Trois Pièces were written for the inauguration of the large organ at the Trocadéro at the exhibition in 1878. The Fantaisie in A major has four themes; the first and second themes are sounded simultaneously toward the end. The Cantabile in B major alternates a two-measure chordal theme with a lyric one of the same length in the beginning

section. Franck used a canon as a unifying device in this
composition, too. Pièce Héroïque is one of the most popular
organ pieces written by Franck. The principal theme is
martial in quality and suggests orchestral brasses. The effect of timpani is suggested by alternating tonic and dominant
pitches in the pedal range. A canonic section, alteration of
themes into parallel major or minor keys, and a full organ
harmonization of the second principal theme at the close--
all contribute to maintaining the interest of the listener.

Franck's final major works for the organ are the
three chorals composed during the last year of his life (1890).
These three fantasias of large design are not built upon a
pre-existing chorale melody, but they do contain sections
which suggest hymn writing. The Choral No. 1 in E major
opens with a stately harmonized melody which Franck developed according to the cellule génératrice technique, in which
the entire piece grows from the same motivic material. The
dignified "choral" theme, which enters in measure 46, is
diatonic and presented in phrases of approximately equal
length. Some of the ways in which the thematic material is
varied are as solo and accompaniment in the original key
and in the parallel minor mode and as alternating phrases
of the theme progressing back and forth from the soprano
range to the tenor range. The First Choral closes with a
climactic version of the choral theme, in which the first
three phrases of the choral melody are repeated in the pedal
part after their statement in block chords on the full organ
sound.

Choral No. 2 in B minor, like the First Choral, is
in a variation form, that of a modified passacaglia. The
first two chorals also contain interludes in recitative or
free fantasy style, which interrupt the series of variations
but which provide a refreshing, brief change in the musical
material. Two sections, which resemble portions of Franck's
Symphony in D minor, softly close the two large sections
of the Second Choral; these same soft parts are examples
of the type of musical writing which suggests the mysticism
and religious idealism reflected in Franck's works.

Perhaps the most popular of Franck's Trois Chorals
is the Choral No. 3 in A minor. This choral is in large
ternary form. The center section is an extended, lyric
Adagio which contrasts with the fiery first and final sections.
Franck frequently used changes of key in order to keep the
restatements of the themes effective. Chords which demand

wide stretches of the hands are often found in Franck's works
because he had such large hands.

L'Organiste is the title of a collection of 59 short
pieces by Franck for harmonium or organ, which were written, like the chorals, during the last year of his life. [6]

Characteristics which recur frequently in Franck's
organ music are repetition of the same melodic figure with
slight chromatic changes (as from minor to major thirds),
wedge-like, widening melodic interval changes, the use of
sharp keys, canons, pedal points, the frequent use of chromaticism, and rich harmonies.

Félix Alexandre Guilmant (1837-1911) as a composer
owed much to his being a famous recitalist; he was the first
French concert performer to tour in America. He wrote
much for the concert organ repertoire, a number of offertories, elevations, communions on noëls, and some pieces on
Gregorian themes. Guilmant wrote his organ sonatas between 1874 and 1907. He often added a Grand Choeur or a
fugue to the standard group of pieces in the sonatas. Noël
Languedocien (1886) is one of his better known pieces. Guilmant, as a music editor in collaboration with the musicologist
André Pirro, edited with scholarly competence the complete
works of composers such as Titelouze, Clérambault, and
Scherer in the Archives des Maîtres de l'Orgue series.

Charles-Marie Widor (1844-1937), a Romanticist by
nature, wrote for the symphonic organ. Widor had a sense
of style and grandeur which was most appropriate to the instrument. He contrasted sonorities well, changed manuals
for dramatic effect, and, like Lemmens, used a staccato
touch for brilliance. Inverted pedal point and double pedaling
were other devices adopted by him.

Widor wrote ten organ symphonies between 1876 and
1900. The first four (C major, D major, E major, and F
major) make up Opus 13, and the next four (F major, G
major, A major, and B major), Opus 42. Widor, like Guilmant, added other forms such as pastorales, toccata-preludes,
chorals, variations, marches, intermezzos, scherzos, and
finales to the standard set of sonata movements. The last
two symphonies are the Symphonie Gothique, Op. 70 (1895)
and the Symphonie Romane, Op. 73 (1900), which are mature
works of a more liturgical character than the first eight
symphonies. The Christmas introit Puer natus est and the

Easter gradual <u>Haec dies</u> are two Gregorian themes used in these two final large works. Widor wrote <u>Sinfonia Sacra</u>, Op. 81, for organ and orchestra, and <u>Domine salvum fac populorum</u> for organ and brass.

Many French organ composers of the nineteenth century wrote collections of pieces in which less imaginative writing was employed. Théodore Dubois (1837-1924), one time director of the Paris Conservatoire and successor to Saint-Saëns at the Church of the Madeleine, wrote several books of organ pieces. [7] Eugène Gigout (1844-1925), the organist of St. Augustin, Paris, for over 60 years, had a great interest in plainsong. This interest in plainsong inspired him to write some 600 pages of short pieces in Gregorian modes for harmonium or organ. [8] His other compositions include works for pipe organ such as the <u>Toccata</u> in B minor (1892) and the famous <u>Grand-Choeur Dialogué</u>, which was especially effective when divisions of the organ were played antiphonally across the nave in St. Augustin.

Léon Boëllmann (1862-1897) was a student of Gigout who became an adopted member of Gigout's family. He is famous for the <u>Suite Gothique</u>, which was popular in America in the earlier part of the twentieth century. His compositions include other suites, a <u>Fantasia</u> in A major, an <u>Offertoire</u> on two noëls, a <u>Fantasia Dialoguée</u> for organ and orchestra, <u>Heures Mystiques</u>, and many shorter pieces.

Notes

1. Toward the later part of the nineteenth century, small organs for the home called harmoniums or melodians became popular. These instruments did not have a pedal board. A number of French composers wrote collections of pieces for these instruments.
2. Norbert Dufourcq, <u>A. P. F. Boëly: Oeuvres complètes pour Orgue</u>, vol. 1, Paris: Editions musicales de la Schola Cantorum, preface, p. 2.
3. Norbert Dufourcq, <u>La Musique d'Orgue Française de Jehan Titelouze à Jehan Alain</u>, Paris: Librairie Floury, 1949; p. 172.
4. Peter Williams, <u>The European Organ 1450-1850</u>, London: B. T. Batsford Ltd. , 1966; p. 201-203.
5. These "symphonies" are actually sonatas in several movements written for orchestral organs. They incorporate forms commonly found in nineteenth-century symphonic

writing such as movements written in sonata-allegro, variation, or song forms, and dance movements such as scherzos. The symphony of from four to six pieces usually closed with a stirring, brilliant toccata. Organ "symphonies" also equaled some of their orchestral counterparts in length. [See Dufourcq, op. cit., p. 144-158.]

6. Franck had planned to c ompose 91 in all. Four manuscript pieces, which were intended to be published with the 59 but which Franck did not have time to copy for the original publisher (Enoch), are found in Pièces Romantiques Ignorées, No. 17, in the L'Organiste Liturgique series, Schola Cantorum, Paris.

7. In the March of the Magi Kings by Dubois a high pitch is sustained throughout the composition to signify the star leading the wise men to Bethlehem.

8. Dufourcq, op. cit., p. 166.

Bibliography

Cavaillé-Coll, Cécile, and Emmanuel Cavaillé-Coll. Aristide Cavaillé-Coll: Ses Origines, Sa Vie, Ses Oeuvres. Paris: Librarie Fischbacher, 1929.

Davies, Laurence. César Franck and His Circle. Boston: Houghton Mifflin Co., 1970.

Demuth, Norman. César Franck. New York: Philosophical Library, 1949.

Dufourcq, Norbert. A. P. F. Boëly: Oeuvres Complètes pour Orgue, vol. 1. Paris: Editions musicales de la Schola Cantorum, preface.

_____. César Franck. Paris: Editions du Vieux Colombier, 1949.

_____. La Musique d'Orgue Française de Jehan Titelouze à Jehan Alain. Paris: Librairie Floury, 1949.

Gastoué, A. "A Great French Organist: A. Boëly and His Works," Musical Quarterly, vol. XXX, No. 3 (July 1944), p. 336-344.

Grace, Harvey. French Organ Music, Past and Present. New York: H. W. Gray Co., 1919.

_____. The Organ Works of César Franck. London: Novello and Co., 1948.

d'Indy, Vincent. César Franck, translated by Rosa Newman. Reprint, New York: Dover Publ., 1965.

Pruitt, William. "Charles Tournemire and the Style of Franck's Major Organ Works," Diapason (October 1970), p. 17.

Smith, Rollin. "Camille Saint-Saëns," Music/The A. G. O.
    and R. C. C. O. Magazine, vol. 5, no. 12 (December
    1971), p. 24-26.
Sumner, William Leslie. "The French Organ School," Sixth
    Music Book. London: Hinrichsen Edition Ltd. , 1950;
    p. 281-294.
Tournemire, Charles. César Franck. Paris: C. Delagrave,
    1931.
Williams, Peter. The European Organ 1450-1850. London:
    B. T. Batsford Ltd. , 1966; p. 201-203.

15. GERMANY AND AUSTRIA SINCE 1900

In 1896 Albert Schweitzer examined a new organ in the Liederhalle of Stuttgart and drew conclusions that the sound he had heard there was indeed no forward step in organ conception and construction but actually a backward one. This experience encouraged Schweitzer to listen for several years to many instruments and to study organ building practices seriously.   In 1906 Schweitzer wrote of the conclusions and observations he had made in the pamphlet The Art of Organ Building and Organ Playing in Germany and France. This pamphlet condemned the commercialism and indifference of organ builders to craftsmanship and tonality and defined his thoughts about what the ideal organ should be and how it should sound.   Schweitzer's pamphlet became the earliest and basic writing on which the Orgelbewegung, the German organ reform movement, was founded, a movement which has greatly affected organ building in Europe and North America in the twentieth century.   Several factors, which Schweitzer deemed of great importance, were the use of the slider chest, mechanical key action, lower wind pressures, and high and free placement of the instrument.

Another event which gave impetus to the organ reform movement occurred in Germany--the so-called "Praetorius" organ was built in the Music Institute at the University of Freiburg im Breisgau in 1921 under the supervision of Professor Willibald Gurlitt according to specifications given by Praetorius in the Syntagma Musicum, Vol. 2, De Organographia (1619).   The specifications are given below.

Freiburg im Breisgau, Germany.
Music Institute, University.
Built by Walcker Company, 1921.

Oberwerk	Rückpositiv
Principal 8'	Quintadeena 8'
Octava 4'	Blockflöit 4'
Mixtur IV	Gemshörnlein 2'

HISTORICAL BACKGROUND

1870	Franco-Prussian War
1875-1955	Thomas Mann
1898-1956	Bertolt Brecht
1900	Schoenberg Gurre-lieder
1905	R. Strauss Salomé
1912	Schoenberg Pierrot Lunaire
1914-1918	World War I
1916	Freud Introduction to Psychoanalysis
1919-1933	German Republic
1921	Construction of "Praetorius" organ in Freiburg
1923	Rilke Sonette an Orpheus
1923	Hitler's Munich Putsch
1925	Kafka Der Prozess
1925	Berg Wozzeck
1926	Freiburg Organ Conference
1928	Kurt Weill Three-Penny Opera
1933-1939	Thomas Mann Joseph und seine Brüder
1933-1945	Third Reich under Hitler
1939-1945	World War II
1941	Franz Werfel Song of Bernadette
1949	Federal Republic of Germany established
1949-1963	Adenauer, chancellor of Germany
1963	Rolf Hochhuth Der Stellvertreter
1963-1966	Erhard, chancellor of Germany
1966-1969	Kiessinger, chancellor of Germany
1969-	Brandt, chancellor of Germany

Grob Gedact/Rohrflöit 8'
Nachthorn 4'
Schwiegelpfeiff 1'
Rancket oder stille
    Posaun 16'
Gemshorn 4' (added to
    Praetorius specification)

Zimbel doppelt, gar klein
    und scharff
Spitzflöit oder
    Spillflöit 4'
Krumbhorn 8'

In die Brust

Klein lieblich Gedactflöit.
    Rohrflöit 2'
Baerpfeiff 8'
Geigend Regal 4'

Pedal

Untersatz starck 16'
Posaunen Bass 16'
Singend Cornet 2'
Dolzianbass 8' (added to
    Praetorius specification)

This instrument became the center of interest for the famous

Freiburg Organ Conference in 1926. Christhard Mahrenholz, one of the leaders of the conference, emphasized the close relationship of the organ reform to the music and liturgy of the church.

In addition to those factors listed above, which were stressed by Schweitzer in his pamphlet of 1906, the Deutsche Orgelbewegung decided that the following points should also be emphasized: the organ, which is primarily a polyphonic instrument, should be developed for the literature to be played on it; stop names should be appropriate to function, pipe construction, or tone quality; the tonal design should be developed along the "Werk principle" (completeness of each division and contrast between divisions, placement of the divisions, and their architectural appearance); and acoustics of the room should be natural and allow for suitable reverberation.

During the third decade of the twentieth century a few renowned teachers and organists became aware that their Romantic performances had violated the conception and artistic styles of music from early periods of musical composition. One of the most striking admissions of error and of change toward producing a faithful performance enlightened by study was that made by Dr. Karl Straube. In the Foreword to his Neue Folge (new series) of Alte Meister des Orgelspiels (Early Masters of Organ Performance) (1929). Straube admitted that the opinions he had expressed in the preface to his edition of Alte Meister of 1904 were no longer valid and that the real aim of performance should be an artistic reproduction of a work of musical art as it was originally conceived, in direct relation to the precepts of its period of composition and for instruments built according to similar principles of construction of a particular era. Straube's thoughts were shared by Günther Ramin, the organist of St. Thomas Church, Leipzig (the church Bach had served), and Hans Henny Jahnn. These men discovered in 1922 that the St. Jakobi organ built by Arp Schnitger in Hamburg was an excellent example of the best of organ building.

The rise of musicological research and a great reawakening of interest in early music, especially from the Renaissance and Baroque periods, deeply influenced such outstanding twentieth-century German composers as Distler and Hindemith to write in what might be called a neo-Baroque style. This objective type of composition and organ performance also gained support from a strong reaction against the overemotional and extremely subjective expressions of the nineteenth century at which time organs were unashamedly built as orchestral substitutes.[1]

The specifications given below are those of a new von Beckerath instrument, which was built recently in the United States.

New Haven, Conn. , Dwight Chapel, Yale University.
<u>Built by von Beckerath, 1971.   Mechanical action.</u>

Great	Positiv	Swell
Bourdon 16'	Gedackt 8'	Gedackt 8'
Principal 8'	Quintadena 8'	Principal 4'
Rohrflöte 8'	Principal 4'	Waldflöte 2'
Octave 4'	Rohrflöte 4'	Sifflöte 1'
Spielflöte 4'	Octave 2'	Terzian II
Nasat 2 2/3'	Quinte 1 1/3'	Cymbel III
Octave 2'	Sesquialtera II	Trichterregal 8'
Flachflöte 2'	Scharf IV	Tremolo
Tierce 1 3/5'	Rankett 16'	
Mixture V	Cromorne 8'	
Trumpet 8'	Tremolo	

Pedal

Principal 16'
Subbass 16'
Octave 8'
Gedackt 8'
Octave 4'
Hohlflöte 4'
Nachthorn 2'
Mixture V
Posaune 16'
Trumpet 8'
Schalmei 4'
Tremolo

Two principal composition techniques are evident in twentieth-century German organ music. One is that of traditional polyphonic forms clothed in contemporary counterpoint and harmony. The forms used are those of the prelude, fugue, canon, toccata, chorale-based works such as chorale prelude, fantasia, and partita, variation, passacaglia,

GERMANY AND AUSTRIA: 1900's

1860	1900	1930	1960

1861 Franke, Friedrich Wilhelm 1932
1862 Gulbins, Max-----------1932
    1874 Schoenberg, Arnold(Austrian-Amer.) 1951
    1874 Schmidt, Franz (Austrian) 1939
    1874 Schmid, Heinrich Kaspar----------------1953
    1879 Haas, Joseph--------------------------------1960
        1881 Knab, Armin --------------------1951
        1882 Kodály, Zoltán (Hungarian)-----------------1967
        1883 Hasse, Karl ------------------------------1960
        1883 Stögbauer, Isidor------------------------------------
        1885 Windsperger, Lothar 1935
        1885 Poppen, Hermann Meinhardt ----1956
        1886 Kaminski, Heinrich------1946
        1886 Grabner, Hermann ------------------------------1969
        1887 Landmann, Arno --
            1891 Lechthaler, Josef --1948
            1891 Hoyer, Karl ----1936
            1891 Drischner, Max----------------------------------1971
            1892 Jarnach, Philipp (French-German)------------------------
            1893 Kickstat, Paul---------------------------------------
            1894 Roeseling, Karl ---------------------------1960
            1895 Hindemith, Paul ----------------------------1963

1895 David, Johann Nepomuk (Austro-German)------
1897 Gebhard, Hans ------
1897 Heiss, Hermann------
1897 Weyrauch, Johannes Wilhelm Robert ------
1897 Marx, Karl ------
1898 Eggermann, Fritz ------
1898 Ramin, Günther-------1956
1900 Klotz, Hans ------
1900 Křenek, Ernst (Austro-American)------
1901 Humpert, Hans--1943
1901 Pepping, Ernst------
1902 Poppen, Hermann------
1902 Marckhl, Erich------
1902 Micheelsen, Hans Friedrich------
1903 Raphael, Günter-------1960
1904 Ahrens, Joseph ------
1904 Schroeder, Hermann ------
1906 Bornefeld, Helmut ------
1907 Bialas, Günter ------
1907 Fortner, Wolfgang ------
1907 Höller, Karl ------
1907 Walcha, Helmut ------
1908 Distler, Hugo ---1942
1908 Mohler, Philipp ------
1908 Leinert, Freidrich------
1908 Hessenberg, Kurt------
1908 Wellesz, Egon (Austrian)------
1908 Fiebig, Kurt ------

GERMANY AND AUSTRIA: 1900's (cont.)

1860　　　　1900　　　　1930　　　　1950　　　　1970

1909 Schindler, Walter------
1909 Genzmer, Harald------
1911 Bossler, Kurt------
1911 Stein, Max Martin------
1913 Hiltscher, Wolfgang-1941
1914 Metzger, Hans Arnold------
1914 Zipp, Friedrich Otto Gottfried------
1916 Reda, Siegfried------1968
1916 Eder, Helmut (Austrian)------
1917 Baumann, Max------
1918 Doppelbauer, Josef Fr. (Austrian)------
1918 Baur, Jürg------
1921 Driessler, Johannes------
1923 Schmeel, Dieter------
1923 Manicke, Dietrich------
1923 Heiller, Anton (Austrian)------
1924 Heilmann, Harald------
1925 Klebe, Giselher------
1925 Hummel, Bertold------
1925 David, Thomas Christian------
1926 Schweppe, Joachim------
1926 Kameke, Ernst-Ulrich von------
1927 Schilling, Hans-Ludwig------

1927 Barbe, Helmut ------------------------
1928 Gerlach, Günter -----------------------
1928 Kluge, Manfred -----------------------
1929 Romanovsky, Erich---------------------
1929 Stadlmair, Hans-------------------------
　　1930 Tachezi, Herbert-------------------
　　1930 Voss, Friedrich---------------------
　　1930 Zimmerman, Heinz Werner ---------
　　1931 Stockmeier, Wolfgang---------------
　　1934 Wiemer, Wolfgang-------------------
　　1936 Reimann, Arinert -------------------
　　　　1940 Schoof, Armin ------------------

chaconne, sonata, suite, concerto, and organ Mass, which is sometimes freely composed, sometimes based on plainsong. Hindemith and Distler have exerted the strongest influence in this objective style of writing. Dissonance and lean contrapuntal lines are principal factors in this music. Although a tonal center is usually understood, melodic intervals of seconds, fourths and fifths, quartal harmony, and a modal character are emphasized.

The second principal composition technique is the 12-tone (serial) technique. Schoenberg and Křenek are the chief exponents of this type. This technique ackowledges no tonal center, since each of the 12 tones is of equal value and is used in a predetermined order, either singly or in any combinations desired. In addition to the two principal techniques discussed, contemporary German composers have devised modified forms and styles which incorporate various devices and techniques. Jazz rhythms (one of the chief elements in the composition style of Heinz Werner Zimmermann), modal melodies, and distinctive harmonies are a few examples of some of the characteristics they have chosen to use.

There are few compositions written for organ in the serial technique. Variations on a Recitative, Op. 40 (1940), by Arnold Schoenberg (1874-1951) is based on the 12-tone technique modified, but it suggests a tonal center of D. This work was first performed by Carl Weinrich in March, 1944, for the International Society for Contemporary Music. To choose a recitative melody as a thematic basis for ten variations, a cadenza, and a section beginning in imitative style is unusual. Extremely complex rhythms, constant dissonance, tempo and meter changes, all permit few moments of regularity and normal pulse. A performance of the Variations is an intellectual achievement and a feat of industriousness for an organist.

Ernst Křenek (1900-   ), an Austro-American convert to Schoenberg's dodecaphonic system, has written a Sonata, Op. 92 (1941), in one movement for organ. The form is sonata-allegro with an interpolated Andante section in A-B-A form and a scherzo finale. Although there are many meter changes, the basic time unit is usually a quarter-note, which gives coherence to the composition. The lines are more vocal than those found in Schoenberg's Variations and the rhythms much less complex, both of which allow this piece to be much more easily comprehended. Two young Germans in the contemporary group who write in atonal style are

Giselher Klebe (1925-   ) and Arinert Reimann (1936-   ).

The Sieben Orgelchoräle (Seven Organ Chorales) by
Armin Knab (1881-1951) are tonal settings of familiar chorale
melodies such as "O Sacred Head Now Wounded," "Now
Thank We All Our God," and "How Brightly Shines the
Morning Star." The principal contrapuntal device used is
the canon, and the harmonic background for the counterpoint
is strong. Scarcely any accidentals are found in these
traditionally conceived works. Karl Hasse (1883-   ) and
Heinrich Kaminski (1886-1946) have both written chorale
preludes. Hasse, a pupil of Straube and Reger, has composed in the larger forms of fantasy and fugue, suite, and
sonata. Kaminski was a pupil of Hugo Kaun and was one
of Carl Orff's teachers. In addition to the chorale arrangements, he has written a toccata and fugue, an andante, and
three pieces for organ and violin.

Johann Nepomuk David (1895-   ) has been a prolific
composer for the organ. He has written a large body of
chorale arrangements which he has entitled Choralwerk.
He has also composed in the larger forms of chaconne,
fugue, fantasy, prelude and fugue, ricercar, and toccata and
fugue. His works are tonal but not romantic, and he employs a contemporary contrapuntal style.

Paul Hindemith (1895-1963) as a teacher and composer has been a strong stimulus for neo-Baroque composition in twentieth-century Germany. His own organ contributions are limited to three sonatas and two concertos. The
first two sonatas were written in 1937 and the third in 1940.
The first concerto was written in 1928 for the dedication of
the new organ at the Frankfurt radio station, and the second
was composed in 1962 for the new organ at Lincoln Center
Philharmonic Hall in New York City. [2]

The sonatas were conceived in the neo-Baroque style
with conventional but diversified and energetic rhythmic
character. Lean contrapuntal lines coupled with untraditional
harmonic progressions and phrases of irregular length make
these pieces for organ especially interesting. The melodies
are warm, a quality that many other contemporary works
lack. "Hindemith generally avoided any triadic outlines in
his melodies, and the frequent use of melodic fourths and
seconds (and their inversions, melodic fifths and sevenths)
were an aid to this endeavor."[3] Hindemith frequently employed the device of a melody in octaves, or sometimes

separated a melody in exact parallel motion by two octaves. Incomplete triads and the use of chords constructed of super- imposed fourths are two of his harmonic characteristics. Although the meter is changed from time to time in the so- natas of Hindemith, this practice is quite frequent in his second concerto. Hindemith employed surprising changes of tonal centers.

Forms used by Hindemith in the sonatas include sonata-allegro, binary, ternary, fantasy, rondo, and fugue forms. The Phantasie, frei section from the First Sonata is an exciting one, probably the most passionate movement in all three sonatas. Sonata II ends with a fugue in rondo form, only one example of Hindemith's frequent use of imi- tation.

Hindemith selected three folk songs, "Ach Gott wem soll ich's klagen," "Wach auf, mein Hort," and "So wunsch ich ihr," which are included in his The Craft of Musical Composition, Book II, as bases for the three movements of Sonata III. [4]

There are few registration indications in the first concerto or in the sonatas, but explicit registrations are given for the second concerto. As in many Baroque works, the registration of the sonatas can indicate the structure of the work. Hindemith wanted the tempos exact, even though he allowed divergence in registrations. [5]

Ernst Pepping (1901-   ) has written many organ works which have been influenced by his study of sixteenth- and seventeenth-century music. He is probably best known for his Grosses Orgelbuch (Large Organ Book), which contains chorale settings in both Vorspiel (prelude) and Orgelchoral (organ choral) forms, and Kleines Orgelbuch (Small Organ Book) (1940), which contains shorter and easier chorale set- tings. The chorale melody is clearly set apart in one voice most of the time. These pieces are contrapuntal, contain much rhythmic variety, and the phrasings and articulations are meticulously indicated. Accidentals are frequent, since Pepping does not employ key signatures. He has written several chorale partitas, some manualiter chorale settings, two concertos, fugues, and sonatas.

Hans Friedrich Micheelsen (1902-   ) has composed seven organ concertos, Das Holsteinische Orgelbüchlein (pieces for small organ) and Choralmusik. The concerto

on Es sungen drei Engel has probably received the largest
number of performances.

Joseph Ahrens (1904-   ) has been Professor of Church
Music at the Berlin Hochschule für Musik since 1950.   His
organ works are neo-Baroque in character.   Ahrens' organ
hymn Pange lingua (1936) has settings of four stanzas (two
with the cantus firmus in the pedal, one in motet style, and
a version with the cantus in long notes in the uppermost part
and an Amen section).   Thirteen imaginative variations are
found in the Lobe den Herren partita (1947).   Several bicinia,
a drone bass variation, quick ascending scale passages, rolled chords, and a wide variety of interesting rhythmic treatments are found in the partita.

Hermann Schroeder (1904-   ) is one contemporary
German composer who is well-known in America.   His tonal
compositions in traditional forms are interesting and make
excellent teaching material because most of them are short
and only moderately difficult.   He has written three organ
sonatas.   Cantus firmus works include an organ Mass (Orgel-
Ordinarium) based on the Kyrie Cunctipotens genitor Deus
plainsong, Orgelchoräle in Kirchenjahr, a partita on Veni
Creator Spiritus, and Six Organ Chorales on Old German
Sacred Folksongs, Op. 11, on tunes such as In dulci jubilo
and Schönster Herr Jesu.

Helmut Bornefeld (1906-   ) has limited himself in
organ composition to chorale-based works.   His works are
tonal and are cast in the form of chorale preludes or chorale
partitas.   The three volumes of chorale settings by Helmut
Walcha (1907-   ), the famous teacher and organist at the
Dreikönigskirche, Frankfurt, have been popular in the United
States.   These imaginative chorale preludes are excellent
service and teaching material in contemporary contrapuntal
tonal writing.

Hugo Distler (1908-1942) was one of the most dis-
tinguished twentieth-century German composers.   He wrote
the two splendid partitas Nun komm der Heiden Heiland,
Op. 8, No. 1 (1933), and Wachet auf, Op. 8, No. 2 (1935),
the Kleine Orgelchoral Bearbeitungen, Op. 18, No. 3 (1938)
(Small Chorale Arrangements), the trio Sonate, Op. 18,
No. 2, (1939), and Dreissig Spielstücke (Thirty Pieces),
Op. 18, No. 1 (1938), for the little organ at St. Jakobi
Church in Lübeck.   Distler served this church from 1931
to 1937. [6]   He put a contemporary spirit into Baroque forms

by employing cross-rhythms, complex subdivisons of beats,
and syncopation. The contrapuntal lines are diatonic, modal,
and contain many melodic seconds and fourths. The major
and minor third is avoided in both melody and harmony. The
Spielstücke and Sonate were composed on the little chamber
organ Distler ordered built for use in his home in Stuttgart. 7

        One of Distler's pupils was Siegfried Reda (1916-1968),
who has written similar linear music. Inspired by chorales
Reda's organ works contain four chorale concertos, chorale
preludes, an Adventspartita on Mit Ernst, o Menschenkinder
(1952), and a Choral-Spiel-Buch. Other forms he has used
have been the prelude, fugue, and the sonata. The pains-
taking articulation, the complex subdivisions of the beat,
unbarred sections, the pedal solos, the absence of key signatures and many meter changes are some of the characteristics common to both Reda and Distler.

        The writing of Kurt Fiebig (1908-   ) is more conven-
tional than that of Reda or Distler. His Prelude and Fugue
in B-flat (1948) and the Triosonate utilize regular meters and
common rhythms. The Viennese teacher and concert organist
Anton Heiller (1923-   ) has written sonatas, partitas, and
settings of Ecce lignum crucis and Salve regina melodies.
A very active pedal part, cross-rhythms, frequent meter
changes, a fugal section, and pedal point are factors that
characterize the first sonata, a work in three movements.
The second movement is for manuals alone, and the third is
in toccata style. Heiller's Second Sonata was composed in
1953.

        The Hungarian composer Zoltán Kodály (1882-1967)
wrote a setting of Pange lingua for chorus with a prominent
organ part. Kodály's pupil Josip Slavenski (1896-1955) composed a Sonata religiosa for organ and violin. Two younger
Hungarian composers, who have written in traditional forms
such as the passacaglia, fugue, and sonata, are Erzsébet
Szönyi (1924-   ) and Hidas Frigyes (1928-   ).

                            Notes

1.   Leading organ building forms of the twentieth century in
     Germany are those of Rudolf von Beckerath (Hamburg),
     Karl Schuke (Berlin), and the Walcker company (Lud-
     wigsburg). These builders have erected some distin-
     guished instruments in Germany and in the United States.

The leading Austrian organ builder is the Rieger firm
in Schwarzach.
2. See the unpublished doctoral thesis of Albert George
    Bolitho, "The Organ Sonatas of Paul Hindemith,"
    Michigan State University, 1968, for a longer analysis
    of all the organ works of Hindemith.
3. Ibid. , p. 30.
4. A source of these tunes is Franz M. Böhme Altdeutsches
    Liederbuch, reprinted by Breitkopf und Härtel, Wies-
    baden, 1966. Hindemith composed the complete sonata
    within a day and a half.
5. He had the habit of carrying a pocket metronome to check
    tempos.
6. Not 1933 as is given in Die Musik in Geschichte und
    Gegenwart.
7. Larry Palmer, Hugo Distler and His Church Music,
    St. Louis: Concordia Pub. House, 1967; p. 93.

Bibliography

Brinkmann, Reinhold.   "Einige Bermerkungen zu Schönbergs
    Orgelvariationen," Musik und Kirche, vol. 29, no. 2
    (March-April 1969), p. 67.
Brown, Rayner. "Some New German Organ Music," The
    American Organist, May 1966, pp. 12-14.
_____. "Some More German Organ Music," The Ameri-
    can Organist, July 1969, p. 16-17.
Gehring, Philip. "Distler's Organ Works," The American
    Organist, vol. 46, no. 7 (July 1963), p. 14.
Gibson, Emily Cooper. "A Study of the Major Organ Works
    of Paul Hindemith," Diapason (February 1971), p. 22-
    24.
Newlin, Dika. "Schoenberg's Variations on a Recitative,"
    Organ Institute Quarterly, vol. 6, no. 1 (Spring 1956),
    p. 16-18.
Noss, Luther. "Arnold Schoenberg: Variations on a Recita-
    tive for Organ," Notes, vol. IV, no. 4 (Sept. 1947),
    pp. 485-486.
Walker, John. "Schoenberg's Opus 40," Music/The A. G. O. -
    R. C. C. O. Magazine, vol. IV, no. 10 (October 1970),
    p. 33.

16. FRANCE SINCE 1900

At least five different styles can be identified in twentieth-century French organ composition: symphonic writing, literature based on Gregorian melodies, program music (both religious and secular), colorist or impressionistic composition, and compositions constructed in new, advanced techniques of the twentieth century.

One of the organ works which was composed in a rather free rhythm is the Messe des Pauvres by the unconventional Erik Satie (1866-1925). With one exception, the "Mass" does not employ traditional Mass sections. All of the six movements are of moderate and short duration. In connection with the Kyrie is Dixit Domine, which is followed by the Prière des Orgues, Commune qui Mundi Nefas, Chant Ecclésiastique, Prière pour les Voyageurs et les Marins en Danger de Mort, and Prière pour le Salut de Mon Ame.

Louis Vierne (1870-1937) is the outstanding organ symphonist of the early twentieth century. This blind organist of Notre Dame Cathedral was influenced by Franck, Widor, and Debussy, but he developed his own distinct but not extreme harmonic and melodic idioms. His music is technically demanding, sometimes pianistic, and is consistently orchestral in character. Vierne's compositions are original, well developed, vigorous, and tuneful; most of them are concert music. His harmonies are rich, he shows a skillful use of contrapuntal devices, and his striking themes are evenly balanced.

Vierne's music can be divided into three composition periods. The first period (1895-1905) includes the first two organ symphonies. The second period (1905-1917) encompasses music of more spontaneity and grace than that found in the first period, with themes of greater breadth and picturesque harmony found in the Third Symphony and the 24 Pièces en Style Libre. The third period, during which Vierne's writing seems more active and agitated (1917-1931), includes the last three symphonies and the descriptive Pièces de Fantaisie. [1]

HISTORICAL BACKGROUND

1900	Charpentier Louise
1902	Debussy Pélléas et Mélisande
1902	Curies discovered radium
1904	Rolland Jean Christoph
1905	Cézanne Grandes Baigneuses
1905	Dubussy La Mer
1909	Gide La Porte Etroite
1910	Stravinsky Firebird
1911	Ravel L'Heure Espagnole
1913	Stravinsky Le Sacre du Printemps
1913-1927	Proust A la Recherche du Temps Perdu
1914-1918	World War I
1917	Valéry La Jeune Parque
1919	League of Nations formed
1920	Ravel La Valse
1921	Honegger King David
1929	Cocteau Les Enfants Terribles
1930	Stravinsky Symphonie des Psaumes
1931	Saint-Exupéry Vol de Nuit
1932	Gertrude Stein Matisse, Picasso and Gertrude Stein
1933	Colette La Chatte
1935	Honegger Jeanne au Bucher
1938	Dufy Regatta
1939-1945	World War II
1941	François Mauriac La Pharisienne
1943	Sartre L'Etre et le Néant
1943	Chagall Crucifixion
1946	Giraudoux La Folle de Chaillot
1947-1958	Fourth Republic
1951	NATO formed
1957-1958	Malraux La Métamorphose des Dieux
1957	Poulenc Dialogues des Carmélites
1958-1969	DeGaulle, President of the Fifth Republic
1959	Anouilh Becket
1969-	Pompidou, President

Vierne added extra pieces to the four standard movements generally found in sonatas in his six symphonies,
which were written between 1899 and 1931: a prelude and a
fugue to the First; a choral to the Second; a cantilène to
the Third; a prelude and a menuet to the Fourth; a prelude to the Fifth, and an aria to the Sixth. The slow movements were given titles such as romance, larghetto, and
intermezzo.

The better known selections from the 24 Pièces en
Style Libre are the Carillon, Berceuse, Divertissement,
Arabesque, and Lied. From the larger fantasy pieces come
the beautiful Carillon de Westminster and Naïades.

Charles Arnould Tournemire (1870-1939) was a pupil
of Franck and the organist of Ste. Clotilde, a post he held
for over 40 years. Tournemire was a master of improvisation; the freedom of expression found in improvisation is
also contained in Tournemire's compositions. His originality
was inspired by Gregorian propers in the liberal paraphrases
named L'Orgue Mystique, which he grouped into 51 cycles
(255 pieces) for the liturgical year. These pieces were to
be played at Mass but not in alternation with the choir. Each
individual cycle consists of five pieces: prelude, offertory,
elevation, communion, and postlude. Since the first four
pieces in each cycle were associated with a liturgical function, the length of the music was governed by the function.
The preludes and elevations are brief, the communions
moderately long, the offertories longer than the communions,
and the postludes were as long as Tournemire saw fit to
make them.

The forms used by Tournemire in L'Orgue Mystique
are choral-paraphrases, versets, chorals, interludes, fantasies, fugues, variations, rhapsodies, and free forms. The
improvisatory spirit, which is supported by a rubato style
of playing, seems to flow freely through all these forms.
The music in these pieces is based on the chant modes,
both harmonically and melodically. Tournemire frequently
employed major and minor seconds in harmony and melody
and avoided thirds; his compositions often end on open fifths
or unison pitches. Parallel movement at various intervals
and note clusters are two other musical characteristics of
Tournemire's organ music. [2]

Tournemire's other compositions include some "symphonic" pieces and religious program music based upon the

seven last words of Christ.   Maurice Duruflé has reconstituted five of Tournemire's improvisations.

Joseph Bonnet (1884-1944), like Guilmant, was an organist who was a better performer and teacher than composer.   Most of his compositions are programmatic concert pieces such as Elfes, Chant du Printemps, and Lied des Chrysanthèmes.

Ermend Bonnal (1880-1944) composed a Symphonie "Media Vita" and at least three suites of programmatic "landscapes." Georges Jacob (1877-1950) is best known for his 12 impressionistic, secular pieces Les Heures Bourguignonnes, based on pastoral pictures of Maurice Lena.   Religious program music was composed by Daniel-Jean-Yves Lesur (1908-   ), who was Tournemire's assistant at Ste. Clotilde.   Two titles of compositions by Lesur are Scène de la Passion (1931) and La Vie Intérieure (1932).

One of the finest single organ compositions of the twentieth-century French school is the Pastorale by Jean-Jules-Aimable Roger-Ducasse (1873-1954).   This piece, which is conceived in the Romantic tradition, is a series of variations which contains a masterful use of organ colors and demands a virtuoso technique for performance.   The theme is presented in four different time values simultaneously in one variation, and the pedal part sounds the theme in quick 16th-notes over most of the pedal board while the hands alternate chords in another variation.

The organ works of Henri Mulet (1878-1967) have been warmly received in America.   Especially popular are his Carillon-Sortie and the Tu es Petra toccata from the Esquisses Byzantines (Byzantine Sketches).   This group of programmatic sketches describes different parts of a cathedral such as the nave, stained glass, and rose window, and religious cermonies which take place in such an edifice.

One of the outstanding figures of twentieth-century French organ music is Marcel Dupré (1886-1971).   This internationally renowned musician's career encompassed that of composer, music editor, author, teacher, Director of the Paris Conservatoire, and the successor to Widor as organist of St. Sulpice.   Dupré's non-programmatic works include the Trois Préludes et Fugues (1920).   Religious program music embraces the Vêpres du Commun de la Vierge (1920), Cortège et Litanie (1923), the four-movement Symphonie-Passion

FRANCE SINCE 1900

1870	1900	1930	1970

1866 Satie, Erik----------------------1925

1870 Tournemire, Charles Arnould------1939

1870 Vierne, Louis --------------------1937

1870 Schmitt, Florent---------------------------1958

1873 Quef, Charles ------------------------1931

1873 Roger-Ducasse, Jean-Jules-Aimable ---------------1954

1877 Jacob, Georges---------------------------------1950

1878 Mulet, Henri---1967

1880 Bonnal, Ermend------------------1944

1883 Barié, Augustin--1915

1883 Cellier, Alexandre-Eugène ----------------------1968

1884 Bonnet, Joseph ----------------------------1944

1886 Dupré, Marcel--1971

1886 Saint-Martin, Léonce de----------------------------1954

1892 Honegger, Arthur --------------------------1955

1892 Milhaud, Darius----------------------------------

1893 Benoit, Paul ---

1899 Poulenc, Francis ----------------------------1963
1903 Fleury, André-----------------------
1903 Duruflé, Maurice---------------------
1907 Langlais, Jean ----------------------
1908 Messiaen, Olivier-------------------
1908 Lesur, Daniel-Jean-Yves -----------
1909 Litaize, Gaston ---------------------
1910 Puig-Roget, Henriette --------------
1911 Grünenwald, Jean-Jacques ----------
1911 Alain, Jehan Ariste 1940
1915 Girod, Marie-Louise ----------------
1920 Falcinelli, Rolande------------------
1921 Demessieux, Jeanne 1968
1924 Cochereau, Pierre-------------------
1930 Guillou, Jean ---------------------
1933 Charpentier, Jacques---------------
1934 Darasse, Xavier -----------
1934 Henry, Jean-Claude ----------
1937 Ourgandijian, Raffi (Lebanese-French)
1942 Roth, Daniel F.----

(1924), and Le Chemin de la Croix (1932). His symphonic
works include the organ concerto (1939) and the Deuxième
Symphonie (1929). The popular 11 Variations sur un Noël,
Op. 20, was written in Montreal while Dupré was playing a
series of all-Bach programs there.

Dom Paul Benoit (1893-   ), organist of the Benedictine
Abbey of St. Maurice and St. Maur in Clervaux, Luxembourg,
has composed Noël Basque (eight variations on a familiar
carol tune) and Au Soir de l'Ascension du Seigneur (which
refers to Gregorian melodies supported by richly chromatic
harmonies).

Arthur Honegger (1892-1955) has written two pieces
for organ, a Fugue in C-sharp minor and Choral. The fugue
is a warm, Romantic development of a short, chromatic subject. One of Honegger's associates in the French group
"Les Six," Darius Milhaud (1892-   ), has written a short
Pastorale, Neuf Préludes, and a three-movement Sonata.
Francis Poulenc (1899-1963), another member of the "Six,"
wrote the tuneful and exciting Concerto in G minor in one
movement for organ, string orchestra and timpani.

Maurice Duruflé (1903-   ), organist of St. Etienne-
du-Mont, Paris, has not composed many pieces for the organ.
The Suite (1934) contains three movements, one of them the
brilliant and challenging Toccata. The Prélude et Fugue sur
le Nom d'Alain, which was written in memory of Jehan Alain,
incorporates some strains from Alain's Litanies. The subtle
registration and impressionistic harmonies found in Duruflé's
compositions, such as the three movements based on Veni
Creator, resemble compositions by Fauré, one of Duruflé's
teachers.

Most of the organ works of Jehan Ariste Alain (1911-
1940) were written for the tracker organ built in the home by
Jehan and his father, Albert Alain (1880-   ), who was a student of Guilmant, Dupré, and Bonnet. The father had carefully studied Dom Bédos' writings when he was constructing
the organ and designed it to include classical French stops.

The Postlude pour l'Office de Complies was Alain's
earliest composition and was written for an organ in the
eighteenth-century Abbey of Valloires in northern France
while the composer was there on retreat. In 1932 Alain was
deeply impressed with the displays and performances presented at the French colonial exhibition in Paris. The dances,

unusual rhythms, and melodies which employed microtones he heard and saw there inspired him to write Deux Danses à Agni Vavishta. The Variations sur un Thème de Clément Jannequin are actually written on a tune by an anonymous composer, which Alain found in an early book of French folk songs. Litanies has been extremely popular for use as a toccata in organ recitals.

The composition styles of Alain encompass the free, improvisatory type, impressionistic works, and pieces influenced by plainsong. Although Alain was a composition pupil of Dukas, Alain did not like to be restricted to prescribed forms. In his mind he heard irregular divisions of beats, but found it impossible to transcribe to paper what he heard. Alain disliked the 16' sound in the pedal so he frequently registered sounds in that division at only the 8' level.

Jean Langlais (1907-   ) is the present organist of Ste. Clotilde, Paris. Many of his works have these characteristics: brightly colorful registration; through-composed pieces with sharply contrasting sections; irregular rhythms and meter changes; poetic and directly appealing melodies; rich harmonies (frequent use of harmonic progressions employing chromatic mediants); virtuoso pedal work; bitonality; incorporation of plainsong themes; and early forms treated in contemporary styles.

Most of Langlais' colorful works are pieces of moderate length grouped in suites or collections such as the programmatic Trois Poèmes Evangeliques, Trois Paraphrases Grégoriennes, Neuf Pièces, Suite Brève, Suite Française, and Hommage à Frescobaldi. Fête and Incantation pour un Jour Saint are only two of many individual pieces which are widely used as recital pieces. The Première Symphonie (1941-1942) is his only effort so far in a larger form. Langlais wrote the Suite Médiévale in the form of a low Mass and incorporated incidentally the melodies of the Asperges me (Entrée), Kyrie-Fons bonitatis (Offertoire), Adoro te devote (Elévation), Ubi caritas (Communion), and Christus vincit (Acclamations sur le Texte des Acclamations Carolingiennes).

One of the most significant and influential composers of the twentieth century is Olivier Messiaen (1908-   ), a highly idiomatic and individualistic composer. In the Preface to his book The Technique of My Musical Language Messiaen listed a number of people and things tangible and intangible which have affected him and his music. Among others were

Dukas, Dupré, members of his family, Shakespeare, Claudel,
holy scripture, birds, Russian music, plainsong, Hindu rhythms, the mountains of Dauphiné, and his musical interpre-
ters.

Among the earliest of Messiaen's pieces for organ are
three of short or moderate length: Le Banquet Céleste (1928),
Diptyque (1930), and Apparition de l'Eglise Eternelle (1932).
The Celestial Banquet is based upon the text from the Gospel
according to St. John which begins, "He who eats my flesh
...," which refers to the Holy Eucharist (Holy Communion,
The Last Supper). All three of these pieces conform to
regular pulse (meter). The registration suggested by the
composer for Diptyque and Apparition is rather traditionally
French, but the Banquet calls for Prestant 4' and Piccolo 1'
coupled to the pedal without any pedal stops drawn until the
final chord. Repetition in Messiaen's works provides gather-
ing intensity and the suggestion of eternal concept which
transcends time.

L'Ascension (1933) is a suite in four movements based
upon texts associated with the ascension of Christ and the
Mass of the Ascension. The first and fourth movements are
very slow and majestic. The Serene Alleluias pictures the
soul as it flutters and trembles in joyful anticipation of being
received into spiritual realms. Cross-rhythms and buoyant
melody give this movement its primary motion and interest.
The third movement, Outburst of Joy, contrasts the full
Great organ against the full Swell, sharp, staccato chords
against legato pedal melody and a series of triplets, and,
further, cadenzas, chords alternated between hands in toccata
style, to express the deep happiness of the soul before the
glory of Christ.

La Nativité du Seigneur ("The Nativity of the Lord")
(1935) is a suite of nine meditations which depict various
personages who were present at the nativity (the virgin and
Child, shepherds, angels, wise men) and also several significant meanings of the event (eternal purposes, the Word, God
among us). Messiaen treated his approach to the subject with
emotion and sincerity but also with the attempt to communi-
cate with the listener from three points of view: theological,
instrumental, and musical. Many unusual and perhaps exotic
timbres and colors are indicated. Often the 8' pitch is omitted and various combinations of mutations are desired. Trans-
positions, different modes, and added rhythms are only three
of the musical techniques used by Messiaen in his carefully

defined and intellectual conception of composition.

Les Corps Glorieux (1939) is a group of seven visions of the life of the resurrected ones. These highly imaginative pieces sometimes employ single line, one melody in octaves, or two-part textures for extended portions of the movements. The music in these pieces is constructed from the same musical materials as those used in the Nativity.

Messe de la Pentecôte (1950) was inspired by texts appropriate to Pentecost and deal with subjects such as the tongues of fire which descended upon the apostles; "things visible and invisible" (from the Nicaean Creed); the gift of wisdom; "springs of water and birds of heaven, bless the Lord"; and the rushing wind filled all the house." Three elements used by Messiaen in this suite of five movements are bird calls, changing note durations in ascending and descending degrees, and three Hindu rhythmic modes: one which does not change, one which gains value each time it is presented, and one which diminishes in value each time it is sounded.

Livre d'Orgue (Organ Book) (1951) contains seven pieces which embody a great use of polyrhythms, asymetric and symetric enlargement of rhythmic cells, bird calls, unusual combinations of mutations and stops of octave displacement, along with inspiration of various scriptural texts, and cluster appogiaturas. The most recent organ work by Messiaen is a shorter one, the Verset pour la Fete de la Dédicace (1960), which was composed as a test piece for the Paris Conservatory.

Notes

1. Norbert Dufourcq, La Musique d'Orgue Française de Jehan Titelouze à Jehan Alain, Paris: Librairie Floury, 1949; p. 186.
2. William Pruitt, "Charles Tournemire 1870-1949," The American Organist, August 1970, p. 20-25.

Bibliography

Alain, Marie-Claire. "The Organ Works of Jehan Alain," translated by Irene Feddern, The Diapason, pt I (January 1970), p. 20-21; pt II (February 1970), p. 22-25;

and pt III (March 1970), p. 6-8.

Cohalan, Aileen. "Messiaen: Reflections on Livre d'Orgue,"
   Music/The A. G. O. and R. C. C. O. Magazine, vol. II
   (July 1968), p. 26; November 1968, p. 28; and
   December 1968, p. 28.

Delestre, R. L'Oeuvre de Marcel Dupré. Paris: Procure
   Générale du Clergé, 1952.

Doyen, Henri. Mes Leçons d'Orgue avec Louis Vierne:
   Souvenirs et Témoignages. Paris: Editions Musique
   Sacrée, 1966.

Dreisoerner, Charles, "The Themes of Langlais' Incantation,"
   Music/The A. G. O. -R. C. C. O. Magazine, vol. 6, no.
   4 (April 1972), p. 41-44.

Dufourcq, Norbert. "Panorama de la Musique d'Orgue Fran-
   caise au XXe Siècle," Revue Musicale, vol. XIX, no.
   184 (June 1938), p. 369-376; vol. XIX, no. 185 (July
   1938), p. 35-44; vol. XIX, no. 186 (September 1938),
   p. 120-125; and vol. XX, no. 189 (March 1939),
   p. 103-115.

_____. La Musique d'Orgue Française au XXe Siècle.
   Paris: Librairie Floury, 1939.

_____. La Musique d'Orgue Française de Jehan Titelouze
   à Jehan Alain. Paris: Librairie Floury, 1941 (2 ed. , 1949).

Gavoty, Bernard. Louis Vierne, la Vie et l'Oeuvre. Paris:
   Albin Michel, 1943.

Goléa, Antoine. Rencontres avec Olivier Messiaen. Paris:
   René Julliard, 1960.

Hassman, Carroll. "Messiaen: An Introduction to his Com-
   positional Techniques and an Analysis of 'La Nativité',"
   Diapason, pt 1 (December 1971), p. 22-23; and pt 2
   (January 1972), p. 26-27.

Hesford, Bryan. "Dupré's 'Stations of the Cross'," Musical
   Times, vol. 102, no. 1425 (November 1961), p. 723-
   724.

Kasouf, Richard J. "Louis Vierne and His Six Organ
   Symphonies," The American Organist (November 1970),
   p. 20-26.

Klinda, Ferdinand. "Die Orgelwerke von Olivier Messiaen,"
   Musik und Kirche, vol. 39 (January-February 1969),
   p. 10.

Long, Page C. "Vierne and His Six Organ Symphonies,"
   The Diapason, pt I (June 1970), p. 23; pt II (July
   1970), p. 7; and pt III (August 1970), p. 8.

Lord, Robert Sutherland. "Organ Music of Jean Langlais:
   Comments on performance style," The American Organist, (January 1968), p. 27-32.

_____. "Sources of Past Serve Langlais in Organ Works,"

The Diapason (January 1959), p. 24; and February 1959, p. 24.

Messiaen, Olivier. Technique de Mon Langage Musical, Paris: Leduc, 1944; The Technique of My Musical Language, translated into English by John Satterfield, Paris: Leduc, 1956.

Pruitt, William. "Charles Tournemire 1870-1949," The American Organist (August 1970), p. 20-25.

Raugel, Félix. Les Grandes Orgues des Eglises de Paris. Paris: Librairie Fischbacher, 1927.

Samuel, Claude. Entretiens avec Olivier Messiaen. Paris: Editions Pierre Belfond, 1967.

Sumner, William Leslie. "The French Organ School," Sixth Music Book. London: Hinrichsen Edition Ltd. , 1950; p. 281-294.

Thomerson, Kathleen. "Errors in the Published Organ Compositions of Jean Langlais," American Guild of Organists Quarterly, vol. X, no. 2 (April 1965), p. 47-54.

Wickline, Homer. "Flor Peeters' Organ Works Are Intended to Serve Noble Art," The Diapason (September 1947), p. 22.

17. ENGLAND AND CANADA SINCE 1900

England

During the first half of the twentieth century English organ builders constructed Romantic, orchestral instruments. The organ reform movement, which became strong in Germany in the 1920's, is beginning to affect English organ building slowly. Examples of a more classic concept of organ design than that exhibited earlier in this century are the organs at the Royal Festival Hall, London (1954), and the first new tracker-action organ in London City Church of St. Vedast (1961). The most prominent English organ builders today are Harrison and Harrison, William Hill & Son and Norman & Beard, J. W. Walker & Sons, and N. P. Mander.[1]

Although many twentieth-century English composers have written for the organ, no single composer has composed a great deal. Much of the literature which has been written is based upon hymn-tunes, although the pieces may be called "chorale" preludes and employ the same techniques as those applied to chorale settings for several hundred years. Although it is not true of all contemporary English composition for the organ, there is still much which is conservative, diatonic writing and which employs only the simplest forms of construction.

Ralph Vaughan Williams (1872-1958) composed Three Preludes founded on Welsh Hymn Tunes (Bryn Calfaria, Rhosymedre, Hyfrydol). The first contains pianistic cadenzas and imitative entries in a fantasy treatment. Rhosymedre, a setting of two stanzas of the tune, is a dignified, flowing arrangement. The Hyfrydol prelude is a stirring, majestic one in which the voices generally march forward in stepwise movement; the piece contains scarcely one accidental, but the lines of the accompaniment are vigorous and frequently syncopated.

Sir Walford Davies (1869-1941) is known for his Solemn Melody, a noble and dignified tune. The two Shaw brothers, Martin (1875-1958) and Geoffrey (1879-1943), have

HISTORICAL BACKGROUND

1900	Elgar Dream of Gerontius
1901-1910	Reign of Edward VII
1901	Shaw Caesar and Cleopatra
1903	Shaw Man and Superman
1904	Barrie Peter Pan
1907-	W. H. Auden
1909	Vaughan Williams Fantasia on a Theme of Tallis
1910	Vaughan Williams Sea Symphony
1910-1936	Reign of George V
1910	Masefield The Tragedy of Pompey the Great
1912	Sinking of the Titanic
1914-1918	World War I
1914-1953	Dylan Thomas
1915	Maugham Of Human Bondage
1919	League of Nations formed
1922	Galsworthy The Forsyte Saga
1924	Shaw Saint Joan
1931	Walton Belshazzar's Feast
1935	Eliot Murder in the Cathedral
1936	Reign of Edward VIII
1936-1952	Reign of George VI
1939-1945	World War II
1945	Britten Peter Grimes
1950	Eliot The Cocktail Party
1952-	Reign of Elizabeth II
1962	Britten War Requiem

---

contributed much to church music. Martin Shaw, one of the editors of the Oxford Book of Carols, wrote a Processional for organ, which contains much parallel chordal writing and leads to a fortissimo harmonization of the hymn-tune associated with the text Praise to the Lord, the Almighty (Lobe den Herren).

Three Liturgical Preludes and Three Liturgical Improvisations came from the pen of George Oldroyd (1886-   ). Both sets of pieces are improvisatory, tuneful, and contain many meter changes. Harold Darke (1888-   ) has written A Meditation on Brother James' Air of loose construction, which contains frequent short references to the basic melody.

Herbert Howells (1892-   ) has composed two sets of Three Psalm Preludes, which are improvisatory, rich

harmonically, rhythmically interesting, and which lend themselves to colorful registration.   These pieces were inspired
by psalm verses.   Howells has dedicated six imaginative
pieces of assorted character to Herbert Sumsion.   Sarabande
for the Morning of Easter and Master Tallis's Testament
come from this group.   Howells' composition technique employs tertial harmonies, flowing melodic lines, moderately
frequent meter changes, and many ingenious divisions of the
rhythmic unit.

Percy W. Whitlock (1903-1946) composed Five Short
Pieces, which are short character pieces.   The Folk Tune
and Scherzo are probably the best known compositions from
the group.   Whitlock's first set of Six Hymn-Preludes contains more variety of musical materials than the second.
Alec Rowley (1892-1958) wrote improvisations and chorale
preludes, which often are restless in nature.   Eric Harding
Thiman (1900-   ) has composed both character pieces and
hymn-tune settings.   His compositions are characterized by
pleasant melody and improvisatory style.   Thiman's Tune
for the Tuba continues the English trumpet voluntary tradition.

The Carillon of Herbert Murrill (1909-1952) is a fan-
fare-toccata which contains shifting meters and rhythms,
which are combined with an interesting pedal part.   Benjamin
Britten's one organ composition is a Prelude and Fugue on
a Theme of Vittoria (1946).   The largamente prelude is only
13 measures long and contains a chant-like, free pedal theme
with sustained chords.   The fugue is in four-part texture
most of the time and later reduced to two-part writing, which
is divided between different voices.   Britten's rhythms change
frequently.   The fugue, conceived in a Romantic style, builds
to a fortissimo climax and closes pianissimo.

The Album of Praise collection contains conventional
pieces by Gordon Jacob (1895-   ), George Dyson (1883-1964),
Norman Gilbert, and Healey Willan (1880-1968).   Peter Hurford (1930-   ), master of the music at the Cathedral and
Abbey Church of St. Albans, contributed an interesting Paean
to the volume.   He has also written a Suite 'Laudate Dominum' in six movements, which was inspired by verses of
scripture.

The most interesting and challenging English organ
composition of today is being written by younger composers
who have become sensitive to contemporary musical advances
and techniques.   John McCabe (1939-   ) is an imaginative

composer who often incorporates jagged rhythms and unusual subdivisions of the beat.   Parallel chords often have special articulations indicated.   Traditional styles such as the French overture and toccata styles are incorporated in fresh ways. In the Sinfonia, Op. 6 (1961), a passacaglia theme is introduced in $\frac{14}{8}$ time.   Each time the theme is presented it is altered rhythmically and begins on a different tonal level.

Alleluyas of Simon Preston (1938-) was inspired by the composition techniques of Messiaen.   The Prelude, Scherzo and Passacaglia by Kenneth Leighton (1929-) offers much rhythmic variety and quartal harmonies in both the prelude and passacaglia;   the scherzo uses the gigue rhythm as its unifying element.   Leighton's Paean is a march which is introduced and closed by a section which consists principally of four-note broken chords.

The Exultate of Bryan Kelly (1934-) is strongly rhythmic and, for the most part, in a regular meter.   The texture is thin and clear, chords are sometimes treated in a staccato or syncopated manner, and various articulations are all important features of the piece.

Parallelisms of both intervals and chords constitute an important element of the martial Processional by William Mathias (1934-).   The Toccata alla Giga, Op. 37, by Alun Hoddinott (1929-) is rhythmically vigorous and contains a powerful sense of snap and drive within many subdivisions of $\frac{6}{8}$ time.

Peter Racine Fricker (1920-) has written a clever suite of Six Short Pieces, which exhibit a sure control of a modified dodecaphonic system in declamatory, lyric, hymnic, and free styles.

Canada

Canadian organ composition is closely related to the English school because of common heritage, taste, and similarity of training.   The most famous composer of church and organ music who lived in Canada was the English-Canadian Healey Willan (1880-1968).   Willan's music is traditional and seemingly untouched by the newer musical styles and techniques of the twentieth century.   Many of his compositions are well constructed but sometimes lack inspiration and originality.   The largest portion of Willan's organ composition

ENGLAND SINCE 1900

1870	1900	1950	1970

1871 Buck, Percy Carter----------1947
1872 Vaughan Williams, Ralph------1958
1874 Bairstow, Edward Cuthbert 1946
1875 Shaw, Martin E. F. ---------1958
1879 Shaw, Geoffrey Turton ----1943
1879 Bridge, Frank------------1941
1879 Ireland, John Nicholson---------------------1962
1883 Dyson, (Sir) George ------------------1964
1883 Harris, (Sir) William Henry----------------
1885 Porter, Ambrose P.----------------------1971
1886 Dixon, J. H. Reginald-----------
1886 Oldroyd, George----------1951
1887 Ley, Henry George -----------------
1888 Darke, Harold Edwin -------------
1888 Coleman, Henry Pinwell -----------
1889 Rhodes, Harold Williams--------------
1889 Statham, Heathcote Dicken ---------------
1889 Gibbs, Cecil Armstrong ---------------1960
1891 Lang, Craig Sellar -------------
1892 Howells, Herbert Norman ----------------
1892 Rowley, Alec-----------1958
1894 Milner, Arthur Frederick ----------------
1895 Jacob, Gordon P. S. ---------------

(Australian-English)

1895 Waters, Charles Fredrick------
1896 Thalben-Ball, George Thomas------
1896 Slater, Gordon Archbold------
1897 Christopher, Cyril Stanley------
1898 Demuth, Norman------
1899 Sumsion, Herbert Whitton------
1900 Bush, Alan Dudley------
1900 Thiman, Eric Harding------
1902 Walton, (Sir) William------
1903 Whitlock, Percy 1946
1903 Milford, Robin--1959
1904 Downes, Ralph William------
1904 Emery, Wilfred J.------
1904 Tippett, Michael------
1908 Phillips, Gordon------
1909 Butcher, Vernon------
1909 Orr, Robin------
1909 Murrill, Herbert Henry John 1952
1909 Campbell, Sidney Scholfield------
1911 Scott, Anthony Leonard Winstone------
1912 Gilbert, Norman------
1913 Britten, Benjamin------
1914 Rimmer, Frederick------
1914 Webber, William Southcombe Lloyd------
1915 Searle, Humphrey------
1916 Guest, Douglas Albert------
1916 Wolff, Stanley Drummond------
1917 Arnell, Richard------
1917 Ratcliffe, Desmond------

ENGLAND SINCE 1900 (cont.)

1900	1950	1970

1917 Jackson, Francis --------------------------
1920 Bush, Geoffrey ----------------------
1920 Fricker, Peter Racine ----------------
1922 Hamilton, Iain --------------------
1925 Milner, Anthony --------------------
1926 Wills, Arthur William---------------
1926 Brockless, Brian ------------------
1927 Whettam, Graham------------------
1927 Routh, Francis John ----------------
1927 Joubert, John----------------------
1929 Hoddinott, Alun--------------------
1929 Leighton, Kenneth------------------
1930 Hurford, Peter --------------------
1931 Williamson, Malcolm--------------- (Australian)
1933 Naylor, Peter -------------------
1934 Davies, Peter Maxwell------------
1934 Ridout, Alan Jones --------------
1934 Dickinson, Peter ----------------
1934 Kelly, Bryan --------------------
1934 Mathias, William James ---------
1936 Healey, Derek Edward-----------
1937 Crunden-White, Paul-----------
1938 Preston, Simon---------------
1939 McCabe, John---------------
1939 Steel, Christopher Charles -------

lies in hymn-tune settings.   In them there is practically no change of tonality, the harmonies are bland, and the rhythms are conventional.

Willan's free organ works include an early Prelude and Fugue in B Minor and his famous Introduction, Passacaglia and Fugue.   The latter work contains more imaginative and daring writing than his later organ compositions. Key changes, varying rhythms, and rich harmonies of the Romantic era mark the work.   There are 18 variations, some traditional and others theatrical, opulent, rather curiously juxtaposed.   The fugue is in E-flat minor, and the third section moves to the parallel major key for a stretto over a pedal point.   The Nobilmente coda utilizes the passacaglia theme for one final time (the 19th variation) in pedal octaves which is accompanied by grandiose chords on the manuals.

The Toccata on O Filii et Filiae by Lynwood Farnam (1885-1930) is a favorite for many Easter congregations.   The piece contains fast pianistic arpeggios on the manuals with the theme in pedal octaves;   manual triplet figurations on the harmonies make up the middle section.

For convenience organ compositions by twentieth-century Canadian composers can be classified into three general styles: traditional, moderately contemporary, and progressive contemporary styles.   Composers who have written in a conventional fashion by using diatonic melodies and harmonies and simpler forms and rhythms are composers such as Kenneth Meek (1908-   ), Guy Ducharme, Eugene Hill, and William France.

The organ works of Frederick Karam (1926-   ) and Gerald Bales (1919-   ) would be considered contemporary, but they still contain many features of established forms and composition techniques such as regular meters and standard registration practices.   Karam's Divertimento contains a modal flavor;   in this same piece there is alternation of two themes, one lyric and the other sprightly.   Bales maintains interest in his Petite Suite by using such devices as pedal ostinato passages,   mild parallelisms (major triads usually), and some bitonal chords.   The stately and flowing lines of Bales' Prelude in E Minor are in a more traditional vein.

Four Canadians who employ more advanced techniques are François Morel (1926-   ), Keith Bissell (1912-   ), Vernon Murgatroyd, and Maurice Boivin (1918-   ).   All of

HISTORICAL BACKGROUND

1804-1895	Antoine Plamondon, Quebec painter
1810-1871	Paul Kane, painter
1861-1944	Bliss Carman, writer
1867	Confederation of Canada
1869-1944	Stephen Leacock, writer
1873-1932	J. E. H. MacDonald, painter
1879-1941	Emile Nelligan, poet
1882-	A. Y. Jackson, painter
1896	Klondike gold rush began
1914-1918	World War I
1915-	Louis Archambault, sculptor
1920	"Group of Seven" painters formed
1923-	Jean-Paul Riopelle, non-objective artist
1939-1945	World War II
1940	E. J. Pratt Brébeuf and His Brethren
1948	Stratford Festival established
1959	St. Lawrence Seaway opened

CANADA SINCE 1900

1880   1900   1950   1970

1880 Willan, James Healey---------1968 (English-Canadian)
1885 Farnam, W. Lynwood 1930
    1891 Egerton, Arthur Henry   1957
        1902 Brown, Allanson G. Y.----(English-Canadian)
        1908 Piché, Paul Bernard -------
        1908 Meek, Kenneth-------------(English-Canadian)
            1912 George, Graham -------
            1912 Bissell, Keith Warren --
            1913 Archer, Violet B. ------
            1918 Boivin, Maurice--------
            1919 Bales, Gerald Albert ---
                1926 Karam, Frederick--
                1926 Morel, François ---

these men have used metrical indications and parallel treatment of chords (the same type of chord in a series of chords
which appear on different tonal levels). Murgatroyd placed
a free rhythm section in the middle of the Méditation sur un
Thème Grégorien. Boivin employed a number of examples
of bitonality in Deux Pièces, two short pieces inspired by
Latin texts (Laetare Jerusalem, Introit for the Fourth Sunday
of Lent, and Ego sum pastor bonus, Preface for the Second
Sunday after Easter). In the Sonata Keith Bissell utilizes a
style of contemporary counterpoint and both augmentation and
diminution devices. The Prière (1954) by Morel is the most
advanced harmonically of the pieces mentioned; the composer
uses 11th-chords and chords combining as many as seven different pitches. Double pedaling and the chant-like melody
(also played by the feet) occur in this mystic piece.

The Canadian organ-building firm of Casavant Frères
has maintained a reputation for instruments of high quality
for many years. Lawrence I. Phelps, former tonal director of
the Casavant company actively supports the ideals of the
twentieth-century organ reform. The firm of Gabriel Kney
deserves mention for fine instruments, also. The specifications of a smaller instrument built along classic lines is
given below.

Wolfville, Nova Scotia, Manning Memorial Chapel,
Acadia University. Built by Casavant Frères, 1963.

Hauptwerk	Brustwerk	Pedal
Quintaden 16'	Gedackt 8'	Subbass 16'
Prinzipal 8'	Spitzflöte 4'	Prinzipal 8'
Rohrflöte 8'	Prinzipal 2'	Choralbass 4'
Oktav 4'	Quinte 1 1/3'	Mixtur IV (2')
Waldflöte 4'	Sesquialtera II	Fagott 16'
Flachflöte 2'	(2 2/3')	
Mixtur IV (1')	Zimbel II (1/4')	
Trompete 8'	Holzregal 8'	
	Tremulant	

Couplers: Hauptwerk/Pedal; Brustwerk/Pedal;
Brustwerk/Hauptwerk

Note

1.   Clutton, Cecil, and Austin Niland, The British Organ,

London: B. T. Batsford, 1963; p. 107-118.

Bibliography

Beechey, Gwilym.   "Parry and His Organ Music," Musical
    Times, ꞁol. 109, no. 1508 (October 1968), p. 956;
    and vol. 109, no. 1509 (November 1968), p. 1057.
Clutton, Cecil, and Austin Niland.   The British Organ.   Lon-
    don: B. T. Batsford Ltd. , 1963.
Harverson, Alan.   "Britten's Prelude and Fugue," Musical
    Times, vol. 102, no. 1417 (March 1961), p. 175.
Milner, Arthur.   "The Organ Sonata of Herbert Howells,"
    Musical Times, vol. 105, no. 1462 (December 1964),
    p. 924.
Phelps, Lawrence I.   "A Short History of the Organ Revival,"
    reprinted from Church Music 67.1.   St. Louis: Concor-
    dia Pub. House, 1967.
Young, Percy.   "A Survey of Contemporary Organ Music:
    England," Church Music 67.2, p. 25.

18. THE LOWLANDS, SCANDINAVIA, SWITZERLAND, ITALY, AND CZECHOSLOVAKIA SINCE 1800

Several organ builders from Denmark, the Netherlands, and Switzerland have established enviable reputations for distinguished work in constructing new instruments and in restoring older ones. The ideals of these builders are in concord with the aims of the Orgelbewegung, the organ reform movement of the twentieth century. Sybrand Zachariassen became the head of the Marcussen and Son organ building firm in Aabenraa, Denmark, in 1920. The firm gained renown for restoring instruments, for building excellent organ cases, and for constructing mechanical-action instruments, especially in northern Europe. D. A. Flentrop of Zaandam, the Netherlands, has earned distinction for the same reasons. He has built some splendid instruments of high quality in Europe and America. The firm of Metzler & Söhne, Dietikon, Switzerland, built a superb instrument for St. Peter's in Geneva. Poul-Gerhard Andersen has cooperated with the Metzler firm to build several outstanding organs in Switzerland.

Belgium

Jacques Lemmens founded the modern French organ school. In addition to Guilmant and Widor, Lemmens had other students like Joseph Callaerts (1838-1901) and Alphonse Mailly who became composers of character pieces. Because of Belgium's geographical position between France, the Netherlands, and Germany, it is natural that Belgian organ music would have strong spiritual connections with these other schools of composition.

The three most prominent organ composers of modern Belgium have been Jongen, de Maleingreau, and Peeters. The organ compositions of Joseph Jongen (1873-1953) are closely related to the French school. His pieces have appealing melodies (Chant de May) and interesting rhythmic figures. Jongen's pianistic Toccata is in the tradition of Vierne and Widor.

HISTORICAL BACKGROUND

1831	Belgium became independent
1843-1907	Edvard Grieg
1848	Swiss Constitution
1864	International Red Cross established by Swiss
1870	Unification of Italy established
1890-1948	Reign of Queen Wilhelmina, the Netherlands
1905	Norway became independent
1905-1957	Reign of King Haakon VII, of Norway
1907-1950	Reign of King Gustav V, of Sweden
1912-1947	Reign of King Christian X, of Denmark
1914-1918	World War I
1917	Finland declared independent
1918	Czechoslovakia became independent
1919	League of Nations founded
1934-1951	Reign of King Leopold III, of Belgium
1938	Czechoslovakia dismembered by Munich Pact
1939-1945	World War II
1942	United Nations formed
1947-1972	Reign of King Frederick IX, of Denmark
1948--	Reign of Queen Juliana, the Netherlands
1950--	Reign of King Gustav VI, of Sweden
1951--	Reign of King Baudouin, of Belgium
1951	North Atlantic Treaty Organization founded
1956--	Kekkonen, President of Finland
1957	European Common Market established
1957	Reign of King Olav V, of Norway
1968	Democratization of communism in Czechoslovakia halted by Warsaw Pact powers
1972--	Reign of Queen Margarethe, of Denmark

Paul de Maleingreau (1887-1956) composed several large works which are religious program symphonies similar to the Symphonie-Passion of Dupré. The Symphonie de la Passion, Op. 20, was inspired by the pictorial works of Roger de la Pasture (Vander Weyden); its movements are entitled Prologue, Le Tumulte au Prétoire, Marche au supplice, and O Golgotha! The Symphonie de l'Agneau Mystique, Op. 24, inspired by the pictorial works of Hubert and Jean van Eyck, contains three movements named Images, Rhythmes,

and <u>Nombres</u>. de Maleingreau has also written a <u>Symphonie</u>
<u>de Noël</u>, several Masses, and <u>Opus Sacrum</u>.

Flor Peeters (1903-) is famous as a concert organist, teacher, composer, and editor of early organ music,
especially that of the Lowlands. His compositions are a
synthesis of French and Flemish characteristics. English,
American, and Gregorian hymn melodies have been used by
Peeters as the bases for many cantus firmus settings; his
recent series in this genre is entitled <u>Hymn Preludes for the</u>
<u>Liturgical Year</u>, Op. 100, in 24 volumes. The <u>Aria</u> and
<u>Elégie</u> are especially appealing, short melodious works. Ar-
chaic and modal harmonies flavor his works as in the 35
<u>Miniatures</u>, Op. 55, and the <u>Suite Modale</u>, Op. 43. <u>Entrata</u>
<u>Festiva</u>, Op. 93, for organ, two trumpets, and two trom-
bones (timpani and unison chorus ad libitum) is a stirring
piece of moderate length, which incorporates the <u>Christus</u>
<u>vincit</u> melody. Peeters also uses programmatic titles such
as <u>Nostalgia</u> and <u>Morning Hymn</u> for some of his works.

Belgian-born Guy Weitz, who resided in London since
early in the twentieth century, composed two organ symphonies. The first symphony is in three movements, each of
which is based on a melody associated with the Virgin Mary,
<u>Regina pacis</u>, <u>Mater dolorosa</u>, and <u>Stella maris</u>. The
<u>Symphony No. 2</u> is in five movements and includes a passa-
caglia as one movement. Weitz's writing is well-suited to
the organ and has a strong affinity to French composition
style. [1]

The Netherlands

Contemporary Dutch organ composition is deeply influenced by German and French styles of composition. Dutch
folk-songs and Calvinist psalm-tunes are frequently used as
bases for Dutch cantus firmus organ compositions.

C. F. Hendricks (1861-1923) was a late nineteenth-
century Dutch organ composer. His short, simple pieces
were influenced by French organ works of that period.

Perhaps Hendrik Andriessen (1892-) is best known
for his lengthy <u>Toccata</u> and <u>Premier Choral</u>. Andriessen's
organ works have been strongly influenced by the French
school; two of the clearest examples of this French proclivity are shown by manual figurations above pedal themes

BELGIUM: 1820-1970

1820   1850   1900   1950   1970

1823 Lemmens, Jacques (Jaak) 1881
  1833 Mailly, Alphonse-Jean-Ernest----1918
  1838 Callaerts, Joseph--------1901
     1854 Tinel, Edgar----------1912
     1858 Depuydt, Oscar----------1925
          1873 Jongen, Joseph-Marie----------1953
          1875 Dethier, Gaston --------1958
          1875 Moulaert, Raymond----------------1962
             1887 de Maleingreau, Paul------1956
                1898 Hens, Charles----------
                1899 Plum, J. M. ----1944
                   1903 Peeters, Flor ------------
                   1909 van Dessel, Lode------------
                      1911 Huybrechts, Lode----------
                      1914 Froidebise, Pierre-1962
                         1918 de Brabanter, Jos --------
                         1919 Verschraegen, Gabriel --------

and a harmonic palette similar to that of Vierne. The Toccata by Marius Monnikendam (1896-) is a brilliant and
rhythmic work dedicated to Charles Tournemire. An insis-
tent, monotonous quarternote tread is the unifying rhythmic
feature of Monnikendam's Cortège. His compositions are
characterized by a definite tonal center, interesting harmonies,
dissonances used for color, modality, and frequent use of
parallel fourths.

The Concert Etude, Op. 104 (1963) by Anthon van der
Horst (1899-1965) is an intense, dramatic, and virtuoso work,
especially for the pedal technique. This piece is in tripartite form and contains a contrasting middle section in a quiet
mood. Toccata in modo conjuncto (1943), Orgel Partita op
Ps. 8 (1946), and Concerto, Op. 58 (1954) are three larger
compositions by the Amsterdam Conservatorium teacher.

Cor Kee (1900-) is famous for his course in improvisation at the Haarlem Summer Academy for Organists.
The styles of his composition range extend from the conservative, tonal writing of his earliest period to the 12-tone
writing which he practices today. Kee has composed 17 settings of Calvinist psalm-tunes, which are divided into three
volumes. These pieces are tonal, contain meter changes,
and many varieties of rhythmic divisions of the beat. These
pieces also follow several of the general types of chorale-
prelude writing such as fantasy, solo melody and accompaniment, and manualiter settings. Carefully designated articulations, the use of key signatures but few accidentals, scant
ornamentation, and changing tempi also characterize these
works. Drie Inventionen (1967) and Reeks-veranderingen
(Variations on a Tone-Row) (1966/1967), examples of Kee's
more recent writing, contain the following characteristics:
constantly changing rhythms and tempos, no tonal center,
tiny melodic fragments, unusual stop combinations, frequent
stop changes, lean texture, and intensely dissonant chords.

Piet Kee (1927-), son of Cor Kee, has written a
contemporary chorale fantasia on Wachet auf (Wake, Awake)
and a chorale prelude on O Sacred Head Now Wounded (1964).
The first of these two pieces contains a number of toccata
elements and has the chorale melody moving from one voice
to another (sometimes identified as "migrant" form of
chorale prelude). Triptych on Psalm 86 (Chorale, Canon,
Toccata) (1964) makes use of much more dissonance and
free counterpoint. The rhythms are not complex, although
they do change from measure to measure. Piet Kee has

THE NETHERLANDS: 1860-1972

1860	1900	1950	1972

1861 Hendricks, C. F.------1923

1877 Zwart, Jan---------1937

1878 Zagwijn, Henri------------------1954

1880 Bonset, Jacobus----------------------------

1881 Dresden, Sem--------------------------1957

1888 Bunk, Gerard------------------------------

1888 Van den Siegtenhorst-Meyer, Bernhard 1953

1892 Andriessen, Hendrik ------------------------

1896 Monnikendam, Marius ------------------------

1897 Vranken, Jaap---------------1956

1898 Mulder, Ernest Willem-------1959

1899 van der Horst, Anthon----------------------------1965

1900 Kee, Cor------------------------

1900 Schouten, Hennie----------------------

1902 Bijster, Jacob --------------------------

1903 Nieland, Jan --------------------1963

1907 Badings, Henk ----------------------------

1907 Felderhof, Jan

1909 de Braal, Andries

1909 Mudde, Willem-Federik-Antonius

1910 Eraly, Paul

1910 Nieland, Herman

1911 Koetsier, Jan

1911 Mul, Jan Johan

1912 Strategier, Hermann

1913 Koert, Hans van

1916 Toebosch, Louis

1917 de Klerk, Albert

1918 van Dijk, Jan

1919 Maessen, Antoon

1919 Post, Piet

1920 Vogel, Willem

1927 Kee, Piet

1929 Bartelink, Bernard

1930 Dragt, Jaap

1930 Kox, Hans

1934 Bruynèl, Ton

also composed a series of short manualiter settings of the
tune associated with the English text "God Himself Is with
Us" (Arnsberg, a hymn-tune by Neander).

Jacob Bijster (1902-   ), an outstanding Dutch orchestral composer, writes in a conventional Romantic style. The
forms he uses in his organ works are the passacaglia, partita, fantasy, and fugue. Another leading Dutch contemporary
organ composer is Henk Badings (1907-   ), who was the director of the Royal Conservatory at the Hague. His music,
like that of Bijster, is Romantic with little dissonance. One
of his unusual compositions is the Passacaglia for organ and
timpani. Badings has employed such forms as the prelude
and fugue, canzona, toccata, and concerto.

Partita, Op. 41, No. 1 (1954) for English horn and
organ manuals alone by Jan Koetsier (1911-   ) is an effective
work for organ and a solo instrument. The piece incorporates
the chorale tune Wie schön leuchtet der Morgenstern ("How
Brightly Shines the Morning Star"). Koetsier has also composed the Twelve Preludes and Fugues (1946) in a contemporary contrapuntal idiom. These pieces are short, and the
texture is principally that of a trio. There is one prelude
and fugue for each of the 12 chromatic tones.

Two contemporary Dutch organ composers who have
been active in Utrecht are Hermann Strategier (1912-   ) and
Albert de Klerk (1917-   ). Strategier's Toccatina and de
Klerk's Ten Pieces in two volumes are moderately difficult.

Denmark

Martin Radeck (died 1684), one of the earliest Danish
organ composers, is represented by a partita on Jesus
Christus unser Heiland ("Jesus Christ our Saviour). The
Danes also claim Buxtehude as one of their most famous
musicians because he lived in Denmark for approximately
the first half of his life, before he moved to Lübeck, Germany. Another organ composer associated with the North
German Organ School was Melchior Schildt, who served
Christian IV of Denmark from 1626-1629.

Johann Peter Emilius Hartmann (1805-1900) and his
son-in-law Niels Wilhelm Gade (1817-1890) are the chief
Danish organ composers of the nineteenth century. Hartmann
composed free works such as fantasias, marches, a sonata,

DENMARK: 1800-1972

1800	1850	1900	1950	1970

1805 Hartmann, J. P. E. ------------------1900
1817 Gade, Niels W. -------------1890
1848 Malling, Otto Valdemar 1915
1865 Nielsen, Carl August-----1931
1876 Emborg, Jens Laursøn----------1957
1879 Rung-Keller, Paul S. ------------------
1888 Raastad, Niels Otto ------------------
1892 Jeppesen, Knud ------------------
1893 Thomsen, Peter (American-Danish)------------
1893 Langgaard, Rued I. -----1952
1900 Sandberg Nielsen, O. 1941
1903 Møller, Svend-Ove 1949
1906 Christensen, Bernhard------------------
1906 Viderø, Finn------------------
1912 Andersen, Aksel ------------------
1919 Kayser, Leif------------------
1919 Bentzon, Niels Viggo ------------------
1922 Thybo, Leif------------------
1928 Høgenhaven Jensen, Knud ------------------
1931 Nørholm, Ib------------------
1932 Nørgaard, Per------------------

and character pieces in the Romantic tradition. Gade's organ
compositions include three "tone-pieces" and four works based
on chorale melodies. Other nineteenth-century Danish organ
composers were G. Matteson-Hansen, his son Hans, and Otto
Valdemar Malling (1848-1915), who wrote character pieces
with religious programs (Shepherds in the Field, Easter
Morn).

Perhaps the most famous organ composition by a later
Danish composer is the Commotio by Carl August Nielsen
(1865-1931), who is better known for his orchestral works.
The Commotio is one continuous movement which suggests
perpetual motion, even in slower passages. Tonal centers
frequently shift and are rarely established. The writing is
always metrical and contains a use of cross-rhythms such
as six notes against four. Articulations are carefully indicated, and, although the piece is difficult, there are no unusual technical demands.

Other Danish composers of the same period who wrote
shorter works for the organ were Paul S. Rung-Keller
(1879-   ), Niels Otto Raastad (1888-   ), Bernhard Christensen (1906-   ), and Otto Sandberg Nielsen (1900-1941). The
compositions of Jens L. Emborg (1876-   ) resemble those
of Reger and Karg-Elert in style. Knud Jeppesen (1892-   )
and Finn Viderø (1906-   ) are two famous Danish musicolo-
gists and teachers who have written chorale settings in a
traditional vein.

After Nielsen's death musical composition in Denmark
was guided by the works and teaching of the late Romanticist
Rued Langgaard (1893-1952). Leif Kayser (1919-   ), Niels
Viggo Bentzon (1919-   ), and Knud Høgenhaven (1928-   ) are
the principal Danish composers of 12-tone music for the organ. The compositions of Leif Thybo (1922-   ) and Svend-
Ove Møller (1903-1949) contain lean, contrapuntal lines, thin
textures, quartal harmony, and irregular meters. The
Sonata 1969 of Leif Kayser features metrical rhythms and
even divisions of the beats; the tonality also shifts frequently.

Two younger Danish organ composers are Ib Nørholm
(1931-   ) and Per Nørgaard (1932-   ). The Partita Concertante, Op. 23, by Nørgaard is in three movements: Fantasia, Canto variato, and Toccata. The writing is linear
and atonal. Although the notes are metrically distributed in
the measures, they are so complex rhythmically that the
passages are rare when a regular pulse can be felt. Much

of the composition is played high on the manuals and the few dynamic alterations are strongly contrasting. Constant changes in harmony and rhythms give Nørgaard's music a restless character.

Sweden

For the most part Swedish organ compositions are metrical and tonal; few organ compositions have appeared in more advanced twentieth-century techniques. Swedish organ composers have usually employed traditional forms such as cantus firmus compositions based on Swedish hymn-tunes[2] or plainsong,[3] and preludes (or fantasias) and fugues.[4] Gunnar Thyrestam's Preludium och Fuga No. 2 (1947) contains a rhapsodic, sectional prelude followed by a fugue which has a rather square-cut subject eight measures long, which is first sounded in the pedal part. The Triptyk (1951) of Valdemar Söderholm (1909-   ) contains a short toccata, a chromatic Adagio, and rhythmic Allegro energico, which employs an active pedal part.

One of Sweden's leading twentieth-century composers is Hilding Rosenberg. His Fantasia e Fuga (1941) begins with an arresting rhythmic theme which contrasts strongly with the second theme, which is constructed of sixteenth-note triplets; the subject of the fugue is a lyric one, which eventually leads to a manual cadenza. Rosenberg's Praeludium e Fuga (1948) is poetic and pastoral in nature. Rosenberg's harmonic palette remains triadic for the most part.

Bengt Hambraeus (1928-   ), a pupil of Messiaen, is one Swedish composer who uses a serial technique in organ composition. Stig Gustav Schönberg (1933-   ) wrote a Toccata Concertante (1954) which is moderately long, strongly rhythmic, principally for manuals, and contains a Calmato middle section. Schönberg's Lacrimae Domini (1958) is a tone-poem of 18 minutes' duration. At the beginning its brooding principal theme is presented alone in the pedals. The piece contains several sections of contrasting character: brilliant toccata parts, an extremely chromatic, pensive middle section, a short fugal portion, and a broad Grave section at the end.

SWEDISH ORGAN SCHOOL: 1850-1970

1850   1900   1950   1970

1853 Sjögren, Johann G. E. 1918
1867 Hägg, Gustaf Wilhelm 1925
1879 Olsson, Otto Emanuel----------------1964
1882 Fryklöf, H. 1919
1884 Wikander, David----------1955
1886 Bengtsson, Gustav----------1965
1887 Lindberg, Oskar----------1955
1889 Berg, Gottfried----------
1892 Rosenberg, Hilding ----------------
1894 Runbäck, Albert----------------
1898 Olson, Daniel----------------
1900 Thyrestam, Gunnar Olof ----------------
1908 Sörenson, Torsten----------------
1909 Söderholm, Valdemar----------------
1919 Johansson, Sven-Eric----------------
1928 Hambraeus, Bengt----------------
1933 Schönberg, Stig Gustav----------------
1934 Welin, Karl-Erik----------------
1940 Morthenson, Jan W. ----

Norway

The present-day Norwegian school of organ composition seems to be rather conservative, content to continue in simple, diatonic lines and harmony. Even the compositions of the mid-twentieth century have a mild, pastoral character, which is underlined by uncomplicated rhythms and metrical writing. Some Norwegian cantus firmus compositions have been based on plainsong[5] and carols.[6] Knut Nystedt (1915-) and Conrad Baden (1908-) are leading contemporary Norwegian composers who have utilized established organ forms and styles such as the pastorale, toccata, and chaconne.

Finland

One example of Finnish contributions to contemporary organ literature is Ta Tou Theou, Op. 30, by Einojuhani Rautavaara (1928-). This fantasy was inspired by sacred texts and was written in 1966 for the dedication of the new Marcussen organ in the Helsinki Cathedral. The free form of toccata has appealed to other Finns such as Sulo Salonen (1899-), Erkki Salmenhaara, and Jarmo Parvainen (1928-).

Switzerland

Swiss organ composers tend to write in styles similar to the German or French schools. Otto Barblan (1860-1943) was probably the first Swiss composer of modern times to have written much for the organ. Barblan wrote in a Romantic style similar to that of Reger and, like Reger, employed forms such as the chaconne, toccata, fugue, and passacaglia, in addition to smaller character pieces and religious adagios.

Frank Martin (1890-) has composed a Passacaille for organ solo and a Sonata da Chiesa (1938) for either viola d'amore or flute and organ. Martin's writing contains elements of French Impressionism and Franck's style, but his writing is more linear than that usually associated with those styles.

The organ compositions of Walther Geiser (1897-) are Germanic in tendency,[7] while those of his contemporary Albert Moeschinger (1897-) have been influenced by both

NORWAY: 1850-1970

| 1850 | 1900 | 1950 | 1970 |

(1812 Lindeman, L. M. 1887)
1845 Cappelen, Christian
1887 Valen, Fartein Olaf----------1952
1895 Sandvold, Arild----------------
1906 Nielsen, Ludvig--------------
1908 Baden, Conrad----------------
1915 Nystedt, Knut----------------

FINNISH ORGAN SCHOOL: 1860-1970

| 1860 | 1900 | 1950 | 1970 |

1865 Sibelius, Jean J. J. C. ----------------1957
1898 Salonen, Sulo----------------
1911 Bergman, Erik--------------
1918 Stenius, Torsten--------------
1928 Rautavaara, Einojuhani----------
1928 Parvainen, Jarmo Uolevi----------

German Romanticism and French Impressionism.

Paul Müller-Zürich (1898-) has composed a quantity of organ works in larger forms (toccata, fantasy and fugue, canzone, concerto) and for other instruments with organ. Since 1950 he has written chorale toccatas and fantasies on Ein' feste Burg ("A Mighty Fortress"), Wie schön leuchtet ("How Brightly Shines the Morning Star"), Ach Gott vom Himmel ("O God in Heaven"), and Christ ist erstanden ("Christ is arisen") for organ, two trumpets, and two trombones. His organ chorales and chorale preludes date from 1959. Henri Gagnebin (1886-) has also written for the combination of organ and other instruments[8] in addition to his organ solo works.

Mysticism, numerical symbolism, and polymodality play a part in the works of Willy Burkhard (1900-1955), a pupil of Karg-Elert. Many of the organ works by this famous Swiss composer of the first half of the twentieth century are based on chorale melodies; the Choral-Triptychon (1953) is one of his major works in the chorale field. Rudolf Moser (1892-1960), Bernhard Reichel (1901-), and Adolf Brunner (1901-) have also contributed to chorale-based literature for the organ.

Italy

The principal Italian composer of organ pieces about the turn of the twentieth century was Marco Enrico Bossi (1861-1925), an important Italian symphony composer, conservatory director, and concert performer who toured in both Europe and America. Bossi's organ compositions are post-Romantic in style.[9] His Alleluia is similar to mid-nineteenth-century French works of the Romantic era; the piece exhibits contrapuntal writing and composition devices of that period. Bossi also wrote two sonatas for the organ.

Ottorino Respighi (1879-1936), the brilliant orchestrator and composer of The Pines of Rome and The Fountains of Rome, wrote a Preludio for organ which combines chromatic harmonies with contrapuntal imitations and figures. This piece closes with a quick flourish in octaves and large fortissimo chords. Alfredo Casella (1883-1947) composed a Concerto Romano for organ and orchestra which had its first performance in New York on March 11, 1927.

SWITZERLAND: 1860-1970

1860	1900	1950	1970

1860 Barblan, Otto-------------------1943

1883 Mottu, Alexandre ------1943

1886 Gagnebin, Henri (Belgian-Swiss)--------------------------|

1890 Martin, Frank --------------------------------------|

1892 Moser, Rudolf-------------------------1960

1897 Geiser, Walther------------------------|

1897 Moeschinger, Albert--------------------|

1898 Müller-Zürich, Paul---------------------|

1900 Burkhard, Willy 1950

1901 Beck, Conrad---------------------------|

1901 Reichel, Bernhard----------------------|

1901 Brunner, Adolf-------------------------|

1911 Studer, Hans---------------------------|

1913 Segond, Pierre-------------------------|

1922 Wildberger, Jacques--------------------|

1924 Huber, Klaus --------------------------|

1929 Vogler, Ernst--------------------------|

Pietro Yon (1886-1943), the composer of Gesu Bambino and organist of St. Patrick's Cathedral, New York City, for 17 years, composed in the nineteenth-century Romantic style with conventional harmonies and simple forms. The organ works of Oreste Ravanello also derive their principal musical style from that same period.

Czechoslovakia

The modern Czech organ school is an outgrowth of the musical traditions of Smetana and Dvořák, whose primary interest lay in the orchestral medium. Both of these men composed a few organ works in polyphonic style early in their careers. Leoš Janáček (1854-1928), Vítězslav Novák, and Josef Suk were the leading Czech teachers of composition in the early part of the twentieth century. Janáč, as an organ composer, is chiefly known for the demanding Postludium from the Glagolithic Mass. In that same period several virtuoso organist-teachers[10] were instrumental in restoring interest in concert organ music in Czechoslovakia.

Czech organ composers have drawn upon a number of different sources for bases of cantus firmus compositions such as Czech sacred songs (Miloslav Krejčí), folk songs (Otto Albert Tichý), Christmas carols (Josef Blatný), and chorales (František Michálek, Bedřich Wiedermann). Romantic, orchestral qualities and the improvisatory spirit are also very strong in Czech organ music.[11] Mid-twentieth-century composers continued utilizing polyphonic forms such as chaconne,[12] fantasy,[13] and prelude and fugue (or toccata).[14]

A few observations about some of the Czech organ music of the 1960's can be drawn from works by six composers who wrote compositions in conjunction with the Second International Organ Competition at the Music Festival in Prague in 1966. In Laudes Petr Eben (1929-   ) uses standard metrical indications and divides the beat into rhythms made up of notes of small denomination, sometimes in complex juxtapositions.[15] Other devices used by Eben in the same piece are double pedaling, polytonalities, and quick changes for three manuals.

Karel Reiner (1910-   ) in the first (Moderato. Energico) of Three Preludes employs a preponderance of small intervals (half-steps and whole-steps) within a third in

ITALY: 1860-1970

1860	1900	1950	1970

1861 Bossi, Marco Enrico 1925
1866 Busoni, Ferrucio B. 1924
  1871 Ravanello, Oreste----1938
  1872 Perosi, Lorenzo-------------------1956
    1877 Cappelletti, Arrigo--------------------------
    1879 Respighi, Ottorino ----1936
      1883 Casella, Alfredo-----1947
      1885 Mauro-Cottone, M.1938
      1886 Yon, Pietro--------------1943 (Italian-American)
      1887 Manari, Raffaele 1933
        1893 Somma, Bonaventura-----------1960
        1895 Castelnuovo-Tedesco, M. ------1969 (Italian-American)
          1906 Germani, Fernando ----------------
          1911 Rota, Nino----------------------
            1929 Tagliavini, L. F.----------------

CZECHOSLOVAKIA: 1850-1972

1850   1900   1950   1970

1852 Musil, František------------------------1951
  1865 Martinu, Bohuslav -------------------1959
    1883 Wiedermann, Bedrich Antonín-1951
      1895 Michálek, František------1951
        1908 Kabeláč, Miloslav-----------------
        1910 Reiner, Karel ----------------
        1910 Slavický, Klement-------------
        1913 Sokola, Miloš-----------------
        1922 Mácha, Otmar------------
        1926 Zimmer, Ján-------------
        1929 Eben, Petr--------------

---

constructing his melodies.   Reiner also utilizes polytonal
chords in parallel motion, frequent meter changes, and sud-
den dynamic alterations or fast crescendos and dimenuendos
in the same prelude.   In the second prelude (Sostenuto) the
first thematic idea carried out in several voices is that of a
written-out mordent used melodically (another reference to
Reiner's idiomatic use of melodies constructed of small
intervals).   This prelude also contains some nine-note chords,
each note on a different pitch.   Prelude III (Allegro Assai)
utilizes very frequent meter changes and practically constant
use of triplet eighth-notes is the unifying rhythmic element.

        The works of Otmar Mácha (1922-   ), Klement Sla-
vický (1910-   ), and Miloš Sokola (1913-   ) are more traditional in approach than those just considered, although their
compositions are definitely contemporary in nature.   The
Mourning Toccata (Mácha) and Passacaglia Quasi Toccata on
the Theme B-A-C-H (Sokola) are metrical throughout.   The
Passacaglia is evenly constructed upon a triplet figure;   the
coda begins with a pedal cadenza and ends on rolled chords
in which most of the pitches are different.   Rapid meter
changes[16] and chord tones of all different pitches occur frequently in the Slavický Invocation.

        The use of the most advanced twentieth-century com-
position style in these six pieces from the mid-'60's is that
of Miloslav Kabeláč (1908-   ) in his Four Preludes.   These
pieces call for three manuals and pedal, each at a different
dynamic level.   The only registration suggestions are the
pitch level desired by the composer (e. g. +4' -1').   The

tempo is very carefully indicated, and the rhythmic unit is shown by dotted lines arranged at regular intervals (e. g. , 1. 8 cm. apart, 1. 35 cm. , 2. 03 cm.), which specify precisely where each note or chord is played. If notes are held, a horizontal heavy line indicates duration by the length of the line, and tone-clusters are the rule rather than the exception in these pieces.

Notes

1. Several Belgian organ composers moved to the United States: Gaston Dethier, Charles Courboin (organist of St. Patrick's Cathedral, New York City), August Maekelberghe (Organist of St. John's Episcopal Church, Detroit), and Camil van Hulse, who resides in Arizona.
2. Berg: <u>Koralpartita över Lov Vare Dig, o Jesu Krist</u>; Lindberg: <u>Fyra Orgelkoraler</u>; Wikander: <u>Passacaglia över koralen "Jag Ville Lova och Prisa."</u>
3. Runbäck: <u>Sequentia Pentecostes "Veni sancte spiritus."</u>
4. Daniel Olson (1898-   ), Otto Olsson (1879-1964), Hilding Rosenberg (1892-   ), Gunnar Thyrestam (1900-   ), Sven-Eric Johannsson (1919-   ).
5. Sandvold: <u>Två gregorianska melodier</u>.
6. Nielsen: <u>Fantasia pastorale</u> (1946).
7. Chorale preludes, at least two fantasies, and a <u>Sonatine</u>, Op. 26 (1939).
8. <u>Sonata da Chiesa, per la Pasqua</u>, for trumpet and organ.
9. <u>Siciliana, Resignation</u>.
10. Josef Klička (1855-1937), Josef Bohuslav Foerster (1859-1951), Eduard Tregler (1868-1932), Bedřich Antonín Wiedermann (1883-1951), and František Michálek (1895-1951).
11. Example: Jaroslav Kvapil: <u>Fantasy in E Minor</u> (1932).
12. Example: Vladimír Hawlík (1955).
13. Example: Alois Hába, Op. 75 (1951); Miloslav Kabeláč, Op. 32 (1957).
14. Example: František Broz (1949); Emil Hlobil (1948).
15. One example: ten 32nd-notes against seven 16th-notes.
16. $\frac{12}{16}$ $\frac{8}{16}$ $\frac{11}{16}$ $\frac{10}{16}$ $\frac{8}{16}$ $\frac{5}{16}$ $\frac{6}{4}$ $\frac{8}{16}$ $\frac{9}{4}$

Bibliography

Gibbs, Alan. "Carl Nielsen's 'Commotio'," <u>Musical Times</u>, vol. 104, no. 1441 (March 1963), p. 208.

Lade, John. "The Organ Music of Flor Peeters," Musical
    Times, vol. 109, no. 1505 (July 1968), p. 667.
Peeters, Flor. "The Belgian Organ School," Sixth Music
    Book. London: Hinrichsen Edition Ltd., 1950; p. 270-
    274.
Phelphs, Lawrence I. "A Short History of the Organ Revival,"
    reprinted from Church Music 67.1. St. Louis: Con-
    cordia Pub. House, 1967.
Spelman, Leslie P. "20th Century Netherlands Organ Music,"
    Music/The A. G. O. and R. C. C. O. Magazine, vol. 4,
    no. 9 (September 1970), p. 35.
Wickline, Homer. "Flor Peeters' Organ Works Are Intended
    to Serve Noble Art," Diapason (September 1947), p. 22.

19. AMERICAN ORGAN MUSIC: 1700-1970

Section I: Through 1900

Organ music in America was slow to attain what we would consider today a respectable standard. For many years the primitive conditions in the new country forbade most artistic efforts. Music of most kinds was forbidden in some forms of worship. Psalms were practically the only kind of music allowed by the Puritans. If organ music was allowed in worship, its principal (and sometimes only) function was to accompany congregational singing, and sometimes short organ introductions and interludes were permitted in connection with hymn-singing. Organs were costly to have made in Europe and to ship across the ocean. Even if there were organs, few organists were trained to play them. Episcopal churches were the principal kind of church which installed organs as an adjunct to worship. Other churches to use organ music were Roman Catholic, Lutheran, Reformed, and Moravian churches. Up until 1800 there were no more than 20 organs in New England churches. The rest of the country had about the same number in proportion to the population. [1]

English practices, tradition, and taste predominated in early America. Voluntaries were improvised, and the works of Stanley, Greene, Boyce, Felton, and Arne were used. Transcriptions for the organ of such things as Handel choruses and Scotch airs were frequently played. William Selby (1738-1798) was an Englishman who became a merchant in America with a lively interest in music. Selby, as the organist of King's Chapel, Boston, gave concerts which included some of his own compositions. He wrote <u>Voluntaries or Fugues for Organ or Harpsichord</u> and a <u>Concerto for Organ or Harpsichord.</u> [2]

During the first half of the nineteenth century, music in the church improved gradually because there was a general reaction against the florid "fuguing tunes" of William Billings and the frivolous, secular types of music which had crept into church use. Lowell Mason (1792-1872) wrote hundreds

HISTORICAL BACKGROUND

1780	Cornwallis surrendered at Yorktown
1785	Jefferson designed the capitol of Virginia
1787	American Constitutional Convention
1789-1794	Washington, President of the United States
1791	Paine Rights of Man
1791	Bill of Rights
1793	Whitney invented the cotton gin
1803	Louisiana Purchase
1804-1806	Lewis and Clark expedition to the Pacific
1807	Robert Fulton built steamboat
1809-1849	Edgar Allan Poe
1812-1814	War of 1812
1819	Florida purchased from Spain
1823	Monroe Doctrine
1825	Opening of the Erie Canal
1826-1864	Stephen Collins Foster
1826	Cooper Last of the Mohicans
1834	McCormick patented reaper
1837	Morse invented telegraph
1846	Mexican-American War
1848	California gold rush
1850	Hawthorne Scarlet Letter
1850	Longfellow Evangeline
1852	Stowe Uncle Tom's Cabin
1853	Peery opened Japan to world trade
1854	Thoreau Walden
1855	Whitman Leaves of Grass
1857	Currier and Ives published prints
1861-1865	Civil War
1867	Alaska purchased from Russia
1871	Emerson Essays
1876	Bell invented telephone
1877/78	Edison invented microphone, phonograph, and introduced incandescent lamp
1884	Mark Twain Huckleberry Finn
1896	Edward MacDowell Indian Suite
1897	Sousa Stars and Stripes Forever
1898	Spanish-American War

of hymn-tunes such as <u>Bethany</u>, <u>Olivet</u>, and <u>Missionary Hymn</u>.
He also introduced music teaching into the public schools
and organized teachers' conventions, which later became music festivals.   Mason was an organist and directed church
choirs in Savannah, Georgia, and later in Boston.

During the period between 1825 and 1850 so many
organs were built in America that there were not enough
trained organists to play them.   The first organ recitals in
America contained many types of music such as transcribed
vocal arias and choruses, transcribed harpsichord music,
band marches, ballroom waltzes, and improvisations on
popular airs.   Dudley Buck (1839-1909) was probably the
first prominent American organist to play organ recitals with
any frequency.   His own works included <u>Concert Variations</u>
<u>on the Star Spangled Banner</u>, Op. 23, a transcription of the
<u>William Tell Overture</u>, Op. 37, and <u>The Last Rose of Sum-</u>
<u>mer, Varied</u>, Op. 59.

After the Civil War hymn introductions and interludes
were still used and transcriptions were still popular, but
preludes and postludes were regularly played at church services.   Works by Batiste, Lemmens, and Smart were added
to those by Dudley Buck, John H. Willcox (1827-1875), and
George W. Chadwick (1854-1931).   Recitalists often included
dramatic improvisations in their programs. [3]

Many German musicians came to the United States
during the nineteenth century and had a profound effect upon
music in this country.   One of the first to come and live in
America was Karl Theodore Pachelbel (a son of Johann
Pachelbel), who visited Boston in 1732 or 1733.   During the
latter half of the nineteenth century many leading American
musicians such as Dudley Buck, John Knowles Paine (1839-
1906), George Chadwick, Horatio Parker (1863-1919), and
James H. Rogers (1857-1940) pursued musical studies in
Europe with teachers such as Liszt, Moscheles, Rheinberger,
Guilmant, and Widor.   In 1860 Paine composed his <u>Variations</u>
<u>on Austria</u>, which contains the theme, four variations, and
a fugue.   Professor Horatio Parker of Yale University was
one of the leading nineteenth-century American composers of
organ music.   Many of Parker's works are character pieces
with titles such as <u>Wedding Song</u> and <u>Triumphal March</u>, but
he also wrote music similar to Mendelssohn's <u>Songs without</u>
<u>Words</u> and the works of his teacher Rheinberger in forms
such as fugue and canon.

EARLY AMERICAN ORGANISTS AND ORGAN COMPOSERS*

1700   1750   1800   1850   1900

1738 Selby, William-----1798 (English-American)
1745 Jackson, George K. ------------1823 (English-American)
(1746 Billings, William---1800)
1747 Taylor, Rayner ----------1825
1756 Reinagle, Alexander 1809 (English-American)
1757 Read, Daniel----------1836
1768 Carr, Benjamin--------1831
1770 Hewitt, James ---1827 (English-American)
ca.1770 Atwell, Richard ?
1792 Mason, Lowell----------------1872

1800   1850   1900

1827 Willcox, John H. --1875
(1837 Lang, Benjamin ---------1909)
1839 Buck, Dudley ---------1909
1839 Paine, John Knowles --1906
(1840 Whiting, George Elbridge----1923)
(1841 Warren, Samuel Prowse--1915)
(1846 Gilchrist, William ------1916)
(1848 Gleason, Frederick-1903)
1853 Foote, Arthur---------------1937
1854 Chadwick, George -----------1931
1857 Rogers, James Hotchkiss-------1940
1858 Shelley, Harry Rowe ----------1947

*Names in parentheses are of non-composers influential in fields of playing and composition.

AMERICAN ORGAN COMPOSERS BORN 1860-1899

1860	1900	1950	1970

1861 Andrews, George Whitfield 1932
(1861 Woodman, Raymond H. ------------1943)
1863 Parker, Horatio--1919
1863 Middleschulte, Wilhelm------------1943 (German)
(1865 Carl, William Crane ------------1944)
1867 Beach, Amy Marcy Cheney ------1944
1867 Noble, T. Tertius ------------------1953 (English-American)
1867 Douglas, Charles Winfred ------1944
1872 Palmer, Courtlandt--
1872 Borowski, Felix ------------------------1956 (English-American)
1873 Dickinson, Clarence--------------------------------1969
1874 Ives, Charles--------------------------1954
1874 Demarest, Clifford------------1946
1876 Kinder, Ralph --------------------1952
1879 Matthews, Harvey Alexander --
1880 Bloch, Ernest ------------------1959
1880 DeLamarter, Eric ----------1953
1881 Gaul, Harvey Bartlett--1945
1882 Howe, Mary--1964
1882 Bingham, Seth Daniels--1972
1884 Titcomb, Everett --------------------------------1968
1886 Becker, John J. --------------------------1961
1887 Diggle, Roland--------------------------1954

1887 Barnes, Edwin Shippen -------------------------------------
1890 Clokey, Joseph Waddell--------1960
1890 James, Philip --------------------------------
1891 Jacobi, Frederick --1952
1891 Baumgartner, H. Leroy---------1969
1891 Donovan, Richard Frank-----------------
1892 Candlyn, T. Frederick H. ------1964 (English-American)
1892 Nevin, Gordon Balch 1943
1893 Moore, Douglas Stuart ---------1969
1893 Coke-Jephcott, Norman ---------1962 (English-American)
1894 Wagenaar, Bernard (Dutch-American)--1971
1894 Bennett, Robert Russell ------------------
1894 Piston, Walter Hamor------------------------
1894 Sinzheimer, Max (German-American)---------------
1895 Sowerby, Leo-------------------1968
1895 McKinley, Carl------------------1966
1895 Simonds, Bruce----------------------------
1896 Sessions, Roger Huntington ------------------
1896 Weinberger, Jaromir (Czech-American) 1967
1896 Hanson, Howard -------------------------
1896 Thomson, Virgil ----------------------------
1896 Pasquet, Jean ------------------------------
1897 Cowell, Henry Dixon-----------1965
1897 van Hulse, Camil (Belgian-American) -------
1897 Porter, William Quincy ------1966
1898 Harris, Roy ------------------------------
1899 McKay, George Frederick-----------------1970
1899 Thompson, Randall------------------------

Romantic clichés were used by Parker and his contemporaries, but their works were a great improvement upon the hundreds of transcriptions and cheap pseudo-organ music absorbed by church congregations and the audiences at theaters and municipal auditoriums about the turn of the twentieth century. For many years orchestral organs were popular, and the music performed on these instruments had saccharine tunes which could be easily remembered, foot-tapping rhythms, and often earth-shaking volume.

19.   Section II: Twentieth Century

Fortunately a number of factors have improved the general levels of musical taste of not only the American organist, but of the organ builder, and of those who hear organ music frequently.   The American Guild of Organists has labored valiantly since 1896 to raise standards of organ and church choral music.   Universities and colleges have secured fine teachers, who now train splendid performers and composers of both recital and church organ music.

A great exchange of organ music between America and Europe has taken place, and many organ recitalists, both American and European, have crossed the Atlantic to perform music of their own countries.   Many Americans have studied organ playing and organ literature in Germany, France, Belgium, the Netherlands, Austria, Italy, and England.   Many leading European musicians such as Schoenberg, Milhaud, Stravinsky, and Hindemith have come to America to live and teach.

The great improvements in communication media--television, radio, and recordings--have increased appreciation of music in general and of organ music in particular. The ease with which organ music is published and distributed today has also been a large contributing factor to an awareness of better organ music.

Organ Building in the United States

During the early part of the eighteenth century colonists of German background, who lived in Pennsylvania and

HISTORICAL BACKGROUND

1903	Wright brothers' first successful flight
1905	Einstein Theory of Relativity
1906	San Francisco earthquake and fire
1909	Frank Lloyd Wright Robie House, Chicago
1914	Robert Frost North of Boston
1914-1918	World War I
1915	Charles Ives Concord Sonata
1918	Cather My Antonia
1919	League of Nations founded
1922	James Joyce Ulysses
1924	Gerschwin Rhapsody in Blue
1925	F. Scott Fitzgerald The Great Gatsby
1926	Hemingway The Sun Also Rises
1927	Lindbergh flew alone across the Atlantic
1928	First commercial talking films
1928	Benét John Brown's Body
1929	Thomas Wolfe Look Homeward, Angel
1930	Grant Wood American Gothic
1931	Eugene O'Neill Mourning Becomes Electra
1933-1945	Roosevelt President
1934	Virgil Thomson Four Saints in Three Acts
1935	Gerschwin Porgy and Bess
1939-1945	World War II
1939	Roy Harris Third Symphony
1939	John Steinbeck The Grapes of Wrath
1942	United Nations formed
1944	Aaron Copland Appalachian Spring
1945-1953	Truman President
1947	Williams Streetcar Named Desire
1949	Barber Knoxville: Summer of 1915
1949	Arthur Miller Death of a Salesman
1950	Menotti The Consul
1950-1953	Korean War
1950	Stravinsky The Rake's Progress
1951	NATO formed
1953-1961	Eisenhower President
1958	First American satellite in orbit
1961	Viet Nam involvement began
1961	Eliot Carter Double Concerto
1961-1963	Kennedy President
1961	Berlin War raised
1961	First space flights flown by man
1963-1969	Johnson President
1969	Apollo 11 landed Americans on the moon
1969-	Nixon President

neighboring sections of the country, imported small chamber
instruments from Germany.   David Tannenberg (1728-1804)
was the principal organ builder of the German tradition in
Pennsylvania.   English organs were ordered for Anglican
churches in Virginia, New York, and New England.   Organs
of the English type were built in the New York and Boston
areas.

Leading American organ builders of the early nineteenth century were George Jardine, Henry Erben, and the
Hook brothers.   After 1850 the Romantic movement made its
influence felt.   The two prominent builders of this period
were Hilborne Roosevelt and George Hutchings. [4]

John T. Austin and Ernest M. Skinner were two outstanding American builders of the early twentieth century.
Their organs, like those of Roosevelt and Hutchings, were
expressions of the Romantic movement in organ building which
was still in full swing.   The English engineer Robert Hope
Jones made strong inroads against the performance of legiti-
mate organ literature on real pipe organs with two of his
accomplishments, the theater organ (conceived totally in an
orchestral way for amusement and popular music) and the
unit organ, the effects of both achievements which have been
very difficult to overcome. [5]

Although Americans were aware of Albert Schweitzer's
search for a truer performance of Bach through his prefaces
to the Widor-Schweitzer edition of Bach's organ works, the
tonal and mechanical conceptions of the organ reform movements in Europe did not make much headway until organ
builders in America themselves became aware of the wide
difference between what they were building and what kind of
instrument had, in fact, been able to produce the best results
in the performance of classic organ literature.   The credit
for awakening the American organ world to the organ reform
can be given to concert organists such as Lynwood Farnam,
Melville Smith, E. Power Biggs, and Robert Noehren, and
to organ builders such as Walter Holtkamp and the Englishman G. Donald Harrison of the Aeolian-Skinner Company.
Both Holtkamp and Harrison independently studied the construction practices, voicing techniques, and tonal designs of
old European master organ builders and adopted practices
which were harmonious with their own aesthetic ideals.   They
were thus able to produce instruments much superior to those
of the earlier part of the twentieth century. [6]

Herman Schlicker, the German-born builder who established his firm in Buffalo, New York, has made many fine contributions to the art of organ building in America. He has encouraged the use of mechanical action and has ably designed instruments for the true literature of the organ.

Since the late 1940's many mature and student organists have been able to observe the finest European organs first-hand and have demanded that American builders produce instruments of similar quality. A number of foreign firms, which have subscribed to the ideals of the organ reform movement such as von Beckerath, Walcker, Flentrop, Rieger, and Casavant, have built some splendid instruments in America. Some smaller builders in New England such as Charles Fisk and Fritz Noack have also supported the principles of the organ reform. Larger firms such as Schantz, Austin, and Möller have adopted to various degrees some of the guidelines of the European organ reform. Surely the wide interest in a return to the high ideals of the organ reform movement augers well for the musical art of the organ and its literature in America. [7]

There are at least six different types of organ music which have been written in America during the twentieth century thus far. These types may be identified as program music for recital use, an eclectic style which combines two or more rather traditional stylistic elements, French, English, and German (neo-Baroque) oriented works, and, finally, twentieth-century techniques, which include newer styles of composition such as serial, chance (aleatory), atonal, jazz, and combinations of organ with tapes. Some composers have adopted several different styles for different purposes; other composers have chosen one style or technique and have consistently remained within one style or perhaps have developed their own personal adaptation of the style.

Program music

Under the Romantic influence, many organ transcriptions and character pieces were written by American organ composers toward the end of the nineteenth and well into the twentieth century. Their colorful titles suggested a program for the imagination of the listener. These pieces were intended for concert use or for the amusement of the organist, not for church services. Two of the chief exponents of character pieces were Harvey B. Gaul (1881-1945) (Easter

AMERICAN ORGAN COMPOSERS: 1900-1970

1900	1950	1970

1900 Edmundson, Garth--------------------------------1971
1900 Copland, Aaron-------------------------------------
1904 Parrish, Carl-----------------------1965
1905 Friedell, Harold--------------1958
1906 Kettering, Eunice----------------------------------
1906 Lockwood, Normand --------------------------------
1908 Bitgood, Roberta --------------------------------
1908 Casner, Myron-------------------------------------
1909 Bender, Jan (Dutch-American)----------------------
1909 Whitney, Maurice C. ------------------------------
1910 Barber, Samuel ----------------------------------
1910 Berlinski, Herman (German-American)--------------
1910 Crandell, Robert --------------------------------
1910 Noehren, Robert ---------------------------------
1911 Arbatsky, Yury (Russian-American) ---------------
1911 Canning, Thomas ---------------------------------
1911 Hovhaness, Alan ---------------------------------
1912 Fleischer, Heinrich (German-American)-----------
1912 Barlow, Wayne -----------------------------------
1912 Roberts, Myron ----------------------------------
1913 Read, Gardner -----------------------------------
1913 Dello Joio, Norman ------------------------------

1913 Elmore, Robert Hall --------------------------------
1914 Haines, Edmund Thomas -------------------------
1914 Bunjes, Paul --------------------------------------
1914 Kubik, Gail-------------------------------------
1914 Effinger, Cecil ----------------------------------
1914 Held, Wilbur ------------------------------------
1914 Lenel, Ludwig (French-American)------------
1915 Persichetti, Vincent----------------------------
1915 Huston, John -----------------------------------
1916 Kohs, Ellis B. ------------------------------------
1917 Kay, Ulysses Simpson---------------------------
1917 Purvis, Richard ---------------------------------
1917 Keller, Homer----------------------------------
1918 Bouman, Paul ---------------------------------
1918 Wright, Searle-------------------------------
1918 Cook, John (English-American) ----------
1919 Manz, Paul---------------------------------
1919 Williams, David Henry (Welsh-American)--
1919 Young, Gordon-----------------------------
1920 LaMontaine, John -------------------
1920 Wienhorst, Richard ----------------
1921 Goode, Jack C. ---------------------
1921 Wyton, Alec (English-American) ---
1921 White, Louie ------------------
1921 Dirksen, Richard Wayne----------
1922 Johnson, David N. ------------
1922 Foss, Lucas-----------------
1923 Bohnhorst, Frank --------------1956

AMERICAN ORGAN COMPOSERS: 1900-1970 (cont.)

1910	1950	1970

1923 Bristol, Lee Hastings, Jr. ------------
1923 Pinkham, Daniel -------------
1923 Bassett, Leslie -------------
1923 Rorem, Ned ----
1924 Brandon, George-------------
1924 Krapf, Gerhard (German-American)------------
1925 Gehring, Philip -------------
1926 Rohlig, Harald (German-American)-----------
1926 Arnold, Corliss Richard------------
1927 Peek, Richard-----
1929 Hancock, Eugene Wilson-----------
1929 Schalk, Carl-----------
1929 Beck, Theodore-----------
1930 Arnatt, Ronald (English-American)-----------
1930 Felciano, Richard-----------
1932 Stout, Alan-----
1934 Busarow, Donald-----------
1934 Hancock, Gerre-----------
1942 Near, Gerald-----------

Morning on Mt. Rubidoux, Daguerreotype of an Old Mother)
and Joseph Waddell Clokey (1890-1960) (Dripping Spring,
Twilight Moth, The Kettle Boils, Grandfather's Wooden Leg).
As only one example of the taste of audiences and of the
performers of the earliest third of the twentieth century it
has been observed that many organists could not resist the
temptation to include Powell Weaver's The Squirrel on their
recitals.   One illustration of lush Romantic harmonies and
an orchestral conception of organ composition is that of
Richard Purvis (1917-   ), whose Seven Chorale Preludes on
Tunes found in American Hymnals have been popular with
organists who prefer organ music in this vein.

        Several leading musicians have written organ music
of a higher artistic level than that of the early nineteenth
century which has programmatic titles and which is intended
for recital use.   Dr. Seth Bingham (1882-1972) included two
such pieces (Black Cherries, Forgotten Graves) in his Pastoral Psalms.   His Roulade and Rhythmic Trumpet from the
Baroques suite have provided lighthearted and cheerful music
for many organ programs.   The Carnival suite by Robert
Crandell (1910-   ) contains four movements, each of which
depicts one of four characters in Italian comedy: Pulcinella,
Harlequin, Columbina, and the clowns Giangurgolo and Co-
viello.

        Garth Edmundson (1900-1971) also composed music of
this type (March of the Magi, from Christmas Suite No. 1).
Eric DeLamarter (1880-1953) and Leo Sowerby (1895-1968),
two famous Chicago composers, gave colorful titles to some
of their compositions: Festival Prelude in Honor of St.
Louis, King of France (DeLamarter) and Madrigal, Jubilee,
and Comes Autumn Time (Sowerby).   The Bible Poems and
Religious Preludes of Czech-American Jaromir Weinberger
(1896-1967) are suites of short, programmatic pieces inspired by Biblical texts.   These pieces are through-composed;
their rich harmonies and rhapsodic writing call for colorful
registrations.

Eclectic Style

        Many American organ composers have formed individ-
ual styles which are eclectic in nature and which continue
rather traditional composition practices and conventional uses
of the organ's resources.   Dr. Clarence Dickinson (1873-
1969), a founder of the School of Sacred Music at Union

Theological Seminary, New York City, based his works on
German Romanticism of the Mendelssohnian type (The Joy of
the Redeemed, a setting of the hymn-tune O Quanta Qualia).
Carl McKinley (1895-1966), H. Leroy Baumgartner (1891-
1969), and G. Winston Cassler (1906-   ) have set hymn or
chorale melodies in somewhat customary ways. George
Frederick McKay (1899-1970) (Benedictions) and Myron Roberts (1912-   ) (Homage to Perotin, Prelude and Trumpetings)
have each put his own stamp of individuality on their compositions which were constructed of traditional elements.

French Style

        French composition practices have made a strong im-
pression upon many American organ composers. Bruce
Simonds (1895-   ), former dean of the School of Music at
Yale University, chose to write his two plainsong settings in
an impressionistic style. Seth Bingham and Garth Edmundson
were only two Americans who adopted the French toccata type
somewhat resembling those of Vierne and Widor for some of
their pieces (Bingham: Toccata on Leonie; Edmundson:
Gargoyles, Vom Himmel hoch). It is interesting to observe
the style changes which occur in the organ works of Philip
James (1890-   ) between his Méditation à Sainte Clotilde
(published in 1924) in Franckian style; Fête (published in
1924), a joyous, full-bodied work; and the Galarnad (published in 1949), which approaches 12-tone writing in sections.

English Style

        A substantial number of American organist-composers
associated with the Episcopal Church exhibited a marked preference for an English type of composition of the last half of
the nineteenth century. This style might be characterized in
a very general way by conventional harmonies in unsurprising
progressions, uncomplicated rhythms, and standard organ
registration practices. Sometimes this style of writing follows a loosely structured, improvisatory fashion. These composers have often set hymn-tunes and plainsong melodies and
free-accompaniments for congregational singing. Dr. T.
Tertius Noble (1867-1953), an English cathedral organist who
served at St. Thomas Church, New York City, wrote many
hymn-tune settings. T. Frederick H. Candlyn (1892-1964),
Dr. Noble's successor at St. Thomas Church, composed
arrangements of plainsong melodies (Divinum Mysterium,

Sursum Corda) and dignified pieces of the English trumpet
tune genre. Other distinguished organ composers in the English school include Everett Titcomb (1884-1968), Harold Friedell (1905-1958), Winfred Douglas (1867-1944), and M. Searle
Wright (1918-   ).   David N. Johnson (1922-   ) has composed
several Trumpet Tunes patterned after the English trumpet
tunes which alternate a melody played on the solo trumpet
stop with a harmonized version of the same melody.

German Style

       A Germanic, neo-Baroque style has been expressed by
composers within the Lutheran church tradition.   The chorale
and hymn settings of these composers employ the well-
established polyphonic forms and contrapuntal devices of the
German schools of the seventeenth and eighteenth centuries
and combine them with contemporary conceptions of harmony
and melody.   Some of the most practical and interesting
church melody arrangements are the Chorale Improvisations
by Paul Manz (1919-   ).   The Four Organ Chorales by Ludwig Lenel (1914-   ) are much more complex.   Jan Bender
(1909-   ) is an important contributor to this contrapuntal
school of organ works.   The Voluntaries on the Hymn of the
Week by Wayne Barlow (1912-   ) were composed in similar
character for use in the Lutheran Church.

       Two Baroque forms which have been employed as
means of expression by twentieth-century American organ
composers are the passacaglia and the fugue.   Composers
who have used the passacaglia type are Douglas Moore (1893-
1969), Ellis B. Kohs (1916-   ), Leo Sowerby, Virgil Thomson (1896-   ), Gardner Read (1913-   ), and Searle Wright.
Only a few of those who have used the fugue form are Robert
Noehren (1910-   ), Cecil Effinger (1914-   ), and Homer Keller (1917-   ).

Twentieth-Century Techniques

       Seth Bingham introduced such musical devices as a
prominent use of fourths, delayed parallel intervals, unpre-
pared and unresolved discords, cross-relations and false-
relations, bi-tonalisms, augmented and diminished intervallic
leaps, and consecutive and hidden fifths into his Thirty-six
Hymn and Carol Canons in Free Style, Op. 52.   Bingham's
use of these devices, unexpected harmonies, and surprising

rhythmic arrangements in his hymn-tune settings anticipated similar methods of writing by other organ composers.

Some composers have chosen sturdy, folk hymn-tunes, and white spirituals from the South from shaped-note collections such as The Sacred Harp as their cantus firmus material. Gardner Read (1913-) has a collection of Eight Preludes on Old Southern Hymns, Op. 90, sometimes sprightly, sometimes melancholy pieces, which often employ contrapuntal elements. In 1946 Richard F. Donovan (1891-) wrote two contemporary settings of the tunes Land of Rest and Christian Union. Samuel Barber (1910-) selected Wondrous Love for a set of variations, Op. 34, in addition to his own organ transcription of his Silent Night arrangement from Die Natali, Op. 37.

Charles Ives (1874-1954), the eccentric but highly original composer who anticipated many contemporary composition techniques, wrote his amusing and bizarre Variations on America in 1891. It is composed of an introduction, chorale, and five variations, to which he made polytonal additions in 1894.

Virgil Thomson (1896-) employed lean contrapuntal lines for his arrangement of Divinum Mysterium in his Pastorale on a Christmas Plainsong. Thomson's Pange lingua is much more elaborate and contains triple-pedaling, intricate alternation between manuals, polytonalities, many parallel seconds, and complex rhythmic figures.

The name of Leo Sowerby would probably be the first mentioned as the most prominent American organ composer of the mid-twentieth century. Sowerby was associated with St. James Cathedral, Chicago, for a major portion of his life. He was deeply interested in the music of the church, often in demand for Episcopal church music conferences, and was one of the music editors of the Hymnal 1940. His 29 cantus firmus (principally hymn-tune) settings are generally post-Romantic in style. String and orchestral reed stops are often indicated in the registration suggestions of the composer. Sowerby usually placed the tune in a different range and in varying qualities of sound for each stanza of the arrangement. The harmonizations are warm and unashamedly chromatic in nature. Probably the best-known collection of Sowerby's hymn-tune settings is the Meditations on Communion Hymns. One of his best hymn-preludes is the Prelude on Malabar, which he based on David McK. Williams' hymn-tune and

wrote for inclusion in the Modern Anthology, which was edited
by Williams.   In the Malabar prelude, Sowerby employed the
same technique which had proved effective in so many chorale
preludes of the Baroque period, that of using the melodic
elements of the basic material (in this case, the hymn-tune
phrases) in imitation, in sequences, and in anticipation of the
solo treatment of the melody phrase.   Toward the end of this
same prelude Sowerby builds to a splendid climax by the
gradual addition of stops and by playing the hymn-tune melody
in octave chords.   H. W. Gray, the music publishing firm
with which Sowerby had a close relationship, published one-
third of Sowerby's hymn preludes in a series in 1956.   The
settings of Deus tuorum militum and Sine nomine are vigor-
ously martial and aggressive.

     Roughly three-fourths of Sowerby's organ compositions
were designed for concert and recital use.   A number of
free works of moderate length, which were popular in the
late 1930's and 1940's, exhibit Sowerby's use of such traditional forms, devices, and techniques as variations on an
original theme (Arioso, Requiescat in pace), ostinato (Carillon), and use of a rhythmic motive as a unifying factor
(Fanfare).   Much chromaticism is also a recurring characteristic in some of his earlier pieces.   Comes Autumn Time
is a colorful and strongly rhythmic orchestral overture which
Sowerby arranged for organ;   the piece, which is conceived
in sonata-allegro form, was inspired by some lines of the
poet Bliss Carman.   The Toccata (1940) is one of Sowerby's
best pieces of moderate length.   Deft use of manual changes
for echo effects, addition or periodic elimination of the pedal
part to strengthen the listeners' understanding of the construction (sonata-allegro form), and a technically challenging part
for the manuals are features of this work.

     Sowerby's largest single work for organ solo is the
Symphony in G Major (1930), which was dedicated to the
Canadian organ virtuoso Lynwood Farnam.   The first of
three movements (Very broadly) is highly unified by the frequent appearance of the principal theme in many guises;
even the second theme is closely related to the principal
theme.   The second movement (Fast and sinister) has often
been used alone as a recital number.   The thematic material
is in two segments, one chordal segment in the rhythm ♩♩♩
and the other an eighth-note figure which leaps upward in
the intervals of fourths and fifths to and within the range of
an octave.   The pedal part is active and often sounds thematic material under manual figurations.   The final movement

is in the form of a passacaglia (Slowly), which is built upon
an eight-measure melody. The 33 variations contain a wide
variety of rhythmic, harmonic, and contrapuntal effects,
which attest to Sowerby's great command of musical materials. Another large variation work is Pageant (1931), a
pedal concerto-extravaganza designed to exhibit the pedaling
prowess of Sowerby's friend Fernando Germani, the Italian
organ virtuoso. The theme-tune has the lilt and mood of
folk music, a characteristic of many of Dr. Sowerby's compositions.

The Suite (1933-1934) contains examples of Sowerby's
two principal composition styles. The well-known Fantasy
for Flute Stops in tripartite form employs a dry, contemporary, contrapuntal style, which features dissonance for its
color and both melodies and harmonies built upon seconds,
fourths, and fifths. In contrast the Air with Variations from
the same Suite features extreme chromaticism, frequent syncopation, and shifting and quartal harmonies in subjective expression. The registrations call for the use of Romantic
and orchestral colors such as soft strings, clarinet, English
horn, flute with tremolo, and gradual crescendos and dimin-
uendos by addition or retiring of stops or the use of the
Crescendo pedal.

The Sinfonia Brevis (1965) was one of Sowerby's last
major compositions for organ solo. The Sinfonia contains
three movements which are cyclic since themes for the first
and third movements were drawn from the second movement,
which Sowerby had completed first and had originally planned
as a single piece.

Dr. Sowerby contributed generously to literature for
the organ with other instruments in groups or alone. Probably the three most popular of his works in this type were
the Poem (viola and organ) (1942), Ballade (English horn and
organ) (1949), and Festival Musick (two trumpets, two trombones, kettledrums, and organ) (1953). Two of Sowerby's
best composition pupils are Jack C. Goode (1921-) and
Gerald Near (1942-).

Specifications of the organ at St. James Cathedral are
given below as the resources of the instrument were when
Sowerby was the organist and choirmaster from 1927-1962.

Chicago, St. James Cathedral.
Built by Austin Organ Co. , 1920.

Great

Double Open Diapason 16'
Principal Diapason 8'
Second Open Diapason 8'
Doppel Flute 8'
Gemshorn 8'
Gemshorn Celeste 8'
Octave 4'
Harmonic Flute 4'
Trumpet 8'
Chimes

Choir

Open Diapason 8'
Concert Flute 8'
Unda Maris 8'
Dulciana 8'
Flute d'Amour 4'
Flautina 2'
Clarinet 8'
Tremulant

Pedal

Resultant 32'
Open Diapason 16'
Violone 16'
Bourdon 16'
Second Bourdon 16'
Gross Flute 8'
Tuba Profunda 16'
Harmonic Tuba 8'
Contra Fagotto 16'

Swell

Bourdon 16'
Open Diapason 8'
Stopped Diapason 8'
Viole d'Orchestre 8'
Echo Salicional 8'
Vox Celeste 8'
Flauto Traverso 4'
Piccolo 2'
Dolce Cornet III
Contra Fagotto 16'
Cornopean 8'
Oboe 8'
Vox Humana 8'
Tremulant

Solo

Flauto Major 8'
Stentorphone 8'
Gross Gamba 8'
Gamba Celeste 8'
Flute Ouverte 4'
Tuba Profunda 16'
Harmonic Tuba 8'
Harmonic Tuba 4'
Cor Anglais 8'
Chimes

One of the best examples of the use of the serial
technique in American organ compositions is the Chromatic
Study on the Name of Bach by Walter Piston (1894-   ).   The
tone-row is reversed while the second voice presents the
row in its original order.   This process is repeated when
the third and fourth parts enter.   Piston has also contributed
the Prelude and Allegro to instrumental ensemble literature
for organ and strings.

The Chorale No. 1 is a striking piece written by
Roger Sessions (1896-   ), which employs rhapsodic writing
in sophisticated rhythms.   The Sonata, Op. 86 (1961), by
Vincent Persichetti (1915-   ) is an atonal work which is
technically challenging.   Persichetti has also composed a
three-movement Sonatine, Op. 11, for pedals alone.   A number of other famous American composers who are usually
associated with musical media other than the organ who have
written a few pieces for the organ include Henry Cowell
(1897-1965), Aaron Copland (1900-   ), Quincy Porter (1897-
1966), and Norman Dello Joio (1913-   ).

The jazz element has not been used very much in
organ literature, but Robert Russell Bennett (1894-   ) did
employ some jazz rhythms in his Sonata, as did Robert Elmore (1913-   ) in his Rhythmic Suite (Rhumba).

The newer technique of chance (aleatory) music was
used by Lucas Foss (1922-   ) in his Etudes for Organ, in
which tone-clusters are juxtaposed with a hymn-tune, a
combination which might seem strange to traditionalists.   The
use of tapes with organ has made Richard Felciano (1930-   )
one of the pioneers in another twentieth-century attempt to
find new means of musical expression.

A few of the outstanding American works on a larger
scale for organ with other instruments are Howard Hanson's
Concerto for Organ, Strings and Harp, Op. 22, No. 3, Nor-
mand Lockwood's Concerto for Organ and Brass Quartet,
Seth Bingham's Connecticut Suite, Samuel Barber's Toccata
Festiva for organ, strings, trumpet, and timpani, and Daniel
Pinkham's two Concertantes.

Notes

1.   John Tasker Howard, Our American Music, New York:
        Thomas Y. Crowell Co., 1946;   p. 20.
2.   Ibid., p. 137-140.
3.   The "Thunder Storm" (often with lighting effects) and
        the "Midnight Fire Alarm" (produced in one New York
        church with real firemen) are described by Barbara
        Owen in "American Organ Music and Playing, from
        1700," Organ Institute Quarterly, vol. 10, no. 3
        (Autumn 1963), p. 12.
4.   Barbara Jane Owen, "Organ: History," Harvard Diction-
        ary of Music, 2nd ed., Cambridge, Mass.: Harvard

University Press, 1969; p. 618-619.
5.   Ibid. , p. 619
6.   Lawrence I. Phelps, "A Short History of the Organ Re-
      vival," reprinted from Church Music, St. Louis: Con-
      cordia Pub. House, 1967; p. 10-15.
7.   Ibid. , p. 17-20.

Bibliography

Amacker, Marianne. "The Chorale Preludes of Leo Sowerby,"
      The Diapason (August 1970), p. 20-21.
Armstrong, William H. Organs for America: The Life and
      Work of David Tannenberg. Philadelphia: University of
      Pennsylvania Press, 1967.
Barnes, William Harrison. The Contemporary American
      Organ: Its Evolution, Design and Construction, 8th ed.
      Glen Rock, N. J. : J. Fischer, 1964.
Cowell, Henry, and Sidney Cowell. Charles Ives and His
      Music. New York: Oxford University Press, 1955.
Gallo, William K. "Dudley Buck--the Organist," Diapason
      (November 1971), p. 22-24.
Howard, John Tasker. Our American Music. New York:
      Thomas Y. Crowell Co. , 1946.
Osborne, William. "Five New England Gentlemen," Music/
      The A. G. O. and R. C. C. O. Magazine, vol. III, no. 8
      (August 1969), p. 27-29.
Owen, Barbara Jane. "American Organ Music and Playing,
      from 1700," Organ Institute Quarterly, vol. 10, no. 3
      (Autumn 1963).
_____. "Organ: History," Harvard Dictionary of Music,
      2nd ed.   Cambridge, Mass. : Harvard University Press,
      1969.
Phelps, Lawrence I. "A Short History of the Organ Revival,"
      reprinted from Church Music 67. 1.   St. Louis: Concor-
      dia Pub. House, 1967.

Part II

BIOGRAPHICAL CATALOG

NOTES ON THE USE OF THE CATALOG

The purpose of the Catalog is to provide basic information about organ composers and their published works in
a simple, useful form. (Manuscripts are rarely listed since
one of the chief purposes of this catalog is to provide publishing information. The few transcriptions for organ included here are indicated as transcriptions.)

This catalog is limited to composers, selected according to the following criteria: their compositions are frequently found on organ recital programs and church service
lists in the United States and abroad, and they are prominently
listed in national and international dictionaries of composers
and also in both American and foreign organ publishers' recent catalogs. Authors of organ methods and editors of organ
music are not listed. Many composers are listed here with
this biographical information for the first time in a work of
this type. Some composers have not been listed because
biographical information was not available in standard sources,
or some composers did not reply to the author's request for
biographical information.

The following types of information are provided in the
biographical sketches insofar as possible and/or appropriate:
birth and death places and dates, musical training and degrees, important teachers and pupils, and significant church,
teaching, and performing positions.

Titles of organ compositions are listed alphabetically
under the composer's name. In many instances pagination of
the titles is provided from major anthologies of organ music
published by both American and foreign firms. Sources from
historical collections such as the Denkmäler deutscher Tonkunst are included as an aid for reference and study, although
such collections are more commonly found in public libraries
than in private ones. A few important collections, codices,
and tablatures are also listed in order to provide publishing
information. Composition dates, when known, are given in
parentheses along with the composition title; the publisher's

name and catalog number is followed by the copyright date.

Compositions for organ and other instruments, including concertos for organ and orchestra, are listed under the individual composer's name. (No effort has been made to include music for organ and voice nor compositions in which the organ part could be performed by any one of several keyboard instruments as in continuo parts.)

An asterisk (*) before a title indicates an edition which is suggested as authoritative. The German umlaut (¨) over a, o, and u is alphabetized as though the letters were spelled out ae, oe, and ue. If no date of publication can be found, this is indicated by "n.d."

For more complete material about great composers such as Beethoven, Brahms, Liszt, Mendelssohn, and Mozart, to mention only a few, the reader will find abundant sources of information elsewhere.

In case the reader is not able to find a title at first glance, he is encouraged to look through the entire list of compositions under the composer's name, since the title might appear in a different form from that which the reader expects. Example: a prelude in F Minor could be listed under the title Three Preludes (C Minor, F Minor, G Major).

The author will be grateful for corrections or additional biographical information from readers, composers, and publishers about organ composers listed here since such information is not always easily available.

ANTHOLOGIES OF ORGAN MUSIC

The contents of the anthologies of organ music listed below are listed separately under the individual composer's name in the Biographical Catalog.

An Album of Praise. London: Oxford University Press, 1958.
Alte deutsche Weihnachtsmusik, Rudolf Steglich, ed. Kassel, Germany: Nagels Verlag, n.d.
Alte italienische Meister, M. Enrico Bossi, ed. Frankfurt: C. F. Peters Corp., 1936.
Alte Meister, Karl Straube, ed. Leipzig: C. F. Peters Corp. n.d.

Alte Meister des Orgelspiels, Neue Folge, Karl Straube, ed.,
    2 vols. Frankfurt: C. F. Peters Corp. 1929.
Alte Meister aus der Frühzeit des Orgelspiels, Arnold Scher-
    ing, ed. Leipzig: Breitkopf und Härtel, 1913.
Alte Orgelmusik aus England und Frankreich, Flor Peeters,
    ed. Mainz, Germany: B. Schotts Söhne, 1958.
Alte Weihnachtsmusik, Richard Baum, ed. Kassel, Germany:
    Bärenreiter Verlag, 1934.
Altenglische Orgelmusik, Denis Stevens, ed. Kassel, Ger-
    many: Bärenreiter Verlag, n. d.
Altniederlandische Meister, Flor Peeters, ed. Mainz, Ger-
    many: B. Schotts Söhne, 1958.
American Organ Music, Leslie Spelman, ed., 2 vols. Evan-
    ston, Ill. : Summy-Birchard, 1957.
Les Anciens Maîtres Espagnols, Paule Piedelièvre, ed.
    Paris: Schola Cantorum, 1953.
Anthologia Organistica Italiana, Sandro Dalla Libera, ed.
    Milan: G. Ricordi and Co., 1957.
Anthologia pro Organo, Flor Peeters, ed. Brussels: Schott
    Frères, 1949.
Anthology of Early French Organ Music, Joseph Bonnet, ed.
    New York: H. W. Gray Company, 1942.
Antologia de Organistas Clásicos Españoles, Felipe Pedrell,
    ed., 2 vols. Madrid: Union Musical Española, 1968.
Apel, Willi, Masters of the Keyboard. Cambridge, Mass. :
    Harvard University Press, 1947.
Archives des Maîtres d'Orgue des Seizième-Dix-Huitième
    Siècles, Alexandre Guilmant and André Pirro, eds.,
    10 vols. (1898-1910). Reprint, Mainz, Germany: B.
    Schotts Söhne, n. d. ; reprint, Johnson Reprint Corpora-
    tion.
L'Arte Musicale in Italia, Vol. III, Luigi Torchi, ed. Milan:
    G. Ricordi and Co., 1897.
A Brief Compendium of Early Organ Music, Herthe Schweiger,
    ed. New York: G. Schirmer, 1943.
Cantantibus Organis, Flor Peeters, Titus Timmerman, and
    Piet Visser, eds., 2 vols. Utrecht: Van Rossum, 1957-
    1958.
A Century of Czech Music, Karel Paukert, ed., 2 vols.
    Chicago: H. T. FitzSimons Co., 1965.
Chorale Preludes by Masters of the Seventeenth and Eighteenth
    Centuries, Walter E. Buszin, ed. St. Louis:
    Concordia Pub. House, 1948.
Choralvorspiel alter Meister, Karl Straube, ed. Leipzig:
    C. F. Peters Corp. 1951.
The Church Organist's Golden Treasury, Carl F. Pfatteicher
    and Archibald T. Davison, eds., 3 vols. Bryn Mawr,

Pa.: Oliver Ditson Co.   (Theodore Presser sole repre-
   sentative), 1949.
Classici Italiani dell'Organo, Ireneo Fuser, ed.   Padua,
   Italy: Edizioni Zanibon, 1955.
Corpus of Early Keyboard Music, Willi Apel, ed.   American
   Institute of Musicology, 1963 [in progress].
Denkmäler der Tonkunst in Bayern, Adolf Sandberger, ed.,
   36 vols.   Leipzig: Breitkopf und Härtel, 1901-1935.
Denkmäler der Tonkunst in Osterreich, Guido Adler, ed.,
   91 vols.   Graz, Austria: Akademische Druck- und U.
   Verlaganstalt, 1959.
Denkmäler deutscher Tonkunst, Max Seiffert, ed. (1892-1931).
   Reprint, Wiesbaden: Breitkopf und Härtel, 1958-1959.
Early English Organ Music, Margaret Glyn, ed.   London:
   Plainsong and Medieval Society, n. d.
Early Spanish Organ Music, Joseph Muset, ed., New York:
   G. Schirmer, 1948.
Eighty Chorale Preludes: German Masters of the Seventeenth
   and Eighteenth Centuries, Hermann Keller, ed.   Frank-
   furt: C. F. Peters Corp. 1937; reprint, 1951.
Elf Orgelchoräle des siebzehnten Jahrhunderts, Fritz Dietrich,
   ed., Kassel, Germany: Bärenreiter Verlag, 1932.
Das Erbe deutschen Musik, Max Schneider, ed., 49 vols.
   Leipzig: Breitkopf und Härtel, 1937.
European Organ Music of the 16th and 17th Centuries, Finn
   Viderø, ed.   Copenhagen: Wilhelm Hansen Musik Forlag,
   1970.
A Festive Album.   London: Oxford University Press, 1956.
The First Four Centuries of Organ Music, John Klein, ed.,
   2 vols.   New York: Associated Music Publishers, 1948.
The French Organist, Robert Leech Bedell, ed., 2 vols.
   New York: Edward B. Marks Music Corp., 1944.
Frühmeister der deutschen Orgelkunst, Hans Joachim Moser,
   ed.   Leipzig: Kunst (Breitkopf und Härtel), 1930.
Geschichte der Musik in Beispielen, Arnold Schering, ed.
   Leipzig: Breitkopf und Härtel, 1931; reprint, New York:
   Broude Brothers, 1950.
Gleason, Harold, Method of Organ Playing.   F. S. Crofts
   and Co., 1937.   5th ed., New York: Appleton-Century-
   Crofts, 1962.
Historical Anthology of Music, Archibald T. Davison and
   Willi Apel, eds., 2 vols.   Cambridge, Mass.: Harvard
   University Press, 1950 (reprint 1954).
The International Organist, Robert Leech Bedell, ed., 2
   vols.   New York: Edward B. Marks Music Corp., n. d.
Laudamus Dominum, Paul Rosel and Martin Bangert, eds.
   St. Louis: Concordia Pub. House, 1946.

Liber Organi, Ernst Kaller, ed. , 11 vols.   Mainz, Germany:
    B. Schotts Söhne, 1931-1966.
Les Maîtres français de l'orgue, Félix Raugel, ed. , 2 vols.
    Paris: Schola Cantorum, 1951.
Masterpieces of Organ Music, Norman Hennefield, ed. , 67
    folios.   New York: Liturgical Music Press, n. d.
The Modern Anthology, David McK. Williams, ed.   New
    York: H. W. Gray Co. , 1949.
Modern Organ Music, David Willcocks, ed. , 2 vols.   Lon-
    don: Oxford University Press, 1967.
Musica Boemica per Organo, Jiri Reinberger, ed. , 3 vols.
    Prague: Státní Nakladatelství Krásné Literatury, Hudby
    a Umení, 1954.
Musica Organi, 3 vols. , Henry Weman, ed.   Stockholm:
    Nordiska Musikförlaget, 1949, 1954, 1957.
Noel, Willard Irving Nevins, ed. , New York: Carl Fischer,
    1964.
Nuove Composizioni per Organo, Prague: Panton, 1966.
Old Spanish Organ Music, Carl Riess, ed.   Copenhagen:
    Wilhelm Hansen Musik Forlag, 1960.
Organ Book No. 2, C. H. Trevor, ed.   London: Oxford
    University Press, 1967.
Organ Music of Canada, Charles Peaker, ed. , 2 vols.
    Scarborough, Ontario: Berandol Music, 1971.
Organ Music for the Communion Service, Paul Bunjes, ed.
    St. Louis: Concordia Pub. House, 1956.
Organ Music of the Netherlands and Scandinavia, Robert
    Leech Bedell, ed.   New York: Edward B. Marks Music
    Corp. , n. d.
L'Organiste liturgique, Gaston Litaize and Jean Bonfils, eds. ,
    60 vols.   Paris: Schola Cantorum, 1953 [in progress].
Organum, Max Seiffert, ed. , 4th series, 10 vols.   Lippstadt,
    Germany: Kistner and Siegel, n. d.
Die Orgel.   Lippstadt, Germany: Kistner and Siegel, n. d.
Orgelchoräle des 17. und 18. Jahrhunderts, Kurt Wolfgang
    Senn, Wilhelm Schmid, and Gerhard Aeschbacher, eds.
    Kassel, Germany: Bärenreiter Verlag, 1950.
Orgelmeister des Siebzehnten und Achtzehnten Jahrhunderts,
    Karl Matthaei, ed.   Kassel, Germany: Bärenreiter
    Verlag, 1932.
Orgue et Liturgie, Norbert Dufourcq, Félix Raugel, and
    Jean de Valois, eds. , 74 vols.   Paris: Schola Cantorum,
    1953 [in progress].
Oudnederlandse Meesters, Flor Peeters, ed. , 3 vols.   Paris:
    Henry Lemoine et Cie. , 1938.
The Parish Organist, Heinrich Fleischer, Erich Goldschmidt,
    Thomas Gieschen, and Willem Mudde, eds. , 12 vols.

St. Louis: Concordia Pub. House, 1953-1966.

Ricercare, Canzonen und Fugen des 17. und 18. Jahrhunderts,
  Willi Hillemann, ed. Kassel, Germany: Nagels Verlag,
  1956.

Schule des klassischen Triospiels, Hermann Keller, ed.
  Kassel, Germany: Bärenreiter Verlag, 1928.

Sechs-und-vierzig Choräle für Orgel, Gisela Gerdes, ed.
  Mainz, Germany: B. Schotts Söhne, 1957.

Silva Iberica, M. S. Kastner, ed. Mainz, Germany: B.
  Schotts Söhne, 1954.

Spielbuch für die Kleinorgel, Wolfgang Auler, ed. , 2 vols.
  Frankfurt, C. F. Peters Corp. , 1942 (reprint 1951).

Tallis to Wesley, Gordon Phillips, ed. , 33 vols. London:
  Hinrichsen Edition, 1956 [in progress].

Treasury of Early Organ Music, E. Power Biggs, ed. New
  York: Mercury Music Corp. , n. d.

A Treasury of Shorter Organ Classics, E. Power Biggs, ed.
  New York: Mercury Music Corp. , 1955.

Twelve Short Pieces by Old English Composers, John E.
  West, ed. London: Novello and Co. , 1906.

AMERICAN MUSIC PUBLISHERS (Addresses and Agents)
As of January 1972

Abingdon Press, 201 Eighth Avenue, So. , Nashville 2, Tenn.

American Composers' Alliance, 170 West 74th Street, New
  York, N. Y.

American Musicological Society (see Galaxy).

Amsco Music Publishing Co. , 240 West 55th Street, New
  York, New York 10019.

Associated Music Publishers, Inc. , 609 Fifth Avenue, New
  York, N. Y. 10017.

Augsburg Publishing House, 426 South Fifth Street, Minneapolis, Minn. 55415.

Baerenreiter Music Publishers, 443 West 50th Street, New
  York, N. Y. (also P. O. Box 115, Inwood, Station, New
  York, N. Y. 10034).

Belwin-Mills Publishing Corp. , 250 Maple Avenue, Rockville
  Center, N. Y. 11571.

Big 3 Music Corp. , 1350 Avenue of the Americas, New
  York, N. Y. 10036.

Boosey and Hawkes, Inc. , 30 W. 57th St. , N. Y. 10019.

Boston Music Co. , 116 Boylston, Boston, Mass.

Broadcast Music Inc. , 589 Fifth Ave. , New York, N. Y.

Brodt Music Company, P. O. Box 1207, Charlotte, N. C. 28201.

Alexander Broude Inc. , 1619 Broadway, New York, N.Y.
    10019.
Broude Brothers, Ltd. , 6 West 45th Street, New York, N.Y.
    10036.
Canyon Press, Inc. , P.O. Box 1235, Cincinnati, Ohio. 45201.
Concordia Publishing House, 3558 So. Jefferson Ave. , St.
    Louis, Mo. , 63118.
Cos Cobb Press, New York, N.Y. (Boosey and Hawkes).
Da Capo Press, 227 West 17th Street, New York, N.Y. 10011.
Oliver Ditson Co. , Bryn Mawr, Pa. (Theodore Presser).
Edition Musicus-N.Y. Inc. , 333 West 52nd, Brooklyn, N.Y.
    10033.
Elkan-Vogel Inc. , Presser Place and Lancaster Ave. , Bryn
    Mawr, Penn.
Carl Fischer, Inc. , 62 Cooper Square, New York, N.Y.
    10003.
J. Fischer & Bro. , Harristown Road, Glen Rock, N.J.
H. T. FitzSimons Co. , 615 No. La Salle St. , Chicago, Ill.
    60610.
Harold Flammer, Inc. , 251 West 19th St. , New York, N.Y.
    10011.
Galaxy Music Corp. , 2121 Broadway, New York, N.Y. 10023.
Gamble Hinged Music Co. , Inc. , 312 So. Wabash, Chicago,
    Ill.
H. W. Gray Co. , Inc. , 159 E. 48th St. , New York, N.Y.
    10017 (Belwin-Mills).
Gregorian Institute of America, 2115 W. 63rd, Chicago, Ill.
Harvard University Press, Cambridge, Mass.
Hope Publishing Co. , 5707 W. Lake St. , Chicago, Ill. 60644.
Johnson Reprint Corporation, 111 Fifth Avenue, New York,
    N.Y. 10003.
Edwin F. Kalmus, P.O. Box 1007, Opa-Locka, Florida.
Edition Le Grand Orgue, 476 Marion St. , Brooklyn, N.Y.
    10033.
Liturgical Music Press (Theodore Presser).
McLaughlin & Reilly, Co. (Summy-Birchard).
Edward B. Marks Music Corporation, 136 West 52nd St. ,
    New York, N.Y. 10019.
Masterpieces of Organ Music (Theodore Presser).
Mercury Music Corp. (Theodore Presser).
Edwin H. Morris & Co. , Inc. , 31 W. 54th St. , New York,
    N.Y. 10019.
MCA Music, 543 W. 43rd St. , New York, N.Y. 10036.
Edition Musicus, 476 Marion St. , Brooklyn, N.Y. 10033.
Organum (Concordia).
Die Orgel (Concordia).
Oxford University Press, Inc. , Music Dept. , 417 Fifth Ave. ,

New York, N. Y. 10016; also 16-00 Pollitt Drive, Fair Lawn, N. J. 07410.

Peer International Corporation, 1619 Broadway, New York, N. Y. 10019.

C. F. Peters Corporation, 373 Park Ave. , South, New York, N. Y. 10016.

Theodore Presser Co. , Bryn Mawr, Pa. 19010.

Presto Music Service, Box 10704, Tampa, Florida.

R. D. Row (Carl Fischer)

Rubank, Inc. , 16215 N. W. 15th Ave. , Miami, Fla. 33169.

Sacred Music Press, 501 E. Third, Dayton, Ohio.

E. C. Schirmer Music Co. , 600 Washington, Boston, Mass.

G. Schirmer, Inc. , 609 Fifth Ave. , New York, N. Y.

Arthur P. Schmidt Co. (no longer exists).

Schmitt, Hall & McCreary Co. , 527 Park Ave. , Minneapolis, Minn.

Edward Schuberth & Co. , Inc. , 39 W. 60th St. , New York, N. Y. (Amsco).

Southern Music Co. , 1100 Broadway, Box 329, San Antonio, Texas 78206.

Southern Music Publishing Co. , Inc. , 1619 Broadway, New York, N. Y. 10019.

Sprague-Coleman, New York, N. Y.

Summy-Birchard Company, 1834 Ridge Ave. , Evanston, Ill. 60204.

Vitak-Elsnic Co. , 4815 South Ashland Ave. , Chicago, Ill. 60609.

White-Smith, 40 Winchester, Boston, Mass.

Willis Music Co. , 440 Main St. , Cincinnati, Ohio 45201; also 7380 Industrial Highway, Florence, Ky. 41042.

M. Witmark & Sons, 488 Madison Ave. , New York, N. Y.

The B. F. Wood Music Co. , 24 Brookline Ave. , Boston, Mass.

World Library of Sacred Music, 2145 Central Parkway, Cincinnati, Ohio 45214.

FOREIGN MUSIC PUBLISHERS

American agents' names, when known, are given in parentheses. See the list of American Music Publishers, preceding this, for addresses in the United States.

J. Aible, Leipzig.

G. Alsbach & Co. , Leidsegracht 11, Amsterdam (Peters).

Amadeus, Vienna.

J. André, Offenbach, Germany.
Ars Viva Verlag, Mainz, Germany (Associated Music Pub-
    lishers).
Artia, Prague (Boosey & Hawkes).
Ascherberg, Hopwood & Crew Ltd. , 16 Mortimer Street,
    London W. 1 (Brodt).
Edwin Ashdown, Ltd. , London (Boosey & Hawkes; Brodt).
Atelier Elektra, Copenhagen.
Augener Ltd. , Acton Lane, London, W. 4 (Galaxy).
Berandol (BMI-Canada Limited), 41 Valleybrook Drive, Don
    Mills 405, Ontario (Associated Music Publishers).
Bärenreiter Verlag, Heinrich Schütz Allee 35, 35 Kassel-
    Wilhelmshöhe, West Germany (Baerenreiter).
Bahn Musikverlag, Heinrichshofen, Germany.
M. Bahn, Berlin.
Annie Bank, Anna Vondelstraat 13, Amsterdam (World
    Library of Sacred Music).
Musikverlage Anton J. Benjamin, Werderstrasse 44, 2
    Hamburg 13.
H. Beyer & Söhne, Langensalza, Germany.
Edmund Bieler, Cologne-Sülz, Germany.
Billaudot, 14 rue de l'Echiéquier, Paris.
Anton Böhm & Sohn, Lange Gasse 26, 89 Augsburg 2,
    Germany.
F. Bongiovanni, Editore, Bologna (Belwin-Mills).
Albert Bonniers Förlag, Stockholm.
S. Bornemann, 15 rue de Tournon, Paris VI (Belwin-Mills).
Bosworth & Co. , Ltd. , 14/18 Heddon Street, Regent Street,
    London W. 1 (Belwin-Mills).
Ed. Bote & G. Bock, Sonnenbergerstrasse 14, Wiesbaden
    (Associated Music Publishers).
Brattfisch, Nuremberg.
Breitkopf & Härtel, Wiesbaden (Associated Music Publishers).
British and Continental Music, 8 Horse and Dolphin Yard,
    London W. IV 7 L G.
Carisch, S. p. A. , via General Fara 39, Milan (Belwin-Mills).
J. & W. Chester Ltd. , Eagle Court, London E. C. 1
    (Belwin-Mills).
Christophorus Verlag, Freiburg, Germany.
Musikverlag Alfred Coppenrath, Neuöttinger Strasse 32,
    8262 Altötting/Obb. , Germany.
Costallat, 60 Chausée Dantin, Paris.
J. B. Cramer & Co. Ltd. , 99 St. Martin's Lane, London,
    W. C. 2 (Brodt).
A. Cranz, Wiesbaden.
J. Curwen & Sons Ltd. , 24 Berners St. , London, W. 1
    (G. Schirmer).

M. Th. Dahlströms Musikförlag, Stockholm.
Edition Dania, Copenhagen (Peters).
Deichert, Leipzig.
Delrieu & Cie. , Nice, France (Galaxy).
DeRing, Antwerp.
Deutscher Verlag für Musik (Associated Music Publishers).
Edizioni de Santis, Rome (Belwin-Mills).
Musikverlag Ludwig Doblinger, Dorotheergasse 10, A-1011
    Vienna (Associated Music Publishers).
Donemus, Jacob Obrechtstraat 51, Amsterdam Z (Peters).
Librairie E. Droz, 25 rue de Tournon, Paris.
Elkan & Schildknecht, Emil Carelius, Stockholm.
A. Durand & Cie. , Editeurs, 4 Place de la Madeleine,
    Paris (Elkan-Vogel).
Elkin & Company, Ltd. , London (Galaxy).
Engstrøm & Sødring A/S, Palaegade 6, Copenhagen (Peters).
Enoch & Cie. , Paris (Associated Music Publishers).
Rudolf Erdmann, Adolfsallee 34, 62 Wiesbaden.
Eriks Musikhandel, Karlavägen 40, 114 49 Stockholm Ö.
Editions Max Eschig, 48 rue de Rome, Paris (Associated
    Music Publishers).
Edition Fazer, Helsinki.
Edition Foetisch, Lausanne, Switzerland
Dan Fog, Gråbrødretorv 7, Copenhagen.
R. O. Forberg, Bad Godesberg, Germany (Peters).
France Music Co. (Associated Music Publishers).
E. H. Freeman, Ltd. , Brighton, England (Belwin-Mills).
F. W. Gadow & Sohn, Hildburghaussen, Germany.
Galliard Ltd. , London (Galaxy).
Carl Gehrmans Musikförlag, Stockholm (Boosey & Hawkes;
    Southern Music Publishing Co.).
C. Geissler, Heinrichshofen, Germany.
H. Gerig, Geneva (Big 3; M. C. A.).
G. A. Grieshammer, Leipzig.
J. Hamelle, Editeur, 24 Boulevard Malesherbes, Paris VIII
    (Elkan-Vogel).
Wilhelm Hansen Musik Forlag, Copenhagen (G. Schirmer).
Henn, Geneva.
H. Hérelle et Cie. , Editeur, 16 rue de l'Odéon, Paris
    (now owned by Philippo) (Elkan-Vogel).
Max Hesse, Berlin.
Heugel et Cie. , 2 bis, rue Vivienne, Paris I (Theodore
    Presser).
Heuwekemeijer, Amsterdam (Elkan-Vogel).
Hinrichsen Edition, 119-125 Wardour St. , London W. 1
    (Peters)
Abr. Hirsch, Stockholm.

Heinrich Hohler, Landsberg, Germany.

Hofmeister, Hofheim, Germany (Presto).

Hudebni Matice Umelecke Besedy, Prague.

Hüllenhagen & Griehl, Hamburg.

Hug & Co., Limmatquai 26-28, Zürich (Peters).

Huss & Beer, Stockholm.

International Music Co. (Alfred A. Kalmus), 16 Mortimer
    St., London W. 1.

Iroquois Press (Jaymar Music Ltd.), P.O. Box 3083,
    London 12, Ontario.

Janin Frères, Lyons, France.

Junfermann, Paderborn, Germany.

Otto Junne, Munich.

C. F. Kahnt, Lindau/Bodensee, Germany (Associated Music
    Publishers).

Kaiser, Munich.

Kallmeyer, Wolfenbüttel, Germany.

J. S. Kerr, Glasgow.

Fr. Kistner & C. F. W. Siegel & Co., Luisenstrasse 8,
    Lippstadt, Germany (Concordia; Presto).

Körlings Förlag, Stockholm.

Körner, Erfurt, Germany.

G. W. Körner, Leipzig.

Krumpholz & Co., Berne, Switzerland.

Laudy & Co., London.

Editions Musicales Alphonse Leduc, 175 rue St. Honoré,
    Paris (E. B. Marks; Brodt).

Leeds Music Corp., 322 W. 48th St., New York, N.Y.,
    10019.

H. Lemoine, 17 rue Pigalle, Paris IX (Elkan-Vogel).

Alfred Lengnick & Co., Ltd., Purley Oaks Studios, 421a
    Brighton Road, South Croyden, Surrey, England (Belwin-
    Mills).

Leonard, Gould & Bottler, London.

LeRoux, Strasbourg, France.

F. E. C. Leuckart Musikverlag, Nibelungenstrasse 48,
    8 Munich 19 (Associated Music Publishers).

Henry Litolffs Verlag, Braunschweig, Germany (Peters).

Ab Lundeqvistska Bokhandeln, Östra Agatan 31, Uppsala,
    Sweden.

Ab Lundquist, Stockholm.

Harald Lyche & Co., Musikkforlag, Kongensgatan 2, Oslo
    (Peters).

Au Ménestral (Heugel), 2 bis, rue Vivienne, Paris.

Verlag Merseburger Berlin Gmbh, Alemannenstrasse 20,
    1000 West Berlin 38 (Peters).

Metropolis, Frankrijklei 24, Antwerp.

J. B. Metzler, Stuttgart, Germany.
Möseler-Verlag, Wolfenbüttel, Germany.
Willy Müller Edition, Hauptstrasse 85, Heidelberg, Germany
   (Peters).
L. Muraille, Liège.
Musica Rara, London, W. 1 (Rubank).
Musikaliska Konstföreningen, Stockholm.
Editions Musique Sacrée, 3 rue de Mézières, Paris VI.
Adolf Nagel (Associated Music Publishers).
Nagels Musik Archiv (Baerenreiter), Kassel, Germany
   (Associated Music Publishers).
Nederlandsche Orgelmuziek, Zaandam, The Netherlands.
Pierre Noel, Paris.
V. Norbergs Förlag, Västerås, Sweden.
Nordiska Musikförlaget, Stockholm (G. Schirmer).
Det Nordiske Forlag, Copenhagen.
Norsk Musikforlag, Oslo.
Noteria, Mantorp, Sweden.
Novello and Company Limited, 27 Soho Square, London;
   also Borough Green, Sevenoaks, Kent, England (Belwin-
   Mills).
Oesterreichischer Bundesverlag, Vienna (Associated Music
   Publishers).
Oppenheimer, Hameln, Germany.
Orbis-Verlag, Münster, Germany.
L'Organiste Liturgique (Schola Cantorum).
Orgue et Liturgie (Schola Cantorum).
Les Editions Ouvrières, 12 avenue Soeur-Rosalie, Paris XIII
   (Galaxy).
Oxford University Press, 44 Conduit Street, London W. 1
   (Oxford).
Paterson's, London (Carl Fischer).
W. Paxton and Co. , Ltd. , London (Belwin-Mills).
Edition Peters, Forsthausstrasse 101, Frankfurt (Peters).
Philippo, Editeur, 24 Boulevard Poissonières, Paris IX
   (Elkan-Vogel).
Pitault, Paris (no longer exists).
Plainsong and Medieval Society, London.
F. R. Portius, Stuttgart, Germany
Psallite, Bohnhort, Germany.
Publications de la Société Française de Musicologie, (Heugel)
   2 bis, rue Vivienne, Paris I.
F. Pustet, Regensburg, Germany.
Reinhardt, Switzerland, (Peters).
Richards & Co. , London.

G. Ricordi & C., Via Berchet 2, Milan (Belwin-Mills).

Ries & Erler, Berlin (Peters).

Rieter-Biedermann, Leipzig (Peters).

Ritmo S. A., Francisco Silvela 15, Madrid.

Editions Salabert, 22 rue Chauchat, Paris IX (Belwin-Mills).

Sassetti & Cia., Editores de Música, Avenida Visconde
  Valmor 20B, Lisbon 1, Portugal.

M. Schauenburg, Lahr/Bayern, Germany.

R. Schauer (Associated Music Publishers).

Editions Musicales de la Schola Cantorum et de la Procure
  Générale de Musique, 76 bis, rue des Saints Pères,
  Paris VII (Elkan-Vogel; World Library of Sacred Music).

Schott & Co., Ltd., 48 Great Marlborough Street, London
  W. 1 (Associated Music Publishers).

Schott Frères, Brussels (Peters).

Verlag B. Schotts Söhne, Weihergarten 1-9, 65 Mainz,
  Germany (Associated Music Publishers; Belwin-Mills).

J. Schuberth, Wiesbaden.

C. L. Schultheiss Musikverlag, Tübingen, Germany.

L. Schwann, Düsseldorf.

Schweers & Haake, Bremen, Germany.

Maurice Senart, Paris (Belwin-Mills).

Seyffardt, Amsterdam.

C. F. W. Siegel, Munich, Germany.

Musikverlag Hans Sikorski, Hamburg (Belwin-Mills).

Carl Simon (Baerenreiter).

N. Simon, Hamburg.

N. Simrock, Hamburg (Associated Music Publishers).

Sirius Verlag Berlin Margarita Katz, Wiclefstrasse 67,
  1 Berlin 21 (Peters).

Skandinavisk Musikforlag, Borgergade 2, Copenhagen.

Casa Musicale Sonzogno (Belwin-Mills; Associated Music
  Publishers).

Publications de la Société Française de Musicologie (Heugel),
  2 bis, rue Vivienne, Paris I (Theodore Presser).

Stainer and Bell Ltd., Lesbourne Road, Reigate, Surrey,
  England (Galaxy).

Verlag Styria, Vienna.

Edition Suecia, Stockholm.

Süddeutscher Musikverlag (Willy Müller), Hauptstrasse 85,
  Heidelberg (Peters).

Symphonia Verlag, Basel, Switzerland (Belwin-Mills).

Tascher'schen, Kaiserslautern/Bayern, Germany.

Gordon V. Thompson Ltd., 32 Alcorn Ave., Toronto 7,
  Ontario (Big 3).

Editions Musicales Transatlantiques (Theodore Presser).

Ugrino, Elbchausée 499a, Hamburg.

Union Musicale Español, Calle San Jerónimo (Associated
Music Publishers).
United Music Publishers Ltd. , 1 Montague Street, Russell
Square, London, W. C. 1.
Universal-Edition A. -G. , Karlsplatz 5, Vienna (Theodore
Presser).
Wed. J. R. Van Rossum, Utrecht (now owned by Annie Bank)
(Peters; World Library of Sacred Music).
Verbum Förlag, Stockholm.
C. F. Viewig, Berlin (Peters).
Vincent Music Co. , London.
J. A. H. Wagenaar, Utrecht.
Weekes & Co. , London.
Josef Weinberger Ltd. , 10-16 Rathbone St. , London W. 1
(Brodt).
J. Weinberger, Vienna (Brodt).
Westerlund, Helsinki (Southern Music Publishing Co.).
J. C. Willemsen, Amersfoort, The Netherlands.
Jos. Williams Edition, London (Galaxy).
Year Book Press, London.
Zanibon Edition, Padua (Peters; World Library of Sacred
Music).
Edizioni Suvini Zerboni, Milan (Associated Music Publishers).
J. Zwart, Koog/ Zaan, The Netherlands.

ADAMS, THOMAS. born London, Sept. 5, 1785; died London, Sept. 15, 1858. Organist, London; skillful extemporizer.
>Variations on Adeste Fideles, in Master Studies for the Organ, Carl, ed. , G. Schirmer; also Clementi.
>compositions (2) in Twelve Short Pieces by Old English Composers.
>hymn-tune preludes (2) in Hymn-Tune Voluntaries, John West, ed. , Novello.

ÄBEL, DAVID. German. died 1639. Organist, Rostock; probably a pupil of Sweelinck.
>preludes (2) in Organum, Series IV, Vol. 21.

AGUILÉRA DE HERÉDIA, SEBASTIÁN. born Aragon, 1560/1570; died Saragossa, after 1620. 1585-1603, organist, Cathedral, Huesca, Aragon; 1603, priest-organist, Cathedral, Saragossa, Spain.
>Obra de Octavo Tono Alto (Ensalada), in Historical Organ Recitals, Vol. VI, p. 20.
>Obra de Primero Tono, in Liber Organi, Vol. XI, p. 5.
>Tiento de Falsas de Cuarto Tono, in Early Spanish Organ Music, p. 22.
>compositions (3) in Antologia de Organistas Clásicos Españoles, Vol. I, p. 64-76.

AHLE, JOHANN RUDOLF. born Mühlhausen, Germany, Dec. 24, 1625; died Mühlhausen, July 9, 1673. 1646, appointed organist, St. Andreas, Erfurt; 1654, became organist, Divi Blasii, Mühlhausen.
>Ich ruf' zu dir, in Orgel Kompositionen aus alter und neuer Zeit.
>compositions in Das Erbe deutschen Musik, Series I, Vol. 9.
>compositions in Masterpieces of Organ Music, Folio 20.
>chorale preludes (2) in Orgelchoräle um J. S. Bach.

AHRENS, JOSEPH. born Sommersell, Westphalia, Germany, Apr. 17, 1904. Studied with father; 1925, became organist, Berlin; 1950, appointed Professor of Church Music, Musikhochschule, Berlin.
>Cantiones Gregorianae, 3 vols. , Schott 4787/9.
>Canzone in cis, Böhm.
>Canzone in F dur, Böhm.
>Choralpartita über Christus ist erstanden, Schott 2552.
>Choralpartita über Jesu, meine Freude, Böhm.
>Choralpartita über Lobe den Herren, Schott 3813.
>Choralpartita über Verleih uns Frieden, Schott 3814.
>Concertino für Positiv, Müller.
>Concerto, organ and brass, Müller 54.

Dorische Toccata, Böhm.
Fantasie und Ricercare, Müller.
Fünf kleine Stücke, Böhm.
Das heilige Jahr, 3 vols. , Bärenreiter 5194.
Hymnus über Pange lingua (1936), Schott 2551.
Hymnus über Veni creator spiritus, Schott 3815.
Kleine Musik in A moll, Böhm.
O Herr aus tiefer Klage, in Choralvorspiele zum Kirchen-
    lied, Vol. 7.
Orgelmesse (1945), Schott 3841.
Passamezzo und Fuge in G moll, Böhm.
Präludium, Arie und Toccata in A moll, Böhm.
Regina coeli, Böhm.
Ricercare in A moll, Böhm.
Sonata for Viola and Organ, Müller 93.
Toccata eroica und Fuge, Schott 2427.
Toccata und Fugue in E moll, Böhm.
Trilogia Sacra, 3 vols. , Müller.
Triptychon über B-A-C-H, Schott 4194.
Verwandlungen I, II, III, Schott 5397, 1965, 1967, 1967.
Zu Bethlehem geboren, Böhm.
AHRENS, SIEGLINDE. born Berlin, Feb. 19, 1936. Organ pupil
    of Joseph Ahrens and André Marchal; composition pupil of
    Boris Blacher, Oliver Messiaen, and Darius Milhaud; 1950-
    1956, 1961-1962, organist, Salvator-Kirche, Berlin; 1962,
    appointed to faculty, 1970, Professor of Organ, Folkwang-
    Hochschule, Essen, Germany.
    Fantasie, Müller.
    Sonata for Violin and Organ, Müller.
    Suite, Müller.
ALAIN, ALBERT. born St. Germain-en-Laye, France, Mar. 1,
    1880. Father of Jehan, Marie-Claire, and Olivier Alain;
    since 1924, organist, St. Germain-en-Laye; pupil of Alexandre
    Guilmant.
    Andante, Hérelle, 1927.
    Deux séries de Trois pièces (Rhapsody on Christmas Carols),
        Vol. 4, Sénart (Hérelle), 1914.
    Final (G Major): Cantemus Domino, Varia II, in Orgue et
        Liturgie, Vol. 46, p. 16.
    Messe basse, organ and harmonium, Hérelle, 1919.
    Offertoire pour la fête de l'Assomption, in The International
        Organist, Vol. II, p. 9.
    Pièces pour harmonium ou orgue, Consortium Musical
        (Hérelle), 1930.
    Scherzo, Senart (Philippo).
    Trois Pièces (Cortège; Andantino; Rapsodie sur des Noëls),
        Philippo.
ALAIN, JEHAN ARISTE. born St. Germain-en-Laye, France,
    Feb. 3, 1911; died Petit Puy, June 20, 1940. At age 13,
    assistant organist, St. Germain-en-Laye; pupil of Dupré, Paul
    Dukas, and Roger-Ducasse; organist, Maisons-Laffite; 1936,
    prize for composition, Les Amis de l'Orgue; 1939, honorary
    mention in Performance and Improvisation, Les Amis de l'Orgue.

Oeuvres, 3 vols., Leduc, 1943:
    Vol. 1: Suite--Introduction et Variations-Scherzo-
        Choral; Trois Danses: Joies-Deuils-Luttes (1939).
    Vol. 2: Variations sur un thème de Clément Janne-
        quin; Le Jardin suspendu; Aria; Deux danses à
        Agni Yavishta; Prélude et Fugue; Intermezzo;
        Litanies (1938).
    Vol. 3: 1er Prélude; 2e Prélude; Climat (1930);
        1re Fantaisie; 2e Fantaisie; Lamento; Petite
        Pièce; Monodie; Berceuse sur deux notes qui
        cornent; Ballade en mode Phrygien; Grave; Varia-
        tions sur Lucis Creator; Postlude pour l'Office de
        Complies; Page 21 de 8e Cahier de notes de Jehan
        Alain.
    Deux Chorals, (Hérelle) Philippo.
ALAIN, OLIVIER. born St. Germain-en-Laye, France, Aug. 3,
    1918. License-en-lettres, Sorbonne; since 1960, Director,
    Ecole César Franck, Paris.
    Lacrymae, in Le Tombeau de Gonzalez, Orgue et Liturgie,
        Vol. 38, p. 21.
    Offertoire--Fantaisie pour le 2e dimanche après l'Epiphanie,
        in Offertoires, Orgue et Liturgie, Vol. 52, p. 5.
    Prélude, Introït-Récitatif pour le 2e dimanche après
        l'Epiphanie, in Préludes à l'Introït, Orgue et Liturgie,
        Vol. 48, p. 3.
    Récit pour l'Elévation, in Elévations, Orgue et Liturgie,
        Vol. 57, p. 5.
    Suite (Prélude; Impromptu; Ricercare; Air; Final), Leduc.
ALBERTI, JOHANN FRIEDRICH. German. born 1642; died 1710.
    Organist, Cathedral, Merseburg, Germany.
    Der du bist, in Choralvorspiel alter Meister, p. 5; also
        in Seasonal Chorale Preludes, Book II.
    Herr Gott dich loben wir, in Chorale Preludes by Masters
        of the XVII and XVIII Centuries.
    Herzlich lieb, in The Church Organist's Golden Treasury,
        Vol. II; The First Four Centuries of Organ Music,
        Vol. II, p. 315; also in Orgel Choräle Sammlung.
    Te Deum, in Orgelchoräle um J. S. Bach.
    compositions in Elf Orgelchoräle des siebzehnten Jahrhun-
        derts.
    compositions in Das Erbe deutschen Musik, Series I, Vol. 9.
    compositions in Eighty Chorale Preludes of the Seventeenth
        and Eighteenth Centuries.
    compositions (2) in Orgel Kompositionen aus neuer und alter
        Zeit.
ALBINONI, TOMMASO. born Venice, June 8, 1671; died Venice,
    Jan. 17, 1750. Violinist; composer of opera, instrumental
    music; both Walther and Bach made transcriptions for organ
    of his works.
    Sonata opera sesta (no. 6), Bärenreiter.
    Three Sonatas for Violin and Clavier, Bärenreiter.
    compositions in Masterpieces of Organ Music, Folio 39.
    see Konzert in F dur, arranged for organ by J. G. Walther

in Walther Orgelkonzerte, Bärenreiter, 1920.
ALBRECHTSBERGER, JOHANN GEORG. born Klosterneuburg, Germany, Feb. 3, 1736; died Vienna, Mar. 7, 1809. A student with Michael Haydn in Vienna; organ-clavier maker; 1772, court organist, Vienna; successor to Mozart, assistant choirmaster, 1792, director, St. Stephen's Cathedral, Vienna.
Fugen (12), Op. 1, Leuckart.
Fuge (C Major), Op. 4, Leuckart.
Fuge über den Thema do, re, mi, fa, sol, la, Op. 5, Leuckart.
Fugen und Präludien (6), Op. 6, Leuckart.
Fugen (6), Op. 11, Leuckart.
Fugen (6), Op. 18, Leuckart.
Fuge (B-flat Major), Königliche Adademie der Künste, Auswahl vorzüglicher Musik-Werke No. 33.
Fugue (D Minor), C. S. Lang, ed. , Cramer.
Fugue (E-flat), C. S. Lang, ed. , Cramer.
Fugues (12), Novello.
Ite, Missa est, Alleluia, in Pâques, Vol. 1, p. 17.
Prelude, in Organ Book No. 2, p. 18.
Prelude and Fugue (D Major), Universal Edition 9578.
Six Trios, Novello.
Twelve Trios, Novello.
Versetten (44) oder kurze Vorspiele, Leuckart.
chorale preludes (3) in Preludien Buch (Reinbrecht).
chorale preludes (2) in Zorn's Preludien, Heinrichshofen.
fugues on Easter Themes (2), Böhm.
ALCOCK, JOHN. born London, Apr. 11, 1715; died Lichfield, Feb. 23, 1806. Chorister under Charles King at St. Paul's Cathedral; at age 14, pupil of John Stanley; 1737, organist, St. Andrews, Plymouth; 1742, organist, St. Lawrence, Reading; 1750, organist, Lichfield Cathedral; 1755, B. Mus. degree; 1761, Doc. Mus. , Oxford; 1761-1786, organist, Parish Church, Sutton Coldfield; 1766-1790, organist, St. Editha's, Tamworth.
Four Voluntaries, in Tallis to Wesley, Vol. 23 (1961).
ALCOCK, WALTER GALPIN. born Edenbridge, Kent, England, Dec. 29, 1861; died Salisbury, Sept. 11, 1947. 1896-1916, assistant organist, Westminster Abbey; 1902, organist, Chapels Royal; 1916, organist, Salisbury Cathedral; Doc. Mus. , Durham University; Member of the Victorian Order; 1933, knighted.
Fantasia Impromptu, Novello.
Introduction and Passacaglia, Oxford, 1934.
Marche Triomphale, Novello.
Twelve Short Introductory Voluntaries, Novello.
ALDROVANDINI, GIUSEPPE ANTONIO VINCENZO. born Bologna, Italy, 1665; died Bologna, Feb. 9, 1707. Pupil of Perti; 1695, began teaching, Bologna Accademia Filarmonica and in 1702 became principal of that body; choirmaster to Duke of Mantua.
Pastorale, in Classici Italiani dell'Organo, p. 139.
ALVORADO, DIOGO DE. Spanish. died 1643.
Tiento (Pange Lingua), in Old Spanish Organ Music, p. 5.

ALWOOD (ALLWOOD, ALWOODE), RICHARD. English. born ca.
1550.
  In Nomine, in Liber Organi, Vol. X, p. 6.
  Voluntary; Claro paschali gaudio, in Altenglische Orgel-
      musik, pp. 16, 20.
  compositions (4) in The Mulliner Book
AMELLÉR, ANDRÉ-GABRIEL. born Arnaville (Meurthe et Moselle),
France, Jan. 2, 1912. Composition pupil of Roger-Ducasse
and Tony Aubin at the Conservatory, Paris; 1937-1953,
contrabassist, Opéra, Paris; 1953, became Director, Ecole
Nationale de Musique et d'Art Dramatique, Dijon.
  Suite pour Claviers dans le style ancien, Philippo.
  Toccata, in Toccata, Orgue et Liturgie, Vol. 10, p. 19.
AMMERBACH, ELIAS NIKOLAUS. born Naumburg, Germany, ca.
1530; died Leipzig, Jan. 27, 1597. 1560-1595, organist,
Thomaskirche, Leipzig; Orgel oder Instrument Tabulatur
(Leipzig, 1571); Ein new künstlich Tabulaturbuch (Leipzig,
1575); re-edition Orgel oder Instrument Tabulaturbuch (Nürn-
berg, 1583).
  O Welt, ich muss, in Orgelmusik der Reformationzeit.
  Passamezzo, in Historical Anthology of Music, Vol. 1,
      p. 171.
ANDERSEN, AKSEL. born Ruskin, Nebraska, Mar. 1, 1912. 1932,
organist, Vartov, Denmark; 1933-1948, organist, St. Jacobi,
Varde; 1948-1955, organist, St. Paul's Church, Aarhus;
1956-1959, organist, Eliaskirken; 1955, appointed Professor,
Conservatory, Copenhagen; since 1959, organist, Christians-
borg Castle Church.
  Fantasi över koralen "Krist stod op af döde," in Musica
      Organi, Vol. 3, p. 29.
ANDREWS, GEORGE WHITFIELD. born Wayne, Ohio, Jan. 19,
1861; died Honolulu, Hawaii, Aug. 18, 1932. 1879, graduated,
Oberlin Conservatory; pupil of Jadassohn, Rheinberger, Guil-
mant, and d'Indy; 1886, became teacher, 1892, Professor of
Organ and Composition, Oberlin Conservatory; 1903, Mus. D.,
Oberlin Conservatory; founder, American Guild of Organists.
  Con grazia, J. Fischer.
  Fugue (A Minor), in The International Organist, Vol. I, p. 9.
  Processional March, J. Fischer.
  Three Pieces, J. Fischer.
ANDRIESSEN, HENDRIK. born Haarlem, The Netherlands, Sept. 17,
1892. Studied at the Conservatory, Amsterdam; pupil of
Zweers and dePauw; 1916-1936, organist, Haarlem; 1934,
became teacher, 1937, Director, Utrecht Conservatory; Pro-
fessor of composition, Conservatory, Amsterdam; 1949, ap-
pointed director, Royal Conservatory, The Hague; 1934-1949,
organist, Roman Catholic Cathedral, Utrecht.
  Chorale No. 1 (1913), H. W. Gray; Van Rossum R. 273.
  Chorale No. 4, Donemus 952; Van Rossum R. 259.
  Concerto, organ and orchestra, miniature score, Donemus
      173.
  Deuxième Choral, Van Rossum R. 535.
  Intermezzi (1943), 2 vols., Van Rossum R. 204 and R. 255.

Intermezzo, in Cantantibus Organis, Vol. II, p. 14.
O Filii et Filiae, in Anthology of Organ Music, Vol. 2,
    Hinrichsen.
Offertoire "Assumpta est Maria," in A la Vierge, Orgue et
    Liturgie, Vol. 14, p. 25.
Passacaglia (1929), Marks; Van Rossum R. 172.
Pezzo Festoso (1962), Donemus 290.
Quattro Studi (1953), Van Rossum R. 376.
Quiet Interlude, in Preludes-Interludes-Postludes, Vol. 2,
    Hinrichsen 600b.
Sinfonia (1940), Van Rossum R. 232.
Sonata da Chiesa (1927), Marks; Van Rossum R. 184.
Suite, Van Rossum R. 548, 1969.
Thema met Variaties (1949), Van Rossum R. 341.
Third Choral (1920), Edition Le Grand Orgue; also Leduc;
    Van Rossum R. 465.
Toccata (1917), in The International Organist, Vol. I, p. 51;
    Van Rossum R. 277.
compositions in Advent to Whitsuntide, vols. 1 and 2, Hin-
    richsen 741A and 741B.
D'ANGLEBERT, JEAN-HENRI. born Paris, 1628; died Paris Apr.
    23, 1691. Pupil of Chambonnières; organist to Duke of
    Orleans; clavecinist to Louis XIV; wrote Pièces de clavecin
    ... avec le maniere de les jouer (1689).
    Fugue, in Liber Organi, Vol. I, p. 16.
    Fugue, in The First Four Centuries of Organ Music, Vol.
        II, p. 278.
    Quatuor sur le Kyrie, à trois sujets tirés du plein-chant,
        in Les Maîtres français de l'orgue, Vol. II, p. 33.
ANGLÈS, (PADRE) RAFAEL. born Rafales, Spain, 1731; died
    Valencia, Feb. 19, 1816. 1762-1772, organist, Cathedral,
    Valencia.
    composition in Elkan-Vogel Organ Series, Vol. 5.
ANNIBALE PADOVANO. born Padua, Italy, 1527; died Graz, Aus-
    tria, Mar. 15, 1575. 1552-1566, Second organist, San Marco,
    Venice; 1566, appointed maestro di cappella to Archduke Carl
    of Austria in Graz.
    Organ Compositions, Benetti, ed. , Zanibon 4435.
    Toccata VI tono, in Classici Italiani dell'Organo, p. 51.
    Treize ricercare, Noëlie Pierront, ed. , Paris: Hennebaine,
        1934.
    ricercari (2) in L'Arte Musicale in Italia, Vol. III, p. 79.
ANONYMOUS--English, Fifteenth Century.
    Orgeltabulierung: Puisque m'amour (Dunstable), in Geschichte
        der Musik in Beispielen, p. 31.
    Resurrexi ..., Haec dies ..., Alleluia ..., in Pâques,
        L'Organiste liturgique, Vol. 5.
ANONYMOUS--English, Seventeenth Century.
    Voluntary in D Minor for Double Organ, Watkins Shaw, ed. ,
        Novello EOM 4, 1960.
ANONYMOUS--English, Eighteenth Century.
    Voluntary in A Minor, Walter Emery, ed. , Novello EOM 17,
        1961.

ANONYMOUS--French, Fifteenth Century.
    Le Moulin de Paris, in Anthology of Early French Organ
        Music, p. 3.
ANONYMOUS--French, Seventeenth Century.
    Ave maris stella, 1er Ton (suite) and Pange lingua, in
        Pré-Classiques français, L'Organiste liturgique, Vol.
        18.
    Tombeau de Mazarin, in Cérémonies Funèbres, L'Organiste
        liturgique, Vol. 18, p. 6.
    compositions (9) in Pré-Classiques français, L'Organiste
        liturgique, Vol. 31.
ANONYMOUS--Gothic.
    Christ ist erstanden, in Liber Organi, Vol. VIII, p. 8.
ANONYMOUS--Italian, Seventeenth Century.
    Canzone, Ricercari, in 17th Century Keyboard Music in the
        Chigi MSS. of the Vatican Library, Corpus of Early
        Keyboard Music, No. 32, Vol. 1.
ANONYMOUS--Polish, Sixteenth and Seventeenth Centuries.
    compositions (9) in Keyboard Music from Polish Manuscripts,
        Corpus of Early Keyboard Music, No. 10, Vol. 4.
ANONYMOUS--Spanish, Seventeenth Century.
    Canción para la Corneta con el Eco, in Liber Organi, Vol.
        XI, p. 24.
    Galharda de 1º Tom, in Silva Iberica, p. 14.
    Obra de Quarto Tono, in Liber Organi, Vol. XI, p. 11.
    Obra de Quinto Tono, in Liber Organi, Vol. XI, p. 13.
    Quatro Piezes de Clarines, in Liber Organi, Vol. XI, p. 19.
    Xácara de 1º Tono, in Silva Iberica, p. 14.
ANTEGNATI, COSTANZO. born Brescia, Italy, ca. 1549; died
    Brescia, Nov. 16, 1624. From family of organ builders;
    1584, organist, Cathedral, Brescia; wrote treatise L'Arte
    organica (Brescia, 1608), new edition, Lunelli, ed. , Mainz,
    1938.
    L'Antegnata, Zanibon.
    Intavolatura de Ricercari d'Organo (1608), in Corpus of
        Early Keyboard Music, No. 9.
    ricercari (3), in L'Arte Musicale in Italia, Vol. III, p. 153.
ANTICO, ANDREA. born Montona (Istria), Italy, ca. 1470-1480;
    died Venice, ?. Priest; lived in Rome and Venice; pub-
    lished Frottole intabulate da sonare organi (1517) which was
    the first sixteenth-century printing of Italian tablatures of or-
    gan music.
    Frottola: Non resta in questa valle, in Classici Italiani
        dell'Organo, p. 31.
    Frottole Intabulate da sonare organi, in Knud Jeppesen:
        Die italienische Orgelmusik am Anfang des Cinquecento,
        Vol. 1, p. 3*-25*.
ARAUJO, PEDRO DE. Portuguese. Seventeenth Century.
    See Cravistas Portuguezes, Vol. II.
ARBATSKY, YURY. born Moscow, Russia, Apr. 15, 1911. Pupil
    of Rachmaninoff; 1932, graduated, Leipzig Conservatory;
    worked in Belgrade and Prague; 1944, received doctorate,
    Charles University; 1949, came to United States; organist-

director, Salem Lutheran Church, Chicago, Ill.
Leiturgia, Peters ZM 372.
Partita on Jesu, meine Zuversicht, Merseburger.
Passacaglia, Peters ZM 396.
Sursum Corda (7 chorale preludes), Gertners (Peters ZM
    374).
chorale preludes (3) in The Parish Organist, Vols. 1-4.
ARCHER, VIOLET BALESTRERI.   born Montreal, Canada, Apr. 24,
1913. Studied at McGill University and at Yale University;
pupil of Hindemith and Bartók; 1950-1953, faculty member,
North Texas State College; 1953-1961, faculty member, Univer-
sity of Oklahoma; 1961, returned to Canada; 1962, became
faculty member, University of Alberta, Edmonton.
    Two Chorale Preludes, Peer International Corp. , New York,
        1962.
ARESTI, GIULIO CESARE.   born Bologna, Italy, 1617;   died Bologna,
1692 or 1694.
    Elevazione, Ricercare, in L'Arte Musicale in Italia, Vol.
        III, p. 405.
    Ten Sonatas, (Peters EM 881).
ARMSDORFF, ANDREAS. German. born 1679;   died 1699. Organist, Erfurt, Germany.
    Allein Gott, in The Church Organist's Golden Treasury,
        Vol. I, p. 22.
    Allein Gott, in The First Four Centuries of Organ Music,
        Vol. II, p. 430.
    Herr Jesu Christ, dich zu uns wend, in Chorale Preludes
        by Masters of the Seventeenth and Eighteenth Centuries,
        p. 4.
    Komm, heiliger Geist, in Eighty Chorale Preludes of the
        Seventeenth and Eighteenth Centuries, p. 81;   also in
        Orgelspiel im Kirchenjahr, Vol. 1.
    Komm, heiliger Geist, in Laudamus Dominum, p. 8.
    Wie schön leuchtet, in The Church Organist's Golden
        Treasury, Vol. III, p. 171;   also Körner.
    chorale prelude in Elf Orgelchoräle des siebzehnten Jahr-
        hunderts.
    chorale preludes (4) in Orgelchoräle um J. S. Bach.
    compositions in Das Erbe deutschen Musik, Series I, Vol. 9.
ARNATT, RONALD. born London, Jan 16, 1930. Attended Westminster Abbey and King's College, Cambridge, choir schools;
1945, went to Trent College; 1954, B. Mus. , Durham University; after 1947, served several Washington, D. C. , churches;
1951-1954, taught at American University, Washington, D. C. ;
since 1954, Organist-Choirmaster, Christ Church Cathedral,
St. Louis, Mo. ; 1968, Associate Professor of Music, University of Missouri, St. Louis; 1970, honorary Doc. Mus. ,
Westminster Choir College.
    Five Preludes on Hymn Tunes (Slane, Lancashire, Malabar,
        Down Ampney, Innocents), Concordia.
    Prelude on Nicholson, in Deo Gloria, McLaughlin and Reilly.
    Procession, H. W. Gray (St. Cecilia Series 860).
    Three Plainsong Preludes (Divinum Mysterium, Antiphon to

the Benedictus for Good Friday Tenebrae, Victimae
Paschali), H. W. Gray, 1970.
Three Preludes on Hymn Tunes in the Worship Supplement
(Gloria, Love Unknown, Jam Lucis), Concordia.
Two Preludes on Plainsong Melodies (Pange lingua, Christe
Redemptor), H. W. Gray (St. Cecilia Series 945).
Variations on a Theme by Leo Sowerby (Palisades), H. W.
Gray, 1970.
compositions in The Parish Organist, vols. 11 and 12.
ARNE, THOMAS AUGUSTINE. born London, March 12, 1710; died
London, March 5, 1778. Studied at Eton; wrote music for
dramatic works; 1759, received honorary Doc. Mus. , Oxford;
wrote Six Favourite Concertos for the Organ, Harpsichord, or
Piano Forte, 1787.
Air (A), Cramer.
Ayre and Gavot, Cramer.
Concerto V (G Minor), organ and strings, Bärenreiter NMA
210; also in English Organ Music of the Eighteenth
Century, Vol. II, Vernon Butcher, ed. , Hinrichsen 293.
Flute Solo, in Elkan-Vogel Organ Series, Vol. 2, 1947.
Gig, Cramer.
Invention, Cramer.
Maggot, Cramer.
Two Tunes, Cramer.
ARNELL, RICHARD. born London, Sept. 15, 1917. Pupil of John
Ireland; 1935-1938, studied at the Royal College of Music;
1939-1947, conducted in New York; 1948, returned to London.
Andantino, Peer International Corp. , New York.
Baroque Prelude and Fugue, H. W. Gray (Contemporary
Organ Series 20).
Choral Variations on Ein' feste Burg, Hinrichsen 551 E.
Classical Sonata, Hinrichsen 551 B.
Ein' feste Burg, in Organ Preludes Ancient and Modern.
Fugal Flourish, Hinrichsen 551 C.
Sonata, Op. 21, No. 2, Hinrichsen 551 A.
Three Related Pieces, Hinrichsen 6001.
ARNOLD, CORLISS RICHARD. born Monticello, Ark. , Nov. 7,
1926. 1946, B. Mus. , Hendrix College; 1948, M. Mus. ,
University of Michigan; 1948-1952, organist-director of music,
First Methodist Church, El Dorado, Ark. ; 1954, Sac. Mus.
Doc. , Union Theological Seminary, New York City; 1954-1959,
Director of Music-organist, First Methodist Church, Oak Park,
Ill. ; 1956-1957, Fulbright Fellow to France; pupil of Glenn
Metcalf, Charles Peaker, Vernon de Tar, André Marchal, and
Nadia Boulanger; composition pupil of Leo Sowerby, Seth
Bingham, and Normand Lockwood; since 1959, faculty mem-
ber, Michigan State University; since 1959, Director of Music-
Organist, Peoples Church, East Lansing, Mich.
Fantasy, Choral, and Toccata on Veni Emmanuel, in Ameri-
can Organ Music, Vol. I, p. 9.
ATTAINGNANT, PIERRE. French. born end of fifteenth century;
died probably in Paris, before July, 1553. Music printer,
seller.

Deux livres d'orgue parus en 1531, Yvonne Rokseth, ed. ,
    Series I, No. 1 of Publications de la Société Française
    de Musique, Heugel, Paris, 1925 (reprint 1967).
Sanctus, in Geschichte der Musik in Beispielen, p. 88.
Treize motets et un prelude pour orgue ... parus en 1531,
    Yvonne Rokseth, ed. , Series I, No. 5 of Publications
    de la Société Française de Musique, Heugel, Paris,
    1930 (reprint 1968).
Troisième verset du Magnificat du 8e ton, in Les Maîtres
    français de l'orgue, Vol. II, p. 1.
Tu devicto mortis, in Harold Gleason, Method of Organ
    Playing, p. 60.
ATWELL, RICHARD. American. born ca. 1770; died ?
    Christmas Suite (The Shepherds; The Angel Gabriel; The
    Chorus of Angels).
AVISON, CHARLES. baptised Newcastle-on-Tyne, England, Feb. 16,
    1709; died Newcastle-on-Tyne, May 9, 1770. Studied in Lon-
    don; 1736, became organist, St. John's Church, Newcastle.
    Second Organ Concerto, arr. Mathew, Oxford.

BABOU. French. Eighteenth Century.
    compositions (13) in Treize Pièces de Babou, Orgue et
        Liturgie, Vol. 43.
BACH, CARL PHILIPP EMANUEL. born Weimar, Germany,
    March 8, 1714; died Hamburg, Dec. 14, 1788. Fine cem-
    balist; served Fredrick of Prussia; lived in Berlin, Potsdam,
    Hamburg; published Versuch über die wahre Art, das Clavier
    zu spielen, Berlin, 1753 and 1762.
    Choral Fugue on Alles was Odem hat, Cramer.
    Concerto in E-flat Major, organ and strings, Wotquenne-
        Verzeichnis Nr. 35, Silorski 639, Berlin.
    Concerto in G Major, organ and strings, Wotquenne-
        Verzeichnis Nr. 34, Silorski 638.
    Fantasi och fuga (c-moll), in Musica Organi, Vol. I, p. 127.
    Fuga on the Letters of his Name, Oxford.
    Organ Sonatas, Jean Langlais, ed. , FitzSimons.
    Orgelwerke, Traugott Fedtke, ed. , 2 vols. , Peters 8009 a/b.
        Vol. 1: Six Sonatas.
        Vol. 2: Preludes in D Major, F Major, D Minor,
            Fantasies and Fugues in C Minor, F Major, and
            E-flat Major.
    Prelude and Six Sonatas, (Peters H U 569).
    Six Pieces for a Musical Clock, Ludwig Altman, ed. , World
        Library of Sacred Music.
    Solfeggio, Cramer.
    Wer weiss wie nahe mir mein Ende, in Reinbrecht Prelu-
        dien Buch, Viewig.
    compositions in Masterpieces of Organ Music, Folios 12 and
        30.
BACH, HEINRICH. born Wechmar, Germany, Sept. 16, 1615; died

Arnstadt, July 10, 1692. 1641, became organist, Liebfrauen-
und Oberkirche, Arnstadt; Stadtmusikus, Arnstadt.

    Christ ist erstanden, in The Church Organist's Golden
        Treasury, Vol. I, p. 77; in Orgel Choräle Sammlung.

    Have Mercy, Lord, Historical Recital Series, H. W. Gray.

    compositions in Masterpieces of Organ Music, Folio 19.

BACH, JOHANN BERNHARD. born Erfurt, Germany, Nov. 23,
1676; died Eisenach, June 11, 1749. ca. 1695, became
organist, Kaufmanns-Kirche, Erfurt; went to Magdeburg;
1703, became organist, ducal chapel, Eisenach, at court of
Duke Johann Wilhelm; also organist, St. Georg.

    Du Friedefürst, Herr Jesu Christ, in The Church Organist's
        Golden Treasury, Vol. I, p. 123.

    Four Variations on Thou Prince of Peace, H. W. Gray.

    Partita über Du Friedefürst, in Choralvorspiel alter Meister,
        p. 12.

    Vom Himmel hoch, in The Church Organist's Golden Trea-
        sury, Vol. III, p. 90.

    chorale preludes (2) in Orgelchoräle um J. S. Bach.

    compositions in Das Erbe deutschen Musik, Series I, Vol. 9.

    compositions in Masterpieces of Organ Music, Folio 12.

BACH, JOHANN CHRISTIAN. born Leipzig, Germany, Sept. 5,
1735; died London, England, Jan 1, 1782. Studied under C.
P. E. Bach in Berlin; later went to Bologna to study with
Padre Martini; 1760-1762, organist, Cathedral, Milan; opera
composer; 1762, went to England; appointed music master to
the queen.

    Concerto in F Major, organ strings, Op. 7, No. 2, Asso-
        ciated Music Publishers.

    Fuga (c-moll), in Musica Organi, Vol. I, p. 127.

    chorale prelude in The Church Organist's Golden Treasury,
        Vol. II, p. 147.

BACH, JOHANN CHRISTOPH. born Arnstadt, Germany, Dec. 8,
1642. died Eisenach, March 31, 1703. Son of Heinrich Bach
in Arnstadt line; 1665, became organist, Georgenkirche,
Eisenach; 1700, appointed court musician, Eisenach.

    Eleven Chorale Preludes, in Masterpieces of Organ Music,
        Folio 41.

    In Gottes Namen fahren (Dies sind die heiligen Zehn Gebot),
        in Choralvorspiele zum Kirchenlied, Vol. 2.

    Präludium und Fuge (E-flat Major), in Historical Anthology
        of Music, Vol. II, p. 106.

    Vater unser, in Notre Père, Orgue et Liturgie, Vol. 24,
        p. 7.

    44 Choräle zum Präambulieren (all manualiter), Bärenreiter
        285; also Kalmus 3095.

    Wenn wir in höchsten Nöthen sein, in Gleason, Method of
        Organ Playing, p. 136.

    Wie schön leuchtet, in Organ Preludes Ancient and Modern,
        Vol. 3.

    chorale preludes (4) in Chorale Preludes by Masters of the
        Seventeenth and Eighteenth Centuries.

    chorale preludes (2) in The Church Organist's Golden

Treasury, Vol. III, pp. 136, 177.
chorale preludes (5) in Eighty Chorale Preludes: German
    Masters of the Seventeenth and Eighteenth Centuries.
chorale preludes (2) in Laudamus Dominum.
chorale preludes (4) in Orgel Choräle Sammlung.
chorale preludes in Orgelspiel im Kirchenjahr, Vol. I (4);
    Vol. 2 (2).
chorale preludes (2) in The Parish Organist, Vol. 1-4.
chorale preludes in Seasonal Chorale Preludes, Book 1 (1);
    Book 2 (1).
chorale preludes (2) in Zorn's Preludien, Heinrichshofen.
BACH, JOHANN CHRISTOPH FRIEDRICH. born Leipzig, Germany,
    June 21, 1732; died Bückeburg, Jan. 26, 1795. 1750-1795,
    served Count Wilhelm of Bückeburg; pupil of Agricola, Homi-
    lius, Kirnberger, Altnikol, Kittel, and Müthel.
    Warum sollt ich mich, in Orgel Choräle Sammlung
        chorale preludes (2) in The First Four Centuries of
        Organ Music, vol. II, p. 306.
    chorale preludes (4) in Laudamus Dominum.
    composition in Anthologia Antiqua, Vol. 2, J. Fischer.
BACH, JOHANN MICHAEL. born Arnstadt, Germany, Aug. 9, 1648;
    died Gehren, May 1694. 1673-1694, organist, Gehren (near
    Arnstadt); father of J. S. Bach's first wife, Maria Barbara.
    Von Gott, in Choralvorspiel alter Meister, p. 17.
    Wenn mein Stündlein vorhanden ist, in The Church Organist's
        Golden Treasury, Vol. III, p. 132; Eighty Chorale
        Preludes: German Masters of the Seventeenth and
        Eighteenth Centuries, p. 116; The First Four Cen-
        turies of Organ Music, p. 336; also in Choralvorspiele
        zum Kirchenlied, Vol. 3; also in Orgel Choräle
        Sammlung; also H. W. Gray.
    Wenn wir in höchsten Nöthen sein, in The Parish Organist,
        Vol. 1-4, p. 188; also in Chorale Preludes by Mas-
        ters of the Seventeenth and Eighteenth Centuries, p.
        15; also in Orgelspiel im Kirchenjahr, Vol. 2.
    chorale preludes (2) in Orgelchoräle um J. S. Bach, Frot-
        scher, ed. , M. Litolff.
    composition in Elf Orgelchoräle des siebzehnten Jahrhunderts.
    composition in Masterpieces of Organ Music, Folio 12.
    compositions in Das Erbe deutschen Musik, Series I, Vol. 9.
BACH, JOHANN SEBASTIAN. born Eisenach, Germany, Mar. 21,
    1685; died Leipzig, July 28, 1750. (For a more detailed
    sketch of J. S. Bach's life, see the chapter in Part I on his
    works.)
    Note: The works listed below are found in the anthologies
    whose titles are given at the beginning of this catalog, arrange-
    ments of Bach's works for organ and other instruments, col-
    lections arranged for the organ such as The Art of the Fugue,
    and various organ works of Bach in separate editions whose
    titles are found in current catalogs of organ music publishers.
    Also see the appendix Organ Works of Bach: Pagination in
    Standard Editions.
    (The) Art of the Fugue, Bärenreiter 5193; also Schurich,

ed. , Müller 6 and 7; also see Kunst der Fuge.
Complete Organ Works, 10 vols. , Augener.
Composizioni scelti, 5 vols. , Matthey-Ferrari, ed. , Ricordi
    2271-2275: Composizioni facili; Composizioni di me-
    dia difficoltà; Corali; Preludi e fughe; Composizioni
    difficili.
Drei Orgelchoräle (Wer nur; Vor deinen Thron; Vater
    unser), Merseburger SM 8.
Eight Short Preludes and Fugues, Straube, ed. , Peters
    4442; also Widor and Schweitzer, eds. , G. Schirmer
    1456.
Fantasia C-dur, BWV 573, Merseburger 811.
Fantasy and Fugue in G Minor, in Geschichte der Musik in
    Beispielen, p. 421.
Four Duets, Peters 4465.
Fuga (G-dur), in Musica Organi, Vol. I, p. 60.
In dulci jubilo, in Alte Meister, p. 4; all three settings
    arranged as a group, Peters 356.
In dulci jubilo, in Musica Organi, Vol. I, p. 34.
Kleine Präludien und Fugen, BWV 553-560, Werner Tell,
    ed. , Merseburger 807.
(Der) Kunst der Fuge, Helmut Walcha, ed. , Litolff, 1967.
Lord Jesus Chirst, We Humbly Pray, in Organ Music for
    the Communion Service, p. 45.
(The) Musical Offering, Peters 219; also H. Walcha, ed. ,
    Peters 4835; also Falcinelli, ed. , (Peters SCH 105).
My Spirit, Be Joyful, organ and two trumpets, E. Power
    Biggs, ed. , Mercury Music Press.
Now Thank We All Our God, organ and trumpet, E. Power
    Biggs, ed. , Mercury Music Press.
Orgelbüchlein, Bärenreiter 145; also Kalmus 3094.
(Die) Orgelchoräle aus der Leipziger Original-handschrift,
    Bärenreiter NBA 5009.
Orgelchoräle manualiter, Bärenreiter NBA 378.
Prelude, Trio and Fugue in B-flat, Walter Emery, ed. ,
    Novello EOM 12, 1959 (No BWV catalog number was
    assigned to this composition because it had not been
    discovered at the time Schmieder was making the
    catalog.)
Preludium (B-flat Major), in Musica Organi, Vol. I, p. 52.
Preludium (G Major), in Musica Organi, Vol. I, p. 56.
Sechs Choräle (Schübler), BWV 645-650, Hans Schmidt-
    Mannheim, ed. , Merseburger 870.
Three Wedding Chorales, organ and two trumpets, E. Power
    Biggs, ed. , Mercury Music Press.
Trio (Aria), in Schule des klassischen Triospiels, p. 16.
Two Fanfares and Chorale, organ, three trumpets, timpani,
    E. Power Biggs, ed. , Mercury Music Press.
Vater unser, in Historical Anthology of Music, Vol. II,
    p. 15.
Works for the Small Organ, H. Keller, ed. , Peters 4510.
chorale preludes (11) in The Church Organist's Golden
    Treasury, Vol. I.

chorale preludes (14) in The Church Organist's Golden
Treasury, Vol. II.
chorale preludes (13) in The Church Organist's Golden
Treasury, Vol. III.
chorale preludes (2) in Laudamus Dominum.
compositions (11) in Harold Gleason, Method of Organ
Playing.
compositions in The Parish Organist, Vols. 1-4, 5, 6, 7,
8. 10.

BACH, WILHELM FRIEDEMANN. born Weimar, Germany, Nov. 22,
1710; died Berlin, July 1, 1784. Son and student of J. S.
Bach; Forkel indicates that Bach wrote the six sonatas for
W. F. Bach; pupil of Graun; 1733-1747, organist, Sophien-
kirche, Dresden; 1747-1764, organist, Liebfrauenkirche,
Halle; concertized.
Complete Works for Organ, E. Power Biggs, ed. , Mercury
Music Press, 1947; also Kalmus 3110; also Orgue
et Liturgie, Vol. 37.
Fuga (F Major), G. Ramin, ed. , Breitkopf & Härtel 6241.
Fughetta (G Minor), in A Brief Compendium of Early Organ
Music, p. 66; also in Musica Organi, Vol. I, p. 124.
Fugues (7), Peters (HU 558).
Huit fugues sans pédale, de Nys, ed. , Orgue et Liturgie,
Vol. 45.
Nun komm, in Viens, Sauveur, Orgue et Liturgie, Vol. 19,
p. 24.
Organ Works, 2 vols. , Traugott Fedtke, ed. , Peters 8010a/b.
Was mein Gott will, in The Church Organist's Golden Trea-
sury, Vol. III, p. 129; also in Orgel Choräle Samm-
lung.
Wir danken dir, in Historical Recital Series, H. W. Gray.
chorale preludes (3) in Choralvorspiel alter Meister.
chorale preludes (2) in Orgelchoräle um J. S. Bach.
compositions in Das Erbe deutschen Musik, Series I, Vol. 9.
compositions in Masterpieces of Organ Music, Folio 12.

BACHELET, ALFRED ANDRÉ. born Paris, France, Feb. 26, 1864;
died Nancy, Feb. 10, 1944. Studied at Conservatory, Paris;
student colleagues were Dukas, Gedalge, and Debussy; 1914-
1944, Director, Conservatory, Nancy.
Fantasy and Fugue (E-flat Minor), Durand, 1943.

BACKES, LOTTE. born Cologne, Germany, 1901. Studied at the
Academy of Arts, Berlin; concert pianist and organist.
Fantasia "De Ascensione Domini," Sirius.
Improvisation on an Original Theme, Novello.
In Sacratissima Nocte, Deutscher Verlag für Musik 8022.
Praeludium and Toccata, Novello.
Two Fantasies, Associated Music Publishers.
Zwei Orgelstücke, ("... et Spiritus Dei"; "... et repleti
sunt omnes"), Sirius.

BADEN, CONRAD. born Drammen, Norway, July 31, 1908. 1931,
completed organ studies, Oslo; 1932, studied in Leipzig and
Paris; music critic; since 1943, organist, Strømsø Church;
teacher, Conservatory, Oslo.

Fantasie and Fugue on Ljoset yver landet dagna, Norsk
Musikforlag.
Fem Orgelkoraler on melodies by Lindeman, Lyche 285.
Four Choral Preludes, Lyche 152.
Korset vil jeg (Toccata, Choral and Fugue), Lyche 432.
Lux illuxit (Toccata, Choral, and Fugue), Lyche 121.
Preludium, Pastoral och Chaconne, in Musica Organi,
Vol. III, p. 58.
Twelve Organ Chorales, Lyche 544.
BADINGS, HENK. born Banding, Java, Jan. 17, 1907. Studied
composition with Pijper at Technical University, Delft, Nether-
lands; 1934, became Professor of composition, Amsterdam;
1937, became Director, Musieklyzeum, Amsterdam; 1941-
1945, Director, Royal Conservatory, Den Haag.
Canzona, C trumpet and organ, Donemus, 1971.
Canzona, oboe and organ, Donemus 128.
Concerto, organ and orchestra, miniature score, Donemus
177.
Dialogues, flute and organ, Donemus 474.
Intermezzo, violin and organ, Donemus 154.
It Is Dawning in the East, organ and guitar, Donemus 456.
Music for Organ and Electronic Tape (1971), World Library.
Passacaglia, organ and timpani, Donemus 172.
Passacaglia per Timpani e Organo (1970), Donemus 172.
Prelude and Fugue I (1952), Donemus 422.
Prelude and Fugue II (1952), Donemus 419.
Prelude and Fugue III (1953), Donemus 247.
Prelude and Fugue IV (1956), Donemus 288.
Preludium (1938), Donemus 420.
Preludium (from Preludium en Fuga II), in Cantantibus
Organis, Vol. II, p. 26.
Toccata (1929), Donemus 421.
BAIRSTOW, (SIR) EDWARD CUTHBERT. born Huddersfield, Eng-
land, Aug. 22, 1874; died York, May 1, 1946. 1894, Mus.
B., 1900, Mus. Doc., Durham University; 1899-1906, organ-
ist, Wigan; 1906-1913, organist, Leeds; organist, York
Minster; 1929, became Professor of Music, Durham Univer-
sity; honorary doctorates from Oxford and Leeds.
Legend (A-flat Major), Stainer & Bell.
Prelude (C), Cramer.
Prelude, Elegy and Toccata, Augener.
Prelude on Veni Emmanuel, Oxford.
Scherzo (A-flat Major).
Sonata (E-flat Major), Oxford, 1938.
Three Short Preludes, Oxford, 1947.
preludes (2) on plainsong melodies in Modern Organ Com-
posers, Vol. 3.
BALBASTRE, CLAUDE-BÉNIGNE. born Dijon, France, Jan. 22,
1727; died Paris, May 9, 1799. Pupil of his father and of
Rameau; 1756, became organist, St. Roch; 1760, made one
of several organists of Notre Dame, Paris; taught members
of the royal family; one of the organists, Versailles chapel.
Christmas Music, 2 vols., Kalmus 3116 and 3117.

Livre de Noëls, 3 vols., L'Organiste liturgique, Vols. 48,
    52, 55/56.
Noël with variations on Josef est bien marié, in A Treasury
    of Shorter Organ Classics, p. 27.
Prelude on Two Old French Noels, C. Dickinson, arranger,
    H. W. Gray.
Two noëls, in Les Maîtres français de l'orgue, Vol. I.
BALES, GERALD ALBERT. born Toronto, Canada, May 12, 1919.
Studied at Conservatory, Toronto; pupil of Healey Willan;
organist-choirmaster, St. Ann's Anglican Church and Rosedale
United Church, Toronto; 1959, became organist and choir-
master, St. Mark's Cathedral, Minneapolis, Minn.; 1971,
appointed to faculty, University of Ottawa, Ontario.
Fanfare for Easter Day, brass and organ, in Organ Music
    of Canada, Vol. I, p. 39.
Festival Fanfare, 3 trumpets, 3 trombones, snare drum,
    cymbal, organ, Summa (Art Masters).
Petite Suite, in Organ Music of Canada, Vol. II, p. 7.
Prelude (E Minor), in Organ Music of Canada, Vol. II,
    p. 68.
Three Ceremonial Fanfares, 3 trumpets, 3 trombones,
    timpani, Summa (Art Masters).
Two Preludes, H. W. Gray.
BALLARD, ROBERT. French. Sixteenth-seventeenth centuries.
Lutenist to Maria de Medici.
Courante, in Huit courantes, L'Organiste liturgique, Vol.
    58-59, p. 18.
BANCHIERI, ADRIANO. born Bologna, Italy, Sept. 3, 1568; died
Bologna, 1634. Pupil of Guami; became a monk in Monte
Oliveto monastery; 1588-1595, second organist, San Marco,
Venice (G. Gabrieli, first organist); 1596, organist, St.
Michele, Bosco (near Bologna); 1601-1607, at Santa Maria in
Regola, Imola; 1609, returned to Monte Oliveto where he
became abbot in 1620; wrote church music, madrigals, trea-
tises, dramatic works; wrote L'Organo suonarino (two editions,
1605, 1611) which contains organ music and exact rules for
figured bass accompaniment; he also wrote organ music found
in Diruta's Il Transilvano, Part II.
Dialogo, in Liber Organi, Vol. IV, p. 24; also in The
    First Four Centuries of Organ Music, Vol. I, p. 183.
Fantasia in Eco, in Cantantibus Organis, Vol. I, p. 9.
Orgelpreludia (6), Annie Bank.
Ricercare del quarto tono and seven other compositions,
    L'Arte Musicale in Italia, Vol. III, p. 353.
compositions (2) in Classici Italiani dell'Organo.
BARBE, HELMUT. born Halle (Saale), Germany, 1927. Pupil of
Ernst Pepping; 1952, appointed Kantor, St. Nicolai, Berlin-
Spandau; since 1955, instructor, Evang. Kirchenmusikschule,
Berlin-Spandau; 1970, became chairman, Protestant Church
Music Society, West Berlin.
Sonate (1964), Hänssler FH XVI, 7.
chorale preludes in Orgelbuch zum Evangelischen Kirchen-
    gesangbuch, Book 16 (1); Book 20 (1).

chorale preludes (6), in Orgelvorspiele.
BARBER, SAMUEL. born West Chester, Pa., Mar. 9, 1910.
Nephew of Louise Homer; studied at Curtis Institute, Philadelphia; pupil of Fritz Reiner; 1935, won Pulitzer Prize;
won American Rome prize; composer of orchestral and operatic works.
> Chorale Prelude on Silent Night, G. Schirmer, 1961.
> Toccata Festiva, organ, strings, trumpet, timpani, G.
> Schirmer.
> Variations on Wondrous Love, Op. 34 (1959), G. Schirmer,
> 1959.
BARBLAN, OTTO. born Scanfs, Engadin, Switzerland, Mar. 22,
1860; died Geneva, Dec. 19, 1943. 1878-1884, studied at the
Conservatory, Stuttgart; pupil of Lebert (organ) and Faisst
(organ and composition); 1885, teacher of voice, Canton school
in Chur; 1887, became organist, Cathedral of St. Pierre,
Geneva; 1888, appointed to composition and organ faculty,
Conservatory, Geneva.
> Andante mit Variationen, Op. 1, Rieter-Biedermann.
> Chaconne on B-A-C-H, Op. 10, Leuckart.
> Cinq Pièces, Op. 5, Peters 3878.
> Drei Stücke, Op. 22, Böhm (Augsburg).
> Gebet, Op. 8, Hug.
> Largo in the style of Handel, in The International Organist,
> Vol. II, p. 40.
> Passacaglia, Op. 6, Peters 3878 A
> Toccata, Op. 23.
> Variationen und Tripelfuge über B-A-C-H, National-Ausgabe,
> Hug.
> Vier Stücke, Op. 21, Peters 3878 B.
BARIÉ, AUGUSTIN. born Paris, 1883; died Antony, 1915. Studied
at the Institut des Jeunes Aveugles; pupil of Guilmant and
Vierne; 1906-1915, organist, St. Germain-des-Prés.
> Symphonie, Op. 5 (Prelude and Fugue in B-flat Minor;
> Adagio; Intermezzo; Finale), Durand, 1911.
> Trois Pièces, Op. 7 (Marche; Lamento; Toccata), Durand,
> 1911.
BARLOW, WAYNE. born Elyria, Ohio, Sept. 6, 1912. Studied at
Eastman and appointed to faculty there in 1937; pupil of
Schoenberg.
> Three Christmas Tunes, Concordia 97-4476.
> Voluntaries for the Hymn of the Week, 2 vols., Concordia
> 97-1453 (1963); 97-1456 (1964).
> chorale preludes (11) in Harold Gleason, Method of Organ
> Playing.
> hymn preludes (2) in The Parish Organist, Vols. 11 and 12.
BARNES, EDWIN SHIPPEN. born Seabright, N. J., Sept. 14, 1887.
Pupil of Horatio Parker, Vierne, and d'Indy; 1911, became
organist, Church of the Incarnation, New York City; organist,
Rutgers Presbyterian Church; Organist, St. Stephen's Church,
Santa Monica, Calif.
> Allegro Risoluto (D), H. W. Gray.
> Deux Pièces (Prélude solennel; Offertoire), Op. 5, Durand.

Petite Suite, Op. 23, Durand.
Prelude (C Major), in American Organ Music, Vol. I, p. 3.
Prelude and Festal Hymn, in The Modern Anthology, p. 1.
Scherzo.
Symphony I, G. Schirmer.
BARRAINE, ELSA. born Paris, Feb. 13, 1910. 1929, won Prix
de Rome; pupil of Busser and Dukas; studied at the Conser-
vatory, Paris.
Prélude et Fugue, Durand.
Deuxième Prélude et Fugue, Durand.
BARRETT, JOHN. English. born ca. 1674; died ca. 1735. Pupil
of John Blow.
Voluntary in C Major, in Tallis to Wesley, Vol. 21, p. 2.
BARTELINK, BERNARD. Dutch. born 1929. 1954, won Prix
d'excellence, Conservatory, Amsterdam; 1961, won improvisa-
tion competition, Haarlem; teacher, Institute of Church Music,
Utrecht; organist, Concertgebouw Orchestra, Amsterdam;
1971, became organist, St. Bavo's Roman Catholic Cathedral,
Haarlem.
Musica pro offertorio et sub communione, Gooi & Sticht
(Hilversum), 1970.
Partita Piccola super Lumen ad revelationem gentium, Van
Rossum R 460.
Prelude, Trio and Fugue, Donemus, 1960.
Toccata, Van Rossum R 400.
BASSANI, GIOVANNI BATTISTA. born Padua, Italy, ca. 1657;
died Bergamo, Oct. 1, 1716. Pupil of Castrovillari in Venice;
1677, became organist-choirmaster, Confraternità della Morte,
Ferrara; 1680, became choirmaster to Duke Alexander II of
Mirandola; 1682-1683, principe, Accademia dei Filarmonici;
1685, maestro di cappella, Accademia della Morte, Ferrara;
1688, became maestro, Cathedral, Ferrara; 1712, became
maestro, Basilica di Santa Maria Maggiore, Bergamo.
Larghetto, in Alte italienische Meister, p. 3.
composition in Masterpieces of Organ Music, Folio 25.
BASSETT, LESLIE. American. born 1923.
Toccata, American Composers Alliance, 2121 Broadway,
New York City, 10023.
BATISTE, ANTOINE-EDOUARD. born Paris, Mar. 28, 1820; died
Paris, Nov. 9, 1876. Taught at the Conservatory, Paris;
1842-1854, organist, St. Nicolas-des-Champs; organist, St.
Eustache.
Quatre Grands Offertoires de Ste. Cécile, Op. 7, 8, 9, 10,
G. Schirmer 891.
BATTISHILL, JONATHAN. born London, May 1738; died Islington,
Dec. 10, 1801. Choirboy, St. Paul's Cathedral, London;
organist, St. Clement, Eastcheap, and Christ Church, Newgate
St. , London.
Andante quasi allegretto, in Elkan-Vogel Organ Series,
Vol. 2, 1947.
Allegretto (A), Cramer.
Corant and Minuet, Cramer.
compositions (2) in Twelve Short Pieces by Old English

Composers.
BAUMANN, MAX. born Kronach/Oberfranken, Germany, Nov. 20,
1917. Composition pupil of Konrad Friedrich Noetel and Boris
Blacher at the Hochschule, Berlin; organ pupil of Otto Dunkel-
berg; 1949, appointed teacher of theory and composition, later
professor, Hochschule für Musik, Berlin.
Drei Stücke (Pesante; Vivo; Allegro rigoroso), Merse-
burger 863.
Fasciculus, Merseburger 864.
Invocation, Op. 67, No. 5, Sirius, 1962.
Konzert, organ, strings, and timpani, Op. 70, Merseburger
862.
Orgel-Suite, Op. 67, No. 1, Sirius, 1962.
Postludium über Es ist ein Ros', Op. 66, No. 2, Sirius,
1961.
Postludium über Nun lobet Gott, Op. 67, No. 4, Sirius,
1962.
Psalmi, organ and piano, Op. 67, No. 2 (also with baritone
solo), Sirius, 1962 (1968).
Sonatine, Merseburger 861.
BAUMGARTNER. Sixteenth century. Organ compositions by this
unknown composer are found in the Buxheimer Orgelbuch.
BAUMGARTNER, HENRY LEROY. born Rochester, Ind. , Aug. 6,
1891; died Sept. 18, 1969. Studied at Elkhart, Ind.; 1912,
graduated, Indianapolis Conservatory of Music; pupil of Jepson
and Horatio Parker at Yale University; 1916, B. Mus. , Yale;
taught harmony, counterpoint at Yale; organist-director,
Church of the Redeemer, New Haven, Conn.
Four Preludes, Op. 40 (E-flat, G Minor, C, F), Associated
Music Publishers.
Idyll, H. W. Gray.
Seven Preludes on Familiar Hymn Tunes, J. Fischer, 1957.
Solemn Procession, H. W. Gray.
Vision, in The Modern Anthology, p. 11.
BAUR, JÜRG. born Düsseldorf, Germany, Nov. 11, 1918. 1937,
studied at Staatlichen Hochschule für Musik, Cologne; com-
position pupil of Philipp Jarnach, organ pupil of Michael
Schneider; 1946, became teacher, 1964, Director, Robert-
Schumann-Konservatorium, Düsseldorf; 1952-1960, Kantor-
Chorleiter, Pauluskirche, Düsseldorf.
Partita über Aus tieffer Not, Breitkopf & Härtel 6505.
Toccata (1950), Breitkopf & Härtel 6230.
Trio und Passacaglia (1950), Breitkopf & Härtel 6289.
chorale preludes (4) in Orgelbuch zum Evangelischen
Kirchengesangbuch, Books 5, 12, 17, and 20.
BAUSTETTER, J. T. Netherlandish. Eighteenth Century.
Sarabande, in Oudnederlandse Meesters, Vol. I, p. 111.
BEACH, AMY MARCY CHENEY (MRS. H. H. A.) born Henniker,
New Hamp. , Sept. 5, 1867; died New York City, Dec. 27,
1944. Prodigy; concert pianist.
Prelude on an Old Folk Tune "The Fair Hills of Eire, O",
H. W. Gray (Contemporary Organ Series 15), 1943.
BEAUVARLET-CHARPENTIER, JEAN-JACQUES. born Abbeville,

France, June 28, 1734; died Paris, May 6, 1794. Organist,
St. Paul, Lyon; organist, Abbaye St. Victor, St. Paul, Notre
Dame, all in Paris.
> Fugue (G Minor), in Les Maîtres français de l'orgue, Vol.
> II, p. 82.

BEAUVARLET-CHARPENTIER, JACQUES-MARIE. born Lyon,
France, July 31, 1766; died Paris, Sept. 7, 1834. Became
organist at the following churches: St. Paul, Lyon; St.
Germain-l'Auxerrois, St. Germain-des-Prés, St. Eustache,
St. Paul-St. Louis, all in Paris.

BECK, CONRAD. born Schaffhausen, Switzerland, June 16, 1901.
Studied at the Conservatory, Zürich; pupil of Honegger and
Lévy; lived in Paris and Berlin; 1939, appointed radio con-
ductor, Basel, Switzerland.
> Choral Sonata, Schott 4149.
> Sonatina, Schott 2132.
> Two Preludes, Schott 2244.

BECK, THEODORE. born Oak Park, Ill. , 1929. Professor of
Music, Concordia Teachers College, Seward, Neb.
> Forty-Seven Hymn Intonations, Concordia 97-5018.
> Intonations for the Hymn of the Week, Concordia 97-4899.
> Soul, Adorn Thyself with Gladness, in Organ Music for the
> Communion Service, p. 20.
> chorale preludes in The Parish Organist, Vols. 10, 11, and
> 12.

BECKER, JOHN J. born Henderson, Ky. , Jan. 22, 1886; died
Wilmette, Ill. , Jan. 21, 1961. Pupil of Middleschulte; taught
and conducted, Notre Dame University and University of St.
Paul; 1939, became director, Federal Music Project, Minneapolis, Minn. : 1943, became Director of Music, Barat College
of the Sacred Heart, Lake Forest, Ill.
> Fantasia Tragica, H. W. Gray (Contemporary Organ Series
> 29).

BÉDOS DE CELLES, (DOM) FRANÇOIS. born Caux, France,
Jan. 24, 1709; died St. Denis, Nov. 25, 1779. Member of
the Benedictine Order; served in various cloisters, especially
the Cloister St. Croix, Bordeaux; wrote L'Art du Facteur
d'Orgues (1766-1778).

BEETHOVEN, LUDWIG VAN. born Bonn, Germany, Dec. 16, 1770;
died Vienna, Mar. 26, 1827. Pupil of Van den Eeden and
Neefe, court organists; 1784-1792, assistant organist at court
of Elector Max Franz; 1792, went to Vienna to perform and
compose; pupil of Haydn, Schenk, and Albrechtsberger; supported to some extent by Viennese nobility and aristocracy;
deafness and family problems caused great anguish; celebrated
composer of sonata, concerto, string quartet, operatic, and
symphonic forms.
> Orgelwerke, Ludwig Altman, ed. , Hinrichsen 1438, 1962:
>> Suite: Three Pieces for a Mechanical Organ (Adagio;
>> Scherzo; Allegro).
>> Two Preludes through the major keys for organ,
>> Op. 39.
>> Organ Fugue in D Major (1783).

Pièces en trio de claviers, Tournemire, ed. , Eschig.
Prélude circulaire, Op. 39, No. 1, Marcel Dupré, ed.
Prelude in E Minor, Marcel Dupré, ed.
Two Preludes in All Major Keys, Op. 39, Oesterreichischer
  Bundesverlag.
compositions in Masterpieces of Organ Music, Folio 48
  supplement.
BELL'HAVER (BELL'AVERE), Vincenzo. born Venice, Italy, 1530?;
  died Venice, Oct. 1587. Pupil of A. Gabrieli, whom he suc-
  ceeded in 1586 as first organist, San Marco, Venice; wrote
  organ Toccata found in Diruta's Il Transilvano, Part I.
  Toccata, in Anthologia Organistica Italiana, p. 16.
  Toccata, in L'Arte Musicale in Italia, Vol. III, p. 179.
BENCINI, GIUSEPPE. Tuscan? first half, eighteenth century.
  Fuga in G Major, in Classici Italiani dell'Organo, p. 168.
  Fuga; Sonata, in L'Arte Musicale in Italia, Vol. III, p. 409.
BENCRISCUTTO, FRANK. born Racine, Wis. , 1928. Director of
  Bands, University of Minnesota, Minneapolis, Minn.
  composition in The Parish Organist, Vol. 12.
BENDER, JAN. born Haarlem, The Netherlands, 1909. Pupil of
  Hugo Distler; organist-director of music, St. Jakobi, Frank-
  furt, Germany; Cantor, St. Michaelis, Lüneburg; Professor
  of composition, Wittenburg University, Springfield, Ohio;
  Professor of composition, Concordia College, Seward, Neb.
  Dreissig kleine Choralvorspiele, 3 vols. , Bärenreiter 2431,
    2434, 2429, 1949.
  Fantasy on Awake, my heart, with gladness, Concordia
    97-4467.
  Festival Preludes on Six Chorales, Concordia 97-4608, 1963.
  Four Variations on Down Ampney, Op. 47, Augsburg 11-
    0807, 1971.
  Hymn of the Week Organ Settings, Concordia 97-1444.
  Introduction, Fugue and Variations on Kremser, Abingdon.
  Lobe den Herren, in Voluntaries for the Christian Year,
    Vol. 1.
  New Organ Settings, 2 parts, Concordia 97-1454, 97-1461.
  O God, O Lord of Heaven and Earth, Augsburg 11-827.
  Partita on Our Father, Thou in Heaven Above, Augsburg,
    11-829.
  Phantasy on Come, Holy Ghost, God and Lord, organ,
    brass, cymbals, timpani, Concordia 97-1443 (parts
    97-4535/40 and 97-4566).
  Processional on All Glory, Laud and Honor, Concordia
    97-1396, 1956.
  Toccata, Aria and Fugue, Concordia 97-4396.
  Triptych (Toccata, Fugue and Aria), Concordia 97-4721.
  Twenty Short Organ Pieces, Concordia 97-3948.
  chorale preludes (2) in Organ Music for the Communion
    Service, pp. 18 and 35.
  chorale preludes (5) in Orgelbuch zum Evangelischen
    Kirchengesangbuch, Books 2, 5, 6, 10, and 14.
  chorale preludes (5) in Orgelvorspiele.
  chorale preludes in The Parish Organist, Vols. 1-4, 5, 6,
    7, 8, 9, 11, and 12.

BENGTSSON, GUSTAV. born Vadstena, Sweden, Mar. 29, 1886; died 1965. 1909-1912, pupil of H. Riemann and Paul Juon; 1916-1936, Director, Östagöta Singing Society; 1921, became teacher in the seminary, Karlstad; since 1942, in Linköping.

Korta förspel till samtliga koraler i 1921 års psalmbokstillägg, Abr. Lundquist.

Miniatyrer (5), Abr. Lundquist.

Preludier till samtliga koraler till svenska psalmboken av ar 1819, 2 vols., Abr. Lundquist.

Preludier till de nya koralerna av år 1937, Abr. Lundquist.

Preludier (33) till alternativa koraler i 1921 års psalmbokstillägg, Abr. Lundquist.

Preludiebok för skola och hem, Abr. Lundquist.

BENNETT, JOHN. English. born 1735; died 1784.

For Diapasons, Cramer.

Fugue (D Major), Transcriptions for Organ, Marchant, ed., 1895.

Prelude, Cramer

Voluntaries IX and X, H. Diack Johnstone, ed., Novello, 1966.

Voluntaries, No. 9, Patrick Williams, transcriber, Cramer, 1967.

BENNETT, ROBERT RUSSELL. born Kansas City, Mo., June 15, 1894. Student of Carl Busch; pupil of Nadia Boulanger; 1927, won Guggenheim Fellowship; studied in Paris, Berlin, and London; 1930, began working in Hollywood, Cal., as composer, conductor, pianist, arranger, and orchestrator.

Sonata, Cos Cob.

BENOIST, FRANÇOIS. born Nantes, France, Sept. 10, 1794; died Paris, May 6, 1878. 1811-1815, studied at the Conservatory, Paris; 1815, won Prix de Rome; 1819, became first organist at court; 1819-1872, Professor of organ, Conservatory, Paris.

compositions (3) in Les Maîtres français de l'orgue, Vol. II.

BENOIT, (DOM) PAUL. born Nancy, France, Dec. 9, 1893. 1925, became priest; 1933, became organist, Benedictine Abbaye St. Maurice et St. Maur, Clervaux, Luxembourg; pupil of M. Pierson (organist, Cathedral, Versailles).

Au Soir de l'Ascension, J. Fischer 7934, 1943.

Cantilène Pascale sur l'Alleluia, J. Fischer 8359.

(Le) Chant Interieur, J. Fischer 8841.

Deux Fantaisies (sur l'Introit Gaudeamus de l'Assomption; Sur l'alleluia du Dimanche de Pâques), Hérelle, 1946, Philippo.

Diptyque en l'honneur de Sainte Thérèse de l'Enfant Jésus (Evocation; 14 septembre 1897), Philippo.

Entrée Pontificale sur Resurrexi, J. Fischer 8362.

Esquisses Liturgiques, J. Fischer 9517.

Fifty Elevations on Modal Themes, J. Fischer 8323.

Forty-one Elevations for Harmonium, J. Fischer 8984.

Liturgical Suite for Easter, J. Fischer 8362, 8455, 8359, 8360.

Noël Basque, J. Fischer 7961, 1943.

Ode pour la Paix, J. Fischer 9286.

Pièces d'orgue, J. Fischer 8774.

Quatre Préludes, J. Fischer 8509.
Sept Pièces, Philippo.
Six Elévations pour la Messe XI, Philippo.
Sixty Devotional Pieces of Modal Themes, J. Fischer 9185.
Sortie on Ita, Missa est, J. Fischer.

BENTZON, NIELS VIGGO. born Copenhagen, Aug. 24, 1919. Pupil
of Knud Jeppesen and Emilius Bangert at Royal Conservatory,
Copenhagen; 1945, became teacher at the Conservatory, Aarhus; 1949, became a teacher at the Conservatory, Copenhagen.
Variationer, Op. 103, Hansen 28481.

BERG, GOTTFRID. born Stockholm, Jan. 29, 1889. 1909, graduated in organ and pedagogy (1915), Conservatory, Stockholm;
1916-1954, organist-choirmaster, Helga Trefaldighets Church,
Gävle; 1918-1944, music teacher, Gävle; 1931-1943, music
critic.
Lov vare dig, o Jesu Krist, koralpartita, in Musica Organi,
Vol. III, p. 135.

BERGMAN, ERIK. born Nykarleby, Finland, Nov. 24, 1911. 1931-
1933, studied at Helsingfors University and at Sibelius Music
Academy, and in Berlin, Vienna, and Paris; organist-
choirmaster, Catholic Church, Helsingfors; since 1947, music
critic.
Passacaglia och fuga c-moll, in Musica Organi, Vol. III,
p. 78.

BERLINSKI, HERMAN. born Leipzig, Germany, Aug. 18, 1910.
Studied at the Leipzig Conservatory and at the Ecole Normale
de Musique, Paris; pupil of Cortot and Boulanger; M. S. M.
and D. S. M., Seminary College, Jewish Theological Seminary
of America; Director of Music and Organist, Hebrew Congre-
gation, Washington, D. C.
(The) Burning Bush, H. W. Gray, 1957.
From the World of My Father, Mercury Music Corp.
In Memoriam (Prelude, 1958), Associated Music Publishers.
Kol Nidre, Mercury Music Corp.
Processional Music, Mercury Music Corp.
Sinfonia No. 3 (Sounds and Motions), H. W. Gray.
Three Preludes for Festivals, Mercury Music Corp.
Two Preludes for the High Holy Days, Mercury Music Corp.

BERLIOZ, HECTOR. born La Côte-Saint-André, Isère, France,
Dec. 11, 1803; died Paris, Mar. 8, 1869. Studied at the
Conservatory, Paris; pupil of Reicha and Lesueur; 1830,
won Prix de Rome; wrote for Paris newspapers; 1839, be-
came a Conservator, 1852, Librarian, of the Conservatory,
Paris; toured in Germany, Austria, Hungary, Russia, and
England; famous composer of operatic, oratorio, and sym-
phonic works.
Sérénade Agreste, Toccata, Hymn pour l'Elévation, in
Pièces romantiques ignorées, Organiste liturgique,
Vol. 17.

BERMUDO, JUAN. born Ecija (Seville), Spain, ca. 1510; died
after 1555. Franciscan Minorite friar; sixteenth-century
theorist; wrote Comiença el libro primero de la Declaración
de Instrumentos (Juan de Leon, Osuna, 1549, 1555).

Ave maris stella, in Organ Book, No. 1.
Oeuvres d'orgue, Orgue et Liturgie, Vol. 47.
Organ Pieces (13), Kalmus 3219.
Veni Creator Spiritus, in Harold Gleason, Method of Organ
    Playing.
compositions in Elkan-Vogel Organ Series, Vol. 5.
BERTELIN, ALBERT. born Paris, July 26, 1872; died Paris,
    June 19, 1951. Pupil of Théodore Dubois, Massenet, and
    Widor at the Conservatory, Paris; 1902, won Prix de Rome.
    Ave Maria, in Notre Dame, Orgue et Liturgie, Vol. II,
        p. 19.
BERTHIER, PAUL. born Auxerre, France, 1884; died 1953. Pupil
    of d'Indy; organist, Cathedral, Auxerre.
    Jam heims, in A la Vierge, Orgue et Liturgie, Vol. 14,
        p. 28.
    Passacaille sur Christus vincit, in Pâques, L'Organiste
        liturgique, Vol. 5, p. 16.
BEST, WILLIAM THOMAS. born Carlisle, England, Aug. 13, 1826;
    died Liverpool, May 10, 1897. Greatest English concert or-
    ganist of the nineteenth century; 1855-1894, organist, St.
    George's Hall, Liverpool.
    Chorale Preludes (3), Novello.
    Christmas Fantasies on Old Christmas Carols, Kalmus 3220.
    Christmas Fantasy on English Melodies, Augener.
    Fantasie on a Chorale from the Scotch Psalter, Augener.
    Fantasie on Dundee and Old 81, Augener.
    Introduction, Four Variations, and Finale on God save the
        Queen, Op. 29, Hinrichsen 260, 1953.
    Prelude on America, Boston Music Co.
    Sonata in G, Op. 38, Novello.
    Twelve Short Preludes on English Psalm Tunes, Augener;
        also Kalmus 3221.
BEYER, MICHAEL. German. born 1927. Church Music Director,
    Berlin, Germany.
    Orgelvorspiele, Merseburger.
    Sonata, viola and organ, Bärenreiter BA 4145.
    Toccata in Re, Sirius.
    Toccata Sub Communione (1970), Bote und Bock.
    chorale prelude in The Parish Organist, Vol. 12.
    chorale preludes (12) in Orgelvorspiele.
BIALAS, GUNTER. born Bielschowitz, Germany, July 19, 1907.
    1939, teacher of theory, Hochschulinstitut für Musikerziehung,
    University of Breslau; 1945, became Director of the Bach
    Society, Munich; 1947, became composition teacher, Musik-
    hochschule, Weimar; 1947, became composition teacher, di-
    rector, Northwest German Music Academy, Detmold.
    Sieben Meditationen, Bärenreiter 3976, 1965.
BICHSEL, M. ALFRED. born La Chaux-de-Fonds, Switzerland,
    1909. Professor of Music, Valparaiso University, Valparaiso,
    Ind.
    chorale prelude in The Parish Organist, Vol. 1-4.
BIJSTER, JACOB. born Haarlem, The Netherlands, Nov. 7, 1902;
    died 1958. Studied at the Conservatory, Haarlem; 1922,

became organist in Haarlem; 1924, received Prix d'excellence; 1929, appointed to faculty, Conservatory, Amsterdam.

Chorale, Trio, Introduction and Fugue on Song 217, Ars Nova.

Deuxième Choral, Ars Nova.

Eight Pslams with Preludes, Ars Nova.

Fantasy and Fugue on Psalm 68, Ars Nova.

Fantasy on Komt nu met zang (Gezang 146), Ars Nova.

Koraal, Trio en Fuga, (Gezang 227), Ars Nova.

Paraphrase on Gelukkig is het land, Ars Nova.

Partita on Gezang 45, Ars Nova.

Partita on My Saviour hangs upon the Cross, Ars Nova.

Passacaglia, Metro Muzik.

Prelude and Fughetta on Gezang 174 en 228, Ars Nova.

Ricercare, Ars Nova.

Toccata, Ars Nova.

Triptyque, Ars Nova.

Variations on Ich wil mij gaan vertroosten, Ars Nova.

Variations on Komt wilt u spoeden naar Bethlehem, Ars Nova.

Variations on Stort tranen uit, Ars Nova.

BINGHAM, SETH DANIELS. born Bloomfield, N. J., Apr. 16, 1882; died New York City, June 21, 1972. Pupil of Horatio Parker, d'Indy, Widor, Guilmant, and Jepson; 1908, B. Mus., Yale University; became music faculty member at Yale until 1919; 1912, appointed organist-choirmaster, Madison Avenue Presbyterian Church, New York City; 1920-1954, teacher of theory, Columbia University, New York City; faculty member, Union Theological Seminary, New York City.

Adoration, Op. 9, No. 2, H. W. Gray (St. Cecilia Series 273).

Agnus Dei (Communion), Op. 36, No. 2 (1939), J. Fischer 7508; H. W. Gray (St. Cecilia Series 922).

Annunciation, H. W. Gray

Aria, Op. 9, No. 5, H. W. Gray.

At the Cradle of Jesus (1943), Belwin-Mills

Baroques (Overture; Rondo Ostinato; Sarabande; Rhythmic Trumpet; Voluntary), Op. 41 (1944), Galaxy, 1944.

Bells of Riverside, Op. 36, No. 5 (1939), J. Fischer 7509.

Canonic Etude on Greensleeves, H. W. Gray.

Carillon de Chateau Thierry (Memories of France) (1936), H. W. Gray.

Concerto (G Minor), Op. 46 (1946), organ and orchestra, H. W. Gray.

Concerto, Op. 57, brass, snare drum, and organ, Belwin-Mills.

Connecticut Suite, Op. 56 (1953), organ, strings, optional parts for trumpet and trombone, H. W. Gray.

Counter-theme, Op. 9, No. 6, H. W. Gray (St. Cecilia Series 292).

Fantasy (C Major), Op. 50 (1949), in The Modern Anthology, p. 18.

First Suite, Op. 25 (1926) (Cathedral Strains; Intercession; Rhythm of Easter; Toccata), G. Schirmer.

(The) Good Shepherd, Galaxy, 1966.
Harmonies of Florence, Op. 27 (1929) (Florentine Chimes;
    Primavera; Savonarola; Twilight at Fiesole; March
    of the Medici), H. W. Gray.
He Is Risen, Op. 62 (1962), H. W. Gray.
Hymn Fantasy on Riverton (1957), in American Organ Music,
    Vol. 2.
Introit on Elton (1962), World Library of Sacred Music.
Modal Trio, in Harold Gleason, Method of Organ Playing,
    p. 140.
Nativity Song (1941), H. W. Gray (St. Cecilia Series 683).
Night Sorrow, Op. 36, No. 4 (1939), J. Fischer 7505.
Offertoire sur une chanson espagnole, in Le Tombeau de
    Gonzalez, Orgue et Liturgie, Vol. 38, p. 5.
Passacaglia, Op. 40 (1939), J. Fischer 7529.
Pastoral Psalms, Op. 30, Carl Fischer, 1938.
Pastorale (Memories of France), Op. 16, H. W. Gray
    (Contemporary Organ Series 11).
Pioneer America, Op. 26 (1928) (Redskin Rhapsody; Along
    the Frontier; Sailing over Jordan; Puritan Proces-
    sion), H. W. Gray.
Prelude and Fughetta (F Major), Op. 36, No. 1 (1939),
    J. Fischer 7504.
Prelude on St. Kevin (1962), Galaxy.
Roulade, Op. 9, No. 3, H. W. Gray (St. Cecilia Series
    264), 1920.
St. Flavian, Op. 9, No. 4, H. W. Gray (St. Cecilia Series
    255).
Seven Preludes or Postludes on Lowell Mason Hymns, Op.
    42, H. W. Gray, 1945.
Six Pieces, Op. 9 (1920-1923) (Prelude and Fugue in C;
    Adoration; Roulade; St. Flavian; Aria; Counter-
    theme), H. W. Gray.
Sonata of Prayer and Praise, Op. 60 (1960), H. W. Gray,
    1959.
Thirty-six Hymn and Carol Canons in Free Style, Op. 55
    (1952), H. W. Gray, 1952.
Toccata on Leonie, Op. 36, No. 3 (1939), J. Fischer,
    1940; H. W. Gray (St. Cecilia Series 858).
Twelve Hymn Preludes, Op. 38 (1942), 2 sets, H. W. Gray,
    1942.
Ut queant laxis: Hymn to St. John the Baptist (1962), Peters
    6289, 1962.
Variation Studies, Op. 54 (1950), Witmark.
BINKERD, GORDON W. born Lynch, Neb., May 22, 1916. Com-
    position pupil of Bernard Rogers and Walter Piston; 1949,
    became faculty member, University of Illinois; 1959, won
    Guggenheim Fellowship.
    Andante (1956), Associated Music Publishers.
    Arietta, Associated Music Publishers.
BISSELL, KEITH WARREN. born Meaford, Ontario, Canada, 1912.
    B. Mus., University of Toronto; 1947, began teaching in
    British Columbia; 1948-1955, Supervisor of Music, organist,

Christ Church, Edmonton, Alberta; 1955, appointed Chief
Supervisor of Music, Scarborough, Ontario; 1960, pupil of
Carl Orff (Munich).

 Sonata, in Organ Music of Canada, Vol. II, p. 47.

BITGOOD, ROBERTA. born New London, Conn., Jan. 15, 1908.
Studied at Conn. College for Women, Guilmant Organ School,
and Columbia University; Sac. Mus. Doc., Union Theological
Seminary, New York City; organist-choirmaster at Holy
Trinity Lutheran Church, Buffalo, New York, First Presby-
terian Church, Riverside, Cal., Redford Presbyterian Church,
Detroit, Mich., First Presbyterian Church, Bay City, Mich.,
and First Congregational Church, Battle Creek, Mich.

 Chorale Prelude on God Himself Is with Us, H. W. Gray
  (St. Cecilia Series 793).

 Chorale Prelude on Jewels, H. W. Gray (St. Cecilia Series
  746), 1949.

 Chorale Prelude on O Master, Let Me Walk, Sacred Music
  Press.

 Chorale Prelude on Siloam, H. W. Gray (St. Cecilia
  Series 778).

 Noel (Carol of the Birds), H. W. Gray.

 Offertories from Afar, Flammer, 1964.

 On an Ancient Alleluia, H. W. Gray (St. Cecilia Series
  894).

 Prelude on Covenanters' Tune, Flammer, 1958.

 Postlude on an Old Spanish Hymn, Sacred Music Press.

BLACKBURN, JOHN. Canadian. Twentieth century.

 Chorale Improvisation on Old 124th, Galaxy.

 Chorale Prelude on Croft's 136th, Concordia 97-3946.

 Prelude on Beata Nobis Gaudia, Galaxy.

 Prelude on Lobe den Herren, Galaxy.

 Prelude on Seelenbräutigam, Concordia.

 Prelude on St. Thomas, H. W. Gray (St. Cecilia Series
  785).

 Two Chorale Preludes (Divinum Mysterium; Gelobt sei
  Gott), Galaxy.

BLANCO, JOSEF. Spanish. born after 1750.

 Concerto No. 1, for two organs, M. S. Kastner, ed.,
  Schott.

BLITHEMAN, WILLIAM. English. born ?; died London, Whit-
sunday, 1591. 1564, Master of Choristers, Christ Church,
Oxford; 1586, B. Mus., Cambridge University; taught John
Bull; 1585, one of the organists (with Bull) at the Chapel
Royal; wrote six compositions found in the Mulliner Book.

 Gloria tibi trinitas VI, in Altenglische Orgelmusik.

 Jesu, Redemptor Omnium, in Cantantibus Organis, Vol. 12,
  F. Pustet.

BLOCH, AUGUSTYN. Polish. Twentieth century.

 Organ Sonata, Zaiks, Warsaw (Universal, London).

BLOCH, ERNEST. born Geneva, Switzerland, July 24, 1880; died
Portland, Oregon, July 15, 1959. Pupil of Dalcroze; studied
in Brussels, Frankfurt, and Munich; 1897-1899, violin pupil
of Ysaÿe; pupil of Thuille, Munich; 1904, 1911-1915, taught

composition, Conservatory, Geneva; 1917, came to the United States; taught at the David Mannes School, New York City; 1920-1925, Director, Institute of Music, Cleveland, Ohio; 1925-1930, Director, Conservatory, San Francisco.

Four Wedding Marches (1946-1950), G. Schirmer, 1951.

Processional, G. Schirmer, 1961.

Six Preludes, G. Schirmer, 1948.

BLOW, JOHN. born North Collingham Notts, England, February, 1649; died London, Oct. 1, 1708. Pupil of Christopher Gibbons; 1668, appointed organist, Westminster Abbey; 1674, became Master of the Children, Chapel Royal; taught Henry Purcell; 1677, received Mus. Doc. (Lambeth) from Dean of Canterbury Cathedral; 1695-1708, reappointed organist, Westminster Abbey.

Complete Organ Works, H. W. Shaw, ed., Schott 10595.

Prelude, Cramer.

Selected Organ Music, Vernon Butcher, ed., Hinrichsen 100.

Three Vers, in Alte Orgelmusik aus England und Frankreich.

Toccata, in Toccata, Orgue et Liturgie, Vol. 10, p. 13.

Two Old English Pieces (No. 2), Cramer.

Two Voluntaries, Hugh McLean, ed., Novello E. O. M. No. 23.

Verse, in Liber Organi, Vol. 10, p. 13.

Voluntary in C Major, in Tallis to Wesley, Vol. 21, p. 1.

BODA, JOHN. born Boyceville, Wis., Aug. 2, 1922. Studied at Eastman School of Music; 1946, appointed to faculty, Florida State University, Tallahassee, Fla.

compositions in The Parish Organist, Vol. 12.

BÖHM, GEORG. born Hohenkirchen (Ohrdruf), Germany, Sept. 2 (not 3), 1661; died Lüneburg, May 18 (not 8), 1733. 1698-1733, organist, St. Johannis, Lüneburg.

Allein Gott, in Chorale Preludes by Masters of the Seventeenth and Eighteenth Centuries, p. 20.

Choral and Variations on Christe, der du bist, in Alte Meister, p. 8.

Christe, der du bist, in Musica Organi, Vol. I, p. 24.

Collected Keyboard Works, 2 vols., Breitkopf und Härtel.

Five Preludes and Fugues, in Organum, Series IV, Vol. 4, Concordia 97-4336.

Gelobet seist du, in Alte Weihnachtsmusik.

Gelobet seist du, in Noël, Orgue et Liturgie, Vol. 4, p. 15.

Harpsichord and Organ Works, 2 vols., Johannes and Gesa Wolgast, eds., Bärenreiter 5200.

Herr Jesu Christ, dich zu uns wend, in The First Four Centuries of Organ Music, Vol. II, p. 397.

Prelude and Fugue in C Major, in Alte Meister des Orgelspiels, Vol. I; also Sumner, ed., Peters 4301D.

Prelude and Fugue in C Major, in Anthologia pro Organo, Vol. II, p. 38.

Prelude and Fugue in A Minor, in Anthologia pro Organo, Vol. IV, p. 34.

Trio on Christe, der du bist, in Schule des klassischen Triospiels, p. 10.

Variations on Christe der du bist Tag und Licht, Peters.
Vater unser, in Notre Père, Orgue et Liturgie, Vol. 24,
    p. 18.
Vom Himmel hoch, in Harold Gleason, Method of Organ
    Playing, p. 168.
chorale preludes (3) in Choralvorspiel alter Meister.
chorale preludes (7) in The Church Organist's Golden Trea-
    sury, Vol. I.
chorale preludes in The Church Organist's Golden Treasury,
    Vol. II.
chorale preludes (2) in The Church Organist's Golden Trea-
    sury, Vol. III.
chorale preludes (5) in Orgel Choräle Sammlung.
chorale preludes (2) in Orgelchoräle des 17. und 18. Jahr-
    hunderts.
chorale preludes (4) in Orgelmeister des Siebzehnten und
    Achtzehnten Jahrhunderts.
chorale preludes in The Parish Organist, Vols. 5 and 6.
compositions in Masterpieces of Organ Music, Folios 6,
    19, 28, and 56.
BOËLLMANN, LÉON. born Ensisheim, France, Sept. 25, 1862;
    died Paris, Oct. 11, 1897. Pupil of Gigout at Niedermeyer
    School, Paris; 1896, became organist, St. Vincent-de-Paul,
    Paris.
    Adoro te; Paraphrase sur Laudate Dominum; Canzona dans
        la tonalité grégorienne.
    Album of Loud Voluntaries, Rowley, ed. , Boosey and
        Hawkes.
    Album of Soft Voluntaries, Rowley, ed. , Boosey and Hawkes.
    Carillon (Douze Pièces), in The French Organist, Vol. I,
        p. 71, Leduc.
    Communion, Leduc.
    Deuxième Suite, Op. 27, Leduc, 1896.
    Douze Pièces, Op. 16, Leduc, 1890.
    Elévation, Bornemann; also Boosey and Hawkes.
    Fantaisie, Leduc, 1906.
    Fantaisie Dialogué, Op. 35, Durand.
    Four Recital Pieces, Rowley, ed. , Boosey and Hawkes.
    Fugue, in The French Organist, Vol. II, p. 64.
    (Les) Heures Mystiques, 2 vols. , Enoch, 1896; also Boosey
        and Hawkes.
    Offertory on Noëls, in The French Organist, Vol. I, p. 31;
        also Durand, 1898.
    Prelude, in The French Organist, Vol. II, p. 59.
    Ronde Française, Op. 37 (transcribed by Choisnel), Durand,
        1911.
    Six Characteristic Pieces, Rowley, ed. , Boosey and Hawkes.
    Suite Gothique, Op. 25, Durand, 1895; also Boosey and
        Hawkes.
    Suite No. 2, Boosey and Hawkes.
    Suite No. 3, Boosey and Hawkes.
    Suite No. 4, Boosey and Hawkes.
    Tema, Rowley, ed. , Boosey and Hawkes.

Toccata (D Minor), Boosey and Hawkes.
Two Pieces, in Organ Book No. 2, p. 28.
Two Pieces, Rowley, ed. , Boosey and Hawkes.
Verset, Rowley, ed. , Boosey and Hawkes.
BOËLY, ALEXANDRE-PIERRE-FRANÇOIS. born Versailles, France,
     Apr. 19, 1785; died Paris, Dec. 27, 1858. Organist, St.
     Germain-l'Auxerrois.
     Eight Preludes on Carols by Denizot, in Organ Music for
          Christmas, Vol. 1.
     Fourteen Preludes based on sixteenth-century hymns and
          carols, Op. 45, Costallat et Billaudot.
     Muses soeurs de la peinture, in Organ Music for Christmas,
          Vol. 2.
     O Filii et Filiae, in Seasonal Voluntaries for Easter, W.
          Paxton.
     Oeuvres complètes, 2 vols. , Pièces d'orgue pour le service
          liturgique, Kalmus 3236, 3237.
     Préludes, Fugues, Canons, 2 vols. , A. Gastoué and N.
          Dufourcq, eds. , Procure du Clergé, Paris.
     Toccata, Novello.
     composition in Cecilia, Book XII, Augener.
     compositions (4) in Historical Organ Recitals, Vol. III.
     compositions (2) in Les Maîtres français de l'orgue, Vol. II.
BOHNHORST, FRANK RUNYAN. American. born 1923; died 1956.
     Pupil of Grant Fletcher and Normand Lockwood; M. S. M. ,
     Union Theological Seminary, New York City; 1951-1956, com-
     poser in residence, Illinois Wesleyan University.
     Prelude on Slane, in American Organ Music, Vol. I, p. 19.
BOIVIN, MAURICE. born Ottawa, Canada, Oct. 11, 1918. Studied
     at the University of Ottawa; pupil of Ernest MacMillan,
     Healey Willan, and Jean Papineau-Couture; 1949, B. Mus. ,
     Conservatory, Toronto; studied at University of Montreal;
     1960, became faculty member, Conservatory, Quebec; 1953,
     appointed choir director, St. Bernadette, Quebec; studied in
     the United States.
     Deux Pièces, in Organ Music of Canada, Vol. II, p. 40.
BONFILS, JEAN-BAPTISTE. born St. Etienne, France, 1921. Pupil
     of Dupré, Messiaen, and Milhaud; editor, L'Organiste liturgique
     series, published by Schola Cantorum; organist, Grande Syna-
     gogue, Paris; assistant to Messiaen, Trinité.
     Communion on Beata Viscera, in A la Sainte Vierge,
          L'Organiste liturgique, Vol. 2, p. 22.
     Fantaisie (manuscript).
BONNAL, ERMEND. born Bordelaux, France, 1880; died 1944.
     Pupil of Tournemire and Vierne; Director, Ecole de Musique,
     Bayonne; organist, St. André, Bayonne.
     Noël landais, Durand, 1938.
     Paysages euskariens (La Vallée du Béhorléguy, au matin;
          Le Berger d'Ahusquy; Cloches dans le ciel), Durand,
          1930.
     Paysage landais, Durand, 1904.
     Petite rhapsodie bretonne, Eolian, 1898.
     Réflets solaires, Leduc, 1905.

Symphonie "Media Vita" (1932), organ part, Leduc 1932.
BONNET, JOSEPH. born Bordeaux, France, Mar. 17, 1884; died
    St. Luce-sur-Mer, Quebec, Canada, Aug. 2, 1944. Virtuoso
    pupil of Guilmant; 1906, appointed organist, St. Eustache,
    Paris.
    Chant triste, Leduc, 1925.
    Clair de lune, Leduc.
    Douze Pièces, Op. 5, Leduc, 1909.
    Douze Pièces, Op. 7, Leduc, 1910.
    Douze Pièces, Op. 10, Leduc, 1913.
    Epithalame, Leduc.
    Etude de Concert, Leduc.
    Fantaisie sur Deux Noëls, Leduc.
    Legende en Ré mineur, Leduc.
    Romance sans paroles, Leduc.
    Trois Poèmes d'Automne (Lied des Chrysanthèmes; Matin
        Provençal; Poème du Soir), Leduc, 1906.
    Variations de Concert, Leduc, 1906.
BONPORTI, FRANCESCO ANTONIO. Baptized Trento, Italy,
    June 11, 1672; died Padua, Dec. 19, 1749. Priest; served
    at Cathedral, Trento.
    Concerto (B Major), organ and strings, Schott.
BONSET, JAC (JACOBUS). born Amsterdam, Aug. 1, 1880. Pupil
    of Schultz and Zweers; 1911, became organist, Old Lutheran
    Church, Amsterdam.
    Drei Stücke, Alsbach.
    Fantasie en koraal op Psalm 118, Alsbach.
    Fantasie op Op bergen en in dalen, Op. 172, Alsbach.
    Fantasie op Een vaste burg is onze God, Op. 73, Alsbach.
    Fantasie op Psalm 25, Op. 227, Alsbach.
    Fantasie op Psalm 68, Op. 134, Alsbach.
    Intermezzo, Op. 113, in Organ Music of the Netherlands
        and Scandinavia, p. 38.
    Marche funèbre, Op. 58, Alsbach.
    Partita op Psalm 128, Op. 224, Alsbach.
    Psalm 75, Op. 225, Alsbach.
    Sechs Stücke, Op. 52, Alsbach.
    Triptiek, Op. 186, Alsbach.
    Variaties en Fuge op een thema van Purcell, Op. 155,
        Alsbach.
    Variaties op Nu sijt wellekomme, Alsbach.
    fantasies (2) in Te Deum Laudamus, Vol. 2 and Vol. 3,
        Willemsen.
BORNEFELD, HELMUT. born Stuttgart-Untertürkheim, Germany,
    Dec. 14, 1906. Studied at the Musikhochschule, Stuttgart;
    1931, became Director, Kammerchors, Esslingen; 1937, pas-
    sed Church Musician examination; Cantor-organist, Heidenheim-
    Brenz.
    Choralpartita I über Wir glauben, Bärenreiter 2435, 1949.
    Choralpartita II über Der Herr ist mein getreuer Hirt,
        Bärenreiter 2436, 1949.
    Choralpartita III über Nun komm, Bärenreiter 2437, 1950.
    Choralpartita IV über Mit Fried und Freud, Bärenreiter

2438, 1951.

Choralpartita V über Gott der Vater wohn uns bei, Bärenreiter 3975.

Choralpartita VI über Komm, Gott Schöpfer, Bärenreiter,
2654, 1953.

Choralpartita VII über Christus, der ist mein Leben,
Bärenreiter 2439.

Choralpartita VIII über Herr Gott, dich loben wir, Bärenreiter 2420.

Choralsonate I, Auf meinen lieben Gott, German (transverse)
flute and organ, Bärenreiter 3481.

Choralvorspiele, 2 vols., Bärenreiter 3515-3516.

(Das) Choralwerk, 6 vols., Bärenreiter 2212-2217.

Orgelstücke (Intonationen) (1948-1949), Bärenreiter 2440,
1949.

chorale preludes (5) in Orgelbuch zum Evangelischen
Kirchengesangbuch, Books 7, 12, 13, 15, and 20.

BOROWSKI, FELIX.   born Burton, England, Mar. 10, 1872; died
Chicago, Ill., Sept. 6, 1956.   1897, became head, theory-
composition, 1916-1925, president, Chicago Musical College;
music critic; 1937-1942, taught musicology, Northwestern
University, Evanston, Ill.

First Suite, E. B. Marks, 1955.

Sonata No. 3, A. P. Schmidt, 1924.

BORRIS, SIEGFRIED.   born Berlin, Germany, Nov. 4, 1906.   Pupil
of Hindemith and Schering; 1945, became instructor, Musikhochschule, Berlin.

Canzone, viola and organ, Op. 110, No. 1, Sirius.

Drei Orgel-Canzonen, Sirius.

Concerto, organ, flute, oboe, bassoon, and strings, Sirius.

Lauda, oboe and organ, Op. 110, No. 2, Sirius.

Orgel-Phantasie in D dur, Op. 79, No. 3, Sirius.

Te Deum, oboe and organ, Op. 110, No. 4, Sirius.

Zwei Orgel-Phantasien, Op. 79, Sirius.

chorale preludes (2) in Orgelbuch zum Evangelischen
Kirchengesangbuch, Books 15 and 20.

BOSSI, MARCO ENRICO.   born Salô, Brescia, Italy, Apr. 25, 1861;
died at sea going from America to Europe, Feb. 20, 1925.
Studied at Bologna, Milan (with Fumagalli, organ); 1881-1889,
organist, Cathedral, Como; 1889-1896, Professor of harmony
and organ, Royal Conservatory San Pietro, Naples; 1896-1902,
Professor of advanced composition and organ, Liceo Benedetto
Marcello, Venice; 1902-1912, Director, Liceo Musicale,
Bologna; 1916-1923, Director, Music School, St. Cecilia
Academy, Rome; toured Europe and America as organist and
pianist.

Alleluia (Final), in The International Organist, Vol. II,
p. 68.

Ave Maria, Offertoire, Edition Musicus, New York.

Composizione (10), Op. 118, Carisch, S. A., Milan.

Concerto in A Minor, Op. 100, organ, string orchestra,
four horns, and timpani, (organ part), Peters 3597A.

Entrée Pontificale, Op. 104, No. 1, Peters 3584A.

Fantaisie, Durand.
Fünf Stücke, Op. 104, Peters.
Fünf Stücke, Op. 113, Sten (Turin).
Fünf Stücke im freien Stil, Op. 132, Peters.
Gebet (B Major), Ricordi.
Giga, V. Fox, ed., H. W. Gray (St. Cecilia Series 903).
Hora Mystica, Op. 132, No. 4, Peters 3585D.
Marche héroïque, Durand.
Meditation and Prayer, violoncello and organ, Le Grand
    Orgue.
Offertorium (D Major), Ricordi.
Organ Works, 2 vols., Peters 3590 A and B.
Redemption, Op. 104, No. 5, Peters 3584 E.
Res severa magnum gaudium.
Resignation, in The International Organist, Vol. I, p. 34.
Scherzo (G Minor), United Music Publishers.
Siciliana, in Historical Organ Recitals, Vol. V, p. 78;
    also Ricordi.
Six Pieces (Prelude; Musette; Choral; Scherzo; Cantabile;
    Alleluia final), Durand (Boston Music Company).
Sonata No. 2, Op. 71, Novello.
Three Short Pieces (Pedal Study; Little Chorale; Ricercare),
    (Peters N 3974).
Zehn Stücke, Op. 118, Carisch.
Zwei Scherzi, Op. 49, Sten (Turin).
BOSSLER (BOSZLER), KURT. born Duisburg, Germany, July 10,
    1911. 1936, appointed organist, Salvator Church, Duisburg;
    1937-1941, composition pupil of Helmut Degen and attended the
    Music Teachers' Academy, Conservatory, Duisburg; 1941,
    became organist, Protestant Church, Bad Rappenau (Baden);
    1943, appointed organist, St. Paul's Church and composition
    teacher, Music School, Freiburg-im-Breisgau; 1963, appointed
    instructor, Protestant Church Music Institute, Heidelberg.
    Acht Choralvorspiele, 2 vols., Merseburger 892/893.
    Choral-partita über Heut singt, in Die Orgel, Kistner &
        Siegel, 1961 (Concordia 97-4565).
    Drei Orgelstücke (Praeludium und Fuge, Op. 37; Toccata,
        Op. 40; Chaconne, Op. 50), Merseburger 821, 1956.
    Freiburger Orgelbuch, in Die Orgel, Op. 1, No. 9, Kistner
        & Siegel, 1965 (Concordia 97-4751).
    Heidelburger Orgelbuch, Kistner & Siegel, 1968 (Concordia
        97-4924).
    chorale preludes (6) in Neue Orgelvorspiele, Merseburger.
    chorale preludes (5) in Orgelvorspiele, Merseburger.
BOULNOIS, JOSEPH. born Paris, Jan. 28, 1884; died Chalaines,
    Oct. 20, 1918. Studied at the Conservatory, Paris; pupil of
    Louis Vierne and Alexandre Guilmant; organist, St. Louis
    d'Antin, Paris.
    Trois Pièces (Fugue; La Toussaint; Choral) (transcribed
        by Michel Boulnois).
BOULNOIS, MICHEL. born Paris, Oct. 31, 1907. Studied at the
    Conservatory, Paris; organ pupil of Marcel Dupré; composi-
    tion pupil of Nadia Boulanger and Henri Busser; 1937, ap-

pointed organist, St. Philippe-du-Roule, Paris.

Communion pour l'Anonciation, in Communions, Orgue et
   Liturgie, Vol. 62, p. 20.

Elévation pour la fête de l'Anonciation, in Elévations, Orgue
   et Liturgie, Vol. 57, p. 8.

Offertoire pour la fête de l'Anonciation ou le IVe dimanche
   l'Avent, in Offertoires, Orgue et Liturgie, Vol. 52,
   p. 12.

Pièce terminal pour la fête de l'Anonciation, in Orgue et
   Liturgie, Vol. 75.

Prélude à l'Introit pour la fête de l'Anonciation sur l'Introit
   et la deuxième antienne des vêpres, in Préludes à
   l'Introit, Orgue et Liturgie, Vol. 48, p. 5.

Symphonie, Lemoine, 1949.

compositions (3) in Au Saint Sacrement, Orgue et Liturgie,
   Vol. 18.

BOUMAN, PAUL. born Hamburg, Minn. , 1918. Organist-Director
   of Music, Grace Lutheran Church, River Forest, Ill.

chorale preludes in The Parish Organist, Vols. 1-4, 10,
   11, and 12.

BOURDON, ÉMILE. born Lapalisse, France, 1884. Pupil and
   assistant to Vierne at Notre Dame, Paris; organist, Cathedral,
   Monaco.

Choral Varié, Leduc, 1920.

Dix Pièces, Op. 7, Leduc, 1921.

Dix Nouvelles Pièces, Op. 18, Lemoine, 1952.

Marche solennelle, Bornemann.

Saboly sur Noël 33ter, in Noëls variés, Orgue et Liturgie,
   Vol. 40, p. 6; also in Christmas Music by Various
   French Composers, Kalmus.

Symphonie, Leduc, 1926.

BOUVARD, JEAN. Founder, Les Amis de l'Orgue, Lyon, France;
   organist, Ste. Thérèse, Lyon; Professor of Music History,
   Conservatory, Lyon.

Noël Provençal, Muva (Lyon), 1938.

Noël Vosgien, in Noëls variés, Orgue et Liturgie, Vol. 40,
   p. 9, also in Christmas Music by Various French
   Composers, Kalmus.

BOYCE, WILLIAM. born London, England, 1710; died Kensington,
   Feb. 7, 1779. Choirboy, St. Paul's Cathedral, London; organ
   pupil of Maurice Greene; organist, St. Michael's, Cornhill;
   1758, appointed organist, Chapel Royal.

Excerpts from Ten Voluntaries, Gordon Phillips, ed. ,
   Hinrichsen, 1966.

Four voluntaries, in Tallis to Wesley, Vol. 26, 1966.

Gavotte (G), Cramer.

Short Prelude and Fugue, Cramer.

Suite, S. Drummond Wolff, ed. , Concordia 97-4848.

Three Trios in Dance Form, Cramer.

Two Minuets, Cramer.

Two Voluntaries (A Minor; D Minor), Hinrichsen 336.

Two Voluntaries, Novello.

Voluntary in A Minor, in Liber Organi, Vol. 10, p. 23.

Voluntary in A Minor, in Twelve Short Pieces by Old Eng-
lish Composers, p. 11.
Voluntary in G Major, in Tallis to Wesley, Vol. 1, p. 14,
Hinrichsen 1713.
Voluntary I in D Major and Voluntary No. 4 in G Minor,
in English Organ Music of the Eighteenth Century,
Hinrichsen, 1951.
BOYVIN, JACQUES. born Paris, ca. 1649; died Rouen, June 30,
1706. Student of Lebègue, Richard, or Nivers; organist,
Notre Dame, Rouen; wrote Premier livre d'orgue (1689).
Oeuvres complètes d'orgue, in Archives des maîtres d'orgue
des seizième-dix-huitième siècles, Vol. VI.
Plein jeu continu du 7e ton, in Les Maîtres français de
l'orgue, Vol. II, p. 37.
*Premier livre d'orgue, Jean Bonfils, ed. , Ouvrières, 1969.
Suite de Septième ton, in European Organ Music of the
16th and 17th Centuries, p. 60.
compositions (5) in Les Maîtres français de l'orgue, Vol. I.
BOZYAN, H. FRANK. born New York City, Nov. 19, 1899; died
New Haven, Conn. , Dec. 29, 1965. 1920, graduate, 1954,
organist, and professor of organ, Yale University; Hindemith's
Sonata II written for him.
BRAAL, ANDRIES DE. born Beilen (Drente), The Netherlands,
Dec. 9, 1909. Studied at the Conservatory, Amsterdam;
composition pupil of Hendrik Andriessen; 1941-1947, Director,
Muziekschool, Deventer; 1947-1956, Director, Muziekschool,
Arnhem; 1956-1963, Director, Stedlijk Muzieklyceum, Arnhem;
1963-1965, Director, Stichting Muziekschool, Zeeuw; since
1965, Director, Stedelijk Muziekschool, Breda.
Koraalvoorspelen.
Passacaglia en fuga.
Sonate.
Varieties over een adventslied.
BRABANTER, JOS DE. born Liederkerke, near Brussels, 1918.
Studied at the Institute for the Blind, Woluwe; graduated from
Institute of Religious Music, Malines, as laureat; pupil of
Flor Peeters and de Jong.
Passacaglia and Allegro, H. W. Gray.
Sonata, Novello.
BRACQUEMOND, MARTHE HENRIOD-. born Paris, Apr. 9, 1898.
Composition pupil of Charles-Marie Widor; organ pupil of
Louis Vierne, Marcel Dupré, and Henri Busser; 1937-1962,
organist, Eglise Reformée de la rue Cortembert, Paris.
Ombres (Suite sur la Passion), Leduc.
Noël avec variation, Schola Cantorum.
BRAHMS, JOHANNES. born Hamburg, Germany, May 7, 1833;
died Vienna, Apr. 3, 1897. Pupil of Marxsen; 1853, made
concert tour with Remenyi; conductor of Prince of Lippe-
Detmold's orchestra; 1858-1862, studied in Hamburg; 1863-
1864, conductor, Singakademie, Vienna; 1864-1869, toured;
1871-1874, conducted Gesellschaft der Musikfreunde concerts;
1878-1897, lived in Vienna; 1881, received honorary Dr. phil. ,
Breslau University; great composer of works for orchestra,

chorus, voice, and piano, as well as organ.
  Complete Organ Works, 2 vols. , Walter E. Buszin and
      Paul Bunjes, eds. , Vol. I: Four Early Compositions;
      Vol. 2: Op. 122, Peters 633A and B, 1964.
  Chorale Prelude and Fugue on O Trauerigkeit, O Herzeleid,
      in Historical Organ Recitals, Vol. V, p. 24.
  Eleven Chorale Preludes, Op. 122, E. Power Biggs, ed. ,
      Mercury Music Press, 1949; also Novello; also
      Simrock.
  Organ Works, 2 vols. , Vol. I: chorale preludes; Vol. 2:
      miscellaneous compositions, E. B. Marks, 1948.
  Sämtliche Werke: Orgelwerke, Vol. 16, Breitkopf und
      Härtel 6062, 1926-1927; also Kalmus 3247.
  St. Anthony chorale, in The Parish Organist, Vol. 9, p. 21.
  Trio on Schmücke dich, in Schule des klassischen Triospiels,
      p. 34.
  chorale preludes in The Parish Organist, Vols. 1-4, 5, 6,
      7, 8, and 10.
  compositions (5) in Musica Organi, Vol. I, p. 184-197.
BRANDON, GEORGE. born Stockton, Calif. , Feb. 4, 1924. Studied
    at University of the Pacific; 1952, M. S. M. , Union Theolo-
    gical Seminary, New York City; pupil of Searle Wright,
    Robert Baker, and Harold Friedell; served churches in Stock-
    ton, Calif. , Burlington, N. Car. , Forest Hills, N. Y. , Oska-
    loosa, Iowa, and Davis, Calif. ; 1957-1959, taught, Eureka
    College, Eureka, Ill. : 1959-1962, taught, William Penn Col-
    lege, Oskaloosa, Iowa.
  Canonic Partita on Duke Street, Brodt.
  Eureka Suite, Brodt.
  Fantasy on Old Hundredth, Brodt.
  Four Liturgical Preludes, J. Fischer, 1969.
  Organ Variations, Carl Fischer, 1970.
  Organ Variations on Barnby's Tune Sandringham, Brodt.
  Variations on Five Plainsong Hymntunes, Augsburg, 1966.
  Variations on the Hymn-tune Dix, Brodt.
  Variations on Two Spirituals, Brodt.
BREMNER, JAMES. American. born ?; died Philadelphia, 1780.
    1763, founded music school and organist, Christ Church,
    Philadelphia; taught Francis Hopkinson.
  Trumpet Air, in Early American Compositions for Organ,
      Jon Spong, ed.
BREMOND D'ARS, PHILIPPE DE. born Royan (Charente-Maritime),
    France, Sept. 22, 1889. Composition pupil of Vincent d'Indy
    and Paul Dukas; organ pupil of Abel Decaux and Louis Vierne;
    organist, St. Antoine des Quinze-Vingts, Church of the Domin-
    icans, Paris, St. Médard, St. Pierre-de-Montrouge; organ
    teacher, Ecole César Franck and at the Institut de Musique
    liturgique.
  Air sur le hautbois, Philippo, 1938.
BRÉVILLE, PIERRE DE. born Bar-le-Duc, France, 1861; died
    Paris, 1949. Pupil of Franck and Dubois; music critic.
  Prelude and Fugue, Rouart, Lerolle & Cie.
  Suite Brève.

BRIDGE, FRANK. born Brighton, England, Feb. 26, 1879; died
     Eastbourne, Jan. 10, 1941. Studied at the Royal College of
     Music; pupil of Stanford; violist, opera conductor, and com-
     poser.
     Minuet (1939).
     Organ Pieces, Book I (1905), Boosey and Hawkes.
     Organ Pieces, Book II (1912), Boosey and Hawkes.
     Prelude (1939).
     Processional (1939).
     Sonata in D Minor, Novello.
     Three Pieces (Andante moderato in C Minor; Adagio in E
          Major; Allegro con spirito in B-flat Major), H. W.
          Gray.
BRIEGEL, WOLFGANG CARL. born Nürnberg, Germany, 1629;
     died Darmstadt, Nov. 19, 1712. 1650, court Cantor, Gotha;
     1671-1709, court Kapellmeister, Darmstadt.
     Acht Fugen durch die Kirchentöne, Fuga über Dies sind die
          heilgen zehn Gebot, Concordia 97-4646.
     Chorale Prelude on Christ lag in Todesbanden, Koerner.
     Vom Himmel hoch, in Harold Gleason, Method of Organ
          Playing; also in Organ Chorales by Old Masters,
          Ars Nova.
BRIGNOLI, GIACOMO. Italian. Sixteenth century.
     Fuga di canzon francese, in Anthologia pro Organo, Vol. III,
          p. 17.
BRISTOL, LEE HASTINGS, JR. American. born 1923. 1962-1969,
     President, Westminster Choir College, Princeton, N. J.
     Chorale Prelude on Stuttgart, Harold Flammer.
     Variations on Old 100th, J. Fischer, 1951.
BRITTEN, BENJAMIN. born Lowestoft, Suffolk, England, Nov. 22,
     1913. Pupil of Frank Bridge and John Ireland; studied at
     the Royal College of Music.
     Prelude and Fugue on a theme of Vittoria (1946), Boosey
          and Hawkes, 1952.
BRIXI, FRANZ XAVER (FRANTISEK XAVER). born Prague,
     Jan. 2, 1732; died Prague, Oct. 14, 1771. Organist, St.
     Gallus; 1756, choirmaster, Cathedral, Prague.
     Concerto (F Major), organ and chamber orchestra, Bären-
          reiter MAB 26.
     Fantasy (A Minor); Fugue (F Major), in Old Bohemian
          Masters, Quoika, ed. , Breitkopf und Härtel.
     Fugue (C Minor), in A Century of Czech Music, Vol. I,
          p. 16.
     Toccata in A Minor, in A Century of Czech Music, Vol. II,
          p. 17.
BROCKLESS, BRIAN. born London, 1926. Pupil of Herbert
     Howells at the Royal College of Music; Professor, Royal
     Academy of Music; Head, Music Department, University of
     Surrey; Director of Music, St. Bartholomew the Great Priory,
     Smithfield, London; organist, St. Mary Aldermary.
     Introduction, Passacaglia and Coda, Novello, 1967.
     Prelude, Toccata and Chaconne, Novello.
BROSIG, MORITZ. born Fuchswinkel, Upper Silesia, Germany,

Oct. 15, 1815; died Breslau, Jan. 24, 1887. 1842, became
organist, Cathedral, Breslau.
> Acht Stücke, Op. 58, Leuckart.
> Acht Stücke verschiedenen Charakters, Op. 46, Leuckart.
> Ausgewählte Orgelkompositionen, 6 vols., Leuckart.
> Drei Präludien und Zwei Postludien, Op. 11, Leuckart.
> Eight Pieces, Op. 58, Leuckart.
> Fantasie on Christ ist erstanden, Leuckart.
> Five Chorale Preludes, Op. 4, Leuckart.
> Fünf Präludien, Op. 21, Schlesinger (Berlin).
> Fünf Stücke, Op. 15, André.
> Fünf Stücke, Op. 47, Leuckart.
> Funf Tonstücke, Op. 61, Leuckart.
> Melodies for the Catholic Hymnbook, Op. 30, Leuckart.
> Prelude on O Traurigkeit, Op. 12, No. 2, Koerner.
> Preludien und Fugen (3), Op. 1, Leuckart.
> Sechs Präludien und Fugen, Op. 60, Leuckart.
> Sieben Stücke, Op. 14, André.
> Stücke (5), Op. 3, Leuckart.
> Twenty-one Short Preludes on Hymns, Op. 8b, Leuckart.
> Twelve Pieces, Op. 52, Leuckart.
> Valet, in Der Praktische Organist, Part I, Tascherchen;
>   also in Orgel Choräle Sammlung.
> Vier Stücke, Op. 12, Leuckart.
> Vier Stücke, Op. 13, André.
> chorale preludes (4) in Anthologie.
> chorale preludes (9) in Cantus Firmus Praeludien, Vol. 3,
>   Schott, 1928.

BROUGHTON, RUSSELL. American. born 1895; died Feb. 7, 1969.
Graduate, Oberlin Conservatory of Music; pupil of Boulanger
and Dupré; Head, Music Department, St. Mary's Junior College, Raleigh, N. Car.
> Divinum Mysterium, in American Organ Music, Vol. I,
>   p. 22.

BROWN, ALLANSON G. Y. born York, England, May 31, 1902.
1915, became organist, St. Maurice, York; 1925, became
Fellow of the Royal College of Organists; pupil of Edward
Bairstow; organist, Belfast, Northern Ireland; 1932, appointed organist, Dominion United Church, Ottawa, Canada;
organist, Leamington, Ontario.
> Chant Religieux, H. W. Gray.
> (A) Festive Alleluia, A. P. Schmidt.
> Fragrance, A. P. Schmidt.
> Improvisation on Pange lingua, H. W. Gray (St. Cecilia
>   Series 953).
> Improvisation on Two Chorales for Palm Sunday, H. W.
>   Gray (St. Cecilia Series 719).
> Improvisation on Urbs beata, B M I--Canada, Ltd.
> Prelude on Austria, A. P. Schmidt.
> Three Religious Pieces, McLaughlin & Reilly.
> Two Meditations on Themes by Palestrina, A. P. Schmidt.

BROWN, JAMES CLIFFORD. born Ipswich, England, 1923. Studied
at Cambridge University; Fellow of the Royal College of

Organists; 1948, became Assistant Lecturer, 1951, Lecturer, 1948, University Organist, Leeds University.
Andante sospirando, Oxford.
BROWN, RAYNER. American. Faculty member, Biola College.
Chorale Prelude Aus tiefer Not, viola and organ, Western International Music.
Concerto, organ and band, Western International.
Concerto No. 2, organ and orchestra, Western International.
Prelude and Fugue, violin and organ, Western International.
Sonata, cello and organ, Western International.
Sonata, clarinet and organ, Western International.
Sonata, flute and organ, Western International.
Sonata for two players, Western International.
Sonata, oboe and organ, Western International.
Sonata, viola and organ, Western International.
BRUCKNER, JOSEF ANTON. born Ansfelden, Upper Austria, Sept. 4, 1824; died Vienna, Oct. 11, 1896. 1856, became organist, Cathedral, Linz; 1867, appointed court organist, Vienna; toured in France and England, especially as an improviser; intimately associated with St. Florian Monastery, Austria.
Fuge in D moll (1861/1862).
Orgelwerke, Doblinger.
Prelude and Postlude (Fugue), Peters D-943.
Prelude in C Major and Fugue in D Minor, Wöss, ed. , Universal 8752.
Prelude in E-flat Major (ca. 1836).
Prelude in E-flat Major (ca. 1837).
Volledige Orgelwerken, Annie Bank.
Vorspiel und Fuge in C moll (ca. 1847), Filser (Augsburg).
Zwei Orgel Stücke in D moll (ca. 1846), Böhm.
BRUHNS, NICOLAUS. born Schwabstedt, Germany, in Advent, 1665; died Husum, Mar. 29, 1697. Student of Buxtehude; organist, Copenhagen; 1689, became organist, Cathedral, Husum.
Complete Organ Works, Stein, ed. , Peters 4855.
Nun komm, in Alte Meister des Orgelspiels, p. 23.
Prelude and double Fugue in E Minor, in La Fugue au XVIIIe siècle, Orgue et Liturgie, Vol. 15, p. 3.
Prelude and Fugue in E Minor, in The First Four Centuries of Organ Music, Vol. II, p. 408.
Prelude and Fugue in G Major, in Alte Meister des Orgelspiels, Vol. I, p. 13.
Three Preludes and Fugues (G Major; E Minor; E Minor), in Organum, Series IV, Vol. 8, Concordia 97-4340.
BRUIN, BRAM. Dutch. Twentieth century.
Beveel gerust Uw wegen, Willemsen.
Daar ruist langs de wolken, Willemsen.
De dag door Uwe gunst, Willemsen.
Drie Koraalbewerkingen, Alsbach.
Fantasie op Psalm 75, Alsbach.
Jesu meine Freude, Willemsen.
Preludium op Psalm 24, Alsbach.
Preludium op Psalm 105, Alsbach.

Preludium op Psalm 146, Alsbach.
Psalm 19, Willemsen.
Psalm 68, Willemsen.
Psalm 89, Willemsen.
Psalm 97, Willemsen.
Psalm 99, Willemsen.
Psalm 122, Willemsen.
Psalm 150, Willemsen.
Toccata, Alsbach.
Toccata No. 2, Alsbach.
Vier Koraalbewerkingen, Alsbach.

BRUMANN, KONRAD (CONRAD VON SPEYER). died Speyer, Germany, Oct. 31, 1526. Pupil of Hofhaimer; 1513, at the latest, became organist and vicar, Cathedral, Speyer; compositions found in Klebers Tabulaturbuch.
 compositions (2) in Frühmeister der deutschen Orgelkunst.

BRUMEL, ANTON (ANTOINE). Flemish. Fifteenth and sixteenth century. Pupil of Okeghem; 1498-1500, choirmaster and canon, Notre Dame, Paris; served at court in Lyon and Ferrara.
 Benedictus (1508), in Geschichte der Musik in Beispielen, p. 63.
 Bicinium, in Oudnederlandse Meesters, Vol. III, p. 9.
 Regina coeli, in Alte Meister aus der Frühzeit des Orgelspiels, p. 26.
 plainsong hymn in Oudnederlandse Meesters, Vol. II, p. 10.

BRUNA, PABLO (PAU). Spanish. Seventeenth century. Blind musician who served King Philipp IV.
 Tiento de Falses de Sisé To, in Early Spanish Organ Music, p. 62.

BRUNCKHORST, ARNOLD MELCHIOR. German. born ca. 1670; died 1720. City organist, Celle, Germany.
 Prelude, in Organum, Series IV, Vol. 7.

BRUNNER, ADOLF. Swiss. born 1901.
 Pfingstbuch über Nun bitten wir (Praeambulum; Choral; Partita; Passacaglia; Choral), Bärenreiter 2432, 1949.

BRUYNÈL, TON. born Utrecht, The Netherlands, Jan. 26, 1934. Studied at the Conservatory, Utrecht; composer of electronic music; associated with Electronic Music Studio, Rijksuniversiteit, Utrecht, and with the Technische Hogeschool, Delft.
 Arc, organ and four electronic instruments (1966-1967), Donemus, 1967.
 Milieu, organ and electronic instruments (1965-1966).
 Reliëf, organ and four electronic instruments (1964), Donemus.

BUCHNER, HANS (HANS OF CONSTANCE). born Ravensburg, Germany, Oct. 26, 1483; died Constance, 1538. Pupil of Hofhaimer; studied in Vienna; 1506, organist, 1512, officially installed, Cathedral, Constance; member of court orchestra to Maximilian I; taught Fridolin Sicher; 1526, organist, Cathedral, Überlingen; wrote Fundamentum ca. 1525.
 Kyrie eleison, in Alte Meister aus der Frühzeit des

Orgelspiels, p. 36.
Quem terra, pontus, in Geschichte der Musik in Beispielen, p. 78.
compositions (4) in Frühmeister der deutschen Orgelkunst.
BUCK, DUDLEY. born Hartford, Conn., Mar. 10, 1839; died Orange, N. J., Oct. 6, 1909. 1858, studied in Europe; pupil of Moscheles and Friedrich Schneider; taught Harry Rowe Shelley; 1862, became organist, Park Church, Hartford, Conn.; 1869, appointed organist, St. James' Church, Chicago; organist, St. Paul's Church, Boston; ca. 1875, became organist, St. Ann's, New York City; organist, Holy Trinity, Brooklyn.
At Evening.
Four Tone Pictures.
Grand Sonata.
Holy Night, G. Schirmer.
Impromptu and Pastorale.
Rondo-Caprice.
Second Organ Sonata, Op. 77 (1877), Novello.
Six Short Chorale Preludes, Op. 49, Ed. Schuberth-White Smith.
Triumphal March.
Variations on a Scotch Melody, Op. 51, G. Schirmer.
Variations on The Last Rose of Summer, Op. 59, G. Schirmer.
Variations on The Star Spangled Banner, Op. 23, G. Schirmer.
BUCK, (SIR) PERCY CARTER. born West Ham (London), England, Mar. 25, 1871; died London, Oct. 3, 1947. Studied at the Royal College of Music; 1891-1894, organist, Worcester College, Oxford; 1897, Mus. Doc., Oxford; 1897, M.A.; 1896-1899, organist, Cathedral, Wells; 1899-1901, organist, Cathedral, Bristol; 1901-1927, music director, Harrow School; taught at universities of Dublin, Glasgow, and Sheffield; 1925-1937, Professor of Music, London University.
Sonata No. 1 (E-flat), Breitkopf und Härtel, 1896.
Two Christmas Preludes, Op. 35, in Noel, C. Fischer.
BULL, JOHN. born Somersetshire, England, ca. 1563; died Antwerp, Mar. 12/13, 1628. ca. 1572, choirboy, Chapel Royal; 1582, appointed joint organist, Hereford Cathedral; 1586, B. Mus., Oxford; 1591, organist, Chapel Royal; 1589?, Mus. Doc., Cambridge; 1592, Mus. Doc., Oxford, by incorporation; student of William Blitheman; 1601, left England; 1613, began service to Archduke in Brussels; 1617, appointed organist, Cathedral, Antwerp.
Fantasy, in Anthologia pro Organo, Vol. I, p. 36.
Five Pieces from the Flemish Tabulatura, (Peters N 3075).
Keyboard Music, Vol. I, in Musica Britanica, Vol. 14, Stainer and Bell, 1960.
Noëls Flamands, in L'Organiste liturgique, Vol. 60.
Prelude, in Alte Orgelmusk aus England und Frankreich, p. 9.
Prelude and Carol on Laet ons met herten Reijne, in

Musica Britanica, Vol. 14, p. 151; also in Historical
Organ Recitals, Vol. I, p. 26; also in Treasury of
Early Organ Music, p. 13; also in The First Four
Centuries of Organ Music, Vol. I, p. 148; also in
Old English Organ Music, J. E. West, ed. , Novello.
Salve regina, in Salve regina, L'Organiste liturgique, Vol.
21, p. 21.
Two Fantasies, in Anthologia pro Organo, Vol. III.
Vexilla Regis prodeunt, in Passion, L'Organiste liturgique,
Vol. 8, p. 13; also Novello.
BUNJES, PAUL G. American. born 1914. M. Mus. , University
of Michigan; Ph. D. , Eastman School of Music; faculty mem-
ber, Concordia Teachers' College, River Forest, Ill.
Chorale Concerto on A Mighty Fortress, organ, three trum-
pets, and chorus, Concordia 97-1412, 1957.
Chorale Trio on All My Heart, Concordia 97-3206.
chorale preludes (3) in The Parish Organist, Vol. 1-4.
BUNK, GERARD. born Rotterdam, Mar. 4, 1888. Studied at the
conservatories of Rotterdam and Hamburg; 1910-1945, taught
at the Conservatory, Dortmund; taught at the Conservatory,
Bielefeld; since 1925, organist, St. Reinoldi, Dortmund.
Eight Character Pieces, Op. 12, Leuckart.
Fantasie, Op. 57, Breitkopf und Härtel 5639.
Introduction, Variations and Fugue on an old Dutch Folk-
song, Tischer & Jagenberg (Cologne).
Musik für Orgel, Op. 81, Breitkopf und Härtel 5724.
BURKHARD, WILLY. born Évillard sur Bienne, Switzerland,
Apr. 17, 1900; died Zürich, June 18, 1955. Studied at the
conservatories of Berne, Leipzig, and Munich; pupil of Karg-
Elert; 1928-1933, taught piano and composition, Berne; 1942,
began teaching at the Conservatory, Zürich.
Choral Variations, Op. 28, No. 1 (Aus tiefer Not), Schott
2241.
Choral Variations, Op. 28, No. 2 (In dulci jubilo), Schott
2242.
Choral-Triptychon (1953), Bärenreiter 2655, 1954.
Concerto, Op. 74, organ, strings, percussion, Bärenreiter
2037.
Fantasie, Op. 32, Schott 2243.
Fantasie und Choral über Ein' feste Burg, Op. 58, Bären-
reiter 2057.
Hymn, Op. 75, organ and orchestra, Bärenreiter 2791.
Partita über Grosser Gott, wir loben dich, Bärenreiter
2647.
Partita über Wer nur, Bärenreiter 2648.
Präludium und Fuge, Bärenreiter 2646.
Sonatine, Op. 52 (Toccata; Trio und Tema con variazioni
e Fughetta), Bärenreiter 2056.
BURNEY, CHARLES. born Shrewbury, England, Apr. 7, 1726;
died Chelsea, Apr. 12, 1814. 1744-1747, pupil of Arne;
author of General History of Music; 1749-1751, organist,
St. Dionis-Backchurch; 1751-1760, organist, King's Lynn,
Norfolk; B. Mus. , 1769, Mus. Doc. , Oxford University.

composition in Masterpieces of Organ Music, Folio 60.

BUSAROW, DONALD. born Racine, Wis., Apr. 10, 1934. 1956, Concordia Teachers College, River Forest, Ill., University of Michigan, 1964, M. Mus., Cleveland Institute of Music, and Michigan State University; Organist-Director of Music, Bethany Lutheran Church, Detroit; Minister of Music, Outer Drive-Faith Lutheran Church, Detroit; organ pupil of Henry Fusner, Victor Hildner, Robert Noehren, and Corliss Arnold.

> Chorale Prelude on Nun freut euch, Concordia 97-5001, 1971.
> chorale prelude in The Parish Organist, Vol. 12.

BUSCH, ADOLPH GEORG WILHELM. German. born 1891; died 1952.

> Eight Chorale Preludes, G. Schirmer.
> Fantasie on a Recitative of Bach and Aus tiefer Not, Op. 19, Breitkopf und Härtel.
> Freu dich sehr, in Das Organistenamt, Vol. 2, Breitkopf und Härtel.

BUSH, ALAN DUDLEY. born London, 1900. Mus. B., University of London; Fellow of the Royal Academy of Music; 1925, appointed Professor of composition, Royal Academy of Music; 1958, made Extension Lecturer, University of London; 1957, Visiting Professor of Composition, Deutsche Hochschule für Musik, Berlin.

> Three English Song Preludes, Jos. Williams.
> Two Occasional Pieces, Op. 56, Novello, 1962.

BUSH, GEOFFREY. born London, Mar. 23, 1920. 1928-1933, choirboy, Salisbury Cathedral; studied at Lancing College and at Balliol College, Oxford; 1940, B. Mus., 1946, Doc. Mus.; Lecturer in Music, Extra-Mural Delegacy, Oxford.

> Carillon (Es ist ein Ros'), in A Christmas Album, Oxford.
> Toccata, in A Festive Album, Oxford, 1956, p. 16.

BUSONI, FERRUCCIO BENVENUTO. born Empoli, Tuscany, Italy, Apr. 1, 1866; died Berlin, July 27, 1924. 1888-1889, Professor of piano, Conservatory, Helsingfors; 1890, taught, Conservatory, Moscow; 1891-1894, taught at the New England Conservatory of Music, Boston, and concertized in America; 1913, became Director, Liceo Musicale, Bologna; 1915-1920, lived in Zürich; 1920, became Professor of composition, Academy of Arts, Berlin.

> Fantasie contrappuntistica (1910/1911), Breitkopf und Härtel 6342.
> Prelude on a ground and Fugue (double fugue on a chorale), Op. 7 (published, 1881).

BUSSER, HENRI-PAUL. born Toulouse, France, Jan. 16, 1872. Studied at the Conservatory and Ecole Niedermeyer, Paris; pupil of Widor, Gounod, and Franck; 1893, won Prix de Rome; 1892, became organist, St. Cloud; Director, Ecole Niedermeyer; 1921, appointed Professor of composition, Conservatory, Paris; choirmaster, Opéra-Comique, Paris.

> Canzone (Suite Brève), Choudens.
> Deux pièces sur des Noëls populaires, Op. 82, No. 2 (Il est né; Accourez pastoureaux), Durand, 1931.
> Magnificat, Lemoine.

Marche de Fête, Op. 36, Durand, 1908.

(Le) Sommeil de l'enfant Jésus, violin (or 'cello), harp, and organ, (Peters C55).

BUTCHER, VERNON. born East Rudham, Norfolk, England, 1909. M. A., D. Mus., Oxford University; Fellow, Royal College of Music; 1930-1941, Music Master, Chigwell School; 1946-1948, Organist, Llandaff Cathedral; 1949-1953, Director of Music, Wreckin College; 1953, became Music Master, Worcester College for the Blind.

Introduction and Fugue in E-flat Major, Oxford University Press.

Three Postludes on Hymn Tunes, Hinrichsen 192.

Three Versets on Diva Servatrix, Oxford University Press.

Two Improvisations on Anglican Chants, Hinrichsen 191.

BUTTSTETT (BUTTSTEDT), JOHANN HEINRICH. born Bindersleben (Erfurt), Germany, Apr. 25, 1666; died Erfurt, Dec. 1, 1727. By 1684, organist, Reglerkirche, Erfurt; pupil of Pachelbel; 1687, became organist, Kaufmannskirche, Erfurt; 1691-1727, organist, Predigerkirche, Erfurt.

Gelobet seist du, in The First Four Centuries of Organ Music, Vol. II, p. 423.

Nun lasst uns Gott dem Herrn, in Kleemeyer Book, Op. 17, Siegel.

Nun komm, in Viens, Sauveur, Orgue et Liturgie, Vol. 19, p. 16.

chorale prelude in Choralvorspiel alter Meister, p. 47.

chorale prelude in Eighty Chorale Preludes: German Masters of the Seventeenth and Eighteenth Centuries, p. 56.

chorale prelude in The Church Organist's Golden Treasury, Vol. II, p. 9.

chorale prelude in The Parish Organist, Vol. 1-4, p. 120.

chorale preludes (4) in Alte Weihnachtsmusik.

chorale prelude in Elf Orgelchoräle des siebzehnten Jahrhunderts.

chorale prelude in Das Erbe deutschen Musik, Series I, Vol. 9.

chorale prelude in Masterpieces of Organ Music, Folio 26.

chorale preludes (3) in Orgelchoräle des siebzehnten und achtzehnten Jahrhunderts.

chorale preludes (4) in Orgelchoräle um J. S. Bach.

chorale preludes (2) in Orgelspiel in Kirchenjahr, Vols. I and II.

chorale preludes (2) in Ritter Sammlung, Ries & Erler.

BUUS, JAKOB (JACQUES, JACHET). born Flanders, ca. 1500; died probably Vienna, late July 1565. Possibly a pupil of Willaert; 1541, became assistant organist, San Marco, Venice; 1551-1564, organist, court chapel, Vienna; wrote Intabolatura d'Organo di Ricercari M. Giacques Buus, Organista dell'illustrissima Signoria di Venetia in San Marco (1549).

Ricercari III and IV, (Peters HU1185).

BUXHEIMER ORGELBUCH. A collection of organ pieces in manuscript dated ca. 1470 which contains many arrangements of Burgundian chansons, about thirty preludes, and a copy of the

Fundamentum organisandi by Paumann.
Salva regina, in Salve regina, L'Organiste liturgique, Vol.
    21, p. 3.
complete transcription in 3 vols., Das Erbe deutschen
    Musik, Vols. 37, 38, 39, Bärenreiter.
composition in Apel, Masters of the Keyboard praembulums
    (2) in Historical Anthology of Music, Vol. I.
transcription by Booth, 2 vols., Hinrichsen 585 A and B.
BUXTEHUDE, DIDERIK (DIETRICH).   born Oldesloe (Holstein),
    1637, died Lübeck, Germany, May 9, 1707.   Probably studied
    with father; 1657-1658, organist, Marienkirche, Helsingborg;
    1660, became organist, Marienkirche, Helsingör; 1668, suc-
    ceeded his father-in-law, Franz Tunder, as organist, Marien-
    kirche, Lübeck; 1673, established Abend Musiken.
    Ausgewählte Orgelwerke, Hermann Keller, ed., Peters 4449,
        4457, 1938/1939.
            Vol. 1: Preludes and Fugues.
            Vol. 2: Chorale settings.
    Ausgewählte Werke, Walter Haacke, ed., Breitkopf und
        Härtel 6281.
    Danket dem Herrn, in Seasonal Chorale Preludes (with
        pedal).
    Ein' feste Burg, Cramer.
    Erschienen ist, in Anthologie.
    Free Compositions and Chorale Transcriptions, Max Seiffert,
        ed., 2 vols., Bärenreiter 5201.
    Herr Christ der einig, in Master Studies for the Organ,
        G. Schirmer.
    Nun bitten wir, in Chorale Preludes by Masters of the
        Seventeenth and Eighteenth Centuries, p. 24.
    Nun komm, in Harold Gleason, Method of Organ Playing,
        p. 176.
    Nun komm, in Viens, Sauveur, Orgue et Liturgie, Vol. 19,
        p. 3.
    Orgelcompositionen, Philipp Spitta and Max Seiffert, eds.,
        4 vols., Breitkopf und Härtel, 1940; also Kalmus
        3277, 3278, 3279, and 3280.
            Vol. 1: Passacaglia; Two Chaconnes; Prelude,
                Fugue, and Chaconne; Ten Preludes and
                Fugues.
            Vol. 2: Seven Preludes and Fugues; Four Fugues;
                Five Toccatas; Two Canzons; Four Partitas.
            Vol. 3: Chorale Preludes.
            Vol. 4: Chorale Preludes.
    Passacaglia in D Minor, in The First Four Centuries of
        Organ Music, Vol. II, p. 295.
    Präludium und Fuge C-dur, Dietrich Kilian, ed., Merse-
        burger 836.
    Präludium und Fuge (F Major, transposed from E Major),
        in European Organ Music of the 16th and 17th Cen-
        turies, p. 99.
    Prelude and Fugue in E Minor, in Geschichte der Musik in
        Beispielen, p. 249.

Preludium och fuga (F Major), in Musica Organi, Vol. I,
    p. 44.
Sämtliche Orgelwerke, Josef Hedar, ed., Hansen 3921/3922,
    3927/3928, Copenhagen, 1952.
    Vol. 1: Passacaglia, Ciaconen, Canzonen.
    Vol. 2: Preludes and Fugues.
    Vol. 3: Chorale Variations
    Vol. 4: Organ chorales.
Six Organ Preludes on Chorales, Ley, ed., Oxford 31.123.
Trio on Vater unser, in Schule des klassischen Triospiels,
    p. 8.
Vater unser, in Notre Père, Orgue et Liturgie, Vol. 24,
    p. 8.
chorale preludes (6), Seth Bingham, ed., in Anthologia
    Antiqua, Vol. 5, J. Fischer.
chorale preludes (4) in Chorale Preludes, Sets 1 and 2,
    Novello.
chorale preludes (2) in Choralvorspiel alter Meister.
chorale preludes (3) in Choralvorspiele zum Kirchenlied,
    Vol. 2.
chorale preludes (2) in Eighty Chorale Preludes: German
    Masters of the Seventeenth and Eighteenth Centuries.
chorale preludes (2) in The Church Organist's Golden
    Treasury, Vol. I.
chorale preludes (2) in The Church Organist's Golden
    Treasury, Vol. II.
chorale preludes (2) in The Church Organist's Golden
    Treasury, Vol. III.
chorale preludes (3) in Neue Werke, Seiffert, ed., Breitkopf
    und Härtel.
chorale preludes in Organ Preludes, Ancient and Modern,
    W. Sumner, ed., Vols. 1 (1) and 3 (1), Hinrichsen.
chorale preludes (2) in Orgelchoräle des siebzehnten und
    achtzehnten Jahrhunderts.
chorale preludes (7) in Orgelmeister des siebzehnten und
    achtzehnten Jahrhunderts.
chorale preludes in Orgelspiel im Kirchenjahr, Vol. 1 (3),
    Vol. 2 (1).
compositions (3) in Alte Meister.
compositions (4) in Alte Meister des Orgelspiels, Vol. I.
compositions (5), Seth Bingham, ed., in Anthologia Antiqua,
    Vol. 8, J. Fischer.
compositions (2) in Anthologia pro Organo, Vol. II.
compositions (2) in Anthologia pro Organo, Vol. IV.
compositions in Elf Orgelchoräle des siebzehnten Jahrhun-
    derts.
compositions in Elkan-Vogel Organ Series, Vol. 4.
compositions in Historical Anthology of Music, Vol. II,
    pp. 14, 99.
compositions (2) in Historical Organ Recitals, Vol. I.
compositions in Masterpieces of Organ Music, Folios 2, 14,
    17, 20, 30.
compositions in The Parish Organist, Vols. 5, 6.

compositions (2) in Treasury of Early Organ Music, pp. 47,
52.

preludes and fugues (2) in Liber Organi, Vol. 1.

preludes and fugues (2) in Liber Organi, Vol. 6.

BYRD, WILLIAM. English. born in Lincolnshire?, England, 1543;
died Stondon Massey, Essex, July 4, 1623. Pupil of Tallis;
1563-1572, organist, Cathedral, Lincoln; 1569, Gentleman in
Chapel Royal; end of 1572, organist's duties of Chapel Royal
shared with Tallis; 71 pieces in Fitzwilliam Virginal Book.

(The) Bells (passacaglia), in Anthologia pro Organo, Vol.
III, p. 22.

Eight Organ Pieces, Ledger, ed. , 1543A.

Fantasy, in Anthologia pro Organo, Vol. 1, p. 20.

Miserere; Praeludium, in Alte Orgelmusik aus England und
Frankreich.

Pavan, Cramer.

Pavanna, The Earl of Salisbury, in The First Four Centuries of Organ Music, Vol. I, p. 117.

Selected Works (Ausgewählte Werke), Hinrichsen 1543 A.

compositions (2) in Alte Orgelmusik aus England, Peeters,
ed.

compositions (2) in Liber Organi, Vol. 10.

CABANILLES, JUAN (JOAN) BAUTISTA JOSÉ. born Algemesi
(Valencia), Spain, Sept. 6, 1644; died Valencia, Apr. 29,
1712. 1655-1712, priest-organist, Cathedral, Valencia;
taught José Elias.

Intermèdes de V^e ton (Messe de Angelis), in Les Anciens
Maîtres Espagnola, p. 23.

Intermedios de Quinto tono para la Misa de Angelis, in
Antologia de Organistas Clásicos Españoles, Vol. I,
p. 80.

Musici Organici Iohannis Cabanilles, 3 vols. , Hyginii Angles,
ed. , Biblioteca de Cataluna, 1927-1936.

Opera Selecta pro Organo, Arnould Tournemire and Flor
Peeters, eds. , 3 vols. , Schott Frères.

Organ Works, Climent, ed. , Union Musical Española.

Organistas Españoles, Escuela Valencia, Climent, ed. , (2
tientos, 2 passacaglias, galliard), Union Musical
Española, Madrid, 1963.

Paseos, in Historical Anthology of Music, Vol. II, p. 111.

Passacalles in first mode, in Chacones et Passacailles, Orgue
et Liturgie, Vol. 22, p. 19.

Tiento, in Anthologia pro Organo, Vol. II, p. 12.

Tiento, in Anthologia pro Organo, Vol. IV, p. 22.

Tocata en Do Major de Ma Esquerra, in Early Spanish Organ
Music, p. 37.

tientos (3) in Historical Organ Recitals, Vol. VI.

tientos (3) in Old Spanish Organ Music.

CABEZÓN, ANTONIO DE. born Castrillo de Matajudíos (Burgos),

Spain, 1510; died Madrid, Mar. 26, 1566. Blind organist-
cembalist for King Philip II of Spain; 1526, became organist-
clavichordist to Empress Isabella, consort of Charles V; after
1539, Cabezón served Prince Philip and his family; friend of
Tomás de Santa Maria at Spanish court at Villadolid; 1548-
1551, 1554-1556, accompanied Philip in his travels.

Dic nobis, in Early Spanish Organ Music, p. 1.
Diferencias sobre el Canto del Caballero, in Historical Organ
    Recitals, Vol. I, p. 5.
Fuga al contrario (Tiento), in Geschichte der Musik in
    Beispielen, p. 112.
Himno a 3, in Silva Iberica, p. 2.
Magnificat on the Seventh Tone, in The First Four Cen-
    turies of Organ Music, Vol. I, p. 78.
Nun danket all, in Orgel Choräle Sammlung.
Oeuvres d'orgue, in Orgue et liturgie, Vols. 30 and 34.
Salve regina, from Libro de Cifra, Henestrosa, ed. , in
    Salve Regina, L'Organiste liturgique, Vol. 21, p. 15.
Tiento, in Alte Meister des Orgelspiels, Vol. I, p. 82.
Tientos et Fugues, M. S. Kastner, ed. , Schott 4948.
Veni Creator Spiritus, in Organ Book No. 1.
Versos del sexto tono and Diferencias sobre le Pavana
    Italiana (D Minor), in Apel, Masters of the Keyboard.
Versus, in Anthologia pro Organo, Vol. I, p. 14.
compositions (15) in Antologia de Organistas Clásicos
    Españoles, Vol. 1, pp. 1-27.
compositions (14) in Cabezón, Orgue et Liturgie, Vol. 30.
compositions (3) in Les Anciens Maîtres Espagnols.
compositions in Elkan-Vogel Organ Series, Vol. 5.
compositions (3) in Harold Gleason, Method of Organ
    Playing.
compositions (4) in Historical Organ Recitals, Vol. VI.
compositions (8) from Obras de Musica, Schott 4286.
diferencias (3) in Schule des klassischen Triospiels, Vol. I.
versi (4) in Anthologia pro Organo, Vol. III, p. 14.
CABEZÓN, HERNANDO DE. baptized Madrid, Sept. 7, 1541; died
    Valladolid, Oct. 1, 1602, son of Antonio de Cabezón.
    Glosado, in Antologia de Organistas Clásicos Españoles,
        Vol. I, p. 32.
CABEZÓN, JUAN DE. Spanish, sixteenth century. Brother of
    Antonio de Cabezón.
    Glosado, in Antologia de Organistas Clásicos Españoles,
        Vol. I, p. 28.
CALVIÈRE, GUILLAUME-ANTOINE. born Paris, France, 1700;
    died Paris, April 1755. Great improviser; 1730, organist,
    St. Germain-des-Prés, Ste. Marguerite; 1739, organist,
    Chapelle Royale.
    Récit de Cromorne en taille, Paul Brunold, ed. , Sénart,
        Paris, 1931.
CAMIDGE, MATTHEW. born York, England, 1758; died York,
    Sept. 21, 1859. Son of Matthew Camidge; 1812, Mus. B. ,
    Mus. Doc. , Cambridge; 1842, became organist, York
    Minster.

Concerto No. 2 in G Minor, Op. 13, No. 2, Francis Jackson, ed., Novello, 1966; also T. T. Noble, ed., H. W. Gray.

CAMONIN, PIERRE. born Bar-le-Duc (Meuse), France, Feb. 2, 1903. Organ pupil of Louis Vierne and Marcel Dupré, priest, organist, Eglise des Carmes; organist, Cathedral, Verdun.

Communion (Fête-Dieu), in Communions, Orgue et Liturgie, Vol. 62, p. 14.

Messe de la Fête-Dieu-Pange Lingua, in Orgue et Liturgie, Vol. 75.

Offertoire pour la Fête-Dieu sur Lauda Sion, in Offertoires, Orgue et Liturgie, Vol. 52, p. 17.

Panis angelicus (Fête-Dieu) sur Sacris solemniis, in Elévations, Orgue et Liturgie, Vol. 57, p. 13.

Prélude à L'Introit pour la fête de la Fête-Dieu, in Préludes à l'Introit, Orgue et Liturgie, Vol. 48, p. 8.

CAMPBELL, SIDNEY SCHOLFIELD. born London, England, 1909. Pupil of Ernest Bullock and Harold Darke; Mus. D., Durham University; 1931-1936, organist, West Ham Parish Church; 1936, became organist, St. Peter's Croyden; 1943-1947, St. Peter's Collegiate Church, Whampton; 1949-1953, organist, Ely Cathedral; 1953-1956, Southwark Cathedral, London Bridge; 1954-1956, Director of Studies, Royal School of Church Music; 1956-1960, Organist and Master of the Choristers, Canterbury Cathedral; Organist and Master of the Choristers, St. George's Chapel, Windsor.

Canterbury Interlude, in Preludes, Interludes, Postludes, Hinrichsen 600 F.

Epilogue on A Gallery Carol, in A Christmas Album, Oxford.

Exultate, Oxford.

Gaudeamus, in A Festive Album.

Pageantry, Novello.

Variations on Vexilla Regis, Novello.

CAMPION, FRANÇOIS. French. born 1680? died 1748.

suites (3) in Campion, Orgue et Liturgie, Vol. 13.

CAMPRA, ANDRÉ. born Aix (Provence), France, Dec. 4, 1660; died Versailles, June 29, 1744. Composer of opera; conductor.

Rigaudon, in A Treasury of Shorter Organ Classics, p. 30.

CANDLYN, T. FREDERICK H. born Davenham, Cheshire, England, Dec. 17, 1892; died Point Lookout, N. Y., Dec. 16, 1964. B. Mus., University of Durham; 1912, came to United States; Head, Music Department, N. Y. State College for Teachers, Albany; organist, St. Paul's Church, Albany, for twenty-eight years; 1943-1954, organist-choirmaster, St. Thomas' Church, New York (succeeded Noble); 1954, became organist-choirmaster, Trinity Church, Roslyn, L. I., N. Y.

Easter Prelude on O Filii et Filiae, Oliver Ditson.

Elegy, in The Modern Anthology, p. 34.

Fanfare-Procession (Tuba Theme), C. Fischer, 1934; 1960.

Fantasy on Veni Emmanuel, in American Organ Music, Vol. 2.

Festal Rhapsody on Christ ist erstanden, Abingdon.

Finale on a Tonic Pedal, H. W. Gray (St. Cecilia Series
    224).
(An) Indian Legend, H. W. Gray (St. Cecilia Series 211).
Marche Héroïque, H. W. Gray (St. Cecilia Series 251).
March of the Three Kings (Provençale), H. W. Gray (St.
    Cecilia Series 127).
Prelude on Divinum Mysterium, Arthur P. Schmidt, 1930;
    (Concordia 97-4659); H. W. Gray (St. Cecilia Series
    912).
Prelude on Flavian, Abingdon, APM-186.
Prelude on Hyfrydol, Abingdon, APM-187.
Rhapsody on Sursum Corda, H. W. Gray (St. Cecilia Series
    749), 1949.
Scherzo Caprice, H. W. Gray (St. Cecilia Series 140).
Scherzo on In dulci jubilo, Oliver Ditson.
Six Hymn Preludes, Abingdon.
Sonata Dramatica, H. W. Gray.
Sonata-Rhapsody, Arthur P. Schmidt.
Song of Autumn, H. W. Gray.
Three Christmas Preludes, Abingdon.
Toccata on Neander, Arthur P. Schmidt.
Tuba Theme, C. Fischer, 1934.
CANNING, THOMAS. American. born 1911. Professor of Music,
    Eastman School of Music, Rochester, N. Y.
    I Come, O Savior, to Thy Table, in Organ Music for the
        Communion Service, p. 47.
    chorale preludes in The Parish Organist, Vol. 1-4, 11, and 12.
    compositions (2) in Harold Gleason, Method of Organ Playing.
CAPOCCI, FILIPPO. Italian. born May 11, 1840; died Rome,
    July 25, 1911. Pupil of father; 1875, became organist and in
    1898 became choirmaster (successor to father) St. John Lateran,
    Rome.
    Adoro te devote, Carisch & Jänichen.
    Allegretto in Olden Style, Junne.
    Dix Pièces, Leduc.
    Fantasy on Veni Creator Spiritus, in Organ Works of
        Modern Masters, Vol. 2.
    Original Pieces, 12 Vols. , Augener.
    Sonata No. 2 (G Major), Augener.
    Sonata No. 3, Augener.
    Sonata No. 4 (E-flat), Kistner and Siegel.
    Sonata No. 6 (E Major), G. Schirmer.
    Ten Pieces, Carisch.
CAPPELEN, CHRISTIAN. Norwegian. born 1845, died 1916.
    Fantasie on Lover den Herre, Norsk Musikforlag.
    Grand Chorus, in Organ Music of the Netherlands and
        Scandinavia, p. 42.
    Improvisation on Den store hvide flok, Norsk Musikforlag.
    Legende (A Major), Norsk Musikforlag.
    Lette praeludier (20), Op. 19, NMO Hansen.
    Orgelstykker (2), NMO Hansen.
    Postludier (12), Op. 28, 2 Vols. , NMO Hansen.
    Six Chorale Preludes, Norsk Musikforlag.

Vier lyrische Stücke, Norsk Musikforlag.
Zwei Stücke (Hymne; Elegie), Norsk Musikforlag.
Zwei Stücke, Norsk Musikforlag.

CAPPELLETTI, ARRIGO. born Como, Italy, Jan. 16, 1877. Pupil of Pozzolo and of Cesare Dal'Olio; studied at the Accademia Filarmonica, Bologna, and at the Conservatory, Milan; organist-chorimaster, Chiesa di S. Fedele, Como.
Offertoire in A Minor, in The International Organist, Vol. II, p. 34.

CAPRICORNUS (BOCKSHORN), SAMUEL FRIEDRICH. German. born probably 1629; died Stuttgart, Nov. 10, 1665. 1651, appointed to Driefaltigkeitskirche, Pressburg; 1655, Opus Musicum published.
Lüneburg Tablatures, John R. Shannon, ed. , Vol. II, Concordia.

CARL, WILLIAM CRANE. born Bloomfield, N. J. , Mar. 2, 1865; died New York, Dec. 8, 1936. 1882, appointed organist, First Presbyterian Church, Newark, N. J. ; 1890, became pupil of Guilmant; 1899, Director and founder, Guilmant Organ School, New York; until 1936, organist, Old First Presbyterian Church, New York; founder of American Guild of Organists.
Master Pieces, G. Schirmer, 1938; also Kalmus 3284.
Master Studies, G. Schirmer, 1907.
Thirty Postludes, Kalmus 3283.

CARR, BENJAMIN. born London, England, Sept. 12, 1768; died Philadelphia, May 24, 1831. Pupil of Charles Wesley; 1793, went to America and established the first American music store; influential in early American musical life.
Andante, in Three Pieces by Early American Composers.
Aria, in Early American Compositions for Organ, p. 7.
Voluntary (Prelude; Aria; Andante).

CARREIRA, ANTONIO. born probably Lisbon, Portugal, ca. 1525; died between July 15, 1587/1597. Choirmaster for King Sebastian and Cardinal King Henry; represented in anthology: Manuscript musical, 242 of the Biblioteca General, U. de Coimbra, Portugal.
Three Fantasies, (Peters HU 1695).

CARVALHO, JOAO DE SOUZA. born Estremoz, Portugal, Feb. 22, 1745; died Borba?, 1798. Studied in Italy, sent by José I; ca. 1767, returned to Portugal to compose and teach.
Allegro, in Silva Iberica, p. 22.

CASANOVAS, NARCISO. born Sabadell (Barcelona), Spain, Feb. 17, 1747; died Montserrat, Apr. 1, 1799. Monk at Montserrat; virtuoso organist, master improviser.
Paso en Do Major, in Early Spanish Organ Music, p. 83.

CASELLA, ALFREDO. born Turin, Italy, July 25, 1883; died Rome, Mar. 5, 1947. Pupil of Fauré in Paris; toured as pianist; 1912-1915, taught piano, Conservatory, Paris; professor of piano, Santa Cecilia, Rome; 1927-1929, conductor, Boston Pops Orchestra; 1938-1947, lived in Italy.
Concerto romano, for organ and orchestra.

CASINI, GIOVANNI MARIA. born Florence, Italy, ca. 1670; died
  Florence, 1715. Priest-organist; 1703-1714, organist, Cathedral, Florence; maestro di cappella at the court; pupil of
  Pasquini; wrote Pensieri per l'organo (J. Guiducci e S. Fran-
  chi, Firenze, 1714.
     Pensiero Decimo, in Cérémonies Funèbres, L'Organiste
       liturgique, Vol. 15, 3.
     Pensiero musicale VIII, in Classici Italiani dell'Organo,
       p. 150.
     Triple Fugue (Pensiero Terzo), in La Fugue au dixhuitième
       siècle, Orgue et Liturgie, Vol. 15, p. 21.
     compositions in Archives des maîtres d'orgue des seizième-
       dixhuitième siècles, Vol. 10.
     pensieri (2) in L'Arte Musicale in Italia, p. 417.
CASNER, MYRON. born Williamsport, Pa., 1908. B.A., M.A.,
  Wesleyan University, Middletown, Conn.; studied at Royal
  College of Music and Royal College of Organists; chairman,
  department of languages, organist, St. John's Episcopal Church,
  Sturgis, Michigan.
     Prelude, Offertory, and Postlude on Schmücke dich, Con-
       cordia 97-4627.
     compositions in The Parish Organist, Vols. 11 and 12.
CASSLER, G. WINSTON. born Moundridge, Kansas, Sept. 3, 1906.
  Graduate, McPherson College, Kansas; B. Mus., Oberlin Con-
  servatory of Music; studied, College of St. Nicholas, Kent,
  England; pupil of Ernest Bullock; studied at Royal College of
  Music, Eastman School of Music; taught, Oberlin Conservatory
  of Music; 1949-, faculty, St. Olaf College, Northfield, Minn.
     Hymn-preludes, 4 vols., Augsburg, 1960-1962.
     Hymntune Duets, C Instruments and Organ, Augsburg 11-
       9238, 1970, Supplement for B-flat and F Instruments
       11-9239.
     Organ Music for the Church Year, Augsburg, 1959.
CASTELNUOVO-TEDESCO, MARIO. born Florence, Italy, Apr. 3,
  1895; died Hollywood, Calif., Mar. 16, 1968. Pupil of Piz-
  zetti; studied, Cherubini Institute; 1939, settled in America.
     Fanfare, H. W. Gray (Contemporary Organ Series 28).
     Fugue on the Name of Albert Schweitzer, McLaughlin and
       Reilly M-2881.
     Introduction, Aria and Fugue (1967), World Library.
     Prelude on the Name of Frederick Tulan, McLaughlin and
       Reilly M-2880.
CATO, DIOMEDES. Italian origin, died after 1615. ca. 1570,
  active in Polish royal court; organ compositions found in the
  tablature of Johannes Fischer (ca. 1595).
     compositions (2) in Keyboard Music from Polish Manuscripts,
       Corpus of Early Keyboard Music, No. 10, Vol. 4.
CAURROY, FRANÇOIS EUSTACHE DU, see DuCaurroy.
CAVACCIO, GIOVANNI. born Bergamo, Italy, 1556; died Bergamo,
  Aug. 11, 1626. 1581-1604, choirmaster, Cathedral, Bergamo;
  1604-1626, choirmaster, Santa Maria Maggiore, Bergamo.
     compositions (3) in L'Arte Musicale in Italia, Vol. III,
       p. 191.

CAVAZZONI, GIROLAMO. born Bologna (not Urbino), Italy, 1525;
    died Venice ?, 1560. Son of Marco Antonio Cavazzoni; or-
    ganist, San Marco, Venice; taught Costanzo Antegnati.
        Ad coenam, in Anthologia pro Organo, Vol. III, p. 20;
            also in Geschichte der Musik in Beispielen, p. 99.
        Christe Redemptor, in Organ Music for Christmas, Vol. 2.
        Dal I e II libro di Intavolatura per Organo, in I Classici
            della Musiche Italiana, Quaderno 23027.
        Magnificat and Gloria Patri, in The First Four Centuries
            of Organ Music, Vol. I, p. 71.
        Missa Apostolorum, in Harold Gleason, Method of Organ
            Playing.
        Organ Book, Kalmus 3285.
        Orgelwerke, 2 vols. Mischiati, ed. , Schott 4991 and 4992.
                Vol. 1: Four Ricercars; Two Canzonas; Four
                    Hymns; Two Magnificats.
                Vol. 2: Three Masses; Eight Hymns; Two
                    Magnificats; Two Ricercars.
        Second Livre d'Orgue, in L'Organiste liturgique, Vols. 34,
            38, 41.
        composition in Elkan-Vogel Organ Series, Vol. 1.
        compositions (3) in Classici Italiani dell'Organo.
        compositions (3) in Historical Anthology of Music, Vol. I.
        compositions in L'Arte Musicale in Italia, Vol. III.
CAVAZZONI, MARCO ANTONIO. born probably in Urbino before
    1490; died Venice, ca. 1570. Organist, Venice; 1520, or-
    ganist for Pope Leo X in Rome; 1528-1531, returned to Ven-
    ice; 1536-1537, organist, Cathedral, Chioggia; 1545-1559,
    singer, San Marco, Venice.
        Recerchari, Motetti, Canzoni, Libro Primo, in Jeppesen:
            Die italienische Orgelmusik, Vols. I and II.
        Ricercare, in Classici Italiani dell'Organo, p. 32.
        composition in I Classici Musicali Italiani, Vol. I.
CELLIER, ALEXANDRE-EUGÈNE. born Molières-sur-Cèze,
    France, June 17, 1883; died Paris, Mar. 4, 1968. Pupil
    of Guilmant and Widor at the Conservatory, Paris; 1910,
    organist, Temple de l'Etoile; organist, Société Bach.
        Choral-prélude sur la mélodie du Ps. 65, in Le Tombeau
            de Gonzalez, Orgue et Liturgie, Vol. 38, p. 3.
        Concerto.
        Eglises et paysages, 2 parts, Heugel.
        Etude in E Minor, Leduc, 1916.
        (Les) Pèlerinages Suite, Leduc, 1923.
        Prélude et Fugue, in L'Orgue Néo-Classique, Orgue et
            Liturgie, Vol. 33, p. 16.
        Quatre pièces brèves, in Maîtres contemporains de l'orgue.
        Suite Symphonique (G Major), Leduc, 1906.
        Theme et variations sur Ps. 149 "Sing unto the Lord a
            new song," trumpet and organ, in Varia, Orgue et
            Liturgie, Vol. 66, p. 16.
        Trois choral-paraphrases sur les mélodies des Psaumes
            de la Renaissance (Douleur, Esperance, Joie),
            Heugel, 1936.

Chorale No. 1, Psalm 77.
Chorale No. 2, Psalm 90.
Chorale No. 3, Psalm 138.
CHADWICK, GEORGE WHITEFIELD. born Lowell, Mass. , Nov. 13,
1854; died Boston, Apr. 4, 1931. 1877-1878, studied at Conservatory, Leipzig; pupil of Rheinberger; 1880, became organist South Congregational Church, Boston; professor of
harmony and composition, 1897, director, New England Conservatory of Music, Boston; 1905, honorary Ll. D. , Tufts
College. (Organ works by Chadwick are no longer in print;
photocopies may be procured from the Library of Congress
and the libraries of Harvard and Yale Universities.)
    Canon in C Minor.
    Pastorale, Introduction and Theme, Requiem, Canzonetta,
        J. B. Millet, 1895/1896.
    Progressive Pedal Studies, A. P. Schmidt, 1890.
    Suite in Variation Form, H. W. Gray, 1923.
    Ten Canonic Studies, Op. 12, A. P. Schmidt, 1885.
    Theme, Variations and Fugue, Boston, 1923 (transcription).
CHAIX, CHARLES. born Paris, Mar. 26, 1885. Studied at Ecole
Niedermeyer, Paris, and at Conservatory, Geneva; 1909,
began teaching, Conservatory, Geneva.
    Six Chorals figurés pour orgue, Op. 1, Leuckart, 1907.
    chorale preludes (2) in The French Organist, Vol. II, p. 56.
CHAMBONNIÈRES, JACQUES CHAMPION DE. born Paris or Cham-
bonnières, France, after 1601; died Paris or Chambonnières,
between 1670 and 1672. Court clavecinist to Louis XIV; wrote
Pièces de Clavessin (1670).
    Chacone (G Minor), in Chacones et Passacailles, Orgue et
        Liturgie, Vol. 22, p. 7.
    Oeuvres complètes, Brunold and Tessier, eds. , Sènart,
        1925.
    Pavanne, in Anthology of Early French Organ Music, p. 13.
    Sarabande, in Les Maîtres français de l'orgue, Vol. I,
        p. 6.
CHARPENTIER, JÂCQUES-GEORGES-PAUL. born Paris, Oct. 18,
1933. Studied at the Conservatory, Paris; pupil of Tony
Aubin; since 1966, Inspector of Music Instruction.
    (L')Ange à la Trompette, Leduc, 1962.
    Cinq Offertoires, Leduc, 1964.
    Messe de Minuit, Lemoine.
    Messe pour tous les temps, Leduc, 1966.
    Six Offertoires, Leduc (including Offertoire pour la fête de
        la Ste. Trinité).
    Te Deum, Costallat et Billaudot.
CHARPENTIER, MARC-ANTOINE. born Paris, France, 1634; died
Paris, Feb. 24, 1704. Pupil of Carissimi; associated with
Molière at Théâtre-Français; served the dauphin, Princesse
de Guise, Jesuits, Duke of Orléans; 1698, maître-de-musique,
Sainte Chapelle (succeeded F. Couperin); composer of opera,
Masses, and oratorios.
    Transcriptions pour orgue, in Orgue et Liturgie, Vol. 53;
        also Kalmus 3286.

CHAUMONT, LAMBERT. French, Seventeenth century. Wrote
Pièces d'orgue (1694).
  Chaconne Grave, in Cantantibus Organis, Vol. II, p. 11.
  Livre d'orgue, in Monumenta Leodiensium Musicorum,
    Vol. 1; also Heugel.*
CHAUSSON, ERNEST-AMEDÉE. born Paris, France, Jan. 20,
  1855; died Limay (Mantes), June 10, 1899. Pupil of Franck
  and Massenet; opera and orchestral composer.
  Vespers of Virgins (Versets pour les Vêpres des Vierges),
    Schola Cantorum.
CHAUVET, CHARLES-ALEXIS. born Marines (Seine-et-Oise),
  France, July 7, 1837; died Argentan (Orne), Jan. 28, 1871.
  Studied at the Conservatory, Paris; organist, St. Thomas-
  d'Aquin; 1863, became organist, St. Bernard-de-la-Chapelle;
  1866, organist, St. Merry; 1869, organist, La Trinité.
  Neuf offertoires destinées au temps de Noël, Durand, 1880.
  Recueil de sept pièces, Heugel.
  Vingt célèbres pièces, Théodore Dubois, ed. , Heugel, 1896.
CHERUBINI, LUIGI. born Florence, Italy, Sept. 14, 1760; died
  Paris, Mar. 15, 1842. Famous opera composer.
  Sonata, in Die Orgel, Concordia 97-4910.
CHRISTENSEN, BERNHARD. born Copenhagen, March 9, 1906.
  1929, graduated, Royal Conservatory, Copenhagen; 1932-
  1945, choirmaster, Christiansborg Castle; since 1945, or-
  ganist, Vangedekerke.
  Fantasie, Engstrom & Sødring.
  Glaeden hun er født i dag, Engstrom & Sødring.
  Koralbearbejdelser til gudstjenestebrug, Engstrom &
    Sødring.
CHRISTOPHER, CYRIL STANLEY. born Oldbury, Worcestershire,
  England, June 23, 1897. Pupil of Hollins and Bairstow;
  teacher, conductor.
  Fantasy on tune from Ravenscroft Psalter of 1621 (Old
    104th), Op. 20, No. 1, Hinrichsen 198 A.
  Homage Hymn, in Preludes, Interludes, Postludes,
    Hinrichsen 600 A.
  Psalm Prelude on Verses from Psalm 139, Op. 35, No. 2,
    Hinrichsen 552B.
  Rhapsody on a Ground, Hinrichsen 53.
  Scherzo-Fugue, Op. 20, No. 2, Hinrichsen 198 B.
  Sonata Brevis, Op. 34, Hinrichsen 552 A.
  Three chorale improvisations, Hinrichsen 52.
CIAMPI, LEGRENZIO VINCENZO. Italian. born 1719; died 1762.
  Six Concertos, organ or harpsichord and strings, Op. 7,
    score in Library of Congress.
CIMA, GIOVANNI PAOLO. born Milan, Italy ca. 1570; died
  during first half of seventeenth century.
  Canzone alla francese: La novella, in Classici Italiani
    dell'Organo, p. 98.
  Ricercare, in L'Arte Musicale in Italia, Vol. III, p. 141.
CLARKE, JEREMIAH. born London, probably ca. 1670; died
  London, Dec. 1, 1707. Sang under Blow at the Chapel
  Royal; 1692, organist, Winchester College; 1699, appointed

vicar-choral and organist, St. Paul's Cathedral, London;
1704, appointed joint organist with William Croft, Royal
Chapel; 1705, Vicar Choral, St. Paul's Cathedral.
> Three harpsichord pieces, in Varia, Orgue et Liturgie,
> Vol. 25.
> Trumpet Voluntary, in The Parish Organist, Vol. 9, p. 15.
> Trumpet Voluntary, trumpet solo, duet, or trio and organ,
> H. W. Gray.
> compositions (4) in Alte Orgelmusik aus England und
> Frankreich.

CLAUSSMANN, ALOYS. born Uffholtz (Haut-Rhin), France, July 5,
1850; died Clermont-Ferrand (Puy-de-Dome), France, Nov. 6,
1926. 1867-1872, studied at Ecole Niedermeyer; 1887(1890?)-
1926, organist, Cathedral, Clermont-Ferrand; 1881, founded
Philharmonic Orchestra, Clermont-Ferrand; 1908-1922, Director, Conservatory, Clermont-Ferrand.
> Cent Pièces, Op. 66, Lemoine.
> Introduction and Fugue, Op. 30, Lemoine.
> Sonata No. 1, Op. 44, Lemoine.

CLAUSSNITZER, PAUL. born Nieder-Schöna bei Freiberg, Germany, Dec. 9, 1867; died Borna (Leipzig), Apr. 6, 1924.
Studied at the Conservatory, Dresden; 1889, became music
teacher, Seminary, Grimma; 1894, went to Nossen; 1910,
became royal music director and professor, Seminary, Borna.
> Ach Gott vom Himmel, in Anthologie.
> Choral Sonata, Op. 30, Simrock.
> Drei Charakterstücke, Op. 23, Schweers & Haake.
> Dreizig kleine Stücke, Op. 36, Leuckart.
> Eighty Organ Pieces, F. W. Gadow.
> Eleven Chorale Preludes, Op. 29, Leuckart.
> Fifty Chorale Preludes, F. W. Gadow.
> Nine Preludes for Penitence and Grace, Op. 27, Leuckart.
> Nine Variations on Christus der ist mein, Op. 20, Leuckart.
> One-hundred Chorale Preludes, Op. 9, 7, 17, 10, 14, 16,
> 18, 19, 20, F. W. Gadow.
> One-hundred Interludes, Op. 21, Leuckart.
> Sixty Chorale Preludes, Op. 46, 48, 49, 50, Simrock.
> Sixty-one Preludes, Op. 7, 10, 14, 16, 18, 19, Leuckart.
> Ten Chorale Preludes, Op. 26, Leuckart.
> Thirty Short and Easy Preludes, Op. 9 and 17, Leuckart.
> Vier-und-zwanzig ganz leichte und kurze Stücke, Op. 44,
> Benjamin.
> Vom Himmel hoch, in Noël, p. 40.
> Zehn Choralvorspiele, Leuckart.
> Zwei feierliche Märsche, Op. 22, Schweers & Haake.
> chorale preludes (3) in The Lutheran Organist, Concordia.
> chorale preludes (4) in Organ Pieces by Modern Masters,
> O. Junne.

CLAVIJO DEL CASTILLO, BERNARDO. Spanish, born late sixteenth century; died Feb. 1, 1626. No knowledge of training;
after 1588, royal choirmaster and organist, Naples; taught at
University of Salamanca; 1603, became organist, royal chapel.
> Tiento de Segundo tono, por Gsolrend, in Antologia de

Organistas Clásicos Españoles, Vol. I, p. 77.
CLEMENT DE BOURGES. born Bourges, ca. mid-sixteenth century; died ?. Choirboy, St. Martin de Tours; 1538, at Lyon; served Henri II, François II; several pieces in Orgel-Tabulaturbuch of Paix.
    Fantaisies, in L'Organiste liturgique, Vol. 29-30.
CLÉRAMBAULT, LOUIS-NICOLAS. born Paris, France, Dec. 19, 1676; died Paris, Oct. 26, 1749. Father was one of the 24 violons du Roi; pupil of André Raison; organist, Maison Royale de St.-Louis, St. Cyr; succeeded Raison at church of the Jacobins; music director to Mme. de Maintenon; 1704-1710, organist, St. Sulpice.
    Basse et dessus de trompette, in Historical Organ Recitals, Vol. 1, p. 122; also in Les Maîtres français de l'orgue, p. 50; also in Treasury of Early Organ Music, p. 68.
    Capriccio, in Liber Organi, Vol. II, p. 30.
    Deux Suites, Schott 1874; also published by Schola Cantorum*.
    Premier Livre d'Orgue (Suite du premier ton; Suite du Deuxième ton), in Archives des maîtres d'orgue des seizième-dix-huitième siècles, Vol. III, also Kalmus 3308.
    Récits, in The First Four Centuries of Organ Music, Vol. II, p. 446.
    composition in Anthologia Antiqua, Vol. 1.
    composition in Masterpieces of Organ Music, Folio 31.
    compositions (2) in Anthologia pro Organo, Vol. II.
    compositions (2) in Anthologia pro Organo, Vol. IV.
CLOKEY, JOSEPH WADDELL. born New Albany, Ind., Aug. 28, 1890; died Covina, Calif., Sept. 14, 1960. 1912, B.A., Miami University, Oxford, Ohio; 1915, graduate of Cincinnati Conservatory; 1915-1926, taught music theory, Miami University; 1919-1921, taught theory and organ, Western College for Women; 1926-1939, professor of organ, Pomona College, Claremont, Calif.; 1939-1946, Dean, School of Fine Arts, Miami University.
    Ballade in D, H. W. Gray (St. Cecilia Series 709).
    Bell Prelude, H. W. Gray (St. Cecilia Series 692).
    Cantabile, in The Modern Anthology, p. 41.
    Canyon Walls, H. W. Gray (St. Cecilia Series 307).
    In a Norwegian Village, H. W. Gray (St. Cecilia Series 147).
    Jagged Peaks, H. W. Gray (St. Cecilia Series 305), 1924.
    Legend, H. W. Gray (St. Cecilia Series 191).
    Partita (G Major), organ and piano, H. W. Gray.
    Partita (G Minor), organ and string orchestra (quartet), H. W. Gray.
    Ten Meditations on Hymn Melodies, J. Fischer 8824.
    Ten Preludes based on Plainsong Kyries, Flammer.
    Thirty-five interludes on Hymn-tunes, J. Fischer 9100.
    Trio, violin, 'cello, and organ, H. W. Gray.
    Wind in the Pine Trees, H. W. Gray (St. Cecilia Series

306).

Woodland Idyl, H. W. Gray (St. Cecilia Series 198).

COCHEREAU, PIERRE-EUGÈNE CHARLES. born Saint Mandé,
France, July 9, 1924. 1943-1950, studied at Conservatory,
Paris; organ pupil of Marcel Dupré and composition pupil of
Tony Aubin; since 1955, organist, Notre-Dame-de-Paris;
since 1962, Director, Conservatory, Nice.
> Micro-Sonate, Leduc.
> Trois variations sur un thème chromatique, Leduc.

COELHO, MANOEL RODRIGUEZ. born Elvas, Portugal, 1583; died
1635. Priest; 1603, organist, master, Lisbon Cathedral chapel
royal; wrote Flores de musica para o instrumento de tecla e
harpa (Lisbon, 1620), a collection of twenty-four tentos, the first
instrumental work published in Portugal.
> Ave maris stella, in Orgel Kompositionen aus alter und neuer
> Zeit, also in The Progressive Organist, Bk. 3.
> Five Tentos, M. Kastner, ed. , Schott 2506.
> Four Susanas on the song Suzanne un jour, M. Kastner, ed. ,
> Schott 4633.
> Verse do primero tono, voice and organ, in Historical Anthol-
> ogy of Music, Vol. II, p. 32.

COKE-JEPHCOTT, NORMAN. born Coventry, England, Mar. 11,
1893; died New York City, Mar. 14, 1962. Choirboy, Holy
Trinity Church, Coventry; 1911, came to America; served
Church of the Holy Cross, Kingston, N. Y. , Church of the Messiah, Rheinbeck, N. Y. , Grace Church, Utica, N. Y. ; 1932-1953,
organist and master of the Choristers, Cathedral Church of St.
John the Divine, New York City.
> Bishops' Promenade, H. W. Gray (St. Cecilia Series 800).
> Fugue on GAE, H. W. Gray (St. Cecilia Series 784).
> Fugue Final, Oxford.
> Londonderry Air, H. W. Gray (St. Cecilia Series 810).
> Miniature Trilogy, A. P. Schmidt.
> Symphonic Toccata, H. W. Gray.
> Variations and Toccata on America, H. W. Gray (St. Cecilia
> Series 670).

COLEMAN, RICHARD HENRY PINWILL. born Dartmouth, England,
1888; died Feb. 17, 1965. 1908, Sub-organist, Manchester
Cathedral; organist, Blackburn and Derry; 1921, appointed organist, Petersborough Cathedral for twenty-three years; Doc.
Mus. , Dublin University; organist, Eastbourne and Brighton.
> Alla Marcia, in Simple Organ Voluntaries, Oxford.
> Chorale Preludes, J. S. Kerr.
> Chorale Preludes, Leonard, Gould & Bottler.
> Festal Finale, in A Festive Album, p. 8.
> Festival March, Cramer.
> Finale on Hyfrydol, in Hymn Tune Voluntaries, Oxford.
> Prelude, in An Easy Album, Oxford.
> Rhapsody on King's hymn, Bosworth.
> Ten Hymn Tune Voluntaries, 2 books, Stainer & Bell.
> Twenty-four Interludes based on Communion Hymns, Oxford.
> Two Interludes, Novello, 1931.
> Variations and Toccata, Novello.

Voluntary in G, Cramer, 1966.

COMMETTE, EDOUARD. born Lyon, France, Apr. 12, 1883; died
Apr. 24, 1967. Pupil of Widor; 1900-1952, organist, Cathedral,
Lyon; professor, Conservatory, Lyon.

Adoration, in The International Organist, Vol. I, p. 48.

Deux Méditations, Philippo.

Douze pièces, 2 vols., (Prélude; Campanile; Versets;
Cantilène; Intermezzo; Absolution; Pastorale; Sur le
Lac; Toccata; Rêverie; Minuet; Marche solennelle)
Leduc, 1935/1936.

Offertoire, H. W. Gray.

Quatorze Pièces brèves, Durand.

Scherzo, in The French Organist, Vol. 1, p. 43.

Six pièces (Offertoire sur des Noëls; Fughetta; Allegretto;
Adoration; Aspiration religieuse; Scherzo), Bornemann.

COOK, JOHN. born Maldon, England, Oct. 11, 1918. 1939, Mus.
B., University of Cambridge, organ pupil of Boris Ord and
David Willcocks; 1948, Associate Royal College of Music;
1951, Fellow, Royal College of Organists; 1958, Mus. D.,
University of Durham; 1949-1954, organist, Collegiate Church
of the Holy Trinity, Stratford-on-Avon; 1954-1962, organist,
St. Paul's Cathedral, London, Ontario; 1962-1968, organist,
Church of the Advent; since 1965, Music Department, M.I.T.,
Cambridge, Mass.

Capriccio, for organ and strings (1964).

Fanfare, Novello, 1952.

Flourish and Fugue, H. W. Gray.

Improvisation on Veni Creator Spiritus, Novello.

Invocation and Allegro Giojoso, Novello.

Mr. Purcell's Wedding March, Novello.

Scherzo, Reflection and Dance, H. W. Gray.

Two hymn-preludes, in Festal Voluntaries (Christmas,
Ascension), Novello.

Variations on Alles ist an Gottes segen, H. W. Gray.

Variations on Alles ist an Gottes segen, Novello.

COPLAND, AARON. born Brooklyn, N.Y., Nov. 14, 1900. Pupil
of Boulanger; noted orchestral composer, lecturer, writer,
has won many awards.

Episode (1940), H. W. Gray (Contemporary Organ Series).

Preamble for a Solemn Occasion, Boosey and Hawkes.

Symphony for Organ and Orchestra (1924), Boosey and
Hawkes.

CORELLI, ARCANGELO. born Fusignano (Imola), Italy, Feb. 17,
1653; died Rome, Jan. 8, 1713. Composer, virtuoso violinist; taught Locatelli; founded modern violin technique;
created concerto grosso.

Pastorale for Violin and Organ, C. F. Peters FK4.

Preludio, in Anthologia pro Organo, Vol. IV, p. 46.

transcription in Anthologia Antiqua, Vol. 1.

CORNET, PIERRE (PETER, PIETER). Flemish. born ca. 1562;
died 1626. Organist to Infanta Clara Eugenia during the Spanish occupation.

Ad te clamamus, in Ricercare, Canzonen und Fugen, p. 8.

Courante, in Oudnederlandse Meesters, Vol. II, p. 56.
Fantasia, in Anthologia pro Organo, Vol. III, p. 30.
Salve Regina, in Historical Organ Recitals, Vol. I, p. 48;
    also in Hymnes et Antiennes, Orgue et Liturgie,
    Vol. 8, p. 10.
Toccata, in Anthologia pro Organo, Vol. I, p. 24.
Toccata; Fantasie, in Oudnederlandse Meesters, Vol. III.
composition in Archives des maîtres d'orgue des seizième-
    dix-huitième siècles, Vol. 10.
compositions (3) in Oudnederlandse Meesters, Vol. I.
compositions (2) in Altniederlandische Meister.
CORRADINI, NICOLÒ. born Bergamo, Italy, end of sixteenth cen-
    tury; died ?, 1620. Organist, Cathedral, Cremona; wrote
    book of twelve ricercari found in Martini library, Bologna.
    Ricercare IX tono, in Classici Italiani dell'Organo, p. 101.
CORREA DE ARAUXO, FRANCISCO. born Seville, Spain, 1575/
    1577; died ?, 1663. Dominican monk; studied in Seville;
    1598-1630, organist, San Salvador, Seville; 1626, published
    Facultad orgánica (Alcalá de Henares, 1626) which contains
    seventy compositions for organ (tientos, glosses, variations);
    became Bishop of Segovia.
    Facultad Orgánica, in Monumentos de la Música Española,
        Vol. 6, 12.
    Libro de Tientos y Discursos, M. S. Kastner, ed. , Insti-
        tuto Español de Musicologia, Barcelona, Vol. 1.
    Tiento de IV⁰ Tono por E la mi a modo de canción, in
        Historical Organ Recitals, Vol. 6, p. 30.
    Tiento y Discurso, in Antologia de Organistas Clasicos
        Españoles, Vol. II, p. 1.
    tientos (3) in Old Spanish Organ Music.
CORRETTE, GASPARD. French. Seventeenth and eighteenth cen-
    turies. 1706, organist, St. Herbland, St. Pierre-le-Portier,
    St. Denis, St. Jean, all in Rouen, France.
    *Missa Octavi Toni, in Orgue et Liturgie, Vols. 50 and 51;
        also published by Kalmus 3313.
    compositions (3) in Les Maîtres francais de l'orgue,
        Vol. II.
CORRETTE, MICHEL. born Rouen, France?, 1709; died Jan. 22,
    1795. 1737, became organist, Grosspriors of France; 1750,
    appointed organist, Jesuits; 1759, became organist for Prince
    of Condé; 1780, organist for Duke of Angoulême.
    Concerto in D Minor, for organ and strings (flute ad lib.),
        Bärenreiter (NMA 201).
    Noël sur Vous qui desirez sans fin, in Les Maîtres français
        de l'orgue, Vol. II, p. 78; also in L'Organiste litur-
        gique.
COSTELEY, GUILLAUME. born probably in Pont-Audemer, France,
    1531; died Evreux, Feb. 1, 1606. Organist, valet de chambre
    to Henry II and Charles IX of France; 1560, "Estat des pen-
    sionnaries du roy en son espargne"; 1570, "organiste ordinaire
    et vallet de chambre du roy"; wrote Fantasie sus orgue ou
    espinette.
    Fantaisie "Une jeune fillette," in Anthology of Early French

Organ Music, p. 7.

COSYN, BENJAMIN. English. Flourished 1622-1643. Organist,
Alleyn's College, Dulwich; organist, Charterhouse; his anthol-
ogy, Benjamin Cosyn's Virginal Book, contained pieces by Bull,
Gibbons, and himself.

> Three Voluntaries, John Steele, ed., Novello EOM 14, 1959.

COUPERIN, FRANÇOIS ("LE GRAND"). born Paris, Nov. 10, 1668;
died Paris, Sept. 12, 1733. Pupil of his father Charles, his
uncle François, and Jacques-Denis Thomelin; 1685, became
organist, St. Gervais, the position saved for him; 1693, appointed organist, royal chapel at Versailles.

> Benedictus, in Organ Music for the Communion Service,
> p. 58.
> Domine Deus and Agnus Dei, in The First Four Centuries of
> Organ Music, Vol. II, p. 290.
> Fugue on Kyrie, in Historical Organ Recitals, Vol. I, p. 66;
> also in Treasury of Early Organ Music, p. 66.
> *Messe des Convents, Norbert Dufourcq, ed., Schola Can-
> torum, Paris.
> *Messe des Paroisses, Norbert Dufourcq, ed., Schola Can-
> torum, Paris, 1963.
> Pièces d'orgue, Archives des maîtres d'orgue des seizième-
> dix-huitième siècles, Vol. 5; also published by Schott
> 1878.
> *Pièces d'orgue consistantes en Deux Messes, Paul Brunold,
> ed., Editions L'Oiseau-Lyre, Louise B. M. Dyer,
> Monaco, 1949; also Kalmus 3314 and 3315.
> Suite from Solemn Mass for Parish Use, Seth Bingham, ed.,
> in Anthologia Antiqua, Vol. 7, J. Fischer.
> compositions in Anthologia Antiqua, Vols. 4 and 7.
> compositions in Denkmäler deutscher Tonkunst, Vol. 4.
> compositions in Masterpieces of Organ Music, Folios 29,
> 33, 37.
> compositions in The Parish Organist, Vols. 7 and 8.
> Mass movements (2) in Anthology of Early French Organ
> Music.
> Mass movements (2) in Anthologia pro Organo, Vol. II.
> Mass movements (5) in Liber Organi, Vol. I.
> Mass movements (3) in Liber Organi, Vol. II.
> Offertoire (G Major), in Anthologia pro Organo, Vol. IV,
> p. 29.

COUPERIN, LOUIS. born Chaumes, France, ca. 1626; died Paris,
Aug. 29, 1661. Pupil of Chambonnières; 1653, became organ-
ist, St. Gervais, Paris; court musician, Louis XIV; uncle of
François.

> Chaconne (F Major), in Les Maîtres français de l'orgue,
> Vol. II, p. 15.
> Chaconne (G Minor), in Anthology of Early French Organ
> Music, p. 16.
> *L'Oeuvre d'orgue, in Orgue et Liturgie, Vol. 6.
> compositions (2) in Alte Orgelmusik aus England und Frank-
> reich.

COURBOIN, CHARLES-MARIE. born Antwerp, Belgium, Apr. 2,

1886.   Pupil of Blockx at Conservatory, Brussels;   1902, appointed organist, Cathedral, Antwerp;   organist, Oswego and
Syracuse, New York;   1917-1918, organist in Springfield, Mass. ;
1919, appointed organist, Wanamaker Auditoriums, New York
City and Philadelphia;   1943-1970, organist, St. Patrick's Cathedral, New York City.
> Belgian Mother's Song (Benoit), H. W. Gray (St. Cecilia
> Series 696).

COWELL, HENRY DIXON.   born Menlo Park, Calif. , Mar. 11,
1897;   died 1965.   Studied at University of California and Institute of Applied Music, New York;   won Guggenheim prize to
study in Berlin;   pupil of R. Huntington Woodman;   taught at
Stanford, New School for Social Research, University of California, Mills College, Columbia University;   1951, Director, Composition Department, Peabody Institute, Baltimore.
> Hymn and Fuguing Tune No. 14 (1962), Associated Music
> Publishers.
> Prelude, Associated Music Publishers, 1958.
> Processional, H. W. Gray (Contemporary Organ Series 16).

COXSUN, ROBERT.   English.   Sixteenth century.
> Laetamini in Domino, in Altenglische Orgelmusik, p. 38.

CRANDELL, ROBERT EUGENE.   born Hornell, N. Y. , Jan. 10,
1910.   1932, B. M. , University of Michigan;   1936, S. M. M. ,
Union Theological Seminary, New York City;   organ pupil of
Paul Alwardt, Clarence Dickinson, and Hugh Porter;   composition pupil of Hunter Johnson, Edwin Stringham, Nadia Boulanger,
and Roy Harris;   1932-1934, taught theory, University of Michi-
gan;   1936-1941, organist-choirmaster, First Baptist Church,
Bridgeport, Conn. ;   1941-1944, Central Congregational Church,
Brooklyn;   1944-1953, Cadman Memorial Church, Brooklyn;   1953-
1966, First Presbyterian Church, Brooklyn;   faculty member,
Roosa School of Music, Brooklyn for twelve years;   1963, appointed Lecturer in composition and theory, Union Theological
Seminary;   1951, appointed to faculty, since 1963, Director of
Music Department, Packer Collegiate Institute, Brooklyn.
> Carnival Suite, H. W. Gray, 1950.

CROFT, WILLIAM.   baptized Nether Ettington, England, Dec. 30,
1678;   died Bath, Somerset, Aug. 14, 1727.   Chorister in
Chapel Royal under Dr. Blow;   1700, organist, St. Anne, Soho;
1707, joint organist with Jeremiah Clarke, Chapel Royal;   1708,
became organist, Westminster Abbey;   1713, Doc. Mus. , Oxford.
> Trumpet Tune, in Alte Orgelmusik aus England und Frank-
> reich, p. 6.
> Voluntaries, Simpson, ed. , Hinrichsen 221, 223-226.
> Voluntary in C Major, Hinrichsen.
> Voluntary in D Major, Hinrichsen.
> Voluntary in D Minor, Hinrichsen.
> Voluntary in D Major, Hinrichsen.
> Voluntary in C Major, Hinrichsen.
> Voluntary in D Minor, Hinrichsen.

CROTCH, WILLIAM.   born Norwich, England, July 5, 1775;   died
Taunton, Dec. 29, 1847.   Child prodigy, played the organ at
very early age;   studied at Oxford;   1790, organist, Christ

Church, Oxford; 1794, Mus. B., Oxford; 1797, organist, St. John's College; 1797-1847, Professor of Music, St. John's College; organist, St. Mary's Church; 1799, Mus. Doc., Oxford; ca. 1807, became organist, Oxford; 1822, appointed Principal, Royal Academy of Music.
Introduction and Fugue on a Chant by Dr. P. Hayes.
CRUNDEN-WHITE, PAUL. English, born November, 1937. Studied at the Worcester College for the Blind; pupil of Priaulx Ranier and Paul Steinitz at the Royal Academy of Music; 1960, won Italian government scholarship to study with Goffredo Petrassi.
Theme and Variations, Novello.
Three Christmas Pieces, Novello.
CRUZ, AGOSTINHO DA. born Braga, Portugal, ca. 1590; died Coimbra, June 19, 1633. 1609, entered Monastery of Santa Cruz, Coimbra; choirmaster, royal monastery, St. Vincent de Fora, Lisbon.
Verso de 8º tom por d-sol-re, in Silva Iberica, p. 11.
CURRY, W. LAWRENCE. American, born 1906, died 1966.
Chorale prelude on Dundee, H. W. Gray (St. Cecilia Series 727), 1947.
Fantasia on Ein' feste Burg, H. Flammer.
Improvisations on Schönster Herr Jesu, Abingdon.
Prelude on Bremen, Abingdon.
CURTIS, EDGAR.
Concerto, Organ and String Orchestra, Peters 6638.
CZERNOHORSKY, BOHUSLAV. born Nimburg, Czechoslovakia, Feb. 16, 1684; died Graz, July 1, 1742. 1703, became Minorite friar; Magister musicae, Padua; organist, Franciscan cloister, Assisi; Kapellmeister, Teinkirche, Prague, and St. Jacob's Cloister.
Fugue in A Minor, in La Fugue au dix-huitième siècle, Orgue et Liturgie, Vol. 15, p. 28; also in Anthologia pro Organo, Vol. II, p. 55.
Fugue in A Minor, in A Century of Czech Music, Vol. I, p. 3; in Musica Organi, Vol. I, p. 48.
Fugue in D Minor, in A Century of Czech Music, Vol. I, p. 7.
Orgelstücke (8) Bärenreiter MAB 3.
Toccata in C Major, in A Century of Czech Music, Vol. II, p. 5.
compositions (3) (Toccata in C Major, Fugue in A Minor, Fugue in D Minor), in Altböhmische Meister, Rudolf Quoika, ed., Breitkopf und Härtel 5925, 1948.

DAGINCOUR (D'AGINCOUR), FRANÇOIS. born Rouen, France, 1684; died Rouen, Apr. 30, 1758. Pupil of Boyvin and Lebègue; 1701-1706, organist, Ste. Madeleine-en-la-Cité; 1706, became organist, Cathedral, Rouen; organist, royal Abbey of St. Ouen; 1726, appointed organist, St. Jean, Rouen; organist, Chapelle Royale.
L'Orgue d'autrefois. François Dagincour, Panel, ed., Hérelle.

Pièces d'orgue, in Orgue et Liturgie, Vol. 31.
compositions (2) in Les Maîtres français de l'orgue, Vol. II.
DALLIER, HENRI. born Rheims, France, 1849; died Paris, 1934.
1865, organist for choir, Rheims; pupil of Franck; improviser;
1879, became organist, St. Eustache, Paris; 1905, appointed
organist, la Madeleine, succeeded Fauré; 1905-1934, professor
of harmony, Conservatory, Paris.
Cinq invocations, Lemoine, 1926.
In Deo caritas, Leduc, 1895.
Offertoire: O Filii et Filiae, La Schola Paroissiale, 1896.
Six grands préludes d'orgue pour la Tousaint, Op. 19, Leduc,
1891.
DANDRIEU, JEAN-FRANÇOIS. born Paris, France, 1682; died
Paris, Jan. 16, 1738. 1705, appointed organist, St. Merry,
Paris; 1721, became organist, royal chapel; 1733, succeeded
his uncle Pierre as organist, St. Barthélemy.
Fugue sur Ave maria stella, in Les Maîtres français de
l'orgue, Vol. I, p. 72.
Fugue sur l'Hymne des Apôtres Exultet, in Les Maîtres
français de l'orgue, Vol. II, p. 64.
Magnificat, in Noël, p. 3.
Muzete, in The First Four Centuries of Organ Music,
Vol. II, p. 457.
*Noëls, 4 vols., in L'Organiste liturgique, Vols. 22, 16, 12,
19-20.
Noëls, in Christmas Music, Kalmus 3366.
Offertoire pour le jour de pâques sur O Filii et Filiae, in
Pâques (I), p. 10; also in Offertoire for Easter, Biggs,
ed., McLaughlin and Reilly; in The Parish Organist,
Vol. 8.
(Le) petit nouveau né, in Douze noëls anciens, p. 11, Schott
Frères, 1938.
*Pièces d'orgue, Alexandre Guilmant and André Pirro, eds.,
Schott 1880.
Premier Livre de Pièces d'orgue, in Archives des maîtres
d'orgue des seizième-dix-huitième siècles, Vol. 7.
Puer nobis nascitur, in Venite Adoramus, McLaughlin &
Reilly.
compositions in The Parish Organist, Vols. 5, 6 and 7.
noëls (2) in Orgue et Liturgie, Vol. 4.
DANDRIEU, PIERRE. French. born ca. 1660; died Paris, Oct.
1733. Priest and organist, St. Barthélemy; wrote Noëls variés
(1715).
composition in Orgue et Liturgie, Vol. 4, p. 15.
noëls (3) in Les Maîtres français de l'orgue, Vol. II.
DANIEL-LESUR (see Lesur, Daniel-Jean-Yves).
DAQUIN, LOUIS-CLAUDE. born Paris, France, July 4, 1694;
died Paris, July 15, 1772. Student of Marchand; organist,
Cloître de Petit St. Antoine; 1727-1772, organist, St. Paul.
Chartres, in New Book of Noëls, E. Power Biggs, ed.,
Music Press.
Livre de Noëls, in Archives des maîtres d'orgue des
seizième-dix-huitième siècles, Vol. III; also Schott

1875; also Orgue et Liturgie, Vol. 36, Schola Can-
torum. *
Noël (D Minor), in Liber Organi, Vol. II, p. 33.
Noël sur les flûtes, in Les Maîtres français de l'orgue,
Vol. I, p. 81.
Noëls, in Christmas Music, Kalmus 3368.
Swiss Noël, in Treasury of Early Organ Music, p. 70.
Twelve Noëls, E. Power Biggs, ed., 2 vols, Mercury
Music Press.
compositions in The Parish Organist, Vols. 5 and 6.
noëls (7) in Douze Noëls anciens, Schott Frères.
DARASSE, XAVIER-FRANÇOIS. born Toulouse, France, Sept. 3,
1934. Studied at Conservatory, Toulouse, and Conservatory,
Paris; winner of seven Premier Prix: harmony, counterpoint,
fugue, organ, improvisation, analysis, composition; pupil of
Duruflé, Falcinelli, and Messiaen; 1962-1965, organist, St.
Pierre de Neuilly; 1964, won Prix de Rome; 1965, professor
of organ, Conservatory, Toulouse.
Prélude; Largo; Choral et Variations, in Pièces Brèves
contemporains, L'Organiste liturgique, Vol. 42.
DARKE, HAROLD EDWIN. born Highbury, London, Oct. 29, 1888.
Scholarship student at Royal College of Music; pupil of Parratt
and Stanford; 1906, organist, Emmanuel Church, West Hamp-
stead; organist, St. James, Paddington; assistant to Walford
Davies, Temple Church; since 1916, organist, St. Michael's
Church, Cornhill; Fellow, Royal College of Organists; faculty
member, Royal College of Music; 1919, Mus. Doc., Oxford
University; 1941-1945, organist King's College, Cambridge;
taught, Cambridge University.
Andantino, in Little Organ Book.
Bridal Procession, Ascherberg, Hopwood & Crew Ltd.
Chorale Prelude on a Theme by Tallis, Novello, 1919.
Elegy, in Simple Organ Voluntaries, Oxford.
(A) Fantasy, Oxford.
In Green Pastures, in An Easy Album, Oxford.
(A) Meditation on Brother James' Air, Oxford.
Rhapsody.
Three Chorale Preludes, Op. 20, Novello.
DAVID, JOHANN NEPOMUK. born Eferding, Upper Austria,
Nov. 30, 1895. Choirboy, St. Florian monastery; 1920-1923,
studied at Vienna Academy; 1924-1933, organist-choirmaster,
Wels, Upper Austria; 1934, became professor of composition,
1939, appointed director, Leipzig Conservatory, Director of
Chorale, Leipzig; 1945-1947, Director, Mozarteum, Salzburg;
1947, appointed professor of composition, Musikhochschule,
Stuttgart.
Chaccone (A Minor) (1927), Breitkopf und Härtel 5593.
Chaccone und Fuge (1962), Breitkopf und Härtel 6402.
Choralwerk (1932-   ), Vols. 1-19, Breitkopf und Härtel
5571 A-T (1968).
Concerto for Organ and Orchestra, Op. 61 (1965), Breitkopf
und Härtel 6569.
Fantasie über L'Homme armé, (1929) Breitkopf und Härtel

5550.
Introit, Chorale and Fugue on a theme by Bruckner, organ and nine wind instruments, Op. 25, Breitkopf und Härtel 5725.
Partita (1970), Breitkopf & Härtel.
Partita on Two Christmas Songs, Breitkopf und Härtel.
Partita über B-A-C-H (1964), Breitkopf und Härtel 6464.
Partita über Innsbruck (1955), Doblinger.
Passamezzo und Fuge (G Minor) (1928), Breitkopf und Härtel 5595.
Praeambel und Fuge (D Minor) (1930), Breitkopf und Härtel 5549.
Ricercar (A Minor), Breitkopf und Härtel 6242.
Ricercare (C Minor) (1925), Breitkopf und Härtel 5596.
Toccata und Fuge (1962), Breitkopf und Härtel 6401.
Toccata und Fuge (F Minor) (1928), Breitkopf und Härtel 5597.
Zwei Fantasien und Fugen (1931), Breitkopf und Härtel 5599.
Zwei Hymnen (1928), Breitkopf und Härtel 5594.
Zwei kleine Präludien und Fugen (1931), Breitkopf und Härtel 5591.
Zwölf Orgelfügen, Breitkopf und Härtel 6560 a/m.
DAVID, THOMAS CHRISTIAN. German. born 1925.
Fantasie über Dux Michael (1965), Associated Music Publishers.
Fünf Orgelchoräle (1961), Doblinger.
Fünf Orgelchoräle (1963), Doblinger.
Variations on a German Folk Song, organ and viola, Doblinger.
DAVIES, (SIR) HENRY WALFORD. born Oswestry, England, Sept. 6, 1869; died Wrington, Somerset, Mar. 11, 1941. 1890-1894, student at Royal College of Music, pupil of Parratt and Stanford; 1892, Mus. Bac., 1898, Mus. Doc., Cambridge; 1895-1903, teacher of counterpoint, Royal College of Music; 1890-1891, organist, St. Anne's Church, Soho; 1898-1923, organist-choirmaster, Temple Church; 1919-1926, professor, University of Wales; 1924, appointed organist, St. George's Windsor.
Jesu, dulcis memoria, in memory of Parry (1924) Year Book Press.
Memorial Melody (1936).
Solemn Melody (1908), arr. West, Novello, 1910.
DAVIES, PETER MAXWELL. born Manchester, England, Sept. 8, 1934. Studied at Royal Manchester College of Music; pupil of Petrassi, Rome; 1959-1962, Director of Music, Cirencester Grammer School; pupil of Roger Sessions at Princeton University.
Fantasy on O Magnum Mysterium, Schott 10826.
DECAUX, ABEL. born Auffay, France, 1869; died Paris, 1943.
Pupil of Guilmant; 1903-1926, organist, Sacré Coeur; professor

of organ, Schola Cantorum.
Fugue sur Ave maris stella.
DECKER, JOHANN. German. born 1598; died 1668.
    Präambulum, from Lüneburg Tablature, in Organum, Series
        IV, Vol. 2.
DEGEN, HELMUT. born Aglasterhausen (Heidelberg), Germany,
    Jan. 14, 1911. Pupil of Jarnach; 1937, began teaching at
    Conservatory, Duisburg; 1947, began teaching at Hochschulin-
    stitut, Trossingen.
    Kommt ihr Hirten, in Christmas Music, Bärenreiter 1869.
    Konzert, organ and brass choir, Schott 3682.
    chorale preludes (4) in 73 leichte Choralvorspiele, alter und
        neuer Meister, H. Fleischer, ed. , Leuckart.
DE KLERK, ALBERT. Dutch. born 1917. Organist, St. Joseph's
    Roman Catholic Church, Haarlem; municipal organist, Grote
    Kerk, Haarlem (along with Piet Kee).
    Christe du bist licht ende dag, Van Rossum.
    Concerto for Organ and Brass, (Peters D 448).
    Eight Fantasies on Gregorian Themes, Van Rossum.
    Sonata, (Peters D221).
    Twelve Images, Novello (Original Compositions 351-New
        Series).
    Variations on O Jesu soet, Annie Bank.
DE LAMARTER, ERIC. born Lansing, Mich. , Feb. 18, 1880; died
    Orlando, Fla. , May 17, 1953. Pupil of Middleschulte, Guil-
    mant, and Widor; organist, Chicago; 1918-1936, assistant con-
    ductor, Chicago Symphony Orchestra; Chicago music critic.
    Carillon, H. W. Gray (St. Cecilia Series 154)
    Chorale Prelude on a Melody by Hassler, Witmark.
    Concerto No. 1 (E Major), organ and orchestra (1920) H. W.
        Gray.
    Concerto No. 2 (A Major), organ and orchestra (1922) H. W.
        Gray.
    Festival Prelude, Witmark & Sons, 1945.
    Intermezzo, H. W. Gray (St. Cecilia Series 149).
    (A) Gothic Prelude, G. Schirmer, 1937.
    March, H. W. Gray (St. Cecilia Series 150).
    Nocturnes (Nocturne at Sunset; Fountain; Nocturne at Twilight),
        H. W. Gray, 1943.
    Stately Procession, H. W. Gray, 1943.
    Suite, Witmark & Sons, 1945.
    Toccatino H. W. Gray (St. Cecilia Series 153).
DELBOS, CLAIRE (pseudonym of Louise Justine Delbos).
    French. died April 1959. Violinist; first wife of Oliver
    Messiaen.
    Deux Pièces, Hérelle, 1935 (Lemoine).
    L'Offrande à Marie, Hérelle, 1935.
    Paraphrase pour la fête de tous les Saints, le jour des Morts,
        les dimanches 24e après la Pentecôte et le 1er de
        l'Avent, Lemoine.
DELLO JOIO, NORMAN. born New York, N. Y. , Jan. 24, 1913.
    Pietro Yon was his godfather; pupil of B. Wagenaar and Hinde-
    mith; 1944-1946, won two Guggenheim fellowships; 1944-1950,

faculty, Sarah Lawrence College.
> Antiphonal Fantasia on theme of Albrici, organ, brass, and
> strings, E. B. Marks.
> Laudation, E. B. Marks, 1965.

DELVINCOURT, CLAUDE. born Paris, France, Jan. 12, 1888;
died Bivio di Albinia, Orbetto, Italy, April 5, 1954. Pupil of
Boëllman, Busser, Plé-Caussade, and Widor; 1931-1941, Director, Conservatory, Versailles; 1941-1954, Director, Conservatory, Paris.
> Trois Pièces (Marche d'Eglise; Méditation; Sortie de Fête),
> Durand.

DEMAREST, CLIFFORD. born Tenafly, N. J. , Aug. 12, 1874;
died Tenafly, May 13, 1946. Pupil of Woodman; organist,
Church of the Messiah, New York.
> Air Varié, organ and piano, H. W. Gray.
> Andante Religioso, H. W. Gray.
> Cantabile, H. W. Gray.
> Cantilena, G. Schirmer.
> Canzona, H. W. Gray.
> Chorale Prelude on Amsterdam, O. Ditson.
> Fantasy in C Minor, organ and piano (1917).
> Pastoral Melody, A. P. Schmidt.
> (A) Pastoral Suite, H. W. Gray, 1913.
> Prelude on Materna, G. Schirmer.
> Rhapsodie, G. Schirmer.
> Rip Van Winkle (1925) G. Schirmer.
> Sunset, harp and organ, H. W. Gray.

DEMESSIEUX, JEANNE. born Montpellier, France, Feb. 14, 1921;
died Nov. 11, 1968. Pupil of Dupré; organist, St. Esprit;
organist, La Madeleine; 1952, appointed professor of organ,
Conservatory, Liège.
> Douze chorals et Praeludien, McLaughlin and Reilly 1662.
> Poème, Op. 9, organ and orchestra, Durand, 1952.
> Prélude et fugue en ut, Bornemann.
> Repons pour le temps de Pâques, Durand.
> Sept Méditations sur le Saint-Esprit, Durand, 1947.
> Six Etudes, Bornemann, 1946.
> Te Deum, Durand.
> Triptyque (Prélude; Adagio; Fugue), Durand.
> Twelve Chorale Preludes on Gregorian Themes, McLaughlin
> and Reilly M-1661.

DEMUTH, NORMAN. born London, July 15, 1898. Pupil of Parratt
and Dunhill at the Royal College of Music; organist, London
churches; 1930, appointed Professor of composition, Royal
Academy of Music; writer.
> Processional Fanfare, Novello 305 0. C. (N. S.).

DENIS, JEAN. French. died Paris, 1672. Organist, St. Séverin,
Paris.
> Prélude "pour sonder si l'accord est bon partout," in Les
> Maîtres français de l'orgue, Vol. II, p. 13.

DES PREZ, JOSQUIN. born Hainault or Henegouwen (Burgundy),
ca. 1440; died Condé-sur-Escaut, Aug. 27, 1521. Singer,
later canon and choirmaster, St. Quentin; perhaps a pupil of

Okeghem; 1475, served as a singer at the court of Duke Sforza, Milan; ca. 1486-1494, singer, papal choir; lived in Florence, Modena, and Ferrara; provost, Cathedral chapter, Condé-sur-Escaut.

Agnus Dei (2), in Anthologia pro Organo, Vol. I, p. 8.

Agnus Dei, in The First Four Centuries of Organ Music, Vol. I, p. 30.

Canzona, in Oudnederlandse Meesters, Vol. I, p. 20.

Mass movements (4) in Oudnederlandse Meesters, Vol. II.

Trio and Two Agnus Dei, in Oudnederlandse Meesters, Vol. III.

composition in Alte Meister aus der Frühzeit des Orgelspiels.

composition in Liber Organi, Vol. 8.

composition in Masterpieces of Organ Music, Folio 65.

DESSEL, LODE VAN. (see Van Dessel, Lode).

DETHIER, GASTON-MARIE. born Liège, Belgium, Apr. 18, 1875; died New York, May 26, 1958. Studied at Conservatory, Liège; pupil of Guilmant; 1894, came to United States; Organist, St. Xavier, New York; teacher, New York Institute of Musical Art.

Albumleaf, J. Fischer.

Allegro Giocoso, J. Fischer.

Allegro Appasionato, J. Fischer.

Andante Cantabile, J. Fischer.

Andante Grazioso, J. Fischer.

Aria, J. Fischer.

Ave Maria, J. Fischer.

Barcarolle, J. Fischer.

Cantilène Pastorale, J. Fischer.

Caprice (The Brook), J. Fischer.

Christmas, J. Fischer.

Con Amore, G. Schirmer.

Elegy, J. Fischer.

Festal Prelude, J. Fischer.

Gavotte, G. Schirmer.

Impromptu, J. Fischer.

Intermezzo, J. Fischer.

Lied, J. Fischer.

Menuet, J. Fischer.

Nocturne, J. Fischer.

Passacaglia, J. Fischer.

Pastoral Scene, J. Fischer.

Pensée Printanière, J. Fischer.

Prelude in E Major, J. Fischer.

Prelude on Dies irae, Edition Le Grand Orgue; also Leopold Muraille.

Procession Solenelle, J. Fischer.

Reverie, J. Fischer.

Scherzo, J. Fischer.

Theme and Finale, in The French Organist, Vol. II, p. 70.

Variations on an Ancient Christmas Carol, J. Fischer.

DICKINSON, CLARENCE. born Lafayette, Ind., May 7, 1873; died New York, N.Y., Aug. 2, 1969. Pupil of Harrison Wild, Riemann, Guilmant, Widor, Vierne, and Moskowski; organist-choirmaster, St. James' Episcopal Church, Chicago; founder, American Guild of Organists; 1912, named professor of church music, 1945, Director, School of Sacred Music, Union Theological Seminary, New York; organist-choirmaster, Brick Presbyterian Church, New York.

Andante Serioso, H. W. Gray (St. Cecilia Series 80).
Berceuse, H. W. Gray (St. Cecilia Series 830).
Canzona, H. W. Gray (St. Cecilia Series 81).
Exaltation, H. W. Gray (St. Cecilia Series 799).
Intermezzo ("Storm King" Symphony), H. W. Gray, (St. Cecilia Series 497).
Joy of the Redeemed, in The Modern Anthology, p. 47.
Meditation on Herzliebster Jesu, H. W. Gray (St. Cecilia Series 625).
Memories, H. W. Gray (St. Cecilia Series 357).
Ninety Interludes, H. W. Gray.
Old Dutch Lullaby, organ and harp, H. W. Gray.
Preludes on Two Ancient Melodies, H. W. Gray.
Reverie, H. W. Gray (St. Cecilia Series 79).
Romance, H. W. Gray (St. Cecilia Series 205).
Storm King Symphony, H. W. Gray.

DICKINSON, PETER. born Lytham St. Anne's, Lancashire, Nov. 15, 1934. 1962-1966, Lecturer, College of St. Mark & St. John, Chelsea, London; since 1966, Staff Tutor in Music, Extra-Mural Department, University of Birmingham; M. A. , Cambridge University; 1958-1960, studied at Juilliard School of Music; Associate, Royal College of Music, Fellow, Royal College of Organists.

Carillon (1964).
Fanfares and Elegies, three trumpets, three trombones, and organ, Novello (1967).
Organ Concerto (1971).
Paraphrase 1 (1967).
Postlude on Adeste Fideles, Novello.
Study in Pianissimo (1959).
Three Statements, Novello, 1966.

DIERCKS, JOHN H. born Montclair, N. J. , 1927. Chairman, Music Department, Hollins College, Va.

Six Sacred Compositions, Abingdon.
Two Chorale Preludes (A Mighty Fortress; O Christ, Thou Lamb of God).
composition in The Parish Organist, Vol. 12.

DIGGLE, ROLAND. born London, England, Jan. 1, 1887; died 1954. 1904, came to United States; 1907-1911, organist-choirmaster, St. John's Episcopal Church, Wichita, Kansas; 1911-1914, organist, St. John's Cathedral, Quincy, Ill. ; 1914-1949, organist, St. John's Church, Los Angeles, Calif.

Allegretto Grazioso, H. W. Gray (St. Cecilia Series 232).
Alleluia, Theodore Presser.
Alleluia, King of Glory, in Easter Hymns, Ed. Schuberth.
American Fantasy, White-Smith.
California Suite, G. Schirmer.
Carol Fantasy, Theodore Presser.

Carol Fantasy, Theodore Presser.
Carol Prelude on God Rest Ye, G. Schirmer.
Choral Symphonique on Nicaea, O. Ditson.
Chorale Fantasie, White-Smith.
Chorale Prelude on Forest Green, Ed. Schuberth.
Chorale Prelude on Racine, Ed. Schuberth.
Christmas Carologue, White-Smith.
Christmas Fantasy in March Form, J. Fischer.
Christmas Rhapsody, Ed. Schuberth.
Concert Fantasie on Materna, O. Ditson.
Concert Fantasie on Neander, E. H. Morris.
Epic Ode on Halifax, Ed. Schuberth.
Exulte Deo, E. H. Morris.
Fantasy on Komm, süsser Tod, Amsco.
Fugal Fantasy on Mine Eyes Have Seen, G. Schirmer.
In Olden Times, H. W. Gray.
(The) King's Highway, Ed. Schuberth.
Mother's Evening Prayer, E. H. Morris.
Nocturne, in The Modern Anthology, p. 54.
Prelude on All Through the Night, Ed. Schuberth.
Prelude Jubilant on Leoni, Ed. Schuberth.
Prelude, Variations and Fugue on Dundee, H. W. Gray,
        (St. Cecilia Series 624).
Rejoice, Ye Pure in Heart, Gamble Hinged Music Co.
Rhapsody, Gothique, H. W. Gray.
Scherzo Fantastique, H. W. Gray.
Solemn Epilogue on Canticum Refectionis, Leeds.
Song of the Good Shepherd, Theodore Presser.
Song of Victory, Ed. Schuberth.
Toccata Gregoriano, H. W. Gray (St. Cecilia Series 747).
Toccata on St. Theodulph, H. W. Gray (St. Cecilia Series
        643), 1937.
Toccata Pomposa, Galaxy, 1940.
Will o' the Wisp, H. W. Gray (St. Cecilia Series 578).
chorale preludes (15) in Everybody's Favorite Series, Amsco.
DIJK, JAN VAN. Dutch. born 1918.
    Concerto, music for organ and small orchestra, miniature
        score, Donemus 178.
DIRKSEN, RICHARD WAYNE. American. born 1921. Studied at
    Peabody Conservatory, Baltimore, Md.; Instructor of organ,
    American University; since 1942, Associate Organist and Choir-
    master, Washington Cathedral.
    Prelude on Urbs Beata, Novello.
DIRUTA, GIROLAMO. Italian. born Deruta, Italy, 1550; died ?.
    Pupil of Zarlino, A. Gabrieli, and Merulo; 1574, was a Friar
    Minor in monastery at Correggio; ca. 1582-1593, organist,
    Venice; 1593, probably organist, Santa Maria dei Frari, Venice;
    1597, organist, Cathedral, Chioggia; 1609-1622, organist,
    Cathedral, Gubbio; 1597, published first edition of Il Transilvano
    (Giacomo Vincenti, Venice, 1597), a method of organ playing,
    in two parts, containing registration instruction and organ pieces
    by Merulo, both Gabrielis, Luzzaschi, Antonio Romanini, Paolo
    Quagliati, Bell'haver, Guami; part two, music by G. Gabrieli,

Antonio Mortaro, Gabriele Fotorini, Banchieri, and Diruta himself.
Ricercare VIII tono, in Classici Italiani dell'Organo, p. 90.
Ricercare on the Seventh Tone, in The First Four Centuries
    of Organ Music, Vol. I, p. 125.
compositions (2) in Harold Gleason, Method of Organ Playing.
compositions in L'Arte Musicale in Italia, Vol. III, p. 165.

DISTLER, HUGO. born Nürnberg, Germany, June 24, 1908; died
    Berlin, Nov. 1, 1942 (suicide). Studied at Leipzig Conservatory;
    pupil of Ramin (organ); 1931-1937, organist, St. Jacobi, Lübeck;
    1937-1940, Director, taught organ and composition, Musikhoch-
    schule, Stuttgart; 1940-1942, Director, taught organ and com-
    position, Hochschule für Musik, Berlin; 1941-1942, Director of
    choir, Cathedral, Berlin.
    Dreissig Spielstücke, Op. 18, No. 1 (1938), Bärenreiter 1288.
    Jesus Christus, unser Heiland, in Orgelbuch zum Evangelis-
        chen Kirchengesangbuch, Book 13.
    Kleine Orgelchoralbearbeitungen, Op. 8, No. 3 (1938),
        Bärenreiter 1222.
    Orgelsonate (Trio), Op. 18, No. 2 (1939), Bärenreiter 1308.
    Partita über Nun komm, Op. 8, No. 1 (1933), Bärenreiter
        637.
    Partita über Wachet auf, Op. 8, No. 2 (1935), Bärenreiter
        883.
    Wie schön leuchtet, in Das Organistenamt, Vol. 2.
    composition in The Parish Organist, Vol. 5.

DIXON, J. H. REGINALD. born England, 1886. 1909, became
    organist, St. Peter's Cathedral, Lancaster (60 years).
    Baroque Suite, Hinrichsen 592 A.
    Berceuse, Hinrichsen 592 B.
    Festive Postlude, in Preludes, Interludes, Postludes, Hin-
        richsen 600 E.

DOLES, JOHANN FRIEDRICH (SENIOR). born Steinbach-Hallenberg,
    Germany, Apr. 23, 1715; died Leipzig, Feb. 8, 1797. 1740-
    1744, pupil of J. S. Bach; 1756-1789, Cantor, St. Thomas
    school, Leipzig.
    Three Chorale Preludes, C. F. Kahnt.
    Three Chorale Preludes, Edition Musicus.
    Zwei-und-dreissig singbare und leichte Choralvorspiele,
        G. A. Grieshammer.
    chorale preludes (2) in Chorale Preludes by Masters of the
        Seventeenth and Eighteenth Centuries.

DONATO, ANTHONY. born Prague, Nebraska, Mar. 8, 1909;
    Studied at Eastman School of Music; pupil of Hanson and Rogers;
    1947, Ph. D. , Eastman; 1931-1937, taught, Drake University;
    1937-1939, taught, Iowa State University; 1939-1946, taught,
    University of Texas; since 1947, professor of composition,
    Northwestern University; 1951-1952, received Fulbright scholar-
    ship to study in England.
    Two Pastels, Mercury Music Press.

DONOVAN, RICHARD FRANK. born New Haven, Conn. , Nov. 29,
    1891. 1922, Mus. Bac. , Institute of Musical Art, New York;
    pupil of Widor; studied at Yale; 1923, appointed to faculty,
    Smith College; organist-choirmaster, Christ Church, New

Haven, Conn.; 1928, became faculty member, 1945, professor, School of Music, Yale University.

Paignon, H. W. Gray (Contemporary Organ Series 18).

Two Chorale Preludes, Mercury Music Press.

DOPPELBAUER, JOSEF FRIEDRICH, born Wels, Upper Austria, Aug. 5, 1918. 1938-1940, studied at the Konservatorium and Musikhochschule, Graz, as pupil of Karl Marx (composition) and Franz Illenberger (organ); 1947-1957, organist and choirmaster, Stadtpfarrekirche, Wels; 1955-1956, studied at the Mozarteum, Salzburg; 1957-1960, theory teacher, Bruckner-Konservatorium, Linz; since 1960, professor of organ and composition, Mozarteum, Salzburg; winner of many composition prizes.

Acht kurze Stücke, Coppenrath.

Concerto (1958), organ and string orchestra, Doblinger.

Drei kleine Präludien und Fugen, Doblinger.

Fünf Orgelchoräle, Doblinger.

Kleine Stücke, Doblinger.

Ornamente, Doblinger.

Partita in C (1955), Doblinger.

Partita über Ave maris stella (1963), Doblinger.

Partita über Vater unser, Doblinger.

Sieben Choralvorspiele, Coppenrath.

Sonatine, Coppenrath.

Suite brève (1961), Doblinger.

Toccata und Fuge (in memory of Maurice Ravel) (1951), Doblinger.

Toccatina in G Minor (1954), Doblinger.

Vier neue Stücke, Coppenrath.

Zehn Pedaletüden, Doblinger.

DORNEL, ANTOINE. French. born ?, ca. 1685; died Paris, 1765. 1716, substitute for André Raison; 1719, became organist, Abbey Ste. Geneviève.

Livre d'orgue, 2 vols., Orgue et Liturgie, Vols. 68-69, 71-71.

Organ Book, 2 vols., Kalmus 3415, 3416.

compositions (4) in Les Maîtres français de l'orgue.

DOUGLAS, CHARLES WINFRED. born Oswego, New York, Feb. 15, 1867; died Evergreen, Colo., Jan. 18, 1944. 1891, B. Mus., Syracuse University; 1891, appointed instructor of vocal music, Syracuse University; 1892, appointed organist-choirmaster, Church of Zion and St. Timothy, New York City; 1894, illness forced him to move to Colorado; 1903-1906, studied and taught church music (especially plainsong) in England, France, and Germany; 1906-1944, director of music, Community of St. Mary, Peekskill, N.Y., 1917, Doc. Mus., Nashotah Seminary, Wisconsin; 1923, founded Evergreen Conference; 1937-1943, vicar, Mission of the Transfiguration, Evergreen, Colo., musical editor, Hymnal 1940.

Two Advent Hymn Preludes, H. W. Gray (St. Cecilia Series 734).

Two Lenten Preludes, H. W. Gray (St. Cecilia Series 684).

DOWNES, RALPH WILLIAM. born Derby, England, 1904. Studied

at the Royal College of Music; B. Mus., M.A., Oxford University; 1928-1935, Director of Music, Lecturer, Princeton
University, New Jersey; 1936, became Organist, London Ora-
tory; 1954, named Professor of Organ, Royal College of Music;
1954, appointed Curator-Organist, Royal Festival Hall, London.
  Jubilate Deo, H. W. Gray (St. Cecilia Series 616).
  Paraphrase on O Filii et Filiae, (Hinrichsen 1012), H. W.
      Gray (St. Cecilia Series 743).
DOYEN, (CANON) HENRI. born Soissons (Aisne), France, Oct. 3,
  1905. Studied at Collège de Conflans and Institut Catholique de
  Paris; pupil of Louis Vierne, Charles Tournemire, Joseph
  Bonnet, and Marcel Dupré; 1930-1955, Maître de Chapelle,
  Cathedral, Soissons; 1954, became organist, Cathedral, Sois-
  sons; 1950, named editor of L'Organiste; 1967, made editor
  of Musique Sacrée.
  Evocations liturgiques.
  Messe et Vêpres de la Sainte Vierge.
  Noël ancien, in Noëls variés, Orgue et Liturgie, Vol. 40,
      p. 11; also in Christmas Music by Various French
      Composers, p. 11, Kalmus.
  Suite Latine, Op., Procure Générale, n. d.
DRAGT, JAAP. Dutch. born 1930. Organ pupil of Jacob Bijster
  and counterpoint pupil of Ernest W. Mulder at the Conservatory,
  Amsterdam; 1955, won Prix d'Excellence in composition; organ
  teacher, Muzieklyceum, Zwolle.
  De profundis clamavi, Ars Nova.
  Deux Noëls en Toccata, Ars Nova.
  Deux Préludes, Ars Nova.
  Diptyque (1966), (Peters HU 1866).
  Four Chorale Preludes, Ars Nova.
  (A) Mighty Fortress (1966), Ars Nova.
  Prelude and Fugue on Psalm 122 (1968).
  Prelude, Choral et Fugue op Gezang 103, Ars Nova.
  Psalm 89, in Six Preludes on Ps. 89, Ars Nova.
  Psalm 146, and Herr Jesu Christ (1966), Ars Nova.
  Three Chorale Preludes, Ars Nova.
  Variations on Nu sijt willekomme, Ars Nova.
  Vijf Koraalpreludes, Vol. I, Alsbach.
  Vijf Koraalpreludes, Vol. II, Alsbach.
DRESDEN, SEM. born Amsterdam, Netherlands, Apr. 20, 1881;
  died The Hague, July 31, 1957. Studied at Amsterdam Conser-
  vatory and in Berlin; 1919, became theory teacher, Conserva-
  tory, Amsterdam; 1924-1929, Director, Royal Conservatory,
  The Hague; 1929-1937, Director, Amsterdam Conservatory;
  Director, Conservatory, The Hague.
  Concerto (1953).
  Toccata, Chorale and Fugue, Donemus 220.
DRIESSLER, JOHANNES. born Friedrichsthal (Saarbrücken), Ger-
  many, Jan. 26, 1921. Pupil of Rahner; studied at Hochschule
  für Musik, Cologne; 1946, faculty member, Northwest Music
  Academy, Detmold.
  Orgelsonaten durch das Kirchenjahr, Vol. 1, Advent, Bären-
      Vol. 1, Advent, Barenreiter 2795: Sonata I (Toccata

über Nun komm; Aria über Es kommt; Fuga über O
Heiland), Sonata II (Allegro über Macht hoch; Andante über Wie soll; Vivace über Gottes Sohn ist
kommen).

Vol. 2, Christmas, Bärenreiter 2796: Sonata III (Toc-
cata über Gelobet seist du; Canzona über Es ist ein
Ros'; Passacaglia über Da Christus geboren war),
Sonata IV (Andante über Vom Himmel; Allegro über
Der Tag, der ist; Moderato über Den die Hirten),
Sonata V (Prelude über Lobt Gott; Fantasia über Wir
Christenleut).

Vol. 3, New Year, Epiphany, Bärenreiter 2797: Sonata
VI (Prelude über Freut euch; Bicinium über Das alte
Jahr; Fantasia über Jesu, nun sei gepreiset; Fuga
über Hilf, Herr Jesu), Sonata VII (Adagio über Herr
Christ, der einige; Allegro über O Jesu Christe,
wahres Licht; Andante über O süsser Herr; Vivace
über Lobt Gott den Herrn).

Vol. 4, Passion, Bärenreiter 2798.

Vol. 5, Easter, Bärenreiter 2799.

Vol. 6, Ascension and Whitsuntide, Bärenreiter 2800.

Vol. 7, Trinity and Saints' Days, Bärenreiter 2813.

Vol. 8, End of the Church Year, Bärenreiter 2814.

Toccata and Hymn on Wach auf, wach auf, du deutsches land,
Op. 46, No. 1, Breitkopf und Härtel 6434.

Twelve Chorale Preludes on Great Hymns, J. Fischer.

chorale preludes (2) in Orgelbuch zum Evangelischen Kirchen-
gasangbuch, Books 8 and 10.

DRISCHNER, MAX. German. born Jan. 31, 1891; died Apr. 26,
1971. Kantor-Organist, Nikolaikirche, Brieg, Germany.

Chaconne (F Minor), Schultheiss.

Choralfantasie über Lobe den Herren, Schultheiss.

Choralvorspiele (18), Schultheiss.

Choralvorspiele (61) für Dorforganisten, Schultheiss.

Glatzer Variationen, Schultheiss.

Nordische Fantasie (A Minor), Schultheiss.

Nordische Toccata und Fuge (G Minor), Schultheiss.

Nordische Kanzonen, Schultheiss.

Norwegische Variationen, Schultheiss.

Norwegische Volkstonsuiten, Schultheiss.

Partiten über zwei Weihnachtslieder (Es ist ein Ros' entsprungen; In dulci jubilo), Schultheiss (Peters D 624).

Passacaglia (C Minor), Schultheiss.

Passacaglia (E Major), Schultheiss.

Präludium und Fuge (A Minor), Schultheiss.

Vom Himmel hoch (Choralfantasie), Schultheiss.

Wachet auf (Choralfantasie), Schultheiss.

DUBOIS, FRANÇOIS-CLÉMENT-THÉODORE. born Rosnay (Marne),
France, Aug. 24, 1837; died Paris, June 11, 1924. Studied at
Conservatory, Paris, pupil of Benoist and Ambroise Thomas;
1855-1858, organist, Invalides; organist, Ste. Clotilde; 1861,
won Prix de Rome, 1863, choirmaster, Ste. Clotilde; 1869,
choirmaster, La Madeleine; 1877-1896, organist, Madeleine

(succeeded Saint-Saëns); 1871, appointed professor of harmony,
1891, professor of composition, 1896, director, Conservatory,
Paris.
>   Alleluia, organ, three trumpets, trombone, H. W. Gray.
>   Bénédiction (Messe de Mariage), in The French Organist,
>   Vol. I, p. 84.
>   Cantilène Nuptiale, Leduc (Heugel).
>   Dix Pièces, Heugel; also published by G. Schirmer 1479.
>   Dix pièces pour orgue et harmonium, Leduc, 1889.
>   Douze Pièces, Leduc, 1886.
>   Douze pièces nouvelles d'orgue, Leduc, 1892.
>   Entrée, Heugel.
>   Fantasietta with Variations on a Provençale Theme, G.
>   Schirmer.
>   In Paradisum, Leduc, 1925.
>   Interludium, Novello.
>   March of the Magi Kings, Oliver Ditson, 1899.
>   Messe de Mariage, Leduc.
>   Offertoire pour l'Ascension, Heugel.
>   Preludium Grave, in The International Organist, Vol. II,
>   p. 2.
>   Quarante-deux pièces, organ or harmonium, Heugel, 1926.
>   Toccata, Leduc.

DU CAURROY, FRANÇOIS-EUSTACHE. baptized Beauvais, France,
Feb. 4, 1549; died Paris, Aug. 7, 1609. Canon, Ste. Chapelle;
1599, became superintendent of King's music to Henri IV; wrote
Fantaisies in three, four, five, six voices, which could be
played on the organ; some themes were borrowed from plainsong or folksong.
>   Fantasies a III, IIII, V, et VI, Parties, Norbert Dufourcq,
>   ed. , Schola Cantorum.
>   Fantaisie sur Une jeune fillete, or Je crois Vierge Marie,
>   in Anthology of Early French Organ Music, p. 7.
>   Fantaisie sur Ave maris stella, in A la Vierge, Orgue et
>   Liturgie, Vol. 14, p. 10.
>   Requiem aeternam, in Pièces funèbres, Orgue et Liturgie,
>   Vol. 23, p. 4.
>   Treisiesme Fantasie a l'imitation de Salve regina, in Salve
>   regina, L'Organiste liturgique, Vol. 21, p. 18; also
>   fragment in Les Maîtres français de l'orgue.

DÜBEN, ANDERS (ANDREAS), the elder. born Germany, ca. 1590;
died Stockholm, Sweden, July 7, 1662. Studied at University of
Leipzig; 1614-1620, pupil of Sweelinck; 1620 or 1621, court
organist, Stockholm; 1625, organist, German church, Hofkapell-
meister.
>   Allein Gott, in 20 Chorale Variations of the German Sweelinck
>   School, Bärenreiter.
>   Wo Gott der Herr, in Chorale Arrangements and Free Com-
>   positions of the German Sweelinck School, Moser, ed. ,
>   Bärenreiter.
>   chorale preludes (3) in 46 Choräle.
>   compositions (2) in Organum, Series IV, Vol. 21.

DUFAY, GUILLAUME. born probably near Hainault, Belgium,

ca. 1400; died Cambrai, Nov. 27, 1474. Choirboy, Cathedral, Cambrai; 1419-1426, was in Rimini and Pesaro; 1426-1428, choirmaster, Cathedral, Cambrai; served in Rome, Cambrai, Florence, Bologna, and Savoy; 1445, became canon, Cathedrals of Cambrai and Mons.

Alma Redemptoris Mater, in Liber Organi, Vol. 8, p. 6;
    also in The First Four Centuries of Organ Music,
    Vol. I, p. 7.
compositions (3) in Oudnederlandse Meesters, Vol. III.
plainsong hymn in Anthologia pro Organo, Vol. I, p. 6.
plainsong hymn in Anthologia pro Organo, Vol. III, p. 8.
plainsong hymns (4) in Oudnederlandse Meesters, Vol. II.

DUFOUR. French. died 1786.
Prelude in A minor, in Les Maîtres français de l'orgue,
    Vol. II, p. 80.

DU MAGE, PIERRE. born Beauvais, France, ca. 1676; died Laon, Oct. 2, 1751. 1708, Premier livre d'orgue published, contains a suite in first tone; pupil of Louis Marchand; 1703, became organist, St. Quentin Cathedral.

Grand jeu, in Historical Organ Recitals, Vol. I, p. 126;
    also in Les Maîtres français de l'orgue, p. 47; also
    in The First Four Centuries of Organ Music, p. 467.
Livre d'orgue: Suite on the 1st Tone, in Archives des
    maîtres d'orgue des seizième-dix-huitième siècles,
    Vol. 3; also published by Schott 1872.*
Récit, in Alte Orgelmusik aus England und Frankreich,
    p. 34.
compositions in Masterpieces of Organ Music, Folio 38.

DU MONT, HENRI. born Villers l'Evêque, France, 1610; died Paris, May 8, 1684. Until 1638, served at Notre Dame Church, Liège; served St. Lambert Cathedral, Liège; 1639-1684, organist, St. Paul Church, Paris; served Duke of Anjou; 1673-1681, director of queen's music.

Allemande, in Les Maitres français de l'orgue, Vol. II,
    p. 14.
(L')Oeuvre pour Clavier, in L'Organiste liturgique, Vol. 13.
Pièce du 1er ton, in Les Maîtres français de l'orgue, Vol. I,
    p. 1.

DUNSTABLE, JOHN. born probably at Dunstable, Bedfordshire, England, between 1380 and 1390; outstanding fifteenth-century English composer; lived in France, served Duke of Bedford.

Agincourt hymn, in Treasury of Early Organ Music, p. 6
    (transcription).
Puisque m'amour, in Geschichte der Musik in Beispielen,
    p. 35 (transcription).
Veni, creator spiritus, in The First Four Centuries of Organ
    Music, Vol. I, p. 4 (transcription).
organ arrangement in Arnold Schering, Studien zur Musik-
    geschichte der Frührenaissance, p. 163.
unnamed composition in Early English Organ Music, p. 1;
    also in Treasury of Early Organ Music, p. 5.

DUPONT, GABRIEL-EDOUARD-XAVIER. born Caen, France, Mar. 1, 1878; died Vésinet, Aug. 2, 1914. Pupil of Massenet,

Gédalge, and Widor at Conservatory, Paris.

Méditation, in French Masterworks for Organ, Alexander
    Schreiner, ed. , J. Fischer, Glen Rock, N. J. , 1958,
    p. 31.

Pour la Toussaint, Demets, 1902.

DUPRÉ, MARCEL. born Rouen, France, May 3, 1886; died
Meudon, May 31, 1971. Pupil of Vierne, Guilmant, and Widor
at Conservatory, Paris; 1916-1922, substituted for Vierne at
Notre Dame; 1906, became assistant to Widor at St. Sulpice;
1926, succeeded Gigout as professor of organ, 1954, director,
Conservatory, Paris; 1934-1971, organist, St. Sulpice (succeeded Widor); 1947, became general director, American Conservatory, Fontainebleau.

Angélus, Op. 34, Hérelle, 1938 (Philippo).

Annonciation, Op. 56, Bornemann, 1961.

Ballade, Op. 30, organ and piano, H. W. Gray, 1932.

(Le) Chemin de la Croix, Op. 29 (fourteen stations),
    Durand, 1932.

Choral et Fugue, Op. 57, 2 vols. , Bornemann, 1962.

Concerto (E Minor), organ and orchestra, Op. 31, Borne-
    mann, 1943.

Cortège et Litanie, Op. 19, Leduc, 1923.

Cortège et Litanie, Op. 19, No. 2, organ and orchestra,
    Leduc, 1921.

Deux Esquisses, Op. 41 (E Minor; B-flat Minor), Borne-
    mann, 1946.

Deuxième Symphonie (C-Sharp Minor), Op. 26, Sénart, 1929.

Eight Short Preludes on Gregorian Themes, McLaughlin and
    Reilly.

Evocation, Op. 37 (1941), Bornemann, 1942.

Fantaisie (B Minor), Op. 8, organ and piano, Leduc, 1912.

Fifteen Pieces founded on Antiphons, Op. 18, H. W. Gray.

In Memoriam, Op. 61, 2 vols. , Bornemann, 1965.

Lamento, Op. 24, Leduc, 1926.

Miserere mei, Op. 45, Bornemann, 1949.

Offrande à la Vierge, Op. 40 (Virgo mater; Mater dolorosa;
    Virgo mediatrix), Bornemann, 1945.

Paraphrase on Te Deum, in The Modern Anthology.

Poème Héroïque, Op. 33, organ and brass, H. W. Gray,
    1936.

Prélude, Intermezzo, et Toccata, Sénart.

Psaume XVIII, Op. 47, Bornemann.

Quatre Fugues Modales, Op. 63, Bornemann, 1968.

Scherzo (F Minor), Op. 16, Leduc, 1917.

Sept Pièces, Op. 27 (Souvenir; Marche; Pastorale; Carillon;
    Légende; Canon, Final), H. W. Gray-Bornemann, 1931.

Sinfonia, Op. 42, piano and organ, H. W. Gray, 1946.

Six Antiennes pour le Temps de Noël, Op. 48, Bornemann.

Soixante-dix-neuf Chorals, Op. 28, H. W. Gray, 1931.

Sonata (A Minor), organ and cello, H. W. Gray.

Suite, Op. 39, Bornemann, 1945.

Suite Bretonne, Op. 21, Leduc, 1924.

Symphonie en Sol Mineur, Op. 25, Sénart, 1927 and 1928,

organ and orchestra.

Symphonie-Passion, Op. 23, Leduc, 1924.

Toccata on Ave maris stella, Leduc.

(Le) Tombeau de Titelouze, Op. 38, Bornemann-H. W. Gray,
     1942 and 1943.

Triptyque, Op. 51, Bornemann, 1957.

Trois Elévations, Op. 32, Hérelle, 1935 (Philippo).

Trois Hymnes, Bornemann.

Trois Préludes et Fugues, Op. 7 (B Major, F Minor, G
     Minor), Leduc, 1920.

Trois Préludes et Fugues, Op. 36 (E Minor, A-flat Major,
     C Major), H. W. Gray-Bornemann, 1940.

Two Chorales, Op. 59, Galleon Press.

Variations à deux thèmes, Op. 35, organ and piano, H. W.
     Gray, 1938.

Variations sur un Noël, Op. 20, Leduc, 1922.

Vêpres du Commun de la Sainte Vierge, Op. 18 (15 ver-
     sets), H. W. Gray, 1919.

Vingt-quatre Inventions, Op. 50, 2 vols., Bornemann, 1956.

Vision, poème symphonique, Op. 44, Bornemann, 1947.

Vitrail, Op. 65, Bornemann, 1969.

DUPUIS, THOMAS SANDERS.   English.   born 1733; died 1796.

Fugue in G Minor, in Tallis to Wesley, Vol. 22, p. 8.

Introduction and Fugue in D Major, in English Organ Music
     of the Eighteenth Century, Hinrichsen, 1951.

DURÓN, SEBASTIÁN.   born Brihuega (Guadalajara), Spain, Apr. 19,
     1660; died Cambo, Aug. 3, 1716.   Pupil of Andres de Sola;
     1679, became assistant organist, Seo, Saragossa; 1680, ap-
     pointed second organist, Cathedral, Seville; 1684, appointed
     organist, Cathedral, Burgo de Osma; 1686-1691, organist,
     Cathedral, Palencia; 1691, appointed organist, Chapel Royal.

tientos (3) in Six Tientos, Orgue et Liturgie, Vol. 74, p. 19.

DURUFLÉ, MAURICE.   born Louviers (Eure), France, Jan. 11,
     1902.   Pupil of Tournemire, Vierne, Gigout, Dukas, and Guil-
     mant; 1929-1931, assistant to Vierne at Notre Dame; 1930,
     appointed organist, St. Etienne-du-Mont; 1944, became pro-
     fessor of harmony, Conservatory, Paris.

Prélude, Adagio et Choral varié sur Veni Creator, Op. 4,
     Durand, 1931.

Prélude et Fugue sur le nom d'Alain, Op. 7, Durand, 1943.

Prélude sur l'Introït de l'Epiphanie, in Préludes à l'Introit,
     Orgue et Liturgie, Vol. 48, p. 10.

Scherzo, Op. 2, Durand, 1929.

Suite, Op. 5 (Prélude; Sicilienne; Toccata), Durand, 1934.

DYSON, (SIR) GEORGE.   born Halifax, Yorkshire, England, May 28,
     1883; died Winchester, Sept. 29, 1964.   Studied at Royal
     Academy of Music, in Italy, and in Germany; music master,
     Royal Naval College, Osborne, Marlborough College, Wellington
     College, and Rugby School; 1918, Mus. Doc., Oxford; 1924-
     1938, Music Director, Winchester College; 1937-1952, Director,
     Royal College of Music.

Fantasia and Ground Bass, Novello.

Prelude and Postlude, in Novello Organ Music Club 3, 1956.

Two Pieces, Novello.
Variations on Old Psalm Tunes, 3 books, Novello.
Voluntary in D Major, in An Album of Praise, p. 9.

EBEL (see Abel).
EBERLIN, JOHANN ERNST. born Jettingen (Burgau), Austria,
    Mar. 27, 1702; died Salzburg, June 19, 1762. 1729, ap-
    pointed organist, Cathedral, Salzburg; 1749, made Kapell-
    meister to the Prince-Archbishop, Salzburg.
        Aus meines Herzens Grunde, Concordia.
        Es wolle Gott uns, in Anthologie.
        Fugue (A Minor), Cramer.
        Fugue (G Minor), Cramer.
        Nine toccatas and fugues, Kalmus 3429; also in Vol. IV,
            Süddeutschen Orgelmeister des Barok, R. Walter, ed.,
            Coppenrath.
        Three Toccatas and Fugues in D, Novello.
        Toccata and Fugue in D Minor, in A Treasury of Shorter
            Organ Classics, p. 10.
        Toccata and Fugue in G Minor, H. Diack Johnston, ed.,
            Novello EOM 7, 1959.
EDER, HELMUT. born Linz, Austria, Dec. 26, 1916. Pupil of
    Hindemith, Carl Orff, and Johann Nepomuk David.
        Choral-Suite, Doblinger.
        Concerto "L'Homme armé," Op. 50, organ and orchestra,
            Doblinger.
        Five pieces, Op. 40, Associated Music Publishers.
        Partita on a theme by J. N. David, Op. 42, Breitkopf und
            Härtel 6507.
        Partita über Ach wie flüchtig, Op. 47, No. 2, Doblinger.
        Partita über Es sungen drei Engel, Op. 47, No. 3, Doblinger.
        Partita über O Heiland, reiss die Himmel auf, Op. 47,
            No. 1, Doblinger.
        Vox Media, Op. 53, Doblinger.
EDMUNDSON, GARTH. born Pittsburgh, Pa., May 11, 1900; died
    New Castle, Penn., Apr. 2, 1971. Studied at the Conservatory,
    Leipzig; pupil of Harvey Gaul, Lynnwood Farnam, and Joseph
    Bonnet; 1943-1968, organist, First Presbyterian Church, New
    Castle, Penn.; teacher, honorary Doc. Mus., Westminster
    Choir College.
        Apostolic Symphony, J. Fischer.
        Ariel, H. W. Gray (St. Cecilia Series 760).
        Bells through the Trees, J. Fischer.
        (A) Carpenter is Born, (Apostolic Symphony No. 1), J.
            Fischer.
        Chorale Prelude on In dulci jubilo, H. W. Gray.
        Christmas Suite No. 1 (March of the Magi; The Virgin's
            Slumber Song, Carillon), H. W. Gray, St. Cecilia
            Series 581), 1932.
        Christmas Suite No. 2 (Adeste fideles; Veni Emmanuel;

In dulci jubilo; Vom Himmel hoch--St. Cecilia Series
635), H. W. Gray (St. Cecilia Series 633), 1937.
Christus Crucifixus, H. W. Gray.
Christus Nocte, H. W. Gray (St. Cecilia Series 678), 1941.
Christus Resurrexit, H. W. Gray.
Concert Variations, H. W. Gray.
(An) Easter Spring Song, J. Fischer.
Eucharistia, H. W. Gray (St. Cecilia Series 774).
Folk Song Prelude, H. W. Gray.
For Passiontide, H. W. Gray (St. Cecilia Series 699).
Four Modern Preludes on Old Chorals, Galaxy.
From the Western Church, H. W. Gray.
Humoresque Fantastique, J. Fischer.
Imagery in Tableaux, J. Fischer 0335, 1934.
Impressions Gothiques (Passacaglia, Silence Mystique;
    Gargoyles), J. Fischer; (Gargoyles available separately,
    J. Fischer 8998, 1933).
In Modum Antiquum, 2 vols. , J. Fischer.
Oremus, H. W. Gray (St. Cecilia Series 786).
Prelude on Spanish Chant, in Gleason, Method of Organ
    Playing.
Sequentia, J. Fischer.
Seven Classic Preludes on Old Chorals, J. Fischer 7466,
    1938.
Seven Contrapuntal Preludes, J. Fischer.
Seven Modern Preludes on Ancient Themes, J. Fischer.
Seven Polyphonic Preludes on Christian Liturgy, J. Fischer.
Seven Service Preludes, J. Fischer.
To the Setting Sun, J. Fischer.
Toccata Brillante, in The Modern Anthology, p. 70.
Toccata on Wie schön leuchtet, H. W. Gray (St. Cecilia
    Series 815).
EFFINGER, CECIL. born Colorado Springs, Colo. , July 22, 1914.
Pupil of Boulanger and Wagenaar; oboist; 1945, taught at
American University, Biarritz; 1936-1941, 1945-1948, faculty
member, Colorado College; 1948, appointed head of theory de-
partment, University of Colorado.
    Prelude and Fugue, H. W. Gray (Contemporary Organ Series
        17).
EGERTON, ARTHUR HENRY. born Montreal, Canada, 1891; died
1957. B. Mus. , McGill Conservatory of Music; Fellow of the
Royal College of Organists, London; Doc. Mus. , University of
Toronto; Professor of Music, Wells College, Aurora, N.Y. ;
Supervisor of Music Schools, Outremont, Quebec; organist,
Christ Church Cathedral, Montreal; organist, Trinity Memorial
Church, Montreal.
    Prelude and Fugue on Iste Confessor, H. W. Gray.
    Prelude Improvisation on Veni Emmanuel, Oxford.
    Prelude on O Filii et Filiae, Oxford.
EGGERMANN, FRITZ. born Steyr, Austria, Oct. 29, 1898. Self-
taught composer; 1921-1938, teacher, Volksschule, Steyr;
ca.1945, became Gymnasial-Professor, Steyr; since 1957, has
devoted himself to composition.

Orgelstücke (1961-1962), 6 vols., Breitkopf und Härtel
      6341 A-F, 1962-1966.
ELGAR, (SIR) EDWARD WILLIAM. born Broadheath, Worcester,
   England, June 2, 1857; died Worcester, Feb. 23, 1934. 1885-
   1889, organist, St. George's Roman Catholic Church, Worcester; 1900, honorary doctorate, Cambridge, the first of many;
   1905-1906, Professor of Music, University of Birmingham;
   1924, Master of the King's Musick; influenced by Mendelssohn,
   Berlioz, and Wagner.
      Chanson de Matin, Op. 15, No. 2, Novello.
      Chanson de Nuit, Op. 15, No. 1, Novello.
      'Nimrod' from the 'Enigma' Variations, Op. 36, William H.
         Harris, arranger, Novello.
      Piacevole (String Quartet), Op. 83, Novello.
      Prelude 'The Kingdom', Op. 51, Novello.
      Sonata in G Major, Op. 28 (1895), Breitkopf und Härtel;
         also British and Continental Music Agencies, Ltd.,
         London, 1941.
ELÍAS, JOSÉ (JOSEPH). born Catalonia, Spain, 1675; died 1749.
   1715, organist, San Justo y Pastor, Barcelona; 1725, became
   Discalced monk in Cloister, Madrid; pupil of Cabanilles; wrote
   some compositions in Música de Órgano which contains chorals,
   toccatas, tientos, and passacaglias.
      Preludi (Andante; Allegro), in Early Spanish Organ Music,
         p. 58.
      compositions (5) in Antologia de Organistas Clásicos
         Españoles, Vol. II, pp. 12-96.
      compositions (3) in Liber Organi, Vol. 11.
ELMORE, ROBERT HALL. born Ramapatnam, India, Jan. 2, 1913.
   1933, received Licentiate, Royal Academy of Music, London,
   England; 1926-1933, pupil of Yon; 1937, B. Mus., University
   of Pennsylvania; 1942, became organist-director of music,
   Holy Trinity Church, Philadelphia, Pa.; 1940, appointed teacher
   of composition, University of Pennsylvania; professor of piano
   and organ, Clarke Conservatory of Music, Philadelphia; 1956-
   1969, organist-choirmaster, Central Moravian Church, Bethlehem, Pa.; 1969, appointed organist-choirmaster, Tenth Presbyterian Church, Philadelphia.
      Chorale Prelude on Lancashire; Choral Meditation on More-
         cambe, in Mixture IV, Flammer.
      Chorale Prelude on Seelenbräutigam, in The Modern Anthology,
         p. 78.
      Concerto for Brass, Organ and Percussion, H. W. Gray, 1969.
      Contemporary Chorale Preludes, Sacred Music Press.
      Donkey Dance, H. W. Gray (St. Cecilia Series 676).
      Meditation on an Old Covenanter's Tune, H. W. Gray.
      Meditation on Veni Emmanuel, J. Fischer.
      (The) Night of the Star, Galaxy.
      Rhythmic Suite (Pavane; Rhumba), Saint Mary's Press, New
         York, Gentry (Presser).
      Three Meditative Moments on Moravian Hymns, H. Flammer.
      Three Minatures, H. Flammer.
      Two Chorale Preludes, Elkan-Vogel.

Two Pieces, H. W. Gray (St. Cecilia Series 693).
EMBORG, JENS LAURSØN. born Ringe, Denmark, Dec. 22, 1876;
    died Copenhagen, Apr. 18, 1957. Organ pupil of Otto Malling;
    since 1906, organist, Vordingborg; 1897-1939, teacher, semin-
    ary, Vordingborg; 1939-1947, State Inspector of Singing.
        Koralforspil (26), Op. 32, Hansen.
        Toccata och Fuga, Op. 44, No. 4, Musica Organi, Vol. 3,
            p. 24.
EMERY, WILFRED J. English. born 1904.
        (A) Christmas Prelude on This Endris Night, Oxford.
        Hymn Prelude on Hanover, Cramer.
        Paen, Cramer.
        Prelude on the Psalm Tune Windsor, Cramer.
        Prelude on the Psalm Tune York, Cramer.
ENGEL, JAMES. born Milwaukee, Wis. , 1925.
        Two Chorale Preludes, Concordia.
        composition in The Parish Organist, Vol. 10.

ENGELMANN, JOHANNES. German. Twentieth century. Resides
    in Leipzig.
        Fantasia, Passacaglia, und Fuge (G Minor), Op. 34, VEB
            Breitkopf und Härtel 5500, Leipzig.
        Fantasia, Passacaglia und Fuge über den Namen B-A-C-H,
            VEB Breitkopf und Härtel 5528, Leipzig.
ÉRALY, PAUL. born Leuven, The Netherlands, 1910. Studied at
    the Lemmens School, Malines; pupil of Paul Gilson and André
    Marchal; made concert tours in Austria and France; organist,
    St. Servaaskerk, Schaarbeek.
        Pastoraal, in Cantantibus Organis, Vol. I, p. 30.
ERB, MARIE-JOSEPH. born Strasbourg, France, Oct. 23, 1858;
    died Andlau, July 9, 1944. 1880-1940, organist, St. Jean,
    Strasbourg; pupil of Widor, Saint-Saëns, Loret, Gigout, and
    Boëllmann; studied at Ecole Niedermeyer.
        Achtzig kurze Orgelstücke über Choralmontinen, Op. 74,
            Le Roux.
        Pieces (20) (organ and harmonium) Op. 73, Schwann, Dussel-
            dorf, 1906; also Le Roux, Strasbourg, 1907.
        Postlude on Ite Missa est, in Orgel Kompositionen aus alter
            und neuer Zeit.
        Sonata, Leduc.
        Sorties et Postludes sur des airs de cantiques populaires
            allemands, Schwann, Dusseldorf, 1907; also Le Roux,
            Strasbourg, 1925.
        Suite (1919), Boston Music Company, Boston, 1921.
        Suite Liturgique (1913).
        Suite sur la Kyriale de la Vierge, Janin, Lyon, 1911.
        Three Sonatas based on plainsong melodies
            Sonata 1, Otto Junne, Brussels, 1908.
            Sonata 2, Leduc, Paris, 1921.
            Sonata 3, Sénart, Paris, 1930.
        Zwanzig Orgelstücke, Schwann.
        chorale preludes in Organ Works of Modern Masters, Vol. 1
            (4); Vol. 2 (1).

ERBACH, CHRISTIAN. born Hesse, Germany, 1573; died Augsburg, summer, 1635. 1602, organist, St. Moritz, Augsburg;
ca. 1600, became organist for Fugger family, organist and city
music director, Augsburg; 1625, became organist, Cathedral,
Augsburg.
> Acht Canzonen, Alfred Reichling, ed. , Merseburger 844.
> Kyrie Versetten, in Liber Organi, Vol. 1, p. 4.
> Kyrie Versetten, in Liber Organi, Vol. 6.
> Lucis Creator optime, in Cantantibus Organis, Vol. 12,
>   F. Pustet.
> Pange lingua, in Pange lingua, Reichling, ed. , Coppenrath.
> compositions in Masterpieces of Organ Music, Folio 44.
> compositions (Drei Introitus mit Versus) in Orgel, Series II,
>   No. 11, Concordia 97-4471.
> compositions in Ricercare, Canzonen und Fugen.
ERICH, DANIEL. German. Early eighteenth century. Organist,
Güstrow; pupil of Buxtehude.
> Allein Gott, in Choralvorspiel alter Meister, p. 61.
> Es ist das Heil, in Elf Orgelchoräle des siebzehnten Jahr-
>   hunderts.
ESLAVA, MIGUEL HILARIÓN. born Burlada, Spain, Oct. 21, 1807;
died Madrid, July 23, 1878. 1827, pupil of Secanilla; 1828,
became choirmaster, Cathedral, Burgo de Osma; 1832-1847,
served Cathedral, Seville; organist, royal chapel, Madrid;
professor of composition, Conservatory, Madrid.
> Postlude, in Dickinson, The Technique and Art of Organ
>   Playing, H. W. Gray, New York, 1922, p. 54.
ETLER, ALVIN DERALD. born Battle Creek, Iowa, Feb. 19, 1913.
Oboist; studied at University of Illinois, Western Reserve, and
Yale (B. Mus. , 1944); 1938-1940, oboist, Indianapolis Symphony
Orchestra; 1942-1946, taught at Yale; 1946-1947, taught at
Cornell; 1947-1949, taught at University of Illinois; 1949, be-
came faculty member at Smith College.
> Prelude and Toccata (1950), Associated Music Publishers.
EWALDT. (No biographical information available.) Compositions
found in additions to the Pelplin tablatures (which were written
no later than 1630). Organ Book (MS I/220), Polish, ca. 1580.
> Allein zu dir, in Corpus of Early Keyboard Music, No. 10,
>   Vol. 1.
EZNARRIÁGA, CÁNDIDO. Spanish, seventeenth century.
> Tres versillos de Segundo Tono, in Early Spanish Organ
>   Music, p. 34.

Faenza Manuscript. Musica Disciplina, Vol. XIII (1959), pp. 79-
107, Vol. XIV (1960), pp. 64-104; and Vol. XV (1961),
pp. 65-104.
FALCINELLI, ROLANDE. born Paris, France, Feb. 12, 1920.
Studied at Conservatory, Paris; pupil of Dupré; 1946, became
organist, Sacré-Coeur de Montmartre, Paris; 1948, professor
of organ, American Conservatory, Fontainebleau, professor of

organ, Conservatory, Paris.

Chorale Prélude No. 2 à l'Introit de la Messe de Christ-Roi, in Préludes à l'Introit, Orgue et Liturgie, Vol. 48, p. 12.

Cinq Chorals d'orgue, Op. 28, Bornemann, 1952.

Communion pour la Fête de Christ-Roi, in Communions, Orgue et Liturgie, Vol. 62, p. 7.

Cor Jesu Sacratissimum, Editions Musicales Transatlantiques.

Cortège Funèbre, in Orgue et Liturgie, Vol. 75.

Elévation pour la Messe de Notre Seigneur Jésus-Christ-Roi, in Elévations, Orgue et Liturgie, Vol. 57, p. 21.

Offertoire pour la Fête de Christ-Roi, in Offertoires, Orgue et Liturgie, Vol. 52, p. 31.

Petit Livre de Prières, Op. 24, Bornemann, 1948.

Prélude à l'Introit de la Messe du Sacré-Coeur de Jésus, in L'Orgue Néo-Classique, Orgue et Liturgie, Vol. 33, p. 10.

Rosa mystica, Op. 29, in Notre Dame, Orgue et Liturgie, Vol. 11, p. 28.

FARNAM, W. LYNNWOOD. born Sutton, Quebec, Canada, Jan. 13, 1885; died New York, Nov. 23, 1930. Studied at Royal College of Music, London; pupil of James Higgs; organist of churches in Montreal and Boston; 1904, came to United States; organist, Church of the Holy Communion, New York.

Toccata on O Filii et Filiae, Presser.

FASOLO, GIOVAN BATTISTA. born Asti, Italy, first half of the seventeenth century. Franciscan monk; choirmaster to the Archbishop of Moneale.

Ad coenam agni, in Cantantibus Organis, Vol. 8.

Annuale: Versetten, Ricercaten, Canzonen und Fugen durch das ganze Kirchenjahr (Venice, 1645), Rudolf Walter, ed., Willy Müller 71, 1965.

Judex crederis, in Harold Gleason, Method of Organ Playing, p. 62.

Kyrie, in The First Four Centuries of Organ Music, Vol. I, p. 218.

Pange lingua, in Hymnes et Antiennes, Orgue et Liturgie, Vol. 8, p. 8.

Salve regina, in Salve regina, Orgue et Liturgie, Vol. 21, p. 26.

compositions (3) in Liber Organi, Vol. 4.

FATORINI, GABRIEL. (FATTORINI, GABRIELE). born Faenza, Italy, latter part of the sixteenth century; died, ?. Choirmaster, Faenza.

ricercari (2) in L'Arte Musicale in Italia, p. 161.

FAUCHARD, (CANON) AUGUSTE-LOUIS-JOSEPH. born Laval, France, 1881; died 1957. Pupil of Vierne, Guilmant, and d'Indy; organist, Cathedral, Laval.

In memoriam, in Pièces funèbres, Orgue et Liturgie, Vol. 23, p. 25.

(Le) Mystère de Noël sur Jesu, Redemptor omnium (1940), in Orgue et Liturgie, Vol. 12.

Symphonie No. 1, Symphonie mariale (on motets or hymns

to the virgin).
Symphonie No. 2, Symphonie Eucharistique (on Latin hymns), 1944.

FAULKES, WILLIAM. born Liverpool, England, Nov. 4, 1863; died Liverpool, Jan. 25, 1933. From 1886, organist and teacher in Liverpool.

Alleluja-Postlude on Lässt uns erfreuen, Novello.
Ballade (C Major), Novello.
Barcarolle, G. Schirmer.
Cantilena, G. Schirmer.
Capriccio, G. Schirmer.
Christmas Meditation on Adeste fideles, Op. 183, No. 3, G. Schirmer.
Communion, Fantasy, Little Toccata, Op. 128, A. P. Schmidt.
Concert Prelude on a Chorale, Op. 154, No. 1, Laudy.
Fantasia on Urbs beata, Op. 112, Novello.
Fantasy on Christmas Carols, Op. 121, No. 2, G. Schirmer.
Fantasy on Christmas Carols, Op. 103, Novello.
Fantasy on Welsh Airs, Op. 178, Paxton.
Festival Prelude on Ein' feste Burg, Novello.
Funeral March, Novello.
Hallelujah, Op. 183, No. 1, G. Schirmer.
Hosanna, Op. 183, No. 4, G. Schirmer.
Meditation, Novello.
Minuet and Trio, Op. 142, No. 2, G. Schirmer.
Nocturne, Novello.
Overture (C Minor), Op. 152, A. P. Schmidt.
Paraphrase on a Christmas Hymn, Op. 151, No. 1, A. P. Schmidt.
Pastoral-Overture, Novello.
Postlude, Novello.
Prelude and Fugue, Novello.
Rhapsody on an Ancient Christmas Carol, Novello.
Rhapsody on Old French Carols, Vincent.
Rhapsody on Pentecost, G. Schirmer.
Six Pieces, Op. 135, A. P. Schmidt.
Sonata No. 2, Op. 106, G. Schirmer.
Symphonic Concert Scherzo, Novello.
Theme and Variations (E Major), Novello.
Three Pieces, A. P. Schmidt.
Toccata (F Major), G. Schirmer.
Toccata on the God of Abram Praise, Schott.
Variations in E-flat Major, G. Schirmer.
Variations in F, Op. 143, G. Schirmer.
Wedding Bells, Op. 183, No. 2, G. Schirmer.
Wedding March, Novello.
Wedding March (E Major), G. Schirmer.

FELCIANO, RICHARD. born Santa Rosa, Calif., Dec. 7, 1930. Organ pupil of Gordon Dixon and Raymond White; composition pupil of Darius Milhaud and Luigi Dallapiccola; 1955, M.A., Mills College; 1959, Ph.D., University of Iowa; held Fulbright scholarship and grants from French and Italian governments, and the Wooley and Copley Foundations; 1964, Ford Foundation composer-in-residence, Detroit Public Schools; 1959-1967, Chairman, Department of Music, Lone Mountain College, San Francisco; since 1967, Professor of Music, University of California, Berkeley.

Glossolalia, electric tape, percussion, baritone (or dramatic tenor), and organ, World Library of Sacred Music, Soverign Series, No. III.

God of the Expanding Universe, organ and electronic tape, E. C. Schirmer, 1970.

I Make My Own Soul of All the Elements of the Earth, organ and electronic tape, E. C. Schirmer, 1971.

Litany, organ and electronic tape, E. C. Schirmer, 1971.

FELDERHOF, JAN. born Amsterdam, The Netherlands, Sept. 25, 1907. Studied at Amsterdam Conservatory; pupil of Sem Dresden; 1934, became instructor of harmony, Amsterdam Conservatory.

Aria, violin and organ, Donemus 153.

Epos, Donemus 424.

FELTON, WILLIAM. born Drayton, Salop (Shropshire), England, 1715; died Dec. 6, 1769. Studied at St. John's College, Cambridge; 1741, became vicar-choral, Cathedral, Hereford; one of the stewards, Three Choirs Festival.

Air, Op. 1, No. 3, Vernon Butcher, arr., Cramer, London, 1938.

Allegro, Op. 2, No. 5, Wall, arr., Cramer, London, 1936.

Allegro, Op. 4, No. 1, Wall, arr., Cramer, London 1938.

Allegro, Op. 5, No. 1, Wall, arr., Leonard, Gould and Boultter, London, 1948.

Concerto, Op. 1, No. 5 (E Minor), John E. West, arr., Novello, London, 1904.

Concerto, Op. 2, No. 3 (B-flat Major), E. Power Biggs, arr., H. W. Gray, New York, 1942.

Concerto in B-flat, Hugh McLean, arr., Oxford.

Little Trio, Cramer.

Little Tune, Cramer.

Three movements from Concertos, Wall, arr., Oxford University Press, London, 1939.

FERRARI, GUSTAVE. born Geneva, Switzerland, Sept. 28, 1872; died Geneva, July 29, 1948. Studied at Geneva Conservatory and in Paris; lived in London; 1917-1925, conducted operetta in America; toured as accompanist and singer, lecturer.

Sortie-Improvisation, in American Organ Monthly, Vol. 1, no. 5 (September, 1920), Boston Music Co.

FETLER, PAUL. born Philadelphia, Pa., 1920. Professor of theory and composition, University of Minnesota, Minneapolis, Minn.

composition in The Parish Organist, Vol. 12.

FÉVRIER, PIERRE. born France, 1715; died ca. 1780. Organist and maître de clavecin; 1754, became organist, royal Jesuits College; appointed organist, Sainte Chapelle and St. Roch.

Fugue in B Minor (Suite Three), from Pièces de Clavecin, in Les Maîtres français de l'orgue, Vol. II, p. 73.

FIEBIG, KURT.   born Berlin, Germany, Feb. 28, 1908.   Choirboy,
   Cathedral choir, Berlin; pupil of Arnold Dreyer (organ), became his assistant; pupil of Schrecker; 1926, organist-cantor
   in Berlin; organist, Cathedral, Quedlinburg; 1941-1950, Director, Evangelical Church Music School, Halle; 1951, became
   organist and Cantor in Hamburg.
      Acht-und-vierzig leichte Choralvorspiele, Hüllenhagen &
         Friehl.
      Choral Fantasie über du dich hab' ich gehoffet, Sirius.
      Prelude and Fugue in B-flat Major (1948), Peters 4548, 1951.
      Schmückt das Fest, in Orgelvorspiele, Merseburger.
      Triosonate (G Major), Peters 4616, 1952.
      chorale preludes in Orgelbuch zum Evangelischen Kirchen-
         gesangbuch, Book 12 (1), Book 17 (1).
      chorale preludes (7) in 73 leichte Choralvorspiele alter und
         neuer Meister.
FINCK, HEINRICH.   born Bemberg, Germany, 1445; died Vienna,
   June 9, 1527.   Served three Polish kings; 1510-1513, Kapell-
   meister to Duke Ulrich in Stuttgart; court musician to Maxi-
   milian I in Augsburg; 1520, became composer to chapter,
   Cathedral, Salzburg; 1525-1526, court Kapellmeister to Ferdi-
   nand I in Vienna.
      Orgelbearbeitung eines choralen Cantus firmus ca. 1490, in
         Geschichte der Musik in Beispielen, p. 53.
      Three Mass movements, in Alte Meister aus der Frühzeit
         dea Orgelspiels.
FINKBEINER, REINHOLD.   born Stuttgart, Germany, Aug. 6, 1929.
   Studied at the Knittel Conservatory, Berlin; composition pupil
   of Kurt Hessenburg and Hermann Heiss; Kantor, Frankfurt-am-
   Main; staff member, Hessischen Rundfunks.
      Choralfantasie über Wachet auf, Breitkopf und Härtel 6592,
         1968.
      Klangflächen (1963) Breitkopf und Härtel AV, 1963.
      Partita über In dich hab' ich (1957), Breitkopf und Härtel
         6303, 1958.
      Toccata und Fuge (1953), Breitkopf und Härtel 6459, 1965.
FIOCCO, JOSEPH HECTOR.   born Brussels, January, 1703; died
   Brussels, June 22, 1741.   1731-1737, Music director, Cathe-
   dral, Antwerp; 1737-1741, Music director, Ste. Gudule, Brussels.
      Andante, in Oudnederlandse Meesters, Vol. II, p. 100.
      Gavotte and Adagio, in Oudnederlandse Meesters, Vol. I,
         p. 114.
      Werken voor Clavecimbel, Joseph Watelet, ed. , Broude Bros. ,
         1971.
FISCHER, JOHANN KASPAR (CASPAR) FERDINAND.   German.
   born ?, between 1665 and 1670; died Rastatt, Germany,
   Mar. 27, 1746.   1696-1716, Kapellmeister to Margrave Ludwig
   of Baden in Bohemia; wrote Ariadne musica neo-organoedum
   (1702) which contained twenty preludes and fugues in twenty keys
   (suggesting the same idea Bach carried out in the Wohl-temperirte
   Clavier) plus five ricercari on Ave Maria klare; Der Tag; Da
   Jesus an dem Kreuze; Christ ist erstanden; Komm, heiliger

Geist.
  Ariadne musica neo-organoedum, in Liber Organi, Vol. 7,
    Schott 2267.
  Ave Maria klare, in South German Christmas Music, p. 7.
  Blumenstrauss (Musical Bouquet), Kalmus 3440; also Vol. I,
    Süddeutsche Orgelmeister des Barok, R. Walter, ed.,
    Coppenrath.
  Christ ist erstanden, in Pâques, Vol. I, p. 8; also in The
    First Four Centuries of Organ Music, p. 393.
  Präludium and Fuge (E Major), in Geschichte der Musik in
    Beispielen.
  Präludium und Fuge (E Major), in Historical Anthology of
    Music, Vol. II, p. 129.
  Präludium und Fuge (F Major), in A Brief Compendium of
    Early Organ Music, p. 46; also in Musica Organi,
    Vol. I, p. 43.
  Sämtliche Werke für Klavier und Orgel, von Werra, ed.,
    Breitkopf und Härtel, 1901.
  Selected Pieces, Schott 2479.
  (Der) Tag der ist so freudenreich, In Ritter, Zur Geschichte
    des Orgelspiels, Max Hesse's Verlag, Leipzig, 1884;
    also in Orgel Choräle Sammlung.
  chorale prelude in Eighty Chorale Preludes: German Masters
    of the Seventeenth and Eighteenth Centuries.
  chorale preludes (2) in Choralvorspiele zum Kirchenlied,
    Vol. 3.
  chorale preludes (3) in The Church Organist's Golden Trea-
    sury, Vol. I.
  chorale preludes (2) in The Church Organist's Golden Trea-
    sury, Vol. III.
  chorale preludes (2) in Choralvorspiele zum Kirchenlied,
    Vol. 3.
  composition in Elkan-Vogel Organ Series, Vol. 3.
  compositions (2) in Harold Gleason, Method of Organ Playing.
  compositions in Masterpieces of Organ Music, Folios 7 and
    55.
  compositions in The Parish Organist, Vols 5, 6, 7, and 8.
  ricercare (5) in Orgelmeister des siebzehnten und achtzehnten
    Jahrhunderts.
FISCHER, JOHANN. German. Sixteenth/seventeenth century. 1594-
  1596, Künstlich Tabulatur-Buch; organist at Morungen; 1595,
  organist at Angerburg.
FISCHER, MICHAEL GOTTHARDT. born Albach (Erfurt), Germany,
  June 3, 1773; died Erfurt, Jan. 12, 1829. Studied in Erfurt
  and Jena; pupil of Johann Christian Kittel; became organist,
  Barfüsserkirche, Erfurt (succeeded J. W. Hassler); organist,
  Predigerkirche, Erfurt (succeeded Kittel).
  Eight Chorales with Canon, Op. 16, G. W. Körner.
  Ein' feste Burg, Op. 18, G. W. Körner.
  Prelude, in Organ Book No. 2, p. 19.
  Prelude on O Jesulein süss, in Organ Music for Christmas,
    C. H. Trevor, ed., Vol. I, Oxford.
  Six Chorales with Variations, G. W. Körner.

chorale preludes (15) in Anthologie, Concordia.
chorale preludes (6) in Cantus firmus Präludien, B. Schott.
chorale preludes (32) in Chorale Preludes, F. Billig, ed. ,
   C. F. W. Siegel.
chorale preludes (9) in Organ Album, Volkmar, ed. , Peters.
chorale preludes (2) in Orgel Vorspiele zu den Melodien des
   Choralbuchs, Grosse-Weischede, ed. , Leuckart.
chorale preludes (5) in Seasonal Chorale Preludes, C. H.
   Trevor, ed. , Vol. 1 and 2, Oxford.
Fitzwilliam Virginal Book, John Alexander Fuller-Maitland and W.
   Barclay Squire, eds. , 2 vols. , London, 1899 (Reprint, Dover,
   New York, 1949).
FLEISCHER, HEINRICH. born Eisenach, Germany, 1912. Ph. D. ,
   University of Leipzig; Professor of Music, Valparaiso Univer-
   sity, Valparaiso, Ind. ; Professor of Music, University of Minne-
   sota, Minneapolis, Minn.
   Our God, Our Help, in Wedding Music, Vol. II, p. 50, Con-
      cordia.
   chorale preludes (4) in The Parish Organist, Vol. 1-4.
FLETCHER, PERCY E. born Derby, England, Dec. 12, 1879; died
   London, Sept. 10, 1932. 1899, conducted in London theaters.
   Festal Offertorium.
   Festival Toccata, H. W. Gray (St. Cecilia Series 23).
   Fountain Reverie.
   Lyra Davidica, in Hymn Tune Voluntaries, Curwen.
   Matinale.
FLEURET, EUGÈNE-ALBIN-DANIEL. born Dole (Jura), France,
   Mar. 1, 1869; died Lyon (Rhône), July 12, 1915. Studied at
   Conservatory, Lyon, professor of harmony and counterpoint
   and 1912, began organ class at Conservatory, Lyon; ca. 1896,
   organist, Saint-Pothin, Lyon; 1899-1915, organist, La Rédemp-
   tion.
   Invocation, in The International Organist, Vol. I, p. 42.
   Toccata, in The French Organist, Vol. II, p. 77.
FLEURY, ANDRÉ. born Neuilly-sur-Seine, France, July 25, 1903.
   Pupil of Vierne and Dupré; assistant to Gigout, Huré, and
   Tournemire; 1930, appointed organist, St. Augustin; 1943,
   became professor, Ecole Normale de Musique; 1949, appointed
   organist, St. Bénigne Cathedral, Dijon; 1949, became pro-
   fessor, Conservatory, Dijon.
   A solis ortus, in Hymnes et Antiennes, Schola Cantorum.
   Allegro symphonique, Hérelle, 1928, 1947, Philippo.
   Choral sur Vexilla regis, in Pâques, Vol. I, p. 25.
   Communion, in Communions, Orgue et Liturgie, Vol. 62,
      p. 27.
   Divertissement sur un Noël, Pastorale, Variations sur
      Adeste fideles, in L'Organiste, Decembre, 1941.
   Elévation pour le XVIe dimanche après la Pentecôte, in
      Elévations, Orgue et Liturgie, Vol. 57, p. 18.
   Offertoire, in Offertoires, Orgue et Liturgie, Vol. 52, p. 26.
   Postlude, Hérelle, 1935, Philippo.
   Postlude pour le XVIe dimanche après la Pentecôte, in Orgue
      et Liturgie, Vol. 75.

Prélude à l'Introit, in Préludes à l'Introit, Orgue et Litur-
gie, Vol. 48, p. 14.
Prélude, Andante, et Toccata, Lemoine, 1935.
Prélude et Fugue, Hérelle, 1929, Lemoine.
Première Symphonie, Lemoine, 1946.
Seconde Symphonie, Lemoine, 1949.
Variations sur un Noël bourguignon, in Christmas Music by
Various French Composers, p. 15, Kalmus; also in
Noëls variés, Orgue et Liturgie, Vol. 40, p. 15.
Versets sur A solis ortus, in Hymnes et Antiennes, Orgue
et Liturgie, Vol. 8, p. 26.
Vingt-quatre pièces (orgue et harmonium), Hérelle, 1936.
FLOR, CHRISTIAN. born Neukirchen (Eutin), Germany, 1626; died
Neukirchen, 1697. Probably studied in Lübeck or Hamburg;
1652, became organist, St. Lamberti Church, Lüneburg; 1676,
appointed organist, St. Johannis, Lüneburg.
composition in Masterpieces of Organ Music, Folio 45.
compositions (3) in Lüneburg Tablatures.
preludes (2) in Organum, Series IV, Vol. 2.
FOGLIANO, GIACOMO. born Modena, Italy, 1468; died Modena,
Apr. 10, 1548. 1489-1497 and 1504-1548, organist, Cathedral,
Modena.
Ricercare, in Anthologia Organistica Italiana, p. 2.
FONTANA, FABRIZIO. born Turin, Italy, ?; died Rome, Dec. 28,
1695. 1650, became member, Roman Congregazione di S.
Cecilia; organist, Santa Maria, Vallicella; 1657, made organ-
ist, St. Peter's, Rome; 1692, appointed organist, S. Maria
dell'Anima.
Ricercare X, in Classici Italiani dell'Organo, p. 137.
composition in Archives des maitres d'orgue des seizième-
dix-huitième siècles, Vol. 10.
ricercari (3) in L'Arte Musicale in Italia, p. 201.
FONTANA, GIOVANNI BATTISTA. born Brescia, Italy, ?; died
Brescia (Padua?), 1630.
Fugue in F Minor, in The International Organist, Vol. II,
p. 20.
Sonata in One Movement (D Minor), in The International
Organist, Vol. II, p. 16.
FOOTE, ARTHUR WILLIAM. born Salem, Mass., Mar. 5, 1853;
died Boston, Apr. 8, 1937. Pupil of Stephen Emery at New
England Conservatory; 1874, graduated, 1875, received first
A.M. degree in music in America from Harvard; pupil of
John Knowles Paine; 1878-1910, organist, First Unitarian
Church, Boston; 1909-1912, President, American Guild of
Organists.
Canzonetta (A Minor), Op. 71, No. 4 (1912).
Christmas, Op. 80, Schmidt, 1919.
Night, Op. 61, Schmidt, 1909.
Oriental Sketch, Schmidt, 1899 (transcription).
Seven Pieces, Op. 71, Schmidt, 1912.
Six Pieces, Op. 50, Schmidt, 1902.
Suite in D Major, Op. 54, Schmidt, 1904.
Three Compositions for Organ, Op. 29, Schmidt, 1894.

FORAY, PIERRE. born Blois, France, Sept. 22, 1905. Studied at
Caen; composition pupil of M. Dequin; 1930-1932, organist,
St. Pierre, Caen; 1941-1944, teacher, Ecole d'orgue, Caen;
1947-1958, organist, St. Ouen, Caen; since 1967, organist,
Cathédrale St. Michel, Draguignan.
  "Et Marie conservait ...," Op. 49 (1957), in Varia III,
      Orgue et Liturgie, Vol. 60, p. 16.
  "Ils ne sonts pas perdus ...," Op. 47 (1956), in Varia III,
      Orgue et Liturgie, Vol. 60, p. 18.
  "Tu aimeras ton prochain comme toi-même," Op. 47 (1956),
      in Varia III, Orgue et Liturgie, Vol. 50, p. 14.
FORTNER, WOLFGANG. born Leipzig, Germany, Oct. 12, 1907.
1927-1931, studied at the Conservatory, Leipzig; 1931, became
teacher, Evangelical Church Music Institute, Heidelberg; 1954,
appointed teacher of composition, Northwestern Music Academy,
Detmold; 1957, appointed lecturer, Musikhochschule, Freiburg.
  Concerto (1932), organ and string orchestra, Schott.
  Intermezzo, Schott 4718.
  Praeambel und Fuge, Schott 2269.
  Toccata und Fuge, Schott 2101.
FOSS (originally FUCHS), LUKAS. born Berlin, Aug. 15, 1922.
1933, began study in Paris with Lazare Levy and Noel Gallon;
1937, came to the United States; studied at the Curtis Institute
of Music, Philadelphia; pupil of Randall Thompson, Fritz
Reiner, Koussevitzky (Berkshire Music Center), and Hindemith
(Yale); 1945, won Guggenheim Fellowship; 1944-1950, pianist,
Boston Symphony Orchestra; 1950-1952, won Fulbright Fellow-
ship to Rome; 1953, appointed professor of composition and
conductor, University Orchestra, University of California, Los
Angeles; 1960, toured Russia with Aaron Copland; 1959-1960,
won second Guggenheim Fellowship; 1963, appointed conductor,
Buffalo Symphony Orchestra.
  Etudes (4), in Source Music of the Avant Garde, Vol. 2,
      No. 2 (July, 1968), p. 29-33, (Composer/Performer
      Edition, 330 University Ave., Davis, Calif. 95616.
FRANCK, CÉSAR-AUGUSTE-JEAN-GUILLEAUME-HUBERT. born
Liège, Belgium, Dec. 10, 1822; died Paris, Nov. 8, 1890.
1835, family moved to Paris; pupil of Benoist at Paris Con-
servatory; 1844, returned to Paris from Belgium; 1847, be-
came organist, Notre-Dame-de-Lorette; 1851, became organist,
St. Jean-St. François au Marais; 1858, appointed choirmaster,
1859, organist, Ste. Clotilde; 1872, appointed professor of
organ, Conservatory, Paris (succeeded Benoist); taught Duparc,
Pierné, d'Indy, Ropartz, Chausson, Samuel, Rousseau, Augusta
Holmès, Pierre de Bréville, and Guillaume Lekeu.
  Andantino (1858), Costallat.
  Complete Organ Works, 4 vols., Peters 3744 A, B, C, D.
  Easy Service Music from Franck's The Organist, L. Robinson,
      arr., Hope Publishing Company, Chicago, Ill.
  Grand Chorus on Two Carols, in Venite Adoremus, McLaugh-
      lin & Reilly; also Peters 3744 E and H.
  Noël angevin, in Organ Music for Christmas, Vol. 2, C. H.
      Trevor, ed., Oxford.

*Oeuvres Complètes, 4 vols., Durand; also Kalmus, 4 vols.,
    3443-3446; also M. Dupré, ed., 4 vols., Borne-
    mann.
  Vol. 1: Six pièces (Fantaisie [C Major]; Grande
          Pièce Symphonique; Prélude, Fugue, et
          Variation).
  Vol. 2: Trois pièces (Pastorale; Prière; Finale).
  Vol. 3: Trois pièces (Fantaisie in A Major;
          Cantabile in B Major; Pièce Héroïque).
  Vol. 4: Trois chorals (E Major, B Minor, A
          Minor).
(L')Organiste, Cinquante-neuf pièces posthumes (organ and
    harmonium), Enoch; Durand; also Boosey and Hawkes.
Pastorale, Boosey and Hawkes.
Pièce héroïque, Boosey and Hawkes.
Pieces for organ or piano, Peters 4529.
Prelude, Fugue and Variation, Boosey and Hawkes; also in
    Musica Organi, Vol. I, p. 174.
Quarante-quatre pièces posthumes (organ and harmonium),
    Enoch, Paris, 1900.
Selected Works for Organ, Edwin Shippen Barnes, G. Schir-
    mer 1491, 1925.
Suite, in Pièces romantiques ignorées, L'Organiste liturgique,
    Vol. 17, p. 23.
Three Chorales, Gerard Alphenaar, reviser, E. B. Marks
    Organ Library 66, 1948.
Three Chorales, Harvey Grace, ed., Novello.
Trois Antiennes (1859).
Vieux Noël, in Noël, p. 8, C. Fischer.
compositions in The Parish Organist, Vols. 5, 6, 7, and 8.
FRANK, PAUL. born Vienna, Austria, 1905. Studied at the Con-
    servatory, Vienna; 1940, came to United States; Ph. D.,
    University of Chicago; from 1946, faculty member, Otterbein
    College, Westerville, Ohio.
    Offertory, in American Organ Music, Vol. I, p. 5.
FRANKE, FRIEDRICH WILHELM. born Barmen, Germany, June 21,
    1861; died Cologne, Apr. 3, 1932. Studied at Musikhochschule,
    Berlin; organist, Stralsund and Preetz; 1891-1924, teacher of
    organ, harmony, and counterpoint, Conservatory, Cologne;
    organist, Gürzenichkonzerte.
    Cantus-firmus Präludien, 4 vols. B. Schott & Söhne, 1928.
    Choral-variationen über Was Gott tut, Schott 2083.
    Choral-variationen über Wer nur, Schott, 1896.
    Chorale Fantasies, 2 vols., Schott.
    Durch Adams Fall, in Orgel Choräle Sammlung.
    Mein Leben ist ein Pilgrimstand, in Orgel Vorspiele zu den
        Melodien des Choralbuchs, Leuckart.
FREIXANET. born Catalonia, Spain, ca. 1730; died ?.
    Sonata, in Silva Iberica, p. 20.
FRESCOBALDI, GIROLAMO. Christened Ferrara, Italy, Sept. 9,
    1583; died Rome, Mar. 1, 1643. Pupil of Luzzaschi and Ban-
    chieri; 1604, organist, singer, Accademia di Santa Cecilia,
    Rome; traveled to Flanders; lived in Brussels; 1607, became

organist, Santa Maria in Trastevere; 1608, appointed organist,
St. Peter's, Rome; 1628-1634, court organist in Florence;
1634-1643, organist, St. Peter's, Rome; taught Froberger.
Aria detta la Frescobalda con variazion, in Cantantibus
    Organis, Vol. II, p. 8.
Canzona, in Alte Meister des Orgelspiels, Vol. I, p. 86.
Canzona, in Historical Anthology of Music, Vol. II, p. 22.
Canzona in C Major, in Geschichte der Musik in Beispielen,
    p. 239.
Capricci, Canzoni, Fuga, in Corpus of Early Keyboard
    Music, No. 30, Vol. 2.
Composizione per Organo e Cembalo, in I Classici della
    Musica Italiana, Quaderno 43-47.
Fantaisie (12), in Orgue et Liturgie, vols. 32 and 35.
Fiori Musicali, Fernando Germani, ed. , De Santis.
Fugue (G Minor), Cramer.
Hymns, Partitas, in Corpus of Early Keyboard Music,
    No. 30, Vol. 3.
Nove Toccate Inedite, S. dalla Libera and L. F. Tagliavini,
    eds. , Bärenreiter, 1962.
Organ Works, Hermann Keller, ed. , 2 vols. , C. F. Peters
    4514, 4515.
        Vol. 1: Fiori Musicali.
        Vol. 2: Toccatas, canzonas, ricercars, capriccios.
*Orgel und Klavier Werke, Pierre Pidoux, ed. , 5 vols. ,
    Bärenreiter 2201-2205, 1954.
        Fantasie und Canzoni alla Francese, Bärenreiter 2201.
        Capriccios, Ricercari, und Canzoni, Bärenreiter 2202.
        Toccatas und Partitas, Bärenreiter 2203.
        Toccata, Canzoni und Hymns, Bärenreiter 2204.
        Fiori Musicali, Bärenreiter 2205.
Ricercare, in Treasury of Early Organ Music, p. 29.
Sixty-eight Selected Pieces, 2 vols. , Breitkopf und Härtel.
Three Fugues, Cramer.
Toccata, in Historical Anthology of Music, Vol. II, p. 19.
Toccata avanti la Messa delli Apostoli, in Organ Music for
    the Communion Service, p. 60.
Toccata in G Major, in The First Four Centuries of Organ
    Music, Vol. I, p. 197.
Toccata per l'Elevazione, in Historical Organ Recitals,
    Vol. I, p. 34.
Toccatas, 2 vols. , in Orgue et Liturgie Vol. 26 (12) and
    Vol. 41 (11).
Toccatas heretofore unpublished, Dalla Libera, ed. , Bären-
    reiter.
Toccatas, Partitas, 2 vols. , Kalmus 3452/3453.
canzonas (2) in Anthologia pro Organo, Vol. I.
capriccios (2) in Anthologia Organistica Italiana.
composition in Elkan-Vogel Organ Series, Vol. I.
compositions (4) in Alte italienische Meister.
compositions (2) in Anthologia pro Organo, Vol. III.
composition in Archiv von Musikwissenchaft, No. 42.
compositions (7) in Classici Italiani dell'Organo.

compositions (8) from Messa della Madonna, in A la Sainte Vierge, L'Organiste liturgique, Vol. 2, p. 3.

compositions in Masterpieces of Organ Music, Folio 24.

compositions in The Parish Organist, Vols. 7 and 8.

compositions (4) in Spielbuch für die Kleinorgel, Vol. I.

compositions (3) in L'Arte Musicale in Italia, Vol. III, p. 223.

passacaglias (2) in Chacones et passacailles, L'Organiste liturgique, Vol. 22.

toccatas (2) in Harold Gleason, Method of Organ Playing.

toccatas (23) in Keyboard Compositions Preserved in Manuscript, Corpus of Early Keyboard Music, No. 30, Vol. 1.

toccatas (2) in Liber Organi, Vol. 5, p. 4.

FRICKER, HERBERT AUSTIN. English or Canadian. born 1868; died 1943.

Adagio (A-flat Major), Chester.

Cantilena Nuptiale, Beal Stuttard and Co.

Concert Overture (C minor), Novello, 1906.

Fantasie-Overture (G Minor), G. Schirmer.

Romance (G-flat Major), G. Schirmer.

Scherzo Symphonique, Beal Stuttard and Co.

Suite, H. W. Gray.

Three Organ Pieces, J. Broadbent.

FRICKER, PETER RACINE. born London, England, Sept. 5, 1920. Studied at Royal College of Music; 1952, became music director, Morley College, London; 1951, began teaching, Royal College of Music; 1964-1965, faculty member, University of California, Santa Barbara.

Chorale, Schott 10564.

Pastorale, Schott 10742.

Praeludium, Oxford.

Ricercare, Op. 40, Schott, 1965.

Six Short Pieces, Augsburg 11-9415, 1971.

Sonata (1947).

Toccata-Gladius Domini, Augsburg.

Wedding Processional, Schott 10741.

FRIEDELL, HAROLD. born Jamaica, Long Island, N. Y., May 11, 1905; died February 17, 1958. Pupil of Wagenaar and David McK. Williams; 1934-1946, organist-choirmaster, Calvary Episcopal Church, New York; 1946-1958, organist-choirmaster, St. Bartholomew's Church, New York; taught at Juilliard School of Music, Union Theological Seminary, and Guilmant Organ School, New York.

Elegy, Violin, Harp and Organ, H. W. Gray.

Verses for the Nunc dimittis, in The Modern Anthology, p. 83.

FROBERGER, JOHANN JACOB. born Stuttgart, Germany, May 18, 1616; died Héricourt, near Montbeliard, May 7, 1667. Court organist to Ferdinand III in Vienna who sent Froberger to study with Frescobaldi for four years (1637-1641); 1641-1645, 1653-1657, court organist in Vienna; toured a great deal.

Ausgewählte Orgelwerke, Karl Matthaei, ed., Bärenreiter

381.
Canzona (F Major), in Spielbuch für die Kleinorgel, Vol. I,
     p. 40.
Capriccio (Canzona), in Historical Organ Recitals, Vol. I,
     p. 69.
Keyboard Works, 3 vols., Bärenreiter 5197.
Nun danket alle Gott, in Orgel Chorale Sammlung, Metzler.
Organ Works, Auler, ed., in Denkmäler der Tonkunst in
     Osterreich, Vol. 8 (Jg. IV/1); Vol. 13 (Jg. VI/2);
     Vol. 21 (Jg. X/2), Breitkopf und Härtel, 1897.
Organ-clavier works, 2 vols., Breitkopf und Härtel.
Ricercare, in The First Four Centuries of Organ Music,
     Vol. II, p. 246.
Toccata, in Liber Organi, Vol. 5, p. 12.
Toccata (D Minor), in Treasury of Early Organ Music,
     p. 41.
Toccata II (D Minor), in Historical Anthology of Music,
     Vol. II, p. 64.
Various Organ Works, Kalmus 3455; also Vol. 8, Süd-
     deutsche Orgelmeister des barok, R. Walter, ed.,
     Coppenrath.
composition in Elkan-Vogel Organ Series, Vol. 3.
composition in The Parish Organist, Vol. 8.
compositions (3) in Alte Meister des Orgelspiels, Vol. I.
compositions (4) in Anthologia pro Organo, Vol. I.
compositions (2) in Anthologia pro Organo, Vol. III.
compositions in Masters of the Cembalo, Schultz, ed.,
     C. F. Peters 4407 A.
compositions in Masterpieces of Organ Music, Folios 35
     and 62.
compositions (10) in Organum, Series IV, Vol. 11 (Con-
     cordia 97-4343).
ricercars (2) in European Organ Music of the 16th and 17th
     Centuries, p. 124, 126.
FROIDEBISE, PIERRE. born Ohey (Namur), Belgium, May 15,
     1914; died Liège, October 28, 1962. Pupil of Jongen,
     Moulaert, and de Maleingreau at Royal Conservatory, Brussels;
     pupil of Tournemire; 1954, appointed Professor of harmony,
     Royal Conservatory, Liège; organist, Stiftskirche, St. Jâcques,
     Liège.
     Diptique (1939), published by himself.
     Petit livre d'orgue en style ancien, Schola Cantorum.
     Prélude et Fugue (1939), published by himself.
     Sonatine (1939), published by himself.
FRYKLÖF, HARALD. Swedish. born 1882, died 1919. From 1908,
     organist, Storkyrkan, Stockholm.
     Passacaglia, in Musica Organi, Vol. III, p. 100.
FUENLLANA, MIGUEL DE. born Navalcarnero (Madrid), Spain,
     early sixteenth century; died ?. Blind vihuela virtuoso and
     composer; chamber musician to Marquesa de Tarifa, Philip II,
     and Queen Isabel de Valois; wrote fantasies; wrote Libro de
     música para vihuela, intitulado Orphenica Lyra.
     composition in Elkan-Vogel Organ Series, Vol. 5.

FUMET, DYNAM-VICTOR. born Toulouse, France, May 4, 1867;
died Paris, Jan. 2, 1949. Pupil of Franck at Conservatory,
Paris; played the choir organ at Ste. Clotilde for a time;
1910, became organist, St. Anne, Paris.
Adam et Eve, Schola Cantorum.
Canticum novum, Schola Paroissale, Procure de musique
religieuse, Saint-Leu-le-Foret, France.
FUX, JOHANN JOSEPH. born Hirtenfeld, Styria, 1660; died Vienna,
Feb. 14, 1741. 1696, theorist, appointed organist, Schotten-
kirche, Vienna; 1698, became court composer, 1704, Kapellmeister, St. Stephen's, Vienna; 1713-1741, court Kapellmeister.
composition in Masterpieces of Organ Music, Folio 30.

GABRIELI, ANDREA. born Venice, Italy, between 1510 and 1520;
died Venice, 1586. Pupil of Willaert; 1558, organist, S.
Geremia, Venice; 1566-1586, outstanding organist at San
Marco, Venice, succeeded Merulo; taught G. Gabrieli, Hassler, and Aichinger; founder of Italian organ school; prolific
composer: fifteen pieces in B. Schmidt's Tabulaturbuch, five
toccatas in Diruta's Il Transilvano, Pt. I, one piece in Woltz's
Nova musica; began type of preludial intonazione and canzona
da sonar; worked towards ricercari and fantasie based on one
theme; wrote Canzoni alla francese, Book I (1571), Canzoni
alla francese, Book II (1605), G. Gabrieli, ed., Intonazioni
d'organo (1593), G. Gabrieli, ed., also contains four toccatas,
Ricercari per l'organo (1595), G. Gabrieli, ed., in three
volumes.
Canzona, in Anthologia pro Organo, Vol. I, p. 16.
Canzona, in Historical Organ Recitals, Vol. I, p. 10.
Intonations, Vol. III, Kalmus.
Intonazione settimo tono, in Historical Anthology of Music,
Vol. I, p. 146.
Orgelwerke, Pierre Pidoux, ed., 5 vols., Bärenreiter 1779-
1783, 1953; also Kalmus 3459-3463.
Vol. 1: Intonationen.
Vol. 2: Ricercari.
Vol. 3: Ricercari.
Vol. 4: Canzonen; Ricercari ariosi.
Vol. 5: Canzoni alla francese.
Pass'e Mezzo Antico, in The First Four Centuries of Organ
Music, Vol. I, p. 88.
Toccata, Dalla Libera, ed., Ricordi 2659.
Tre Messe, Dalla Libera, ed., Ricordi 129954.
composition in Archives des maitres d'orgue des seizième-
dix-huitième siècles, Vol. X.
compositions (4) in Anthologia Organistica Italiana.
compositions (5) in Classici Italiani dell'Organo.
compositions in Masterpieces of Organ Music, Folio 66.
compositions (4) in L'Arte Musicale in Italia, Vol. 3, p. 6.

intonations (2) in Treasury of Early Organ Music, p. 29.
GABRIELI, GIOVANNI. born Venice, Italy, ca. 1555; died Venice, Aug. 12, 1612. Nephew of Andrea Gabrieli; 1575-1579, court organist, Munich; 1584, made substitute second organist, 1585, appointed second organist, San Marco, Venice; taught Heinrich Schütz; wrote music found in Diruta's Il Transilvano, Parts I and II; wrote Intonazioni e ricercari per l'organo (1593, 1595).

Canzon Septimi Toni a 8, organ and brass quartet, Concordia 97-4841.

Composizioni per Organo, 3 vols. , Dalla Libera ed. , Ricordi 2573, 2598, 2612, 1957-1959.

Fantasy on the Sixth Tone, in The First Four Centuries of Organ Music, Vol. I, p. 131.

In ecclesiis, in Historical Anthology of Music, Vol. I, p. 175.

Intonation on the Ninth Tone, in Harold Gleason, Method of Organ Playing, p. 65.

Intonazioni and Toccata, in L'Arte Musicale in Italia, Vol. III, p. 131.

Ricercar and Canzon, in Ricercare, Canzonen und Fugen des 17, und 18. Jahrhunderts.

Sonata Pian e Forte, arranged for brass choir and organ, Peters 4267.

Works for Keyboard, Bärenreiter 2819.

compositions (2) in Anthologia Organistica Italiana.

compositions (3) in Classici Italiani dell'Organo.

intonations (3) in Treasury of Early Organ Music, p. 28.

GADE, NIELS WILHELM. born Copenhagen, Feb. 22, 1817; died Copenhagen, Dec. 21, 1890. 1844, teacher, Conservatory, Leipzig; director Gewandhauskonzerte, Leipzig (succeeded Mendelssohn); 1858, appointed organist, Holmens Church, Copenhagen; 1866, director, Conservatory, Copenhagen.

Fantasi on Lover den Herre, Hansen 11700.

Lobe den Herren, in Organ Fantasies on Ancient Hymns and Chorales, Lorenz.

Orgelkompositioner, (Tre Tonestykker, Op. 22; Tre Choralforspil; Festligt praeludium over Choralen Lover den Herre, Sørgemarsh), Wilhelm Hansen 4158, 1969.

Three Compositions, Op. 22, Breitkopf und Härtel.

GAGNEBIN, HENRI. born Liège, Belgium, Mar. 13, 1886. Studied at Lausanne, Berlin, Geneva, and Paris; pupil of d'Indy and Vierne; 1910-1916, organist, Eglise de la Rédemption; 1916-1925, organist, St. Jean, Lausanne; 1926, became Director, Conservatory, Geneva.

Carillon, Leduc.

Monologue et Fugue, in Liturgie et Concert, Orgue et Liturgie, Vol. 70, p. 17.

Pastorale, Leduc.

Pièces d'orgue sur les Psaumes huguenots, 8 vols. , Henn, Ouvrières, 1966.

Sonata da Chiesa per la Pasqua, trumpet and organ, in Orgue et cuivres, Orgue et Liturgie, Vol. 9, p. 25.

GAL, HANS. Austrian. born 1890. Writer on music; since 1945, teacher, University of Edinburgh.

> Concertino, organ and string orchestra, Op. 55, in Musica Organi, Vol. II, p. 101.

GARDNER, JOHN LINTON. born Manchester, England, March 2, 1917. Studied at Wellington College; 1939, B. Mus., Exeter College, Oxford; assistant conductor, Covent Garden; 1955, became instructor, Morley College.

> Five Hymn-tune Preludes, Novello.

GAUL, HARVEY BARTLETT. born New York, N. Y., Apr. 11, 1881; died Pittsburgh, Dec. 1, 1945. 1898, assistant organist, St. John's Chapel, New York; organist, St. Luke's Chapel, Paris; 1910, became organist, Calvary Church, Pittsburgh; pupil of Widor, d'Indy, Guilmant, and Dudley Buck.

> Ancient Hebrew Prayer of Thanksgiving, J. Fischer 7105, 1936.
>
> April, H. W. Gray (St. Cecilia Series 72).
>
> Ascension Fiesta, H. W. Gray (St. Cecilia Series 620).
>
> (La) Brume, H. W. Gray (St. Cecilia Series 67).
>
> Chant for Dead Heroes, H. W. Gray (St. Cecilia Series 110).
>
> Children's Easter Festival, J. Fischer.
>
> Christmas Dance of the Little Animals, H. W. Gray, St. Cecilia Series 679).
>
> Daguerrotype of an old Mother, J. Fischer.
>
> Easter Morning on Mt. Rubidoux, J. Fischer 5713-9, 1926.
>
> Easter Morn with the Pennsylvania Moravians, J. Fischer.
>
> Easter Procession of the Moravian Brethren, H. W. Gray (St. Cecilia Series 705).
>
> Fantasy on Easter Kyries, H. W. Gray (St. Cecilia Series 665).
>
> Four Bach Transcriptions, J. Fischer.
>
> From the Southland, H. W. Gray (St. Cecilia Series 68).
>
> Fughetta, H. W. Gray (St. Cecilia Series 14).
>
> Hymn of the American Navy, H. W. Gray (St. Cecilia Series), 1945.
>
> Lenten Meditation, H. W. Gray (St. Cecilia Series 13).
>
> Little Bells of Our Lady, J. Fischer.
>
> March of the Wise Men, H. W. Gray (St. Cecilia Series 658).
>
> Moravian Evening Hymn, H. W. Gray (St. Cecilia Series 736).
>
> Moravian Morning Star, H. W. Gray (St. Cecilia Series 686).
>
> (A) Negro Once Sang, H. W. Gray (St. Cecilia Series 690).
>
> Sketch in D-flat, H. W. Gray (St. Cecilia Series 12).
>
> Sketch in F Minor, H. W. Gray (St. Cecilia Series 11).
>
> Song for the Golden Harvest, H. W. Gray (St. Cecilia Series 694).
>
> Songs of Early Patroits, J. Fischer.
>
> (La) Sortie des Trois Rois, J. Fischer.
>
> To Martin Luther's Christmas Carol, J. Fischer.
>
> Vesper Processional, J. Fischer.
>
> Wind and the Grass, H. W. Gray (St. Cecilia Series 107).

Yasnaza Polyana, H. W. Gray (St. Cecilia Series 47-48).
GAUTIER (GAULTIER), DENIS. born Marseilles, France, 1603;
died Paris, late January, 1672. Lute pupil of Racquet.
Courante, in Huit Courantes, L'Organiste liturgique, Vols.
58-59, p. 14.
Pavanne ou Tombeau de Mr Raquette, in L'Organiste litur-
gique, Vols. 29-30.
GAY, MAURICE. born Montpellier, 1897. Organ pupil of Albert
Decaux and composition pupil of Vincent d'Indy at the Schola
Cantorum, Paris; professor of organ and music history, Con-
servatory, Aix-en-Provence; organist, Cathedral, Aix-en-
Provence.
Béthléem, in Varia, Orgue et Liturgie, Vol. 66, p. 3.
Entrée de Jésus à Jérusalem, in Orgue et Liturgie, Vol. 60,
p. 3.
GEBHARD, HANS. German. born 1897.
Fantasie, Op. 18, Schott 2245.
GEHRING, PHILIP. born Carlisle, Pa., Nov. 27, 1925. A.B.,
Mus. B., Oberlin; M. Mus., Ph. D., Syracuse University;
Associate of the American Guild of Organists; organ pupil of
Fenner Douglass, Arthur Poister, and André Marchal; com-
position pupil of Herbert Elwell and Ernst Bacon; 1950-1953,
organist-choirmaster, Kimball Memorial Lutheran Church,
Kannapolis, N. Car.; 1952-1958, taught Davidson College,
Davidson, N. Car.; since 1958, faculty member, Valparaiso
University, Valparaiso, Ind.
Four Pieces in the Manner of an Organ Mass, Augsburg
11-9176, 1969.
Six Hymn Tune Preludes, Concordia 97-4768, 1966.
GEHRKE, HUGO. born Mayville, Wis., 1912. Professor of Music,
California Concordia College, Oakland, Calif.
chorale preludes (3) in The Parish Organist, Vol. 1-4.
chorale preludes in The Parish Organist, Vols. 5, 6, 10,
and 12.
GEISER, WALTHER. born Zefingen, Switzerland, May 16, 1897.
Pupil of Busoni; 1924, violist, Basel orchestra and string
quartet; since 1924, teacher of composition, instrumentation,
ensemble playing, and conducting, director of orchestra, Con-
servatory, Basel.
Concert Piece, organ and chamber orchestra, Bärenreiter
2034.
Drei Choralvorspiele, Op. 17b (1931) Bärenreiter.
Fantasie I, Op. 17a (1931), Bärenreiter 2059, 1948.
Fantasie II, Op. 28 (1939), Bärenreiter 2060, 1949.
Sonatine, Op. 26 (1939), Bärenreiter 2061, 1948.
GENZMER, HARALD. born Blumenthal (Bremen), Germany, Feb. 9,
1909. Pupil of August Wagner, Thuille, and Hindemith at
Hochschule für Musik, Berlin; chorus master, Opera House,
Breslau; 1938, at Folk Music School, Berlin; 1946, ap-
pointed teacher of composition, 1948, Director, Hochschule für
Musik, Freiburg; 1957, appointed faculty member, Hochschule
für Musik, Munich.
Adventskonzert, Peters P5938.

Dritte Sonate (1963), Litolff (Peters 5970).
Preludium, Intermezzo, und Fuge (1950), Schott 3842.
Sonate (1952), Schott 4489.
Sonate Nr. 3, Peters 5970.
Tripartita in F Major, Schott 3842.
Toccata, Trio, und Chaconne, Schott 4489, 1953.
Zweite Sonate (1956), Litolff (Peters 5856).
chorale preludes (5) in 73 leichte Choralvorspiele, alter und
    neuer Meister, Leuckart.
GEOFFROY, JEAN-NICOLAS. French. born ?; died Perpignan,
    France ?, end of the seventeenth century. Organist, St.
    Nicholas-du-Chardonnet, Paris; organist, Cathedral, Per-
    pignan.
        compositions (2) in Les Maîtres français de l'orgue, Vol. II.
GEORGE, GRAHAM. born Norwich, England, April 11, 1912. 1932-
    1933, studied at McGill University, Montreal; 1936, Mus. B.,
    1939, Mus. Doc., University of Toronto; composition pupil of
    Paul Hindemith, conducting pupil of Willem van Otterloo; since
    1932, organist and choirmaster of churches in Montreal, Sher-
    brooke, Que., and Kingston, Ont.; 1938-1941, teacher of
    school music in Quebec; Professor of Music, Head, Music
    Department, Queen's University, Kingston, Ont., Canada.
        Elegy (to Vaughan Williams), H. W. Gray (St. Cecilia
            Series 948).
        Passacaglia on Lobe den Herren, H. W. Gray.
        Three Fugues (1964), Berandol.
        Two Preludes on King's Majesty, H. W. Gray (St. Cecilia
            Series 898).
GERBER, HEINRICH NIKOLAUS. born Wenigen-Ehrich (Sondershau-
    sen), Germany, Sept. 6, 1702; died Wenigen-Ehrich, Aug. 6,
    1775. Studied at University of Leipzig; pupil of J. S. Bach
    and Kirnberger; 1728, made organist, Heringen; 1731, be-
    came organist, Sondershausen.
        Es ist gewisslich, in 73 leichte Choralvorspiele, alter und
            neuer Meister, Leuckart.
        chorale preludes (2) in Orgelchoräle um J. S. Bach, Litolff.
        composition in Das Erbe deutschen Musik, Series I, Vol. 9.
GERLACH, GUNTER. German. born 1928.
        Das Gastmahl des Herrn (5 chorale arrangements), Merse-
            burger 884.
        Meditation on Te lucis ante, viola and organ, Merseburger
            854.
        Partita on Nun bitten wir, Merseburger 856.
        Prelude on O Gott, der frommer Gott, Rieter-Biedermann.
        Sonate, Merseburger 855.
GERMANI, FERNANDO. Italian. born Rome, April 5, 1906. 1934,
    taught at Conservatory, Rome; 1936-1938, taught organ, Curtis
    Institute, Philadelphia; 1939, taught at Accademia Chigiana,
    Siena; 1948, appointed organist, St. Peter's Basilica, Vatican.
        Toccata, Op. 12, De Santis, 1937.
GHEIN (GHEYN), MATHIAS VAN DEN. born Tirlemont, Belgium,
    Apr. 7, 1721; died Louvain, June 22, 1785. 1741, appointed
    organist and carilloneur, St. Peter's Church, Louvain.

compositions (2) in Anthologia pro Organo, Vol. II.
compositions (2) in Anthologia pro Organo, Vol. IV.
compositions (2) in Oudnederlandse Meesters, Vol. II.
compositions (3) in Oudnederlandse Meesters, Vol. III.
GIBBONS, CHRISTOPHER. baptized London, Aug. 22, 1615; died
    London, Oct. 20, 1676. Son of Orlando Gibbons; singer,
    Chapel Royal; 1638, became organist, Cathedral, Winchester;
    1660, appointed organist, Chapel Royal and Westminster Abbey;
    1663, Mus. Doc., Oxford.
        compositions (7) in Keyboard Compositions, Corpus of Early
            Keyboard Music, No. 18.
GIBBONS, ORLANDO. baptized Oxford, England, Dec. 25, 1583;
    died Canterbury, June 5, 1625. 1596, choirboy, King's College;
    1605-1625, organist, Chapel Royal; 1606, Mus. B., Cambridge;
    1623, organist, Westminster Abbey; 1607, M. A., Oxford;
    1622, Mus. Doc., Oxford (honorary); keyboard works found in
    Fitzwilliam Virginal Book and other virginal books.
        Complete Keyboard Works, 5 vols., Margaret Glyn, ed.,
            Stainer and Bell, London, 1924-1925.
        (A) Fancy for Double Orgaine, Hinrichsen 1583A.
        Fancy, Voluntary, and Fantasy, in Tallis to Wesley, Vol. 9.
        Fantasy, in Alte Orgelmusik aus England und Frankreich,
            p. 12.
        Hymn Prelude, Cramer.
        In Nomine, Cramer.
        Keyboard Compositions, Clare G. Rayner, ed., Corpus of
            Early Keyboard Music, No. 18, American Institute of
            Musicology, 1967.
        Keyboard Music, Gerald Hendrie, ed., Musica Britanica,
            Vol. 20, published for the Royal Musical Association,
            Stainer and Bell, Ltd., London, 1962.
        (The) Queen's Command, in The First Four Centuries of
            Organ Music, Vol. I, p. 192; also Cramer.
        Voluntary, in Liber Organi, Vol. 10, p. 8.
GIBBS, CECIL ARMSTRONG. born Great Baddow (Chelmsford),
    Essex, England, Aug. 10, 1889; died Chelmsford, May 12,
    1960. Studied at Trinity College, Cambridge (A. A., Doc.
    Mus.) and at Royal College of Music; taught at Royal College
    of Music.
        Minuet in Classic Style, in An Easy Album, Oxford.
        Prelude on Coventry Carol (Lullay, Thou little tiny Child),
            in Christmas Album, Oxford.
        Postlude in D Major, in A Festive Album, Oxford Univer-
            sity Press, London, 1956, p. 4.
        Six Adjectives, Hinrichsen 818.
        Six Sketches, Oxford University Press.
                Book I: Lyric Melody; Elegy; Jubilate Deo.
                Book II: Quiet Thoughts; Folk Song; Processional
                    March.
GIGAULT, NICOLAS. born Paris ?, 1624-1625; died Paris,
    August, 1707. 1646, became organist, St. Honoré; 1652,
    made organist, St. Nicolas-des-Champs; 1672, appointed
    organist, Sainte Chapelle; 1673, became organist, St. Martin-

des-Champs; 1685, made organist, Hôpital du St. Esprit; appointed one of four organists to the king; 1683, became organist, St. Germain-l'Auxerrois; 1687, appointed organist, St. Benoît.

Fugue et verset, in Les Maîtres français de l'orgue, Vol. II, p. 22.

Livre de musique pour l'orgue, in Archives des maîtres d'orgue des seizième-dix-huitième siècles, Vol. IV.

Preludio, in The First Four Centuries of Organ Music, Vol. II, p. 267.

Prélude du cinquième ton, in Organ Book No. 2, p. 30.

Qui tollis, in Liber Organi, Vol. I, p. 18.

composition in The Parish Organist, Vol. 1-4.

preludes (2) in Les Maîtres français de l'orgue, Vol. I.

GIGOUT, EUGÈNE. born Nancy, France, Mar. 23, 1844; died Paris, Dec. 9, 1925. 1857, began studying at Niedermeyer School, Paris; pupil of Saint-Saëns; taught Fauré, Périlhou, Erb, and Boëllmann; 1863-1885, 1900-1905, taught at Niedermeyer School; from 1863, organist, St. Augustin for sixty-two years; 1911, appointed professor of organ and improvisation, Conservatory, Paris (succeeded Guilmant).

Album grégorien, 2 vols. , Leduc, 1895 (E. B. Marks).

Cent pièces brèves (grégoriennes), Heugel, 1889.

Cent pièces nouvelles, Chester, 1922.

Communion, in The French Organist, Vol. I, p. 13.

Deux pièces, Durand, 1898.

Dix pièces, Amsterdam, 1923, Leduc.

Dix pièces en recueil, Leduc, 1892.

Douze pièces, Seyffert, Amsterdam, 1923; Leduc.

Grand-Choeur dialogué, G. Schirmer, 1908.

Grand Choeur dialogué and Toccata in B Minor, in French Masterworks for Organ, Alexander Schreiner, ed. , J. Fischer, Glen Rock, N. J. , 1958.

Interludium (F Major), Junne (Leipzig).

Marche de Fête, in The International Organist, Vol. II, p. 24.

Nouveau recueil de douze pièces, Leduc, 1912.

(L') Orgue d'église, (interludes), 2 vols. , Enoch, 1902.

Pièce jubilaire, Schola Cantorum, 1918.

Pièces diverses, Durand, 1891.

Pièces diverses, London and Leipzig, 1895.

Poèmes mystiques, Durand, 1893.

Prélude et Fugue en si mineur, Durand.

Prélude et Fugue en mi majeur, Durand.

Rapsodie sur des airs catalans, Durand.

Rapsodie sur des airs populairs du Canada, Durand.

Rhapsody on Noëls, in The French Organist, Vol. II, p. 28.

Six pièces (Introduction et Theme fugué; Communion; Marche religieuse; March funèbre; Andante symphonique; Grand Choeur dialogué), Durand, 1881.

Suite de six pièces, Costellat, 1872.

Suite de trois morceaux, Rosenberg, 1888.

Soixante-dix pièces, Leduc, 1912.

Toccata (B Minor), E. B. Marks, Leduc.
Trois pièces, Durand, 1896.
GILBERT, NORMAN. born Halifax, England, 1912. 1931, Licen-
tiateship, Royal Academy of Music; 1935, Fellow of the Royal
College of Organists; 1937, B. Mus.; pupil of Sir Edward
Bairstow, organist-choirmaster, St. John's Church, Warley,
Halifax; organist-choirmaster, St. Paul's Church, Llandudno;
since 1948, Music Master, Headlands Grammar School, Swin-
don.
    Epilogue, in An Album of Praise, Oxford University Press,
        1958, p. 14.
    Postlude, Cramer.
    Two hymn-preludes, in Festal Voluntaries (Lent, Ascension),
        Novello.
GILLES, JOSEPH. born Darnetal, France, May 21, 1903; died
Paris, Oct. 12, 1942. Pupil of Dupré; organist-choirmaster,
St. Pierre-de-Chaillot; Professor, Ecole Normale de Musique.
    Symphonie en mi majeur, Bornemann, 1937.
GINASTERA, ALBERTO EVARISTO. born Buenos Aires, Argentina,
Apr. 11, 1916. Studied at National Conservatory, Buenos
Aires; 1946-1947, Guggenheim Fellowship to United States;
1953, became Professor, National Conservatory, Buenos Aires;
composer of symphony and opera.
    Toccata, Villancico y Fuga, Barry, 1955 (Boosey and
        Hawkes).
GIROD, MARIE-LOUISE. born Paris, France, Oct. 12, 1915.
Studied at Conservatory, Paris; organ pupil of Henriette Puig-
Roget and Marcel Dupré; from 1940, one of the organists,
Oratoire du Louvre, Paris.
    Complainte, in Le Tombeau de Gonzalez, Orgue et Liturgie,
        Vol. 38, p. 18.
    Cortége, Procure du Clergé, 1958.
    "Estans assis aux rives aquatiques" (Psalm 137), in Varia,
        Orgue et Liturgie, Vol. 66, p. 9.
    Fantaisie sur un Psalm de Claude LeJeune (1954).
    Fugue sur un thème de Claude LeJeune, in La Fugue, Orgue
        et Liturgie, Vol. 20, p. 5.
    Noël, Procure du Clergé, 1959.
    Prélude, Choral, et Fantaisie, in Au Saint Sacrement, Orgue
        et Liturgie, Vol. 18, p. 23.
    Suite sur le psaume 23, in Orgue et Liturgie, Vol. 64.
    Tryptique sur Sacris solemnis (1953).
    Variations sur le noël, Dans une étable obscure, Procure
        du Clergé, 1963.
GIROUD, JEAN. French. Twentieth century. Organist, St. Louis,
Grenoble, France.
    Six Méditations sur la Passion.
    Toccata, in Toccata, Orgue et Liturgie, Vol. 10, p. 17.
GLAZOUNOW, ALEXANDRE. born St. Petersburg, Russia, Aug. 10,
1865; died Paris, France, Mar. 21, 1936. Pupil of Rimsky-
Korsakov; symphonic composer; 1905-1928, Director, Conser-
vatory, St. Petersburg; 1928, moved to Paris; honorary Mus.
Doc., Cambridge, Oxford.

Prelude and Fugue, in The International Organist, Vol. I,
        p. 68.
GOEDICKE, ALEKSANDR FIORDOROVICH. Russian. born 1877.
        Concerto (D Major) for organ and string orchestra, Op. 35
        (1926), Universal.
GOLLER, VINCENT (VINZENZ). Austrian. born 1873; died 1953.
        Alleluia lässt uns singen, in Organ Works by Modern Mas-
        ters, Vol. 1, O. Junne.
        Christmas Night, Boston Music Co.
        chorale preludes (2) in Orgel Kompositionen aus alter und
        neuer Zeit, Coppenrath.
GOODE, JACK C. American. born Marlin, Texas, Jan. 20, 1921.
        B. Mus., Baylor University; M. Mus., American Conserva-
        tory of Music, Chicago, Ill.; composition pupil of Leo Sowerby,
        Bella Rósza, Joseph Ahrens, and Ernst Pepping; organ pupil
        of Edward Eigenschenk; faculty member, Wheaton College,
        Wheaton, Ill.; from 1952, organist-choirmaster, First Baptist
        Church, Evanston, Ill.; faculty member, American Conser-
        vatory of Music, Chicago.
        Improvisations on Hymn Tunes, Hope Publishing Co.,
                Chicago, Ill.
        Magnificat, Abingdon.
        Processional, Abingdon.
        Sonata (Manuscript).
        Sonata from Joel, trumpet and organ.
        Three Tableaux (1969) (Manuscript).
GOODMAN, JOSEPH. American. born 1918.
        Fantasy (1968), Broude.
        Fantasy on Windsor, Mercury.
        Three Preludes on Gregorian Melodies, Presser.
GORE, RICHARD T. born 1908. American. Teacher, Wooster
        College, Wooster, Ohio.
        Canonic Toccata on Ye Watchers and Ye Holy Ones, H. W.
                Gray.
        Chorale and Variations on Nun sich der Tag, J. Fischer.
        Coventry Carol, J. Fischer.
        Herzlich lieb hab' ich, in The Parish Organist, Vol. 10.
        Variations on O Heiland, reiss die, Augsburg.
        Variations on Welwyn, Galaxy.
GRABNER, HERMANN. born Graz, Austria, May 12, 1886; died
        July 3, 1969. Studied at Conservatory, Leipzig; 1910, went
        to study with Reger in Leipzig; 1918, became teacher, Mann-
        heim Hochschule and Heidelberg Akademie; 1924, became di-
        rector of composition class, Conservatory, Leipzig; 1938,
        appointed teacher of composition, Hochschule für Musik, Berlin-
        Charlottenburg.
        Concerto, Op. 59, organ and strings, Bärenreiter 2063.
        Fantasie on the Liturgical Pater noster, Op. 27, Kahnt.
        Hymn 'Christus ist erstanden', Op. 32, Kistner & Siegel.
        Meditation über ein geistliches Lied von J. S. Bach, in
                Die Orgel, Concordia 97-4607.
        Orgelchoralbuch zum Evangelischen Kirchengesangbuch,
                Merseburger 810.

Orgeltrio, NMS Hansen.
Partita sopra Erhalt uns, Herr, bei deinem Wort, Op. 28,
    Kistner & Siegel.
Prelude, Passacaglia and Fugue on the Antiphon Media vita
    in Morte sumus, Op. 24, in 20th Century Series
    No. 2, Kistner & Siegel.
Psalm 66, Jauchzt, alle Lande, Gott zu ehren, in 20th
    Century Series, Kistner & Siegel.
Sonata, Op. 40.
Toccata über Wir glauben all, Op. 53, Kistner & Siegel.
chorale preludes (4) in Das Organistenamt, Vol. 2, Breit-
    kopf und Härtel.
chorale preludes (2) in Orgelbuch zum Evangelischen
    Kirchengesangbuch, Book 2 and Book 3, Bärenreiter.
chorale preludes (13) in Orgelvorspiele, Poppen, Reich &
    Strube, Merseburger.
chorale preludes (4) in 73 leichte Choralvorspiele, alter und
    neuer Meister, Leuckart.
GRACE, HARVEY. born Romsey, England, Jan. 25, 1874; died
    Bromley, Kent, Feb. 15, 1944. Organist at London churches;
    directed St. Cecilia festivals; 1918-1944, editor, Musical
    Times.
    Chorale Prelude on London New, Schott.
    Chorale Prelude on Martyrs, Schott.
    Chorale Prelude on Old Hundredth, Schott.
    Christmas Postlude, Richard & Co.
    Cradle Song, Schott.
    Monologues: Meditation, Caprice, Schott.
    Reverie on University, Schott.
    Rhapsody, Op. 17, No. 1, Schott.
    Ten Compositions, 2 vols., Schott.
    Toccatina on Kings Lynn, Schott.
GRANDJANY, MARCEL. born Paris, Sept. 3, 1891. Studied at
    the Conservatory, Paris; pupil of Hasselmans, Renié, Caus-
    sade, and Vidal; 1921-1935, taught at the American Conser-
    vatory, Fontainebleau; 1938, became teacher, Juilliard School
    of Music, New York City; 1943, appointed professor, Conser-
    vatory, Montreal.
    Aria in Classic Style, harp and organ, Associated Music
        Publishers.
GRAUN, KARL HEINRICH. born Wahrenbruck (Dresden), Germany,
    May 7, 1704; died Berlin, Aug. 8, 1759. Composer of opera
    in Italian style and church music.
    Concerto, organ and string orchestra, Willy Müller 1.
GRAY, ALAN. born York, England, Dec. 23, 1855; died Cam-
    bridge, Sept. 27, 1935. Graduated from Trinity College,
    Cambridge; 1883-1892, musical director, Wellington College;
    1892-1912, conductor, Cambridge University Musical Society;
    1892-1930, organist, Trinity College.
    Chorale Preludes (5), Augener.
    Chorale Preludes (6), Stainer and Bell.
    Fantasie on Christmas Carols, in 33 Favorite Organ Pieces,
        G. Schirmer.

    Fantasie on O Filii et Filiae, Novello.

    Fantasy (D), No. 4, Cramer.

    Introduction and Fugue (F Minor), Augener, 1925.

    Prelude on Abridge, Augener, 1920.

    Twelve Short Preludes, sets 1 and 2, Augener.

GREAVES, RALPH CHARLES JOHNSTONE. born Lymington, Hampshire, England, 1889. Studied at Harrow and Royal College of Music.

    Christmas Overture, Oxford.

GREENE, MAURICE. born London, ca. 1695; died London, Dec. 1, 1755 (not 1775). Sang under Jeremiah Clarke at St. Paul's Cathedral; 1716-1718, organist, St. Dunstan's-in-the-West; 1717-1718, organist, St. Andrews, Holborn; 1718, appointed organist, St. Paul's Cathedral; 1730, Mus. Doc. , Cambridge; Professor of Music, Cambridge; friend of Handel.

    Four Voluntaries, in Tallis to Wesley, Vol. 15, Hinrichsen 1695 B.

    Introduction and Trumpet Tune, in Anthologia pro Organo, Vol. IV, p. 50.

    Minuet (G), Cramer.

    Three Voluntaries, in Tallis to Wesley, Vol. 4, Hinrichsen 1695 A.

    Trumpet Tune, Cramer.

    Two Short Pieces (Fancy and Almand), Cramer.

    Voluntaries, 2 sets, Hinrichsen 1695 A and B.

    Voluntary in C Minor, in Liber Organi, Vol. 10, p. 20.

    Voluntary in C Minor, in Three Eighteenth-Century Voluntaries, Sidney S. Campbell, ed. , Oxford.

    Voluntary XIII, Walter Emery, ed. , Novello EOM 18, 1961.

GRIFFITHS, THOMAS VERNON. born West Kirby, Cheshire, England, 1894. M. A. , Mus. B. , Pembroke College, Cambridge; 1922-1923, Senior Music Master, Downside School; 1923-1926, Music Master, St. Edmund's School, Canterbury; 1926-1933, Lecturer in Music, Teachers College, Christchurch, New Zealand; 1933-1942, Director of Music, Dunedin Technical College; Mus. Doc. , University of New Zealand; Professor, University of Canterbury, New Zealand; received Order of the British Empire.

    Meditation on Maria zu lieben, Novello.

    Preludes on Nicaea and St. George's, Windsor, in Festal Voluntaries (Trinity, Harvest), Novello.

    Short Suite, Novello.

GRIGNY, NICOLAS DE. born St. Pierre-le-Vieil, France, Sept. 8, 1672; died Rheims, Nov. 30, 1703. Studied with Lebègue; 1693-1695, organist, St. Denis Abbey Church; 1697-1703, organist, Cathedral, Rheims; it is possible that Bach copied his Livre d'orgue (P. A. LeMercier, Paris, 1699, second edition, C. Ballard, Paris, 1711).

    A solis ortus, in Liber Organi, Vol. 2, p. 29.

    Dialogue de flûtes pour l'élévation, in Les Maîtres français de l'orgue, Vol. II, p. 38.

    Fugue à 5 (Pange lingua), in Anthologia pro Organo, Vol. II, p. 48.

Fugue en la mineur, in Geschichte der Musik in Beispielen, p. 388.

Grand Chorus on a Pedal Point, in The First Four Centuries of Organ Music, Vol. II, p. 434.

Pange lingua, in Anthologia pro Organo, Vol. IV, p. 38.

*Premier livre d'orgue, Noëlie Pierront and Norbert Dufourcq, eds. , Schola Cantorum.

Premier livre d'orgue, in Archives des maîtres d'orgue des seizième-dix-huitième siècles; also published by Schott 1877. *

Récit de tierce en taille, in Historical Organ Recitals, Vol. I, p. 118.

compositions (4) in Anthology of Early French Organ Music.

compositions (2) in Alte Orgelmusik aus England und Frankreich.

compositions (3) in Les Maîtres français de l'orgue.

GRONAU, DANIEL MAGNUS. died Danzig, Feb. 2, 1747. 1717-1719, organist, St. Ann's Chapel, Danzig; 1719-1724, organist, St. Katharinenkirche; 1724-1730, choirmaster-organist, St. Marienkirche; 1730-1747, organist, St. Johanniskirche.

Four Chorale Variations, Bärenreiter.

chorale preludes (4) in Masterpieces of Organ Music, Folio 15.

GRÜNENWALD, JEAN-JACQUES. born Annecy, France, Feb. 2, 1911, of French-Swiss background. Studied at the Conservatory, Paris; pupil of Dupré and Busser; 1936-1945, assistant to Dupré at St. Sulpice; organist, St. Pierre-de-Montrouge, Paris.

Adoratorio, Bornemann.

Berceuse, Salabert, 1939, Bornemann.

Cinq pièces pour l'office divin, Rouart, 1951.

Deux suites, Leduc, 1936-1938.

Diptyque liturgique, H. W. Gray.

Fugue sur les jeux d'anches, in La Fugue, Orgue et Liturgie, Vol. 4, p. 34.

Hommage à Josquin des Prés, Bornemann.

Hymne à la splendeur des clartés, Salabert, 1944.

Hymne aux Mémoires héroïques.

Introduction and Aria, in Le Tombeau de Gonzalez, Orgue et Liturgie, Vol. 38, p. 14.

Mass of the Sacred Sacrament, Kalmus 3489; also in L'Organiste liturgique, Vol. 26.

Pastorale-mystique, in Varia, Orgue et Liturgie, Vol. 66, p. 12.

Pièce en Mosaïque, Bornemann, 1966.

Quatre élévations, Salabert, 1939, 1946.

Sonate, Salabert, 1965.

Tu es petra, Bornemann.

Variations brèves sur un noël du XVIe siècle, in Noël, Orgue et Liturgie, Vol. 4, p. 34.

GUAMI, GIUSEPPE (GIOSEFFO). born Lucca, Italy, between 1530 and 1540; died Lucca, 1611. Probably a pupil of Willaert; 1568-1579, organist to Bavarian court in Munich; 1579,

probably returned to S. Michele, Lucca; 1582, named to
Cathedral of S. Martino, Lucca; 1585-1588, second organist,
1588-1591, first organist, San Marco, Venice; 1591, became
organist, Cathedral of San Martino, Lucca; wrote one piece
found in Diruta's Il Transilvano, two pieces in Woltz's Nova
musicae (Basel, 1617).

> Toccata, in L'Arte Musicale in Italia, Vol. III, p. 183.
> compositions (2) in Classici Italiani dell'Organo.

GUEST, DOUGLAS ALBERT. born Mortomley, Yorks, England,
1916. Bus. B. , M.A. , Kings College, Cambridge; 1945-
1950, Director of Music, Uppingham School; 1950-1957, organist, Salisbury Cathedral; 1957-1963, organist, Worcester
Cathedral; 1957-1963, Conductor, Three Choirs Festival;
Fellow of the Royal College of Music; since 1963, Organist
and Master of the Choristers, Westminster Abbey.

> (A) Voluntary for Easter, in A Festive Album, p. 12.

GUILAIN, JEAN-ADAM-GUILLAUME (born Freinsberg, Wilhelm).
born Germany, ?; died Paris (?), 1702. Friend of Marchand.

> Grand Jeu, in Liber Organi, Vol. II, p. 27.
> Pièces d'orgue, Suites pour le Magnificat, in Archives des
>> maîtres d'orgue des seizième-dix-huitième siècles,
>> Vol. VII; also published by Schott 1883. *

GUILLET, CHARLES. born Bruges, Belgium, end of the sixteenth
century; died Bruges, 1654. Wrote Vingt quatre Fantaisies
a quatre parties disposees selon l'ordre des douze modes
(Ballard, Paris, 1610).

> Fantasie, in Altniederlandische Meister, p. 35.
> Fantasies, in L'Organiste liturgique, Vols. 33, 37, 49-50;
> also Kalmus 3490.
> Werken voor Orgel of 4 Speeltuigen, in Monumenta Musicae
>> Belgicae, Vol. 4.
> fantasies (2) in Oudnederlandse Meesters, Vol. II.
> fantasy in Oudnederlandse Meesters, Vol. III, p. 90.

GUILLOU, JEAN-VICTOR-ARTHUR. born Angers, France, Apr. 18,
1930. Pupil of Dupré, Duruflé, and Messiaen; taught organ
and composition, Lisbon; worked in West Berlin; organist,
St. Eustache, Paris.

> Dix-huit Variations, Leduc.
> Fantaisie, Leduc.
> Inventions, organ and orchestra, Leduc.
> Pour le Tombeau de Colbert, Leduc.
> Sinfonietta, Leduc.
> Toccata, Leduc, 1966.

GUILLOU, RENÉ ALFRED OCTAVE. born Rennes (Illes-et-Vilaine),
France, Oct. 8, 1903; died Paris, Dec. 14, 1958. Studied at
the Conservatory, Paris; composition pupil of Charles-Marie
Widor; 1926, won Grand Prix de Rome; orchestra director,
Monte-Carlo and Radiodiffusion Française.

> Andante symphonique, Lemoine.
> Colloques No. 2, Leduc.
> Cortège de nonnes, Lemoine.
> Loetitia Pia, Lemoine.
> Nocturne mystique, Lemoine.

(L')Offrande Musicale, Leduc.
GUILMANT, FÉLIX-ALEXANDRE. born Boulogne-sur-mer, France,
Mar. 12, 1837; died Meudon, Mar. 29, 1911. 1857, became
organist, St. Nicolas, Boulogne; 1860, was pupil of Lemmens;
1863, became organist, St. Sulpice, Paris; 1868, appointed
organist, Notre Dame, Paris; 1871, became organist, Trinité,
Paris (succeeded Alexis Chauvet) for 30 years; founder, Schola
Cantorum; 1896, appointed professor of organ, Conservatory
(succeeded Widor); taught René Vierne, Bonnet, Decaux,
Georges Jacob, Nadia Boulanger, Cellier, Dupré, and Bonnal.
Allegro (F Major), Op. 81, organ and orchestra, Schott.
Cantilena Pastorale (B Minor), Schott.
Caprice (B-flat Major), Schott.
Chant du Matin, Schott.
Chant du Roi René (Noël provençal), Op. 60, in Noël, p. 14.
Chorale on O Salutaris Hostias, O. Ditson.
Chorales and Two Noëls, Op. 93, Schott.
Chant du soir, Op. 85, Durand.
Communion No. 2 (G Major), Schott.
Communion on Ecce Panis Angelorum, O. Ditson.
Dix-huit pièces nouvelles, Op. 90, Schott 2978 a-g.
Fantasy on Two English Melodies, Novello.
Final alla Schumann, Op. 83, organ and orchestra, Schott.
Fugue (D Major), Op. 25, No. 3, Schott.
Fugue élégiaque, Op. 44, No. 2, Schott.
Grand Choeur, Schott.
Grand Chouer en forme de Marche, Op. 84, G. Schirmer.
Interludes (60), Op. 68, Schott.
March on a theme of Handel, Schott.
Marche, Op. 76, No. 4, Durand.
Marche élégiaque, Op. 74, organ and orchestra, Schott.
Marche-Fantaisie, Op. 44, organ and orchestra, Schott.
Marche funèbre et Chant Séraphique, Schott.
Marche funèbre, No. 2, Op. 41, organ and orchestra, Schott.
Méditation sur le Stabat Mater, Op. 63, organ and orches-
     tra, Schott.
Noël, in Organ Voluntaries, J. Fischer.
Noëls, Op. 60, 4 vols. , Schott 2981 a-d.
Offertory on Adoro te devote, in Orgel Kompositionen aus
     alter und neuer Zeit, Coppenrath.
Offertory on Two Christmas Hymns, G. Schirmer.
Organ Albums: Selected Pieces, Carl, ed. , Schott 1123.
Organ Concerto, Op. 29, Schott.
(L')Organiste liturgique, Op. 65, 10 books in 4 vols. ,
     Schott 2979 a-d.
(L')Organiste pratique, Schott 2980 a-h, k, 1870-1881.
Pièces dans different styles (25 books)
     Book 2, Schott 2976 b.
     Book 3, Schott 2976 c.
     Book 4, Schott 2976 d.
     Book 7, Schott 2976 g.
     Book 16, Schott 2976 q.
Postlude on Induant Justitiam, G. Schirmer.

Prelude and Amen on Ave maris stella, Op. 65, G. Schirmer.
Prelude and Amen on Crudelis Herodes, G. Schirmer.
Première Méditation (A Major), Schott.
Première Symphonie, Op. 42, organ and orchestra, Schott.
Premières Vêpres des Apôtres, Schott.
Prière et Berceuse, Op. 27, Schott.
Répertoire des Concerts du Trocadéro, 2 vols. , Schott.
Scherzo (F Major), Schott.
Sept morceaux, Novello.
Sonata No. 1 (D Minor), Op. 42, Schott 1861.
Sonata No. 2 (D), Op. 50, Schott 1862.
Sonata No. 3 (C Minor), Op. 56, Schott 1863.
Sonata No. 4 (D Minor), Op. 61, Schott 1864.
Sonata No. 5 (C Minor), Op. 80, Schott 1865.
Sonata No. 6 (B Minor), Op. 86, Schott 1866.
Sonata No. 7 (F), Op. 89, Schott 1867.
Sonata No. 8 (A), Op. 91, Schott 1868.
Strophes on Pange lingua, Op. 54, in Liturgical Organist,
    Book 4, Schott.
Tempo di Minuetto (C Major), Schott.
Two Preludes and Amen on Iste Confessor, Op. 65, G.
    Shirmer.
Valet, in Carl, Master Studies for the Organ, G. Schirmer.
Was Gott tut, in The Lutheran Organist, Concordia.
compositions (3) in Historical Organ Recitals, Vol. 5.
compositions in Organ Album, Vol. 1 (3) and Vol. 3 (2),
    Schott Frères.
compositions (5) in Pièces pour orgue, Books 2, 4, 5, 9,
    and 12, Durand.
noëls (3) in Noël, C. Fischer.
GUINALDO, NORBERTO. Argentine. Twentieth century.
Five Spanish Carols, Concordia 97-4855.
Three Litanies, J. Fischer.
GULBINS, MAX. born Kammetschen, East Prussia, July 18, 1862;
died Breslau, Feb. 19, 1932. Studied at the Hochschule,
Berlin; 1900-1908, organist, Elbing; organist, St. Elizabeth,
Breslau.
Aus meines Herzens, Op. 87, No. 2, Leuckart.
Bible Pictures, Op. 73, 2 vols. , Oppenheimer.
Chorale Preludes, Op. 41, Schweers & Haake.
Fantasie on Ein' feste Burg, Op. 101, Oppenheimer.
Fantasie on Wenn meine Sünd mich, in Four Pieces, Op. 31,
    Leuckart.
Fifteen Pieces, Op. 55, 3 vols. , Rieter-Biedermann.
For Passiontide, Op. 58, R. Forberg.
Four Christmas Fantasies, Op. 104, Oppenheimer.
Four Fantasies, Op. 108, Oppenheimer.
Four Pieces, 'cello and organ, Op. 14, Leuckart.
Jesu, meine Zuversicht, in The Lutheran Organist, Concor-
    dia.
Sonata No. 1 (C Minor), Op. 4, Leuckart.
Sonata No. 2 (F Minor), Op. 18, Leuckart.

Thirty-six Chorale Preludes, Op. 16, Leuckart.
Three Fantasies, Op. 110, Oppenheimer.
Three Festival Fantasies, Op. 105, Oppenheimer.
Vier Charakterstücke, Op. 31, Leuckart.
Zwei Stücke, Op. 17, Leuckart.
chorale preludes (5) in Anthologie, Concordia.
GURIDI, JESÚS. born Vitoria (Basque Alava), Spain, Sept. 25, 1886;
    died Madrid, Apr. 7, 1961. Studied in Madrid, Paris, Brus-
    sels, and Cologne; pupil of Jongen; 1909-1939, organist,
    Bilbao; 1944, appointed Professor of Music, Conservatory,
    Madrid.
        Escuela Española, Union Musical Española.
        Prelude and Fantasy, Union Musical Española.
        Triptico del buen Pastor, Union Musical Española.

HAAPALAINEN, VÄINÖ. Finnish. born 1893; died 1945. Com-
    poser and organist, Helsingfors.
        Passacaglia, in Musica Organi, Vol. III, p. 92.
HAAS, JOSEPH. born Maihingen, Germany, Mar. 19, 1879; died
    Munich, Mar. 31, 1960. Organ pupil of Reger and Straube;
    1911, appointed teacher of composition, Conservatory, Stutt-
    gart; 1921, became Professor, Institute of Church Music and
    Hochschule für Musik, Munich.
        Chorale Prelude on Lobe den Herren, in Orgel Kompositionen
            aus alter und neuer Zeit, Coppenrath.
        Eight Pieces, Op. 15, Augener.
        Impromptu und Fughetta, Schweers & Haake.
        Kirchensonate in f dur, Op. 62, No. 1, organ and violin,
            Schott 1963.
        Kirchensonate in d moll, Op. 62, No. 2, organ and violin,
            Schott 1964.
        Passacaglia (Suite in A), Op. 25, No. 5, Leuckart.
        Sonata, Op. 12, (Peters F 72), R. Forberg, 1907.
        Suite, Op. 20, R. Forberg, 1908.
        Suite in A, Op. 25, Leuckart, 1919.
        Ten Chorale Preludes, Op. 3, O. Forberg.
        Three Preludes and Fugues, Op. 11, R. Forberg.
HÄGG, GUSTAF WILHELM. born Wisby, Sweden, Nov. 28, 1867;
    died Stockholm, Feb. 7, 1925. Studied at the Conservatory,
    Stockholm, in Germany, and in France; taught theory and
    organ at the Conservatory, Stockholm.
        Aftonfrid (Even-Song), in Organ Music of the Netherlands
            and Scandinavia, p. 15.
        Festhymn (Festal Song), in Organ Music of the Netherlands
            and Scandinavia, p. 19.
        Fünf Kompositionen, Op. 16 and 22, Gehrmans Vorlag.
        Sechs leichte Tonbilder, Lundquist.
        Sechs Tonbilder, Op. 32, Lundquist.
HAINES, EDMUND THOMAS. American. born 1914. Ph.D.,
    University of Rochester; 1941-1946, taught, University of

Michigan; 1946-1948, taught, Bard College; since 1947, teacher, Sarah Lawrence College.

Promenade, Air, and Toccata, J. Fischer 8392, 1948.

HALL, RICHARD. born York, England, 1903. Associate of the Royal College of Music; 1938-1956, professor of composition, Royal College of Music, Manchester; 1947-1967, Examiner, Associate Board of the Royal School of Music.

Intermezzo, Oxford.

Nocturne, Oxford.

Pastorale du Nord, Oxford.

Three Cathedral Voluntaries, Novello.

HAMBRAEUS, BENGT. Swedish. born 1928. Graduated in musicology, University of Uppsala; head, Music Department, Swedish Radio; composes in serial technique.

Concerto, organ and harpsichord, Nordiska Musikförlaget.

Konstellationer I-III, organ and tape, Nordiska Musikförlaget.

Musik för orgel, Nordiska Musikförlaget.

HAMILTON, IAIN. born Glasgow, Scotland, June 6, 1922. 1947-1951, studied at the Royal College of Music; lecturer on orchestration, Morley College, and at the University of London; 1962, appointed professor of music, Duke University, Durham, N. Car.

Fanfares and Variants, Schott 10785, 1960.

HANCOCK, EUGENE WILSON. born St. Louis, Mo. , Feb. 17, 1929. 1951, B. Mus. , University of Detroit; 1956, M. Mus. , University of Michigan; 1966, Associate of the American Guild of Organists; 1963-1966, Assistant Organist and Choirmaster, Cathedral Church of St. John the Divine, New York City; 1967, Doc. Sac. Mus. , Union Theological Seminary, New York City; organ pupil of William I. Green, Alle Zuidema, Alec Wyton, Marilyn Mason, and Vernon de Tar; composition pupil of Seth Bingham and Joseph Goodman; 1967-1970, Minister of Music, New Calvary Baptist Church, Detroit; since 1970, faculty member, Manhattan Community College, and organist-choirmaster, St. Martin's Church, New York City.

(An) Organ Book of Spirituals, Lorenz, 1966.

HANCOCK, GERRE. born Lubbock, Texas, Feb. 21, 1934. 1955, B. Mus. , University of Texas; 1961, M. Sac. Mus. , Union Theological Seminary, New York City; Fellow of the American Guild of Organists; organ pupil of E. William Doty, Hugh Porter, Robert Baker, Jean Langlais, Marie-Claire Alain, and David Willcocks; composition pupil of Nadia Boulanger and Searle Wright; 1960-1962, assistant organist, St. Bartholomew's Church, New York City; 1962-1971, Organist-Choirmaster, Christ Church, Cincinnati, Ohio; 1964-1971, faculty member, College-Conservatory of Music, University of Cincinnati; 1971, appointed organist and master of the choir, St. Thomas Church, New York City.

Air, H. W. Gray (St. Cecilia Series 897), 1963.

HÄNDEL, GEORGE FRIDERIC (HÄNDEL, GEORG FRIEDRICH). born Halle, Germany, Feb. 23, 1685; died London, Apr. 14, 1759. 1694, pupil of Zachau; 1702-1703, studied law, University of Halle; organist, Calvinistic cathedral, Moritzburg; 1703,

became violinist di ripieno, Berlin opera; 1706-1710, traveled
and composed in Italy; 1710, became Kapellmeister to the
Elector of Hanover (who became George I of England in 1714);
1712, received such success in England that he remained there
against his patron's wishes; 1718, became organist and composer to the Duke of Chandos; appointed Director, Royal
Academy of Music; composed many operas and oratorios.

Concerto (E-flat), Op. 4, No. 6, organ and strings, (Peters
V 11).

Concerto (G Minor), in English Organ Music of the Eighteenth
Century, Hinrichsen, 1951.

Four Voluntaries, in Tallis to Wesley, Vol. 19, Hinrichsen
1685 B.

Fugue (A Minor), Cramer.

Fugue (C Minor), Cramer.

Fugue (E Minor), Leuckart.

Largo et Allegro (D Major), in Varia, Orgue et Liturgie,
Vol. 25, p. 20.

Organ Concerto No. 13, Phillips, ed., Hinrichsen 1685 C;
also Merseburger 839 (score and parts).

Organ Concertos, Op. 4 and Op. 7, arranged for organ
solo, Hermann Keller, ed., 4 books, Müller 4, 5,
17, and 18.

Organ Concertos, arranged for organ solo, C. S. Lang and
J. Dykes Bower, eds., 2 books, Novello.

Orgelkonzerte, Series IV, Vol. 2, in Hallische Händel-
Ausgabe, Schneider and Steglich, eds., Bärenreiter
4006, 1955.

Orgelkonzerte, Op. 4, 2 vols., Matthaei, ed., Bärenreiter,
1894-1895.

Orgelkonzert Nr. 1 (G Minor), Bärenreiter 359.

Orgelkonzert Nr. 2 (B-flat), Bärenreiter 360.

Orgelkonzert Nr. 3 (G Minor), Bärenreiter 361.

Orgelkonzert Nr. 4 (F Major), Bärenreiter 362.

Orgelkonzert Nr. 5 (F Major), Bärenreiter 363.

Orgelkonzert Nr. 6 (F Major), Bärenreiter 364.

Pieces for Musical Clock, Spiegl, ed., Schott 10393.

Prelude and Fugue (A Minor), Heinrich Fleischer, ed.,
Concordia 97-4497.

(La) Rejouissance, Concordia 97-4823.

Sechs Fugen, Breitkopf und Härtel 6310.

Six Fugues or Voluntaries, in Tallis to Wesley, Vol. 19,
Hinrichsen 1685B.

Six Little Fugues, Concordia 97-4626.

Six Organ Concertos, 121-124 installment in The Works of
Handel, J. M. Coopersmith, ed.

Six Organ Concertos, 124-128 installment in The Works of
Handel, J. M. Coopersmith, ed.

Six Organ Concertos, Kalmus 3511.

Six Organ Concertos, Op. 4, Peters 3627.

Sixteen Organ Concertos, Marcel Dupré, ed., 3 vols.,
Bornemann.

Three Fugues (F Major, B Minor, C Minor), Breitkopf und

Härtel.
Twelve Organ Concertos, in G. F. Händels Werke, Chry-
    sander, ed. , Vol. 28, Breitkopf und Härtel, 1881.
Voluntaries, 2 sets, Hinrichsen 1685 A and B.
Zwölf Konzerte, Helmut Walcha, ed. , Schott: scores
    3826-3837; organ parts, 3801-3812.
compositions in Anthologia Antiqua, Vol. 2.
compositions in Masterpieces of Organ Music, Folios 49
    and 50.
compositions (2) in Musica Organi, Vol. I.
HANFF, JOHANN NICOLAUS. born Wechmar (Thuringia), Germany,
    1665; died Schleswig, winter 1711-1712. 1696, organist,
    Eutin; court organist, Eutin; 1706-1711, organist, Hamburg;
    1711, appointed organist, Cathedral, Schleswig.
    Ein' feste Burg, in Organ Preludes Ancient and Modern,
        Hinrichsen.
    Erbarm' dich mein, Kallmeyer.
    chorale preludes (6) in Choralvorspiel alter Meister.
    chorale preludes (3) in The Church Organist's Golden
        Treasury, Vol. I.
    composition in Masterpieces of Organ Music, Folio 61.
HANSON, HOWARD. born Wahoo, Neb. , Oct. 28, 1896. Studied
    at Luther College, Wahoo, Neb. , and Institute of Musical Art,
    New York City; pupil of Percy Goetschius; 1916, graduated,
    Northwestern University; 1916, appointed instructor, 1919-
    1921, dean, College of the Pacific, San Jose, Calif. ; 1921,
    won Prix de Rome, American Academy; 1924-1964, first
    director, Eastman School of Music.
    Concerto, Op. 22, No. 3, organ, strings, and harp,
        C. Fischer, New York City, 1947.
HARK, FRIEDRICH. German. born 1914; died 1943. Organist,
    Versöhnungskirche, Dresden.
    Chemnitzer Orgelbuch, Kistner & Siegel.
    Neues Orgelbuch, Kistner & Siegel.
    Nun danket all, in The Parish Organist, Vol. 1-4.
    chorale preludes (2) in 73 leichte Choralvorspiele, alter
        und neuer Meister, Leuckart.
HARKER, F. FLAXINGTON. born Aberdeen, Scotland, Sept. 4,
    1876; died Richmond, Va. , Oct. 23, 1936. Organ pupil and
    assistant organist to T. Tertius Noble at York Minster; 1901,
    came to the United States; organist in churches in Biltmore,
    N. Car. , and Richmond, Va.
    Christmas-Pastoral on Silent Night, Op. 52, G. Schirmer.
    Noël on an Old French Carol, Harold Flammer.
HARRIS, ROY. born Lincoln County, Okla. , Feb. 12, 1898. 1919,
    entered University of California; organ pupil of Charles De-
    marest; orchestration pupil of Arthur Bliss; pupil of Nadia
    Boulanger; 1927-1928, won Guggenheim Fellowship; 1934-
    1938, head, composition department, Westminster Choir Col-
    lege; 1941-1943, composer-in-residence, Cornell University;
    1943-1948, composer-in-residence, Colorado College, Colorado
    Springs; 1948-1949, composer-in-residence, Utah State Agri-
    cultural College, Logan, Utah; 1949-1951, composer-in-

residence, Peabody College for Teachers, Nashville; 1951-
1956, taught at Pennsylvania College for Women, Pittsburgh;
1957-1960, professor of composition, Indiana University; 1960-
1961, professor of composition, Inter-American University,
San Germán, Puerto Rico; 1961, became faculty member,
University of California, Los Angeles; received honorary Mus.
Doc. from Rutgers University and University of Rochester.
>   Chorale, organ and brass (1943).
>   Etudes for Pedals (1964), World Library.
>   Fantasy, organ, brasses, and timpani, Associated Music
>   Publishers, 1966.
>   Toccata, organ and brass (1944).

HARRIS, (SIR) WILLIAM HENRY. born London, Mar. 28, 1883.
Studied at the Royal College of Music; organ pupil of Parratt;
composition pupil of Walford Davies; 1910, Mus. D., Oxford;
1919-1928, organist, New College, Oxford; 1928-1933, organist, Christ Church Cathedral, Oxford; 1933-1961, organist,
St. George's Chapel, Windsor; Knight Commander of the Voc-
torian Order.
>   Epilog on Dix, Novello 270 O. C. (N. S.).
>   (A) Fancy, Novello, 204 O. C. (N. S.).
>   Fantasy (Postlude) on Campion's tune Babylon's Streams,
>   Stainer and Bell, 1922.
>   Fantasy on Easter Hymns, Novello 249 O. C. (N. S.).
>   Fantasy on the English Folk Tune Monks Gate, Oxford.
>   Flourish for an Occasion, Novello.
>   Four Short Pieces (Preludes; Reverie; Interlude; Scherzetto),
>   Novello.
>   Improvisation on the Old 124th (Genevan Psalter), Stainer
>   and Bell, 1925.
>   Miniature Suite, Novello.
>   Processional March, Novello.
>   Saraband Processional, Novello.
>   Sonata (A Minor), Novello.
>   Three Opening Voluntaries, Novello.
>   Three Preludes, Novello.
>   two hymn-preludes in Festal Voluntaries (Christmas, Easter),
>   Novello.

HART, PHILIP. born ?; died London, July 17, 1749. Organist of
the following London churches: St. Andrew Undershaft, St.
Mary Axe, St. Michael Cornhill, and St. Dionis Backchurch;
wrote Fugues for the Organ or Harpsichord (London, ca. 1720).

HARTMANN, JOHANN PEDER EMILIUS. born Copenhagen, May 14,
1805; died Copenhagen, Mar. 10, 1900. Pupil of his father
and Ludwig Spohr; 1843-1900, organist, Cathedral, Copenhagen;
1867-1900, Director, Royal Conservatory, Copenhagen.
>   Fantasie (F Minor), Hofmeister (Leipzig).
>   Samtlige Orgelvaerker, Dan Fog Musikforlag.
>   Sonata (G Minor), Op. 58, Hansen, 1892.

HARWOOD, BASIL. born Woodhouse, Gloucestershire, England,
Apr. 11, 1859; died London, Apr. 3, 1949. Studied at Ox-
ford; pupil of Reinicke and Jadassohn at the Conservatory,
Leipzig; 1883-1887, organist, St. Barnabas Church, Pimlico;

1887-1892, organist, Ely Cathedral; 1892-1909, organist, Christ Church Cathedral, Oxford; 1900-1909, choral director, Oxford University.

Andante, in Historical Organ Recitals, Vol. 5, p. 75.

Andante tranquillo (E-flat) on the hymn-tune Bedford, Op. 15, No. 6, Novello.

Capriccio, Op. 16, Novello.

Christmastide (Fantasia), Op. 34, Novello.

Communion in F Major on the Hymn-tune Irish, Op. 15, No. 1, Novello.

Concerto in D Major, Op. 24, Novello.

Dithyramb, Op. 7, Novello.

Eight Pieces, Op. 58 (Invocation; Eventide; Communion; Rest; Prelude for Lent; Diapason Movement; Benediction; The Shepherds at the Manger), Novello.

Fantasy on Oldown, C. Fischer.

In an Old Abbey, Op. 32, Novello.

In Exitu Israel, Op. 46, Novello.

Lullaby, Op. 50, Novello.

Paean, Op. 15, No. 3, Novello.

Prelude, Larghetto, and Finale, Op. 51, Novello.

Processional, Op. 44, Novello.

(A) Quiet Voluntary for Evensong, Novello.

Requiem aeternam, Op. 15, No. 5, Novello.

Rhapsody, Op. 38, Novello.

Short Postlude for Ascensiontide on the Old 25th Psalm Tune, Op. 15, No. 4, Novello.

Six Chorale Preludes, Novello.

Sonata No. 1 (C-sharp Minor), Op. 5, Schott

Sonata No. 2 (F-sharp Minor), Novello.

Three Cathedral Preludes, Op. 25, Novello.

Three Preludes on Anglican Chants, Op. 42, Novello.

Three Short Pieces, Op. 45, Novello.

Toccata, Op. 49, Novello.

Two Meditations, Oxford.

Two Preludes on Old English Psalm Tunes, Oxford.

Two Sketches, Op. 18, Nos. 1 and 2, Novello.

Voluntary in D-flat, Op. 43, left hand and pedal obbligato, Novello.

Wedding March, Op. 40, Novello.

HASSE, KARL. born Dohna (Dresden), Germany, Mar. 20, 1883; died Dresden, July 31, 1960. Choirboy, St. Thomas, Leipzig; studied at the University of Leipzig; pupil of Kretzschmar and Riemann; pupil of Straube at the Conservatory, Leipzig, and of Reger at the Academy, Munich; 1907, assistant to Ph. Wolfrums, Heidelberg; 1909, appointed organist-cantor, Johanneskirche, Chemnitz; 1910, became Director of Music Society, Osnaburg; 1919, appointed professor, University Music Director, Tübingen; 1923, received Ph.D.; 1935, appointed Director, Hochschule für Musik, Cologne.

Chorale Preludes, Op. 53, Willy Müller 72.

Choralvorspiele, Op. 9, No. 1, Freiburg, 1926.

Drei Phantasien und Fugen, Op. 6, Rieter-Biedermann.

Drei Fantasien und Fugen, Op. 34.
Fantasie und Fuge, Op. 100.
Festival Prelude on Ein' feste Burg, Op. 14, Willy Müller
46.
Festliches Vorspiel in E dur, Op. 57.
Fifteen Chorale Preludes, Op. 13, Leuckart.
Kanzone (C Minor), Schweers & Haake.
Nun danket alle, in Organ Works of Modern Masters,
Vol. 3, O. Junne.
Preludes and Postludes, Op. 86, Willy Müller 49.
Sechs Stücke, Op. 9, Peters.
Seventeen Chorale Preludes, Op. 7, Rieter-Biedermann.
Sonata in G dur, Op. 16, Mannheim, 1921.
Sonata in c moll, Op. 19, Tübingen, 1924.
Sonata in g moll, Op. 72, Fulda, 1951.
Suite in e moll, Op. 10, Leuckart.
Thirty-six Chorale Preludes, Op. 53, Willy Müller.
Twelve Chorale Preludes, Op. 4, Rieter-Biedermann.
Twenty-three Chorale Preludes, Op. 74, Willy Müller 73.
chorale preludes (3) in Das Organistenamt, Vol. 3, Breit-
kopf und Härtel.
HASSE, NICOLAUS. born Lübeck, Germany, ca. 1617; died 1672.
1642, appointed organist, Church of St. Mary, Rostock.
chorale preludes (4) in Corpus of Early Keyboard Music,
no. 10.
HASSE, PETER (PETRUS), the elder. born Franken, Germany,
ca. 1585; buried, Lübeck, June 16, 1640. 1616, became
organist, Marienkirche, Lübeck (predecessor of Tunder).
Allein Gott in der Höh, in Orgelspiel im Kirchenjahr,
Vol. 2, Schott.
Praeambulum pedaliter (P. H.), in Organum, Series IV,
Vol. 21.
organ verses in three voices (2) on Allein Gott, in Sechs-
und-vierzig Choräle für Orgel.
organ verses (2) on Allein Gott, in Zwanzig Orgelvariation
der deutschen Sweelinck-Schule, Hans Joachim Moser,
ed., Bärenreiter, 1953.
HASSE, PETER, the younger. Christened, Lübeck, Germany,
Feb. 18, 1659; died Lübeck, Oct. 16, 1708.
Praeludium, in Organum, Series IV, Vol. 21.
HASSLER, HANS LEO. born Nürnberg, Germany, Oct. 25, 1564;
died Frankfurt-am-Main, June 8, 1612. Pupil of his father,
Isaak, and A. Gabrieli; 1585, became organist to Octavian
Fugger, Augsburg; 1601, appointed organist, Frauenkirche,
Nürnberg; 1609, organist to Elector of Saxony, Dresden.
Canzona, in The First Four Centuries of Organ Music,
Vol. I, p. 175.
O Living Bread from Heaven, in Organ Music for the
Communion Service, p. 54.
Ricercar and Canzon, in Ricercare, Canzonen und Fugen.
compositions in Denkmäler der Tonkunst in Bayern, Vol. IV,
No. ii (16 organ works).
compositions in Masterpieces of Organ Music, Folio 34.

HAVINGHA, GERHARDUS. born Groningen, The Netherlands,
    1753; 1722, appointed organist, St. Laurensker,
    Alkmaar.
        Giga, in Cantantibus Organis, Vol. I, p. 11.
HAYDN, FRANZ JOSEPH. born Rohrau, Austria, Mar. 31, 1732;
    died Vienna, May 31, 1809. Choirboy, St. Stephen's Cathe-
    dral, Vienna; organist, Church of Sacred Heart brothers;
    1761, entered service to Esterhazy family; great symphony
    and oratorio composer.
        Concerto (C Major) (1756), organ, strings and two oboes,
            Breitkopf und Härtel.
        Concerto (C Major), organ, strings, two horns, and tim-
            pani.
        Eight Pieces for Musical Clocks, Desmond Ratcliffe, ed.,
            Novello.
        Musical Clocks, E. Power Biggs, ed., H. W. Gray, 1946.
        Works for Flute Clock, Concordia 97-4626.
HEALEY, DEREK EDWARD. born Wargrave, Berks, England,
    1936. B. Mus., Durham University; Fellow of the Royal
    College of Music; studied at the Accademia Chigiana, Siena,
    Italy; 1959-1962, Director of Music, Shiplake College; since
    1964, Music Master, Gordon School, Maidenhead.
        Introduzione, Aria e Passacaglia, Novello.
        Partita-'65, Novello, 1967.
        Three Preludes on French Hymn-tunes, Novello, 1965.
        Variants, Op. 23, Novello, 1967.
HEEREMANS, HAROLD. born Bristol, England, 1900. After 1918,
    worked in Canada; 1928, became organist, First Methodist
    Church, Seattle, Washington; organist, University Methodist
    Temple; 1931, appointed to faculty, University of Washington;
    1936, became staff member, New York University; organist,
    Memorial Presbyterian Church, New York; 1941, appointed,
    organist-choirmaster, Unitarian Church of the Saviour,
    Brooklyn; 1958-1964, President, American Guild of Organists;
    1967, appointed organist-choirmaster, Universalist-Unitarian
    Church, Brockton, Mass.
        Aria, H. W. Gray (St. Cecilia Series 619).
        Thirty Trios, M. Witmark, 1948.
HEGER, ROBERT. born Strasbourg, Aug. 19, 1886. Studied in
    Zürich and Munich; opera conductor in Strasbourg, Nürnberg,
    Vienna, Berlin, and Munich (since 1950).
        Trio Sonate über O Ewigkeit, Op. 36, Leuckart.
HEILLER, ANTON. born Vienna, Sept. 15, 1923. 1941-1942,
    studied at the Academy of Music, Vienna; 1945, became
    teacher, Department of Church Music, Academy of Music,
    Vienna; 1952, winner, improvisation contest, Haarlem.
        Concerto, Positive Organ, Harpsichord and Chamber
            Orchestra (1972), Doblinger.
        Ecce Lignum Crucis, in Modern Organ Music, David Will-
            cocks, ed., Oxford University Press, London, 1967,
            Book 2, p. 19.
        Fantasie über Salve regina, Associated Music Publishers.
        In Festo Corporis Christi, Doblinger.

Orgelkonzert, organ and orchestra, Doblinger, 1964.
Partita über Freu dich sehr, Ars Viva Verlag 15.
Sonate, Universal 11689, 1946.
Sonate II (1953), Doblinger, Vienna, 1956.
Zwei kleine Partiten, Ars Viva Verlag, 1967.
Tanz-Toccata (1970), Doblinger.

HEILMANN, HARALD. born Aue, Sachsen, Germany, April 9, 1924.
Studied at the Staatlichen Hochschule für Musik, Leipzig; composition pupil of Johannes Weyrauch, J. N. David, and Wilhelm Weismann; 1950, choir and orchestra director, Berlin;
1951, appointed professor, Deutschen Hochschule für Musik,
Berlin; 1953, pupil of Frank Martin, Staatliche Hochschule
für Musik, Cologne; 1954-1959, staff member of various music publishers; since 1959, devoted himself to composition
and conducting.
    Diptychon (1959), Breitkopf und Härtel 6322, 1960.
    Fantasie, 'cello and organ, Sirius.
    Partita über Christ ist erstanden (1961), Breitkopf & Härtel
        6336, 1962.
    Pentasia, Sirius.
    chorale preludes (2) in Neue Orgelvorspiele, Merseburger.

HEISS, HERMANN. born Darmstadt, Germany, Dec. 29, 1897.
1923, studied twelve-tone technique in Vienna; 1946, became
lecturer, Musik Institut, Kranichstein; 1953, named composition teacher, Akademie für Tonkunst; 1955, appointed director,
Studio for Electronic Composition, Kranichstein.
    Drei Choralpartiten (1948), Breitkopf & Härtel 5983.

HELD, WILBUR. born DesPlaines, Ill. , Aug. 20, 1914. M. Mus. ,
American Conservatory of Music, Chicago; S. M. D. , Union
Theological Seminary, New York City; Fellow, American
Guild of Organists; organ pupil of Frank Van Dusen, Marcel
Dupré, and André Marchal; composition pupil of John Palmer;
1946, became Professor of Music, Ohio State University; 1949,
appointed organist-choirmaster, Trinity Episcopal Church,
Columbus, Ohio.
    Built on a Rock, Augsburg.
    (A) Nativity Suite, Concordia 97-4461.
    Partita on O Sons and Daughters, Concordia 97-4697.
    Prelude on Psalm 42, in Library of Organ Music. Vol. III,
        Enid and Henry Woodward, eds. , Schmitt, Hall and
        McCreary, 1966.
    Six Carol Settings, Concordia, 1970.
    (A) Suite of Passion Hymn Settings, Concordia 97-4843.
    Two Traditional Carols, organ and C instrument, Augsburg
        11-0831.

HELFRITZ, HANS. born Hilbersdorf, Germany, July 25, 1902.
Pupil of Hindemith and Wellesz; 1936, did folklore research in
Chile.
    Concerto, organ and string orchestra, Schott.

HELMONT, CHARLES-JOSEPH VAN. born Brussels, Belgium,
    Mar. 19, 1715; died Brussels, June 8, 1790. Pupil of Pierre
Bréhy; 1733, appointed organist, Ste. Gudule Cathedral,
Brussels; 1741-1777, maître de chant, Ste. Gudule, Brussels.

Fuga, in Altneiderlandische Meister, p. 28.
Werken voor Orgel en Clavecimbel, Joseph Watelet, ed.,
    in Monumenta Musica Belgicae, Vol. VI.
HENDRIKS, C. F. (jun.). Dutch. born 1861; died 1923. Com-
    poser, editor.
    Canonic Preludes (24), Op. 7, Alsbach.
    Deux Pièces, Leduc.
    En forme de canon, Op. 23, No. 2, in Organ Music of the
        Netherlands and Scandinavia, p. 30.
    Feuillet d'Album, Op. 23, No. 3, in Organ Music of the
        Netherlands and Scandinavia, p. 35.
    Prelude and Fugue (C Minor), Alsbach.
    Regrets, Op. 23, No. 1, in Organ Music of the Netherlands
        and Scandinavia, p. 27.
    Sonata (E Minor), Op. 4, Alsbach, 1892.
    Toccata, in The International Organist, Vol. I, p. 14.
    Trois Pièces, Leduc.
HENNIG, WALTER. German. born 1903; died 1965.
    (Die) Abendmahlslieder des Evangelischen Kirchengesangbuch,
        Merseburger 835.
    Präludium und Fuge C-dur, Merseburger 857.
    Sonate über O dass ich tausend Zungen hatte, organ and
        brass, Merseburger 858.
HENRY, JEAN-CLAUDE-JULES. born Paris, Dec. 30, 1934. Won
    five first prizes at the Conservatory, Paris; pupil of Rolande
    Falcinelli, Tony Aubin, and Olivier Messiaen; 1960, won
    Grand Prix de Rome; 1967, appointed professor of counter-
    point, Conservatory, Paris; 1970, became organist, St. Pierre
    de Neuilly.
    Chacone, Leduc.
    Communion pour l'office du dimanche de Sexagésime, in
        Communions, Orgue et Liturgie, Vol. 62, p. 24.
    Elévation pour l'office du dimanche de Sexagésime, in
        Communions, Orgue et Liturgie, Vol. 57, p. 6.
    Offertoire pour l'office du dimanche de Sexagésime, in
        Orgue et Liturgie, Vol. 52, p. 8.
    Postlude pour l'office du dimanche de Sexagésime, in Orgue
        et Liturgie, Vol. 75.
    Prélude pour l'office du dimanche de Sexagésime, in Orgue
        et Liturgie, Vol. 48, p. 16.
    Quatre pièces brèves (pour un office funèbre; pour un temps
        de pénitence; pour un temps d'allegresse; pour tous
        les temps), in Pièces brèves contemporains, L'Organ-
        iste liturgique, Vol. 42, p. 3.
HENS, CHARLES. born St. Gilles-les-Bruxelles, Belgium, 1898.
    1925, graduated from the Conservatory, Brussels; pupil of
    Marcel Dupré; professor of organ, Conservatory, Brussels;
    organist, St. Michel et Ste. Gudule, Brussels.
    Concerto, organ.
    Passacaglia, in Cantantibus Organis, Vol. II, p. 16.
HERZOG, JOHANN GEORG. born Hummendorf (near Kronach),
    Germany, Aug. 5, 1822; died Munich, Feb. 3, 1909. Studied
    at the music school, Schmölz; 1843, became organist, Munich;

taught Rheinberger; 1854, went to Erlangen; 1861-1865,
established historical organ recitals, Erlangen.
Acht Tonstücke, Op. 78, Leuckart.
Achtzehn Stücke, Op. 83, Beyer.
Achtzehn Tonstücke, Op. 52, Viewig.
Dreizig Stücke, Op. 43, Kahnt.
Fünf-und-vierzig Stücke, Op. 84, Böhm.
Fugue and Chorale, Op. 47, No. 2, Rieter-Biedermann.
Jesus, Creator of the World, in In Nativitate Domine,
    McLaughlin & Reilly.
Lobt, Gott, ihr Christen, Breitkopf & Härtel.
Neunzehn Stücke, Op. 87, Beyer.
One hundred nineteen Chorale Preludes, Op. 30, Vol. 2,
    Peters.
One hundred sixty-two Chorale Preludes, Op. 57, Deichert
    (Leipzig).
Schmücke dich, in Six Chorale Preludes, Rieter-Biedermann.
Sechs Stücke, Op. 19, Bosworth.
Sei Lob und Ehr, in Twenty Organ Pieces, Leuckart.
Sieben Tonstücke, Op. 61, Deichert.
Sieben Tonstücke, Op. 79, Leuckart.
Sonata No. 1 (D Minor), Op. 46, Kahnt.
Sonata No. 2 (G Minor) ("Passionsonate"), Kahnt, 1879.
Sonata No. 3 (C Minor), Op. 47.
Sonatas (7), Op. 62, Deichert, 1889.
Sonata (F Minor), Op. 69, O. Forberg, 1896.
Stücke (in churchlike style), Op. 67, Beyer.
Ten Tone Pieces, Op. 67, Leuckart.
Veni Redemptor Gentium, in Orgel Kompositionen aus alter
    und neuer Zeit, Coppenrath.
Vier Festpräludien, Op. 85, Beyer.
Vier Tonstücke, Op. 47, Kahnt.
Vierzehn Stücke, Op. 73, Eichert.
Wer nur den lieben Gott, Op. 43, in Album für Orgelspieler,
    Vol. I, Kahnt.
Zehn Tonstücke, Op. 67, Leuckart.
Zwanzig meist leicht ausführbare Tonstücke, Op. 55, Cop-
    penrath.
Zwanzig Tonstücke, Op. 60, Coppenrath.
Zwanzig Tonstücke, Op. 80, Leuckart.
Zwölf leicht ausführbare Tonstücke, Op. 54, Coppenrath.
Zwölf Stücke, Op. 17, Bosworth.
Zwölf Tonstücke, Op. 53, Gadow.
Zwölf Tonstücke, Op. 65, Forberg.
chorale preludes (17) in Anthologie, Concordia.
chorale preludes (6) in 18 Organ Pieces, Op. 83, Beyer.
chorale preludes (8) in Orgel Choräle Sammlung, Metzler.
chorale preludes (9) in Der Praktische Organist, Part 1,
    Tascher'schen.
chorale preludes (7) in Preludes for Hymns of the Lutheran
    Hymnal, Kittaase.
chorale preludes (8) in Preludes on 192 Chorales, Bädeker.
chorale preludes (3) in Ten Chorale Preludes, Rieter-
Biedermann.

HERZOGENBERG, HEINRICH VON. born Graz, Austria, June 10,
1843; died Wiesbaden, Oct. 9, 1900. Studied in Munich,
Dresden, Graz, and Vienna; 1862-1864, pupil of Dessoff at
the Conservatory, Vienna; lived in Graz; 1874, became one
of the founders of the Bach Society, Leipzig; 1885, became
professor of composition, Berlin.

Erschienen ist der herrliche Tag, in Seasonal Chorale Preludes (with Pedals), Book 2, Oxford.

Fantasie on Nun komm der Heiden Heiland, Op. 39, Rieter-
Biedermann.

Fantasie on Nun danket alle Gott, Op. 46, Rieter-Biedermann.

Nun danket alle Gott, in Organ Works of Modern Masters,
Vol. 3, O. Junne.

Nun komm der Heiden Heiland, Merseburger EV 17.

Pastorale on Nun danket alle Gott, Op. 46, in Organ Book
No. 2, p. 14.

Six Chorale Preludes, Op. 67, Rieter-Biedermann.

HESSE, ADOLPH FRIEDRICH. born Breslau, Germany, Aug. 30,
1808; died Breslau, Aug. 5, 1863. Pupil of his father, an
organ builder; organist, Breslau; 1851, gave organ playing
demonstrations, London; conductor, Symphony Orchestra,
Breslau.

Acht leichte Stücke, Op. 51, Leuckart.

Chorale Preludes, Op. 26, 2 vols., Leuckart.

Drei Präludien, Trio und Vorspiel zu Aus tiefer Not, Op.
74, Breitkopf & Härtel.

Easy Organ Preludes, Op. 25, Leuckart (Hinrichsen 2881).

Fantasie (C Minor), Op. 22, Leuckart.

Fantasie (E Major), Op. 76, Leuckart.

Fantasie (G Minor), Op. 87, Leuckart.

Fantasie nebst Präludium und Fuge über den Namen Hesse,
Hofmeister.

Fantasie No. 1 (F Minor), Op. 57, Leuckart.

Fantasie No. 2 (D Major), Op. 58, Leuckart.

Fantasie und Fuge (D Major), Op. 73, Leuckart.

Fünf Stücke, Op. 81, Leuckart.

Fantasia in D Minor for Four Hands, Op. 87, Leuckart.

Fantasie-Sonate, Op. 83, Hofmeister (Leipzig), 1849.

God Save the King, Op. 68, Leuckart.

Hesse-Album (18 compositions), Leuckart.

Introduktion und Fuge (D Major), Breitkopf & Härtel.

Jesu meine Zuversicht, in Der Praktische Organist, Part 1,
Tascher'schen.

Leichte Vorspiele, Leuckart.

Präludium und Fuge (B Minor), Op. 86, Breitkopf & Härtel.

Präludium und Fuge (D Minor), Op. 66, Breitkopf & Härtel.

Sechs Kompositionen, Op. 70, Breitkopf & Härtel.

Sechs Stücke, Op. 77, Bote & Bock.

Sechszehn leichte Vorspiele, Leuckart.

Sieben Tonstücke, Op. 60, Leuckart.

Six Chorale Preludes, Op. 71, Leuckart.

Toccata, Op. 85, Bote & Bock.

Variations on an Original Theme, Schlesinger (Berlin).
Variationen über den Choral Sei Lob' und Ehr', Op. 54.
Variations on Vater unser, Op. 57, Hofmeister.
Vier Stücke, Op. 63, Leuckart.
Vorspiele (12), Op. 24, Leuckart.
Vorspiele (8), Op. 27, Cranz.
Vorspiele (8), Op. 31, Cranz.
Vorspiele (6), Op. 32, Schlesinger.
Vorspiele (6), Op. 33, Schlesinger.
Vorspiele, Op. 48, Schlesinger.
Vorspiele (5) und ein variierte Choral, Op. 53, Leuckart.
Zwei Fugen und Drei Vorspiele, Op. 62, Leuckart.
Zwei Präludien, Leuckart.
chorale preludes (2) in Anthologie, Concordia.
chorale preludes (3) in The Lutheran Organist, Concordia.
chorale preludes (3) in Orgel Choräle Sammlung, Metzler.
compositions (6) in Ausgewählte Orgel Compositionen,
    Leuckart (Vols. 2, 4, 9, 26, 28, and 33).
HESSENBERG, KURT. born Frankfurt, Germany, Aug. 17, 1908.
Studied at Landesconservatorium, Leipzig; pupil of G. Raphael;
1933, appointed teacher of theory, Hochschule, Frankfurt.
    Fantasie über Sonne der Gerechtigkeit, Op. 66 (1956),
        Merseburger 846.
    Partita über An Wasserflüssen Babylon, Op. 5 (1933).
    Präludium und Fuge, Op. 63, No. 1 (1952), Litolff (Peters
        5864).
    Toccata, Fuge und Chacona, Op. 63, No. 2 (1952), Litolff
        (Peters 5865).
    Trio-Sonate in B dur, Op. 56, Schott 4535, 1955.
    Zwei Partiten, Op. 43: Von Gott will ich (1947-1948),
        Schott 4293 (1952); O Welt, ich muss (1948), Schott
        4294.
    chorale preludes (4) in Orgelbuch zum Evangelischen
        Kirchengesangbuch, Books 5, 14, 16, and 20, Bären-
        reiter.
    chorale preludes (8) in Orgelvorspiele, Merseburger.
    chorale preludes (6) in 73 leichte Choralvorspiele, alter und
        neuer Meister, Leuckart.
HEUSCHKEL, JOHANN. German. Seventeenth century.
    Vom Himmel hoch, in Alte Weihnachtsmusik, p. 36.
HEWITT, JAMES. born Darmoor, England, June 4, 1770; died
Boston, Mass. , Aug. 1, 1827. Violinist; director, court
orchestra for George III; 1792, went to New York, twenty
years violinist, director, composer, organist, concert manager,
music printer; 1812, took musical post at Federal St. Theater,
and as organist, Trinity Church, Boston; 1818, returned to
New York City.
    (The) Fourth of July (A Grand Military Sonata):
        Assembling of the People--Bells.
        Cannon--Distant March--Trumpet--March.
        The Artillery--Rifle Men.
        Quick Step--Infantry.
        Quick March--Shouts of the Populace--Hail, Columbia!

Quiet Verses for Holy Communion, in Early American Compositions for Organ, p. 8.

HIDAS, FRIGYES. Hungarian. born 1928. Conductor, National Theater, Budapest; composer of film and theater music, concertos and chamber music; 1959, awarded Erkel Prize.

Sonata, in Magyar Orgonazene, Sebestyén Pécsi, ed., Editio Musica Budapest, Zenemükiadó Vállalat, Budapest, 1966, Vol. I, p. 17.

HILDNER, VICTOR. American. born 1917. Professor of Music, Concordia Teachers College, River Forest, Ill.

Prelude on Anthes, in The Parish Organist, Vol. 1-4.

HILL, LEWIS EUGENE. Canadian. born 1909.

Four Chorale Preludes, Waterloo Music Co.

Sonatina in G Minor, in Organ Music of Canada, Vol. I, p. 52.

HILLEMACHER, PAUL-JOSEPH-GUILLAUME. born Paris, Nov. 29, 1852; died Versailles, Aug. 13, 1933. Studied at the Conservatory, Paris; 1876, won Grand Prix de Rome; composer of opera.

Album: Prélude funèbre; Méditation; Fughetta a Tre Voci; Four Short Pastorales; Prélude; March; Interludes; Prélude archaïque.

HILLERT, RICHARD. born Granton, Wis., 1923. Professor of Music, Concordia Teachers College, River Forest, Ill.

chorale preludes in The Parish Organist, Vols. 9 and 11.

HILTSCHER, WOLFGANG. German. born 1913; died in Russia (war casualty), 1941. Studied church music and organ, Academy of Music, Leipzig; composition pupil of J. N. David; organist-choirmaster, Heilandskirche, Leipzig.

chorale preludes (5) in 73 leichte Choralvorspiele, alter und neuer Meister, Leuckart.

compositions in The Parish Organist, Vols. 7 and 8.

HINDEMITH, PAUL. born Hanau, Germany, Nov. 16, 1895; died Frankfurt, Dec. 28, 1963. Studied at Hoch Conservatory, Frankfurt; 1915-1923, concertmaster, Frankfurt Opera House; 1927-1935, Director and teacher of composition class, Hochschule für Musik, Berlin; 1937, wrote Craft of Musical Composition; 1935-1937, worked in Turkey; 1937-1940, made several trips to America; 1940-1953, taught at Yale University; 1947, concertized in Mexico, Europe, and South America; 1950-1951, taught at Harvard University; 1951, became professor at the University of Zürich.

Concerto, organ and orchestra (1962), Schott 5388, miniature score, Schott 5033.

Konzert, organ and chamber orchestra, Op. 46, No. 2, Schott 1897.

Sonata No. 1 (1937), Schott 2557.

Sonata No. 2 (1937), Schott 2558.

Sonata No. 3 (1940), Schott 3736.

HINE, WILLIAM. born Brightwell, Oxfordshire, England, 1687; died Gloucester, Aug. 28, 1730. Pupil of Jeremiah Clarke; organist, Gloucester Cathedral.

Finale (Voluntary), in Twelve Short Pieces by Old English

Composers, p. 15.
HODDINOTT, ALUN. born Bargoed, Wales, Aug. 11, 1929. Studied
at University College of South Wales, Cardiff; 1951, joined
staff, Cardiff College of Music and Drama; 1959, appointed
lecturer in music, 1967, Professor, University College of
South Wales; Doc. Mus., University College of South Wales.
Concerto, organ and orchestra, Oxford.
Intrada, in Easy Modern Organ Music, Book 1, Oxford.
Toccata alla Giga, Op. 37, in Modern Organ Music, Oxford,
1965, Book 1, p. 13.
HODEIR, ANDRÉ. born Paris, Jan. 22, 1921. Pupil of Olivier
Messiaen at the Conservatory, Paris; 1954, began The Jazz
Group of Paris.
Fugue sur les douze sons, in La Fugue, Orgue et Liturgie,
Vol. 20, p. 20.
HØGENHAVEN JENSEN, KNUD. Danish. born Mar. 31, 1928.
Pupil of N. V. Bentzon; 1951, became staff member, Royal
Theatre.
Fra himlen høyt, Op. 2, No. 3, in Orgelkoralfantasi,
Atelier Elektra.
Koralspil og Fantasi (2).
Praeludium, Koral, Postludium, Dan Fog.
Toccata og Passacaglia, Op. 7 (1949), Viking Music
(Copenhagen).
chorale preludes (2) in 47 Orgelkoraler, Hansen.
HÖGNER, FRIEDRICH. German. born 1897. Landeskirchenmusik-
director, Bavaria, Germany.
Dreissig Choralvorspiele, Merseburger 894.
chorale preludes (2) in 73 leichte Choralvorspiele, alter und
neuer Meister, Leuckart.
compositions in The Parish Organist, Vols. 5 and 6.
HÖLLER, KARL. born Bamberg, Germany, July 25, 1907. 1932-
1945, taught at Hoch Conservatory, Frankfurt; 1945, became
professor, Musikhochschule, Munich.
Chorale Variations on Helft mir Gottes Güte preisen,
Op. 22, No. 1, Leuckart.
Chorale Variations on Jesu, meine Freude, Op. 22, No. 2,
Leuckart.
Choral-Passacaglia, Schott 5288, 1963.
Ciacona, Op. 54, Schott 4346, 1952.
Fantasie, violin and organ, Op. 49, Peters 5868.
Improvisationen, Op. 55, 'cello and organ, Peters.
Partita on O wie selig, Op. 1, Leuckart.
chorale preludes (4) in 73 leichte Choralvorspiele, alter
und neuer Meister, H. Fleischer, ed., Leuckart.
HOELTY-NICKEL, THEODORE. born Güstrow, Germany, 1894.
Head, Music Department, Valparaiso University, Valparaiso,
Ind.
chorale preludes (2) in The Parish Organist, Vol. 1-4.
HOFHAIMER (HOFHAYMER), PAUL. born Radstadt, Austria,
Jan. 25, 1459; died Salzburg, 1537. Organist of international
repute; 1480, began serving Archduke Sigmund, Innsbruck;
1490, became court organist to Emperor Maximilian I; taught

Kotter, Buchner, Sicher, and Kleber ("Paulomimes"); ca.1520-1537, organist to Prince-Archbishop of Salzburg, M. Lang.
> Ave maris stella, in Liber Organi, Vol. 8, p. 18; also in
> > A la Vierge, Orgue et Liturgie, Vol. 14, p. 5.
> Fantasie über On freudt verzer, in Historical Organ Recitals,
> > Vol. I, p. 3; also in Varia, Orgue et Liturgie,
> > Vol. 25, p. 4.
> Salve regina, in Notre Dame, Orgue et Liturgie, Vol. 11,
> > p. 3; also in The First Four Centuries of Organ
> > Music, Vol. I, p. 41; also Hinrichsen 584.
> compositions (6) in Frühmeister der deutschen Orgelkunst.
> compositions in Masterpieces of Organ Music, Folio 65.

HOFLAND, SIGVART A. born Bergen, Norway, 1889. Professor of Music, Luther College, Decorah, Iowa.
> chorale preludes (4) in The Parish Organist, Vol. 1-4.

HOLLINS, ALFRED. born Hull, England, Sept. 11, 1865; died Edinburgh, Scotland, May 17, 1942. Studied at Wilberforce Institute, York, and Royal Normal College for the Blind, Upper Norwood; pupil of Hans von Bülow; 1884, became organist, St. John's Church, Redhill; toured America three times; studied in Frankfurt; 1888, became organist, Peoples Palace and organist, St. Andrew's Presbyterian Church, Upper Norwood; taught at Royal Normal College; 1897, appointed organist, Free St. George's Church, Edinburgh; 1922, received honorary Mus. Doc., Edinburgh University.
> Christmas Cradle Song, Novello.
> Concert Toccata (B-flat Major), Novello, 1926.
> Prelude on Angelus ad Virginem, Novello.
> Spring Song, Novello, 1904.
> (A) Trumpet Minuet, Novello.

HOLMES, AUGUSTA. born Paris, Dec. 16, 1847; died Paris, Jan. 28, 1903. Pupil of Franck.
> Prelude (Ce que l'on entendit), in Noël, p. 26.

HOMILIUS, GOTTFRIED AUGUST. born Rosenthal (Königstein), Germany, Feb. 2, 1714; died Dresden, June 5, 1785. 1733, became organist, St. Anna, Dresden; 1735, matriculated at the University of Leipzig where he studied with J. S. Bach; 1742, appointed organist, Frauenkirche, Dresden; 1755, Cantor (Music Director) at principal Dresden churches (Kreuzkirche, Frauenkirche, Sophienkirche).
> Ach Herr mich armen Sünder, in Neues Orgel Journal,
> > Körner.
> Durch Adams Fall, organ and oboe (or trumpet), E. Power
> > Biggs, ed., Mercury Music Press.
> Fünf Choralbearbeitungen und Sechs Choralvorspiele, Kistner
> > & Siegel, 1957.
> Orgel Trio in G dur, in Schule des klassischen Triospiels,
> > Breitkopf & Härtel, 1928, 1950.
> Prelude on O Haupt voll Blut, Körner.
> Sechs Choral Vorspiele, in Die Orgel, Series II, No. 2,
> > Kistner und Siegel (Concordia 97-4419).
> chorale preludes (5) in Die Orgel, Series II, Vol. 11,
> > Concordia 97-4418.

transcription of chorale prelude for oboe and organ, <u>Durch</u>
<u>Adams Fall</u>, in <u>Treasury of Early Organ Music</u>, p. 60.
HONEGGER, ARTHUR OSCAR. born LeHavre, France, Mar. 10,
1892; died Paris, Nov. 27, 1955. Pupil of Widor and d'Indy;
member of French "Six."
<u>Fugue et Choral</u>, Chester, London, 1917.
HORST, ANTHON VAN DER. born Amsterdam, June 20, 1899; died
1965. Studied at the Toonkunst Conservatory, Amsterdam; pupil of de Pauw; organist, Waalse en Engelse Kerk, Amsterdam;
organist, Grote Kerk, Naarden; 1936, became head teacher of
organ and conducting, Conservatory, Amsterdam; 1948, received honorary doctorate, Rijksuniversiteit.
<u>Concert Etude</u>, Op. 104 (1963).
<u>Concerto</u>, Op. 58, organ and orchestra (1954), miniature
score, Donemus 95.
<u>Dialogo</u>.
<u>Orgel-Partita op Ps. 8</u> (1947), Ars Nova.
<u>Psalm 121</u>.
<u>Suite in modo conjuncto</u> (1945), Ars Nova, 1945.
<u>Variations</u>, Op. 64: Sinfonia, Bach Cantata No. 4 (1953),
Donemus 59.
HOVHANESS, ALAN. born Somerville, Mass., March 8, 1911. Pupil of Converse and Martinu; composition style influenced by
Indian, oriental systems, and unusual monodic texture.
<u>Dawn Hymn</u>, Peters 6488.
<u>Sanahin</u> (Partita), Peters P66225.
<u>Sonata</u>, flute and organ, Peters 6563.
<u>Sonata</u>, oboe and organ, Peters 6151.
<u>Sonata</u>, trumpet and organ, Peters 6648.
<u>Sonata</u>, two oboes and organ, Peters 6578.
HOWE, MARY. born Richmond, Va., Apr. 4, 1882; died Washing-
ton, D.C., Sept. 14, 1964. Studied at Peabody Conservatory;
pupil of Ernest Hutcheson; on boards of Friends of Music,
Library of Congress, and National Symphony Orchestra, Washington, D.C.
<u>Elegy</u>, Gray.
HOWELLS, HERBERT NORMAN. born Lydney, Gloucestershire,
England, Oct. 17, 1892. 1912-1917, studied at the Royal
School of Church Music, London; pupil of Stanford and Parry;
substitute organist, Salisbury Cathedral; 1920, appointed teacher of composition, Royal College of Music; 1936, became
director of music, St. Paul's Girls' School (succeeded Gustav
Holst); 1937, received honorary D. Mus., Oxford; 1953, received the order of Commander of the British Empire.
<u>Prelude on Sine Nomine</u>, Novello.
<u>Siciliano for a High Ceremony</u>, Novello.
<u>Six Pieces</u> (Sine Nomine; <u>Sarabande for the Morning of</u>
<u>Easter</u>; <u>Master Tallis's Testament</u>; <u>Fugue</u>, <u>Chorale</u>
<u>and Epilogue</u>; <u>Saraband</u>; <u>Paean</u>), Novello.
<u>Sonata</u> (1938), Novello.
<u>Sonata</u> (C Minor), Op. 1 (1933), Novello.
<u>Three Psalm Preludes</u>, Sets I and II, Op. 32, Novello.
<u>Three Rhapsodies</u>, Op. 17, Novello.

HOYER, KARL. born Weissenfels, Germany, Jan. 9, 1891; died
Leipzig, June 12, 1936. Pupil of Reger and Straube at the
Conservatory, Leipzig; 1911, became organist, Ritter-und-
Domkirche, Revel; 1912, appointed first organist, St.
Jacobi, Chemnitz; since 1926, teacher of organ and theory, Conser-
vatory, Leipzig; organist, Nikolaikirche.
Acht Pedal-Etuden, Op. 42, Breitkopf & Härtel 5490.
Chorale Preludes on Melodies of the Evangelischen Kirchen-
gesangbuch, Op. 57, 2 vols., F. R. Portius.
Concertino im alten Stil, organ and string orchestra, Op.
20, Klemm (Leipzig), 1922.
Drei kleine Präludien und Fugen.
Fantasie and Fugue on Wunderbarer König, F. R. Portius.
Fantasie on the Dutch hymn Wir treten zum beten, Leuckart.
Introduktion und Chaconne (D Minor), organ and orchestra,
Breitkopf & Härtel.
Introduction, Variations and Fugue on Jerusalem, du hoch-
gebaute Stadt, Leuckart.
Kanonische Variationes und Fugen über Nun bitten wir,
Op. 44, Breitkopf & Härtel.
Konzertino im alten Stil, Op. 20 (see Concertino above).
Memento mori, Op. 22, Klemm (Leipzig).
Passacaglia und Doppelfuge (F Minor), Leuckart.
Pastorale, Op. 26, violin and organ, Oppenheimer.
Präludium, Chaconne und Doppelfuge.
Sonata (D Minor), Op. 19, Benjamin (Leipzig), 1921.
Ten Easy Chorale Preludes, Leuckart.
Three Chorale Paraphrases, Op. 17, Oppenheimer.
Toccata and Fugue (C Minor), Op. 36, Benjamin (Leipzig).
Twenty Easy Chorale Preludes, Op. 60, Leuckart.
Variations (A Major), Op. 33, Oppenheimer.
Vier Charakterstücke, Op. 35, Oppenheimer.
Weihnachtskanzone, Op. 34, violin (flute) and organ,
Oppenheimer.
chorale preludes (2) in Das Organistenamt, Vol. 2, Breit-
kopf & Härtel.
HUBER, KLAUS. born Berne, Switzerland, Nov. 30, 1924. Pupil
of Willy Burkhard (Zürich Conservatory) and Boris Blacher
(Berlin); 1950-1960, teacher of violin, Conservatory, Zürich;
1960-1963, instructor of music history and literature, Conser-
vatory, Lucerne; 1961-1964, Instructor of Music Theory,
director of classes in composition and instrumentation, Music
Academy, Basel.
Cantus cancricans (1965), Bärenretier 5486, 1968.
In Memoriam Willy Burkhard, Zwei Orgelstücke (1955),
Bärenreiter 4462, 1965.
In te domine speravi, Invention (1964), Bärenreiter 4463,
1966.
HULSE, CAMIL VAN (see van Hulse, Camil).
HUMMEL, BERTOLD. born Hüfingen (Baden), Germany, Nov. 27,
1925. Winner of composition prizes given by Stuttgart (1960)
and Düsseldorf (1961); 1950-1963, Kantor, St. Konrad,
Freiburg-im-Breisgau; since 1963, composition teacher,

Bayerischen Staatskonservatorium, Würzburg, and Director, Studios für neue Musik.

Adagio, Simrock.

Fantasie, Simrock.

Magnificat, 2 vols., Verlag Herder, Freiburg-im-Breisgau, 1961.

Marianische Fresken, Simrock.

Tripartita, Simrock.

HUMMEL, JOHANN NEPOMUK. born Pressburg, Austria, Nov. 14, 1778; died Weimar, Oct. 17, 1837. Pupil of Mozart, Albrechtsberger, and Haydn.

Präludium, Zwischenspiel und zwei Fugen (Ricercare), Heinrich Poos, ed., Merseburger 880.

Zwei Präludien und Fugen (C Minor, E-flat Major), Breitkopf & Härtel.

HUMPERT, HANS. born Paderborn, Germany, Apr. 19, 1901; died Salerno, Italy, Sept. 15, 1943. Pupil of Cordes, Cathedral organist, Paderborn; 1924-1925, studied at Hoch Conservatory, Frankfurt; pupil of Walther Gmeindl; friend of Hindemith and Pepping; 1940, became teacher of composition, Musikschule, Münster.

Choralvariationen über Da Jesus an dem Kreuze (1934), Bärenreiter, 1949.

Doppelfuge.

Fuge.

Fuge in d moll (1925).

Fughette über B-A-C-H (1919).

Kleine Präludien (1934).

Konzert (Concerto for organ) (1932), Bärenreiter, 1949.

Orgelmusik in Drei Sätzen (1928).

Orgelstück (1934).

Präludium, Canzone und Fuge über Der Tag (1934), Schott.

Präludium und Toccata über Nun bitten wir (1934), Schott.

Präludium und Trio (1930).

Second Concerto, organ and orchestra (1937).

Third Concerto, organ (1942), Bärenreiter.

Zwolf Orgelstücke (1934), Schott.

HURÉ, JEAN. born Gien (Loiret), France, Sept. 17, 1877; died Paris, Jan. 27, 1930. Pupil of Guilmant; musicologist, theoretician, composer, improviser; organist, Notre-Dame-des-Blancs-Manteaux, Angers; organist, St. Martin-des-Champs, Paris; 1925, appointed organist, St. Augustin (succeeded Gigout); substituted for Saint-Saëns at St. Séverin and Decaux at Sacré-Coeur; wrote Technique de l'orgue, Esthetique de l'orgue (1923).

Communion pour une Messe de Noël, Sénart, 1914 (Gray).

Prélude, violin ('cello) and organ, Le Grand Orgue.

Prélude pour une messe pontificale, in Varia, Orgue et Liturgie, Vol. 46, p. 3.

HURFORD, PETER. born Minehead, Somerset, England, Nov. 22, 1930. Studied at the Royal College of Music; 1953, won degrees in music and law, Jesus College, Cambridge University; Master of the Music, Cathedral and Abbey Church of

St. Albans; 1963, founded St. Albans International Organ Festival; 1967-1968, organist-in-residence, University of Cincinnati, Cincinnati, Ohio.

(A) Fancy, in For Manuals Only, Oxford.
Fanfare on Old 100th, in Ceremonial Music.
Five Short Chorale Preludes, Oxford.
Five Verses on a Melody from the Paderborn Gesangbuch, Oxford.
Meditation, in An Album of Preludes and Interludes, Oxford.
Paean, in An Album of Praise, p. 22.
Passingala, Novello, 1961.
Suite 'Laudate Dominum,' Oxford, 1961.
Two Dialogues, Novello.

HUSTON, JOHN. born Greenville, Texas, Aug. 13, 1915.   1947, B. Mus. , University of Texas; 1949, M. S. M. , Union Theological Seminary, New York City; organ pupil of William Doty and Clarence Dickinson; composition pupil of Kent Kennan and Harold Friedell; organist, Highland Park Methodist Church and Temple Emanu-El, Dallas, Texas; organist, Church of the Holy Trinity, Brooklyn, and Stephen Wise Free Synagogue, New York City; since 1957, organist and director of music, First Presbyterian Church, New York City; since 1961, Chief Organist, Congregation Emanu-El, New York City; organ faculty member, Union Theological Seminary, New York City.

Meditations on the Seven Last Words of Christ, Gray, 1956.
Prelude in the Style of an Improvisation on Aberystwyth, Gray (St. Cecilia Series 866), 1959.
Psalm Prelude, Gray (St. Cecilia Series 791), 1953.

HUTCHINGS, CHARLES.   English.   born 1910.

Ostinato, Elegy and Paean, Novello.
Two pieces: Pastorale;   Processional, Oxford.

HUYBRECHTS, LODE (LOUIS).   born Stabroek, Belgium, 1911. Studied at the Lemmens School and at the Conservatory, Antwerp; organist, Rochester, N. Y.

Prelude and Fugue, (Peters D 87).
Rêverie, in Cantantibus Organis, Vol. II, p. 30.

IBERT, JACQUES.   born Paris, Aug. 15, 1890;   died Paris, Jan. 5, 1962.   Studied at the Conservatory, Paris;   friend of Milhaud; pupil of Gédalge, Fauré, and Vidal;   1937-1955, Director, Academy of Rome;   1955-1957, Director, Opéra and Opéra Comique.

Justorum animae in manu Dei sunt, in Grands Maîtres Modernes, R. Lebrun, Brussels, 1921, p. 41.
Trois Pièces (Pièce solennelle; Musette; Fugue), Heugel.

ILEBORGH, ADAM.   Rector of Franciscan monastery, Stendal, Germany.   His tablature is dated 1448.

compositions in Corpus of Early Keyboard Music, No. 1, pp. 28-30; also in Historical Anthology of Music, Vol. I, p. 88.

D'INDY, PAUL-MARIE-THEODORE-VINCENT. born Paris, Mar. 27,
1851; died Paris, Dec. 2, 1931. Pupil of Franck; 1872-
1876, organist, Eglise de St. Leu-la-Forêt; 1894, became
founder of the Schola Cantorum with Bordes and Guilmant;
1899, appointed inspector of musical instruction, Paris.
Huit interludes sur ancient modes, Edition Musicus.
Prélude et petit canon, Op. 38, Durand, 1893-1894.
Prélude ou Pièce (E-flat Minor), Op. 66, Durand, 1911.
Versets pour les vêpres du commun des martyrs, Op. 51
          (eight antiphons), Schola Cantorum, 1899.
INGEGNERI, MARCANTONIO (Marco Antonio). born Verona,
Italy, 1545; died Cremona, July 1, 1592. Pupil of Cyprien
de Rore; 1576, became maestro di cappella, Cathedral, Cre-
mona; maestro di cappella to Duke of Mantua; taught Monte-
verdi.
Aria di canzon francese, in Anthologia Organistica Italiana,
          p. 25.
IRELAND, JOHN NICHOLSON. born Inglewood, Bowdon, Cheshire,
England, Aug. 13, 1879; died Washington, Sussex, England,
June 12, 1962. 1893, entered Royal College of Music; pupil
of Stanford; 1904-1926, organist, St. Luke's, Chelsea; 1905,
Mus. B. , Durham; 1932, honorary Doc. Mus. , Durham;
taught at Royal College of Music; taught Benjamin Britten and
Alan Bush.
Capriccio, Stainer.
Elegiac Romance, Novello.
Meditation on John Kebel's Rogationtide Hymn, Freeman.
Miniature Suite.
Sursum Corda and Alla Marcia, Novello.
ISAAK, HEINRICH (ISAAC, HENDRIK). born Flanders ?, ca.1450?;
died Florence, Italy, 1517. 1480-1492, served Lorenzo de
Medici; organist, Cathedral, Florence; 1486, lived in Inns-
bruck; served Maximilian I in Vienna; lived in Augsburg and
Constance; 1514-1517, lived in Florence.
Herr Gott, lass' dich erbarmen, in Anthologia pro Organo,
          Vol. III, p. 6; also in Peeters, Little Organ Book
          for Beginners in Organ Playing, p. 92.
Süsser Vater, Herre Gott, in Liber Organi, Vols. 8 and 9;
          also in The First Four Centuries of Organ Music,
          Vol. I, p. 26.
composition in Frühmeister der deutschen Orgelkunst.
compositions (2) in Alte Meister aus der Frühzeit des
          Orgelspiels.
compositions in Oudnederlandse Meesters, Vol. I (2),
          Vol. II (2), and Vol. III (3).
IVES, CHARLES EDWARD. born Danbury, Conn. , Oct. 20, 1874;
died New York City, May 19, 1954. Organist, Baptist Church,
Danbury, Conn. ; 1894, entered Yale University; pupil of
Horatio Parker and Dudley Buck; 1899-1902, organist, Central
Presbyterian Church, New York City; 1947, won Pulitzer
Prize for Third Symphony (1911).
Adeste fideles (1891), Mercury Music Press.
Variations on America (Introduction, chorale and five

variations) (1891), polytonal additions (1894), Mercury
Music Press, 1949.

JACKSON, FRANCIS. born Malton, Yorkshire, England, 1917.
1929-1933, chorister, York Minster; 1937, B. Mus., Durham;
1937, Fellow of the Royal College of Organists; 1937, won
Limpus Prize; 1946, became organist and Master of the Mu-
sic, York Minster; 1957, Doc. Mus., Durham University.
  (The) Archbishop's Fanfare, in Ceremonial Music, Oxford.
  Division on Nun danket, Novello 261 O. C. (N. S.).
  Fanfare, in A Festive Album, p. 2.
  Impromptu for Sir Edward Bairstow on his Seventieth
    Birthday, Oxford.
  Recessional, in An Album of Postludes, Oxford.
  Scherzetto Pastorale, in A Christmas Album, Oxford.
  Three Pieces (Procession; Arabesque; Pageant), Novello.
  Three Pieces (Toccata; Choral; Fugue), Novello 4 N. O. M. C.
  Toccata, Chorale and Fugue, Novello 275 O. C. (N. S.).
  Two Hymn Preludes, in Festal Voluntaries (Advent, Har-
    vest), Novello.
JACKSON, GEORGE K. born Oxford, England, 1745; died Boston,
  Mass., Nov. 18, 1823. Pupil of James Nares; 1791, Mus.
  Doc., St. Andrew's College; 1796, went to Norfolk, Va.;
  1804, named music director, St. George's Chapel, New York
  City; from 1812, organist at various churches, Boston.
  Short Psalms of Joy.
JACOB, (DOM) CLÉMENT. born Bordeaux, Jan. 13, 1906. 1923,
  became member of the group of French musicians called
  L'Ecole d'Arcueil; 1927, became an Israelite convert to
  Catholicism; became monk and priest, organist, Benedictine
  monastery, En Calcat.
  Christe Redemptor Omnium, in Orgue et Liturgie, Vol. 75.
  Communion on Viderunt (Jour de Noël), in Communions,
    Orgue et Liturgie, Vol. 62, p. 31.
  Elévation pour le jour de Noël, in Elévations, Orgue et
    Liturgie, Vol. 57, p. 3.
  Liturgical Interludes, Leduc.
  Livre d'orgue, Ouvrières, 1966.
  Prélude à l'Introit pour la fete de la Nativité sur Puer
    natus est, in Préludes à l'Introit, Orgue et Liturgie,
    Vol. 48, p. 18.
  Suite in C Major, Leduc.
  Tui sunt caeli (Nativité de Notre Seigneur), in Offertoires,
    Orgue et Liturgie, Vol. 52, p. 3.
  Twenty Easy Pieces on Gregorian Melodies, Enoch.
  Versets sur Veni Creator, in Hymnes et Antiennes, Orgue
    et Liturgie, Vol. 8, p. 29.
JACOB, GEORGES. born Paris, Aug. 19, 1877; died Paris,
  Dec. 28, 1950. Pupil of Guilmant, Vierne, and Widor; or-
  ganist, St. Louis d'Antin; organist, St. Ferdinand.

Douze pièces, Leduc.
(Les) Heures bourguignonnes, Leduc, 1909.
Prélude funèbre, Fugue et Variation, Leduc, 1906.
Religious Suite No. 1, G. Schirmer.
Religious Suite No. 2, G. Schirmer.
Symphonie, Leduc, 1907.
Veni Creator Spiritus, G. Schirmer.
JACOB, GORDON PERCIVAL SEPTIMUS. born Norwood (London), England, July 5, 1895. Studied at the Royal College of Music; pupil of Stanford; 1926, appointed professor of composition, Royal College of Music; Doc. Mus., London.
Festal Flourish, in An Album of Praise, p. 5.
Prelude, Meditation, and Fanfare, Novello.
JACOB, WERNER. born Mengersgereuth-Hämmern, Thuringia, Germany, 1938. Organ pupil of Walter Kraft; composition pupil of Wolfgang Fortner; 1961, appointed Kantor, Luther- kirche, Freiburg-im-Breisgau; 1963, appointed Kantor, Dreieinigkeitskirche, Nürnberg; since 1969, Kantor, St. Sebalduskirche, and director, Bach orchestra, Nürnberg.
Fantasie, Adagio und Epilog (1963), Breitkopf & Härtel 6579, 1968.
JACOBI, FREDERICK. born San Francisco, Calif., May 4, 1891; died New York City, Oct. 24, 1952. Studied in New York City and Berlin; pupil of Bloch; 1913-1917, coach, Metropolitan Opera; lived with American Indians in New Mexico and Ari- zona; 1927, became teacher, Master School of United Arts, New York City; wrote for the Jewish service; 1936-1950, teacher, Juilliard School of Music, New York City.
Prelude, Gray (Contemporary Organ Series 6).
Three Quiet Preludes, Gray (Contemporary Organ Series 24).
JACQUEMIN, (ABBE) CAMILLE. Belgian. born 1899. Lived in Béarn, Belgium; pupil of Louis Vierne.
Choral sur un thème grégorien de l'office des vierges, (Hérelle) Philippo.
Symphonie en si mineur, (Hérelle) Philippo.
Trois tableaux de pèlerinage, (Hérelle) Philippo.
JAMES, JOHN. English. born 16--; died 1745.
Echo Voluntary in D Major, Hinrichsen 228.
JAMES, PHILIP. born Jersey City, N. J., May 17, 1890. Studied at City College of New York; pupil of Bonnet; musical direc- tor of theatrical productions; orchestral conductor; taught at Columbia University two years; 1923, appointed professor of music, 1934, head, department of music, New York University (succeeded Percy Grainger); 1946, received Mus. Doc., New York College of Music.
Alleluia-Toccata (1949), C. Fischer, 1955.
Christmas Suite, Gray.
Dithyramb (1921), Gray (St. Cecilia Series 310), 1923.
Fête (1921), Gray (St. Cecilia Series 311), 1923.
First Organ Sonata (1929), Gray, 1930.
Galarnad, in The Modern Anthology, p. 110.
Meditation à Ste. Clotilde (1916), Ditson, 1916.
Novelette (1946), Gray (St. Cecilia Series 732), 1946.

Ostinato (1928), Gray (St. Cecilia Series 503), 1931.
Pantomime (1941), Gray (Contemporary Organ Series 8), 1941.
Passacaglia on an old Cambrian Bass (1951), C. Fischer, 1957.
Pastorale (1949), Southern, 1955.
Pensée d'Automne (1910), Gray, 1923.
Perstare et Praestare (1944), Gray (St. Cecilia Series 733), 1947.
Requiescat in pace (1949), Summy-Birchard, 1957.
Il Riposo, Suite (1950), Gray, 1952.
Solemn Prelude (1948), Southern.

JANÁCEK, LEOŠ. born Hukvaldy, East Moravia, Czechoslavakia, July 3, 1854; died Ostrau (Moravia), Aug. 12, 1928. Chorister, Old Brünn Monastery; succeeded Krizkowsky as conductor of that choir; studied at Organ School, Prague; 1875, became teacher, Teachers' School, Brünn; 1879, went to the Conservatory, Leipzig, and later to the Conservatory, Vienna; 1881, founder and teacher, Brünn Organ School for forty years; Professor, State Conservatory, Prague; 1925, honorary Ph. D., University of Brünn.

Compositions for Organ, Books I and II, 1884.
Glagolithic Mass organ solo, Universal.
Two Adagios, in Musica Boemica per Organo, Vol. I, Jiří Reinberger, ed. , Státní Nakladatelství krásné literatury, hudby a umění, Prague, 1954.
Two Chorale Preludes, Oxford, 1966.

JARNACH, PHILIPP. born Noisy, France, July 26, 1892. Studied at the Conservatory, Paris; pupil of Busoni; 1927-1949, professor of composition, Conservatory, Cologne; 1950, became Director, Conservatory, Hamburg.

Konzertstück, Op. 21, Schott 2087.

JENNE, NATALIE. born Milwaukee, Wis. , 1934. Professor of Music, Concordia Teachers College, River Forest, Ill.

Wo Gott zum Haus, in The Parish Organist, Vol. 9, p. 31.

JEPPESEN, KNUD. born Copenhagen, Aug. 15, 1892. Pupil of Thomas Laub and Carl Nielsen; organist, St. Stephen's Church, Copenhagen; studied at the University of Copenhagen; pupil of Adler in Vienna; 1920-1946, professor of musicology, Royal Danish Conservatory, Copenhagen; 1922, Ph. D. , University of Vienna; 1946-1957, Professor of Musicology, University of Aarhus.

Fünfzig Choralvorspiele, Hansen 27480, 1957.
Intonazione boreale, Hansen 27570.
Passacaglia, Hansen 28642.
Preludium och fuga e-moll, in Musica Organi, Vol. III, p. 6.

JIMÉNEZ (XIMENES), JOSÉ. Spanish. born 1601; died 1672.
Batalla; Verset du VIe Ton, in Les Anciens Maîtres Espagnols, pp. 10 and 18.
compositions (3) in Antologia de Organistas Clásicos Españoles, Vol. I, p. 40-54.

JIRÁK, KAREL BOLESLAV. born Prague, Czechoslavakia, Jan. 28,

1891; died Chicago, Ill., Jan. 30, 1972. Studied in Prague
and Vienna; 1915-1918, Director, Hamburg Opera; 1920-
1930, professor of composition, Conservatory, Prague; 1930-
1945, conductor, Radio Orchestra, Prague; since 1947, active
in Chicago; taught at Chicago Conservatory College; chairman, Theory Department, Roosevelt University, Chicago.
　　Five Little Preludes and Fugues, Novello.
JOHANSSON, SVEN-ERIC. born Västervik, Sweden, Dec. 10, 1919.
1943, graduated in teaching and in organ (1946) from the Conservatory, Stockholm; pupil of H. Rosenberg; 1944-1950,
organist-choirmaster, Missions Church, Uppsala; 1952, became organist, Hagens Chapel, Göteborg; 1954, became teacher, Conservatory, Göteborg.
　　Praeambulum et Fuga, in Musica Organi, Vol. III, p. 150.
JOHNSON, DAVID N. born San Antonio, Texas, June 28, 1922.
1950, B. Mus., Trinity University; studied at Curtis Institute,
Philadelphia; organ pupil of Alexander McCurdy, Arthur Pois-
ter, and Donald Willing; 1951, M. Mus., 1956, Ph. D., Syra-
cuse University; composition pupil of Ernest Bacon and Rosario
Scalero; 1956-1960, Chairman, Music Department, Alfred Uni-
versity; 1960-1965, Chairman, Department of Music, St. Olaf
College, Northfield, Minn.; 1967-1969, professor of music,
Syracuse University; since 1969, professor of music, Arizona
State University, Tempe, Ariz.; organist-choirmaster, Trinity
Episcopal Cathedral, Phoenix.
　　Beautiful Saviour, Gray (St. Cecilia Series 935), 1967.
　　Chorale Prelude on Ein' feste Burg, Augsburg 11-0822.
　　Chorale Prelude on Faith of Our Fathers, Augsburg 11-0820.
　　Chorale Prelude on Wondrous Love, Augsburg 11-0821, 1965.
　　Deck Thyself, My Soul, with Gladness (15 hymn preludes),
　　　　Augsburg 11-9157, 1968.
　　Easy Trios (Music for Worship), Augsburg 11-9291.
　　Festival Pieces (3), brass and organ (Processional; Allegro
　　　　maestoso; Sinfonia), Augsburg, 1962-1964.
　　Lord, Keep Us Steadfast, Augsburg 11-0839, 1967.
　　Music for Worship for Manuals, Augsburg 11-9297, 1969.
　　Of the Father's Love, Augsburg 11-0841, 1967.
　　Three Trumpet Tunes, Augsburg 11-0816.
　　Trumpet Tune, in An Album of Postludes, Oxford, 1964.
　　Trumpet Tune in E Major, Augsburg.
　　Variations on Puer nobis nascitur, in Library of Organ
　　　　Music, Vol. 2, Schmitt, Hall & McCreary, 1966.
　　chorale preludes (2) in The Parish Organist, Vols. 11 and
　　　　12.
JONGEN, JOSEPH-MARIE-ALPHONSE-NICOLAS. born Liège, Bel-
gium, Dec. 14, 1873; died Sart-les-Spa, July 12, 1953.
Studied at the Conservatory, Liège; organist, Collegiate Church
of St. Jacques, Liège; friend of d'Indy, Chausson, and Fauré;
1902, became professor of harmony, Royal Conservatory,
Liège; 1920, appointed professor of fugue, 1925-1939, Director, Conservatory, Brussels.
　　Cantilène, in Orgel-Kompositionen, Vol. III, Gauss, ed.
　　Chant de May, Op. 53, No. 1, Chester, 1917.

Grand Choeur, in The International Organist, Vol. I, p. 20.
In Memoriam Regis, Lemoine.
Larghetto, Edition Musicus, Philippo.
Marche religieuse; Meditation and Prayer; Prélude religieux, in The French Organist, Vol. II.
Minuet-Scherzo, Op. 53, No. 2, Chester, 1917.
Offertoire (Prière du matin), in The French Organist, Vol. I, p. 59.
Offertoire sur Alma redemptoris, Sénart, 1911.
Petit Prélude, Cebedem, Brussels, 1935.
Prélude Elégiaque et Pensée d'Automne, Op. 47, Augener, 1915.
Prélude et Fugue, Op. 121, Cebedem, 1941.
Quatre pièces, Op. 5, Muraille.
Quatre pièces, Op. 37 (Cantabile; Improvisation-Caprice; Prière; Choral), Durand, 1911.
Scherzetto et Prière, Op. 108, Oxford, 1938.
Sonata eroica, Op. 94, Leduc, 1930.
Toccata, Op. 104, Lemoine, 1935.

JOSQUIN DES PRES (see des Pres).

JOUBERT, JOHN. born Cape Town, South Africa, Mar. 20, 1927. Studied at the South African College of Music and at the Royal Academy of Music, London; 1950, B. Mus., University of Durham; lecturer, University College, Hull.
Passacaglia and Fugue, Op. 35, Novello, 1963.
Prelude on the Old Hundredth, Oxford.

JOULAIN, JEANNE-ANGÈLE-DESIRÉE-YVONNE. born Paris, July 22, 1920. 1934-1943, studied at the Conservatory, Amiens; 1941-1944, studied at Ecole César-Franck, Paris; 1947-1952, studied at the Conservatory, Paris; organ pupil of Marcel Dupré; composition pupil of Guy de Lioncourt; since 1951, professor, Conservatory, Lille; 1952-1961, professor, Conservatory, Roubaix; since 1954, organist, St. Maurice de Lille; 1961-1969, professor, Conservatory, Douai.
Communion pour tous les temps, in Communions, Orgue et Liturgie, Vol. 62, p. 3.
Elévation pour le saint jour de Pâques sur Victimae paschali, in Elévations, Orgue et Liturgie, Vol. 57, p. 11.
Noël flamand, in Noëls variés, Orgue et Liturgie, Vol. 40, p. 22; also in Christmas Music by Various French Composers, Kalmus, p. 22.
Paraphrase pour la fête de la Toussaint sur Justorum animae in manu Dei sunt, in Offertoires, Orgue et Liturgie, Vol. 52, p. 34.
Postlude, in Orgue et Liturgie, Vol. 70.
Pour la Fête des Rameaux sur Hosanna Filio David, in Préludes à l'Introit, Orgue et Liturgie, Vol. 48, p. 20.

JULLIEN, GILLES. French. born ca. 1653; died Chartres, Sept. 14, 1703. 1663-1703, organist, Cathedral, Chartres.
*Livre d'orgue, Société française de Musicologie, Serie I, Vol. 13, Heugel, 1952.
compositions (9) in Les Maîtres français de l'orgue, Vol. I.

KABELÁČ, MILOSLAV. born Prague, July 1, 1908. Pupil of
Karel Jirák.
Fantasy I.
Fantasy II.
Four Preludes, in Nuove Composizioni per Organo, Vol. II.
Symphony III, Op. 33, organ, brass, and timpani.
KAMEKE, ERNST-ULRICH VON. born Potsdam, Germany, 1926.
Organ pupil of Helmut Tramnitz; composition pupil of Wolf-
gang Fortner; 1949-1954, organist and director of music,
Eberbach on the Neckar; 1954-1959, organist and director of
music, Friedenskirche, and instructor, Rheinischen Landes-
kirchenmusikschule, Düsseldorf; since 1959, director of music,
St. Petri, Hamburg.
Toccata, Strophen und Fuge, Breitkopf & Härtel 6568,
1968.
Toccata variata (1959), Breitkopf & Härtel 6325, 1961.
KAMINSKI, HEINRICH. born Tiengen, Baden, Germany, July 4,
1886; died Ried, Bavaria, June 21, 1946. Studied at Heidel-
berg; 1909, pupil of Hugo Kaun; taught Carl Orff; 1930,
became professor, director of master class, Prussian Academy
of Arts, Berlin; 1933, taught in Ried.
Andante, Bärenreiter 2055, 1939.
Canon, organ and violin, 1934.
Canzona, organ and violin, 1917.
Choralsonata, Universal 8608, 1926.
Choralvorspiele über Meine Seele ist stille, Bärenreiter
2142, 1947.
Drei Choralvorspiele, Universal, 1928.
Kanzone, violin and organ, Universal.
Präludium und Fuge, organ and violin, 1929.
Toccata, Universal 7458.
Toccata über Wie schön leuchtet, Universal, 1923.
Toccata und Fuge, Bärenreiter 2054, 1939.
KAPI-KRÁLIK, JENÖ. Hungarian. born 1908. Organist, Protes-
tant church, Budapest-Kelenföld.
Toccata (dorisch), in Musica Organi, Vol. II, p. 74.
KARAM, FREDERICK. born Ottawa, Canada, Mar. 26, 1926. Mus.
Bac., University and Royal Conservatory, Toronto; pupil of
Gerald Bales, Drummond Wolff, and Healey Willan; assistant
professor, University of Ottawa; organist-choirmaster, St.
Elijah Orthodox Church, Ottawa.
Divertimento, in Organ Music in Canada, Vol. II, p. 29.
Gigue, B M I--Canada, Ltd.
(The) Modal Trumpet, B M I--Canada, Ltd.
KARG-ELERT, SIGFRID. born Oberndorf, Swabia, Germany,
Nov. 21, 1877; died Leipzig, Apr. 9, 1933. Studied at the
Conservatory, Leipzig; pupil of Reinecke, Jadassohn, and
Homeyer; taught at Magdeburg Conservatory; 1919, professor
of composition (succeeded Reger), Conservatory, Leipzig.
For harmonium:

Aquarellen, Op. 27, Carl Simon.
Five Miniatures, Op. 9, Carl Simon.
Innere Stimmen, Op. 58, Carl Simon.
Impressions, Op. 102, Peters.
Intarsien, Op. 76, Carl Simon.
Interludes, in The Practical Organist, Peters.
Madrigale, 2 vols. , Op. 42, Carl Simon.
Monologe, Op. 33, Carl Simon.
Partita (D Major), Op. 37 (includes Bourée et Musette),
    Carl Simon.
Portraits, Op. 101, 2 vols. , Peters.
Seven Idylls, Op. 104, Peters 3812.
Six Pièces Romanesques, Op. 103, Seyffardt (Amsterdam).
Six Sketches, Op. 10, Forberg (Leipzig).
Three Sonatinas, Op. 14, Carl Simon.
Tröstungen, Op. 47, Carl Simon.
For Pipe Organ:
Auswahl aus Op. 65, 2 vols. , Carl Simon.
Benediction, Op. 34, No. 4, Marks, 1941.
Bourée et Musette, in The International Organist, Vol. I,
    p. 4.
Canzona on Nearer, My God, to Thee, Op. 81 (1913),
    Carl Simon.
Cathedral Windows (on plainsong melodies), Op. 106, (1923),
    Elkin.
Chaconne, Fugue and Trilogy, Op. 73 (1912), Novello.
Choral Improvisations on In dulci jubilo, Der Hölle Pforten
    sind zerstört, Gelobt sei Gott, Op. 75 (1910), Novello.
Chorale Improvisation on Näher, mein Gott zu dir, Simrock.
Cycle of Eight Short Pieces, Op. 154, Arthur P. Schmidt.
Drei Choral Studien, Edition Le Grand Orgue.
Drei Stücke, Op. 142, Breitkopf & Härtel, 1936.
Fantasie, Kanzone, Passacaglia und Fuge (C Minor), Op. 85,
    No. 2, Leuckart.
Four Baroque Miniatures, Edition Musicus.
Four Interludes, Hinrichsen 600C.
Homage to Handel, Op. 75 (1913), Peters.
Improvisation (E Major), Op. 34B, Breitkopf & Härtel.
Interludes, Hinrichsen 93.
Kaleidoscope, Op. 144 (1930), Oxford.
Kanzone und Toccata (E-flat Minor), Op. 85, No. 1,
    Leuckart.
Modal Interludes, Hinrichsen 114.
Music for Organ, Op. 145, Oxford.
Nun danket alle Gott, Op. 65, No. 59, Breitkopf & Härtel
    6238.
Partita (E Major), Op. 100 (1922), Novello.
Passacaglia (E-flat Minor), Op. 25B (1905-1908), Carl
    Simon.
Passacaglia, Variationen und Fuge über B-A-C-H, Op. 150,
    Hinrichsen 92.
Pastels from Lake Constance, Op. 96 (1919), (Spirit of the
    Lake; Landscape in Mist; Legend of the Mountain;

Reed-grown Waters; Sun's Evensong; Mirrored Moon;
Hymn to the Stars), Novello.
Pastorale, Op. 48, No. 2, violin and organ, Breitkopf &
Härtel.
Pax Vobiscum, Op. 86, No. 5, Novello; also Leuckart.
Pedal Studies, Op. 83 (1913), Peters 3458.
Phantasia und Fuge in D dur, Op. 39B (1905), Carl Simon.
Sanctus, Op. 48, No. 1, violin and organ, Breitkopf &
Härtel.
Sequenz No. 1 (A Minor), Hinrichsen 94.
Sequenz No. 2 (C Minor) (1910), Otto Junne.
Sempre Semplice, Op. 142, 2 vols. , Paxton.
Seven Chorale Improvisations, Paxton.
Sixty-six Choral Improvisations, 6 vols. , Marks; also
Breitkopf & Härtel.
> Vol. I: Advent and Christmas;
> Vol. 2: Passiontide;
> Vol. 3: New Year, Easter, Various Feast Days;
> Vol. 4: Ascension and Whitsuntide;
> Vol. 5: Reformation, Days of Penitence, The
> Lord's Supper, and Funerals;
> Vol. 6: Confirmation, Weddings, Baptisms,
> Harvest Festival.
Sketch Book I, Hinrichsen 117.
Sketch Book II, Hinrichsen 149.
Sonatina (A Minor), Op. 74 (1909), Novello.
Ten Characteristic Pieces, Op. 86 (1911), 2 vols. , Leuc-
kart.
Three Choral-Improvisations, Schweers and Haake.
Three Impressions (Harmonies du Soir; Clair de Lune;
La Nuit), Op. 72 (1911), Novello.
Three Impressions (Sunset; Starlight; Elegiac Poem),
Op. 108 (1922), Arthur P. Schmidt.
Three Pastels, Op. 92 (1912), Augener.
Three Symphonic Canzonas, Op. 85 (1910), Leuckart.
Three Symphonic Chorales, Op. 87 (1913), Carl Simon
7611 a/b.
Triptych, Op. 141 (1930), Elkin.
Twenty Preludes and Postludes (Choral Studies), Op. 78
(1912), Carl Simon 7610.
chorale preludes (3) in Die Orgel, Kistner & Siegel.
interludes (4) in Preludes, Interludes, Postludes, Hinrichsen
600C.
KARGES, WILHELM. born ?, Germany, 1613 or 1614; died Ber-
lin, Nov. 27, 1699. Perhaps a pupil of Abel, Haase the elder,
or Siefert; Adjunkt to A. Düben; 1645, served court in
Königsberg; served Great Elector Frederick Wilhelm of Brandenburg; organist, Cathedral, Berlin for 53 years.
Allein Gott in der Höh sei Ehr, in 20 Chorale Variations of
the German Sweelinck School, Bärenreiter.
Capriccio; Prelude; Fantasy, in Organum, Series IV,
Vol. 21.
chorale preludes (2) in Chorale Arrangements and Free

Compositions of the German Sweelinck School, Bären-
reiter.
KAUFFMANN, GEORG FRIEDRICH. born Ostermondra, Germany,
Feb. 14, 1679; died Merseburg, beginning of March, 1735.
Pupil of Buttstett and Alberti; substitute organist for Alberti
(organist at court and Cathedral, Merseburg); 1733, published
Harmonische Seelenlust.
   Allein zu dir, Herr Jesu Christ, in Hering's Orgel Musik,
      Rieter-Biedermann.
   Aus tiefer Not, in Cérémonies funèbres, L'Organiste
      liturgique, Vol. 15, p. 10.
   Choräle (62) mit beziffertem Bass, Bärenreiter 1925.
   Du hast, O Herr, dein Leben, in Choralvorspiele zum
      Kirchenlied, Vol. 3, Christophorus.
   Ein' feste Burg, in Orgel Choräle Sammlung, Metzler.
   Harmonische Seelenlust, Pierre Pidoux, ed. , Bärenreiter
      1924, 1951.
   Herr Gott, dich loben alle wir, in Seasonal Chorale Pre-
      ludes, Book 2, Oxford.
   Nun danket alle Gott, in The First Four Centuries of Organ
      Music, Vol. II, p. 450.
   Nun komm, in Viens, Sauveur, Orgue et Liturgie, Vol. 19,
      p. 10.
   O Gott du frommer Gott, in The Progressive Organist,
      Book 6, Oxford.
   O heiliger Geist, in Zorn's Prelude Collection, M. Bahn.
   O Jesulein süss, in Organ Music for Christmas, No. 2,
      Oxford.
   Six Chorales, from Harmonische Seelenlust, Richard Gore,
      ed. , organ and oboe, clarient or trumpet in B-flat,
      Concordia 97-4388.
   Six Chorale Preludes, Walter Emery, ed. , Novello.
   Valet, in Orgelspiel im Kirchenjahr, Vol. 2, Schott.
   Vater unser, in Notre Père, Orgue et Liturgie, Vol. 24,
      p. 21.
   chorale preludes (10) in Alte Weihnachtsmusik.
   chorale preludes (3) in Anthologie, Concordia.
   chorale preludes (3) in 18 Chorale Preludes, Pierre Pidoux,
      ed. , Ed. Foetisch.
   chorale preludes (2) in Eighty Chorale Preludes: German
      Masters of the Seventeenth and Eighteenth Centuries.
   chorale preludes (2) in Masterpieces of Organ Music,
      Folios 17 and 18.
   chorale preludes (2) in Orgelchoräle um J. S. Bach,
      G. Frotscher, ed. , Litolff.
   chorale preludes in The Parish Organist, Vol. 1-4.
   chorale preludes (3) in Reinbrecht's Sammlung, Viewig.
   chorale preludes (2) in Reinhard's Cecilia, Simon.
   chorale preludes (4) in 25 Chorale Preludes, Pierre Pidoux,
      ed. , Ed. Foetisch.
   compositions in Das Erbe deutschen Musik, Series I, Vol. 9.
KAUN, HUGO. born Berlin, Mar. 21, 1863; died Berlin, Apr. 2,
1932. 1879, studied at Musikhochschule, Berlin; 1887-1901,

came to the United States and lived in Milwaukee, Wis. ; encouraged by Theodore Thomas, Frederick Stock, and Wilhelm
Middleschulte; 1902, returned to Berlin to teach privately;
1912, became member, Academy of Arts, Berlin; 1922, became teacher of composition, Klindworth-Scharwenka Conservatory, Berlin;   taught Kaminski.

> Dir, dir, Jehova, in The International Organist, Vol. II,
> p. 12; also Kahnt.
> Fantasie über Morgenglanz der Ewigkeit, Kahnt.
> Fantasie und Fuge (C Minor), Op. 62, No. 2, Kahnt.
> Introduktion und Doppelfuge (D Minor), Op. 62, No. 1,
> Kahnt.
> Poetische Stimmungsbilder, Op. 110, 2 vols. , Zimmer-
> mann (Leipzig).
> Prelude on Gottlob es geht nun mehr, Kahnt.
> compositions (2) in Album für Orgel Spieler, Vol. 5, Kahnt.

KAY, ULYSSES SIMPSON. born Tucson, Ariz. , Jan. 7, 1917.
1938, B. M. , University of Arizona; studied at Eastman
School of Music; pupil of Hanson, Rogers, and Hindemith;
1949-1952, won Rome prize and Fulbright scholarship; since
1953, staff member, Broadcast Music, Inc.

> Two Meditations, Gray (Contemporary Organ Series 27).

KAYSER, LEIF. born Copenhagen, June 13, 1919. Studied at the
Royal Conservatory, Copenhagen; pupil of Hilding Rosenberg;
1936, became organist, St. Anthoni Kapel; 1937-1942, organist, St. Ansgar, Copenhagen; priest; 1942, studied in
Rome.

> Julesalmelege, Engstrom & SøEdring.
> Sonata 1969.
> Variazoni sopra In dulci jubilo, Op. 14, Skandinavisk.

KEBLE (see Keeble).
KEE, COR. born Zaandam, The Netherlands, Nov. 24, 1900. Pupil of Jan Zwart and dePauw; organist, Ronde Lutheran Church,
Amsterdam, and Lutheran Oude Kerk, Amsterdam; teacher of
improvisation, Summer Academy for Organists, Haarlem.

> Avondzang, Willemsen.
> Drie Inventionen, Donemus 478, 1967.
> Easter Song, Ars Nova.
> Ein' feste Burg (Een vaste Burgt), manualiter, Ars Nova
> 184.
> Fantasie on De Heer is God, Ars Nova.
> Fantasy on Now Thank We, Ars Nova.
> Fazen, Donemus.
> Hymn, Psalm 116, Willemsen.
> Inleidend Orgelspiel over Van u zyn alle dingen, Ars Nova.
> Kleine Partita op een oud Nederlandse lied.
> (De) Lofzang van Maria, in Cantantibus Organis, Vol. I,
> p. 19.
> Merck toch hoe sterck, con Variazioni, Alsbach.
> Onze Psalmen en Gesangen, Seyffardt.
> Paaslied op Jezus leeft, Partita, Alsbach.
> Partita op Psalm 106, Ars Nova.
> Partita op Psalm 116 (1914-1915), Ars Nova.

Postlude op Psalm 145 en Preludium op Psalm 22, Ars
    Nova.
Psalm 24, Willemsen.
Psalm 33, Willemsen.
Psalm 43, Willemsen.
Psalmen 46 an 47, Ars Nova.
Psalm 84, Willemsen.
Psalmen, 3 vols., Alsbach 15, 16, and 17.
Reeks Veranderingen, Donemus 476, 477, 1966-1967.
Scheepke onder Jezus hoede, Alsbach.
Six Psalm Tune Preludes, Edition Musicus.
Suite, Donemus, 1971.
Ten Psalms (to be played or sung at home, accompanied
    by little organ manual work, for two flutes) (with
    Piet Kee).
Three Psalms, Ars Nova.
Two Little Partitas on Psalm 26 and Psalm 33, Ars Nova.
Two Preludes and Fugues, Ars Nova 288.
U kan ik niet missen, Willemsen.
Variatie-Postludium en Reeks-Postludium, Donemus 479,
    1963.
Variations (4) on a tone-row, 1965-1966.
chorale preludes (5) in Christmas Music, Ars Nova.
KEE, PIET. born Zaandam, The Netherlands, Aug. 30, 1927.
Pupil of father, Cor Kee; studied at the Conservatory, Amster-
dam; pupil of Anthon van der Horst; 1953, became organist,
St. Laurens, Alkmaar; professor, Musieklyceum, Amsterdam;
since 1956, municipal organist, Sankt Bovokerk (Grote Kerk),
Haarlem; three-time winner, International Improvisation Com-
petition, Haarlem.
Four Manual Pieces, Donemus 480.
Inleidend Orgelspel over Gezang 265, God is tenenwoordig,
    Ars Nova 330, 1953.
Music and Space (1969), rondo for two organs and brass,
    Donemus.
Partita on Gott ist gegenwärtig, Hinrichsen.
Triptych on Psalm 86 (Chorale, Canon, and Toccata),
    Hinrichsen 810a, 1964.
Two Pieces (Fantasy on Sleepers, Wake; Passion Chorale),
    Hinrichsen 810b, 1964.
KEEBLE, JOHN. born Chichester, England, ca.1711; died London,
Dec. 24, 1786. Student of Pepusch; 1737, became organist,
St. George's, Hanover Square, London; 1742, appointed or-
ganist, church, Ranelagh.
Double-fugue (C Major), in Tallis to Wesley, Vol. 22, p. 5.
Forty Interludes, Novello, ca.1850.
Introduction and Allegro, in Old English Organ Music, John
    E. West, ed., Novello, ca. 1909.
Select Pieces, in English Organ Music of the Eighteenth
    Century, Vol. II, Vernon E. Butcher, ed., Hinrichsen
    293, 1953.
KELLER, HEINRICH MICHAEL. German. born 1638; died 1710.
Gelobet seist du, Jesus Christ, in Orgelchoräle um J. S.

Bach, G. Frotscher, ed. , Litolff.
composition in Das Erbe deutschen Musik, Series I, Vol. 9.
KELLER, HOMER. American. born 1917.
Fantasy and Fugue, Gray (Contemporary Organ Series 22).
KELLNER, JOHANN PETER. born Gräfenroda, Germany, Sept. 28,
1705; died Gräfenroda, Apr. 19, 1772. 1728, assistant Can-
tor, 1732, appointed Cantor, Gräfenroda.
Ausgewählte Orgelwerke, in Die Orgel, Series II, Vol. 7,
Concordia 97-4441.
Was Gott tut, in The Church Organist's Golden Treasury,
Vol. III, p. 122; also in Everybody's Favorite Series
No. 65, AMSCO.
chorale preludes (2) in Choralvorspiel alter Meister, pp. 80
and 84.
KELLY, BRYAN. born Oxford, England, 1934. Associate of the
Royal College of Music; 1958-1961, teacher, Royal Scottish
Academy of Music; since 1964, teacher, Royal College of
Music.
Exultate, in Modern Organ Music, Book I, p. 2.
Introduction and Allegro, Oxford.
Nativity Scenes, Stainer & Bell, 1966.
Prelude and Fugue, Novello, 1963.
KERCKHOVEN (KERKHOVEN), ABRAHAM VAN DEN. Christened
Brussels, May 2, 1627; died Jan. 9, 1702. 1647, became
court musician to Archduke Leopold Wilhelm of Austria; 1656,
appointed first organist, royal chapel.
Cinq versets pour le Salve regina, in Salve regina,
L'Organiste liturgique, Vol. 21, p. 28; also in
Altniederlandische Meister, Schott Frères.
Fantasia pro duplici organo, in European Organ Music of
the 16th and 17th Centuries, p. 29.
Fuga, in Anthologia pro Organo, Vol. II, p. 70.
Fuga, fantasie, in Oudnederlandse Meesters, Vol. III.
Fugue, Fantasy, in Anthologia pro Organo, Vol. I.
Werken voor Orgel, in Monumenta Musicae Belgicae,
Vol. 2.
compositions (2) in Oudnederlandse Meesters, Vol. I.
KERLL, JOHANN KASPAR. born Adorf, Germany, Apr. 9, 1627;
died Munich, Feb. 13, 1693. Studied in Vienna with Valentini;
pupil of Carissimi and perhaps Frescobladi; 1647, became
organist to Archbishop Leopold Wilhelm, Brussels; 1656-1674,
court musician, Munich; 1677-1684, became organist, St.
Stephen's Cathedral, Vienna; taught Murschhauser and Johann
Pachelbel; 1684, returned to Munich to be court organist.
Capriccio cucu, in The First Four Centuries of Organ
Music, Vol. II, p. 270.
Modulatio Organica, Kalmus 3576; also Süddeutsche Orgel-
meister des Barok, R. Walter, ed. , Vol. II, Coppen-
rath.
Passacaglia, in Alte Meister, p. 42; also in Chacones et
Passacailles, Orgue et Liturgie, Vol. 22, p. 8.
Toccata and Canzona, in Alte Meister des Orgelspiels,
Vol. I.

compositions in <u>Denkmäler der Tonkunst in Bayern</u>, Vol. II, p. 2.

compositions in <u>Masterpieces of Organ Music</u>, Folios 10 and 60.

compositions in <u>Ricercare, Canzonen und Fugen des 17. und 18. Jahrhunderts.</u>

compositions (4) in <u>Spielbuch für die Kleinorgel</u>, Vol. I.

KETTERING, EUNICE. American. born 1906. Graduate of Oberlin Conservatory of Music; pupil of Bartók, Lockwood, and Labunski; since 1935, professor of music literature, Ashland College, Ashland, Ohio.

    <u>(The) House of the Lord</u>, in <u>American Organ Music</u>, Vol. I, p. 24.

    <u>(The) Lord into His Garden Comes</u>, H. Flammer.

    <u>Paraphrase on an American Folk Hymn</u>, Gray.

KICKSTAT, PAUL. born Bochum, Germany, 1893; died 1959. Director of Church Music, Altona, Germany; Instructor, Church Music School, Hamburg; 1924-1954, organist-choirmaster, Christianskirche, Hamburg-Altona.

    <u>Choralvorspiele</u>, 7 vols., Moseler, 1952.

    <u>Ten Organ Postludes</u>, (Merseburger 803).

    <u>Quem Pastores</u>, in <u>The Parish Organist</u>, Vol. 6.

    chorale preludes (2) in <u>73 leichte Choralvorspiele, alter und neuer Meister</u>, H. Fleischer, ed., Leuckart.

KINDER, RALPH. born Stalybridge (Manchester), England, Jan. 27, 1876; died Bala (Philadelphia), Nov. 14, 1952. Studied in America; pupil of Lemare in London; organist in Philadelphia, Bristol, and Providence.

    <u>Aphrodite</u>, J. Fischer.

    <u>Arietta</u>, J. Fischer.

    <u>Berceuse</u>.

    <u>Caprice</u>.

    <u>Easter Hymn</u>, Theodore Presser.

    <u>Evensong</u>, J. Fischer.

    <u>Exultemus</u>, J. Fischer.

    <u>Fantasia on the Battle Hymn of the Republic</u>, J. Fischer.

    <u>Fantasia on Duke Street</u>, G. Schirmer.

    <u>Festival March</u>.

    <u>Grand Choeur</u>, G. Schirmer.

    <u>In Springtime</u>, J. Fischer.

    <u>Jour de printemps</u>, J. Fischer.

    <u>Jubilate Amen</u>, J. Fischer.

    <u>Moonlight</u>, J. Fischer.

    <u>Prelude and Fugue</u> (E Minor), J. Fischer.

    <u>Souvenir</u>, J. Fischer.

    <u>(A) Summer Morning</u>, J. Fischer.

    <u>Toccata</u> (D Major), J. Fischer.

    <u>Twilight Musings</u>, Theodore Presser.

KINDERMANN, JOHANN ERASMUS. born Nürnberg, Germany, Mar. 29, 1616; died Nürnberg, Apr. 14, 1655. Organist, Nürnberg; 1634, went to Italy where he might have studied with Frescobaldi; 1636, became second organist, Frauenkirche, Nürnberg; 1649-1655, organist, St. Egidienkirche, Nürnberg.

Fugue on Three Chorals, in Denkmäler deutscher Tonkunst,
Zweite Folge, Vol. 13.
Gloria, in Orgelchoräle des siebzehnten und achtzehnten
Jahrhunderts.
Harmonia Organica (1645), Süddeutsche Orgelmeister des
Barok, R. Walter, ed. , Vol. 9, Coppenrath.
Magnificat Cycle, in South German Christmas Music, p. 25.
Was mein Gott will, in The First Four Centuries of Organ
Music, Vol. II, p. 241; also in Eighty Chorale Pre-
ludes: German Masters of the Seventeenth and Eigh-
teenth Centuries.
chorale preludes (3) in The Parish Organist, Vol. 1-4.
compositions in Hirschberger Orgelbuch, Vol. 2, Reusch,
ed. , Littmann, 1936.
compositions (3) in Orgelwerke alter Meister aus Süddeutsch-
land, Metzger, ed. , Schultheiss, 1953.
KIRNBERGER, JOHANN PHILIPP. born Saalfeld, Germany, Apr. 24,
1721; died Berlin, night of July 26 and 27, 1783. Pupil of
Kellner and J. S. Bach; 1741-1751, served several Polish
nobles; violinist in royal chapel, Potsdam; 1745, served
Heinrich, Rheinsberg; 1758, became chief musician to Prin-
cess Anna Amalia; associated with C. P. E. Bach, J. Chris-
tian Bach, and Agricola.
Es ist das Heil, in Masterpieces for Organ, William C.
Carl, ed. , G. Schirmer.
Gelobet seist du, in Alte Weihnachtsmusik; also in Orgel-
spiel im Kirchenjahr, Vol. I, Schott.
Herr Jesu Christ, dich zu uns wend, Schott.
Herzlich tut mich verlangen, in Graveyard Gems, St.
Mary's Press.
Orgelchoräle, in Die Orgel, Series II, Vol. 14, Kistner &
Siegel (Concordia 97-4532).
Wer nur den lieben Gott lässt walten, Schott.
chorale prelude in The Church Organist's Golden Treasury,
Vol. II.
KITTEL, JOHANN CHRISTIAN. born Erfurt, Germany, Feb. 18,
1732; died Erfurt, Apr. 18, 1809. 1748, pupil of J. S. Bach,
Leipzig; 1751, became organist, Langensalza; 1756, ap-
pointed organist, Predigerkirche, Erfurt (Pachelbel, Buttstett,
and Adelung had been his predecessors); taught M. G. Fischer
and J. H. Chr. Rinck.
Christus der ist mein Leben, in Cäcilia, Breitkopf &
Härtel.
Ein' feste Burg, in Orgel Choräle Sammlung, Metzler.
Mache dich, mein Geist, in Seasonal Chorale Preludes
(with pedals), Book 2, Oxford.
Mir nach spricht, in Choralvorspiele zum Kirchenlied,
Vol. 3, Christophorus.
Prelude, in Harold Gleason, Method of Organ Playing,
p. 143.
Three Preludes, Walter Emery, ed. , Novello, 1958.
Twenty-four Chorale Preludes, Simrock.
Twenty-four Chorales, André.

Variations on Two Chorales, Hofmeister.
Wie schön leuchtet, in Der Praktische Organist, Part I,
Tascher'schen.
chorale prelude in The Church Organist's Golden Treasury,
Vol. I.
chorale preludes (3) in Anthologie, Concordia.
chorale preludes (2) in The Church Organist's Golden
Treasury, Vol. II.
chorale preludes (2) in Seasonal Chorale Preludes (for
Manuals), Book 1, Oxford.
KLEBE, GISELHER. born Mannheim, Germany, June 28, 1925.
Studied at the City Conservatory, Berlin; pupil of Rufer;
1946-1951, pupil of Boris Blacher; won several important
prizes for compositions.
Introitus, Aria ed Alleluja, Bote und Bock.
KLEBER, LEONHARD. born presumably in Württemberg, Germany,
ca. 1495; died Pforzheim, Mar. 4, 1556. 1524, date of organ
tablature book of collected organ and clavier music of different
composers, containing 112 pieces; 1517, became organist,
St. Dionys, Esslinger; 1521, appointed organist, St. Michaels,
Pforzheim.
Komm, Heiliger Geist, in Ritter's Sammlung, Ries & Erler.
Pange lingua, in Pange lingua, Reichling, ed. , Coppenrath.
Praeambulum in re, in Harold Gleason, Method of Organ
Playing, p. 132.
compositions (13) from Kleber's Tabulaturbuch, in Früh-
meister der deutschen Orgelkunst.
praeambula (2) in Historical Anthology of Music, Vol. I,
p. 89.
KLERK, ALBERT DE. born Haarlem, Oct. 4, 1917. Assistant
organist in Haarlem church as a boy; organist, St. Joseph's
Church, Haarlem; pupil of Anthon van der Horst; studied at
the Conservatory, Amsterdam; 1946, became teacher, Church
Music School, Utrecht; 1956, appointed city organist (with
Piet Kee), Haarlem.
Christe du bist licht ende dag, in Cantantibus Organis,
Vol. I, p. 40.
Concerto, organ and brass (2 horns, 2 trumpets, 2 trom-
bones), Donemus 448.
Fantasia primi toni: Ave maris stella, in Cantantibus
Organis, Vol. II, p. 36.
Fantasia septimi toni: Auctor beate saeculi, in Cantantibus
Organis, Vol. II, p. 38.
Inventionen (1945), Ars Nova.
Octo Fantasie on Gregorian Themes (1954), Van Rossum
R. 378 (Peters D 957).
Postludium, Annie Bank.
Prelude en Fuga (1940), Van Rossum R. 229.
Ricercare (Hommage à Sweelinck) (1954), Van Rossum
R. 342.
Sonata (1942), Donemus 221.
Ten Pieces, 2 vols. , Heuwekemeijer 288.
Variaties op O Jesu soet, Annie Bank.

KLOTZ, HANS. born Offenbach, Germany, Oct. 25, 1900. Studied
at Hoch Conservatory, Frankfurt; pupil of Straube and Widor;
1927, Ph. D. , Frankfurt; 1914-1918, organist, Christuskirche,
Frankfurt; served in Aachen, Flensburg; 1950-1953, teacher,
Schleswig-Holstein Music Academy, Lübeck; 1954, appointed
professor, director, Regional Hochschule für Musik, Cologne;
1958, became director of organ training, Evangelical Church,
Rheinland.
  Neunzehn Vorspiele zu Evangelischen Kirchenliedern,
      Bärenreiter 241, 1947.
  O du Liebe, in The Parish Organist, Vol. 1-4.
KLUGE, MANFRED. born Unna, Westphalia, Germany, July 16,
1928. Organ pupil of Hans Klotz; composition pupil of Olivier
Messiaen, Johannes Driessler, and Jens Rohwer; organist,
Hamburg-Eppendorf; since 1955, instructor in theory and or-
gan, Norddeutschen Orgelschule, and organist, St. Aegidien,
Lübeck.
  Fantasie in drei Rhythmen (1956), Breitkopf & Härtel
      6282, 1957.
  Vater unser (1963), Breitkopf & Härtel 6444, 1964.
KNAB, ARMIN. born Neu-Schleichach, Germany, Feb. 19, 1881;
died Bad Wörishofen, June 23, 1951. Studied at the Conser-
vatory, Würzburg; was a lawyer; 1934, appointed professor
of composition, Hochschule für Musikerziehung und Kirchen-
musik, Berlin.
  Sieben Orgel Choräle, Schott 3728, 1941.
  chorale preludes (2) in Orgel Vorspiele zu den Melodien des
      Choralbuchs, Leuckart.
KNECHT, JUSTIN HEINRICH. born Biberach, Germany, Sept. 30,
1752; died Württemberg, Dec. 1, 1817. Teacher, writer,
composer of theater music.
  Freu dich sehr, in The New Organist, Part II, J. Schu-
      berth.
  Herzliebster Jesu, in Zorn Sammlung, Bahn.
  O Lux beata, in Orgel Kompositionen aus alter und neuer
      Zeit, O. Gauss, ed. , Coppenrath.
  chorale preludes (3) in Reinbrecht's Sammlung, Viewig.
KNELLER (KNÜLLER), ANDREAS. born Lübeck, Germany,
Apr. 23, 1649; died Hamburg, Aug. 24, 1724. 1667, became
organist, Marktkirche St. Jakobi-St. Georgii, Hanover (suc-
ceeded Melchoir Schildt); 1685, appointed organist, St. Petri,
Hamburg (succeeded J. Schade); J. A. Reincken was his
father-in-law.
  Nun komm, in Choralvorspiel alter Meister, p. 88; also
        in Viens, Sauveur, Orgue et Liturgie, Vol. 19, p. 14.
  Präludium und Fuge (D Minor), in Organum, Series IV,
      Vol. 7.
KOCH, JOHANNES H. E. born Preusz, Börnecke, Germany, 1918.
Lecturer, Westfälische Landeskirchenmusikschule, Herford,
Germany.
  Da Christus geboren war, in The Parish Organist, Vol. 12.
  Einfache Vorspiele für Orgel, 2 vols. , Merseburger.
  Five Intradas and Chorales on Easter Hymns, organ and

trumpet, Concordia 97-4628, 1963.

chorale preludes in Orgelbuch zum Evangelischen Kirchengesangbuch, Books 11 (1), 13 (1), 17 (2), and 20 (1),
Bärenreiter.

KODÁLY, ZOLTÁN. born Kecskemet, Hungary, Dec. 16, 1882;
died Mar. 6, 1967. Studied at the University of Budapest;
deeply interested in folk music; associated with Béla Bartók;
pupil of Widor; 1919, became assistant director, Academy of
Music, Budapest.

Organoedia ad Missam lectam, Martin Hall, ed., Boosey &
Hawkes, 1966.

Praeludia (5), Universal 7941a.

Pange lingua, Universal 7941; also Boosey & Hawkes.

KOECHLIN, CHARLES. born Paris, Nov. 27, 1867; died Villa
Le Canadel (Var), Dec. 31, 1950. Studied at the Conservatory, Paris; classmate of Panel and Roger-Ducasse; taught
in the United States; taught Poulenc.

Adagio, Op. 201 (1944).

Adagio, Op. 201B (1944).

Adagio d'orgue, Op. 211 (1947).

Cent thèmes pour improvisations à l'orgue, Op. 192 (1943).

Choral, L'Oiseau-Lyre, 1924.

Deux sonatines, Op. 107 (1929).

Fugue, Op. 126 (1933).

Prélude No. XIV en canons, Procure du Clergé.

Première Sonatine, L'Oiseau-Lyre, 1929.

Quatre chorals en canon, Procure du Clergé.

Sonatine, L'Oiseau-Lyre.

Vingt-quatre petits chorals, 2 vols., Procure du Clergé.

KOERT, HANS VAN. born Den Haag, The Netherlands, 1913. 1937,
received Staatsdiploma in organ; pupil of Monnikendam; organist and teacher, Den Haag.

Fantasia, in Cantantibus Organis, Vol. II, p. 33.

KOETSIER, JAN. born Amsterdam, Aug. 14, 1911. Studied in
Berlin; 1942-1948, assistant conductor, Concertgebouw
Orchestra, Amsterdam; taught, Royal Conservatory, The
Hague; 1950, became orchestral conductor, Munich.

Choral Fantasy, Op. 42 (1955), Donemus 129.

Partita, Op. 41, No. 1, English horn and organ (manuals
only), Donemus 130, 1955.

Twelve Preludes and Fugues, Op. 32, Universal 11917,
1953.

KOHS, ELLIS BONOFF. born Chicago, Ill., May 12, 1916. Studied
at the Conservatory, San Francisco, and at the University of
Chicago; studied at Juilliard School of Music; pupil of Wagenaar and Piston; 1946-1948, joined faculty, Wesleyan University; 1948-1950, taught at the Conservatory, Kansas City;
since 1950, faculty member, University of Southern California.

Capriccio (1948), Mercury Music Corporation.

Passacaglia, organ and string orchestra (or organ and
piano), Gray, 1946.

Three Chorale Preludes on Hebrew Hymns, Mercury.

KOLB, KARLMANN. German. born 1703; died 1765. Organist,

Abbey, Aspach, Bayern, Germany;   tutor of Count Tatten-
bach's children, Munich.
> Certamen Aonium (1733), Willy Müller 22;   also Kalmus
>   3593;   also Süddeutsche Orgelmeister des Barok,
>   Vol. V, R. Walter, ed. , Coppenrath.
> compositions in Masterpieces of Organ Music, Folio 45.

KOTTER, HANS (JOHANNES).   born Strasbourg, Germany, ca. 1480;
died Berne, Switzerland, 1541.   1498-1500, pupil of Paul Hofhaimer;   1504-1522, organist, St. Nicholas Church, Freiburg,
Switzerland;   1532, returned after exile to become schoolmaster, Berne.
> Aus tiefer Not, in Orgelmusik der Reformationszeit, Jost
>   Harro Schmidt, ed. , Merseburger.
> Praeambulum in fa, in Historical Anthology of Music,
>   Vol. I, p. 89.
> Praeludium in fa, in Harold Gleason, Method of Organ
>   Playing, p. 138.
> Salve regina, in Salve regina, L'Organiste liturgique,
>   Vol. 21, p. 9.
> Uss tieffer nodt schry ich zw dir, in Geschichte der Musik
>   in Beispielen, p. 78.
> compositions (6) in Frühmeister der deutschen Orgelkunst.

KOX, HANS.   born Arnhem, The Netherlands, May 19, 1930.
Studied at the Conservatory, Utrecht;   pupil of Henk Badings;
director, music school, Doetinchem.
> Prelude and Fugue (1954), Donemus 171.

KRAFT, WALTER WILHELM JOHANN.   born Cologne, Germany,
June 9, 1905.   Studied at Vogt Conservatory, Hamburg;   organ
pupil of Hannemann;   studied with Hindemith at Musikhochschule, Berlin;   1924, became organist, Markuskirche, Hamburg;   organist, Lutherkirche, Altona-Bahrenfeld;   1929, appointed organist, Marienkirche, Lübeck, until it was destroyed
in 1942;   1945, became organist, St. Nikolai, Flensburg;   1947,
appointed director of organ class, professor, Musikhochschule,
Freiburg;   1950-1955, Director, Schleswig-Holsteinischen
Musikakademy and North German Organ School, Lübeck.
> Fantasia über Dies Irae, Schott, 1968.
> Partita über das Abendlied von Heinrich Schütz.
> Nun will sich scheiden Nacht und Tag, Bärenreiter 2430,
>   1949.

KRAPF, GERHARD.   born Meissenheim-bei-Lahr, Germany, Dec. 12,
1924.   Studied in Karlsruhe;   pupil of Pisk at the University of
Redlands, California;   organist-teacher in Michigan, Missouri,
and Wyoming;   head, organ department, University of Iowa.
> All Praise to Thee Eternal God, Augsburg 11-9075, 1966.
> Chorale Partita on Lord Jesus Christ, with us abide,
>   Concordia 97-4923.
> Christmas Sonata da Chiesa, J. Fischer.
> Come, Your Hearts and Voices Raising, Augsburg 11-9126.
> Dear Christians, One and All, Rejoice, Augsburg 11-0833,
>   1970.
> Little Organ Psalter, Carl Fischer.
> Partita on A Lamb Goes Uncomplaining Forth, Concordia

97-4952.
Partita on Lobe den Herren, Concordia 97-4748, 1965.
Partita on Mit Freuden zart, Concordia 97-4689, 1965.
Partita on Wie schön leuchtet, Concordia.
Reformation Suite, Concordia 97-5002.
Saviour of the Nations, Come, Augsburg 11-9367.
Shirleyn, in Voluntaries for the Christian Year, Vol. I,
    Abingdon.
Sonata I, "Historia Nativitatis," Concordia.
Sonata II, "Thanksgiving," J. Fischer.
Trumpet Tune, J. Fischer, 1962.
chorale preludes (5) in Organ Vespers, Augsburg.
chorale preludes in The Parish Organist, Vol. 11 (2) and
    Vol. 12 (2).

KREBS, JOHANN LUDWIG. born Büttelstädt, Germany, Oct. 10,
    1713; died Altenburg, Jan. 2, 1780. Pupil of his father;
    1726-1735, pupil of J. S. Bach in Leipzig; 1744, became
    organist, Zeitz; 1756, appointed organist, Altenburg.
    Ach Gott, in Choralvorspiel alter Meister, p. 90.
    Ach Gott, erhör mein, Cramer; also in Choral Vorspiele
        alter Meister, Peters.
    Ausgewählte Orgelwerke, Zollner, ed. , Peters 4179, 1938.
    Ausgewählte Orgelwerke, 3 vols. , in Die Orgel, Series II,
        Vols. 18, 20, and 21, Concordia 97-4645, 97-4683;
        organ and oboe, Concordia, 97-4807.
    Choral Vorspiele (15), C. Geissler.
    Choral Vorspiele (5), Koerner.
    Es ist gewisslich, in Eighty Chorale Preludes: German
        Masters of the Seventeenth and Eighteenth Centuries,
        p. 52; also in Chorale Preludes by Masters of the
        Seventeenth and Eighteenth Centuries, p. 38.
    Eight Chorale Preludes, organ and trumpet (or oboe),
        E. Power Biggs, ed. , Mercury Music Press, 1947.
    Fantasie (F Minor), oboe and organ, Breitkopf & Härtel
        4177.
    Fugue (G Major), Peters 4301G; also Hinrichsen 67.
    Ich steh' an deiner, in Organ Music for Christmas, Vol. 1,
        Oxford.
    Klavierübung, Hinrichsen 4178.
    O Ewigkeit, in Geschichte der Musik in Beispielen, p. 455;
        also in Organ Book No. 1, Ch. H. Trevor, ed. ,
        Oxford.
    Präludium und Fuge (C Major), in Historical Organ Recitals,
        Vol. III, p. 45; also Kahnt; also Mercury Music
        Press.
    Prelude and Fugue (F Minor), in Organ Book No. 2, p. 22.
    Preludes and Fugues and Trios, Kistner & Siegel.
    Sei Lob und Ehr, in Seasonal Chorale Preludes, Book 2,
        Oxford.
    Sleepers, Awake!, in A Treasury of Shorter Organ Classics,
        p. 4.
    Toccata (F), Cramer.
    Trio, in Harold Gleason, Method of Organ Playing, p. 152.

Trio (A Minor), in Organ Book No. 2, p. 25.
Two Trios, Cramer.
chorale preludes in The Church Organist's Golden Treasury,
    Vol. I (5), Vol. II (2), Vol. III (7).
chorale preludes (3) in Orgel Choräle Sammlung, Metzler.
chorale preludes (6) in Orgelchoräle um J. S. Bach, G.
    Frotscher, ed. , Litolff.
compositions in Elkan-Vogel Organ Series, Vol. 3.
compositions in Das Erbe deutschen Musik, Series I,
    Vol. 9.
compositions in Masterpieces of Organ Music, Folios 9,
    18, and 43.
compositions (6) in Musica Organi, Vol. I.
trios (5) in Schule des Klassischen Triospiels.
KREBS, JOHANN TOBIAS. born Heichelheim, Germany, July 7,
    1690; died Buttstädt, Feb. 11, 1762. Student of J. G.
    Walther in Weimar and J. S. Bach; 1721, became organist,
    Michaeliskirche, Buttstädt.
    Prelude and Fugue (C Major) and Trio (C Minor), under
        Johann Ludwig Kreb's name in Orgelwerke, J. L.
        Krebs.
    Wo Gott der Herr nicht bei uns, in Die Orgel, Series II,
        Vol. 20, Kistner & Siegel.
    compositions in Das Erbe deutschen Musik, Series I,
        Vol. 9.
KRECKEL, PHILIP G. born ?, 1897; died Rochester, N. Y. ,
    Nov. 9, 1964. Studied at the Conservatory, Munich; pupil
    of Reger and Ludwig Thuille; organist, St. Boniface Church,
    Rochester, N. Y. , for 55 years.
    Chorale Prelude on O Holy Name, McLaughlin & Reilly.
    Chorale Prelude on Lord, Bless Us All, McLaughlin &
        Reilly.
    Concordi Laetitia: O Sacrum Convivium, in Harold Gleason,
        Method of Organ Playing.
    Gloria, laus, et honor, in The Parish Organist, Vol. 1,
        J. Fischer.
    Melodia Sacra, 2 vols. , J. Fischer.
    Musica Divina, 3 vols. , J. Fischer.
    (The) Parish Organ Book, 2 vols. , , J. Fischer.
KŘENEK, ERNST. born Vienna, Austria, Aug. 23, 1900. Pupil of
    Schrecker; friend of Hermann Scherchen and Artur Schnabel;
    1939-1942, professor of music, Vassar College, Poughkeepsie,
    N. Y. ; 1942-1947, professor of music, Hamline University,
    St. Paul, Minn. ; 1947, affiliated faculty member, Chicago
    Musical College; 1954, became American citizen; 1947-1950,
    lived in Los Angeles.
    Sonata (1941), Op. 92, No. 1, Gray (Contemporary Organ
        Series 10), 1942.
    Toccata and Chaconne, Op. 13.
KRETSCHMAR, PAUL. born 1905. Director, Church Music,
    Evangelical Lutheran Freikirche, Germany; lives in Wittingen
    (Hannover), Germany.
    chorale preludes (2) in The Parish Organist, Vol. 1-4.

KRIEGER, JOHANN. born Nürnberg, Germany, Dec. 28, 1651;
died Zittau, July 18, 1735. After 1672, court organist,
Bayreuth; went to Halle; 1678, Kapellmeister to Count Heinrich I, Greiz; 1680, Kapellmeister to Duke Christian von
Sachsen, Eisenberg; 1682, appointed director, Chori Musici,
organist, St. Johanniskirche, Zittau; 1699, organist, St. Petri
and St. Pauli, Zittau.

   Christus der uns selig macht, in 73 leichte Choralvorspiele,
      alter und neuer Meister, H. Fleischer, ed. , Leuckart.

   Herr Christ, der einig Gottes Sohn, in The First Four
      Centuries of Organ Music, Vol. II, p. 347.

   Preludes and Fugues, in Die Orgel, Series II, Vol. 3,
      (Concordia 97-4407).

   Ricercar and Fugue, in Historical Anthology of Music,
      Vol. II.

   Vater unser, in Eighty Chorale Preludes: German Masters
      of the Seventeenth and Eighteenth Centuries, p. 108;
      also in Laudamus Dominum, p. 19; also in Nagel's
      Musik Archives.

   Vater unser, in Harold Gleason, Method of Organ Playing,
      p. 139.

   Vom Himmel hoch, in The New Organist, Part II, J.
      Schuberth.

   chorale preludes (2) in Masterpieces of Organ Music,
      Folios 15 and 17.

   chorale preludes (6) in Orgelchoräle um J. S. Bach, G.
      Frotscher, ed. , Litolff.

   chorale preludes (2) in Orgelspiel im Kirchenjahr, Vols. 1
      and 2, Schott.

   chorale preludes (3) in The Parish Organist, Vol. 1-4.

   compositions in Denkmäler der Tonkunst in Bayern, Vol. 18.

   compositions in Das Erbe deutschen Musik, Series I,
      Vol. 9.

   compositions (3) in Freie Orgelvorspiele vorbachischer
      Meister, Vol. I, Max Seiffert, ed. , Schultheiss, 1948.

   compositions (7) in Organum, Series IV, Vol. 17.

   compositions (6) in Spielbuch für die Kleinorgel, Vol. II.

KRIEGER, JOHANN PHILIPP, the elder. born Nürnberg, Germany,
Feb. 25, 1649; died Weissenfels, Feb. 7, 1725. Brother of
Johann; studied in Copenhagen; 1670, appointed court organist
and composer, Bayreuth; studied in Venice; friend of Carissimi; 1677-1680, chamber musician, organist, Halle; 1680,
appointed court conductor, Halle and Weissenfels.

   Ricercar; Fuga, in Historical Anthology of Music, Vol. II,
      p. 132.

   Sieben ausgewählte Orgelstücke, in Organum, Series IV,
      Vol. 17, (Concordia 97-4349).

   Toccata and Fugue (A Minor), in Spielbuch für die Klein-
      orgel, Vol. II, p. 16.

   Vater unser, in Notre Père, Orgue et Liturgie, Vol. 24,
      p. 17.

   compositions in Denkmäler der Tonkunst in Bayern,
      Vol. 18.

KROPFREITER, AUGUSTINUS FRANZ.   Austrain.   Twentieth cen-
   tury.   Organist, St. Florian Monastery, Austria.
   Ave regina coelorum (1964), Doblinger.
   Dreifaltigkeits-Triptychon (1959), Doblinger.
   (Ein) geistlich Konzert über Der Grimmig Tod, Doblinger.
   Four Pieces (1962), Doblinger.
   Introduction and Passacaglia (1961), Doblinger.
   Kleine Partita über Ach wie nichtig (1964), Doblinger.
   Kleine Partita über Ich wollt (1961), Doblinger.
   Kleine Partita über Wenn mein Stündlein (1961), Doblinger.
   Partita über Maria durch ein Dornwald ging (1959),
        Doblinger.
   Sonata I, Doblinger.
   Sonata II, Doblinger.
   Toccata francese, Oxford.
   Triplum super Veni creator spiritus (1969), Doblinger.
   Variationen über Freu dich, du Himmelskönigin, Doblinger.
KUBIK, GAIL.   born South Coffeyville, Okla., Sept. 5, 1914.
   Studied at the American Conservatory, Chicago; Studied at
   Eastman School of Music; composed for documentary pictures;
   1948, won a Guggenheim fellowship; 1950-1951, won American
   Rome prize; 1970, Visiting Professor of Music and Composer
   in Residence, Scripps College, Claremont, Calif.
        Quiet Piece, Gray (Contemporary Organ Series 19).
KUCHAŘ (KUCHARCZ), JAN KŘITAL.   born Chotecz, Czechoslovakia,
   Mar. 5, 1751; died Prague, Feb. 18, 1829.   Pupil of Seger;
   transcribed Mozart operas; organist, Heinrichskirche; later
   organist, Strahov Monastery; 1791-1800, conductor, Opera
   Theater.
        Pastorale, in A Century of Czech Music, Vol. I, p. 20.
KUHNAU, JOHANN.   born Geising, Germany, Apr. 6, 1660; died
   Leipzig, June 5, 1722.   Organist, St. Johanniskirche, Zittau;
   1684, appointed organist, St. Thomas, Leipzig; lawyer; 1688,
   founded Collegium Musicum, Leipzig; 1700, appointed music
   director, University of Leipzig; 1701-1722, Cantor, St.
   Thomas, Leipzig, and at St. Nicholas (predecessor of J. S.
   Bach).
        Ach Herr, in Historical Organ Recitals, Vol. I, p. 106.
        chorale prelude in The Church Organist's Golden Treasury,
            Vol. II.
        chorale prelude in The Parish Organist, Vol. 1-4.
        chorale preludes (2) in Choralvorspiel alter Meister.
        compositions in Denkmäler deutscher Tonkunst, Vol. IV.
        compositions in Organum, Series IV, Vol. 19, (Concordia
            97-4351).
KUNC, PIERRE.   born Toulouse, France, Oct. 28, 1865; died
   Toulouse, Dec. 29, 1941.   Choirmaster, St. Sulpice, Paris.
   Grande Pièce Symphonique, Leduc.

LA BARRE, DE.   French family.   Sixteenth and seventeenth centuries.

allemandes (2) in Les Maîtres français de l'orgue, Vol. II.

compositions (7) in Pré-Classiques français, L'Organiste liturgique, Vol. 18.

compositions (3) in Pré-Classiques français, L'Organiste liturgique, Vol. 31.

courantes (3) in Huit Courantes, L'Organiste liturgique, Vols. 58 and 59.

LABOLE, G.   French.   Twentieth century.   Pupil of Dupré; organist, Bordeaux.

Symphonie (B Minor), Bornemann, 1940.

LA CASINIERE, YVES DE.   born Angers, France, 1897. 1925, won Prix de Rome;   1953, principal inspector of music instruction.

Fugue, in L'Orgue Néo-classique, Orgue et liturgie, Vol. 33, p. 24.

Prélude et chorale, in Varia, Orgue et Liturgie, Vol. 66, p. 24.

LA GROTTE, NICOLAS DE.   French.   Sixteenth century.   Organist for Henry III of France.

Fantaisie, in L'Organiste liturgique, Vols. 29 and 30.

LA LANDE, MICHEL-RICHARD DE.   born Paris, Dec. 15, 1657; died Paris, June 18, 1726.   Chorister, St. Germain l'Auxerrois;   organist at the following churches in Paris: St. Gervais, St. Jean-en-Grève, Petit St. Antoine, Jesuits of the Maison Professe;   court organist to Louis XIV.

Suite Factice (transcription), in Orgue et Liturgie, Vol. 36.

LA MONTAINE, JOHN.   born Oak Park, Ill., Mar. 17, 1920. Studied at American Conservatory, Chicago;   pupil of Ganz; studied at Eastman School of Music;   pupil of Hanson and Bernard Rogers;   pupil of Wagenaar at the Juilliard School of Music;   1959, won a Pulitzer prize;   pupil of Boulanger;   1959, 1960, won two Guggenheim fellowships in composition;   1962, Composer-in-Residence, American Academy, Rome;   1964-1965, visiting professor, Eastman School of Music.

Elegy.

Even Song, Gray (St. Cecilia Series 889).

Processional, Gray (St. Cecilia Series 910).

LA MOTTE, DIETHER DE.   born Bonn, Germany, Mar. 30, 1928. Pupil of Conrad Hansen and composition pupil of Wilhelm Maler;   1950-1959, instructor of composition, form, and piano, Evangelischen Landeskirchenmusikschule, Düsseldorf;   1959-1962, Verlagslektor on the staff of B. Schott's Söhne, Mainz; since 1962, instructor of composition, 1964, Professor, Staatlichen Musikhochschule, Hamburg.

Präludium (1965), Bärenreiter 4144, 1967.

LANDMANN, ARNO.   born Blankenhain (Thuringia), Germany, Oct. 23, 1887.   Studied, Grossherzogliche Musikschule, Weimar;   pupil of Degner, Straube, and Reger;   1911-1942, organist, Christuskirche, Mannheim;   1942, organ teacher, Städtischen Hochschule für Musik und Theater, Mannheim; 1952, became organist, Rosengartens, Mannheim.

Choral Fantasien, Op. 13, Simrock.

Fantasie über Herzliebster Jesu, Op. 4a, Schott 1886.
In Memoriam, Op. 2, Pabst (Leipzig).
Passacaglia (C-sharp Minor), Op. 7, Benjamin.
Passacaglia und Fuga, Op. 11, Schott 1891.
Six Choral-improvisations, Op. 4b, Schott 1887.
Sonate in b moll, Op. 9, Schott 1889.
Variationen über Wer nur den lieben Gott, Op. 12, Schott 1892.
Vier Vortragstücke, Op. 10, Schott 1890.

LANG, CRAIG SELLAR. born New Zealand, 1891; died London, 1971. Associate, Royal College of Music; Mus. Doc., Durham University; 1929-1945, Director of Music, Christ's Hospital.

Chorale Prelude on Come, Holy Spirit, Stainer & Bell.
Chorale Prelude on Tallis' Canon, Year Book Press.
Introduction and Fugue on Redhead 46, Oxford.
Introduction and Passacaglia (A Minor), Novello, 1952.
Prelude, in An Album of Preludes and Interludes, Oxford.
Prelude and Fugue (G Minor), Novello.
Procession, in An Album of Postludes, Oxford.
Ten Short Preludes and Fugues, Op. 70, 2 books, Augener, 1956.
Three Chorale Preludes, Oxford.
Toccata in C Minor, Oxford.
Tuba Tune (D Major), Cramer.
Twenty Hymn-Tune Preludes, Op. 91, two sets, Oxford, 1966.
Two hymn-preludes, in Festal Voluntaries (Advent, Easter), Novello.

LANGGAARD, RUED IMMANUEL. born Copenhagen, July 28, 1893; died Ribe, July 10, 1952. Pupil of Johann Svend and C. F. E. Horneman; 1926-1930, organist of the church at Christiansborg Castle, Copenhagen; 1940, became organist, Cathedral, Ribe.

Fantasia patetico, Hansen 15086.
Toccata, Hansen 25088.
Toccata, Hansen 15092.

LANGLAIS, JEAN. born La Fontenelle, France, Feb. 15, 1907. Pupil of Dupré, Dukas, Marchal, and Mahaut; 1934, appointed organist, St. Pierre de Montrouge; since 1945, organist, Ste. Clotilde, Paris, (succeeded Tournemire); professor, Institut des Jeunes Aveugles.

American Suite (1959), Gray.
Concerto No. 1, organ, strings, 2 flutes, 2 oboes, 2 clarinets, 2 bassoons, Gray.
Concerto No. 2, organ and string orchestra, Gray.
Deux offertoires pour tour les temps sur des textes grégoriens (1943), (Durand, 1944) Elkan-Vogel, 1943.
Dominica in Palmis, in Passion, L'Organiste liturgique, Vol. 8, p. 21.
Douze Petites pièces pour orgue ou harmonium (1962).
Essai (1962), Bornemann, 1962.
Fête (1946), in The Modern Anthology, p. 118; also Gray (St. Cecilia Series 884-885).

Fête de la Sainte Famille (1958).

Folkloric Suite (Fugue sur O Filii; Legende de Saint
 Nicolas; Cantique; Canzona sur Adams Fall; Rhapsodie sur deux Noëls) (1937,1952), FitzSimons.

Homage à Frescobaldi (Prélude au Kyrie; Offertoire;
 Elévation; Communion; Fantaisie; Antienne; Thème
 et Variations; Epilogue) (1951-1952), Bornemann, 1952.

Homage à Rameau (1963), Elkan-Vogel.

Huit pièces modales (1956), Philippo, Elkan-Vogel, 1957.

Incantation pour un jour saint (1949), in Pâques, Orgue et
 Liturgie, 1949, Vol. I, p. 27.

In Dei Palmarum (1954).

Livre Oecuménique (12 pices), Bornemann (Gray).

Miniature (1958), Gray.

Missa Salve Regina, Costallat et Billaudot.

Neuf Pièces (Chant de peine; Chant de joie; Chant de paix;
 Chant héroïque; Dans une douce joie; De profundis;
 Mon âme cherche une fin paisible; Prélude sur une
 antienne; Rhapsodie grégorienne) (1942-1943), Bornemann, 1945.

Office pour la sainte famille (1957).

Organ Book (Prelude; Pastoral Song; Choral in E Minor;
 Flutes; Musette; Choral in F Major; Scherzando;
 Andantino; Epithalamium; Pasticcio) (1956), Elkan-
 Vogel, 1957.

Piece in Free Form, organ and string quartet (or string
 orchestra), Gray, 1960.

Poem of Happiness (1966), Elkan-Vogel.

Poem of Life (1965), Elkan-Vogel.

Poem of Peace (1966), Elkan-Vogel.

Poèmes évangeliques (L'Annonciation; La Nativité; Les
 Rameaux) (1932), Hérelle, 1936.

Prelude on Coronation (1963), in Modern Organ Music,
 Book 2, p. 16.

Prélude à la messe Orbis factor (1956), in Cantantibus
 Organis, Vol. I, p. 27.

Première Symphonie (1941-1942), (Hérelle) Philippo, 1944.

Quatre postludes (1950), McLaughlin and Reilly.

Rhapsodie Savoyarde (1960).

Scherzo-Cats (American Suite), Gray (St. Cecilia Series
 933).

Sonate en Trio, Bornemann, 1968 (Gray).

Suite Brève (Prélude; Cantilène; Plainte; Dialogue sur les
 mixtures) (1947), Bornemann, 1947.

Suite française (Prélude sur les grands jeux; Nazard; Contre-
 point sur des jeux d'anches; Française; Choral sur la
 voix humaine; Arabesque sur les flûtes; Méditation sur
 les jeux de fonds; Trio; Voix céleste; Final rhapsodique)
 (1948), Bornemann, 1948.

Suite médiévale (Prélude: Entrée; Tiento: Offertoire; Improvisation: Elévation; Méditation: Communion; Acclamations) (1947), Salabert, 1950.

Thème, variations et final, organ and string orchestra,

trumpets, trombones.
Three Characteristic Pieces (1956-1957), Novello.
Three Voluntaries, FitzSimons, 1970.
Triptyque (1954-1956), Novello.
Trois Méditations sur la sainte Trinité (1962), Philippo.
Trois paraphrases grégoriennes (Ave Maris, Ave maris
    stella; Mors et resurrectio; Te Deum) (1933-1934),
    (Hérelle) Philippo, 1933-1934.
Vingt-quatre pièces pour orgue ou harmonium (1933-1939),
    Hérelle, Vol. I, 1939; Vol. II, 1942.
LANGSTROTH, IVAN SHED. born Alameda, Calif., Oct. 16, 1887;
    died New York City, Apr. 25, 1971. Studied in San Francisco
    and Berlin; pupil of Humperdinck and Lhevinne; 1916, became
    organist, American Church, Berlin; 1917-1920, toured Scan-
    dinavia as concert pianist; 1921-1928, teacher, New Conser-
    vatory, Vienna; 1943-1945, lecturer, Brooklyn College, New
    York.
    At the Cradle, Novello 278 O. C. (N. S.).
    Chorale-Toccata and Fugue, Novello, 1956.
    Fantasy and Fugue, Novello, 1956.
    Four Chorale Preludes, Gray (St. Cecilia Series 668).
    Interlude on Winchester Old, Novello.
    Introduction and Fugue, Gray.
    Theme with Variations, Novello.
    Three Chorale Preludes, Novello.
    Toccata (A Major), Gray (St. Cecilia Series 861).
    Two Hymn Preludes, in Festal Voluntaries (Christmas,
        Harvest), Novello.
LASCEUX, GUILLAUME. born Poissy, France, Feb. 3, 1740;
    died Paris, 1831. Organist, Chevreuse; before 1769, organist
    of the Mathurins, Cloister Ste. Aure; organist, St. Etienne-
    du-Mont.
    Fugue de l'office du Très Saint Sacrement, in Les Maîtres
        français de l'orgue, Vol. I, p. 93.
    compositions in Les Maîtres français de l'orgue, Vol. II.
LASSUS, ROLAND DE (ORLANDUS) (ORLANDO DI LASSO). born
    Mons, Belgium, 1532; died Munich, June 14, 1594. Chorister,
    Church of St. Nicolas, Mons; kidnapped three times because
    of his beautiful voice; 1544, began service to several nobles;
    1556-1594, served court of Albert V of Bavaria.
    Christ ist erstanden, in Cantantibus Organis, Vol. 6,
        F. Pustet.
    Ricercar, in Oudnederlandse Meesters, Vol. II, p. 40.
    Ricercar (Regina coeli laetare), in Oudnederlandse Meesters,
        Vol. II, p. 40.
    chorale prelude in The Parish Organist, Vol. 1-4.
LA TOMBELLE, FERNAND DE (FRANÇOIS DE). born Paris,
    Aug. 3, 1854; died Château de Fayrac, Aug. 13, 1928. Pupil
    of Guilmant, Saint-Saëns, and Dubois; studied at the Conser-
    vatory, Paris; 1885-1898, assistant to Dubois at La Madeleine;
    1896-1904, taught at Schola Cantorum.
    Elegy and Festal March, G. Schirmer.
    Meum ac vestrum, Hérelle.

Offertory for Pentecost, Durand.
Pastorale offertoire, Durand.
Six pièces, 2 vols. , Janin (Lyon), 1912.
Six versets, Durand
Toccata, Edition Musicus.
Vêpres d'un confesseur pontife, Schola Cantorum.
Voces Belli, Ledent-Malay, Brussels, 1921.
LA TORRE, F. DE. Spanish. ca. 1500.
　　Alta, in Historical Anthology of Music, Vol. I, p. 103.
LA VIGON (melody)
　　courantes (2) in Huit Courantes, L'Organiste liturgique,
　　　　Vols. 58-59.
LAZARE-LÉVY (LÉVY, LAZARE). born Brussels, Jan. 18, 1882;
　　died Paris, Sept. 20, 1964. Professor of piano, Ecole Nor-
　　male and Conservatory, Paris.
　　Adagio.
　　Allegro molto.
LEBÈGUE, NICOLAS. born Laon, France, 1631; died Paris,
　　July 6, 1702. Perhaps pupil of Chambonnières and Etienne
　　Richard; one of four organists of the Chapelle Royale; 1664-
　　1702, organist, St. Merry; taught de Grigny and Dagincourt.
　　Chacone grave (G Major), in Chacones et Passacailles,
　　　　Orgue et Liturgie, Vol. 22, p. 16.
　　(Les) Cloches, in Anthology of Early French Organ Music,
　　　　p. 35; also in The First Four Centuries of Organ
　　　　Music, Vol. II, p. 283.
　　Noël: Cette journée, in Brief Compendium of Early Organ
　　　　Music.
　　Noël sur Une vierge pucelle, in Historical Organ Recitals,
　　　　Vol. I, p. 64; also in Historical Anthology of Music,
　　　　Vol. II, p. 96; also in Organ Music for Christmas,
　　　　Vol. 2, Oxford.
　　Noëls variés, in Orgue et Liturgie, Vol. 16.
　　Messe (Second livre d'orgue), in Orgue et Liturgie, Vol. 29,
　　　　p. 3.
　　Offertoire (F Major), in Passion, L'Organiste liturgique,
　　　　Vol. 8, p. 18.
　　Puer nobis nascitur, in Organ Music for Christmas, Vol. 3,
　　　　Oxford; also Gray.
　　Symphony in B-flat Major, in Anthology of Early French
　　　　Organ Music, p. 40.
　　Trois livres d'orgue, in Archives des maîtres d'orgue des
　　　　seizième-dix-huitième siècles, Vol. IX; also Schott.
　　compositions (4) in Douze Noels anciens, Schott Frères.
　　compositions (4) in Liber Organi, Vol. I.
　　compositions (5) in Les Maîtres français de l'orgue, Vol. I.
　　compositions in The Parish Organist, Vols. 5 and 6.
　　Mass movements (2) in Harold Gleason, Method of Organ
　　　　Playing, pp. 65 and 66.
　　noels (2) in Les Maîtres français de l'orgue, Vol. II.
LE BOUCHER, MAURICE-GEORGES-EUGÈNE. born Isigny-sur-
　　Mer, France, May 25, 1882. Pupil of Fauré; 1920, ap-
　　pointed director, Conservatory, Montpellier.

Symphonie en mi majeur, Leduc, 1917.
LECHNER, KONRAD.   born Nürnberg, Germany, Jan. 24, 1911.
   Pupil of Carl Orff, J. N. David, and W. Fortner; 1941-1945,
   teacher, Mozarteum; 1948, became professor, Musikhoch-
   schule, Freiburg; 1953, appointed director, Music Academy,
   Darmstadt.
   Drei Orgelstücke, Gerig.
LECHTHALER, JOSEF.   born Rattenberg, Austria, Dec. 31, 1891;
   died Vienna, Aug. 21, 1948.   Musicologist; pupil of Adler in
   Vienna; 1919, Ph. D.; 1925, began teaching theory, Vienna
   Academy of Music; 1933-1938, 1945-1948, Director, Church
   Music School, Vienna.
   Chorale Fantasie über In dich hab' ich, Op. 31, Oester-
      reichischer Bundesverlag.
   Prelude and Fugue on Gaudeamus omnes, Op. 24, Böhm.
   Six Organ Preludes for Christmas, Op. 17, Böhm.
LE COCQ, ALEXANDRE CHARLES.   born Paris, June 3, 1832;
   died Paris, Oct. 24, 1918.   Studied at the Conservatory,
   Paris; pupil of Halévy and Benoist; operetta composer.
   (La) Berceuse des anges, in Noël, p. 11.
LEFÉBURE-WÉLY, LOUIS-JAMES-ALFRED.   born Paris, Nov. 13,
   1817; died Paris, Dec. 31, 1869.   Pupil of Halévy, Adolphe
   Adam, and Séjan; organist, St. Roch; organ pupil of Benoist
   at the Conservatory, Paris; 1847-1857, organist, La Made-
   leine; 1863, became organist, St. Sulpice.
   Adeste fideles, Schott.
   (L')Office catholique, Regnier-Canaux (Paris), 1860.
   (L')Organiste moderne, Schott.
   Processional on Adoro te devote, Novello.
   Six grandes offertoires, Op. 35, Novello.
LEGUAY, JEAN-PIERRE.   born Dijon, France, July 4, 1939.   Or-
   gan pupil of André Marchal, Gaston Litaize, and Rolande Fal-
   cinelli; composition pupil of Olivier Messiaen; 1961, became
   organist, Notre-Dame-des-Champs, Paris; since 1968, pro-
   fessor of organ and music history, Conservatory, Limoges.
   Au maître de la paix (Maison de Dieu; Christ lien de la
      charité; Moisson de joie), Orgue et Liturgie, Vol. 73.
   Cinq versets sur Veni Creator, in L'Organiste liturgique,
      Vol. 53, p. 10.
LEIDING, GEORG DIETRICH (see Leyding).
LEIGHTON, KENNETH.   born Wakefield, Yorkshire, England,
   Oct. 2, 1929.   Studied at Royal College of Music, Queen's
   College, and Oxford; 1953-1956, Gregory Fellow, Leeds
   University; 1956, became lecturer, University of Edinburgh;
   won many composition prizes.
   Et Resurrexit, Op. 49, Novello, 1968.
   Fanfare, in Easy Modern Organ Music, Book 1, Oxford.
   Festival Fanfare, Carl Fischer.
   Paean, in Modern Organ Music, Book 2, p. 2.
   Prelude, Scherzo and Passacaglia, Novello.
LEINERT, FRIEDRICH OTTO.   born Oppeln, Germany, May 10,
   1908.   Studied in Dresden; 1931, was pupil of Schoenberg in
   Berlin; 1932-1944, chorus master in various theaters; 1945-

1952, organist, St. Marien, Marburg/Lahn; 1954, went to Hannover.

Erste Sonate (1950), Breitkopf & Härtel 5979, 1952.

LE JEUNE, CLAUDE. born Valenciennes, France, ca. 1530; died Paris, Sept. 25, 1600. Composer of chamber music for the king; 1552-1564, possibly studied with Willaert in Italy; 1564, resided in Paris; 1589, fled from Paris since he was Protestant; wrote Fantaisies instrumentales for organ or viole found in a collection entitled Mélanges (1612); 1596, "Maistre compositeur ordinaire de la Musique de nostre chambre" in royal service; 1600, "compositeur de la musicque de la chambre du roy."

Trois instrumental fantasies, from Second Livre des Meslanges, in Orgue et Liturgie, Vol. 39.

LEMARE, EDWIN HENRY. born Ventnor, Wight, Sept. 9, 1865; died Los Angeles, Sept. 24, 1934. Studied at the Royal Academy of Music; head positions in Cardiff and Sheffield; 1892, became organist, Holy Trinity, London; 1897, appointed organist, St. Margaret's, London; 1902-1905, organist and director of music, Carnegie Hall, Pittsburgh; 1917-1921, municipal organist, San Francisco; municipal organist, Portland; 1924-1929, city organist, Chattanooga.

Adeste fideles, Theodore Presser.
Allegro pomposo, Op. 86, Schott.
Andantino (D-flat Major), Novello.
Andantino (D Minor), G. Schirmer.
Arcadian Idyll, Op. 52.
Aria and Variations (B-flat Major), Schott.
Auf der Suche, Op. 92, Schott.
Barcarolle.
Bell Scherzo, Op. 89, Schott.
Berceuse (D Major).
Caprice orientale, organ and orchestra, Novello.
Carillon, Op. 76.
Chant sans paroles.
Christmas Bells, Gray.
Christmas Song, Op. 82, Schott.
Communion, Gray.
Concert Fantasy on Hanover, Novello.
Concert Gavotte, Gray.
Concert Piece No. 2 (Tarantella), Op. 90, Schott.
Concertstücke (Polonaise), Schott, 1911.
Dream Frolic, Gray (St. Cecilia Series 164).
Dream Song, Gray (St. Cecilia Series 165).
Easter Morn, Gray (St. Cecilia Series 193).
Fantasy and Fugue (E Minor), Op. 99, Schott.
Festival Suite, Op. 100, Schott, 1920.
Folk Song, Gray (St. Cecilia Series 146).
Gavotte, Op. 84, Schott.
Improvisation (C Major), op. 91, Schott.
Inspiration, Gray (St. Cecilia Series 181).
Joyful Memory, Op. 87, Schott.
Lament, Op. 79, Schott.

Madrigal.
Marche solennelle.
Meditation (D-flat).
Minuet Nuptiale, Op. 103.
Moonlight, Op. 83, No. 2, Schott.
Moonlight, Op. 104, G. Schirmer.
Morning, Op. 94, Schott.
Morning Serenade, Op. 105, G. Schirmer.
Morning Serenade, Op. 145, A. P. Schmidt.
October Serenade, Gray (St. Cecilia Series 195).
Onward, Christian Soldiers, Theodore Presser.
Rhapsodie (C Minor), organ and orchestra, Novello.
Romance Triste, Gray (St. Cecilia Series 182).
Rondo Capriccioso, Op. 64.
Schlummerlied, Op. 81, Schott.
Second Romance (D-flat), Gray (St. Cecilia Series 144).
Serious Variations, Op. 96, Schott.
Seven Descriptive Pieces, Gray.
Sonata I (F Major), Op. 95, Schott, 1914.
Spring Song, Op. 56.
Symphonie No. 2 (D Minor), Op. 50, organ and orchestra,
    Novello.
Toccata and Fugue (D Minor), Op. 98, Schott.
Twelve Short Pieces, Gray.
Twilight Sketches, Op. 138, A. P. Schmidt.
Victory March, Gray (St. Cecilia Series 131).
Wedding Blessing, Op. 85, Schott.
Weeping and Laughing, Op. 133, J. Fischer.
Woodland Idylle, Op. 135, A. P. Schmidt.
LEMMENS, JACQUES-NICOLAS. born Zoerle-Parwije, Belgium,
    Jan. 3, 1823; died Linterpoort, Belgium, Jan. 30, 1881. Pu-
    pil of Hesse (a pupil of Forkel) and Fétis; 1849, appointed pro-
    fessor of organ, Conservatory, Brussels; introduced Bach and
    German composers of the seventeenth century to organists of
    his time; taught Widor, Guilmant, Loret, and Alphonse Mailly;
    wrote Ecole d'orgue (1862).
    Album (12 pieces).
    Canon, in Harold Gleason, Method of Organ Playing, p. 134.
    Fanfare, Gray.
    Organ School, after Gregorian Chants, Schott.
    Prelude (E-flat Major), in Historical Organ Recitals, Vol. V,
        p. 21.
    Sonata No. 2, O Filii, W. Paxton.
    Three Sonatas (Pontificale; O filii; Pascale), Novello.
    Trois Pièces, Hamelle.
LENEL, LUDWIG. born Strasbourg, France, 1914. Head, Music
    Department, Muhlenberg College, Allentown, Pa.
    Fantasy on In the Midst of Earthly Life, Concordia 97-4783.
    Fantasy (Variations) on Splendor Paternae Gloriae, organ,
        celesta, and chimes.
    Four Organ Chorales, Concordia.
    Prelude to the Quempas Carol, Chantry.
    Three Chorale Fantasies on Pre-Reformation Hymns: Christ

Is Arisen; We Now Implore the Holy Ghost; All Praise to Thee, Eternal God, Concordia 97-4663.

chorale preludes in The Parish Organist, Vols. 1-4, 5, 6, 7, and 8.

LESUR, DANIEL-JEAN-YVES (DANIEL-LESUR). born Paris, Nov. 19, 1908. Studied at the Conservatory, Paris; pupil of Tournemire and, 1927-1937, his assistant at Ste. Clotilde; 1935-1939, professor, Schola Cantorum; organist for the Benedictines, Rue de la Source, Paris; 1957, became director, Schola Cantorum.

Hymnes, Leduc, 1935-1939.

In Paradisum, Leduc, 1933.

Scène de la Passion (1931), Leduc.

Quatre hymnes, in Liturgie et Concert, Orgue et Liturgie, Vol. 70, p. 6.

(La) Vie intérieure (1932), Lemoine.

LETOCART, HENRI. born Courbevoie, France, 1866; died Paris, 1945. Pupil of Franck; 1900, became organist, St. Pierre, Neuilly; music editor.

Trois pièces, Noël, 1907.

LEUPOLD, ANTON WILHELM. born Haber, Austria, Apr. 22, 1868; died Berlin, June 16, 1940. Studied at the Stern Conservatory and Academy of Music, Berlin; 1899-1939, organist, St. Peter's Church, Berlin; taught at the Klindworth-Scharwenka Conservatory.

Legende, Op. 11, violin and organ, Ries & Erler.

Liturgical Chorale Book, Augsburg.

(An) Organ Book, Chantry; also Merseburger 828.

LEUPOLD, ULRICH S. born Berlin, Jan. 15, 1909; died Waterloo, Ontario, Canada, June 9, 1970. Pupil of his father, Anton Wilhelm Leupold; 1932, Ph. D., University of Berlin; 1969, D. D., Knox College, University of Toronto; 1938-1939, Minister of Music, Augsburg Lutheran Church, Toledo, Ohio; 1939-1942, assistant pastor, St. Matthew's Lutheran Church, Kitchener, Ont.; 1942-1945, pastor, Christ Church, Maynooth, Ont.; 1945-1970, Dean, professor of New Testament Theology and Church Music, 1969-1970, Head, Waterloo Lutheran Seminary, Waterloo, Ont.

Rejoice in the Lord, Augsburg.

(The) Two-staff Organ Book, 2 vols., Waterloo Music Co.

Wedding Processional and Air, Augsburg 11-826.

LEY, HENRY GEORGE. born Chagford, England, Dec. 30, 1887. Studied at the Royal College of Music; pupil of Parratt; studied at the Keble College, Oxford; 1909, appointed organist, Christ Church Cathedral, Oxford; 1914, Mus. Doc., Oxford; 1926-1945, Director of Music, Eton College, Windsor; taught at the Royal College of Music.

Adagio, in Book of Simple Organ Voluntaries, Oxford.

Cradle Song on Come rock the cradle for Him, Oxford.

Fantasy on the Welsh Tune Aberystwyth, Oxford.

Jubilate Deo, Oxford.

Prelude on Down Ampney, Oxford.

Prelude on St. Columba, in Hymn Tune Voluntaries, Oxford.

LEYDING, GEORG DIETRICH.   born Bücken bei Hoya an der Weser,
Germany, Feb. 23, 1664;   died Braunschweig, May 10, 1710.
1679-1684, student of Jakob Bölsche in Braunschweig;   heard
Reincken and Buxtehude; substituted for Bölsche;   1684, be-
came organist, St. Ulrich, St. Blasius, and later St. Magnus.
    Praeludium, in Die Orgel, Series II, Vol. 15, Concordia
        97-4551.
    Prelude (E-flat Major);   Prelude (C Major), in Organum,
        Series IV, Vol. 7.
LIBERT, HENRI.   born Paris, Dec. 15, 1869;   died Paris, Jan. 14,
    1937.   Studied at the Conservatory, Paris;   pupil of Franck
    and Widor;   organist, St. Denis;   taught at the American Con-
    servatory, Fontainebleau.
    Duo en forme de canon, Sénart.
    Fugue en re mineur, Sénart.
    Prélude en mi mineur, Sénart, 1912.
    Prière, Leduc, 1894.
    Romance sans paroles, in The French Organist, Vol. I,
        p. 8;   also Leduc, 1894.
    Variations symphoniques en forme de passacaille, Lemoine,
        1925.
LIDON, JOSÉ.   born Béjar, Salamanca, Spain, 1752;   died Madrid,
    Feb. 11, 1827.   Organist, Cathedral, Malaga;   1787, became
    organist, Chapel Royal, Madrid.
    Sonata de 1º Tono, in Silva Iberica, p. 28.
LINDBERG, OSKAR.   born Gagnef, Sweden, Feb. 23, 1887;   died
    Stockholm, April 1955.   Studied at the Conservatory, Stock-
    holm, and in Germany;   1904, became organist, Trefaldighet-
    skirke, Stockholm;   1914, appointed organist, Engelbretktskirke,
    Stockholm;   1919, teacher, 1936, professor, Conservatory,
    Stockholm;   1922, director, Academy Orchestra, Stockholm.
    Bröllopsmusik, Nordiska Musikförlaget.
    Den signade dag, Nordiska Musikförlaget.
    En gammal psalmmelodi från Mora, Elkan & Schildeknecht,
        Emil Carelius.
    Fyra Orgelkoraler, in Musica Organi, Vol. III, p. 118.
    Gammal fäbodpsalm, Nordiska Musikförlaget.
    Introitus solemnis, Nordiska Musikförlaget.
    Jeg haver en gång varit ung, Elkan & Schildeknecht, Emil
        Carelius.
    Marcia funebre, Nordiska Musikförlaget.
    När stormens lurar skalla, Nordiska Musikförlaget.
    Orgelkoraler (3), Carl Gehrmans musikförlag.
    Orgelkoraler (4), in Musica Organi, Vol. III.
    Preludier till den svenska koralbokens samtliga koraler,
        Verbum förlag.
    Sonat (G Minor), Op. 23 (1924), Nordiska Musikförlaget.
    Variationer över en gammal dalakoral, Nordiska Musik-
        förlaget.
LINDEMAN, LUDVIG MATHIAS.   born Trondheim, Norway, Nov. 28,
    1812;   died Christiana (Oslo), May 23, 1887.   1839, became
    organist, Our Saviour's Church, Oslo;   1849, appointed singing
    teacher, University Theological Seminary;   1883, founded music

school.
> Choral variations on Wer nur, Edition Lyche 227.
> Three Fugues on B-A-C-H, Norsk Musikforlag.

LISZT, FRANZ. born Raiding (near Odenburg), Hungary, Oct. 22, 1811; died Bayreuth, July 31, 1886. Pupil of Czerny, Salieri, and Reicha; became famous as concert pianist and teacher; lived in Paris, Geneva, and later Rome; 1848-1859, Kapell- meister, Weimar; created the symphonic tone poem; 1866, Pope Pius IX named him Abbé; 1875, named president of the Academy of Music, Pest.
> Christmas Tree, 2 vols., Peters H88a/b; also Gray.
> Complete Organ Works, K. Straube, ed., 2 vols., Peters 3628A/B.
> Fantasia and Fugue on B-A-C-H, C. H. Trevor, ed., Novello; also in Musica Organi, Vol. I, p. 155.
> Four Compositions, Pécsi, ed., Kultura (Boosey & Hawkes).
> March of the Magi, violin, 'cello, harp, and organ, Gray.
> Nun danket alle Gott, Breitkopf & Härtel.
> Organ Works, 2 vols., Kalmus 3615, 3616; also M. Dupré, ed., Bornemann.
> Organ Works, 2 vols., Peters 3628 a/b: Vol. I: Variations on Weinen, klagen (1863); Evocation; Ave verum (Mo- zart); Ora pro nobis; Hymnus; Ave Maria (Arcadelt); Angelus; Introitus; Trauerode. Vol. II: Fantasy and Fugue on Ad nos (1850); Prelude and Fugue on B-A-C-H (1855; 1870); Adagio; Salve Regina; Ave maris stella; Organ Mass (1879); Organ Requiem (1933); Wedding Music.
> St. François de Paule marchant sur les flots, W. S. Meyer, ed., (Peters F71); also L. Saint-Martin, ed., Leduc.
> Shepherds at the Manger, violin, 'cello, harp, and organ, Gray.
> Thirteen Compositions, Gergely, ed., Kultura (Boosey and Hawkes).

LITAIZE, GASTON. born Menil-sur-Belvite, France, Aug. 2, 1909. Studied at the Institut des Jeunes Aveugles and Conservatory, Paris; pupil of Marty, Dupré, and Busser; organist, St. Léon, Nancy, and organist, St. Cloud; professor, Institut des Jeunes Aveugles; organist, St. François Xavier, Paris.
> Cinq pièces liturgiques pour orgue sans pédales, Schola Cantorum, 1950.
> Cortège, organ and brass, in Orgue et Liturgie, Vol. 9, p. 1 (1951).
> Douze pièces (Variations sur un Noël angevin, and others), 2 vols., Leduc, 1931-1939.
> Fugue sur l'Introit Da pacem, in La Fugue, Orgue et Liturgie, Vol. 20, p. 1.
> Grande Messe pour tous les temps, Schola Cantorum, 1949.
> Grand' Messe, in Orgue et Liturgie, Vol. 29.
> Messe basse pour tous les temps, in Orgue et Liturgie, Vol. 42 (1948).
> Messe de la Toussaint, in L'Organiste liturgique, Vol. 47.
> Noël basque, in Noël, Orgue et Liturgie, Vol. 4, p. 27,

1949.
Organ Suite, McLaughlin and Reilly M-2207.
Passacaille, organ and orchestra, 1947 manuscript.
Prélude et Danse fuguée, Leduc, 1964.
Thème et variations sur le nom de Victor Gonzalez, in
Le Tombeau de Gonzalez, Orgue et Liturgie, Vol. 38,
p. 9.
Toccata sur le Veni creator.
Vingt-quatre préludes liturgiques, in L'Organiste liturgique,
Vols. 1, 4, and 9.
LLUSÁ (LLISSA), FRANCESC (FRANCISCO). Spanish. Seventeenth
century-eighteenth century.
Tres Versillos de 6.º tono para Sanctus, in Antologia de
Organistas Clásicos Españoles, Vol. II, p. 11.
Trois versets de Segon To, in Early Spanish Organ Music,
p. 66.
Trois versets du VIe ton, in Les Anciens Maîtres Espagnols,
p. 21.
LOCKE, MATTHEW. born Exeter, England, ca. 1630; died London,
August 1677. 1638, choirboy at the Cathedral, Exeter; wrote
music for drama.
Melothesia, Organ Voluntaries, Thurston Dart, ed., Stainer
and Bell, 1957.
Seven Voluntaries from Melothesia, Hinrichsen 1630A.
Toccata (A Minor), John E. West, ed., Novello, 1906.
Two Voluntaries, John E. West, ed., Novello, 1905/1906.
LOCKWOOD, NORMAND. born New York City, Mar. 19, 1906.
Studied at the University of Michigan; pupil of Respighi and
Boulanger; 1930, won fellowship to the American Academy,
Rome; 1943-1945, instructor, Oberlin Conservatory; 1943-
1945, won Guggenheim Fellowship; 1945-1953, lecturer,
Columbia University; 1953-1955, faculty member, Trinity
University, San Antonio, Texas; 1955, joined faculty, Univer-
sity of Wyoming; 1959, faculty member, University of Denver;
1960, taught at the University of Hawaii; 1961, appointed
faculty member, University of Denver.
Concerto, organ and brass quartet, Associated Music
Publishers.
LOEILLET, JEAN-BAPTISTE. born Ghent, Belgium, Nov. 18,
1680; died London, July 19, 1730. Traveled in England and
France; played flute, oboe, and harpsichord.
Aire, in Oudnederlandse Meesters, Vol. II, p. 99.
Aria; Giga, in Oudnederlandse Meesters, Vol. I.
Gavotte, in Oudnederlandse Meesters, Vol. III, p. 106.
LÓPEZ DE VELASCO, SEBASTIAN. born Segovia, Spain?, six-
teenth century; died Madrid?, seventeenth century. 1628,
appointed maestro de capilla to Infanta Juana, Madrid.
compositions in Cent Versets de Magnificat, Norbert
Dufourcq et Noëlie Pierront, eds., Bornemann.
LOPEZ, MIQUEL. born Villaroya, Spain, Mar. 1, 1669; died
Saragossa, 1732. Catalonian monk.
Eight versets, in Les Anciens Maîtres Espagnols, p. 26.
Verset de Octáu To, in Early Spanish Organ Music, p. 41.

Versos per l'Entrada de la "Salve," in Hymnes et Antiennes,
Orgue et Liturgie, Vol. 8, p. 19.
compositions in Antologia de Organistas Clásicos Españoles,
Vol. II, pp. 97-106.
LORET, CLÉMENT. born Termonde, France, 1833; died Colombes,
1909. Pupil of Lemmens; 1857, became teacher, Ecole
Niedermeyer, Paris; taught Gigout; organist, St. Louis-
d'Antin; organist, Panthéon; organist, Notre Dame des
Victoires.
Canzone, in The French Organist, Vol. I, p. 37.
Douze Pièces, Leduc.
Easter Day, Gray.
Jubilate Deo, Boston Music Co.
Marche de triomphe, Lemoine.
Offertory: Adeste fideles, in Selected Festival Music,
Christmas, Boston Music Co.
LUBLIN, JOHANNES DE (LUBLINA, JAN). Polish. Sixteenth
century. Presumbaly organist, Cloister, Canonici Regulares,
Crasnyk (near Lublin); might have been a teacher; compiled
Tabulatura Ioannis De Lyublyn Canonic(orum) Regularium De
Crasnyk (1540).
Tablature of Keyboard Music, in Corpus of Early Keyboard
Music, No. 6, 6 vols.: Vol. I: Praeambula (21);
three organ Masses; Mass ordinary sections; Vol. 2:
compositions (31); Vol. 3: compositions (38);
Vol. 4: compositions (27); Vol. 5: compositions (60);
Vol. 6: compositions (9).
chorale preludes (2) in Orgelmusik der Reformationszeit,
Jost Harro Schmidt, ed., Merseburger.
LUBRICH, FRITZ. born Neustädtel, Silesia, 1888. Music lecturer,
director, Hamburg, Germany.
Five Chorale Improvisations, Op. 26, Leuckart.
Ich will dich lieben, in Orgel Kompositionen aus alter und
neuer Zeit, Gauss, ed., Coppenrath.
Rathbun, in The Parish Organist, Vol. 12.
Vom Himmel hoch, in Sphärenmusik in der Weihnacht,
Böhm.
LÜBECK, VINCENT. born Padingbüttel bei Dorum, Germany,
September 1654; died Hamburg, Feb. 9, 1740. 1675, became
organist, Kirche St. Cosmae et Damiani, Stade; 1702-1740,
organist, St. Nicolai, Hamburg.
Four Preludes and Fugues, in Organum, Series IV, Vol. 5,
(Concordia 97-4341).
Klavierübung (1728), Peters 4478.
Lobt Gott ihr Christen, in Altdeutsche Weinachtsmusik,
Nagel's Musik Archives.
Musikalische Werke (6 preludes and fugues), Harms, ed.,
Ugrino Abt. Verlag, Klecken, 1921.
Nun lasst uns Gott, in Choralvorspiel alter Meister, p. 98.
Orgelwerke, Hermann Keller, ed., 2 parts, Peters 4437,
1941: Part 1: Preludes and Fugues; Part 2: Chorale
settings.
Partita über Nun lasst uns Gott, in The Church Organist's

Golden Treasury, Vol. III, p. 18.

Prelude and Fugue (C Major), in The First Four Centuries of Organ Music, Vol. II, p. 364.

Prelude and Fugue (C Minor), in Anthologia pro Organo, Vol. IV, p. 24.

Prelude and Fugue (E Minor), in Anthologia pro Organo, Vol. II, p. 26.

Prelude and Fugue (G Major), Josef Hedar, ed. , Wilhelm Hansen, 1953.

Preludium og fuga, Hansen 27096.

Six Preludes and Fugues, Norbert Dufourcq, ed. , Schola Cantorum, 1953, in Orgue et Liturgie, Vol. 17.

chorale prelude in Alte deutsche Weihnachtsmusik, p. 8.

compositions in Masterpieces of Organ Music, Folios 13 and 52.

LÜNEBURG TABLATURES. A collection of North German tablatures of the new German tablature type dated from the middle of the seventeenth century; it contains chorale preludes, chorale variations, dance pieces, and free organ compositions.

Free Organ Compositions, John Shannon, ed. , 2 vols. , Concordia 97-1414, 97-1419, 1958.

compositions in Das Erbe deutschen Musik, Series I, Vols. 36 and 65, Margarete Reimann, ed. , (Peters KN 208 I and II).

LUGGE, JOHN. English. Seventeenth century. 1634, probably vicar-choral, Exeter; organist, St. Peter's Church, Exeter.

Three Voluntaries for Double Organ, Susi Jeans and John Steele, eds. , Novello.

LUYTHON, KAREL. born presumably Antwerp, ca. 1557/1558; died Prague, August 1620. 1566-1571, choirboy in Vienna; served Emperor Maximilian II and Emperor Rudolph II; composed Fuga suavissima found in Woltz's Nova musices organices tabulatura (Basel, 1617).

Fantasie, in Altniederlandische Meister, p. 30.

Fuga suavissima, in Oudnederlandse Meesters, Vol. III, p. 45.

Ricercar; Fantasie, in Oudnederlandse Meesters, Vol. II.

Ricercar, in Chromatisme, L'Organiste liturgique, Vol. 51, p. 4.

Ricercar, in Ricercaris for the Organ, p. 4.

Werken voor Orgel of 4 Speeltuigen, in Monumenta Musicae Belgicae, Vol. 4.

LUZZASCHI, LUZZASCO. born Ferrara, Italy, 1545?; died Ferrara, Sept. 11, 1607. Pupil of Cypriano de Rore; before 1571-1604, court organist to Alfonso II, Duke of Ferrara; choirmaster, Cathedral, Ferrara; taught Frescobaldi; three compositions found in Diruta's Il Transilvano, Part I.

Canzone, in The First Four Centuries of Organ Music, Vol. I, p. 111.

compositions (2) in Classici Italiani dell'Organo.

ricercari (2) and toccata in L'Arte Musicale in Italia, Vol. III, p. 149.

McCABE, JOHN. born Liverpool, England, 1939. Studied at Manchester University and Royal Manchester College of Music;
pianist; 1962, won Royal Philharmonic Prize and Royal Manchester Institution Medal; 1964-1965, studied at the Hochschule
für Musik, Munich.
    Dies Resurrectionis, Oxford.
    Elegy, Novello.
    Johannis-Partita (1964), Novello.
    Nocturne, in Modern Organ Music, p. 9.
    Pastorale Sostenuto, in Easy Modern Organ Music, Book 1.
    Sinfonia, Novello.
McGRATH, JOSEPH J. American. born 1889; died 1968.
    Cantiones Organi, McLaughlin and Reilly.
    Chorale Prelude on Tantum Ergo, G. Schirmer.
    Eucharistica, McLaughlin and Reilly.
    Postlude on Praise to the Holiest, in Gloria Deo, McLaughlin
       and Reilly.
    Pro Ecclesia, McLaughlin and Reilly.
    Twelve Versets on Pange Lingua, Op. 78, J. Fischer.
MÁCHA, OTMAR. born Ostrava, Czechoslovakia, Sept. 2, 1922.
Studied at the Conservatory and Master School; composition
pupil of Jaroslav Rídký.
    Mourning Toccata, in Nuove Composizioni per Organo,
       Vol. 2.
McKAY, GEORGE FREDERICK. born Harrington, Washington,
June 11, 1899; died Stateline, Nevada, Oct. 4, 1970. Pupil
of Sinding and Palmgren; studied at the Eastman School of
Music; 1927-1968, teacher, University of Washington, Seattle.
    Benedictions, Carl Fischer, 1949.
    Canzone Celesti, McLaughlin and Reilly M-2103.
    Elegiac Poem, Oliver Ditson.
    Hymn of Thanksgiving, Belwin.
    (A) Nativity Trilogy, Oliver Ditson.
    Old Hundredth, Belwin.
    Prelude on Crusaders' Hymn, McLaughlin and Reilly.
    Suite on Easter Hymns, Carl Fischer 9281.
    Suite on Sixteenth-Century Hymn Tunes, Gray.
    Wedding Music, McLaughlin and Reilly M-2159.
McKINLEY, CARL. born Yarmouth, Maine, Oct. 9, 1895; died
Centerville, Mass. , July 25, 1966. 1915, graduated from
Knox College, Galesburg, Ill. , and in 1917, from Harvard
University; 1918-1923, organist, Center Church (Congrega-
tional), Hartford, Conn. ; pupil of Gaston Déthier; 1930-1963,
instructor, New England Conservatory of Music; 1963, honor-
ary Mus. Doc. , New England Conservatory; taught at the
Boston Conservatory of Music; 1927-1929, won Guggenheim
fellowship to study in Paris and Munich; organist-choirmaster,
Old South Church, Boston, for thirty years.
    Scherzo-Fantasia, Gray.
    Ten Hymn-tune Fantasies, Gray, 1933.

MACQUE, JEAN DE (GIOVANNI). born Valenciennes (Belgium),
    ca. 1550; died Naples, 1614. 1563, singer, royal chapel,
    Vienna; pupil of Philippe de Monte; from age 15 spent life
    in Italy; 1586, entered service of Don Fabrizio Gesualdo da
    Venosa; 1590, appointed organist, Annunciation Church, Naples;
    1594, became organist, Chapel of viceroyalty, Naples; taught
    Trabaci, Majone, and Rossi; works found in Woltz anthology.
        Canzon, in Oudnederlandse Meesters, Vol. I, p. 33.
        Canzon alla Francesca, in Oudnederlandse Meesters,
            Vol. III, p. 43.
        Consonanze stravaganti, in Historical Anthology of Music,
            Vol. I, p. 200.
        Werken voor Orgel of 4 Speeltuigen, in Monumenta Musicae
            Belgicae, Vol. 4.
        canzonas (2) in Oudnederlandse Meesters, Vol. II.
        compositions (2) in Altniederlandische Meister.
MAEKELBERGHE, AUGUST. born Oostende, Belgium, Jan. 15,
    1909. Studied at Notre Dame College, Oostende, and at the
    Royal Conservatory of Music, Ghent; 1941, M. Mus., Insti-
    tute of Musical Art, Detroit; 1941, Fellow of the American
    Guild of Organists; organ pupil of Leandre Villain; 1940-
    1947, organist, Church of the Messiah, Detroit; since 1947,
    organist, St. John's Episcopal Church, Detroit.
        De Profundis Clamavi, Gray, 1946.
        Fantasia, J. Fischer.
        Flandria Variations, Gray.
        (A) Flemish Prayer, Gray (St. Cecilia Series 856).
        Impromptu Etude, Associated Music Publishers.
        Improvisation on Puer natus est, Gray (St. Cecilia Series
            944).
        Let All Mortal Flesh Keep Silence, J. Fischer.
        Night Soliloquy, Gray (St. Cecilia Series 839).
        Plainsong Prelude, Gray (St. Cecilia Series 878).
        Three Hymn Preludes, Gray.
        Toccata, Melody in Blue and Fugue, Belwin-Mills.
        Triptych, Gray.
MAESSEN, ANTOON. born the Hague, Apr. 8, 1919. Studied in
    The Hague; pupil of Jaap Vranken; since 1946, organist and
    conductor, music critic, teacher, Roosendaal.
        Prelude and Fugue (1954), Donemus 169.
        Toccata sopra Te Deum laudamus (1958), Van Rossum
            R. 433.
        Variaties op een eigen Choral-thema (1953), Donemus.
MAILLY, ALPHONSE-JEAN-ERNEST. born Brussels, Nov. 27,
    1833; died Brussels, January 1918. Studied at the Conserva-
    tory, Brussels; pupil of Lemmens; 1861, appointed professor
    of organ, Conservatory, Brussels.
        Trois Morceaux (Invocation; Andante con moto; Christmas),
            Lemoine.
MAJONE (MAYONE), ASCANIO. Italian. Late sixteenth-seventeenth
    century. Pupil of Giovanni de Macque.
        Ricercare, in L'Arte Musicale in Italia, Vol. III, p. 145.
        Ricercare su canto fermo di C. Festa, in Classici Italiani

dell'Organo, p. 99.
Secondo libro di diversi capricci per sonate (1609), in
Orgue et Liturgie, Vol. 63, p. 65.
MALEINGREAU (MALENGREAU), PAUL DE. born Trélon-en-
Thiérache, France, Nov. 23, 1887; died Brussels, Jan. 12,
1956. Pupil of Edgar Tinel at the Conservatory, Brussels;
1913, appointed professor of harmony, Conservatory, Brussels;
1929-1953, professor of organ, Conservatory, Brussels; 1946,
elected president, Froissert Academy.

    Chorale Prelude, in An Album of Prelude and Interludes,
      Oxford.
    Deux Pièces (Post partum; Ego sum panis), Philippo.
    Dix-huit Elévations liturgiques, au temps pascal, Op. 27,
      Philippo.
    Low Mass for Christmas, in The French Organist, Vol. II,
      p. 10.
    Méditation pour le temps pascal, Philippo.
    Messe de Pâques, Op. 31, Philippo.
    Offrande Musicale in C, Op. 10, No. 1, Chester.
    Offrande Musicale in G, Op. 10, No. 2, Chester.
    Opus sacrum, Op. 22, Sénart.
    Préludes à l'Introit, Op. 25, 3 vols. , Sénart.
    Préludes de Carême, Oxford.
    Si Consurrexit, Durand.
    Suite, Op. 14 (Prélude; Choral; Pastorale; Toccata),
      Durand.
    Suite of four paraphrases on hymns to the virgin (Choral
      Prelude; Intermezzo; Musette; Toccata), Oxford.
    Suite of four paraphrases on gregorian melodies (Prelude;
      Offertory; Communion; Toccata), Edition Musicus.
    Suite Mariale (L'Annonciation; La Visitation; Les Sept
      Douleurs; La Glorification), Oxford.
    Symphonie de la Passion, Op. 20 (Prologue; Le Tumulte
      au Prétoire; Marche au supplice; O Golgotha!),
      (Sénart) 1923, Leduc.
    Symphonie de l'Agneau mystique, Leduc, 1933.
    Symphonie de Noël, Op. 19, Chester.
    Toccata, Op. 18, No. 3, Chester.
    Triptique pour Noël, Op. 23, (Sénart) Philippo.
MALLING, OTTO VALDEMAR. born Copenhagen, June 1, 1848;
died Copenhagen, Oct. 5, 1915. Pupil of Gade and Hartmann
at the Royal Conservatory, Copenhagen; from 1878, named
organist at several Copenhagen churches; 1885, appointed instructor of theory, 1899, director, Royal Conservatory, Copenhagen; 1900, became organist, Cathedral, Copenhagen.

    Aus dem Leben Christi, Op. 63, 2 vols. , Hansen 11952-
      11953.
    Bei kirchlichen Handlungen, Op. 88, Hansen.
    Easter Morn, in Organ Music of the Netherlands and
      Scandinavia, p. 52.
    Festtage des Kirchenjahres, Op. 66, 2 vols. , Hansen
      12139/12140.
    (Die) Geburt Christi, Op. 48, Hansen.

(Die) Geburt Christi, Op. 48, Hansen.
(Die) heilige Jungfrau, Op. 70, 2 vols., Hansen.
(Die) heiligen drei Könige, Op. 84, 2 vols., Hansen.
Kristi fødsel, Hansen 11167.
Nachklänge aus Davids Psalmen, Op. 89, Hansen.
Paulus, Op. 78, 2 vols., Hansen.
(Ein) Requiem, Op. 75, 2 vols., Hansen 13042.
Shepherds in the Fields (Pastorale), in Organ Music of
    the Netherlands and Scandinavia, p. 48; also in
    Masterpieces for Organ, William C. Carl, ed.,
    G. Schirmer.
(Die) sieben Worte des Erlösers am Kreuze, Op. 81, 2 vols.,
    Hansen.
(Der) Tod und die Auferstehung Christi, Op. 54, Hansen
    11402.
MALVEZZI, CRISTOFORO. born Lucca, Italy, June 28, 1547; died
    Florence, Dec. 25, 1597. Priest; 1562, canon, San Lorenzo,
    Florence; maestro di cappella to Grand Duke of Tuscany; had
    a book of ricercari for four voices printed in 1577; Canzone
    (Mode II) found in B. Schmid's Tabulaturbuch (1607).
    Canzone II tono, in Classici Italiani dell'Organo, p. 73.
MANARI, RAFFAELE. born Carsoli, Italy, 1887; died Rome,
    1933. 1915, became Prefect of Studies, Head of organ depart-
    ment, Pontifical School of Sacred Music, Rome.
    Salve Regina, McLaughlin & Reilly 2459.
MANICKE, DIETRICH. born Wurzen, Germany, Oct. 29, 1923.
    Studied in Dresden and Berlin; 1955, Ph.D.; 1948, became
    teacher, Music Academy, Dresden; 1950-1953, taught at the
    Musikhochschule, Ost-Berlin; 1956, appointed to faculty,
    Church Music School, Berlin-Spandau; 1960, became teacher,
    Music Academy, Detmold.
    Choralpartita über Von Gott will ich nicht lassen, Simrock.
MANSFIELD, PURCELL JAMES. English. born 1899.
    Fantasy-Variations on St. Clement, Paxton.
    Postlude on Cwm Rhondda, Paxton.
    Prelude on Crimond, Paxton.
    Prelude on Rutherford, in Six Short Pieces, Weekes & Co.
    Scherzo-Caprice, Augener, 1922.
MANZ, PAUL. born Cleveland, Ohio, 1919. Studied at North-
    western University; pupil of Flor Peeters and Helmut Walcha;
    1946, became organist-choirmaster, Mt. Olive Lutheran Church,
    Minneapolis, Minn.; chairman, Division of Music and Fine
    Arts, Concordia College, St. Paul, Minn.; Ll. D., Concordia
    Teachers College, Seward, Neb.; President, Lutheran Society
    for Music, Worship, and Arts.
    Choral, Op. 5.
    Seelenbräutigam, in The Parish Organist, Vol. 9, p. 18.
    Ten Chorale Improvisations, Op. 5, Concordia 97-4554,
        1962.
    Ten Chorale Improvisations, Op. 7, Concordia 97-4656,
        1964.
    Ten Chorale Improvisations, Op. 9, Concordia 97-4950,
        1970.

Ten Chorale Improvisations, Op. 10, Concordia 97-4951, 1970.

Ten Short Intonations on Well-known Hymns, Op. 11, Augsburg 11-9492, 1970.

compositions in The Parish Organist, Vols. 9, 11, and 12.

MAQUAIRE, LAZARE-AUGUSTE. born Lyon, France, Oct. 25, 1872; died Grenoble, July 11, 1906. Studied at the Conservatory, Paris; organ pupil and assistant to Charles-Marie Widor at St. Sulpice; chapel organist, Ecole Gerson.

Symphony No. 1 (E-flat), Op. 20, Bornemann.

MARCELLO, BENEDETTO. born Venice, July 24, 1686; died Brescia, July 24, 1739. Pupil of Gasparini and Lotti; composer-poet, studied law, filled government posts; wrote settings of Giustiniani's paraphrases of the first 50 psalms for from one to four voices with basso continuo, a few with 'cello obbligato or two violas.

Composizioni per Cembalo od Organo, in I Classici della Musica Italiana, Quaderno 70-71.

Psalm 18 (transcription), in A Treasury of Shorter Organ Classics, p. 21.

Psalm 19, in The Parish Organist, Vol. 9, p. 8.

Psalms 19 and 20, in Wedding Music, Vol. I, Concordia.

Psalm 19; Prelude in A Minor, in Treasury of Early Organ Music.

MARCHAND, LOUIS. born Lyon, France, Feb. 2, 1669; died Paris, Feb. 17, 1732. Played organ in Nevers Cathedral at the age of 15; organist, Auxerre Cathedral; 1689, became organist, Jesuits' church; 1708-1714, organist, Royal Chapel; 1717, failed to compete in improvisation contest with J. S. Bach in Dresden; organist for Franciscans; taught DuMage and Daquin; published Premier livre de pieces de clavecin (Ballard, Paris, 1702).

Dialogue, Schott.

Dialogue (C Major), in European Organ Music of the 16th and 17th Centuries, p. 71.

Fond d'orgue, in Alte Orgelmusik aus England und Frankreich, p. 28.

Fond d'orgue, in Les Maîtres français de l'orgue, Vol. II, p. 41.

Fond d'orgue, in Organ Book No. 2, p. 32.

Lentemente, in The First Four Centuries of Organ Music, Vol. II, p. 427.

Pièces choisies, in Archives des maîtres d'orgue des seizième-dix-huitième siècles, Vol. III.

Pièces d'orgue, in Archives des maitres d'orgue des seizième-dix-huitième siècles, Vol. V; also Schott 1873.*

Plein jeu, in Harold Gleason, Method of Organ Playing, p. 141.

Plein jeu (6 parts), in Historical Organ Recitals, Vol. I, p. 108.

Premier Livre d'orgue, Schott.

compositions (5) in Liber Organi, Vol. I.

compositions in Masterpieces of Organ Music, Folio 48.
MARCKHL, ERICH. born Cilli (Untersteiermark), Germany,
    Feb. 3, 1902. 1926, Ph. D., University of Vienna; studied
    with F. Schmidt at the Musik Akademie; 1937, became tea-
    cher, Hochschule für Lehrenbildung, Dortmund; 1939, took
    music post, Vienna; since 1948, held different posts in Steier-
    mark; 1957, became director, regional Conservatory, Graz.
    Sieben Choralvorspiele, (1937-1939), Dortmund manuscript.
    Sonata über Der Grimmig Tod, Doblinger, 1955.
    Two Choral Trios, Osterreichische Bundesverlag.
MARESCHAL, SAMUEL. born 1554, Tournai, (Belgium)?; died
    1640. 1576-1640, organist, Basel.
    fugues (3), tones (12), Psalms, in Selected Works,
    Corpus of Early Keyboard Music, No. 27.
MARKWORTH, HENRY J. American. born 1900; died 1953.
    Organist-Director of Music, Trinity Lutheran Church, Cleve-
    land, Ohio.
    Selected Solos, 5 books, Concordia 97-1260.
    chorale prelude in The Parish Organist, Vol. 1-4.
MARPURG, FRIEDRICH WILHELM. born Seehausen (Brandenburg),
    Germany, Nov. 21, 1718; died Berlin, May 22, 1795. Served
    courts of Prussia and France; 1763, director, royal lottery,
    Berlin; author of many books about music including Abhundlung
    von der Fuge.
    Christus der ist mein, in Harold Gleason, Method of Organ
        Playing.
    Eight Chorale Preludes, Walter Emery, ed. , Novello, 1968.
    Five Marpurg Fugues, Robert M. Thompson, ed. , Augsburg,
        1969.
    Herr, ich habe misgehandelt, in Reinbrecht's Sammlung,
        Viewig.
    Twenty-one Chorale Preludes, Robert M. Thompson, ed. ,
        Augsburg.
    Wach auf, mein Herz, in Neues Orgel Journal, G. W.
        Koerner (Erfurt).
    Wer nur den lieben Gott, in Wolckmar's Album, Peters.
    chorale preludes in The Church Organist's Golden Treasury,
        Vol. I and II.
    chorale preludes (3) in The Progressive Organist, Books 1,
        5, and 6, Elkin & Co. , Ltd.
    chorale preludes in Seasonal Chorale Preludes, Book 1 (2),
        and Book 2 (2), Oxford.
MARRIGUES, JEAN-NICOLAS. French. born 1757; died 1834.
    Organist at the following Parisian churches: St. Nicolas-des-
    Champs, St. Thomas d'Aquin, and St. Gervais.
    Fugue, in Les Maîtres français de l'orgue, Vol. II, p. 93.
MARTIN, FRANK. born Geneva, Switzerland, Sept. 15, 1890.
    Studied in Zürich, Rome, and Paris; taught at the Institut
    Jacques-Dalcroze; 1950, went to Amsterdam; 1952-1958,
    taught at the Conservatory, Cologne; returned to Switzerland;
    influenced by Franck and French impressionists; later adopted
    a twelve-tone technique.
    Passacaille, Universal 12470.

Sonata da Chiesa, viola d'amore and organ, Universal
    12118, or flute and organ, Universal 13015.
MARTINI, GIOVANNI BATTISTA (GIAMBATTISTA).   born Bologna,
    Italy, Apr. 24, 1706; died Bologna, Oct. 4, 1784.
    Franciscan friar called "Padre Martini"; pupil of Perti and Predieri;
    violinist, harpsichordist, singer, composer, and music his-
    torian; 1725, maestro di cappella, Church of St.
    Francis, Bologna; member, Accademia dei Filarmonica.
    Aria con variazioni, in Anthologia pro Organo, Vol. II,
        p. 61.
    Aria con variazioni, in Anthologia pro Organo, Vol. IV,
        p. 54.
    Canzona on La Martinella, in Alte Meister aus der Frühzeit
        des Orgelspiels, p. 32.
    Composizioni per cembalo od organo, in I Classici della
        musica italiana, G. F. Malipiero, ed. , Vol. 17.
    Four Pieces, Novello.
    Gavotta, Cramer.
    Prelude and Fugue (E Minor), Walter Emery, ed. ,
        Novello EOM 13, 1959.
    Sonata d'Intavolatura per l'organo e' L Ceembalo, Broude
        Bros.
    Sonata II, in Varia, Orgue et Liturgie, Vol. 25, p. 26.
    Sonata No. 9 (F Minor), Schott, 1901.
    Twenty Original Compositions, I. Fuser, ed. , Zanibon
        4135.
    composition in Elkan-Vogel Organ Series, Vol. I.
    compositions (2) in Alte italienische Meister.
    compositions (2) in Classici Italiani dell'Organo.
MARTINU, BOHUSLAV.   born Polička, Czechoslovakia, Dec. 8,
    1890; died Liestal, Switzerland, Aug. 28, 1959. 1906, be-
    came organ student, Conservatory, Prague; 1913, was violinist,
    Prague Philharmonic Orchestra; pupil of Albert Roussel.
    Vigilia, Eschig.
MARTY, ADOLPHE.   born Albi, France, 1865; died 1942. First
    blind student to enter the organ class at the Conservatory,
    Paris; pupil of Franck; teacher, Institut des Jeunes Aveugles;
    organist, St. François Xavier.
    Cinq pièces, Noël, 1892.
    Deux Sonates (La Pentecôte; Ste. Cécile), Noël, 1903, 1904.
    Dix pièces en style libre, Noël, 1910.
    Offertoire pour la Pentocôte, pour l'Immaculée-Conception,
        Hérelle, 1914.
    Orgue Triomphale (12 pieces), Noël, 1898.
    (La) Resurrection, Noël.
    (Le) Saint Rosaire, Noël, 1941.
    Six Pièces, Mackar & Noël, 1897.
MARX, KARL JULIUS.   born Munich, Germany, Nov. 12, 1897.
    Pupil of Carl Orff; 1924, appointed teacher, Academy of Com-
    position, Munich; 1928, became leader, Bach Society, Munich;
    1939-1946, teacher, Hochschule für Musikerziehung, Graz;
    1946, appointed teacher, Hochschule für Musik, Stuttgart.
    Toccata, Op. 31.

Variationen, Op. 20, Breitkopf & Härtel 5608.
chorale preludes (7) in Orgelbuch zum Evangelischen
  Kirchengesangbuch, Books 2, 3, 4, 6, 7, 16, and 19,
  Bärenreiter.
chorale preludes (2) in 73 leichte Choralvorspiele, alter und
  neuer Meister, H. Fleischer, ed. , Leuckart.
MASCHERA, FIORENZO. born Brescia, Italy, ca. 1540; died
  probably Brescia, 1584. Pupil of Merulo; 1557, succeeded
  Merulo as organist, Cathedral, Brescia; composed one can-
  zona found in B. Schmid's Tabulatur Buch (1607) and ten canzonas in Woltz's Nova musices.
  Canzon XIV, in Anthologia Organistica Italiana, p. 27.
  Canzon on La Capriola, in Spielbuch für die Kleinorgel,
    Vol. I, p. 16.
  Canzone XXI, in Classici Italiani dell'Organo, p. 64.
MASON, DANIEL GREGORY. born Brookline Mass. , Nov. 20, 1873;
  died Greenwich, Conn. , Dec. 4, 1953. Pupil of John K. Paine
  at Harvard; 1895, graduated, Harvard University; pupil of
  Chadwick, Percy Goetschius, and d'Indy; 1910-1942, faculty
  member, later head, music department, Columbia University;
  writer and educator.
  Passacaglia and Fugue, Op. 10, Gray (St. Cecilia Series
    37-38), 1913.
  Two Chorale Preludes on Hymn-tunes of Lowell Mason,
    J. Fischer, 1941.
MASON, LOWELL. born Medfield, Mass. , Jan. 8, 1792; died
  Orange, N. J. , Aug. 11, 1872. Singing school director; 1812-
  1827, banker, Savannah, Ga. ; 1820, became organist-choir-
  master, Presbyterian Church, Savannah, Ga. ; 1827, became
  organist, Boston; 1832, founded Boston Academy of Music;
  1835, honorary Mus. Doc. , N. Y. University; began courses
  for music teachers and in Boston public schools.
  (A) Joyous Voluntary, in Early American Compositions for
    Organ, p. 14.
MATHIAS, WILLIAM JAMES. born Whitland, Carmarthenshire,
  South Wales, 1934. Fellow of the Royal Academy of Music;
  D. Mus. , Wales; studied at the University College of Wales,
  Aberystwyth; 1959-1968, Lecturer in Music, University College
  of North Wales, Bangor; since 1968, Senior Lecturer in Mu-
  sic, University of Edinburgh.
  Chorale, in Easy Modern Organ Music, Book 1.
  Invocations, Op. 35, Oxford, 1967.
  Partita, Oxford.
  Postlude, in An Album of Postludes, Oxford.
  Processional, in Modern Organ Music, p. 28.
  Toccata Giocosa, Op. 36, No. 2 (1967), Oxford, 1968.
  Variations on a Hymn Tune (Braint), Oxford, 1963.
MATTHEWS, HARVEY ALEXANDER. born Cheltenham, England,
  Mar. 26, 1879. Organist, Cheltenham; faculty member,
  University of Pennsylvania; 1925, honorary Doc. Mus. , Uni-
  versity of Pennsylvania.
  Cantilena in D, Gray.
  Chorale Improvisation on In dulci jubilo, Gray (St. Cecilia

79 7).
Chorale Improvisation on O Filii et Filiae, Gray (St.
Cecilia Series 789).
Christmas Pastoral, Theodore Presser.
Concert Overture (D Minor), Gray.
Epithalamium, G. Schirmer.
Five Wayside Impressions in New England, Gray.
Fountains, G. Schirmer.
Paean, G. Schirmer.
Pastorale (G Major), G. Schirmer.
Six Chorale Improvisations on Well-Known Hymns, G.
Schirmer.
Ten Chorale Preludes and a Fantasy on Familiar Hymn
Tunes, Oliver Ditson.
Toccata (G Minor), G. Schirmer.
Twelve Chorale Preludes, Oliver Ditson.
MAURO-COTTONE, MELCHOIRRE. born Palermo, Italy, Dec. 12,
1885; died New York City, Sept. 29, 1938. Graduate, Royal
Conservatory, Palermo; organist, New York Philharmonic
Symphony Orchestra and Holy Trinity Church.
Adoration, Gray (St. Cecilia Series 491).
Aria in the Manner of Bach; Introduction in form of
candenza and Fugue, G. Schirmer, 1930.
Ave Maria on a Gregorian Theme, Gray.
Idilio, Gray.
Melodia Serena, Gray.
Rhapsody of the Sun, Gray (St. Cecilia Series 523).
Sicilian Suite, Gray.
Variations on a Christmas Carol, J. Fischer.
While Shepherds Watched, J. Fischer.
MAYONE (see Majone).
MEEK, KENNETH. born England, May 21, 1908. Pupil of Herbert
Sanders; B. Mus., Toronto Conservatory of Music; faculty,
McGill Conservatorium, Montreal.
Three Preludes, in Organ Music of Canada, Vol. I, p. 30.
Voluntary for St. Crispin's Day, in Organ Music of Canada,
Vol. II, p. 65.
MENALT, GABRIEL. born Metaro, Spain, ?; died Barcelona,
1687. Organist, Santa Maria del Mar, Barcelona.
Tiento de Primer To, in Early Spanish Organ Music, p. 48.
MENDELSSOHN-BARTHOLDY, JACOB LUDWIG FELIX. born Ham-
burg, Germany, Feb. 3, 1809; died Leipzig, Nov. 4, 1847.
Pupil of his mother, Zelter, and Hennings; composed and performed from childhood; 1829, revived the Bach Passion according to St. Matthew; became famous as pianist, organist, conductor, and composer; became very popular in England as
conductor; 1833, appointed City Musical Director, Düsseldorf;
1835, became conductor of Gewandhaus Orchestra, Leipzig;
1836, made honorary Ph.D., University of Leipzig; 1841,
took charge of orchestral and choral concerts in Berlin; organized Domchor, Berlin; named Royal General Musical Director; 1842-1843, organized the Conservatory of Leipzig with
Schumann and others.

Organ Works, Peters 1744; also Lemare, ed. , G. Schir-
mer, 1924; also Kalmus 3670; also M. Dupré, ed. ,
Bornemann.
Six Sonatas, Op. 65, Ivor Atkins, ed. , Novello; also
Augener.
Sonata, Op. 65, No. 2, Sumner, ed. , Peters 1744C.
Sonata, Op. 65, No. 6, Sumner, ed. , Peters 1744F.
Three Preludes and Fugues, Op. 37, Ivor Atkins, ed. ,
Novello; also Breitkopf & Härtel.
Trois fugues, in Pièces ignorées, L'Organiste liturgique,
Vol. 17, p. 3.
Werke für Orgel, Op. 37 and Op. 65, Series VIII, Rietz,
ed. , Breitkopf & Härtel, 1874-1877.
compositions (3) in Musica Organi, Vol. I.
MERKEL, GUSTAV ADOLPH. born Oberoderwitz, Germany,
Nov. 12, 1827; died Dresden, Oct. 30, 1885. 1848-1853,
teacher in Dresden; organ pupil of Johann Schneider; com-
position pupil of Schumann; 1858, became organist, Waisen-
hauskirche, Dresden; 1860, organist, Kreuzkirche, Dresden;
1861, appointed professor of organ, Conservatory, Dresden;
1864-1885, Catholic court organist.
Acht Stücke, Op. 21, André.
Adagio (E Major), Op. 35, Schott.
Album, G. Schirmer 1488.
Album, Westbrook, ed. , Schott.
Chorale Sonata, Op. 137, Rieter-Biedermann.
Drei melodiöse Stücke, Op. 72, Schott.
Einleitung und Doppelfuge (A Minor), Op. 105, Breitkopf &
Härtel.
Fantasie (A Minor), Op. 104, Schott.
Fantasie und Fuge (C Minor), Op. 109, Kahnt.
Fantasie No. 5 (D Minor), Op. 176, Breitkopf & Härtel.
Fünf-und-zwanzig Choralvorspiele, Op. 146, Rieter-
Biedermann.
Fünfzehn leichte und kurze Choralvorspiele, Op. 129,
Breitkopf & Härtel.
Fünfzig leichte und kurze Choralvorspiele, Op. 48, 2 vols. ,
Schott.
Fugue on B-A-C-H, Op. 40, in Organ Book No. 2, p. 2.
Introduction and Double Fugue, in The International Organist,
Vol. II, p. 74.
Neun Stücke, Op. 15, André.
Pastorale (G Major), Op. 103, Schott.
Pastorale (G Major), Op. 49, Viewig.
Prelude, in Organ Book No. 2, p. 18.
Schmücke dich, in The Lutheran Organist, Concordia.
Sechs-und-dreizig kurze und leichte Präludien, Op. 47,
Schott.
Six Trios, Op. 100, Fr. Hofmeister.
Sonata No. 2 (G Minor), Op. 42, Schott, 1918; also
Peters, 1918; also Gray.
Sonata No. 3 (C Minor), Op. 80, Fürstner, Berlin, 1874.
Sonata No. 6, Op. 137 (E Minor), Hinrichsen 38; also

in Everybody's Favorite Series No. 57, AMSCO.
Ten Variations on Wer nur den lieben Gott, Op. 116, Breit-
    kopf & Härtel.
Thirty Preludes and Postludes, Peters 3568.
Three Large Chorale Preludes, Op. 32, Breitkopf & Härtel.
Two Chorales, Op. 12, Koerner.
Variationen über ein Thema von Beethoven, Op. 45, For-
    berg.
Vier melodiöse Stücke, Op. 88, Schott.
Vom Himmel hoch, in Harold Gleason, Method of Organ
    Playing, p. 156.
Weihnachtspastorale, Op. 56, Schott.
Zehn melodische Stücke, Op. 99, 2 vols. , Schott.
Zwölf Fugen zum Studium und kirchlichen Gebrauch, Op. 124,
    Breitkopf & Härtel.
Zwölf Stücke, Op. 102, Schott.
chorale preludes (11) in Anthologie, Concordia.
chorale preludes (4) in Der Praktische Organist, Part I,
    Tascher'schen.
chorale preludes (2) in Organ Preludes Ancient and Modern,
    Hinrichsen.
chorale preludes (9) in Orgel Choräle Sammlung, Metzler.
chorale preludes (2) in Orgelwerke I, Rieter-Biedermann.
chorale preludes in Seasonal Chorale Preludes, Book I (3),
    Book II (2), Oxford.
MERULA, TARQUINIO. born Cremona, Italy, ca. 1600; died ?,
    1665, maestro di cappella, S. Maria Maggiore, Bergamo;
    1624, appointed organist, court of Sigismund II of Poland, in
    Warsaw; 1628, became choirmaster-organist, Sant'Agata,
    Cremona, and maestro, Cathedral, Cremona; 1639, became
    organist again at Santa Maria, Bergamo; 1652, became choir-
    master, Cathedral, Cremona.
    Composizione per organo e cimbalo, Alan Curtis, ed. , in
        Monumenti di musica italiani, Vol. I, No. 1, Brescia,
        1961 (Bärenreiter).
MERULO, CLAUDIO. born Corregio, Italy, Apr. 8, 1533; died
    Parma, May 4, 1604. 1556, organist, Brescia; 1557, be-
    came second organist, 1566-1584, first organist, San Marco,
    Venice; 1586, served as court organist to Duke of Parma;
    1591, became organist, ducal Church of the Steccata, Parma;
    1587, appointed organist, Cathedral, Parma; taught Maschera
    and Diruta; one toccata found in Diruta's Il Transilvano,
    Part 1; one toccata in B. Schmid's Tabulatur Buch; ten can-
    zonas in Woltz's Nova Musices.
    Canzonen 1592, Pierre Pidoux, ed. , Bärenreiter 1759, 1954.
    Missae Virginis Mariae, in Notre Dame, Orgue et Liturgie,
        Vol. 11, p. 11.
    Toccata, in Historical Anthology of Music, Vol. I, p. 168.
    Toccata, V ton, in Geschichte der Musik in Beispielen,
        p. 151.
    Toccata del III tuono, in Anthologia Organistica Italiana,
        p. 19.
    Toccata on the Third Tone, in The First Four Centuries of

Organ Music, Vol. I, p. 103.
Toccata I "XI tono detto V", in Classici Italiani dell'Organo,
   p. 54.
Toccate per Organo, 3 vols. , Sandro dalla Libera, ed. ,
   Ricordi 2626, 2638, and 2629.
compositions in Archives des maîtres d'orgue des seizième-
   dix-huitième siècles, Vol. X.
toccatas (4) in L'Arte Musicale in Italia, Vol. III, p. 91.
MESANGEAU. French. Seventeenth century. Lute composer.
   compositions (2) in Les Maîtres français de l'orgue.
MESSIAEN, OLIVIER. born Avignon, France, Dec. 10, 1908. Son
   of Cécile Sauvage, poetess; studied at the Conservatory,
   Paris; pupil of Dupré and Dukas; 1942, became professor of
   musical analysis, philosophy, and aesthetics, Conservatory,
   Paris; since 1931, organist, Trinité; 1949, taught at Berk-
   shire Music Center, Tanglewood, Mass. ; taught Boulez and
   Stockhausen.
   Apparition de l'église éternelle (1932/1934), Lemoine, 1934.
   (L')Ascension (Majesté du Christ demandant sa gloire à son
      Père; Alléluias sereins; Transports de joie; Prière du
      Christ) (1934), Leduc.
   (Le) Banquet céleste (1926, 1934), Leduc.
   (Les) Corps glorieux (1939), Leduc, 1942, Vol. 1: Subtilité
      des corps glorieux; Les eaux de la grâce; L'ange aux
      parfums; Vol. 2: Combat de la mort et de la vie;
      Vol. 3: Force et agilité des corps glorieux; Joie et
      clarté des corps glorieux; Le mystère de la Sainte
      Trinité.
   Diptyque (1930), Durand, 1930.
   Essai sur la vie terrestre et l'éternité bienheureuse, ₹
      Durand, 1930.
   Livre d'orgue (Reprises par interversion; Pièce en trio,
      pour le dimanche de la Sainte Trinité; Les mains de
      l'abîme, pour les temps de pénitence; Chants d'oiseaux,
      pour le temps pascal; Pièce en trio, pour le dimanche
      de la Sainte Trinité; Les yeux dans les roues, pour le
      dimanche de la Pentecôte; Soixante-quatre durées)
      (1951), Leduc, 1952.
   Méditations sur le mystère de la Sainte Trinité (1969).
   Messe de la Pentecôte (Entrée, Les langues de feu; Offer-
      toire, Les choses visibles et invisibles; Consecration,
      Le don de Sagesse; Communion, Les oise aux et les
      sources; Sortie, Le vent de l'Esprit) (1950), Leduc,
      1951.
   (La) Nativité du Seigneur (1936), 4 vols. , Leduc, Vol. 1:
      La Vierge et l'Enfant; Les bergers; Desseins éternels;
      Vol. 2: Le verbe; Les enfants de Dieu; Vol. 3: Les
      anges; Jésus accepte la souffrance; Les mages;
      Vol. 4: Dieu parmi nous.
   Verset pour la fête de la dédicace, Leduc.
METZGER, HANS ARNOLD. German. born 1914. Director,
   Evangelische Kirchenmusikschule, Esslingen, Germany.
   Neue Choralvorspiele (43), Schultheiss, 1960.

chorale preludes in The Parish Organist, Vols. 1-4, 5, 6,
7, and 12.
MEYER, D. German. Seventeenth century.
Prelude, in Organum, Series IV, Vol. 2.
MEYER, GREGOR. born Säckingen, Switzerland, ca. 1510; died
Basel, November 1576. 1535, became organist, St. Ursus,
Solothurn; 1561, appointed organist, reformed Cathedral,
Basel.
composition in Masterpieces of Organ Music, Folio 67.
Kyrie eleisons (2) in Alte Meister aus der Frühzeit des
Orgelspiels.
MICHAEL, CHRISTIAN. born Dresden, Germany, ?; died Leipzig,
Aug. 29, 1637. Studied at the University of Leipzig; 1633,
became organist, Nikolaikirche, Leipzig.
composition in Masterpieces of Organ Music, Folio 60.
MICHÁLEK, FRANTIŠEK. Czech. born 1895; died 1951. Pupil
of Josef Klička and Vítězslav Novák; professor of organ,
Conservatory, Prague, and Janáček Academy of Music, Brno.
In Memoriam, Leuckart.
Partita on Všichni věrní křest'ané, Hudby a Uměni 308.
chorale preludes (2) in Musica Boemica per Organo, Jiři
Reinberger, ed., Vol. I, p. 76, Státní nakladatelství
krásné literatury, Hudby a Umění, 1954.
MICHEELSEN, HANS FRIEDRICH. born Hennstedt, Dithmarschen,
Germany, June 9, 1902. Pupil of Paul Kickstat and Paul
Hindemith; organist, St. Matthäi; 1938, director, Landes-
kirchenmusikschule, Hamburg; 1954, appointed professor and
director of church music, Hochschule für Musik, Hamburg.
Canzona, in Cantantibus Organis, Vol. I, p. 23.
Choralmusik, Bärenreiter 1311, 1951.
(Das) Grechener Orgelbuch, 2 vols., Müller 105.
(Das) Holsteinische Orgelbuchlein (for small organ),
Bärenreiter 1679.
Organistenpraxis, 3 vols., Hüllenhagen und Griehl.
Orgelkonzert in a moll, Bärenreiter 2058.
Orgelkonzert über Es sungen drei Engel, Bärenreiter 2065.
Orgelkonzert III, Bärenreiter 2748.
Orgelkonzert V über Christe, der du bist Tag und Licht,
Bärenreiter 3974.
Orgelkonzert VI über O dass ich tausend Zungen hätte,
Müller 63.
Orgelkonzert VII über Der Morgenstern, Müller 94.
Ostinato, in Musica Organi, Vol. II, p. 129.
Passacaglia, in Musica Organi, Vol. II, p. 137.
chorale preludes (2) in Neue Orgelvorspiele, Part 2, Haag-
Hennig, ed., Merseburger.
chorale preludes (3) in Orgelbuch zum Evangelischen
Kirchengesangbuch, O. Brodde, ed., Books 5, 14,
and 18, Bärenreiter.
chorale preludes (3) in Orgelvorspiele, Poppen, Reich,
and Strube, eds., Merseburger.
chorale preludes (2) in 73 leichte Choralvorspiele, alter
und neuer Meister, H. Fleischer, ed., Leuckart.

MIDDLESCHULTE, WILHELM. born Werne (Dortmund), Germany, Apr. 3, 1863; died Werne, May 4, 1943. Studied at the Institut für Kirchenmusik, Berlin; 1888-1891, organist, St. Luke, Berlin; 1891-1895, organist, Holy Name Cathedral, Chicago; professor of organ, Wisconsin Conservatory of Music, Milwaukee; 1935, appointed instructor of theory and organ, Detroit Foundation Music School; 1939, returned to Germany.

> Chromatische Fantasie und Fuge (C Minor), Kahnt.
> Kanonische Fantasie über B-A-C-H und Fuge über vier
> Themen von J. S. Bach, organ and orchestra, Kahnt.
> Kanons und Fuge über den Choral Vater unser im Himmel-
> reich, Leuckart.
> Konzert über ein Thema von J. S. Bach (A Minor), organ
> and orchestra, Kahnt.
> Perpetuum Mobile, Virgil Fox, ed. , Gray (St. Cecilia
> Series 775); also Peters 311.
> Tokkata über den Choral Ein' feste Burg, Leuckart.

MIGOT, GEORGES ELBERT. born Paris, Feb. 27, 1891. Studied at the Conservatory, Paris; pupil of Widor, Gigout, Guilmant, and d'Indy; curator of instruments, Conservatory, Paris.

> Premier Livre d'orgue, Leduc.
> Six petits préludes, Leduc.
> (Le) Tombeau de Nicolas de Grigny, Leduc.

MILÁN, LUIS. born Valencia, Spain, ca. 1500; died after 1561. Served court in Valencia; 1535/1536, published Libro de música de vihuela de mano intitulado El Maestro.

> composition in Elkan-Vogel Organ Series, Vol. 5.

MILES, GEORGE THEOPHILUS. English. born 1913. Organist, director of music, St. Peter's Church, Birmingham, England.

> chorale preludes in The Parish Organist, Vols. 1-4, 5, 6,
> 7, and 8.

MILFORD, ROBIN HUMPHREY. born Oxford, England, Jan. 22, 1903; died Lyme Regis, Dec. 29, 1959. Studied with Holst and Vaughan Williams at the Royal College of Music.

> Christmas Tune, Cramer.
> Chorale Prelude on St. Columba, in Wedding Pieces, Oxford.
> Harvest Meditation, Oxford.
> Mr. Ben Jonson's Pleasure, Oxford.
> Prelude, in Preludes, Interludes, Postludes, Hinrichsen
> 600E.
> Seven Seasonal Sketches based on Carol Tunes, Novello.
> Three Christmas Pieces (Unto Us a Boy Is Born; The
> Coventry Carol; On Christmas Night), Oxford.
> Three Pastorales (A Tune for Maundy Thursday; Cradle
> Song for Christmas Day; Traveller's Joy), Oxford.
> Two Chorale Preludes, Op. 14, Oxford.
> Two Easter Meditations, No. 1/2; 3/4; 5/6, Oxford.
> chorale preludes (6) in Advent to Whitsuntide, Vol. 2,
> Hinrichsen.

MILHAUD, DARIUS. born Aix-en-Provence, France, Sept. 4, 1892. Studied at the Conservatory, Paris; pupil of Widor, Dukas, and d'Indy; 1917, went to Rio de Janeiro; 1940, came to the

United States; taught at Mills College, Oakland, Calif.; appointed professor of composition, Conservatory, Paris; member of the French "Six".

Neuf Préludes, Heugel, 1946.

Pastorale, Gray (Contemporary Organ Series 9), 1942.

Petite Suite (1955), Eschig.

Sonata, Gray, 1950.

MILNER, ANTHONY. born Bristol, England, May 13, 1925. Studied at the Royal College of Music; 1947-1962, faculty member, Morley College, London; 1962, appointed to the staff, Royal College of Music; 1965, appointed lecturer, King's College, University of London.

Fugue for Advent, Gray (Contemporary Organ Series 31).

Rondo Saltato, Novello.

MILNER, ARTHUR FREDERICK. born Manchester, England, 1894. D. Mus., University of Durham; Fellow, Trinity College of London; Associate, Royal College of Music; Associate, Royal College of Organists; 1942-1963, Lecturer, King's College, Durham; 1950-1967, music critic, Newcastle Journal.

Arabesque, Edwin Ashdown, 1967.

Diptych, Novello, 1965.

Festal Epilog, Novello, 1964.

Finale, Edwin Ashdown, 1963.

Galliard for a Festive Occasion, Novello.

Meditation on Psalm 62, Stainer & Bell, 1966.

Meditation on Psalm 121, Cramer.

Meditation on Psalm 137, Edwin Ashdown, 1966.

Pastorale, Boosey & Hawkes.

Prelude on a Theme of Palestrina, in Preludes, Interludes, Postludes, Hinrichsen 600F.

Prelude, Siciliano and Ricercare, Novello.

Six Preludes, Novello, 1964.

Solemn Prelude, Edwin Ashdown, 1964.

Solemn Prelude, Boosey and Hawkes.

Three Introductory Voluntaries, Novello.

Three Sketches, Novello.

Threnody, Boosey and Hawkes.

Two Meditations on Psalms, Novello.

MØLLER, SVEND-OVE. born Copenhagen, June 24, 1903; died Viborg, Apr. 16, 1949. Pupil of P. S. Rung-Keller and Thomas Laub; 1933-1947, organist, Nykøbing Falster; 1947, appointed organist, Cathedral, Viborg.

Forspil (60) til Salmemelodier, Op. 27 (1946), Skandinavisk.

Koralvariationen (7) (1942).

Orgelfantasi Nr. 6, Hansen 27338.

Orgelpartita No. 1, in Musica Organi, Vol. 3, p. 34.

Pensée (1937).

Te Deum (1949), Dan Fog.

Variationer (7), Op. 8, Edition Dania.

MOESCHINGER, ALBERT. born Basel, Switzerland, Jan. 10, 1897. Studied at Berne, Leipzig, and Munich; influenced by German neo-Romanticism and French Impressionism.

Introduction und Doppelfuge, Schott 2102.

Sonata, violin and organ.
MOHLER, PHILIPP. born Kaiserslautern, Germany, Nov. 26, 1908.
1934-1940, director at musical posts in Munich, Nürnberg, and
Landau; 1940, succeeded Distler at the Musikhochschule, Stuttgart, 1943, became professor there; 1940, directed Stuttgart
Orchestral Society; 1958, appointed director, Hochschule für
Musik, Frankfurt.
Zwei Canzonen, Op. 17 (1941), Müller 66.
MONNARD FAMILY. French. Seventeenth century. Nicolas Monnard, organist, Jacobins (1624); 1634 until at least 1646,
organist, St. Eustache, Hemery Monnard (Emeric), born
ca. 1611, organist, St. Laurent.
compositions (2) in Les Maîtres français de l'orgue, Vol. I.
suite movements (3) in Pré-Classiques français, L'Organiste
liturgique, Vol. 18.
MONNIKENDAM, MARIUS. born Haarlem, The Netherlands, May 28,
1896. Studied at the Amsterdam Conservatory with Sem Dres-
den and de Pauw; 1924, studied with d'Indy; taught at the Mu-
sic Lyceum, Amsterdam, and at the Conservatory, Rotterdam.
Choral, Annie Bank.
Concerto, organ, brass, and timpani (1958), Donemus 134.
Concerto, organ and orchestra, Donemus 470.
Concerto, organ and strings, miniature score, Donemus 155.
Cortège, Van Rossum R. 522 (World Library of Sacred
Music).
Intrada and Sortie, organ, two trumpets, and two trombones,
World Library of Sacred Music.
Inventiones (1959), Donemus.
Marcia funebre (1959), Donemus.
Overture, organ and orchestra, miniature score, Donemus
202.
Rodeña, timpani and organ, Donemus 246.
Sonata da Chiesa (1961), Donemus 258.
Tema con variazioni per la notte di natale, Annie Bank.
Toccata, Van Rossum R. 206; also Gray (St. Cecilia
Series 855).
Twelve Inventions, World Library of Sacred Music 101.
Twelve More Inventions, World Library of Sacred Music
102.
MONTE, PHILIPPE DE. born Malines, Belgium, 1521; died
Prague, July 4, 1603. 1541-1545, tutor to Pinelli family,
Naples; friend of Roland de Lassus; 1554, went to Rome,
Antwerp, and England; 1555, returned to Italy; 1568-1603,
maestro di cappella to Maximilian II in Vienna.
Canzona, in Oudnederlandse Meesters, Vol. I, p. 31.
MOORE, DOUGLAS STUART. born Cutchogue, Long Island, N.Y.,
Aug. 10, 1893; died Greenport, N.Y., July 25, 1969. Grad-
uate of Yale University; composition pupil of Horatio Parker;
1919-1921, pupil of d'Indy, Bloch, Tournemire, and Boulanger;
1921, appointed Curator of Musical Arts, Cleveland Museum of
Art; 1923-1925, organist, Adelbert Chapel, Western Reserve
University; 1926-1962, faculty member, later head, music
department, Columbia University; 1925, won Pulitzer Prize;

1934, won Guggenheim Fellowship; honorary doctorates from Cincinnati Conservatory, University of Rochester, and Yale University.

Dirge (Passacaglia), Gray (Contemporary Organ Series 4), 1941.

MOREAU, (ABBÉ) FÉLIX. born Aigrefeuille-sur-Maine (Loire-Atlantique), France, Sept. 8, 1922. Pupil of his father, Canon Courtonne, and Maurice Duruflé; 1944-1948, organist, Grand Séminaire, Nantes; since 1954, organist, Cathedral, Nantes; professor of organ, Centre de Musique Sacrée and Séminaire, Nantes, and at the Conservatory, Angers; 1964, appointed director, Sessions for Organists, Québec, Canada.

Incarnation (four meditations for Christmas), Leduc.

MORENO Y POLO, JUAN. Spanish. born ?; died 1776.

Dos Versillos de Segundo Tono, in Early Spanish Organ Music, p. 44.

compositions (2) in Antologia de Organistas Clásicos Españoles, Vol. II, p. 123-138.

MORHARD, PETER. German. born ?; died Lüneburg, Germany, 1685. 1662-1685, organist, Michaeliskirche, Lüneburg.

Orgelwerke, G. Fock, ed.

MORTHENSON, JAN W. Swedish. born 1940.

Eternes, Nordiska.

Pour Madame Bovary (1962), Nordiska.

Some of these (1965), Nordiska.

MOSER, RUDOLF. born Niederuzwyl, St. Gall, Switzerland, Jan. 7, 1892; died near St. Moritz, Aug. 20, 1960. Pupil of Reger; 1912-1914, studied at the Conservatory, Leipzig; choirmaster, Cathedral, Basel.

Rhapsodie dans la mode dorienne, Leduc.

Suite über Der Tag, der ist, Hug & Co.

Suite über Veni, Sancte Spiritus, Hug & Co.

chorale preludes (2) in Das Organistamt, Vol. 2, Breitkopf & Härtel.

chorale preludes in The Parish Organist, Vols. 1-4, 5, 6, 7, and 8.

MOTTU, ALEXANDRE. Swiss. born June 11, 1883; died 1943. Studied at the Conservatory, Geneva, and in Leipzig and Berlin; professor of piano, Conservatory, Geneva; organist, Temple des Eaux Vives, Geneva.

Pièces liturgiques, 4 books, Salabert.

Prelude et Choral, Henn, 1942.

Toccata, Henn.

MOULAERT, RAYMOND. born Brussels, Feb. 4, 1875; died Brussels, Jan. 18, 1962. Studied at the Royal Conservatory, Brussels; 1896-1940, taught at the Conservatory, Brussels.

Alleluia Victimae Paschali Laudes (1927).

Deux pièces, Oertel (Brussels), 1910.

Prelude et Choral (1948).

Sonata in D Minor, Bote und Bock, 1907.

MOZART, WOLFGANG AMADEUS. born Salzburg, Austria, Jan. 27, 1756; died Vienna, Dec. 5, 1791. Pupil of his father, Leopold, and of Haydn; 1762, began touring Europe with his

sister;   became Konzertmeister to the Archbishop of Salzburg;
late 1769-1771, tour of Italy; 1779, appointed court organist,
Salzburg, but soon after left Salzburg permanently to live in
Vienna; 1787, appointed chamber-composer to Emperor;
celebrated performer and composer of operas, symphonies,
clavier and choral works.
Adagio and Allegro (F Minor), K. 594, in Historical Organ
    Recitals, Vol. III, p. 48; also Kalmus 3707.
Adagio and Rondo, glass harmonica and flute, oboe, viola,
    and 'cello (or string quartet), Music Press;   also
    E. Power Biggs, arr., Gray (St. Cecilia Series 768).
Andante in F, Hugh McLean, ed., Oxford.
Church Sonatas, organ and orchestra, in New Edition of
    Collected Works, Series VI, No. 16, Bärenreiter
    4511: Nine Church Sonatas, KV 67-69, 144, 145,
    212, 224, 225, 241, two violins, violoncello (bass),
    and organ, Bärenreiter 4731 (or 401); Five Church
    Sonatas, KV 244, 245, 274, 328, 336, Bärenreiter
    402; Two Church Sonatas, KV 278 and 329, two oboes,
    two violins, bass, two horns, two trumpets, timpani,
    and organ, Bärenreiter 403; Church Sonata, KV 263,
    two trumpets, strings, and organ, Bärenreiter 4735.
Fantasia, K. 594, Henry G. Ley, ed., Novello.
Fantasia, K. 608, Walter Emery, ed., Novello.
Kirchensonaten: Sonaten für Orgel und Orchester, Vol. 16,
    Deutscher Verlag für Musik, Leipzig, 1958.
Mozart auf der Orgel, 2 vols., Merseburger 823A/B.
Phantasie, K. 608, Peters 2415; also Kalmus 3708.
Rondo, K. 616, Sikorski 720.
Single pieces for Orgelwalze, Series IV, No. 27, Inter-
    national Mozarteum Foundation, Salzburg, 195-.
Sonata No. 1 in E-flat Major, in A Treasury of Shorter
    Organ Classics, p. 7 (transcription).
Sonatas, organ and various chamber groups, Mercury Music
    Press.
Sonaten für Orgel mit Begleitung (Nr. 1-15), in Sämtliche
    Werke, Vol. 23, Brahms and others, eds., Breitkopf
    & Härtel 1876-1905.
Three pieces (K. 594, 608, 616), Bärenreiter 1868.
Two Sonatas, K. 278 and K. 329, organ and orchestra,
    Kalmus 3706.
MUDDARA, ALONSO DE. Spanish. born between 1506 and 1510;
    died Seville, Apr. 1, 1580. Lutenist; 1566, appointed canon
    of Cathedral, Seville; wrote Tres Libros de música en cifras
    para vihuela (Juan de Leon, Seville, 1546).
    Tiento para harpa u órgano, in Silva Iberica, p. 2.
MUDDE, WILLEM FEDERIK ANTONIUS. born Amsterdam, Oct. 24,
    1909. Pupil of Jan Zwart, Fritz Heitmann, and Wolfgang
    Reimann; organist, in Purmerend, Hilversum, and Amster-
    dam; 1943, appointed organist-choirmaster, Evangelisch
    Lutherse Kerk, Utrecht.
    Canonische Koraalbewerkingen, J. A. H. Wagenaar.
    Introductie, Koraal en Ciaconna op Psalm 24, Ars Nova.

Organ and Trumpet Accompaniments to Festival Hymns,
  Concordia.
Variaties op Er is een Kindeke geboren op aard, Ars Nova.
Vom Himmel hoch, Augsburg.
chorale preludes (3) in The Parish Organist, Vol. 11.
chorale preludes (2) in Twee Begeleidings Partitas,
  J. Zwart.
MUELLER, GOTTFRIED. German. born 1914. Resident of Dres-
  den, Germany.
    Acht Orgel Choräle, Op. 3, Breitkopf & Härtel.
    Partita über Nun komm der Heiden Heiland, Merseburger
      831.
    chorale preludes in The Parish Organist, Vols. 1-4 and 7.
MÜLLER, SIGFRID WALTHER. born Plauen, Germany, Jan. 11,
  1905; died in Russian prison camp, autumn 1946. Pupil of
  Karg-Elert and Straube; 1929-1932, teacher, Conservatory,
  Leipzig; 1940-1941, teacher, Hochschule für Musik, Weimar.
    Choral Improvationen, Op. 10, Leuckart.
    Choral Vorspiele, Op. 58, 2 vols., Rieter-Biedermann.
    Präludium und Fuge in a moll, Op. 26, No. 1, Breitkopf &
      Härtel 5466.
    Präludium und Fuge in G dur, Op. 26, No. 2, Breitkopf &
      Härtel 5467.
MÜLLER-ZÜRICH, PAUL. born Zürich, Switzerland, June 19,
  1898. 1917-1920, studied at the Conservatory, Zürich and in
  Paris; 1927, appointed to faculty, Conservatory, Zürich;
  1953, won Zürich music prize; 1958, won competition prize
  from the Swiss Composers' Society, of which he became president in 1960.
    Canzone in e moll (1936).
    Choral fantasia über Ach Gott vom Himmel, Op. 56 (1955),
      Bärenreiter 437.
    Choral fantasia über Christ ist erstanden (1957), organ,
      two trumpets, two trombones.
    Choral fantasia über Wie schön leuchtet, Op. 52, No. 2,
      organ, two trumpets, two trombones (1953), Bären-
      reiter 438.
    Choral toccata über Ein' feste Burg, Op. 54, No. 1,
      organ, two trumpets, two trombones (1953), Bären-
      reiter 439.
    Concerto, organ and string orchestra, Op. 28 (1938),
      Schott 2855.
    Fantasie und Fuge in E dur, violin and organ, Op. 45
      (1949), Hug.
    Fünf-und-zwanzig Orgelchoräle (Neue Folge), Krompholz.
    Orgelchoräle und Vorspiele, Op. 58, Op. 63 (1959).
    Präludium und Fuge in e moll, Op. 22 (1934), Schott 2337.
    Toccata I in C dur, Op. 12 (1925), Schott 2116.
    Toccata II in D dur, Op. 38 (1943), Gray (St. Cecilia
      Series 773).
    Toccata III, Op. 50, Schott 4536.
    Zwanzig Orgel Choräle, Krompholz.
    chorale preludes (4) in 21 Orgelchoräler Schweizerischer

Komponisten, Krompholz.

MUFFAT, GEORG. Christened in Mégève, Savoy, France, June 1, 1653; died Passau, Feb. 23, 1704. 1663-1669, studied with Lully in Paris; 1671, appointed organist, Cathedral, Molsheim, Alsace; 1678, court organist to Archbishop Max Gandolf, Salzburg; 1682, Archbishop sent Muffat to Rome to study with B. Pasquini; 1687, named choirmaster, 1690, Kapellmeister, to Bishop of Passau, Johann Philipp von Lamberg.

Apparatus musico-organisticus (1690), Peters 6020; also Kalmus 3686; also Süddeutsche Orgelmeister des Barok, R. Walter, ed. , Vol. 3, Coppenrath.

Fugue on O Gott, du frommer Gott, in Reinbrecht's Sammlung, Viewig.

Passacaglia in G Minor, in Chacones et Passacailles, Orgue et Liturgie, Vol. 22, p. 21; also in Historical Anthology of Music, Vol. II, p. 113.

Toccata, in Historical Organ Recitals, Vol. I, p. 84.

Toccata duodezima, in Alte Meister des Orgelspiels, Vol. I, p. 114.

Toccata XI, in Liber Organi, Vol. V, p. 22.

Toccata in F Major, and Passacaglia in G Minor, in Alte Meister.

Toccata in F Major, in The First Four Centuries of Organ Music, Vol. II, p. 322.

Toccata in F Major, in Toccata, Orgue et Liturgie, Vol. 10, p. 5.

MUFFAT, GOTTLIEB. Christened in Passau, Germany, Apr. 25, 1690; died Vienna, Dec. 10, 1770. Son of Georg; scholar in royal chapel, Vienna; pupil of J. J. Fux; 1714, in charge of musical activities at court, Vienna; 1717, named second organist court organist, 1751, first organist, royal chapel of Maria Theresa of Austria.

Componimenti Musicali, Bärenreiter 5196.

Drei Toccaten, in Die Orgel, Series II, No. 10, (Concordia 97-4460).

Drei Toccaten und Capriccios, Neue Folge, in Die Orgel, Series II, No. 13, (Concordia 97-4515).

Easter Alleluia, in Cantantibus Organis, Vol. 8, F. Pustet.

Fuga pastorella (B-flat Major), in Alte deutsche Weihnachtsmusik, p. 15.

Fuge in g moll, in Liber Organi, Vol. I, p. 38.

Fughetta (A-flat Major), in The Parish Organist, Vol. 1-4, p. 224.

Fugue in G Minor, in Liber Organi, Vol. 6, p. 38.

Partitas and Pieces, Georgii, ed. , Schott 2827.

Praeambulum, in Harold Gleason, Method of Organ Playing, p. 150.

Six Fugues, in Die Orgel, Series II, No. 17.

Three Toccatas and Capriccios, in Die Orgel, Series II, No. 10.

Three Toccatas and Capriccios, in Die Orgel, Series II, No. 13.

Toccata und Fuge, in Liber Organi, Vol. 5, p. 30.

Toccata, Fuge und Capriccio, in Die Orgel, Series II,
No. 8 (Concordia 97-4442).
Twelve Short Preludes, in Die Orgel, Series II, No. 16
(Concordia 97-4552).
72 Versetl samt 12 Toccaten (1726), Bärenreiter 1922
(1952).
compositions in Denkmäler der Tonkunst in Osterreich,
Vol. 58 (Jahrgang 29, No. 2).
compositions in Masterpieces of Organ Music, Folio 58.
MUL, JAN JOHAN. born Amsterdam, Apr. 3, 1911. Studied at
the Conservatory, Amsterdam; pupil of Andriessen and Dres-
den; organist, Overveen (near Haarlem); music critic.
Choral Joyeux, Donemus 170.
Sonate, Annie Bank 28.
MULDER, ERNEST WILLEM. born Amsterdam, July 21, 1898;
died Amsterdam, Apr. 12, 1959. Studied composition with
Bernard Zweers at the Conservatory, Amsterdam; teacher of
theory and composition, Conservatory, Amsterdam.
Enige Voorspelen en Fuga, Alsbach.
Fugue (Ars Contrapunctica), Donemus 222.
Passacaglia, Donemus 223.
Vier Psalmvoorspelen, Alsbach.
MULET, HENRI. born Paris, 1878; died Draguignan, 1967. Pupil
of Pugno and Widor at the Conservatory, Paris; organist,
St. Roch; professor at the Ecole Niedermeyer; 1922-1937,
organist, St. Philippe-du-Roule.
Carillon-Sortie, Gray (Standard Series of Organ Composi-
tions 50); also Schola Cantorum.
Carillon-Sortie; Méditation religieuse, in French Master-
works for Organ.
Esquisses byzantines, Marks, 1943; also Leduc.
Offertoire funèbre, in The French Organist, Vol. II, p. 24.
MULLINER, THOMAS. English Mid-sixteenth century. Compiled
The Mulliner Book, a collection of 121 liturgical organ pieces;
a register belonging to Corpus Christi College, Oxford, dated
1563, designates him a "modulator organorum".
Five Pieces from The Mulliner Book, (Peters N 3076).
(The) Mulliner Book, Denis Stevens, ed. , in Musica
Britannica, Vol. I, Stainer and Bell, 1951.
MURRILL, HERBERT HENRY JOHN. born London, May 11, 1909;
died London, July 24, 1952. 1925-1928, studied at the Royal
Academy of Music; pupil of Stanley Marchant and Alan Bush;
1928-1931, Mus. B. , M.A. , Oxford; 1933-1952, appointed
professor of composition, Royal Academy of Music.
Carillon (1949), Oxford.
Fantasia on Wareham (1950), in Hymn Tune Voluntaries,
Oxford.
Postlude on a Ground (1949), in Simple Organ Voluntaries,
Oxford.
MURSCHHAUSER, FRANZ XAVER ANTON. Christened in Zabern
(Alsace), July 1, 1663; died Munich, Jan. 6, 1738. Pupil of
Kerll; 1691, Chorregent, Unser lieben Frau, Munich.
(Die) ganze Welt, Herr Jesu Christ, in Orgelspiel im

Kirchenjahr, Vol. 2, Schott.
Octi-Tonium novum Organicum, Kalmus 3687; also Süd-
    deutsche Orgelmeister des Barok, R. Walter, ed. ,
    Vol. 6, Coppenrath.
compositions (2) in Alte deutsche Weihnachtsmusik.
compositions in Denkmäler der Tonkunst in Bayern, Vol. 18.
compositions in The Parish Organist, Vols. 1-4, 5, and 6.
compositions (6) in Spielbuch für die Kleinorgel, Vol. II.
fugues (4) in Ricercare, Canzonen und Fugen des 17. und
    18. Jahrhunderts.
variation cycles (2) in South German Christmas Music.
MUSHEL, GEORGI. Russian. Twentieth century.
    Toccata, in Modern Organ Music, p. 24.
MUSIL, FRANTIŠEK. Czech. born 1852; died 1908. Teacher of
    counterpoint and instrumentation, Organ School, Brno; con-
    cert organist.
    Sonata Solemnis (D Minor), in Musica Boemica per Organo,
        Jiří Reinberger, ed. , Státní nakladatelství krásné
        literatury, Hudby a umění, Vol. I, p. 11.

NACHTIGALL, OTHMAR. born Alsace, ca. 1480; died Freiburg-
    im-Breisgau, 1537. Pupil of Hofhaimer; studied in Heidel-
    berg, Louvain, Padua, and Vienna; organist, St. Thomas,
    Strasbourg; professor, University of Strasbourg; taught in
    Augsburg.
    compositions (3) in Frühmeister der deutschen Orgelkunst.
NARES, JAMES. baptized Stanwell, Middlesex, England, Apr. 19,
    1715; died London, Feb. 10, 1783. Choirboy under Croft in
    Chapel Royal; pupil of Pepusch; assistant organist, St.
    George's Chapel, Windsor; 1734, named organist, Cathedral,
    York; 1756, became organist and composer to the Chapel
    Royal (succeeded Greene); 1757, Mus. Doc. , Cambridge;
    1757-1780, Master of the Children, Chapel Royal.
    Fugue (G Minor), Cramer.
NAYLOR, PETER. English. born 1933. Studied at Seaford College
    and Cambridge University; pupil of Herbert Howells and John
    Dykes-Bower; studied at the Royal College of Music.
    Movement, Novello.
NEAR, GERALD. born St. Paul, Minn. , May 23, 1942. Organ
    pupil of Rupert Sircom, Gerald Bales, and Robert Glasgow;
    composition pupil of Bales, Leo Sowerby, and Leslie Bassett;
    served as organist in churches in Illinois, Michigan, and
    Minnesota; Director of Music, Calvary Church, Rochester,
    Minn.
    Passacaglia, Augsburg 11-0837, 1966.
    Prelude on Es ist ein' Ros' entsprungen, in Music for
        Worship with Easy Pedals.
    Preludes on Four Hymn Tunes (Old 113th; Eisenach;
        Seelenbrautigam; Hyfrydol), Augsburg 11-0828, 1969.
    Preludes on Three Hymn Tunes (O Lamm Gottes;

Aberystwyth; Vom Himmel hoch), Augsburg 11-0838, 1967.

Postlude on St. Dunstans, Augsburg 11-0842, 1968.

Roulade, Augsburg 11-0825, 1965.

Suite (Chaconne; Sarabande; Final), Gray, 1966.

Toccata, Augsburg 11-0844, 1971.

(A) Triptych of Fugues, Augsburg 11-0824, 1968.

NEVIN, GORDON BALCH. born Easton, Penn., May 19, 1892; died New Wilmington, Penn., Nov. 15, 1943. Organist in Easton, Penn., Cleveland, Ohio, and Johnstown, Penn.

Fantasie on Jerusalem the Golden, O. Ditson.

Pageant Triumphale.

Sonata Tripartite, Summy.

Will-o'-the-Wisp, Summy, 1914.

NIBELLE, HENRI-JULES-JOSEPH. born Briare, France, Nov. 6, 1883. Pupil of Gigout and Guilmant; studied at the Ecole Niedermeyer and Conservatory, Paris; after 1913, organist, Eglise St. François de Sales.

(Le) Carillon orléannais, Lemoine, 1941.

Cinquante pièces, Procure de misuque religieuse, (Saint-Leu-la Foret), 1935.

Prélude et Fugue, in A la Vierge, Orgue et Liturgie, Vol. 14, p. 13.

Prélude et Fugue sur Ave maris stella, in Hymnes et Antiennes, Orgue et Liturgie, Vol. 8, p. 21.

Toccata, Lemoine, 1947.

NIBLOCK, JAMES. born Scappoose, Oregon, 1917. Ph.D., University of Iowa; Head of Music Department, Michigan State University, East Lansing, Mich.

Rex gloriae, in The Parish Organist, Vol. 12.

NIELAND, HERMAN (HERMANUS JACOBUS JOSEPHUS). born Amsterdam, Nov. 23, 1910. Studied at the Conservatory, Amsterdam; pupil of Van der Horst and Mulder; 1943, passed organists' examination.

Canonische Koraalbewerking op Jesus unser Trost und Leben, Alsbach.

Easy Polyphonic Studies (11), (Peters B 661).

Fantasie op Ontwaak, gij die slaapt, Alsbach.

Koraalbewerkingen op Gez. 112, 184, 300A, Alsbach.

Liedbewerking op Ga niet alleen door 't leven, Alsbach.

Marcia Festiva, Alsbach.

Preludium en Fuga, Alsbach.

Triosonate.

Vier Geestelijke liederen, Alsbach.

NIELAND, JAN (JOHANNES HERMANNUS IGNATIUS MARIA). born Amsterdam, Aug. 17, 1903; died 1963. Pupil of de Pauw and Willem Andriessen; 1924, passed organ examination, 1925, passed piano examination, Conservatory, Amsterdam; teacher, Conservatory, Amsterdam; director, Muzieklyceum, Naarden; organist, Concertgebouw, Amsterdam.

Ciaconna en Fuga.

Fantaisie.

Fantaisie et Fugue sur B-A-C-H.

Marche triomphale.

Organ Hymns for Easter, World Library of Sacred Music.

Organ Hymns for Lent, World Library of Sacred Music.

Paraphrase on Six Christmas Hymns, Van Rossum W. 105.

Prelude, Choral, et Variations, (Peters D 659).

Six Organ Pieces for Low Mass, World Library of Sacred
Music 103.

Toccata, Van Rossum R. 226.

Trois morceaux (Meditation; Cantabile; Pastorale), Schott
Frères.

Twelve Pieces, World Library of Sacred Music 104.

NIELSEN, CARL AUGUST. born Nörre-Lyndelse, Denmark, June 9,
1865; died Copenhagen, Oct. 3 (not 2), 1931. Studied at the
Royal Conservatory, Copenhagen; pupil of Gade; studied in
Germany, France, and Italy; orchestra violinist; 1890-1905,
member of court orchestra, Copenhagen; conductor, Copenhagen Opera; 1915, teacher, 1931, director, Conservatory,
Copenhagen.

Commotio, Op. 58 (1931), Edition Dania 11, 1954.

Festpraeludium ved århundredeskiftet, Hansen 28422.

Smaa Praeludier (29), Op. 51.

NIELSEN, LUDVIG. born Borge bei Fredrikstad, Norway, Feb. 3,
1906. Studied at the Conservatory, Oslo, and at the Conservatory, Leipzig; pupil of Straube and Raphael; 1932, became
organist, Hövik and Ris churches, Oslo; 1935, appointed organist and cantor, Nidarsdom, Oslo; since 1943, teacher,
Conservatory, Trondheim.

Christmas Fantasy on Silent Night, Op. 12,* Edition Lyche
255.

Fantasia pastorale över tre julmelodier, in Musica Organi,
Vol. III, p. 45.

Intrata Gotica, Op. 14, Edition Lyche 256.

Intrata Solemnis on Wachet auf, Edition Lyche 427.

Passacaglia over Draumkvedet, Norsk Musikforlag, 1968.

Pro Organo, 5 vols., Harald Lyche.

chorale preludes (5) in Orgelkoraler, Norsk.

NIVERD, LUCIEN. born Vouziers, France, Sept. 20, 1879. Pupil
of Widor; studied at the Conservatory, Paris; director,
Conservatory, Tourcoing.

Choral, Philippo, 1954.

Légende, in Le Grand Orgue, 1926.

Mouvement Perpetual (Toccata), in The International
Organist, Vol. II, p. 55; also Hérelle, 1954.

Pastorale, in Le Grand Orgue, 1926.

NIVERS, GUILLAUME-GABRIEL. French. born 1632; died Paris,
Nov. 30, 1714. 1654-1714, organist, St. Sulpice; 1686, became organist, St. Cyr; 1678-1708, appointed one of the four
organists of the Chapelle Royale.

Ave maris stella, in A la Sainte Vierge, L'Organiste
liturgique, Vol. 2, p. 13.

Cent préludes (Ier livre d'orgue), Vervoitte, ed., E. Repos.

Hymn of the Nativity, in The First Four Centuries of Organ
Music, Vol. II, p. 249.

Neuf Compositions, Schola Cantorum.

*Premier Livre d'orgue, Norbert Dufourcq, ed. , 2 vols. ,
Bornemann, 1963.

*2e Livre d'orgue, Norbert Dufourcq, ed. , Schola Cantorum,
1956.

*3e Livre d'orgue, Norbert Dufourcq, ed. , Heugel, 1958.

Récit de cromorne du premier ton, in Les Maîtres français
de l'orgue, Vol. II, p. 21.

Victimae paschale, in Pâques, L'Organiste liturgique,
Vol. 5, p. 9.

compositions (9) in Les Maîtres français de l'orgue, Vol. I.

NOBLE, THOMAS TERTIUS. born Bath, England, May 5, 1867;
died Rockport, Mass. , May 4, 1953. 1881-1889, organist,
All Saints, Colchester, England; 1884-1889, studied at the
Royal College of Music; pupil of Parratt, Bridge, and Stan-
ford; 1889, named organist, St. Johns, assistant organist,
Trinity College, Cambridge; 1892, became organist-choir-
master, Ely Cathedral; 1898-1913, became organist, York
Minster; 1913-1947, organist-choirmaster, St. Thomas's
Church, New York City; 1918, established St. Thomas's
Choir School; Fellow of the Royal College of Organists.

Chinese Christmas Carol, Gray, 1945.

Chorale Prelude on Aberystwyth, Galaxy.

Chorale Prelude on Eventide, in The Modern Anthology,
p. 130.

Chorale Prelude on Melcombe, A. P. Schmidt.

Chorale Prelude on Rockingham, A. P. Schmidt.

Chorale Prelude on St. Anne, A. P. Schmidt.

Chorale Prelude on Tallis's Canon, A. P. Schmidt, 1936.

Fantasy on an Italian Melody, A. P. Schmidt.

Fantasy on Leoni, Galaxy.

Fantasy on Ton-y-Botel, A. P. Schmidt, 1927.

Festival Prelude (D Minor), A. P. Schmidt.

Fourteen Chorale Preludes on English Hymns, A. P.
Schmidt.

Hebrew Melodies, Gray (St. Cecilia Series 49).

Introduction and Passacaglia, A. P. Schmidt, 1934.

Pastorale Prelude on A Chinese Christmas Carol, Gray
(St. Cecilia Series 713).

Prelude on Watchman, Galaxy.

Prelude Solennel, Oxford.

Solemn March (E Minor).

Theme with Variations (D-flat Major), Augener, 1936.

Three Chorale Preludes, A. P. Schmidt.

Toccata and Fugue (F Minor), Stainer and Bell, 1907.

Triumphal March, Gray (St. Cecilia Series 62).

Two Chorale Preludes on St. James, Galaxy.

Variations, G. Schirmer.

NOEHREN, ROBERT. born Buffalo, N.Y. , 1910. Organist,
Davidson College, Davidson, North Carolina; B. Mus. , University of Michigan; University Organist, University of Michigan, Ann Arbor, Mich.

Fugue, Associated Music Publishers.

Light Divine, in The Parish Organist, Vol. 8.

NØRGAARD, PER. born Gentofte, Denmark, July 13, 1932. Studied at the Royal Conservatory, Copenhagen; 1956-1957, pupil of Nadia Boulanger; since 1960, music critic, Politikens, Copenhagen.

    Partita Concertante, Op. 32, Hansen 4151, 1969.

    chorale preludes (5) in 47 Orgelkoraler, B. Johnsson, ed., Hansen.

NØRHOLM, IB. born Søborg, Denmark, Jan. 24, 1931. Studied at the Royal Conservatory, Copenhagen; since 1957, assistant organist, St. Olaikirke, Helsingør.

    chorale preludes (5) in 47 Orgelkoraler, B. Johnsson, ed., Hansen.

NÖRMIGER, AUGUST. born presumably in Dresden, Germany, ca. 1550; died Dresden, July 22, 1613. 1581, named organist, Dresden court; 1598, Tabulaturbuch auff dem Instrumente.

    O Welt, ich muss, in Orgelmusik der Reformationszeit, Jost Harro Schmidt, ed., Merseburger.

    compositions (4) in Willi Apel, Masters of the Keyboard.

NOORDT, ANTHONI VAN. Dutch. born ?; buried Zuiderkerk, Amsterdam, Mar. 23, 1675. Until Aug. 20, 1664, organist, Nieuwe Zydskapel, Amsterdam; after 1664, organist, Nieuwe Kerk, Amsterdam; 1673, retained as emeritus organist.

    Fantasie, in Oudnederlandse Meesters, Vol. II, p. 86.

    Psalm Bearbeitungen für Orgel, P. Pidoux, ed., Bärenreiter 380, 1954.

    Psalm 24, in European Organ Music of the 16th and 17th Centuries, p. 21.

    Seventh Psalm, in The First Four Centuries of Organ Music, Vol. II, p. 380.

    Tabulatuur-Boeck van Psalmen en Fantasyen, new edition, Alsbach, 1957.

    Verses on Psalm 22 and Psalm 116, in Hollandse Koraalkunst, Nederlandse Orgelmuziek.

NYSTEDT, KNUT. born Oslo, Norway, Sept. 3, 1915. Pupil of A. Sandvold, Ernest White, and Aaron Copland; organist, Torshov-Kirche, Oslo.

    Christ the Lord Is Risen, Augsburg.

    Deus, Sancta Trinitas, Op. 28, Lyche 316.

    (The) Happy Christmas, Augsburg.

    Introduction and Passacaglia, Peters, 1944.

    Partita on Hos Gud er Idel Glede, Op. 44, Peters.

    Pastorale, Op. 20, No. 1, in Musica Organi, Vol. III, p. 52.

    Pietà, Op. 50, Edition Lyche 441.

    Toccata, Op. 9, Edition Lyche 260.

    Toccata (G), Op. 20, No. 2, in Musica Organi, Vol. III, p. 54.

    Variationer over den norske folketone Med Jesus vil jeg fare, NMO Hansen.

OBRECHT, JACOB. born Berg-op-Zoom, The Netherlands, 1450 or
1451; died Ferrara, Italy, 1505. Took holy orders; 1484,
made maitre des enfants, Cambrai; 1485-1487, was in Bruges;
traveled in Italy; 1491, named music director, Notre Dame,
Antwerp; 1504-1505, served the ducal court, Ferrara.
  Chanson, in The First Four Centuries of Organ Music,
      Vol. I, p. 20.
  Fantasy on Salve Regina, in Oudnederlandse Meesters,
      Vol. III; also in Alte Meister aus der Frühzeit des
      Orgelspiels.
  chansons (2) in Oudnederlandse Meesters, Vol. III.
  compositions in Oudnederlandse Meesters, Vol. I (3) and
      Vol. II (4).
  Mass movements (2) in Alte Meister aus der Frühzeit des
      Orgelspiels.
  trio in Oudnederlandse Meesters, Vol. III.
OCKEGHEM, JAN. born probably in Ockeghem (Dendre), (Belgium),
1430; died Tours, France, 1495. Probably a pupil of Binchois; 1443-1444, choirboy, Antwerp, and later (1446-1448)
for Duke Charles of Bourbon; 1449, became a pupil of Dufay;
1452-1453, chorister, royal chapel, from 1454, composer,
chaplain to Charles VII, Louis XI, and Charles VIII; 1469,
traveled to Spain; taught des Pres.
  Fugue in Epidiatesseron, in The First Four Centuries of
      Organ Music, Vol. I, p. 14.
  Motet; Fuga, in Oudnederlandse Meesters, Vol. I.
OLAGUÉ, BARTOLOMEO DE. Probably in the Catalan school of
the seventeenth century.
  Xácara de 1º Tono, in Silva Iberica, p. 15.
OLDROYD, GEORGE. born Healey, Yorkshire, England, Dec. 1,
1886; died London, Feb. 26, 1951. Pupil of Eaglefield Hull;
1915, organist, English Church, Paris; taught, Trinity Col-
lege; 1949, appointed professor, University of London (suc-
ceeded Marchant).
  Fantasy, Prelude and Chorale, Augener.
  (Le) Prie-Dieu, in Book of Simple Organ Voluntaries,
      Oxford.
  This Endrys Night, in Hymn Tune Voluntaries, Oxford.
  Three Chorale Preludes, Augener.
  Three Liturgical Improvisations, Oxford, 1948.
  Three Liturgical Preludes, Oxford, 1938.
  Two Evening Responds, Oxford.
OLEY, JOHANN CHRISTOPH. born Bernburg, Germany, 1738;
died Aschersleben, Jan. 20, 1789. 1755, appointed organist,
Bernburg; schoolmaster.
  Es wolle Gott, in 73 leichte Choralvorspiele, alter und
      neuer Meister, H. Fleischer, ed. , Leuckart.
  Four Chorale Preludes, Walter Emery, ed. , Novello, 1958.
  Freu dich sehr, in The Church Organist's Golden Treasury,
      Vol. I, p. 169.
  Herzliebster Jesu, in The Parish Organist, Vol. 1-4, p. 64.
  Nun danket alle Gott, in Seasonal Chorale Preludes, Book 2,
      Oxford.

Six Chorale Preludes, Walter Emery, ed. , Novello
    EOM 20, 1964.
Variierte Choräle für Orgel, Reussner.
chorale preludes (3) in Preludien Buch, Reinbrecht, ed. ,
    Viewig.
OLSEN, A. LORAN. born Minneapolis, Minn. , 1930. Professor
    of Music, Washington State University, Pullman, Wash.
    Tidings, in The Parish Organist, Vol. 12.
OLSON, DANIEL. born Norrköping, Sweden, May 7, 1898. 1919,
    graduated from the Folkeskole; 1931-1933, studied organ and
    conducting, Stockholm; organist and teacher, Uppsala; since
    1953, organist and teacher, Sollefteå.
    Preludium och Fuga, in Musica Organi, Vol. III, p. 128.
OLSSON, OTTO EMANUEL. born Stockholm, Dec. 19, 1879; died
    1964. 1897-1901, studied at the Conservatory, Stockholm;
    1908-1956, organist, Gustaf Vasa Church, Stockholm; 1908-
    1945, teacher, 1926, professor, Conservatory, Stockholm.
    Adagio, Elkan & Schildknecht.
    Berceuse, Sestetto och Fantasia chromatica, Augener.
    Canons (5), Op. 18, O. Junne.
    Credo symphoniacum, Op. 50 (1918), Elkan & Schildknecht.
    Entré, in Organistens favoritalbum, Vol. I.
    Fantasi och fuga över Vilove dig, o store Gud, Op. 29,
        (1909), Körlings.
    Good Friday, in The International Organist, Vol. I, p. 58.
    Gregorianska melodier, Op. 30 (1910), Carl Gehrmans.
    Jesus, Thy Name hath power to bless, Op. 36, No. 4,
        in Organ Music of the Netherlands and Scandinavia,
        p. 13.
    Marsch, in Favoritmarscher för Orgelharmonium.
    Marsch funebre, in Organistens favoritalbum, Vol. I.
    Meditation (E Minor), Op. 16b, Elkan & Schildknecht.
    Lätta koralpreludier, Körlings.
    Miniatyrer, Op. 5, Nordiska Musikförlaget.
    Orgelstycken (12) över koralmotiv, Op. 36, Körlings.
    Pedalstudien (5), Op. 26, HOF.
    Pieces (6) on Old Church Songs, Op. 47, Augener.
    Prelude on How Brightly Shines, Gray.
    Preludium och fuga (C-sharp Minor), Op. 39, Hansen.
    Preludium och fuga (F-sharp Minor), Op. 52 (1919-1920),
        Hansen.
    Preludium och fuga (D-sharp Minor), Op. 56, in Musica
        Organi, Vol. III, p. 109.
    Sonat (E Major), Op. 38, Augener, 1924.
    Suite (G Major), Op. 20, Augener.
    Suite för orgelharmonium, Dahlström.
    Trios (5), Op. 44, Augener.
    Two Chorale Preludes (Epiphany, Easter), Edition Musicus.
    Variations on the Dorian plainsong Ave maris stella,
        Op. 42, Augener.
    Vom Himmel hoch, Op. 36, No. 3, in Organ Music of the
        Netherlands and Scandinavia, p. 11.
OLTER, MARCUS. German. Seventeenth century. Organist,

Meldorf.
 Canzon, in Organum, Series IV, Vol. 2.
ORR, ROBIN. born Brechin, Scotland, June 2, 1909. Studied at
  the Royal College of Music and at Cambridge; pupil of Dent,
  Casella, and Boulanger; 1938, became organist, St. John's
  College, Cambridge; 1947-1950, lecturer, Cambridge; 1950-
  1956, taught at the Royal College of Music; 1956, appointed
  professor of music, University of Glasgow.
  Three Preludes on Scottish Psalm Tunes, Set I and II,
   Hinrichsen 720B.
  Toccata alla marcia, Hinrichsen 540A.
ORTO, MABRIANO DE. born Ortho, The Netherlands, ?; died
  Nivelles, Italy, February 1529. 1484-1494, singer in papal
  chapel, Rome, with Josquin des Pres; 1487, made a canon;
  1505, began service to Philip of Burgundy; 1515, began ser-
  vice to Archduke Charles.
  Ave Maria, in Alte Meister aus der Frühzeit des Orgel-
   spiels, p. 24.
OTHMAYR, KASPAR. born Amberg, Germany, Mar. 12, 1515;
  died Nürnberg, Feb. 4, 1553. Studied at the University of
  Heidelberg; 1536, went to monastery school, Heilbronn;
  1548, appointed provost, Ansbach, Germany.
  Mit Fried' und Freud', in 73 leichte Choralvorspiele, alter
   und neuer Meister, H. Fleischer, ed. , Leuckart.
  Wo Gott zum Haus, in The Parish Organist, Vol. 6.
OUCHTERLONY, DAVID. Canadian. born Guelph, Ontario. Pupil
  of Healey Willan; studied in New York and London; Organist-
  choirmaster, Holy Trinity, St. Andrew's, Toronto; music
  master, Appleby College, Oakville, St. Andrew's College,
  Aurora, Upper Canada College, Toronto; 1946, appointed
  organist-choirmaster, Timothy Eaton Memorial Church, Tor-
  onto; faculty member, 1947, Supervisor of Branches, 1969,
  Principal, School of Music, Royal Conservatory, Toronto.
  Trumpet Tune, Gray (St. Cecilia Series 843), 1957.
OURGANDJIAN, RAFFI. born Beirut, Lebanon, Jan. 7, 1937.
  1952-1962, studied at the Conservatory, Paris; pupil of Jean-
  Jacques Grünenwald and Olivier Messiaen; 1962-1970, organist,
  St. Pierre, Neuilly.
  Cinq versets sur Veni creator, in L'Organiste liturgique,
   Vol. 53, p. 3.
  Messe en trois parties, in Orgue et Liturgie, Vol. 67,
   1965.
OUSELEY, (SIR) FREDERICK ARTHUR GORE. born London,
  Aug. 12, 1825; died Hereford, Apr. 6, 1889. 1846, B. A. ,
  1849, M. A. , Oxford University; 1849-1851, curate, St. Paul's,
  Knightsbridge; 1855, appointed professor of music, Oxford.
  Sonata No. 1 (C Minor), Novello.
  Sonata No. 2 (G Major), Novello.
  Two Preludes, Novello 233 O. C. (N. S.).
OXINAGAS, JOAQUIN MARTINEZ. Spanish. Eighteenth century.
  Fuga en Sol Menor, in Early Spanish Organ Music, p. 69.
  fugues (3) in Antologia de Organistas Clásicos Españoles,
   Vol. II, pp. 106-123.

fugues (2) in Les anciens maîtres espagnols.

PACH, WALTER. born Vienna, Aug. 22, 1904. 1929, received
diploma, later professor, Hochschule für Musik und darstel-
lende Kunst, Vienna; pupil of Franz Schmidt (composition)
and Franz Schütz (organ); organist, Votivkirche, Vienna.
Chaconne, Oxford, 1955.
Fantasia brevis, Doblinger, 1965.
Fantasie und fuge, Edition Peschek, St. Martin, Linz
(Austria), 1962.
Introduction and Fugue, Novello.
Introduktion und fuge (F-sharp Minor), Doblinger, 1960.
Partita canonica über Vater unser, Doblinger, 1967.
Partita über O unbesiegter, starker Held, St. Michael,
Doblinger, 1960.
Praeambel und Chaconne, Doblinger, 1966.
Two Chorale Preludes, Oxford.
PACHELBEL, JOHANN. Baptized Nürnberg, Germany, Sept. 1,
1653; died Nürnberg, Mar. 3, 1706. Organist, St. Lorenz,
Altdorf; 1672-1673, studied with Kerll in Vienna; 1674, made
organist, St. Stephen's Cathedral, Vienna; 1677, appointed
court organist to Duke Johann Georg, Eisenach; became
friends with many members of the Bach family; 1678, became
organist, Predigerkirche, Erfurt; 1686, taught J. S. Bach's
brother, J. Christoph, from Eisenach; 1690, named court
musician and organist to Duchess Magdalena Sibylla von Württemberg; 1692, fled from French invaders to Nürnberg; 1692,
appointed city organist and organist for Augustiner and Mar-
garethenkirche, Gotha; 1695, appointed organist, St. Sebald,
Nürnberg.
Ach Herr, mich, in Geschichte der Musik in Beispielen,
p. 344.
Aria Sebaldina, Ciacona (F Major), in Spielbuch für die
Kleinorgel, Vol. I.
Aria Querta, Ciacona, in Spielbuch für die Kleinorgel,
Vol. II.
Ausgewählte Klavierwerke (organ), Dorflein, ed. , Schott
2349; also Peters 4407B.
Ausgewählte Orgelwerke, 4 vols. , Bärenreiter 238, 239,
287, and 1016; also Kalmus 3760-3763.
Choral Vorspiele, Breitkopf & Härtel.
Christmas Pastoral, Vom Himmel hoch, Gray.
Ciaconna (D Minor), in Alte Meister.
Ciaconna (F Major), in European Organ Music of the 16th
and 17th Centuries, p. 129.
Fantasia, in Organ Book No. 2, p. 6.
Fifteen Chorale Preludes (Musica Sacra), Bote & Bock.
Fuga, in Ricercare, Canzonen und Fugen des 17. und 18.
Jahrhunderts, p. 32.
Gelobet seist du, in Altdeutsche Weinachtsmusik, Nagel's

Musik Archives.

Hexachordum Apollinis, Bärenreiter 2818.

Lord Jesus Christ, Thou Living Bread, in Organ Music for the Communion Service, p. 38.

Magnificat Fuga, in Historical Anthology of Music, Vol. II, p. 135.

Magnificat Fugen (Secundi toni, Septimi toni), in Liber Organi, Vol. 6.

Magnificat Fugues (32), Huebsch, ed. , Müller 55.

Ninety-four compositions, Botsiber and Seiffert, eds. , in Denkmäler der Tonkunst in Osterreich, Vol. 17 (Jahrgang VIII, No. 2), Breitkopf & Härtel, 1901.

Nun lob', mein Seel', den Herren, in Organ Book No. 2, p. 8.

O Traurigkeit, in Anthologie, Concordia.

Organ Works, Karl Matthei, ed. , 4 vols. , Bärenreiter, 1931: Vol. I: Prelude, Fantasy, 5 toccatas, 3 fugues, ricercar, 2 chaconnes, Bärenreiter 238; Vol. 2: chorale preludes, Bärenreiter 239; Vol. 3: chorale preludes, Bärenreiter 287; Vol. 4: seven chorale partitas, Bärenreiter 1016.

Organ Works, Max Seiffert, ed. , in Denkmäler der Tonkunst in Bayern, Vol. IV/i, Breitkopf & Härtel, 1903.

Pastorale and Fugue on Vom Himmel hoch, in Historical Organ Recitals, Vol. I, p. 94.

Prelude, Fugue, and Chaconne, in Alte Meister des Orgelspiels, Vol. II.

Quarante versets de Magnificat, Vol. II, Noëlie Pierront et Norbert Dufourcq, eds. , Bornemann.

Sieben Choralvorspiele, Koerner.

Ten Fugues on the Magnificat, Walter Emery, ed. , Novello EOM 5, 1958.

Toccata, in Alte Meister des Orgelspiels, Vol. II.

Toccata (C Minor) und Präludium (D Minor), G. Ramin, ed. , Breitkopf & Härtel 6240.

Toccata and Fugue (D Minor), Sumner, ed. , Peters 4301H.

Toccata in E Minor, in Treasury of Early Organ Music, p. 57.

Toccata (F Major), in Alte Meister.

Twelve Pieces, Schuitema, ed. , (Peters HU 1050).

Vater unser, in Notre Père, Orgue et Liturgie, Vol. 24, p. 14; also in Alte Meister; also in Cantantibus Organis, Vol. I, p. 8.

chaconnes, fugues and ricercar in Organum, Series IV, Vols. 13 and 14 (Concordia 97-4345, 97-4346).

chorale preludes (3) in Alte Meister des Orgelspiels, Vol. II.

chorale preludes (11) in Eighty Chorale Preludes: German Masters of the Seventeenth and Eighteenth Centuries.

chorale preludes (7) in Chorale Preludes by Masters of the Seventeenth and Eighteenth Centuries.

chorale preludes (4) in Choralvorspiel alter Meister.

chorale preludes (3) in Choralvorspiele zum Kirchenlied, Vol. 3, Christophorus.

chorale preludes in The Church Organist's Golden Treasury,
Vol. I (5), Vol. II (2), Vol. III (9).
chorale preludes (3) in Laudamus Dominum, p. 3.
chorale preludes in Masterpieces of Organ Music, Folios 1,
5, 17, and 27.
chorale preludes in Organ Preludes Ancient and Modern,
W. Sumner, ed. , Vols. I and III, Hinrichsen.
chorale preludes in Orgelspiel im Kirchenjahr, Rohr, ed. ,
Vol. I (7) and Vol. 2 (8), Schott.
chorale preludes in Seasonal Chorale Preludes, C. H.
Trevor, ed. , Oxford, Book 1 (4) and Book 2 (3).
compositions (2) in Harold Gleason, Method of Organ Playing.
compositions (5) in Musica Organi, Vol. I.
compositions in The Parish Organist, Vols. 1-4, 5, 6, 7,
and 10.
fugues (2) in Spielbuch für die Kleinorgel, Vol. II.
preludes, fantasies, and toccatas, in Organum, Series IV,
Vol. 12 (Concordia 97-4344).
toccatas (2) in Liber Organi, Vol. 5.
PACHELBEL, WILHELM HIERONYMUS. Christened in Erfurt,
Germany, Aug. 29, 1686; died Nürnberg, 1764. Son of Johann Pachelbel; spent youth in Erfurt; studied with father;
organist in Wöhrd; 1706, became organist, St. Jakobi, Nürn-
berg, and at Egidien-Kirche; 1719-1764, organist, St. Sebald,
Nürnberg.
Fantasie über Meine Seele, lass es gehen, in Spielbuch für
die Kleinorgel, Vol. II, p. 59.
Gesamtausgabe der ehr. Werke für Orgel und Clavier,
Moser und Fedtke, eds. , Bärenreiter 2206, 1957.
Organ Works (Werke für Orgel), Max Seiffert, ed. , in
Denkmäler der Tonkunst in Bayern, Vol. IV, Book I,
Breitkopf & Härtel, 1903.
Toccata (G Major), in Treasury of Early Organ Music,
p. 54; also in Liber Organi, Vol. V, p. 20.
PADOVANO, ANNIBALE (see Annibale).
PAGOT, JEAN. born Paris, June 5, 1920. Organ pupil of Abel
Decaux; studied at the Conservatory, Paris; since 1948,
professor of musical instruction, Paris.
Offertoire pour les fêtes de la Sainte Vierge, in A la
Sainte Vierge, L'Organiste liturgique, Vol. 2, p. 19.
PAINE, JOHN KNOWLES. born Portland, Maine, Jan. 9, 1839;
died Cambridge, Mass. , Apr. 25, 1906. Pupil of Kotzschmar
in Berlin; 1862, appointed professor of music and chapel
organist, Harvard University; was the first person to hold a
chair of music in an American university.
Concert Variations on Old Hundred, Harvard University
Press, 1916.
Concert Variations on the Austrian Hymn, Op. 3, No. 1,
Oliver Ditson, 1876.
Deux Préludes pour l'orgue, Op. 19, A. P. Schmidt, 1892.
Fantasy on A mighty fortress, Op. 13, Harvard University
Press, 1916.
Variations on The Star Spangled Banner, Op. 3, No. 2,

Oliver Ditson, 1876.
PAIX, JAKOB. born Augsburg, Germany, 1556; died ?, probably
   after 1623. 1576, became organist, St. Martin, Lauingen and
   in Donau; 1601-1617, organist, Neuberg.
      Aria de Canzon francese, in Spielbuch für die Kleinorgel,
         Vol. I, p. 12.
PALAFUTI. Italian. Eighteenth century.
      Elevazione, in Alte italienische Meister, p. 30.
PALÉRA (PALERO), FRANCISCO FERNÁNDEZ. Spanish. Sixteenth
   century. Represented in Libro Cifra Nueva para tecla, harpa
   y vihuela (Alcala de Henares, 1557).
      Verset du VIIIe ton, in Les Anciens Maîtres Espagnols,
         p. 19.
      Versillo de Octavo Tono, in Early Spanish Organ Music,
         p. 27.
      versillos (2) in Antologia de Organistas Clásicos Españoles,
         Vol. I, p. 57.
PALESTRINA, GIOVANNI BATTISTA PIERLUIGI DA. born Palestrina (Rome), Italy, ca. 1525; died Rome, Feb. 2, 1594. 1544,
   appointed organist-choirmaster, Cathedral of St. Agapit, Palestrina; 1551, appointed maestro, Cappella Giulia, Rome;
   maestro, St. John Lateran; 1561, became maestro, S. Maria
   Maggiore; 1565-1571, director of music, Roman Seminary;
   1567, entered service of Cardinal Ippolito d'Este; 1571-1594,
   maestro, Cappella Giulia.
      Huit Ricercari, in Orgue et Liturgie, Vol. 3.
      Otto Ricercare sopra li tuoni, Fellerer, ed. , Schott 2310;
         also Kalmus 3766.
      Ricercar, in Anthologia pro Organo, Vol. 3, p. 11.
      Ricercar, in Historical Organ Rectials, Vol. 1, p. 15.
      Ricercare del V tono, in Anthologia Organistica Italiana,
         p. 14.
      Ricercare on the First Tone, in The First Four Centuries
         of Organ Music, Vol. I, p. 96.
      compositions in Masterpieces of Organ Music, Folios 22
         and 25.
PALMER, COURTLANDT. American. born Dec. 17, 1872. Con-
   cert pianist; pupil of Leschetizky, Paderewski, and Sgambati.
      Choral with Interludes, in The Modern Anthology, p. 144.
      Eventide, in The Modern Anthology, p. 137.
PANEL, LUDOVIC. born Rouen, France, Dec. 15, 1887; died
   Paris, Nov. 27, 1952. Studied at the Conservatory, Paris;
   organ pupil of Alexandre Guilmant and Eugène Gigout; 1913-
   1921, organist, St. Jacques-de-Dieppe; 1921-1945, organist,
   Sacré-Coeur-de-Montmartre; 1945-1952, choirmaster, St.
   Martin-des-Champs.
      Canzona, Bornemann, 1947.
      Prélude en forme de canon, Editions Musicales Trans-
         atlantiques.
      Prélude et Fugue (B Minor), Editions Musicales Trans-
         atlantiques.
      Six canons (Communion; Choral; Elévation; Musette en
         canon; Psaume et hymne; Intermezzo), Bornemann,

1942.
compositions in Pièces funèbres, Orgue et Liturgie, Vol.
23.
PAPONAUD, MARCEL. French. born 1893. Organist, St.
Bonaventure, Lyon; professor, Conservatory, Lyon.
Désolation, Lemoine.
Différences, Lemoine.
Pascale, in Communions, Orgue et Liturgie, Vol. 62, p. 19.
Prélude à l'Introit: Deus Israel (Messe de Mariage), in
Préludes à l'Introit, Orgue et Liturgie, Vol. 48, p. 22.
Quelques pages d'orgue (Dialogue; Au pays de Saint-François
de Sales; Carillon), Lemoine.
Récit de trompette et fonds d'orgue (L'Ascension), in
Offertoires, Orgue et Liturgie, Vol. 52, p. 15.
Recueillement sur O salutaris Hostia, in Elévations, Orgue
et Liturgie, Vol. 57, p. 10.
Ricercare pour le temps de Noël, in Noëls variés, Orgue
et Liturgie, Vol. 40; also in Christmas Music by
Various French Composers, p. 26.
Toccata, Philippo.
Triptyque, in Viens, Sauveur, Orgue et Liturgie, Vol. 19,
p. 26.
PARADIES, PIETRO DOMENICO. born Naples, 1707; died Venice,
Aug. 25, 1791. Pupil of Porpora; 1747, went to London as
harpsichord teacher.
Concerto (B-flat Major), organ and strings, Schott.
PARKER, HORATIO WILLIAM. born Auburndale, Mass. , Sept. 15,
1863; died Cedarhurst, N. Y. , Dec. 18, 1919. Studied with
Chadwick in Boston; 1882-1885, pupil of Rheinberger in
Munich; 1885, appointed organist and music teacher at the
Cathedral School of St. John, Garden City, Long Island, N. Y. ,
and at the National Conservatory, New York City; 1886,
named organist-choirmaster, St. Andrew's, New York City;
1888, made organist-choirmaster, Church of the Holy Trinity,
Boston; 1894, appointed to faculty, Yale University; 1901,
became organist, St. Nicholas, New York City; 1902, honorary
Mus. Doc. , Cambridge University.
Concert Piece, G. Schirmer, 1891.
Concerto, organ and orchestra, Op. 55, Novello, 1903.
Five Pieces, Op. 32, Novello.
Five Short Pieces, Op. 68, G. Schirmer, 1908.
Five Sketches, Op. 32, Novello, 1893.
Four Compositions, Op. 17, G. Schirmer, 1890.
Four Compositions, Op. 20, G. Schirmer, 1891.
Four Compositions, Op. 28, G. Schirmer, 1891.
Four Compositions, Op. 36, G. Schirmer, 1893.
Four Compositions, Op. 67, G. Schirmer, 1910.
Postlude; Melody; Marcia religioso, J. B. Millet, 1896.
Recital Pieces, G. Schirmer, 1939.
Sonata in E-flat Major, Op. 65, G. Schirmer, 1908.
Triumphal March, G. Schirmer, 1891.
Wedding Song, Op. 20, No. 1, G. Schirmer.
PARRISH, CARL. born Plymouth, Penn. , Oct. 19, 1904; died

1965. 1939, Ph. D. , Harvard University; 1929-1941, taught, Wells College; 1941-1945, taught, Fisk University; 1945-1949, Westminster Choir College; 1949-1953, taught, Pomona College; 1953-1965, professor of music, Vassar College.

Chorale Preludes, Witmark.

Sketch, in Harold Gleason, Method of Organ Playing, p. 163.

PARRY, (SIR) CHARLES HUBERT HASTINGS. born Bournemouth, England, Feb. 27, 1848; died Knight's Croft, Rustington, Sussex, Oct. 7, 1918. Studied at Eton; B. Mus. , 1874, M. A. , Oxford; pupil of Dannreuther and Elvey; taught, 1894-1918, director, Royal College of Music; 1899-1908, professor of music, Oxford; 1898, knighted; 1883, honorary doctorate, Cambridge University; 1884, honorary doctorate, Oxford; honorary doctorate, University of Dublin.

Elegy, Novello.

Fantasia and Fugue (G Major), Novello, 1913.

(An) Old English Tune, Novello.

Seven Chorale Preludes, Op. 186 and 205 (two sets), Novello, 1912, 1916.

Three Chorale Fantasias (1915), Novello.

Toccata and Fugue (The Wanderer), Novello 76 OC (N. S.).

PARVAINEN, JARMO UOLEVI. born Helsinki, Sept. 6, 1928. 1956, M. A. ; organ pupil of Paavo Raussi and Arno Schönstedt; composition pupil of Aarre Merikanto; 1951-1953, organist, Espoo; 1954-1958, organist, Meilahti, Helsinki.

Choral Partita on a Finnish folk-tune "Aruinko nyt mailleen vaipuu", Edition Fazer, 1971.

Choral Partita on a Finnish folk-tune "Halleluja nyt soikohon", Edition Fazer, 1956.

Koralförspil, Vol. 2, Westerlund.

Toccata and Fugue (1958), Edition Fazer 4816, 1968.

Ten Small Chorale Preludes, Edition Fazer, 1959.

PASQUET, JEAN. born New York City, May 31, 1896. Pupil of T. Tertius Noble; taught at the Chicago Conservatory of Music and Busch Conservatory of Music, Chicago.

Chorales of Our Heritage, Augsburg.

Deck the Halls, Ed. H. Morris; also Gray (St. Cecilia Series 907).

Four Pieces from the Baroque Era, Concordia 97-4761.

In Bethlehem, Gray (St. Cecilia Series 908).

Lo, How a Rose, Gray (St. Cecilia Series 721), 1946.

Meditation on Our Father, E. H. Morris.

Patapan, Leeds, 1944.

PASQUINI, BERNARDO. born Massa di Valdinievole, Tuscany, Italy, Dec. 7, 1637; died Rome, Nov. 21, 1710. Pupil of Vittori and Cesti; probably 1663, organist, S. Maria Maggiore, Rome; taught Gasparini, Krieger, Muffat, Kerll, and Zipoli.

Collected Works, in Corpus of Early Keyboard Music, No. 5, Vols. 1, 4, 5, 6, and 7: Vol. 1: compositions (11); Vol. 4: passagagli (4); Vol. 5: toccatas (19); Vol. 6: Tastatas, toccatas, sonis (2); Vol. 7: Pastorale, ricercari (2), toccatas (2).

Introduzione & Pastorale, (Peters D 204).

Seven Toccatas, Esposito, ed. , Zanibon 4068.
Toccato con lo Scherzo del cuccu, (Peters D 205).
compositions (3) in Classici Italiani dell'Organo.
PAUMANN, CONRAD (KONRAD). born Nürnberg, Germany, ca. 1415;
died Munich, Jan. 24, 1473. Celebrated blind organist; 1446,
became organist, St. Sebald's Church, Nürnberg; served
several ducal courts; served Duke Albrecht III of Munich as
court organist; wrote Fundamentum organisandi (1452).
Elend, du hast umfangen mich, in Geschichte der Musik in
Beispielen, p. 42.
Mit ganczem Willen, in Historical Anthology of Music,
Vol. I, p. 85; also in Willi Apel, Masters of the
Keyboard, p. 29.
compositions (2) in Harold Gleason, Method of Organ Playing.
PEEK, RICHARD. born Mason, Michigan, May 17, 1927. 1950,
B. Mus. , Michigan State University; 1952, M. S. M. , 1958, Sac.
Mus. Doc. , Union Theological Seminary, New York City; organ
pupil of Helen Roberts Sholl, Richard Ross, Vernon de Tar,
and Arthur Poister; composition pupil of Harold Freidell and
Normand Lockwood; 1950-1952, organist-choirmaster, Grace
Episcopal Church, Plainfield, N. J. ; since 1952, organist-
choirmaster, Covenant Presbyterian Church, Charlotte, N. Car.
Blessed Is He that Cometh, organ, violin (flute), and harp
(piano), Brodt, 1968.
Chaconne on Ye Sons and Daughters, organ, brass quartet,
timpani, and cymbals, Brodt, 1970.
Chorale and Toccata, organ and strings, Brodt, 1969.
Chorale-Prelude on Dundee; Partita on Donne Secours, in
Organ Music for Worship, Vol. I, Brodt, 1963.
Church Sonata, Brodt, 1969.
Fanfare, Brodt, 1969.
Fantasia and Fugue on St. Anne, Brodt, 1961.
Hymn Preludes for the Church Year, C. Fischer, 1964.
Partita on Fairest Lord Jesus, Brodt, 1969.
Partita on St. Paul (Aberdeen), Abingdon, 1969.
Pastorale on Innsbruck, C. Fischer, 1959.
Prelude on a Theme by Tallis, Brodt, 1960.
Prelude on St. Michaels, C. Fischer, 1961.
Processional March on Vexilla Regis, in Six Organ Pro-
cessionals, World Library of Sacred Music, 1969.
Rondo Ostinato, Brodt, 1969.
Voluntary on Sine Nomine, in Voluntaries for the Church
Year, Vol. I, Abingdon, 1965.
PEERSON, MARTIN. born Cambridgeshire, England, in March,
between 1571 and 1573; died London, end of December 1650.
1613, B. Mus. , Oxford; 1626, master of the children, St.
Paul's Cathedral, London; shared being organist of St. Paul's
Cathedral with Batten and John Tomkins.
Fall of the Leaf, Primerose (from Fitzwilliam Virginal
Book), in Early English Elkan-Vogel Organ Series,
Vol. 2, 1947.
pieces (4) in Fitzwilliam Virginal Book.
PEETERS, FLOR. born Tielen, Belgium, July 4, 1903. Pupil at

Lemmens Institute, Mechlin; pupil of Depuydt, Dupré, and Tournemire; 1925, named first organist, Cathedral, Mechlin; 1925-1952, professor of organ, Lemmens Institute; 1931-1948, professor of organ, Royal Conservatory, Ghent; 1935-1948, taught organ and composition, Conservatory, Tilburg, The Netherlands; 1948-1969, professor of organ, 1952-1969, director, Royal Flemish Conservatory, Antwerp; 1971, received honorary doctorate, University of Louvain.

Alma redemptoris mater, in Notre Dame, Orgue et Liturgie, Vol. 11, p. 24.

Aria, Op. 51, Heuwekemeijer.

Arioso (Concerto, Op. 74), Gray (St. Cecilia Series 949).

Chorale Fantasy on Christ the Lord Is Risen, organ, two trumpets, two trombones, Gray.

Concert Piece, Op. 52a, Peters 6077.

Concerto, organ and orchestra, Op. 52, Peters 6001.

Concerto, organ and piano, Op. 74, Gray.

Elégie, Op. 38, Elkan-Vogel; also Lemoine.

Entrata Festiva, organ, two trumpets, two trombones, Peters 6159.

Festival Voluntary, Op. 87, in Album of Praise, p. 1.

Flemish Rhapsody, Op. 37, Schott Frères 4; also Associated Music Publishers.

Four Improvisations, McLaughlin and Reilly M-1487.

Four Pieces (Hymn; In Memoriam; Largo; Finale), Op. 71, McLaughlin and Reilly M-2202.

Gavotte Antique, Op. 59, No. 4, Gray (St. Cecilia Series 730).

Hymn Preludes for the Liturgical Year, Op. 100, 24 vols., Peters 6401-6424.

Intieme Stonden.

Légende, in The Modern Anthology, p. 152.

Lied Symphony, Op. 66, 3 vols., Peters 6002 A-C.

Monastic Peace, McLaughlin and Reilly M-1719.

Morning Hymn, Op. 59, No. 1, Gray (St. Cecilia Series 728).

Nostalgia, Op. 59, No. 3, Gray (St. Cecilia Series 729).

Organ Partita, McLaughlin and Reilly M-2443.

Partita on Plainchant Hymn (Urbs beata), Hinrichsen 586.

Passacaglia and Fugue, Op. 42, Schott 3727.

Preludes on Stuttgart and Lässt uns erfreuen, in Festal Voluntaries (Christmas), Novello.

Praeludiale, Op. 114, Schwann.

Praeludien und Hymnen, Op. 90, Schwann.

Preludium, Canzona e Cincona, Op. 83, Novello.

Sinfonia, Op. 48, Elkan-Vogel; also Lemoine.

Six Lyrical Pieces, Op. 116 (Grave; Duo for Flutes and Cromorne; Contemplative Canon; Invocation; Lyrical Canticle; Trumpet Tune), Gray (St. Cecilia Series 937-942.

Sixty Short Pieces, Gray.

Solemn Prelude, Op. 86, in Preludes-Interludes-Postludes, Vol. 2, Hinrichsen 600B.

Speculum vitae, Op. 36, poem for high voice and organ in
   four parts, Elkan-Vogel.
Suite Modale, Op. 43, Elkan-Vogel;   also Lemoine.
Symphonic Fantasy, Op. 13, Gray.
Ten Inventions, Op. 117, Schwann.
Ten Organ Chorales, Op. 39; Schott 2553.
Thirty Chorale Preludes, Op. 68, 69, and 70, 3 vols., of
   ten each, Peters 6023/6025.
Thirty Chorale Preludes on Gregorian Hymns, Op. 75, 76,
   and 77, 3 vols., of ten each, Peters 6088/6090.
Thirty Short Preludes on Well-known Hymns, Op. 95,
   Peters 6195.
Thirty-five Miniatures, Op. 53, 2 vols., McLaughlin and
   Reilly M-1508.
Three Pieces (Morning Song; Gavotte Antique; Nostalgia),
   Op. 59, Gray.
Three Preludes and Fugues, Op. 72, Schott 4334.
Toccata, Fugue and Hymn on Ave maris stella, Op. 28,
   Elkan-Vogel.
Twee Trio's op O Hoofd vol bloed en wonden, in Cantantibus
   Organis, Vol. II, p. 22.
Variation and Finale on an Old Flemish Song, Op. 20, Elkan-
   Vogel.
Variations on an Original Theme, Op. 58, Elkan-Vogel.
compositions in Preludes-Interludes-Postludes, Hinrichsen
   600B.
PELLEGRINI, VINCENZO. born Pesaro, Italy, sixteenth century;
   died Milan, probably in 1631. 1603, priest (canon), Cathedral,
   Pesaro; organist, Pesaro; 1611-1631, maestro di cappella,
   Cathedral, Milan; wrote book of canzonets in organ tablature
   in French style Canzoni de intavolatura d'organo fatte alle
   Francese (Venice, 1599).
   Canzone on La Capricciosa, in Classici Italiani dell'Organo,
      p. 87.
   (La) Serpentina, in Anthologia pro Organo, Vol. III, p. 61.
   canzoni (2) in L'Arte Musicale in Italia, Vol. III, p. 49.
PELOQUIN, C. ALEXANDER. American. Twentieth century. Music
   director, Cathedral of Sts. Peter and Paul, Providence, R.I.;
   composer-in-residence, Boston College.
   Homage à Purcell, McLaughlin and Reilly M-2781.
   Joy: A Suite for Organ, Sacred Music Press.
   March for a Joyous Occasion, McLaughlin and Reilly 2177-6,
      1958.
   Partita on Lourdes Pilgrim Hymn, McLaughlin and Reilly.
   (A) Suite for Organ, Sacred Music Press.
   Toccata, McLaughlin and Reilly M-2323.
PEPPING, ERNST. born Duisberg, Germany, Sept. 12, 1901. Pu-
   pil of Walter Gmeindl, Berlin; teacher, 1947, made professor,
   School of Church Music, Spandau, Berlin; 1953, appointed pro-
   fessor of composition, Musikhochschule, Berlin.
   Böhmisches Orgelbuch, 2 vols., Bärenreiter 2749, 2750,
      1953, 1954.
   Concerto I (1941), Schott 3733.

Concerto II (1941/1942), Schott 3734.
Drei Fugen über B-A-C-H (1943), Schott 3818.
Drei Sonaten (1945/1946).
Fünf-und-zwanzig Orgelchoräle nach Sätzen des Spandauer
    Chorbuches (1960), Schott 4723.
Grosses Orgelbuch, Choralvorspiele und Orgelchoräle
    (1939-1941), Schott 3729-3731.
Hymnen (1954), Bärenreiter 2747.
Kleines Orgelbuch (1940), Schott 3735.
Partita über Ach wie flüchtig (1953), Bärenreiter 2753.
Partita über Mit Fried' und Freud' (1953), Bärenreiter
    2755.
Partita über Wer weiss, wie nahe mir mein Ende (1953),
    Bärenreiter 2754.
Partita über Wie schön leuchtet, Schott 2247.
Praeludia-Postludia I, II, Schott.
Sonata (1957), Bärenreiter 2644.
To Koralforspil, Hansen 23044.
Toccata und Fuge über Mitten wir im Leben sind (1941/
    1942), Schott 3737.
Vier Fugen (D Major, C Minor, E-flat Major, F Minor)
    (1942), Schott 3816.
Vom Himmel hoch, in Musica Organi, Vol. II, p. 94.
Zwei Choralvorspiele, Hansen, 1932.
Zwei Fugen (C-sharp Minor) (1943-1946), Schott 3817.
Zwölf Choralvorspiele (no pedal) (1957), Bärenreiter 2645.
PERAZA, FRANCISCO. born Salamanca, Spain, 1564; died Sevilla,
    June 24, 1598. Served dukes of Calabria, Valencia, Salamanca,
    and Toledo; 1582, became organist, Cathedral, Sevilla.
    Medio Registro Alto de Primer Tono, in Early Spanish
        Organ Music, p. 17; also in Antologia de Organistas
        Clásicos Españoles, Vol. I, p. 54.
PERDIGON, PIERRE. born St. Etienne, France, Dec. 10, 1940.
    Studied at the Conservatory, Lyon; 1962, named organist,
    l'Immaculée-Conception, Lyon.
    Cinq versets sur Veni creator, in L'Organiste liturgique,
        Vol. 53, p. 16.
PÉRILHOU, ALBERT. born Daumazan, France, 1846; died Tain,
    1936. Pupil of Saint-Saëns at the Ecole Niedermeyer; 1889-
    1919, organist, St. Séverin.
    Livre d'orgue, 7 vols., Heugel, 1899.
PEROSI, LORENZO. born Tortona, Italy, Dec. 20, 1872; died
    Rome, Oct. 12, 1956. 1890, organist-choirmaster, Abbazia,
    Montecassino; 1892-1893, studied at the Conservatory, Milan;
    pupil of F. X. Haberl; 1893, choirmaster, Cathedral, Imola;
    1894, became choirmaster, San Marco, Venice; 1896, became
    priest; 1898, assistant choirmaster, 1903, choirmaster, Sis-
    tine Chapel, Vatican.
    Centonum (Interludi per la Messa de Beata; Offertorio;
        Preludio).
    Sechs Orgel-Trios, Coppenrath.
    Thirteen Meditations, World Library of Sacred Music.
PEROTIN (PEROTINUS). French. Twelfth century. Leader of the

Notre Dame School, perhaps organist there.
> Organum triplex, in Anthology of Early French Organ
>> Music, p. 1.
> Point d'orgue, in Anthologia pro Organo, Vol. I, p. 4.
> Point d'orgue, in Anthologia pro Organo, Vol. 3, p. 4.

PERSICHETTI, VINCENT. born Philadelphia, Penn. , June 6, 1915.
Organist, St. Mark's Reformed Church, Philadelphia; 1936,
B. Mus. , Combs College of Music; pupil of Olga Samaroff;
pupil of Fritz Reiner at the Curtis Institute; 1932-1949,
organist-choirmaster, Arch St. Presbyterian Church, Philadelphia; 1939, head of composition department, Combs College; 1942, head, composition department, Conservatory,
Philadelphia; 1945, received doctorate, Philadelphia Conservatory of Music; since 1948, teacher of composition, Juilliard
School of Music, New York City.
> Chorale Prelude on Drop, Drop, Slow Tears, Op. 104,
>> Elkan-Vogel, 1968.
> Parable VI, Op. 117 (1971), Elkan-Vogel.
> Sh'ma B'koli (Ps. 30), Elkan-Vogel.
> Sonata, Op. 85 (1960), Elkan-Vogel, 1961.
> Sonatina for pedal alone, Elkan-Vogel, 1955.

PESCETTI, GIOVAN BATTISTA. born Venice, ca. 1704; died
Venice, Mar. 20, 1766. Pupil of Lotti; opera composer;
1738, went to England to conduct opera; 1752-1766, second
organist, San Marco, Venice.
> Allegro, in Alte italienische Meister, p. 30.

PETIT, PIERRE. born Poitiers, France, April 21, 1922. Studied
at the Conservatory, Paris; 1946, won Prix de Rome; pupil
of Nadia Boulanger and Henri Busser; 1951, became teacher
of history of civilization, Conservatory, Paris; 1960, appointed director, semi-classical music, French Radio and
Television; 1963, named director, Ecole Normale de Musique,
Paris; 1965, became director, musical creations, French
Radio and Television.
> Concertino, organ, string orchestra, and percussion (1961),
>> Leduc.

PHILIP, ACHILLE. born Arles, France, Oct. 12, 1878; died
Béziers (Hérault), Nov. 12, 1959. Pupil of Guilmant; organist, St. Jacques du Haut-Pas, Paris; Director, Conservatoire Claude Debussy, St. Germain-en-Laye; 1951, became
organist, Basilica of St. Aphrodise, Béziers.
> Adagio et Fugue, (Leipzig) 1904.
> Lied, in Anthologia Sacra, Series V, No. 3, Hérelle,
>> 1911, 1923.
> Prélude et Fugue, Demets, 1902.
> Prélude et Fugue, Eschig.
> Toccata et Fugue (A Minor), Durand, 1913.
> Variations on Il est né, in In Nativitate Domine, J. S.
>> Haussler, ed. , McLaughlin and Reilly.

PHILIPS, PETER. born London, 1560 or 1561; died Brussels,
1628. 1582, left England; 1582-1583, organist, English
College, Rome; 1585, musician to Lord Thomas Paget with
whom he traveled to Spain, France, and Flanders; 1590,

settled in Antwerp; 1597, entered the service of Archduke Albrecht of Austria in Brussels; 1606, took holy orders.

Fantazie, in Oudnederlandse Meesters, Vol. III, p. 52.

Intavolata, in Alte Orgelmusik aus England und Frankreich, p. 20.

Trio, in Oudnederlandse Meesters, Vol. II, p. 52.

composition in Archives des maîtres d'orgue des seizième-dix-huitième siècles, Vol. 10.

PHILLIPS, CHARLES GORDON. born Slough, England, 1908. Studied at the University of Nottingham; Fellow of the Royal College of Music; since 1956, organist-director of music, All Hallows by the Tower, London; since 1961, professor of organ and harpsichord, London College of Music.

Finale on Veni Emmanuel, in Anthology of Organ Music, Hinrichsen.

Five Meditations on Evening Hymns, Oxford.

Lullaby, Oxford.

(A) Miniature, in An Album of Preludes and Interludes, Oxford.

Partita on a Plainsong Hymn, Hinrichsen 586.

Postlude for a Festival, in Preludes-Interludes-Postludes, Vol. 6, Hinrichsen 600F.

Six Carol Preludes, Oxford.

Sonata, Oxford.

Suite in F Minor (Pontifical March; Minuet; Toccata), Oxford.

Three Miniatures for Small Organ, Oxford.

Toccata (C Major), Oxford.

chorale and hymn preludes (6) in Advent to Whitsuntide, Vol. 3, Hinrichsen.

PICHÉ, PAUL BERNARD. born Montreal, Canada, Apr. 10, 1908. 1929, laureate, gold medalist, Académie de Musique, Québec; studied at the Royal Conservatory, Brussels; pupil of Maleingreau, Hens, and Tournemire; church organist, Montreal; 1932, appointed organist, Cathédral des Trois Rivières.

Rhapsody on Four Noëls, Gray, 1947.

Scherzo, Gray.

PIÉDELIÈVRE, PAULE. French. born July 7, 1902; died Mar. 11, 1964. Pupil of Abel Decaux and Louis Vierne; taught at Schola Cantorum; organist, Eglise des Etrangers, Paris; editor of organ music.

Prélude sur Vexilla Regis, Verlag-Herder, Freiburg-im-Breisgau.

Suite eucharistique.

Suite grégorienne, Hérelle, 1936-1938.

Toccata on Haec dies, Edition Le Grand Orgue.

PIERNÉ, GABRIEL-HENRI-CONSTANT. born Metz, France, Aug. 16, 1863; died Ploujean, Brittany, July 17, 1937. 1871-1872, studied at the Conservatory, Paris; pupil of Franck, Durand, and Massenet; 1890-1898, organist, Ste. Clotilde (succeeded Franck); 1903, assistant conductor to Colonne; 1910-1932, conductor, Orchestre Colonne.

Choral; Offertoire, Leduc, 1907.

Fugue en sol mineur, Bornemann, 1912.
Prélude-Toccata, in The French Organist, Vol. I, p. 3.
Trois pièces, Op. 29 (Prélude; Cantilène; Scherzando),
Durand, 1893.
PIKÉTHY, TIBOR. born Komárom, Hungary, 1884. Music direc-
tor, Cathedral, Vac, Hungary; professor, National Conserva-
tory, Budapest.
Fantasie über B-A-C-H, Op. 28, Schott Frères.
Kleine Präludien, Op. 27, Coppenrath.
Präludien und Fughetten, Op. 41, Coppenrath.
PINGRÉ, PÈRE. French. Eighteenth century. Compiler of organ
music of his time.
Pièces de différents Auteurs copiées par le père Pingré,
in L'Organiste liturgique, Vols. 45-46; also Organ
Book of Anonymous French Composers, Kalmus 3768.
PINKHAM, DANIEL. born Lynn, Mass., June 5, 1923. Studied
at Phillips Academy, Andover, Mass.; 1943, A. B., 1944,
M. A., Harvard University; pupil of Piston, Copland, Honeg-
ger, Barber, Boulanger, Biggs, Aldrich, and Landowska;
1946, taught, Boston Conservatory of Music; 1950, received
Fulbright scholarship; 1953, became lecturer, Simmons Col-
lege; 1954, teaching associate, harpsichord, Boston Univer-
sity; 1957-1958, visiting lecturer, Harvard; organist, King's
Chapel, Boston.
Concertante, organ, brass, and percussion, Peters 6848.
Concertante, organ, celesta, and percussion, Peters 6507,
1963.
Concertante, organ, guitar, harpsichord, and percussion,
Peters 66293.
Four Short Pieces for Manuals, E. C. Schirmer 1418.
Gloria, organ and brass, Robert King.
Pastorale on Morning Star, Galaxy.
(A) Prophecy, E. C. Schirmer.
Signs in the Sun, two organs, Peters.
Sonata, organ and brasses.
Sonata, two oboes and organ, Peters 6578.
Sonatas No. 1 and No. 2, organ and strings.
Suite.
Revelations.
Variations, oboe and organ, Peters P66296.
PIROYE, CHARLES. French. Eighteenth century. 1708-
1717, organist, St. Honoré.
(La) Béatitude, dialogue à deux choeurs, in Les Maîtres
français de l'orgue, Vol. II, p. 54.
PISTON, WALTER HAMOR. born Rockland, Maine, Jan. 20, 1894.
1924, graduated from Harvard University; pupil of Boulanger
and Dukas; 1926, appointed to faculty, later director of the
Music Department, Harvard, 1960, became emeritus director.
Chromatic Study on the Name of Bach (1940), Gray
(Contemporary Organ Series 3), 1941.
Partita (1944), violin, viola, and organ, Associated Music
Publishers.
Prelude and Allegro, organ and strings, Arrow Music

Press, 1944.

PLANCHET, DOMINIQUE-CHARLES. born Toulouse, France,
Dec. 25, 1857; died Versailles, July 19, 1946. Studied at
the Ecole Niedermeyer, Paris; organist, Versailles; 1898,
became choirmaster, Trinité, Paris.

Méditation religieuse, Bornemann.

Offertoire de Pâques, L. Muraille.

PLÉ-CAUSSADE, SIMONE. born Paris, Aug. 14, 1897. Pupil of
Cortot and Dallier; since 1936, professor of counterpoint and
fugue, Conservatory, Paris.

Communion pour la fête de l'Assomption de la Bienheureuse
Vierge Marie, in Orgue et Liturgie, Vol. 62, p. 30.

Elévation pour la fête de l'Assomption, in Elévations,
Orgue et Liturgie, Vol. 57, p. 20.

Offertoire (Assomption de la Bienheureuse Vierge Marie),
in Offertoires, Orgue et Liturgie, Vol. 52, p. 29.

Pater noster, in Notre Père, Orgue et Liturgie, Vol. 24,
p. 30.

Prélude à l'Introit pour la fête de l'Assomption, in
Préludes à l'Introit, Orgue et Liturgie, Vol. 48,
p. 24.

Regina coeli avec variations, in A la Vierge, Orgue et
Liturgie, Vol. 14, p. 30.

Sonnons les matines, in Varia, Orgue et Liturgie, Vol. 66,
p. 11.

PLUM, P. J. M. Belgian. born 1899; died 1944.

Big Ben (Toccata No. 3), Op. 154, Schott Frères.

Clementissime Domine, Op. 124, A. Cranz.

Etude Concertante, Op. 88, Schott Frères.

Fantaisie, Op. 46, Schott Frères.

Final, Op. 86, Schott Frères.

Messe de Mariage.

Messe de Pâques.

Offertoire sur Lauda Sion, Op. 64, Schott Frères (Henn).

Offertoire sur trois noëls, Henn.

Offertoires, Op. 105, Henn.

Pièce funèbre, Op. 83, Schott Frères (Henn).

Prélude lent, Philippo.

Prière en forme de canon, Philippo.

Procession, Bornemann.

Scherzando (Postludium), Op. 81, Schott Frères.

Sortie on a French Theme.

Sortie sur un thême de choral, Schott Frères.

Sursum corda, Philippo.

Symphonie Eucharistique, A. Cranz.

Thème varié, Schott Frères.

Vingt élévations, Op. 104, Schott Frères.

Vingt offertoires, Op. 105, Schott Frères.

Vingt préludes, Op. 101, Schott Frères.

Vingt sorties, Op. 103, Schott Frères.

PODBIELSKI, JOHANNES. Polish. Member of family of organists
active in Mozavia and East Prussia between 1679 and 1731.

Praeludium, in Keyboard Music from Polish Manuscripts,

Corpus of Early Keyboard Music, No. 10, Vol. 4,
p. 30.

POGLIETTI, ALESSANDRO DE. born probably in Tuscany, Italy,
?; died Vienna, July 1683. Jesuit organist in Vienna, from
1661, court and chamber organist to Emperor Leopold I; as-
sociated with Wolfgang and Markus Ebner and Johann Kaspar
Kerll.
Ricercar über Der Tag, der ist, in South German Christmas
Music, p. 9.
Zwölf Ricercars, 2 vols. , Riedel, ed. , in Die Orgel,
Series II, Vols. 5 and 6 (Concordia 97-4424 and
97-4425).
compositions in Denkmäler der Tonkunst in Osterreich,
Vol. XIII, No. 2.

POLLAROLI (POLLAROLO, POLAROLI), CARLO FRANCESCO. born
Brescia, Italy, ca. 1653; died Venice, end of 1722. Pupil of
Legrenzi; 1665, became chorister, 1690, second organist,
1692, second maestro di cappella, San Marco, Venice; opera
composer.
Fuga, in Alte italienische Meister, p. 6.
Sonata, in L'Arte Musicale in Italia, Vol. III, p. 341.

PONS, CHARLES. born Nice, France, Dec. 7, 1870; died Paris,
Mar. 16, 1957. Organist, Cathedral, Nice; music critic and
opera composer.
Quatre pièces (Prélude; Méditation; Intermède; Communion),
Bornemann.

POPPEN, HERMANN MEINHARDT. born Heidelberg, Germany,
Jan. 1, 1885; died Heidelberg, Apr. 10, 1956. Studied the-
ology in Berlin, Kiel, and Heidelberg; 1911-1912, pupil of
Reger in Meiningen; 1918-1919, chief church music director,
Karlsruhe; 1919-1951, director of music, University of
Heidelberg; 1919, became director of music for Landeskirche
and city of Heidelberg; 1931, gave impetus to founding the
Chruch Music Institute, Heidelberg.
Vierzehn Choralvorspiele zu neueren Liedern, Schott 3726.
Zehn Choralvorspiele, M. Schauenberg.
chorale preludes (4) in Orgelvorspiele, Oppen, Reiche and
Strube, eds. , Merseburger.

PORPORA, NICOLÒ ANTONIO. born Naples, Aug. 17, 1686; died
Naples, Mar. 3, 1768. Opera composer and singing teacher.
Fuga, in Classici Italiani dell'Organo, p. 165.
Fuga, in L'Arte Musicale in Italia, Vol. 3, p. 431.

PORTER, AMBROSE P. English. born 1885; died May, 1971.
1925-1959, organist and master of the choristers, Cathedral,
Lichfield, England.
Bénédiction nuptiale, Oxford.
Chorale Fantasia on St. Magnus, Cramer.
Epithalamium, Oxford.
Introduction, Variation and Finale on Stuttgart, Cramer.
Prelude and Fugue on Easter Hymn, Cramer.
Prelude on a Chorale, Stainer & Bell.
Prelude on Tallis Ordinal, Stainer & Bell.
Two Improvisations, in Modern British Organ Music,

Rowley, ed. , J. Williams.

PORTER, WILLIAM QUINCY. born New Haven, Conn. , Feb. 7,
1897; died Nov. 12, 1966. 1921, Mus. Bac. , Yale University;
pupil of Horatio Parker, d'Indy, and Bloch; 1922-1928, 1931-
1932, taught at the Institute of Music, Cleveland, Ohio; 1928,
won Guggenheim Fellowship; 1932-1938, teacher, Vassar;
1938, appointed dean, 1942, director, New England Conservatory; 1946-1965, professor, Yale.

   Canon and Fugue, Gray (Contemporary Organ Series 12),
      1941.
   Toccata, Andante and Finale (1930), Gray (Contemporary
      Organ Series 35).
   Wedding Prelude and March, Gray (St. Cecilia Series 892).

POST, PIET. Dutch. born Apr. 8, 1919. Pupil of Van der Horst
at the Conservatory, Amsterdam; since 1949, cantor-organist,
Grote Kerk, Leeuwarden.

   Canonische Variaties op Als God, mijn God, Ars Nova.
   Fantasie on Holy, Holy, Holy, Ars Nova.
   Improvisatie op Daar is uit's werelds duist're wolken,
      Ars Nova.
   Partita on a Morning Hymn, Ars Nova.
   Partita op de Avondzang, Ars Nova, 1956.
   Partita op Lofzang van Maria, Ars Nova.
   Partita op Psalm 93, Ars Nova.
   Partita op Psalm 101, Ars Nova.
   Partita op Vater unser, Ars Nova.
   Partita voor Advent en Kerstmis.
   Prelude and Fugue on D'Almachtige is mijn herder, Ars
      Nova.
   Prelude, Koraal, Fugato op Komt zielen, deze dag (Psalm
      84), Ars Nova, 1951.
   Sixteen Chorale Preludes, Series 2, Ars Nova.
   Sixteen Chorale Preludes, Series 3, Ars Nova.
   Triptych (Praise God from Whom All Blessings Flow;
      Blessed Jesus, at Thy Word; Now Thank We All),
      Augsburg 11-835.
   Two Little Partitas on Song 153 and Song 155, Ars Nova.
   Two Partitas on Eastern Hymns, Ars Nova.
   Variaties op Op U, mijn Heiland, blijf ik hopen, Ars Nova.
   Variations on Herzliebster Jesu, Ars Nova.
   Variations on the Lenten Hymn Leer mij, O Heer, Ars
      Nova.

POTIRON, HENRI. born Rézé-les-Nantes, France, Sept. 13, 1882.
1910, appointed choirmaster, Sacré-Coeur-de-Montmartre,
Paris; 1923, became teacher, Institut Grégorien; 1954,
named Docteur de l'Université de Paris.

   Petite Suite sur Puer natus in Bethlehem, Hérelle.
   Suite Brève sur Mass XI (Orbis factor), in Varia, Orgue et
      Liturgie, Vol. 46, p. 8.

POULENC, FRANCIS. born Paris, Jan. 7, 1899; died Paris,
Jan. 30, 1963. Pupil of Ricardo Viñes (piano) and Koechlin
(composition); 1917, joined "Nouveaux Jeunes" from which
evolved "Les Six"; composition influenced by Satie and Ravel.

Concerto en sol mineur (1938), organ, string orchestra,
    and timpani, Deiss, 1939.
POWELL, NEWMAN W. born 1919. Professor of music, Val-
    paraiso University, Valparaiso, Ind.
    chorale preludes (2) in The Parish Organist, Vol. 1-4.
PRAETORIUS, HIERONYMUS. born Hamburg, Germany, Aug. 10,
    1560; died Hamburg, Jan. 27, 1629. 1580, became city
    Cantor, Erfurt; 1582-1629, assistant and later organist,
    Jacobikirche, Hamburg.
    Organ Magnificats on the eight tones, in Corpus of Early
        Keyboard Music, No. 4.
PRAETORIUS, JACOB II. born Hamburg, Germany, Feb. 8, 1586;
    died Hamburg, Oct. 22, 1651. Son and pupil of Hieronymus
    Praetorius; 1603, organist, St. Peter's Church, Hamburg;
    pupil of Sweelinck and D. Scheidemann; Hamburg Cathedral
    chapter named him Domvikar, 1648, Domdekan.
    Allein Gott in der Höh sei Ehr, in 20 Chorale Variations
        of the German Sweelinck School, Bärenreiter.
    Choralbearbeitung (Visbyer Orgeltabulatur), in Die Orgel,
        Kistner & Siegel, 1962.
    chorale preludes (5) in Sechs-und-Vierzig Choräle für Orgel.
    compositions in Masterpieces of Organ Music, Folio 45.
    praeambeln (3) in Organum, Series IV, Vol. 2.
PRAETORIUS, MICHAEL. born Kreuzburg-an-der-Werra (Eisenach),
    Germany, perhaps Feb. 15, 1571; died Wolfenbüttel, Feb. 15,
    1621. Studied in Frankfurt; 1587, became organist, Marien-
    kirche; 1596, served Duke Heinrich Julius in Gröningen; as-
    sociated with organ builders Beck and Compenius, with Scheidt
    and Schütz; traveled to Dresden, Halle, Leipzig, and Nürnberg;
    1612, appointed Kapellmeister, Wolfenbüttel; wrote Syntagma
    Musicum, 3 vols. (1615, 1618, 1620).
    Allein auf Gottes Wort will ich, in The Church Organist's
        Golden Treasury, Vol. I, p. 19.
    Alvus tumescit virginus, in The First Four Centuries of
        Organ Music, Vol. I, p. 187.
    Ein' feste Burg, in Eighty Chorale Preludes: German
        Masters of the Seventeenth and Eighteenth Centuries,
        p. 36.
    Fantasie über Ein' feste Burg, Nagel NMA 40, Hannover,
        1927.
    Fantasy on Ein' feste Burg, Heinrich Fleischer, ed., Con-
        cordia 97-1381, 1954.
    Fantasy on We All Believe in One True God, Heinrich
        Fleischer, ed., Concordia 97-1435, 1960.
    Hymnus, A solis ortus cardine, in Sammlung, Karl Matthaei,
        ed., Bärenreiter.
    Nun komm, in Viens, Sauveur, Orgue et Liturgie, Vol. 19,
        p. 1.
    O lux beata, in Alte Meister des Orgelspiels, Vol. II,
        p. 32.
    Sämtliche Orgelwerke, Karl Matthaei, ed., Kallmeyer-
        Möseler Verlag, Wolfenbüttel, Germany, 1930.
    Veni redemptor, in Anthologie pro Organo, Vol. III, p. 52.

chorale preludes (3) in Orgelchoräle des siebzehnten und achtzehnten Jahrhunderts.
chorale preludes (4) in Masterpieces of Organ Music, Folio 36.
chorale preludes (2) in Organ Preludes Ancient and Modern, W. Sumner, ed. , Vols. 1 and 12, Concordia.
chorale preludes in Orgelspiel im Kirchenjahr, Vol. 1 (1) and Vol. 2 (2), Schott.
chorale preludes (5) in The Parish Organist, Vol. 1-4.

PRESTON, SIMON. born Bornemouth, England, 1938. Studied at the Choir School, King's College, Cambridge, at Canford School, and at the Royal Academy of Music; organ pupil of C. H. Trevor and David Willcocks; Mus. B. , M. A. , King's College, Cambridge; formerly suborganist, Westminster Abbey; 1967-1968, acting Master of the Music, Cathedral and Abbey Church of St. Albans.
Alleluyas, in Modern Organ Music, p. 18.

PRESTON, THOMAS. English. born ?; died 1564. 1543, organist and director of choirsingers, Magdalen College, Oxford; 1558-1563, organist, St. George's Chapel, Windsor.
Veni redemptor gentium; Felix namque, in Altenglische Orgelmusik, Bärenreiter 385, 1954.

PUIG-ROGET, HENRIETTE. born Bastia, Corsica, Jan. 9, 1910. Pupil of Tournemire and Dupré; since 1934, organist, Oratoire du Louvre, Paris; professor of piano accompaniment, Conservatory, Paris.
Cortège funèbre, Durand, 1935/1939.
Deploracion para la semana santa (1949), in Pâques, Orgue et Liturgie, Vol. I, 1949.
Deux Prières, Lemoine.
Fantaisie sur des thèmes hébraïques.
Montanyas del Rosello, Leduc, 1934.
Toccata severa, in Toccata, Orgue et Liturgie, Vol. 10, p. 21.

PURCELL, HENRY. born London ?, ca. 1659; died London, Nov. 21, 1695. 1669, named chorister, Chapel Royal under Henry Cooke and later Pelham Humfrey; pupil of John Blow; 1679, appointed organist, Westminster Abbey; 1682, appointed one of the three organists, Chapel Royal.
Ceremonial Music, trumpet(s) and organ, Music Press.
Echo Voluntary for the Double Organ, in The First Four Centuries of Organ Music, Vol. II, p. 371.
Fanfare in C Major, in A Treasury of Shorter Organ Classics, p. 2.
Four Voluntaries and Symphony, Music Press.
Herr Gott, dich loben wir (Doxology), in Orgel-choräle des siebzehnten und achtzehnten Jahrhunderts, p. 66; also in Twelve Short Pieces by Old English Composers, p. 19.
Organ Works, Hugh McLean, ed. , Novello, 1957.
Praeludium, in Alte Orgelmusik aus England und Frankreich, p. 16.
Prelude, in Historical Organ Recitals, Vol. I, p. 102.

Sonata, trumpet and organ, Corliss R. Arnold, arr., Concordia 97-4819, 1967.
Suite in C Major, in Anthologia pro Organo, Vol. II.
Three Voluntaries, in Tallis to Wesley, Vol. 10, Hinrichsen
1659A.
Trompette en Ut, in Varia, Orgue et Liturgie, Vol. 25,
p. 18.
Voluntary on the 100th Psalm Tune, Gray (Standard Organ
Series 2); also Novello.
compositions (2) in Liber Organi, Vol. 10.
compositions in Masterpieces of Organ Music, Folio 10.
compositions (3) in The Parish Organist, Vol. 9.
PURVIS, RICHARD IRVEN. born San Francisco, Calif., Aug. 25,
1917. 1931-1934, organist, Calvary Presbyterian Church,
San Francisco; 1937-1939, organist, St. James' Church,
Philadelphia; 1939-1940, head, department of music, Episcopal
Academy, Overbrook, Penn.; graduate, Curtis Institute of
Music, Philadelphia; pupil of Joseph Lhevinne, Edward Bair-
stow, Charles Courboin, Alexander McCurdy, and David McK.
Williams; 1939-1969, organ recitalist, California Palace of the
Legion of Honor; 1947-1971, organist and master of the chor-
isters, Grace Cathedral, San Francisco; 1959-1968, head,
music department, Cathedral School for Boys, San Francisco.
(An) American Organ Mass on Carols and Hymns (Prelude
Solennel on Veni Emmanuel; Introit on Christe Re-
demptor; Offertory on Resonet in laudibus; Interlude on
Corner; Elevation on Vom Himmel hoch; Communion on
Gevaert; Carillon on Puer nobis nascitur), Flammer.
Andante Cantabile (Pièce Symphonique), World Library.
Communion, Leeds, 1941.
Dialogue Monastique, two organists at two organs, World
Library.
Five Pieces on Gregorian Themes (Divinum Mysterium;
Vexilla regis; Dies Irae; and others), Leeds.
Four Carol Preludes, Leeds.
Four Dubious Conceits (Cantilena on Green Boughs; Les
Petites Cloches; Nocturne on Night in Monterrey;
Marche Grotesque), Flammer.
Four Prayers in Tone, Witmark.
Larghetto Cantabile, classical guitar and organ, World
Library.
Partita on Christ ist erstanden, Witmark.
Passepied for a Joyous Festival; Sarabande for a Day of
Solemnity, in Mixture IV, Flammer.
Petit Concert Champetre, organ and harp, harpsichord, or
piano, World Library.
Seven Chorale Preludes on Tunes Found in American
Hymnals, C. Fischer, 1949.
(A) Solemn Music, Gray.
PUXOL, LUCAS. Spanish. Seventeenth century. Compiled Libro
de cyfra, a codex of seventeenth-century music written in
Spanish keyboard tablature.
Obra de 6º tom. Tiento, in Silva Iberica, p. 12.

QUAGLIATI, PAOLO. born Chioggia, Italy, ca.1555; died Rome, Nov. 16, 1628. Composer of music drama; represented by compositions in Diruta's Il Transilvano and Schmid's Tabula-turbuch (1607).
Toccata dell'Ottavo tono, in L'Arte Musicale in Italia, Vol. III, p. 175.

QUEF, CHARLES-PAUL-FLORIMOND. born Lille, France, Nov. 1, 1873; died Paris, July 2, 1931. Studied at the Conservatory, Lille, and at the Conservatory, Paris; pupil of Dubois, Widor, and Guilmant; organist at the following churches in Paris: St. Nicolas-des-Champs, St. Laurent, Ste. Marie-des-Batig-nolles; 1901, appointed organist, Trinité (succeeded Guilmant).
Cinq pièces, Hérelle.
Communion, Hérelle.
Deux Rhapsodies, Hérelle.
Douze pièces, Op. 36 (1912), Leduc.
Fugue, in The International Organist, Vol. I, p. 42.
Noël parisien, in The French Organist, Vol. I, p. 51; also Durand.
Prélude-Choral, Op. 25 (1902), Noël.
Rapsodies sur des thèmes bretons, Op. 29, 1908.
Trois pièces (On a Clément Marot tune; Dialogue; Idyl).
Trois pièces, Op. 44 (Paraphrase; Idylle; Dialogue), Durand.

RAASTAD, NIELS OTTO. born Copenhagen, Nov. 26, 1888. 1909-1912, studied at the Royal Conservatory, Copenhagen; 1913-1914, studied at the Conservatory, Leipzig, as a pupil of Reger and Straube; 1924, appointed organist, Cathedral, Copenhagen.
Achtzehn Orgelchoräle, Op. 58, Hansen.
Fünf-und-zwanzig Orgelpreludier over Kendte Salmemelodier, Op. 64, Skandinavisk Musikvorlag.
(De) kirklige Højtider, Op. 11, Skandinavisk Musikforlag.
Orgelfantasi över Christ ist erstanden, in Musica Organi, Vol. III, p. 12.
Orgelfantasie über Christus ist vom Tode, Op. 10, Hansen 18497.
Orgelkoraler (12), Op. 8, No. 1, Hansen 16157.
Orgelkoraler (12), Op. 8, No. 2, Hansen 16158.
Orgelkoraler (18), Hansen 21663.
Orgelkoraler, Op. 81, Engstrom & Södring.
Orgelmesse, Op. 82, Hansen 26575.
Orgelsonate, Op. 16, Hansen 17349.
Partita über Aus tiefer Not, Op. 70, Hansen 24884.
Präludium und Fuge (C Major), Op. 20, Leuckart.
Präludium und Fuge (A Minor), Op. 29, Leuckart.

Requiem, Op. 100, Hansen 27569.
Sonata No. 1 (C Minor), Op. 10, Hansen, 1924.
Sonata (E Minor), Op. 23, Leuckart.
Sonata (D Minor), Op. 33, Leuckart.
Vier-und-zwanzig Orgel Choräle, Op. 46, 2 vols., Breitkopf
    und Härtel 5311a/b.
Vierzig Orgelchoräle, Op. 108, Hansen 28104.
Zwölf kleine Stücke, Op. 51, Kistner & Siegel.
Zwölf Orgelchoräle, Op. 8, 2 vols., Hansen.
chorale preludes in Das Organistenamt, Part 2, Vol. I (4)
    and Vol. 2 (4), Breitkopf & Härtel.
chorale preludes (2) in Slaagt skal Fölge slaagters Gang,
    Bitsch & Peterson, eds., Hansen.
RACQUET, CHARLES. born Paris, 1597; died Paris, Jan. 1,
    1664. 1618-1643, organist, Notre Dame, Paris; cooperated
    with Pierre Thierry on the renovation of the Notre Dame organ.
    compositions (2) in Les Maîtres français de l'orgue, Vol. II.
    fantaisies in L'Organiste Liturgique, Vols. 29-30.
RAICK, DIEUDONNÉ. born Liège, Belgium, 1702; died Antwerp,
    Nov. 30, 1764. Vicar-choral, Notre Dame Cathedral, Antwerp.
    Gavotte, in Oudnederlandse Meesters, Vol. I, p. 108.
    Sicilienne, in Oudnederlandse Meesters, Vol. III, p. 102.
    Sicilienne, in Oudnederlandse Meesters, Vol. III, p. 110.
RAISON, ANDRÉ. French. born second half, seventeenth century;
    died Paris, 1719. Organist, Jacobins' Church, Paris; organist,
    royal abbey, Ste. Geneviève; studied at the seminary, Nan-
    terre; taught Clérambault.
    Da pacem Domine, Kalmus.
    Dernier Kyrie on Dialogue, in The First Four Centuries of
        Organ Music, Vol. II, p. 342.
    Deux pièces du 2me ton, in Les Maîtres français de l'orgue,
        Vol. I, p. 70.
    Masses (2) in First Tone and Second Tone, Kalmus 3823.
    Masses (2) in Fifth Tone and Eighth Tone, Kalmus 3824.
    Offerte sur "Vive le Roy", in Historical Organ Recitals,
        Vol. I, p. 110.
    Premier livre d'orgue, in Archives des maîtres d'orgue
        des seizième-dix-huitième siècles, Vol. 2.
    *Premier livre d'orgue, in Orgue et Liturgie, Vols. 55, 56,
        58, 59, and 61.
    Second livre d'orgue, in L'Organiste liturgique, Vols. 39-
        40, 43-44.
    Trio en chaconne, in Les Maîtres français de l'orgue, Vol.
        II, p. 41.
    Trio en passacaglia (Christe from Messe du Deuzieme Ton),
        in Treasury of Early Organ Music, p. 70.
    Various Compositions, Kalmus 3825.
    compositions (2) in Alte Orgelmusik aus England und Frank-
        reich.
    compositions in The Parish Organist, Vols. 1-4, 7, and 8.
RAMIN, GÜNTER. born Karlsruhe, Germany, Oct. 15, 1898; died
    Leipzig, Feb. 27, 1956. Studied at the Conservatory, Leipzig;
    organ pupil of Straube; 1918, appointed organist, Thomaskirche,

Leipzig; 1939, made Cantor, Thomasschule; conductor, Philharmonic Chorus, Berlin; later conductor, Gewandhaus chorus, Leipzig.

Fantasie (E Minor), Op. 4, Breitkopf & Härtel 5284.

Orgelchoral-Suite, Op. 6, Breitkopf & Härtel 5424.

Präludium, Largo, und Fuge, Op. 5, Breitkopf & Härtel 5380.

Straf mich nicht, in Orgelchoräle Sammlung, Metzler.

chorale preludes (9) in Das Organistenamt, Part 2, Chorale Preludes, 2 vols., Breitkopf & Härtel.

RANSE, MARC DE. born Aiguillon (Lot-et-Garonne), France, Apr. 20, 1881; died Aiguillon, Feb. 13, 1951. Pupil of Alexandre Guilmant and Vincent d'Indy; 1912, appointed professor of accompaniment, Schola Cantorum; choirmaster, St. Louis d'Antin; organist, Cathedral, Agen.

Prélude en re mineur, in Varia II, Orgue et Liturgie, Vol. 46, p. 30.

RAPHAEL, GÜNTHER. born Berlin, Apr. 30, 1903; died Herford, Oct. 19, 1960. Studied at the Musikhochschule, Berlin; organ pupil of Walter Fischer; 1926-1934, teacher of theory and composition, Conservatory, Leipzig; 1934-1944, lived in Meiningen; 1945-1948, lived in Laubach; 1948, won Liszt prize, Weimar, for composition; 1949, appointed teacher of theory and composition, Conservatory, Duisberg; 1957-1960, professor, Musikhochschule, Cologne.

Concerto (Ein' feste Burg), organ, three trumpets, timpani, and strings, Op. 57, Müller 16.

Fantasie in C moll, Op. 22, No. 2 (1928, Breitkopf & Härtel 5491.

Fantasie und Fuge über Christus, der ist mein Leben, Breitkopf & Härtel 6533.

Fantasy and Fugue on a Finnish Choral, Op. 41, No. 1, (1939), Breitkopf & Härtel 5949.

Fünf Choralvorspiele, Op. 1 (1922), Breitkopf & Härtel 5256.

Introduktion und Chaconne (C-sharp Minor) Op. 27, No. 1 (1930), Breitkopf & Härtel 5548.

Klein Partita über Herr Jesu Christ (1958), Augsburg.

Largo (Violin Sonata, Op. 12, No. 1), violin and organ, Breitkopf & Härtel 5547.

Meinen Jesum lass ich nicht, in 73 leichte Choralvorspiele, alter und neuer Meister, H. Fleischer, ed., Leuckart.

Nun lasst uns Gott dem Herrn, in Anthologie, Concordia.

Partita on a Finnish Choral, Op. 41, No. 2 (1939), Breitkopf & Härtel 5950.

Partita über Ach Gott, vom Himmel, Op. 22, No. 1, Breitkopf & Härtel 5449.

Partita über einen finnischen Choral, Op. 41, No. 2, Breitkopf & Härtel 5950.

Partita über Herr Jesu Christ dich zu uns, Augsburg.

Passacaglia on a Finnish Choral, Op. 41, No. 3 (1939), Breitkopf & Härtel 5951; also in Musica Organi, Vol. II, p. 48.

Prelude and Fugue (G Major), Op. 22, No. 3 (1930), Breit-
kopf & Härtel 5492.
Sieben Orgelchoräle, Op. 42, Breitkopf & Härtel.
Sonata (C), Op. 36, violin and organ, Breitkopf und Härtel.
Sonata, Op. 68, Breitkopf & Härtel 6275.
Sonata, violoncello and organ, Hanssler Edition 16. 004.
Toccata, Choral, und Variationen, Op. 53, Müller 51.
Toccata in C moll, Op. 27, No. 3 (1934), Breitkopf &
Härtel 5613.
Variationen über Durch Adams Fall, Op. 27, No. 2, Breit-
kopf & Härtel 5552.
Zwölf Orgelchoräle, Op. 37, 2 vols., Breitkopf & Härtel
5617/ 5618.
chorale preludes (3) in Das Organistenamt, Vol. 2, Breit-
kopf & Härtel.
chorale preludes (6) in Orgelvorspiel, Poppen, Reich, and
Strube, eds., Merseburger.
compositions in The Parish Organist, Vols. 7 and 8.
RATCLIFFE, DESMOND. English. born 1917. 1927-1931, chor-
ister, St. Paul's Cathedral, London; studied at the Royal
Academy of Music; 1946, appointed to the Editorial Depart-
ment, Novello and Company.
Figures Plain & Fancy, Novello.
Flourish on Würtemburg, Novello.
Meditation on 'The Infant King', Novello.
Preamble, Contrast and Hosanna, Novello.
Reflections on the Passion Chorale, Novello.
Three Pieces (Prelude; Interlude; Postlude), Novello.
Two Hymn-preludes, in Festal Voluntaries (Lent, Easter),
Novello.
RATHGEBER, VALENTIN. born Oberelsbach, Germany, 1682; died
1750. 1708, became a Benedictine monk, Monastery of Banz.
Aria pastorella (A Major), in Alte deutsche Weihnachtsmusik,
p. 16.
Musical Pastime (Musikalischer Zeit-Vertreib) (1743), Bären-
reiter NMA 105.
compositions in Das Erbe deutschen Musik, Series I, Vol. 19a.
RAUTAVAARA, EINOJUHANI. born Helsinki, Oct. 9, 1928. 1948-
1954, studied at the University of Helsinki and Sibelius Academy;
1955-1956, pupil of Copland, Sessions, and Persichetti in the
United States; 1957, 1959, taught music theory, Sibelius
Academy.
ta tou theou (... se mikä on Jum alasta), Op. 30 (1966),
Edition Fazer 4930, 1968.
RAVANELLO, ORESTE. born Venice, Aug. 25, 1871; died Padua,
July 1, 1938. Studied at the Liceo Benedetto Marcello; 1893,
appointed second organist, 1895, made first organist, San
Marco, Venice; 1898, named maestro di cappella, San Antonio,
Padua; 1902, appointed professor of organ, Liceo Benedetto
Marcello; 1914, named director, Istituto musicale, Padua.
Adorazione, World Library of Sacred Music; also (Peters
N3092).
Andante cantabile, string orchestra, harp, and organ,

Zanibon 3797.
Due Marcie Religiose, World Library of Sacred Music.
Eight Ancient Pieces, World Library of Sacred Music.
Four Pieces, Op. 39, Augener.
(The) Liturgical Organist, Sten (Turin).
Mystica, World Library of Sacred Music.
Organ Pieces on Choral Melodies, Op. 28, Coppenrath.
Prelude-Berceuse, harp and organ, World Library of
    Sacred Music.
Scene at the Crib, World Library of Sacred Music.
Sette Corali, Ricordi.
Sieben Trios, Op. 25, Schwann.
Six Organ Masses, Op. 57, Sten (Turin).
Six Pieces, Op. 50, J. Fischer 4875.
Tema e variazioni in si minore, World Library of Sacred
    Music.

READ, DANIEL. born Attleboro, Mass., Nov. 16, 1757; died New
    Haven, Conn., Dec. 4, 1836. Surveyor; comb maker; 1782-
    1783, directed a singing school on North River; composed
    four hundred tunes.
        Trumpet Tune for Advent, in Early American Compositions
            for Organ, p. 5.

READ, GARDNER. born Evanston, Ill., Jan. 2, 1913. Studied at
    Northwestern University; 1936, Mus. Bac., 1937, M. Mus.,
    Eastman School of Music; 1938-1939, won Cromwell Fellow-
    ship for travel in Europe; pupil of Copland and Sibelius;
    1943, Second Symphony, Paderewski Prize; 1941-1943, taught
    composition, St. Louis Institute of Music; 1943-1945, teacher,
    Conservatory, Kansas City, Mo.; 1945-1948, composition
    teacher, Cleveland Institute of Music; 1948, appointed pro-
    fessor of composition, Boston University College of Music;
    1957, received State Department grant to lecture and conduct
    in Mexico.
        Chorale-fantasia on Good King Wenceslas, Gray.
        Eight Preludes on Old Southern Hymns (1951), Op. 90,
            Gray, 1952.
        Little Pastorale, Galaxy 2124, 1957.
        Meditation on Jesu, meine Freude, Gray (St. Cecilia Series
            814).
        Passacaglia and Fugue, Op. 34 (1936).
        Poem on De Profundis, organ and French horn, Leeds.
        Quiet Music, Op. 65a.
        Six Preludes on Old Southern Hymns, Op. 112, Gray.
        Suite (1950).

READING, JOHN. English. born 1677; died London, Sept. 2,
    1764. Chorister and pupil of John Blow at the Chapel Royal;
    1700-1702, organist, Dulwich College; 1703, Master of the
    Choristers, Lincoln Cathedral; 1708, organist, Church of St.
    John, Hackeny, London; organist, St. Mary Woolnoth and
    St. Mary Woolchurchhaw, London; organist, St. Dunstan-in-
    the-West.
        Adeste fideles, Theodore Presser.
        Voluntary (G Major), in Tallis to Wesley, Vol. 21, p. 6.

REBOULOT, ANTOINE.   French.   Twentieth century.   Organist,
St. Germain-des-Prés, Paris; pupil of André Marchal; resi-
dent of Canada.
 Chaconne en rondeau, in L'Orgue Néo-Classique, Orgue et
  Liturgie, Vol. 33, p. 3.
 Cinq pièces liturgiques pour l'office des morts, in Céré-
  monies funèbres, L'Organiste liturgique, Vol. 15,
  p. 14.
 Vater unser, in Notre père, Orgue et Liturgie, Vol. 24,
  p. 28.
 compositions (2) in Pâques, L'Organiste liturgique, Vol. 5.
REDA, SIEGFRIED. born Bochum, Germany, July 27, 1916; died
Mühlheim (Ruhr), Dec. 13, 1968.   Studied church music, Dort-
mund; pupil of Pepping and Distler; worked in Gelsenkirchen,
Bochum, Berlin; 1946, became director, Evangelical Church
Music, Essen; 1953, appointed Church Music Director, Petri-
kirche, Mülheim.
 Adventspartita über Mit Ernst, O Menschenkinder (1952),
  Bärenreiter 434.
 Cantus-Firmus-Stücke (1960), Bärenreiter 3973.
 Choral-Konzert IV (1952), Bärenreiter.
 Choralkonzert über O Traurigkeit, o Herzeleid, Bärenreiter
  2653.
 Choralphantasie über Herzlich lieb hab' ich dich (1955),
  Bärenreiter.
 Choral-Spiel-Buch, Bärenreiter 2064, 1946.
 Choralsuite (1941).
 Choralvorspiele (1960), Bärenreiter 1763.
 Christ unser Herr, Bärenreiter 2068.
 Gottes Sohn ist kommen, Bärenreiter 2067.
 In Meditationem über Herzlich lieb, Bärenreiter, 1967.
 Kleine Orgelstücke (1942), Bärenreiter 1678.
 Laudamus Te, Bärenreiter, 1965.
 Marienbilder (1951), Bärenreiter 436.
 Meditation und Fuge über Wir danken dir (1960).
 Meditation zu dem Passionslied Ein Lämmlein geht, Bären-
  reiter, 1964.
 O wie selig, Bärenreiter 2066.
 Orgelkonzert I, Bärenreiter 2069.
 Orgelkonzert II, Bärenreiter 2073.
 Orgelkonzert III (1948), Bärenreiter 2433.
 Präludium, Fuge, und Quadrupelum (1957), Bärenreiter
  3971.
 Psalm-Vorspiele, Bärenreiter 2650.
 Sechs kleine Orgelstücke, Bärenreiter 1678.
 Sieben Monologue, Bärenreiter, 1964.
 Sonate 1960, Bärenreiter 3978, 1963.
 Toccata: Novenaria, Modus vertens, Bärenreiter, 1967.
 Triptychon über O Welt, ich muss (1951), Bärenreiter 1904.
 Vorspiele zu den Psalm-Lieden, Bärenreiter 2650.
 chorale preludes in Orgelbuch zum Evangelischen Kirchen-
  gesangbuch, O. Brodde, ed. , Books 1, 3, 6, 4, 16,
  and 18, Bärenreiter.

REDFORD, JOHN.   English.   born ca. 1485?;   died London, 1547.
1534, organist, St. Paul's Cathedral, London.
> Come, Gentle Saviour, in The First Four Centuries of
> > Organ Music, Vol. I, p. 61.
> Glorificamus, in Treasury of Early Organ Music, p. 8.
> Glorificamus, in Twelve Short Pieces by Old English Com-
> > posers, p. 24.
> Lucem tuam, in Altenglische Orgelmusik, p. 17;   also in
> > Liber Organi, Vol. 10, p. 1.
> O lux on the faburden, in Altenglische Orgelmusik, p. 18.
> compositions (9) in Early English Organ Music.
> compositions (2) in Historical Anthology of Music, Vol. I,
> > p. 128.
> compositions (7) in The Mulliner Book.

REGER, MAX.   born Brand, Bavaria, Germany, Mar. 19, 1873; died
Leipzig, May 11, 1916. 1886-1889, organist, Roman Catholic
Church, Weiden; 1890-1895, pupil of Riemann; friend of Straube;
1905-1906, taught composition, theory, and organ, Königliche
Akademie der Tonkunst, Munich; 1907, appointed music director
and professor of composition, University of Leipzig; 1907-1916,
taught at the Conservatory, Leipzig; 1911-1915, Kapellmeister,
Meiningen; 1908, honorary Ph. D. , University of Jena.
> Ave Maria, Op. 80, No. 5, Peters 3064G.
> Benedictus, Op. 59, No. 9, in The International Organist,
> > Vol. I, p. 83;   also Peters 3114;   also in Musica
> > Organi, Vol. II, p. 22.
> Canzona (E-flat Major), Op. 65, No. 9, Peters 3012G.
> Chorale Preludes, Op. 67, 3 vols. , Hinrichsen De-454-456
> > a/b;   Associated Music Press, 1903.
> Fantasie über Alle Menschen; Wachet auf; Alleluja, Gott zu
> > loben, Op. 52, Universal 1247-1249, 1901.
> Fantasie über Ein' feste Burg, Op. 27, Peters 4404, 1899.
> Fantasie über Freu dich sehr, Op. 30, Universal 1181,
> > 1899.
> Fantasie über Straf' mich nicht, Op. 40, No. 2, Universal
> > 1207, 1900.
> Fantasie über Wie schön leuchtet, Op. 40, Universal 1206,
> > 1900.
> Fantasie und Fuge in c moll, Op. 29, Peters 3981a, 1899.
> Fantasie und Fuge in d moll, Op. 135b, Peters 3981, 1916.
> Fantasie und Fuge über B-A-C-H, Op. 46, Universal 1222,
> > 1900.
> Festival Procession by Richard Strauss, transcribed by
> > Reger, with trombones and timpani, ad. lib. , Peters
> > 6008, 1909.
> Four Preludes and Fugues, Op. 85 (C-charp Minor, G
> > Major, F Major, E Minor), Peters 3110, 1905.
> Fuga (D Major), Op. 59, No. 6, in Musica Organi, Vol. II,
> > p. 6.
> Gloria in excelsis, Op. 59, No. 8, in Musica Organi,
> > Vol. II, p. 6.
> Glorious Things of Thee Are Spoken, Edition Le Grand
> > Orgue.

Herzlich tut mich verlangen, in Festival Music for Lent and
    Easter, Carl, ed. , Boston Music Co. ; also Breitkopf
    & Härtel 5933.
Ich dank' dir, lieber Herr, in Anthologie, Concordia.
Intermezzo, Op. 59, No. 3, in Historical Organ Recitals,
    Vol. 5, p. 107.
Intermezzo, Op. 80, No. 10, Peters 3064H.
Introduction, Passacaglia and Fugue in E Minor, Op. 127,
    Hinrichsen De-451; Associated Music Press, 1913.
Introduktion und Passacaglia in d moll, Breitkopf & Härtel
    2198, 1900.
Komm, süsser Tod, Schott.
Kyrie eleison, Op. 59, No. 7, in Musica Organi, Vol. II,
    p. 12.
Monologues, Op. 63 (Prelude; Fugue; Canzone; Capriccio;
    Introduction; Passacaglia; Ave Maria; Fantasie; Toc-
    cata; Fugue; Canon; Scherzo), Leuckart, 1902.
Nine Pieces, Op. 129, 2 vols. , Vol. 1: Toccata in D
    Minor; Fugue in D Minor; Canon in E Minor; Melodia
    in B-flat Major, Hinrichsen De466a; Vol. 2: Capric-
    cio in G Minor; Basso Ostinato in G Minor; Inter-
    mezzo in F Minor; Prelude in B Minor; Fugue in B
    Minor, Hinrichsen De-466b, 1913.
Orgelstücke, Op. 145, Breitkopf & Härtel 4157-4162.
Präludium über Komm süsser Tod, Schott 1893.
Präludium und Fuge in d moll, Junne, 1902.
Präludium und Fuge (G-sharp Minor), Junne, 1907.
Prelude and Fugue on God Save the King, J. Aible; also
    Universal.
Preludes and Fugues, Op. 56 (E Major, D Minor, G Major,
    B Minor), Universal, 1904.
Sechs Trios, Op. 47 (Canon; Gigue; Canzonetta; Scherzo;
    Siciliano; Fugue), Universal, 1900.
Sonata I (F-sharp Minor), Op. 33 (Fantasie; Intermezzo;
    Introduction and Passacaglia), Universal, 1899.
Sonata II (D Minor), Op. 60, Leuckart, 1902.
Suite in e moll, Op. 16, Schott 310.
Suite in g moll, Op. 92, Forberg, 1906.
Symphonic Fantasia in d moll; Fuge in D dur, Op. 57,
    Universal, 1901.
Ten Pieces, Op. 69, 2 vols. , Vol. 1: Prelude in F Major;
    Prelude in E Minor; Fugue in D Minor; Basso ostinato
    in E Minor; Moment Musical in D Major; Capriccio in
    D Minor, Hinrichsen De-457a; Vol. 2: Toccata in D
    Major; Fugue in D Major; Romanze in G Minor; Prelude
    in A Minor; Fugue in A Minor, Hinrichsen De-457b.
Thirteen Chorale Preludes, Op. 79b, Beyer, 1904; also
    Sikorski 116a/b.
Thirty Short and Easy Chorale Preludes, Op. 135a, Peters
    3980, 1915.
Three Pieces, Op. 7 (Prelude and Fugue in C Major;
    Fantasie in A Minor; Fugue in D Major, Augener,
    1894; Schott 311.

Toccata in d moll, Op. 59, No. 5, in Historical Organ
Recitals, Vol. 5, p. 112; also in Musica Organi,
Vol. II, p. 1.
Trio in E dur, in Schule des klassischen Triospiels, p. 36.
Trio Movements, Gordon Phillips, ed. , Peters 3008c, 1957.
Twelve Compositions, Op. 65, 2 vols. , Vol. 1: Rhapsody in
C-sharp Minor; Capriccio in G; Pastorale in A; Con-
solation in E; Improvisation and Fugue in A Minor;
Vol. 2: Prelude and Fugue in D Minor and D Major;
Canzona in E-flat; Scherzo in D Minor; Toccata and
Fugue in E Minor and E Major, Peters 3012A/B.
Twelve Compositions, Op. 80, 2 vols. , Vol. 1: Prelude
and Fughetta in A Minor; Canzonetta in G Minor;
Gigue in D Minor; Ave Maria; Intermezzo in G Minor;
Vol. 2: Scherzo in F-sharp Minor; Romanze; Per-
petuum mobile; Intermezzo in D Major; Toccata and
Fugue in A Minor, Peters 3064A/B.
Twelve Organ Pieces, Op. 59, 2 vols. , Vol. 1: Prelude
in E Minor; Pastorale in F Major; Intermezzo in A
Minor; Canon in E Major; Toccata in D Minor; Fugue
in D Major, Peters 3008a; Vol. 2: Kyrie eleison
in E Minor; Gloria in excelsis in D Major; Benedictus
in D-flat Major; Capriccio in F-sharp Minor; Melodia
in B-flat Major; Te Deum in A Minor, Peters 3008b.
Variation and Fugue on an Original Theme in F-sharp
Minor, Op. 73, Universal, 1904; also (Peters D458).
Wie schön leuchtet, in The Lutheran Organist, Concordia.
compositions in Preludes, Interludes, Postludes, Hinrichsen
600B.
compositions in The Parish Organist, Vol. 1-4.
REICHA (see Rejcha).
REICHARDT, CHRISTIAN. German. born 1685; died 1775.
Organist, Erfurt.
Wer nur den lieben Gott, in Orgelchoräle um J. S. Bach,
G. Frotscher, ed. , Litolff.
composition in Das Erbe deutschen Musik, Series I, Vol. 9.
REICHEL, BERNHARD. Swiss. born 1901. Professor of harmony,
Institut Jacques Dalcroze, and at the Conservatory, Geneva;
organist, Eglise des Eaux-Vives, Geneva.
Orgel Choräle, Op. 6, Bärenreiter 1309.
chorale preludes (4) in 21 Orgelchoräler Schweizerischer
Komponisten, Krompholz.
REIMANN, ARIBERT. born Berlin, Mar. 4, 1936. 1955-1959,
studied at the Musikhochschule, Berlin; pupil of Boris Blacher;
has won a number of composition prizes in Germany.
Dialog I, Schott, 4822.
REINAGLE, ALEXANDER. Baptized at Portsmouth, England,
Apr. 23, 1756; died Baltimore, Md. , Sept. 21, 1809. 1774,
went to Edinburgh; pupil of Raynor Taylor; 1785, became a
pupil of C. P. E. Bach, Hamburg; 1786, came to the United
States; performer and impressario in Philadelphia, Baltimore,
and New York City.
Sonata in E Major, John Tasker Howard, ed. , in Program

of Easy American Piano Music.
REINCKEN (REINKEN, REINIKE), JOHANN (JAN) ADAM. born
probably in Wilshausen, Alsace, Apr. 27, 1623; died Hamburg,
Germany, Nov. 24, 1722. 1654, pupil of Scheidemann in Ham-
burg; 1657, organist, Berghkercke, Deventer, Holland; 1658,
Scheidemann's substitute, 1663, became organist, St. Katharinen-
kirche, Hamburg.
 An Wasserflüssen Babylon, Hinrichsen; also Sikorski 234.
 Collected Keyboard Works, in Corpus of Early Keyboard
  Music, No. 16.
 Es ist gewisslich, Hinrichsen; also Sikorski.
 Toccata (G Major), in Organum, Series IV, Vol. 5.
 Toccata (G Major), in Varia, Orgue et Liturgie, Vol. 25,
  p. 6.
 Toccata and Fugue, in The First Four Centuries of Organ
  Music, Vol. II, p. 257.
 Was kann uns kommen an für Not (Choralfantasie), Sikorski
  235.
 compositions in Masterpieces of Organ Music, Folio 40.
REINER, KAREL. born Žatec, Czechoslovakia, June 27, 1910.
Graduated from Master School; composition pupil of Josef
Suk and Alois Hába.
 Three Preludes, in Nuove Composizioni per Organo 2.
REJCHA (REICHA), ANTON. born Prague, Feb. 26, 1770; died
Paris, May 28, 1836. 1788, became flute player, electoral
orchestra, Bonn; pupil of Neefe; taught in Hamburg, Vienna,
and Paris; pupil of Haydn; taught Liszt, Gounod, Franck,
and Berlioz.
 Fugue in A Major, in A Century of Czech Music, Vol. I,
  p. 24.
REMBT, JOHANN ERNST. born Suhl, Thuringia, Germany, ca.1749;
died Suhl, Feb. 26, 1810. 1773, became organist, Suhl.
 Fünfzig vierstimmige Fughetten, 2 vols. , R. Walter, ed. ,
  Coppenrath.
 Jesu, meine Freude, in Anthologie, Concordia.
 Nun freut euch, in Cäcilia, Breitkopf & Härtel.
 Leichte Triomässige Choralvorspiele, Breitkopf & Härtel.
 Six Fugued Chorale Preludes, Breitkopf & Härtel.
 Six Trios, Susi Jeans, ed. , Schott 10093.
 Was Gott tut, in The New Organist, Part II, Koerner, ed. ,
  Schuberth.
 chorale preludes (3) in Orgel Choräle Sammlung, Metzler.
REMY, MARCEL. born Nice, France, Mar. 13, 1910. Studied at
the Conservatory, Paris; composition pupil of Henri Busser;
1937, appointed professor of piano, Conservatory, Saint-Etienne.
 Prélude funèbre, in Pièces funèbres, Orgue et Liturgie,
  Vol. 23, p. 22.
RESPIGHI, OTTORINO. born Bologna, Italy, July 9, 1879; died
Rome, Apr. 18, 1936. Pupil of Martucci and Rimsky-
Korsakoff; 1913, appointed composition professor, 1923-1925,
director, Royal Musical Lyceum of St. Cecilia, Rome (suc-
ceeded Bossi).
 Prelude on a Chorale of Bach, Edition Musicus.

Preludio, in The International Organist, Vol. I, p. 27.
Tre Pezzi (1910): Preludio (D Minor); Preludio (B-flat
    Major); Preludio (A Minor), Edizione Bongiovanni
    (Bologna).
REUBKE, JULIUS. born Hausneindorf, Germany, Mar. 23, 1834;
    died Pillnitz (Dresden), June 3, 1858. Pupil of Kullak and
    Liszt; came from family of organ builders.
    Sonata on the 94th Psalm, Casper Koch, ed. , G. Schirmer;
        also Hermann Keller, ed. , Peters 4941; also Elling-
        ford, ed. , Oxford; also Schuberth (Leipzig).
    Trio (E-flat), in Organ Book No. 2, p. 12.
REUSCHEL, EUGÈNE. French. born 1900. Piano virtuoso;
    studied at the Conservatory, Paris.
    Promenades en Provence, 2 vols. , Lemoine, 1938.
REUTTER, GEORG, the elder. Baptized in Vienna, Nov. 4, 1656;
    died Vienna, Aug. 29, 1738. Probably a pupil of Kerll; 1686,
    became organist-choirmaster, St. Stephen's Cathedral; 1697-
    1703, theorbist, court chapel, Vienna; 1700-1703, court or-
    ganist; 1715-1738, appointed first Kapellmeister, St. Stephen's
    Cathedral, Vienna.
    Christ ist erstanden, in Cantantibus Organis, Vol. 13,
        F. Pustet.
    compositions in Denkmäler der Tonkunst in Osterreich,
        Vol. XIII, No. 2.
REVEL, PIERRE. born Nattages (Ain), France, 1901. Studied at
    the Conservatory, Paris; 1948, appointed organist/ and pro-
    fessor of harmony, Conservatory, Paris.
    Méditation, in L'Orgue Néo-Classique, Orgue et Liturgie,
        Vol. 33, p. 22.
REVEYRON, JOSEPH. born Lyon, France, Sept. 2, 1917. Organ
    pupil of Edouard Commette; organist, Cathedral, Lyon.
    Deux chorales à Notre Dame, in Liturgie et Concert,
        Orgue et Liturgie, Vol. 70, p. 1.
    Extraits de la Bible, Lemoine.
    Toccata, Orgeret, Editeur (Lyon).
RHEINBERGER, JOSEPH GABRIEL. born Vaduz, Liechtenstein,
    Mar. 17, 1839; died Munich, Nov. 25, 1901. Organist,
    Vaduz; 1851, entered the Conservatory, Munich; organ pupil
    of Herzog; 1860-1866, organist, St. Michael's Hofkirche,
    Munich; 1859, appointed professor of piano, Conservatory,
    Munich; 1860-1901, professor of composition and organ, Con-
    servatory, Munich; 1899, honorary doctorate, University of
    Munich; taught Humperdinck and Horatio Parker.
    Characteristic Pieces (12), Op. 156, Novello.
    Five Hymns, R. Schaab, arr. , R. Forberg.
    Fughettas (24), 4 vols. , Hinrichsen 47, 48, 96, and 97.
    Herzlich thut mich verlangen, in Anthologie, Concordia;
        also in Seasonal Chorale Preludes, Book 2, C. H.
        Trevor, ed. , Oxford.
    Meditations (12 pieces), Op. 167a, 1892.
    Miszellaneen (12 pieces), Op. 174, Leuckart.
    Monologues (12 pieces), Op. 162, Novello.
    Organ Concerto No. 1 (F Major), Op. 137, Kistner & Siegel.

Organ Concerto No. 2 (G Minor), Op. 177, R. Forberg.
Organ Sonatas, Op. 65, 98, 111, 119, 142, 146, 154, 193,
    Harvey Grace, ed. , Novello, 1932-.
Organ Trios, Op. 49 (1870), Peters F 60.
Organ Works, Martin Weyer, ed. , 2 vols. , Forberg 69/70,
    (Bad Godesberg, Germany), 1965.
Recital and Service Pieces, T. Tertius Noble, ed. , 2 vols. ,
    J. Fischer 8507, 8750.
Selected Compositions, Mansfield, ed. , 3 vols. , Paxton,
    1932.
Selected Trios from Op. 49 and 189, Harvey Grace, ed. ,
    Novello, 1963.
Slow Movements from the Sonatas, Harvey Grace, ed. ,
    2 vols. , Novello.
Sonata (A Major), Op. 188, Novello; also Forberg.
Sonata (A Minor) "Tonus peregrinus," Op. 98 (1876), Gordon
    Phillips, ed. , Hinrichsen 1461, 1966; also Novello;
    also Forberg.
Sonata (A-flat Major), Op. 65 (Fantasy-Sonata) (1871),
    Novello; also Universal.
Sonata (B Major), Op. 181 (Fantasie-Sonata), Forberg 89.
Sonata (B Minor), Op. 146, Forberg 90.
Sonata (B Minor), Op. 148a, Forberg.
Sonata (B-flat Major), Op. 142 (1885), Novello; Forberg.
Sonata (C Major), Op. 165, Forberg.
Sonata (C Minor), Op. 27 (1869), Novello.
Sonata (D Major), Op. 168, Forberg 91.
Sonata (D Minor), Op. 148b (1887), Novello; Forberg.
Sonata (D-flat Major), Op. 154, G. Schirmer; Novello;
    Forberg.
Sonata (E Minor), Op. 132 (1882), Novello; Forberg.
Sonata (E-flat Major), Op. 161, Forberg.
Sonata (E-flat Minor), Op. 119 (1880), Novello.
Sonata (F Major), Op. 196, Hinrichsen 780; Novello;
    Forberg.
Sonata (F Minor), Op. 127 (1881), Novello.
Sonata (F-sharp Minor), Op. 111, Forberg 93.
Sonata (G Major), Op. 88 ("Pastorale"), G. Schirmer,
    1909; Novello; Forberg.
Sonata (G Minor), Op. 193, Forberg.
Sonata (G-sharp Minor), Op. 175 (1893), Forberg 92.
Suite, organ, violin, 'cello, string orchestra, Op. 149.
Suite, violin and organ, Op. 150.
Suite, violin and organ, Op. 166.
Ten Trios, Op. 49, Forberg 60.
Three Pieces for Organ, O. Junne.
Trios, Op. 189 (1898).
Vision, O. Ditson.
Zwei-und-zwanzig Fughetten, Op. 123.
Zwölf Charakterstücke, Op. 156.
RHODES, HAROLD WILLIAM. born Hanley, Staffordshire, England,
    Sept. 15, 1889. Studied at the Royal College of Music, Lon-
    don; pupil of Parratt; assistant organist St. George's,

Windsor; 1908-1910, organist, Chapel, Windsor, Great Park;
Mus. D. , London University; music master, Lancing College;
1912-1928, organist, St. John's Church, Torquay; 1928-1933,
organist and master of the choristers, Cathedral, Coventry;
1933-1949, organist, Cathedral, Winchester.
Interlude (G Minor), in Preludes, Interludes, Postludes,
Hinrichsen 600A.
RHYS, PHILIP AP. Welsh. Sixteenth century. Composed the only
extant English organ Mass using the alternation practice;
organist, St. Mary-at-Hill; 1547, became organist, St. Paul's
Cathedral, London (succeeded Redford).
Missa in die Trinitatis (Deus creator omnium), in Altenglische Orgelmusik, p. 24.
RICHARD, ETIENNE. born Paris, ca. 1621; died Paris, May 1669.
Organ virtuoso; perhaps pupil of Lebègue; organist, St.
Jacques-la-Boucherie.
compositions (2) in Les Maîtres français de l'orgue, Vol. I.
compositions (11) in L'Orgue parisien sous le regne de
Louis XIV, Norbert Dufourcq, ed. , Hansen, 1956.
suite movements (13) in Pré-Classiques français, L'Organiste
liturgique, Vol. 18.
RICHTER, FERDINAND TOBIAS. born Würzburg, Austria, ca. 1649;
died Vienna, Nov. 3, 1711. 1662, Kapellmeister for the bishop,
Würzburg; 1683, appointed court organist, Vienna; 1690,
named first organist, court chapel; taught royal children;
taught Wilhelm Hieronymus Pachelbel.
compositions in Denkmäler der Tonkunst in Österreich, Jahr-
gang XIII, Vol. 2.
RIDOUT, ALAN JOHN. born West Wickham, Kent, England, 1934.
Associate, Royal College of Music; 1960, appointed professor,
Royal College of Music; 1961-1962, taught at the University of
Birmingham; 1963, named to faculty, Cambridge University; since
1964, teacher of composition, Canterbury Cathedral Choir School.
Seven Last Words, Oxford, 1968.
Two Pictures of Graham Sutherland, Oxford.
RIMMER, FREDERICK. born Liverpool, England, 1914. M. A. ,
Cambridge University; B. Mus. , University of Durham;
Fellow of the Royal College of Organists; 1951-1966, lecturer,
organist, Glasgow University; since 1967, Gardiner professor
of music, Glasgow University.
Five Preludes on Scottish Psalm Tunes, 2 sets, Hinrichsen 720C.
Pastorale and Toccata, International Music, 1968.
RINCK, JOHANN CHRISTIAN HEINRICH. born Elgersburg, Germany,
Feb. 18, 1770; died Darmstadt, Aug. 7, 1846. 1786-1789,
pupil of Johann Christian Kittel, in Erfurt; 1790, became city
organist, Giessen; 1805, University director of music; 1805,
appointed Cantor, organist, Stadtkirche, Darmstadt; 1813,
named court organist, 1817, chamber musician, Darmstadt.
Album, Peters.
Choralvorspiele, 5 vols. , Bädecker.
Divertimento, in Organ Book No. 2, p. 20.
Freu dich sehr, in Twenty Preludes and Postludes, A. P.
Schmidt.

Fünfzehn Choralvorspiele, Op. 47, Schott.
Hymne: Preis und Anbetung, in Cäcilia, Breitkopf & Härtel.
Jesu, meine Zuversicht, in Seasonal Voluntaries, Mansfield,
    ed. , Paxton.
Rondo (Concerto for Flute Stop), Gray (Historical Rectial
    Series No. 38), 1925.
Sechs Choräle und Variationen, Op. 78, Simrock.
Sechs Choralvorspiele, Op. 12, Schott.
Sechs Choralvorspiele und Variationen, Op. 40, Schott.
Sechs Choralvorspiele und Variationen, Op. 77, Simrock.
Sechs-und-dreizig Nachspiele, Op. 107, Bädecker (Essen).
Stücke, Op. 38, Breitkopf & Härtel.
Twelve Chorales with Variations, Snow, ed. , New England
    Conservatory.
Vier-und-zwanzig Choräle, Op. 64, Simrock.
Vierzig kleine Präludien, Op. 37, André.
Vor- und Nachspiele, Op. 129, Litolff.
Zwei-und-dreizig Vor- und Nachspiele, Hansen.
Zwölf Choralvorspiele, Op. 53, Schott.
Zwölf fugierte Nachspiele, Op. 48, Breitkopf & Härtel.
Zwölf kurze Präludien, Op. 2, Schott.
Zwölf Präludien, Op. 49, Schott.
Zwölf Stücke, Op. 1, Schott.
Zwölf Stücke, Op. 8, Schott.
Zwölf Stücke, Op. 92, 94, 96, and 100, André.
chorale preludes (24) in Anthologie, Concordia.
chorale preludes (15) in Cäcilia, Breitkopf & Härtel.
chorale preludes (4) in The Lutheran Organist, Concordia.
chorale preludes (2) in The New Organist, Part II, Koerner,
    ed. , J. Schuberth.
chorale preludes (6) in Orgel Choräle Sammlung, Metzler.
chorale preludes (18) in Der Praktische Organist, Part 1,
    Leutzel, ed. , Tascher'schen.
chorale preludes (8) in Preludes for Hymns of the Lutheran
    Church, Kittaase (Concordia).
RITTER, CHRISTIAN. German. born between 1645 and 1650; still
    living in 1725. Probably a pupil of Christian Bernhard in
    Dresden; ca. 1665, was a chamber musician at court, Halle;
    1677, appointed court organist, Halle; 1681, went to Sweden;
    1682, named Vicekapellmeister, Stockholm; 1683, appointed
    Vicekapellmeister, chamber organist, Dresden; 1688, re-
    turned to Stockholm; 1704, went to Hamburg.
    Sonatina in d moll, in Organum, Series IV, Vol. 5.
    compositions in Masterpieces of Organ Music, Folio 25.
ROBERDAY, FRANÇOIS. born Paris, Mar. 21, 1624; died
    Oct. 13, 1680. Organist, Minorite Church, Paris; taught
    Lully.
    Caprice sur le mesme sujet, in The First Four Centuries
        of Organ Music, Vol. II, p. 385.
    Fugue, in Alte Orgelmusik aus England und Frankreich,
        p. 29.
    Fugue, in Liber Organi, Vol. II, p. 14.
    Fugue, in Les Maîtres français de l'orgue, Vol. II, p. 17.

Fugue et Caprice, 2me, in Ricercaris for the Organ, p. 13;
Kalmus; also in Chromatisme, L'Organiste liturgique,
Vol. 51, p. 13.
Fugues et caprices, in Archives des maitres d'orgue des
seizième-dix-huitième siècles, Vol. III.

ROBERT, GEORGES-ALFRED-JEAN. born St. Pol-de-Léon (Finis-
tère), France, Apr. 12, 1928. 1941, studied at the Institut
des Jeunes Aveugles; 1946, studied at the Conservatory, Paris;
pupil of Litaize, Plé-Caussade, Marchal, and Dupré; 1948,
appointed organist, Notre-Dame-de-Versailles; since 1954,
teacher, Institut des Jeunes Aveugles.
Offertoire pour le XIe dimanche après la Pentecôte, in
Offertoires, Orgue et Liturgie, Vol. 52, p. 24.
Pour une communion, in Communions, Orgue et Liturgie,
Vol. 62, p. 10.
Pour une élévation, in Elévations, Orgue et Liturgie,
Vol. 57, p. 15.
Prélude à l'Introit pour le premier dimanche de l'Avent, in
Préludes à l'Introit, Orgue et Liturgie, Vol. 48,
p. 25.
Prélude sur les jeux d'Anches, in Le Tombeau de Gonzalez,
Orgue et Liturgie, Vol. 38, p. 26.
Suite, in L'Organiste liturgique, Vol. 35.

ROBERTS, MYRON J. born San Diego, Calif., Jan. 30, 1912.
1935, B. Mus., College of the Pacific, Stockton, Calif.; 1937,
M. S. M., Union Theological Seminary, New York City; organ
pupil of Warren Allen, Allan Bacon, and Clarence Dickinson;
composition pupil of Edwin Stringham and Roger Sessions;
1940-1968, professor of organ, University of Nebraska; 1957-
1967, organist, Holy Trinity Episcopal Church, Lincoln, Neb.;
since 1968, Foundation professor of organ, University of
Nebraska; since 1969, organist, Cathedral of the Risen Christ,
Lincoln, Neb.
Carillon, Gray (St. Cecilia Series 731).
Dialogue, in Modern Organ Music, Book 2, Oxford.
Homage à Perotin, Gray (St. Cecilia Series 832), 1956.
Improvisation on God Rest You Merry, Gentlemen, Gray
(St. Cecilia Series 663), 1968.
Improvisation on the Agincourt Hymn, Gray (St. Cecilia
Series 904), 1964.
In Memoriam, Gray (St. Cecilia Series 745), 1949.
Litany, Gray (St. Cecilia Series 848), 1958.
Pastorale and Aviary, Gray (St. Cecilia Series 954), 1969.
Prelude and Trumpetings, Gray, 1961.
Three Pieces, Marimba and organ (1970).

ROBERTSBRIDGE CODEX. Earliest keyboard music extant, dated
ca. 1325.
Estampie, in Historical Anthology of Music, Vol. I, p. 62.

ROBINSON, JOHN. English. born 1682; died Apr. 30, 1762.
1710, named organist, St. Lawrence's Church; 1713, appointed
organist, St. Magnus's Church; 1727, became organist, Westminster Abbey.
Voluntary (A Minor), Susi Jeans, ed., Novello, 1966.

RODIO, ROCCO. born Bari, Italy, between 1530 and 1540; died
Naples, shortly after 1615. Served Sforza family; contra-
puntalist in early Neapolitan school; wrote Masses, madrigals,
and a book on counterpoint.
> Five Ricercate, Fantasie, S. Kastner, ed. , Zanibon 4162,
> 1958.

ROESELING, KASPAR. born Cologne, Germany, May 5, 1894; died
Cologne, Jan. 1, 1960. Taught organ and theory, Cologne;
1919, became teacher, Volksschule; studied at universities of
Bonn and Cologne; 1920, Ph. D. , University of Cologne; 1950,
became teacher of theory, Musikhochschule, Cologne; 1952,
became Lektor, University of Cologne.
> Music for Organ, Müller 56.
> Ostinato grave, Schott 2428.
> Partita über Veni Creator, Müller.
> Seven Chorale Preludes, Müller 52.

ROGER-DUCASSE, JEAN-JULES-AIMABLE. born Bordeaux, France,
Apr. 18, 1873; died Taillan-Medoc (Bordeaux), July 19, 1954.
Studied at the Conservatory, Paris; pupil of Fauré and Gedalge;
1909, named inspector of singing, Paris schools and professor
of ensemble, Conservatory, Paris; 1935-1945, professor of
composition, Conservatory, Paris; retired to Bordeaux.
> Pastorale (1909), Durand, 1909.

ROGERS, BENJAMIN. born Windsor, England, May 1614; died
Oxford, June 1698. Choirboy, St. George's, Windsor; 1639-
1641, organist, Christ Church, Dublin; 1660, became organist,
Eton College; 1662, named organist, Windsor; 1664, appointed organist, Informator Choristarum, Magdalen College;
1669, received Doc. Mus. , Oxford.
> Prelude (D Minor), in Twelve Short Pieces by Old English
> Composers, p. 27.
> Voluntary, Susi Jeans, ed. , Novello EOM 11, 1962.

ROGERS, JAMES HOTCHKISS. born Fair Haven, Conn. , Feb. 7,
1857; died Pasadena, Calif. , Nov. 28, 1940. Pupil of
Clarence Eddy, Guilmant, and Widor; 1883, appointed organist,
Euclid Avenue Temple and First Unitarian Church, Cleveland,
Ohio.
> Bride's Song, G. Schirmer.
> Cantilena, G. Schirmer.
> Christmas Pastorale, G. Schirmer.
> Concert Overture.
> Grand Choeur, G. Schirmer.
> Miniature Suite, Theodore Presser.
> Processional March.
> Second Suite, Theodore Presser.
> Sonata No. 1 in E Minor, G. Schirmer.
> Sonata No. 2 in D Minor, G. Schirmer.
> Wedding Procession, G. Schirmer.

ROGET, HENRIETTE PUIG- (see Puig-Roget, Henriette).

ROHLIG, HARALD. born Aurich, Germany, Oct. 6, 1926. 1941-
1943, 1948-1951, organist, Christuskirche, Osnabrück, Germany; 1948, studied at the Royal Academy of Music, London;
1951, graduated, Conservatory, Osnabrück; organ pupil of

Günter de Witt and Fritz Heitman; composition pupil of Karl
Schaefer and Wolfgang Fortner; 1951-1953, organist, Katharin-
enkirche, and professor of organ and piano, Conservatory,
Osnabrück; 1955-1961, organist, Memorial Presbyterian Church,
Montgomery, Ala.; since 1955, professor of music, Huntingdon
College, Montgomery, Ala.; since 1961, organist, St. John's
Episcopal Church, Montgomery, Ala.
All Glory, Laud and Honor, Augsburg, 1967.
All Praise to Thee, Eternal, Augsburg, 1967.
All Praise to Thee, My God, This Night, Augsburg, 1967.
Baroque Canzona, Augsburg, 1964.
Christ Is Arisen, Abingdon, 1964.
Christmas Music, flute and organ, Concordia, 1963.
Concertino, organ and orchestra, Concordia, 1967.
Eight Intradas and Chorales, organ and trumpet, Concordia,
1959.
Fifteen Preludes, Abingdon, 1963.
Fifty-five Hymn Intonations, Abingdon, 1962.
Good Christian Men, Rejoice, three trumpets, flute, and
organ, Abingdon, 1963.
Immortal, Invisible, God Only Wise, Concordia, 1966.
In dulci jubilo, Abingdon, 1962.
(A) Little Shepherd Music, flute and organ, Concordia, 1959.
Now Thank We All Our God, three trumpets and organ,
Abingdon, 1963.
O Come, All Ye Faithful, three trumpets and organ, Abing-
don, 1963.
O How Shall I Receive Thee, Augsburg, 1967.
O Where Are Kings and Empires Now, Concordia, 1966.
Partita: Ah, Holy Jesus, Augsburg, 1964.
St. Michael, Abingdon, 1965.
Seven Little Preludes and Fugues, Augsburg, 1965.
Sonata One, Abingdon, 1966.
Ten Pieces, Abingdon, 1964.
Thirty New Settings of Familiar Hymntunes, Abingdon, 1963.
Three Trumpet Tunes, Concordia, 1963.
chorale preludes (2) in The Parish Organist, Vol. 12.
ROLLAND, PHILIPPE. French. born June 11, 1913. Studied at
the Institut National des Jeunes Aveugles; won second prize in
organ, Conservatory, Paris; organ pupil of Jean Langlais and
Marcel Dupré; organist, Saint-Antoine-des-Quinze-Vingts,
Paris; professor, Institute des Jeunes Aveugles, Paris.
Communion, in L'Orgue Néo-Classique, Orgue et Liturgie,
Vol. 33, p. 12.
ROMAN, JOHAN HELMICH. born Stockholm, Oct. 26, 1694; died
Haraldsmala, Oct. 19, 1758. 1714, pupil of Pepusch in Lon-
don; 1717, entered service of Duke of Newcastle; 1729, ap-
pointed court conductor, Stockholm.
Concerto Grosso, organ and strings, Valdemar Soderholm
(Stockholm).
ROMANINI, ANTONIO. Italian. Seventeenth century. Represented
by music found in Part I of Diruta's Il Transilvano.
Toccata, in L'Arte Musicale in Italia, Vol. III, p. 171.

ROMANOVSKY, ERICH. born Vienna, July 11, 1929. 1953, Ph. D.
in musicology, University, Vienna; organ pupil of Wilhelm
Mück and Anton Heiller; composition pupil of Mück and Ernst
Tittel; 1950-1956, organist and choirmaster, Pfarre Baumgar-
ten, Vienna; since 1955, professor of harmony, counterpoint,
and history of music, Academy of Music, Vienna.
Choralvorspiel O heil'ge Seelenspeise, in Nun singet froh
im weissen Kleid, E. Bieler, 1965.
Nachspiele zum Deo gratias, Coppenrath, 1963.
Sonate, Doblinger, 1960.
Three Chorale Preludes, Böhm, 1960.
Triptychon on Veni Creator Spiritus, Doblinger, 1962.
Vorspiele zum Choralintroitus, 2 vols., Coppenrath, 1956,
1958.
Vor-, Zwischen-, und Nachspiele zu Kirchenliedern, 2 vols.,
Coppenrath, 1957, 1971.
Vor-, Zwischen-, und Nachspiele zu Kirchenliedern, in
Präludienbuch zum Orgelbuch der Erzdiözese Wien,
Verlag der Diözesenkommision für Kirchenmusik, Wien,
1959.
Werkmappe, Coppenrath.
ROOPER, JASPER B. born Penkridge, Staffs, England. Twentieth
century. Associate of the Royal College of Music; 1934-1948,
director of music, Lancing College; 1951-1965, staff music
tutor, Oxford.
Prelude on two Christmas Carols, Cramer.
ROPARTZ, JOSEPH-GUY-MARIE. born Guincamp (Côtes-du-Nord),
France, June 15, 1864; died Lanloup (Plouha), Nov. 22, 1955.
Studied at the Conservatory, Paris; pupil of Franck, Dubois,
and Massenet; 1894-1919, director, Conservatory, Nancy;
director, Conservatory, Strasbourg.
Au pied de l'Autel, Rouart, Lerolle & Cie.
Introduction and Allegro moderato, Durand.
Offertoire pascal, Leduc, 1894.
(L')Office du soir (40 versets), organ or harmonium, Parvy,
1885.
Prélude funèbre, in The French Organist, Vol. I, p. 16.
Rhapsodie sur deux noëls, Durand.
Six pièces, Muraille (Liège, Belgium, 1896-1901).
Sur un thème breton, in Historical Organ Recitals, Vol. V,
p. 84.
Thème varié, in The French Organist, Vol. II, p. 47.
Trois méditations: Introduction et allegro moderato; Rhap-
sodie sur des noëls bretons, Durand, 1917-1919.
Trois pièces (Fugue; Intermède; Sur un thème breton),
Durand.
Versets pour les vêpres des saintes femmes, Schola Can-
torum, 1898.
ROREM, NED. born Richmond, Ind., Oct. 23, 1923. Studied in
Chicago, also at the Curtis Institute of Music, at the Berkshire
Music Center, Tanglewood, and at the Juilliard School of Music;
pupil of Copland, Wagenaar, and Virgil Thompson; 1951-1955,
lived in Europe; 1955, returned to America.

Pastorale, Peer.
ROSEINGRAVE, THOMAS. born Winchester, England, 1690; died
Dublin, June 23, 1766. 1710, sent to Italy to study by the
chapter of St. Patrick's Cathedral, Dublin; acquainted with the
Scarlattis; 1725-1737, organist, St. George's, Hanover Square,
London; lived in Hampstead and later in Dublin.
  Compositions for Organ and Harpsichord, Denis Stevens, ed. ,
    Pennsylvania State University Press, University Park,
    Penn. , 1964.
  Fifteen Voluntaries and Fugues (ca. 1730), A. V. Butcher,
    ed. , Hinrichsen 99.
  Ten Organ Pieces, Williams, ed. , Stainer & Bell, 1961.
ROSENBERG, HILDING. born Bosjökloster, Skåne, Sweden, June 21,
1892. 1909, began study at the Royal Academy of Music,
Stockholm; pupil of H. Scherchen; orchestral conductor;
1940, became faculty member, Academy of Music, Stockholm.
  Fantasia e Fuga, in Musica Organi, Vol. III, p. 164.
  Fantasia e fuga, J. & W. Chester.
  Lover Gud i Himmelshöjd (1966), Eriks.
  Preludio e fuge, J. & W. Chester.
  Preludium e Fuga, in Musica Organi, Vol. III, p. 160.
  Toccata, Aria, Ciaconna (1952), J. & W. Chester.
ROSSI, LUIGI. born Torremaggiore, Foggia, Italy, 1597; died
Rome, Feb. 19, 1653. Pupil of de Macque; opera composer.
  Passacaille "del Seig" Louigi, in Chacones et Passacailles,
    Orgue et Liturgie, Vol. 22, p. 6.
ROSSI, MICHELANGELO. born probably Rome, ca. 1600; died
ca. 1670. Served Cardinal Maurizio di Savoia; also served
Barberini household; 1638, became court musician, Modena;
pupil of Frescobaldi; wrote Toccate e Corenti d'Intavolatura
d'Organo e Cimbalo (Carlo Ricarii, Rome, 1657).
  Settima Toccata, in European Organ Music of the 16th
    and 17th Centuries, p. 85.
  Works for Keyboard, in Corpus of Early Keyboard Music,
    No. 15.
  compositions (2) in Anthologia Organistica Italiana.
  compositions (3) in Classici Italiani dell'Organo.
  correnti (10) in L'Arte Musicale in Italia, Vol. III, p. 331.
ROTA, NINO. born Milan, Italy, Nov. 3, 1911. Studied at the
Conservatory, Milan; pupil of Casella; 1929, received diploma, Conservatorio di S. Cecilia, Rome; 1930-1932, studied
at the Curtis Institute of Music, Philadelphia; 1937-1938, be-
came teacher, Liceo Musicale, Taranto; 1939, named teacher,
1950, director, Liceo Musicale, Bari.
  Sonata (March 1965), Edizioni Curci (Milano).
ROTH, DANIEL FRANÇOIS. born Mulhouse, France, Oct. 31, 1942.
Studied at the Conservatory, Mulhouse, and at the Conservatory,
Paris; 1962, became organist, Collège Fenelon; since 1965,
choir organist, 1963, assistant organist, Sacré-Coeur-de-
Montmartre.
  Cinq versets sur Veni creator, in L'Organiste liturgique,
    Vol. 53, p. 20.
ROUSSEAU, ALEXANDRE-SAMUEL. born Neuve-Maison (Aisne),

France, June 11, 1853; died Paris, Oct. 1, 1904. Pupil of
Franck at the Conservatory, Paris; choirmaster, Ste. Clotilde;
professor of harmony, Conservatory, Paris.
  Douze et quinze pièces, 2 vols., Leduc, 1892.
  (Les) Echos sacrés, 2 vols., Leduc, 1891-1892.
  Fantaisie, Recueil Abbé Hazé, 1894.
ROUSSEL, ALBERT-CHARLES-PAUL-MARIE. born Tourcoing (Nord),
France, Apr. 5, 1869; died Royan, Aug. 23, 1937. Composer
for orchestra; pupil of Gigout and d'Indy; 1902-1914, taught
counterpoint, Schola Cantorum, Paris; taught Satie, de Lion-
court, and Varèse.
  Prélude et Fughetta, Op. 41 (1929), Durand.
ROUTH, FRANCIS JOHN. born Kidderminster, England, 1927.
M.A., King's College, Cambridge; Fellow of the Royal Col-
lege of Organists; studied at the Royal Academy of Music;
since 1962, organist, St. Philip's, Earl's Court Road.
  Fantasia, Hinrichsen 739.
  Five Short Pieces (Prelude; Compline Hymn; Chorale and
      Variation; Voluntary; Fantasia on an Easter Alleluia),
      Hinrichsen 1536, 1967.
  (The) Manger Throne, Boosey & Hawkes.
  chorale preludes (2) in Registration, Hinrichsen.
ROWLEY, ALEC. born London, Mar. 13, 1892; died London,
Jan. 10, 1958. Studied at the Royal Academy of Music;
Fellow and faculty member, Trinity College of Music.
  Album of Organ Pieces, Paxton, 1912.
  Benedictus, Novello.
  Book of Voluntaries, Boosey & Hawkes.
  Chorale Preludes (Four Seasonal Improvisations), Hinrichsen
      620.
  Chorale Preludes based on Famous Hymn Tunes, 5 vols.,
      Ashdown (Boosey & Hawkes), 1952.
  Christmas Suite, Novello.
  Concertino, organ and string orchestra, Heugel; United
      Music Publishers (London).
  Contemplation, in The Modern Anthology, p. 157.
  Extemporizations, Jos. Williams.
  Fantasia on Veni Emmanuel, Novello.
  Fantasie and Fugal Toccata, Joseph Williams.
  Fantasy of Happiness, Boosey & Hawkes.
  Five Improvisations, Novello, 1948.
  Four Seasonal Improvisations, Hinrichsen
  Heroic Suite, Boosey & Hawkes.
  Introduction and Variations on a Ground Bass, Jos. Williams.
  Keltic March, Boosey & Hawkes.
  Meditation, string orchestra and organ, Hinrichsen 43.
  Nine Hymn Tune Voluntaries, Novello.
  Organ Concerto.
  Pavan, Gray (St. Cecilia Series 737).
  Picardy, in Hymn Tune Voluntaries, Oxford.
  Rhapsody, Boosey & Hawkes.
  Second Benedictus, Novello.
  (The) Sixty-fifth Psalm (Thanksgiving), Gray.

Soliloquy, Novello.
Sonatina, Novello.
Sonnet, Oxford.
Suite, Boosey & Hawkes.
Three Quiet Pieces, Mills Music.
Toccata.
Triptych, Novello.
Triumph Song, Novello.
Two Plainsong Preludes, Novello.
hymn-preludes (2) in Festal Voluntaries (Advent, Ascension),
    Novello.
RÜHLING, JOHANNES. Christened Borna (Leipzig), Germany,
    Aug. 30, 1550; died Groitzsch, Apr. 2, 1615. 1572-1575,
    organist, Geithain; organist, Döbeln, and later in Groitzsch;
    wrote Tabulaturbuch/ Auff Orgeln und Instrument (J. Beyer,
    Leipzig, 1583), which contains eighty-six intabulated Latin and
    German motets.
RUNBÄCK, ALBERT. born Gårdby på Øland, Sweden, Aug. 30,
    1894. Studied at the Conservatory, Stockholm; since 1917,
    organist-choirmaster, Båstad.
    Efter sammanringningen, Nordiska Musikförlaget Stockholm.
    Gradualpreludier (1942), Nordiska Musikförlaget Stockholm.
    Modulationer till högmässans slutpsalmer (1943), Nordiska
        Musikförlaget Stockholm.
    Offertoriepreludier (1943, 1944, 1949), Nordiska Musik-
        förlaget Stockholm.
    Orgelmässa, Eriks.
    Salve regina (1955), Nordiska Musikförlaget Stockholm.
    Sequentia pentecostes Veni sancte spiritus, in Musica
        Organi, Vol. III, p. 132.
    Te Deum (1957/1964), for two organs, Eriks.
    Variationer över en estländsk aftonkoral (1960), V. Norbergs
        förlag, Västerås.
    compositions in Introituspreludier, Albert Runbäck and
        Waldemar Ahlén, eds. , 2 vols. , Nordiska Musikförlaget
        Stockholm, Vol. I (17) and Vol. 2 (18).
    compositions (6) in Koralförspel, Reinhold Anderson and
        Rudolf Norrman, eds. , Nordiska Musikförlaget Stock-
        holm, Vol. 2.
    compositions (11) in Orgelmusik vid hogmässans avslutning,
        Albert Runbäck, ed. , Nordiska Musikförlaget Stock-
        holm.
    compositions (11) in Orgelmusik vid Jordfästning, Albert
        Runbäck, ed. , Nordiska Musikförlaget Stockholm.
    compositions (8) in Orgelmusik vid vigsel, Albert Runbäck,
        ed. , Nordiska Musikförlaget Stockholm.
    compositions in Postludier för kyrkoårets samtliga sön- och
        helgdagar, Albert Runbäck and Waldemar Ahlén, eds. ,
        3 vols. , Nordiska Musikförlaget Stockholm, Vol. 1 (2),
        Vol. 2 (6), and Vol. 3 (8).
RUNG-KELLER, PAUL S. Danish. born 1879. 1903-1949, or-
    ganist Vor Frelsers church.
    Chorale and Variations on Den lyse Dag vorgangen er,

Engstrom & Södring.
Ciacona, Op. 24, in Musica Organi, Vol. 3, p. 16.
Variations on Skøn Jomfru hun gang, Op. 43, Skandinavisk
Musikforlag.
chorale preludes (4) in Slågt skal Følge slågters Gang, Bitsch
& Petersen, eds. , Hansen.
RUSSELL, WILLIAM. born London, Oct. 6, 1777; died London,
Nov. 21, 1813. 1789-1793, organist, Chapel, Lincoln's Inn
Fields; pupil of S. Arnold; organist, St. Ann's Limehouse;
1801, became organist, Foundling Hospital; 1809, named
organist, Covent Garden Theatre.
Fugue, Williams, ed. , Cramer, 1954.
Fugue in C Major, Williams, ed. , Cramer, 1958.
Introduction and Fugue, Plant, ed. , in Organ Recitalist,
Ashdown, 1908.
Introduction and Fugue, Wall, ed. , Cramer, 1934.
Largo and Fugue, Ley, ed. , Deane, 1927.
Largo and Fugue, Smith, ed. , Ashdown, 1954.
Largo, Andante and Fugue, Cramer, 1945.
Suite in C Major, Coleman, ed. , Cramer, 1945.
Trumpet Tune, John E. West, ed. , Novello, 1904.
Voluntary in A Major, John E. West, ed. , Novello, 1904.
Voluntary in C Major, John E. West, ed. , Novello, 1904.
Voluntary in D Minor, John E. West, ed. , Novello, 1904.

SABADINI (SABADINO), BERNARDO. Italian. born ca. middle of
the seventeenth century; died Parma, probably in January
1719. Court organist, Parma; opera composer; director of
music for the Farnese family and at the Chiesa della Steccata,
Parma.
Grave, in L'Arte Musicale in Italia, Vol. III, p. 437.
SAINT-MARTIN, LÉONCE DE. born Albi, France, 1886; died
Paris, June 10, 1954. 1924, assistant to Vierne at Notre
Dame, Paris; 1920-1937, organist, Notre Dame des Blancs-
Manteaux; 1937-1954, organist, Notre Dame. Pupil of
Adolphe Marty and Albert Bertelin.
Cantique spirituel, Procure Général du Clergé.
Choral-Prélude pour l'Avent, Procure Général du Clergé.
Genèse, Procure Général du Clergé.
In Memoriam, organ and brass, Durand.
Offertoire pour les fêtes simples de la Sainte Vierge, Leduc.
Paraphrase du Psaume 136, Procure Général du Clergé.
Pastorale, Procure Général du Clergé.
Pièces de Noël (Scherzo), Procure Général du Clergé.
Postlude de fête, Hérelle.
Salve Regina, Procure Général du Clergé.
(Le) Salut à la Vierge, Hérelle.
Suite cyclique (Prélude; Fugue; Cantilène; Carillon), Leduc,
1931.
Symphonie dominicale, Procure Général du Clergé.

Toccata de la libération (1944), Procure Général du Clergé.
Toccata et fugue de la Résurrection, Procure Général du
 Clergé.
SAINT-RÉQUIER, LÉON. born Rouen, France, Aug. 8, 1872; died
 Paris, Oct. 1, 1964. Pupil of d'Indy, Bordes, and Guilmant;
 1900-1934, taught harmony, Schola Cantorum, and at Ecole
 César Franck; 1908-1925, choirmaster, St. Gervais; choir-
 master, St. Nicolas-des-Champs; choirmaster, St. Charles de
 Monceau; conductor, music editor.
SAINT-SAËNS, CHARLES-CAMILLE. born Paris, Oct. 9, 1835;
 died Algiers, Dec. 16, 1921. Studied at the Conservatory,
 Paris; pupil of Benoist and Halévy; organist, St. Séverin;
 1853-1857, organist, St. Merry; 1858-1877, organist, La
 Madeleine; 1861-1865, piano teacher, Ecole Niedermeyer;
 taught Fauré; honorary Mus. D., Cambridge University;
 composed opera and for orchestra.
  Bénédiction nuptiale, Op. 9, Durand, 1866.
  Berceuse, Op. 105.
  Coeli enarrant (Psalm 18), Op. 42, Andantino.
  Elévation ou Communion, Op. 13, Durand, 1865.
  Fantaisie, Op. 101, Durand; also Kalmus 3846.
  Fantaisie (D-flat Major), Durand, 1895-1896.
  Fantaisie (E-flat Major), Costallat and Billaudot.
  Fantasy in E-flat Major, G. Schirmer, 1903.
  Hymne à Victor Hugo, Op. 69, Durand.
  Marche héroïque, Op. 34, Durand.
  Marche religieuse, Op. 107 (1898), Durand.
  Menuet, Op. 56, Durand.
  Pièces (3), Op. 1, Leduc, 1866.
  Prière, organ and violoncello, Durand.
  Rêverie du soir, Op. 60.
  Sept Improvisations, Op. 150, Durand, 1918.
  Six Préludes et Fugues, 2 vols., Vol. 1: E Major; B Major;
   E-flat Major, Op. 99, Durand, 1894; also Kalmus
   3848; Vol. 2: D Minor; G Major; C Major, Op. 109,
   Durand, 1898; also Kalmus 3849.
  Symphonie III, organ part.
  Third Fantaisie, Op. 157, Durand, 1918/1919.
  Trois pièces (1852), Leduc.
  Trois rapsodies sur des cantiques bretons, Op. 7, Durand,
   1866; also Kalmus 3847.
SALMENHARRA, ERKKI. Finnish. Twentieth century.
  Prelude, Interlude & Postlude, Gray (Contemporary Organ
   Series 37).
  Toccata, Edition Fazer 4658, 1966.
SALOMÉ, THÉODORE CÉSAR. born Paris, Jan. 20, 1834; died
 St. Germain-en-Laye, July 1896. Studied at the Conservatory,
 Paris; 1869, assistant organist, Trinité, Paris.
  Dix pièces, Leduc.
  Dix pièces, Leduc.
  Douze pièces nouvelles, Op. 59.
  Douze pièces nouvelles, Op. 63, Leduc.
  Douze versets sur le Magnificat et cinq postludes, Op. 67

and 68, Hamelle.
SALONEN, SULO. Finnish. born 1899.
   Partita över en finsk koral, in Musica Organi, Vol. III,
      p. 68.
   Ten Small Organ Chorales, Op. 29, in Koralförspel, Vol. 3,
      Westerlund.
   Toccata, Op. 24, Westerlund 2954.
   Variations and Fugue on a Finnish Chorale, Gehrmans.
   Zwei Choralpartiten, Breitkopf & Härtel 5805.
SALVATORE, GIOVANNI. born Castelvenere (Benevent), Italy, beginning of the seventeenth century; died probably in Naples,
   ca. 1688. Priest; pupil of G. M. Sabino and Padre Erasmo
   di Bartolo; 1641, became organist, San Severino, Naples;
   later organist and choirmaster, San Lorenzo, Naples; 1662-
   1673, taught at Conservatorio della Pietà dei Turchini; 1675-
   1688, taught at Conservatorio dei Poveri di Gesù Christo;
   ca. 1675, named organist, Chiesa dei Carmine.
   compositions in Corpus of Early Keyboard Music, No. 3.
SAMAZEUILH, GUSTAVE-MARIE-VICTOR-FERNAND. born Bordeaux, France, June 2, 1877. Pupil of Fauré, d'Indy, and
   Chausson; music critic.
   Prélude (1917), Durand.
SAMMARTINI, GIOVANNI BATTISTA. born Milan, Italy, 1701; died
   Milan, Jan. 15, 1775. Organist, Milan; 1730-1770, maestro
   di cappella, Convent of St. Maria Maddalena; taught Gluck;
   wrote symphonies and chamber music.
   Sonata in G, violoncello and keyboard, International Music Co.
   transcription in Anthologia Antiqua, Vol. 2.
SANDBERG NIELSEN, OTTO. Danish. born 1900; died 1941.
   member of board, Danish Organists' Association.
   Präludium, Trio und Ciacona über Auf meinen lieben Gott,
      Edition Dania.
SANDVOLD, ARILD. born Oslo, Norway, June 2, 1895. Since
   1914, organist-choirmaster, Cathedral, Oslo; since 1917,
   organ teacher, Royal Norwegian Music Conservatory, Oslo.
   Pre- og Postludie over Koralmotiv (25), Norsk.
   Six Improvisations on Norse Folktunes, Op. 5, Norsk.
   Tva gregorianska melodier, in Musica Organi, Vol. III,
      p. 42.
SANTA MARÍA, (FRÁY) TOMAS DE. born Madrid, ca. 1510; died
   Valladolid, 1570. Dominican brother from Castile; author of
   keyboard method Arte de Tañer Fantasia, assí para Tecla como
   Vihuela (Valladolid, 1565); pupil of Antonio de Cabezón.
   Cláusulas de 1º Tono, in Harold Gleason, Method of Organ
      Playing, p. 144.
   Fantasia, in Anthologia pro Organo, Vol. I, p. 13.
   Fantasia, in Anthologia pro Organo, Vol. III, p. 16.
   Fantasia on the Sixth Tone, in The First Four Centuries
      of Organ Music, Vol. I, p. 120.
   Octo Fantasiae, in Liber Organi, Vol. III.
   Oeuvres transcrites de l'Arte de Tañer Fantasia (1565), in
      Orgue et Liturgie, Vol. 49.
   Paso Suelto, in Early Spanish Organ Music, p. 8.

clausulas (2) in <u>Historical Organ Recitals</u>, Vol. VI.
clausulas (3) in <u>Old Spanish Organ Music</u>.
fantasias (25) in <u>Arte de Tañer Fantasia</u>, Union Musicale
Español, 1965; also Kalmus 3852.

SANTO ELIAS, MANUEL DE. Portuguese, second half of the
eighteenth century. Organist, composer, Lisbon.
<u>Sonata para Cimbalo</u>, in <u>Silva Iberica</u>, p. 24.

SATIE, ERIK-ALFRED-LESLIE. born Honfleur, France, May 17,
1866; died Paris, July 1, 1925. 1883-1884, studied at the
Conservatory, Paris; friend of Milhaud and Debussy; pupil of
Guilmant, d'Indy, and Roussel.
<u>Messe des Pauvres</u>, Salabert, 1929.

SAXTON, STANLEY. American. Twentieth century. M. Mus.,
Syracuse University; Associate of the American Guild of
Organists; pupil of Dupré, Widor, and Boulanger; organist-
choirmaster, Union Presbyterian Church, Schenectady, N. Y.;
professor of music for 37 years, Skidmore College, Saratoga
Springs, N. Y.
<u>Chorale, Variations and Finale on Nun danket alle</u>, Brodt.
<u>Christ Is Risen</u>, White-Smith.
<u>Christmas Processional on In dulci jubilo</u>, Galaxy.
<u>Easter Alleluia</u>, Brodt.
<u>Echo Carol</u>, White-Smith.
<u>Fughetta on Rise, My Soul</u>, White-Smith.
<u>Pastorale and Cradle Song</u>, Gray (St. Cecilia Series 710),
1936.
<u>Prelude and Fugue on Adeste fideles</u>, Brodt.
<u>Prelude on Laudes Domini</u>, Galaxy.
<u>Prelude on Rise Up, Shepherd</u>, Galaxy.
<u>Prelude on Softly Now the Light of Day</u>, White-Smith.
<u>Prelude on Vater unser</u>, Brodt.
<u>Rejoice, the Lord Cometh</u>, Galaxy.
<u>Song of the Lonely Njeri</u>.
<u>Three Skidmore Pieces</u>.
<u>Toccata on Come, Ye Thankful People</u>, White-Smith.

SCARLATTI, ALESSANDRO. born Palermo, Italy, May 2, 1660;
died Naples, Oct. 24, 1725. Founder of the Neapolitan school
of music; pupil of Carissimi; taught Hasse; 1703, named
assistant maestro, 1707-1709, maestro, S. Maria Maggiore,
Rome; composer of operas, Masses, and oratorios.
<u>Concerto</u> (C Minor), Lionel Salter, arr., Oxford.
<u>Toccata No. 11</u>, Edizione de Santis, 1941.

SCARLATTI, GIUSEPPE DOMENICO. born Naples, Oct. 26, 1685;
died Madrid, July 23, 1757. Son of Alessandro Scarlatti;
1701, appointed organist-composer, royal chapel, Naples;
pupil of Gasparini; 1709-1714, choirmaster, Queen Maria,
Poland; 1714-1719, maestro, Vatican; 1719 or 1720, appointed maestro, royal chapel, Lisbon; 1729, accompanied
Maria Barbara to Madrid when she became queen of Spain;
taught Soler.
<u>Five Sonatas</u>, Douglas Greene, ed., G. Schirmer, 1962.
<u>Quattro Sonati</u>, Edizione de Santis, 1960.
<u>Sonaten und Fugen</u>, Loek Hautus, ed., Bärenreiter 5485.

Two Organ Sonatas, Arnold Goldsborough, ed. , Oxford.
SCHALK, CARL. born Chicago, Ill. , Sept. 26, 1929. 1952, B. S.
Ed. ; 1958, M. Mus. ; 1965, M. A. Rel. ; 1952-1958, director
of music, Zion Lutheran Church, Wausau, Wis. ; 1958-1965,
director of music, The Lutheran Hour; since 1965, associate
professor of music, Concordia Teachers College, River Forest,
Ill. ; editor, Church Music.

> Festival Chorale Settings for the Small Parish (Easter),
> organ and trumpet, Concordia 97-4648.
> Preludes on Now and We Lift Our Hearts, in Worship
> Supplement, Concordia.

SCHEIDEMANN, HEINRICH. born Hamburg, Germany, ca. 1596;
died Hamburg, beginning of 1663. Pupil of his father, David
Scheidemann; 1611, pupil of Sweelinck; successor to father
as organist, St. Catherine's Church, Hamburg; taught J. A.
Reinken; organ inspector; probably was instrumental in com-
piling the Lüneburg Tablatures.

> Gott sei gelobet, in Choralvorspiel alter Meister, p. 116;
> also in Eighty Chorale Preludes: German Masters of
> the Seventeenth and Eighteenth Centuries, p. 62; also
> in Chorale Preludes by Masters of the Seventeenth and
> Eighteenth Centuries, p. 60; also in The First Four
> Centuries of Organ Music, Vol. I, p. 211; also in
> Choralvorspiele zum Kirchenlied, Vol. 2, Christophorus.
> In dich hab' ich gehoffet, in 11 Organ Chorales of the
> Seventeenth Century, Bärenreiter.
> Magnificat-Bearbeitungen, Gustav Fock, ed. , Bärenreiter
> 5480, 1970.
> chorale preludes (3) in Corpus of Early Keyboard Music,
> No. 10, Vol. 2.
> chorale preludes (2) in Orgelchoräle des siebzehnten und
> achtzehnten Jahrhunderts.
> chorale preludes in The Parish Organist, Vols. 7 and 8.
> chorale preludes (10) in Sechs-und-Vierzig Choräle für Orgel.
> compositions in Free Organ Compositions from Lüneburg
> Tablatures, Vol. I, p. 16, and Vol. II, p. 100.
> preludes (2) in Historical Anthology of Music, Vol. II,
> p. 23.
> preludes and fugues (15) in Organum, Series IV, Vol. I
> (Concordia 97-4333).

SCHEIDT, GOTTFRIED. born Halle, Germany, Aug. 20, 1593;
died 1661. 1611-1615, pupil of Sweelinck; 1617-1658, organist,
Altenburg.

> Allein Gott, in Sechs-und-Vierzig Choräle für Orgel; also
> in 20 Chorale Variations of German Sweelinck School,
> Bärenreiter.

SCHEIDT, SAMUEL. Christened Halle, Germany, Nov. 4, 1587;
died Halle, Mar. 24, 1654. 1603 or 1604-1607, organist,
Moritzkirche, Halle; 1607-1608, pupil of Sweelinck; 1609,
organist, Moritzkirche, Halle; 1614, at the latest, became
closely associated with M. Praetorius; 1624-1625, oversaw
the building of the Compenius organ in the Moritzkirche; 1619,
Kapellmeister to Wilhelm; 1624, published Tabulatura Nova

(in three parts), third part devoted to organ music for Lutheran
Masses and vespers; 1628-1630, city Director musices, Halle;
1650, published Tabulatur-Buch. Hundert geistl. Lieder u.
Psalmen ... f. die Herren Organisten (Martin Herman, Görlitz,
1650).

Allein Gott, in Sechs-und-Vierzig Choräle für Orgel, p. 222;
     also in 20 Chorale Variations of the German Sweelinck
     School, Bärenreiter.
Aus tiefer Not, in The First Four Centuries of Organ Music,
     Vol. I, p. 206.
Aus tieffer Not, in Pièces funèbres, Orgue et Liturgie,
     Vol. 23, p. 8.
Ausgewählte Werke Orgel, 2 vols., Peters 4393a/b.
Cantilena Anglica Fortunae, in Historical Organ Recitals,
     Vol. I, p. 40; also Schott.
Cantio sacra über Warum betrübst, in Alte Meister des
     Orgelspiels, Vol. II, p. 49; also in Geschichte der
     Musik in Beispielen, p. 220.
Chorales, Kalmus 3866.
Christ lag in Todesbanden, in Pâques, Vol. I, p. 4.
Da Jesus, in Historical Organ Recitals, Vol. I, p. 36; also
     in Six Chorale Preludes on When Jesus on the Cross
     Was Bound, Concordia 97-1339.
Fantasie über Ich ruf, in Alte Meister, p. 88.
Fuga Contraria, in Alte Meister des Orgelspiels, Vol. II,
     p. 36.
Görlitzer Tabulaturbuch, Bärenreiter 1565; also Peters
     4494.
Liedvariationen, Wolfgang Auler, ed., Schott 2828.
Magnificat first tone, in A la Sainte Vierge, L'Organiste
     liturgique, Vol. 2, p. 8.
Magnificat Octavi Toni, in Liber Organi, Vol. I, p. 7.
Magnificat Octavi Toni, in Liber Organi, Vol. II, p. 7.
Nun komm, in Viens, Sauveur, Orgue et Liturgie, Vol. 19,
     p. 2.
Tabulatura Nova, Max Seiffert, ed., in Denkmäler deutscher
     Tonkunst, Vol. I, Breitkopf & Härtel, 1892; also
     Mahrenholz, ed., 2 vols., Parts I and II, (Peters
     U 16); Part III (Peters U 17).
Ten Chorale Preludes from Tabulatura Nova, Breitkopf &
     Härtel.
Toccata on In te Domini speravi, Breitkopf & Härtel.
Vater unser, in Historical Anthology of Music, Vol. II,
     p. 13.
Vater unser, in Notre Père, Orgue et Liturgie, Vol. 24,
     p. 4.
Vater unser, in Anthologia pro Organo, Vol. III, p. 60.
Wie schön leuchtet, in Organ Preludes Ancient and Modern,
     Vol. 3, W. Sumner, ed., Hinrichsen.
Wir glauben, in Anthologia pro Organo, Vol. I, p. 50.
chorales (3) in Alte deutsche Weihnachtsmusik.
chorales (2) in Noël, Orgue et Liturgie, Vol. 4.
chorale preludes (2) in Anthologie, Concordia.

chorale preludes (2) in Chorale Preludes by Masters of the
Seventeenth and Eighteenth Centuries.
chorale preludes (3) in Choralvorspiel alter Meister.
chorale preludes (3) in Choralvorspiele zum Kirchenlied,
Vol. 2, Christophorus.
chorale preludes (5) in 18 Chorale Preludes of the Seventeenth and Eighteenth Centuries, P. Pidoux, ed.,
Foetisch.
chorale preludes (8) in Eighty Chorale Preludes by German
Masters of the Seventeenth and Eighteenth Centuries.
chorale preludes in Elf Orgelchoräle des siebzehnten
Jahrhunderts.
chorale preludes (2) in Harold Gleason, Method of Organ
Playing.
chorale preludes in The Church Organist's Golden Treasury,
Vol. I (4), Vol. II (4), Vol. III (1).
chorale preludes (2) in Laudamus Dominum.
chorale preludes (3) in Das Organistenamt, Vol. 2,
Breitkopf & Härtel.
chorale preludes (3) in Orgelchoräle des siebzehnten und
achtzehnten Jahrhunderts.
chorale preludes (3) in Orgel Choräle Sammlung, Metzler.
chorale preludes in Orgelspiel im Kirchenjahr, Vol. I (8)
and Vol. 2 (2), Schott.
chorale preludes in The Parish Organist, Vols. 1 and 7.
chorale preludes (8) in 25 Chorale Preludes of the Seventeenth and Eighteenth Centuries, P. Pidoux, ed.,
Foetisch.
compositions in Masterpieces of Organ Music, Folios 4,
5, 15, 17, 18, 19, and 53.
compositions in The Parish Organist, Vols. 1-4, 5, 6, 7,
and 8.
compositions (2) in Organ Music for the Communion Service,
pp. 13 and 43.
compositions (4) in Orgelmeister des siebzehnten und
achtzehnten Jahrhunderts.
courantes (2) in Spielbuch für die Kleinorgel, Vol. I.
toccata in Organum, Series IV, Vol. 21.
SCHERER, SEBASTIAN ANTON. Christened Ulm, Germany, Oct. 4,
1631; died Ulm, Aug. 26, 1712. 1653, appointed vice-
organist, Ulm; 1668, named director of music, Collegium
Musicum; 1671-1712, organist, Cathedral, Ulm.
Intonatis Sexti Toni, in Organ Book No. 2, p. 11.
Oeuvres d'orgue, in Archives des maîtres d'orgue des
seizième-dix-huitième siècles, Vol. VIII.
Thirty-two Intonations for Eight Tones and Eight Toccatas,
Schott 1882.
SCHIEFFERDECKER, JOHANN CHRISTIAN. born Teuchern, Ger-
many, Nov. 10, 1679; died Lübeck, Apr. 5, 1732. 1704,
pupil of Buxtehude; 1707, successor to Buxtehude at the
Marienkirche, Lübeck.
Meine Seele erhebt den Herren, in Orgelchoräle um J. S.
Bach, G. Frotscher, ed., Litolff.

compositions in Das Erbe deutschen Musik, Series I, Vol. 9.

SCHILDT, MELCHOIR. born Hannover, Germany, 1592 or 1593;
    died Hannover, May 18, 1667. 1609-1612, pupil of Sweelinck;
    1623-1626, organist, Hauptkirche, Wolfenbüttel; 1626-1629,
    organist for Christian IV of Denmark; 1629, named organist,
    Marktkirche, Hannover.
    Choralbearbeitungen, in Die Orgel, Series II, Vol. 24
        (Concordia 97-4926).
    Partita on Herr Christ, der einig Gottes Sohn, in Alte
        Orgelmusik, Supper, ed. , Merseburger 811.
    chorale preludes (3) in Sechs-und-Vierzig Choräle für Orgel.
    compositions in Masterpieces of Organ Music, Folio 51.
    praeambeln (2) in Organum, Series IV, Vol. 2.
    (probably by Schildt in Free Organ Compositions from Lüne-
        burg Tablatures, Vol. I, numbers 17-24).

SCHILLING, HANS LUDWIG. born Mayen (Rheinland), Germany,
    Mar. 9, 1927. Studied at the Musikhochschule, Freiburg-im-
    Breisgau; composition pupil of Harald Genzmer and Paul
    Hindemith; 1955-1959, teaching commision, University of
    Freiburg; 1957, Ph. D. ; 1960, appointed to the faculty,
    Badische Hochschule für Musik, Karlsruhe; since 1959, staff
    member, Christophorus Publishing House.
    Canzona über Christ ist erstanden, trumpet and organ,
        (1966), Breitkopf & Härtel 6518.
    Chaconne nouvelle (1968), Breitkopf & Härtel 6605, 1970.
    Fantasia 63 über Veni Creator, Breitkopf & Härtel 6449,
        1965.
    Kleine Suite über Vom Himmel hoch (1962), Breitkopf &
        Härtel 6433, 1964.
    Partita No. 1 (1965), Breitkopf & Härtel 6492, 1966.
    Partita No. 2, Canonische Variationen über Singet, preiset
        Gott mit Freuden (1958), Breitkopf & Härtel 6431,
        1964.
    Partita No. 3, Integration B-A-C-H (1961), Breitkopf &
        Härtel 6432, 1964.
    Versetten über O Welt, ich muss dich lassen (1968),
        Breitkopf & Härtel 6606, 1970.

SCHINDLER, WALTER. German. born 1909.
    Kleine Toccata über Ein' feste Burg, in Die Orgel (Concordia
        97-4500).
    Konzert, organ, 2 oboes, English horn, trumpet, timpani,
        percussion, strings, Sirius.
    Partita über Nun ruhen alle Wälder, in Die Orgel, Kistner
        & Siegel (Concordia 97-4531).
    Partita über Veni Creator Spiritus, Sirius.
    Prelude on Gross ist der Herr, in Die Orgel, Kistner &
        Siegel.

SCHLICK, ARNOLT. born Heidelberg, Germany, ?, before 1460;
    died Heidelberg ?, ca. 1521. Before 1511, became organist to
    Count Palatine, Heidelberg; 1511, published Spiegel der Orgel-
    macher und Organisten; 1512, published Tabulatura etlicher
    Lobgesang und Lidlein uff die Orgeln und Lauten.
    Da pacem Domine, Kalmus.

Maria zart, in Alte Meister des Orgelspiels, Vol. II,
p. 62, also in Harold Gleason, Method of Organ
Playing, p. 164; also in The Church Organist's
Golden Treasury, Vol. II, p. 161; also in Willi
Apel, Masters of the Keyboard, p. 39; also in
Schule des klassischen Triospiels, p. 3; also in
Historical Anthology of Music, Vol. I, p. 101; also
in A la Vierge, Orgue et Liturgie, Vol. 14, p. 7;
also in The First Four Centuries of Organ Music,
Vol. I, p. 49.

Orgelkompositionen, Rudolf Walter, ed. , Schott 5759.

Salve regina, in Historical Anthology of Music, Vol. I,
p. 101; also in Willi Apel, Masters of the Keyboard,
p. 38; also in Hymnes et Antiennes, Orgue et
Liturgie, Vol. 8, p. 5.

Tabulaturen etlicher Lobgesang und Lidlein off die Orgeln
und Lauten, Gottleib Harms, ed. , Ugrino Verlag 28
(Peters).

Verleih uns Frieden, in Orgelmusik der Reformationszeit,
Jost Harro Schmidt, ed. , Merseburger.

SCHMEEL, DIETER. born Hamburg, Germany, Dec. 31, 1923.
Organ pupil of Helmut Tramnitz and Knak; composition pupil
of Hans-Friedrich Micheelsen; since 1951, Kantor and
organist, Hamburg-Winterhude.

Introduktion, Kanon and Toccata über Nun danket (1960),
Breitkopf & Härtel 6338, 1962.

Passacaglia über Aus tiefer Not (1960), Breitkopf & Härtel
6329, 1961.

SCHMID, BERNHARD, the elder. born Strasbourg, 1535; died
Strasbourg, 1592. Organist, St. Thomas, Strasbourg; 1562-
1592, organist, Strasbourg Cathedral; 1577, published Zwei
Bücher einer neuen künstlichen Tabulatur auff Orgeln und
Instrument (B. Jobin, Strasbourg).

Passo Mezzo und Saltarello, in Spielbuch für die Kleinorgel,
Vol. I, p. 10.

SCHMID, BERNHARD, the younger. Christened Strasbourg,
Apr. 1, 1567; died probably in Strasbourg, 1625. 1584,
organist, Niklaus, Undis; 1592, succeeded father as organist,
Cathedral and at St. Thomas, Strasbourg; 1607, published
Tabulatur Buch ... Auff Orgeln und Instrumenten zu gebrau-
chen (L. Zetzner, Strasbourg).

Gagliarda Quinta, in Spielbuch für die Kleinorgel, Vol. I,
p. 13.

SCHMID, HEINRICH KASPAR. born Landau, Germany, Sept. 11,
1874; died Odlung (Munich), Jan. 8, 1953. 1899, studied at
the Academy, Munich; pupil of Thuille; 1903, became teacher, Odeon, Athens; 1905-1921, professor, Academy, Munich;
1921-1924, director, Conservatory, Karlsruhe; 1924-1932,
director, Conservatory, Augsburg; after 1933, served in the
Education Department.

Sonata, organ and violin, Op. 60, Schott, 1965.

SCHMIDT, FRANZ. born Pressburg, Austria, Dec. 22, 1874;
died Perchtoldsdorf (Vienna), Feb. 11, 1939. Pupil of

Leschetizky and Bruckner; studied at the Conservatory,
Vienna; 1914, became teacher, 1925-1927, director, Acad-
emy of Music, Vienna; 1927-1931, rector, Hochschule für
Musik, Vienna.
> Chaconne (C-sharp Minor) (1925), Leuckart, 1926.
> Fantasie und Fuge in D dur, Universal 10895.
> Four Chorale Preludes (O Ewigkeit; Was mein Gott will;
> o wie selig; Nun danket) (1926), Leuckart, 1927.
> Four Little Preludes and Fugues (E-flat Major, C Minor,
> G Major, D Major (1928), Österreichischer Bundes-
> verlag, 1951.
> Fugue (F Major) (1927), Weinberger, 1956.
> Gott erhalte (1933), Weinberger, 1959.
> (Der) Heiland ist erstanden (1934), in Musica Organi,
> Vol. II, p. 26.
> Prelude and Fugue (A Major), A Christmas Pastorale
> (1934), in Musica Organi, Vol. II, p. 39.
> Prelude and Fugue (C Major) (1927), Weinberger, 1955.
> Prelude and Fugue (E-flat Major) (1924), Leuckart.
> Toccata in C Major (1924), Universal 10894, 1937.
> Toccata and Fugue (A-flat Major) (1935), Universal 12295,
> 1955.
> Variationen und Fuge über ein eigenes Thema, Leuckart.

SCHMITT, ALPHONSE. born Koetzingen, Alsace-Lorraine,
France, Dec. 1, 1875; died 1912. Pupil of Alexandre
Guilmant.
> Pièce en forme de canon, in The International Organist,
> Vol. I, p. 37.

SCHMITT, FLORENT. born Blâmont, France, Sept. 28, 1870;
died Neuilly (Paris), Aug. 17, 1958. Pupil of Dubois,
Massenet, and Fauré; composer of orchestral and operatic
works; music critic.
> Marche nuptiale, Op. 108 (1946-1951), Durand.
> Prélude.
> Prière, Op. 11 (1899).

SCHNEIDER, JOHANN. born Oberlauter, Koburg, Germany,
Jan. 15, 1702; died Leipzig, Jan. 15, 1788. 1720, pupil
of J. S. Bach; 1721, became organist, concertmaster for
court, Saalfeld; 1730, became organist, Nikolaikirche,
Leipzig.
> Eins ist Not, in Orgel Choräle Sammlung, Metzler.
> Gott des Himmels, in Der Praktische Organist, Part I,
> Luetzel, ed. , Tascher'schen.
> Herr, ich habe misgehandelt, in Orgel Vorspiele zu den
> Melodien des Choralbuchs, Leuckart.
> Vater unser, in Orgelchoräle des siebzehnten und
> achtzehnten Jahrhunderts, p. 92; also in Notre
> Père, Orgue et Liturgie, Vol. 24, p. 25; also in
> Masterpieces of Organ Music, Folio 17; also in
> Orgelchoräle um J. S. Bach, G. Frotscher, ed. ,
> Litolff.
> compositions in Das Erbe deutschen Musik, Series I,
> Vol. 9.

SCHOENBERG, ARNOLD. born Vienna, Sept. 13, 1874; died Los Angeles, Calif., July 13, 1951. Pupil of von Zemlinsky; 1901, became teacher, Stern Conservatory, Berlin; 1903, taught Webern and Berg in Vienna; 1910, taught at the Imperial Academy for Music, Vienna; 1911, became composition teacher, Stern Conservatory, Berlin; 1925, appointed professor, Prussian Academy of Arts, Berlin; 1933, became teacher, Malkin Conservatory, Boston, Mass.; 1935, appointed professor, University of Southern California; 1936, named professor, University of California, Los Angeles; 1941, became United States citizen.

    Variations on a Recitative, Op. 40 (1940), Gray.

SCHÖNBERG, STIG GUSTAV. Swedish. born 1933.

    Duo (1957), Verbum.

    Festmusik (1958), Verbum.

    Lacrimae domini (1958), Nordiska 5222

    Liten kammarmusik (1962), Verbum.

    Små preludier (10) (1965), Verbum.

    Toccata concertante (1954), Nordiska 5068.

    Trio (1957), Verbum.

    Två väldiga strida om människans själ (1960) in Annorlunda koralförspel, Verbum.

SCHOOF, ARMIN. born Essen, Germany, Apr. 17, 1940. Organ pupil of Helmut Walcha; composition pupil of Kurt Hessenberg; since 1962, Kantor, Protestant Church Parish, Bensheim.

    Passacaglia über Ich wollt, dass ich daheime war (1965), Breitkopf & Härtel 6521, 1967.

SCHOUTEN, HENNIE. born Montfoort, Utrecht, The Netherlands, Nov. 17, 1900. Pupil of Willem Petri, DePauw, and Mulder; organist, Evangelical Lutheran Church, Leyden; teacher, Muziekschool, The Hague and Leyden; since 1945, teacher of harmony and counterpoint, Conservatory, Amsterdam.

    Fuga op Psalm 68.

SCHREM, JOHANNES. German. Fifteenth and sixteenth century. Works found in Fridolin Sicher's Tabulaturbuch and in Leonhardt Kleber's Tabulaturbuch (1524).

    Salve regina, in Frühmeister der deutschen Orgelkunst, p. 28.

    Sancta Maria, in Frühmeister der deutschen Orgelkunst, p. 37.

SCHROEDER, HERMANN. born Bernkastel an der Mosel, Germany, Mar. 26, 1904. 1926-1930, studied at the University of Innsbruck and at the Musikhochschule, Cologne; organ pupil of Bachem; taught at Rhineland Music School; 1938, became organist, Cathedral, Trier; 1940, named director, Landesmusikschule; 1946, taught composition, 1948, became professor, Musikhochschule, Cologne; 1946, became lecturer, University of Bonn; 1956-1960, taught at the University of Cologne; 1958-1961, assistant director, Musikhochschule, Cologne.

    Dritte Sonate, Schott.

    Duplum, piano and organ, Schott 6233.

Fantasie, Op. 5b, Schott 2188, 1931.
Fünf Stücke, organ and violin, Schott 4911.
Gregorianische Miniaturen, Coppenrath.
Kleine Intraden, Schott 5071.
Konzert, Op. 25, organ and orchestra, Schott 2559.
(Die) Marianischen Antiphone, Schott 4538, 1953.
O heiligste Dreifaltigkeit, Schwann.
Orgelchoräle im Kirchenjahr, Schott 5426.
Orgel-Ordinarium, Schott 5281, 1962.
Partita über Veni creator spiritus, Schott 4989, 1958.
Pezzi Piccoli, McLaughlin and Reilly.
Präambeln und Interludien, Schott 4539.
Präludium und Fuge über Christ lag, Schott 2554.
Präludium, Canzone und Rondo, organ and violin,
      Schott 3680.
Sechs kleine Präludien und Intermezzi, Schott 2221.
Sechs Orgelchoräle, Schott 2265.
Sonate, Schott 4941.
Toccata, Schwann, 1930.
Zweite Sonate, Schott, 1959.
chorale preludes (2) in Choralvorspiele zum Kirchenlied,
      Vol. 7, Christophorus.
chorale preludes in The Parish Organist, Vols. 7 and 8.
SCHULTZ, RALPH. born Dolton, Ill., 1932. Professor of
   Music, Concordia Collegiate Institute, Bronxville, N.Y.
      In dir ist Freude, in The Parish Organist, Vol. 9, p. 6.
      Salzburg, in The Parish Organist, Vol. 12.
SCHUMANN, ROBERT ALEXANDER. born Zwickau (Saxony), Germany, June 29, 1810; died Edenich (near Bonn), July 29,
   1856. 1828, entered University of Leipzig as a law student;
   1829, went to Heidelberg; 1830, became piano pupil of
   Friedrich Wieck in Leipzig; devoted himself to composition
   after his pianistic career was ruined by device designed to
   improve his technique; 1844, helped found Neue Zeitschrift
   für Musik; 1840, received the Ph.D., University of Jena;
   1843, invited to teach at the Conservatory founded by Mendelssohn; 1844-1850, composed and taught in Dresden; 1850-
   1853, city musical director, Düsseldorf.
      Sechs Fugen über den Namen BACH, Op. 60 (1845),
         Peters 2382; also Marks; also Breitkopf & Härtel.
      Sechs Studien für den Ped.-Flügel, Op. 56 (1845) also as
         Six Etudes en forme de canon et quatre Esquisses,
         Marcel Dupré, ed., Bornemann, 1949; also Durand.
      Skizzen für den Ped.-Flügel, Op. 58 (1845) also as Four
         Sketches, Gray (Standard Series Organ Compositions
         8); also Mercury; also Durand.
      fugue in Musica Organi, Vol. I, p. 152.
SCHWARZ-SCHILLING, REINHARD. born Hannover, Germany,
   May 9, 1904. 1922, studied in Munich; 1925, began study
   at Musikhochschule, Cologne; pupil of Kaminski; conductor
   and organ teacher, Innsbruck; since 1938, teacher of composition, Musikhochschule, Berlin.
      Concerto per Organo (1957), Merseburger 827, 1959.

Da Jesus an dem Kreuze stund, flute and violin (1942),
        Bärenreiter 2080, 1949.
Präludium und Fuge, Bärenreiter 2075.
Sechs kleine Choralvorspiele mit Intanationen, Merseburger
        825, 1959.
Zwölf Choralvorspiele (1927-1948), Bärenreiter 433, 1953.
chorale preludes (3) in Choralvorspiele zum Kirchenlied,
        Vol. 7, Christophorus.
chorale preludes (4) in Orgelvorspiele, Poppen, Reich and
        Strube, eds. , Merseburger.
SCHWEPPE, JOACHIM. born Kiel, Germany, Mar. 3, 1926.
    Studied church music at the Schleswig-Holsteinischen Musik-
    akademie, Lübeck; composition pupil of Ernst Klussmann;
    since 1960, Kantor and organist, St. Stephanus, Hamburg-
    Eimsbüttel.
        Acht Orgelchoräle (1965), Breitkopf & Härtel 6572, 1966.
        Toccata and Fugue (1963), Breitkopf & Härtel 6571, 1966.
        chorale preludes in Orgelbuch zum Evangelischen Kirchen-
            gesangbuch, O. Brodde, ed. , Book 18 (1) and
            Book 20 (1), Bärenreiter.
SCOTT, ANTHONY LEONARD WINSTONE. born Datchet, England,
    1911. Composition pupil of Herbert Howells at the Royal
    College of Music; since 1953, organist, Lambourn Parish
    Church.
        Prelude and Fugue, Oxford.
        Toccata and Fugue in A Minor, Novello.
SCRONX, FR. GERARD. Lowlands composer. born sixteenth
    century; died seventeenth century. Perhaps a pupil of
    Sweelinck.
        Echo, in Oudnederlandse Meesters, Vol. II, p. 64.
        Echo, in Oudnederlandse Meesters, Vol. III, p. 74.
        composition in Archives des maîtres d'orgue des seizième-
            dix-huitième siècles, Vol. 10.
SEARLE, HUMPHREY. born Oxford, England, Aug. 26, 1915.
    Studied at the Royal College of Music; pupil of John Ireland
    and R. O. Morris; 1937, became a pupil of Webern; 1946-
    1948, member of the music staff of British Broadcasting
    Company; 1964-1965, faculty member, Stanford University,
    Palo Alto, Calif.
        Toccata alla Passacaglia, Op. 31, Schott 10580.
SEEGER (see Seger).
SEGER (SEEGER), JOSEF FERDINAND NORBERT. Czech. born
    Řespín bei Mělník, Bohemia, Mar. 21, 1716; died Prague,
    Apr. 22, 1782. Studied philosophy at the University of
    Prague; singer under Czernohorsky at Jakob-Kirche; vio-
    linist, St. Martin-Kirche (organist was Zach); 1741, ap-
    pointed organist, Teinkirche, Prague; probably was pupil of
    Czernohorsky, Benda, G. Marcello, Caldara, and Fux; 1745-
    1782, organist, Kreuzherrenkirche, Prague.
        Acht Tokkaten und Fugen, Albrecht, ed. , Kistner & Siegel,
            1949; also in Organum, Series IV, Vol. 22, (Con-
            cordia 97-4354); also Peters D 922.
        Drei Tokkaten und Fugen, in Eight Toccatas and Fugues,

Ould, ed. , London, 1910.
Fugue in F Minor, in Ecole Classique, Alexandre Guilmant,
ed. , Schott.
Organ Works, Quoika, ed. , Breitkopf und Härtel.
Orgelwerke, in Musica antiqua bohemica 51 (Bärenreiter).
Orgelwerke altböhm. Meister, Vol. II, Breitkopf & Härtel,
1955.
Phantasie, Toccata, Fuge, Zwei Fugen, in Ausgewählte
Orgelwerke der alt-böhm. Meister, Schlesinger
(Berlin).
Prelude in E-flat Major, in A Century of Czech Music,
Vol. II, p. 3.
Toccata in D Minor, in A Century of Czech Music, Vol. II,
p. 23.
Toccata and Fugue in F Major, in A Century of Czech
Music, Vol. I, p. 10.
SEGNI, GIULIO. born Modena, Italy, 1498; died July 24, 1561.
Pupil of Fogliano and Vincenzo da Modena; 1530-1533,
organist, San Marco, Venice; later served Pope Clement
VII in Rome; three of his intabulated ricercari are found in
the printed Spanish anthology Libro de Cifra Nueva (1557).
Composizioni per Organo, in I Classici musicali italiani,
Vol. I.
Recerchare, in Anthologia Organistica Italiana, p. 4.
SEGOND, PIERRE. born Geneva, Switzerland, Feb. 8, 1913.
Studied at conservatories in Geneva and Paris; pupil of
Roger-Ducasse and Dupré; 1942, became organist, Cathedral
of St. Pierre, Geneva; professor, Conservatory, Geneva.
Aus tiefer Not, in Cérémonies funèbres, L'Organiste
liturgique, Vol. 15, p. 12.
SÉJAN, LOUIS-NICOLAS. born Paris, June 10, 1786; died Eure,
end of March, 1849. Pupil and successor of his father at
both St. Sulpice and St. Louis-des-Invalides; 1819, "organiste
adjoint" of the royal chapel; taught Lefébure-Wély and Adolphe
Adam.
Prelude and Fugue on Kyrie in the First Tone by duMont,
in Les Maîtres français de l'orgue, Vol. I, p. 95.
SÉJAN, NICOLAS. born Paris, Mar. 17, 1745; died Paris,
Mar. 16, 1819. Organist at the following churches in Paris:
St. André-des-Arts, St. Séverin, Notre Dame, Cordeliers,
St. Sulpice, St. Louis-des-Invalides; organist, royal chapel;
1795-1802, first professor of organ, Conservatory, Paris.
Fugue in G Minor, in Les Maîtres français de l'orgue,
Vol. II, p. 85.
SELBY, WILLIAM. English. born 1738; died Boston, Mass. ,
December 1798. Harpsichordist, organist; 1771, went to
America, became merchant, taught, composed; 1774, ap-
pointed organist, Trinity Church, Newport, R. I. ; 1777,
named organist, King's Chapel, Boston.
Fugue in D Major.
Ode for the New Year, in Three Pieces by Early American
Composers, Gray.
Prelude and Fugue in A Major, in A Treasury of Shorter

Organ Classics, p. 23.
Psalm 117.
SENFL, LUDWIG. born Zürich, Switzerland, ca. 1492; died
Munich, Germany, early 1543.   1495, became choir boy in
the court chapel; pupil of Isaak in Constance and his assis-
tant at St. Ann's Church, Augsburg; chamber composer to
Maximilian I; 1523, named "intonator" at Bavarian court
chapel.
Ach holdesligs Maidlein, in The First Four Centuries of
Organ Music, Vol. I, p. 66.
Also heilig ist der Tag, in Liber Organi, Vol. 8, p. 20.
composition in Masterpieces of Organ Music, Folio 65.
SESSIONS, ROGER HUNTINGTON. born Brooklyn, N. Y., Dec. 28,
1896.   1915, B. A., Harvard University; 1917, B. Mus.,
Yale University; pupil of Ernest Bloch and Horatio Parker;
1917-1921, taught at Smith College; 1921, named teacher of
theory and later director, Cleveland Institute of Music; 1926-
1933, won Prix de Rome and two Guggenheim Fellowships;
1944-1952, professor of music, University of California,
Berkeley; 1952, appointed professor of music, Princeton
University.
Chorale No. 1 (1938), Gray, 1941.
Mass for unison voices and organ (1956).
Three Chorale Preludes, Cos Cob, 1934; also Marks.
SÉVERAC, DÉODAT DE. born St. Felix-de-Caraman, Lauragais,
France, July 20, 1872 (not 1873); died Céret, Mar. 24,
1921.   Studied at the Conservatory, Toulouse; pupil of Guil-
mant and d'Indy; 1890-1907, studied at the Schola Cantorum.
Petite Suite Scholastique (harmonium) (F Major), Schola
Cantorum.
Suite in E Minor (Prélude; Choral; Fantaisie; Pastorale;
Fugue), Schola Cantorum.
Versets pour les Vêpres d'un Confesseur non Pontife
(1914), Schola Cantorum.
SHAW, GEOFFREY TURTON. born London, Nov. 14, 1879; died
London, Apr. 14, 1943.   Choirboy, St. Paul's Cathedral,
London; Inspector of Music, National Board of Education;
1932, received doctorate conferred by Archbishop of Canter-
bury.
Chorale Prelude (Trinity Office Hymn), Cramer.
Fantasia on Adeste fideles, Novello.
Two Choral Preludes (St. Patrick's Breastplate; Crux
fidelis), Cramer.
Two More Choral Preludes (Picardy; Wohlauf Thut-nicht),
Cramer.
Variations on an Old Carol Tune, Cramer.
Variations on the Irish Melody Slane, Novello.
compositions in Modern British Composers, Sets 1 and 8,
Cramer.
SHAW, MARTIN EDWARD FALLAS. born London, Mar. 9, 1875;
died Southwald, Sussex, Oct. 24, 1958.   Studied at the Royal
College of Music; organist, London churches; 1932, re-
ceived doctorate conferred by Archbishop of Canterbury.

Noon, Cramer.
Processional, Cramer, 1940.
(The) Ride, Cramer.
SHELLEY, HARRY ROWE. born New Haven, Conn. , June 8, 1858;
died Short Beach, Conn. , Sept. 12, 1947. Organist, Centre
Church, New Haven, Conn. ; after 1877, organist for the
following New York churches: Plymouth Church, Brooklyn;
Church of the Pilgrims, Brooklyn; Fifth Avenue Baptist
Church, New York City; Central Congregational Church,
New York City; pupil of Stoeckel, Dudley Buch, and Dvořák.
Ave Maria, G. Schirmer.
Evening Melody, G. Schirmer.
Spring Song, in Historical Organ Rectials, Vol. V, p. 72.
SHERA, FRANK HENRY. born Sheffield, England, May 4, 1882;
died Sheffield, Feb. 21, 1956. Studied at the Royal College
of Music as a pupil of Stanford, Parratt, and Davies; 1916-
1926, music director, Malvern College; 1928-1950, professor
of music, Sheffield University.
Aubade, Oxford.
Nocturne, Oxford.
SIBELIUS, JEAN JOHAN JULIUS CHRISTIAN. born Tavastehus,
Finland, Dec. 8, 1865; died Järvenpää, Sept. 20, 1957.
Studied at the Conservatory, Helsinki, in Berlin and in
Vienna; famous composer of orchestral works.
Two Pieces (Intrada; Sorgmusik), Hinrichsen 783.
SICHER, FRIDOLIN. born Bischofszell, Switzerland, Mar. 6,
1490; died Bischofszell, June 13, 1546. Organist in
Bischofszell and St. Gall, Switzerland; made a tablature
compilation of a large collection of organ works which were
predominantly intabulations of vocal works; 1503-1504,
studied at Constance with Martin Vogelmaier; 1512, studied
with Hans Buchner at Constance.
In dulci jubilo, in Alte Weihnachtsmusik, p. 42; also in
South German Christmas Music, p. 24; also in The
Parish Organist, Vol. 5.
Pange lingua, in Pange lingua, Reichling, ed. , Coppenrath.
composition in Masterpieces of Organ Music, Folio 67.
compositions (13) from Sicher Tabulaturbuch, in Frühmeister der deutschen Orgelkunst.
compositions in The Parish Organist, Vol. 5.
SIEFERT, PAUL. Christened, Danzig, June 28, 1586; died Danzig,
May 6, 1666. 1607, pupil of Sweelinck; 1611, appointed ad-
junct organist, Marienkirche, Danzig (with C. Schmidtlein);
1616, became organist, Altstädtischen Kirche, Königsberg;
1616-1666, organist, Marienkirche, Danzig.
Dreizehn Fantasien à drei (authenticity unsure), in Organum,
Series IV, Vol. 20 (Concordia 97-4352).
Ein Kind geboren, in Orgelspiel im Kirchenjahr, Vol. 2,
Schott; also in Sechs-und-Vierzig Choräle für Orgel
(under title of Puer natus).
chorale preludes (2) in Chorale Arrangements and Free
Compositions of the German Sweelinck School, Hans
Joachim Moser, ed. , Bärenreiter.

SIEGL, OTTO. born Graz, Austria, Oct. 6, 1896. Conductor;
    1933-1948, taught in Cologne; 1948, appointed professor,
    Academy of Music, Vienna.
    Weihnachts-Sonate, Op. 137, viola and organ, Associated
        Music Publishers.
SIGTENHORST MEYER (see Van den Sigtenhorst Meyer).
SIMON, JOHANN KASPAR. born Schmalkalden, Thuringia, Germany,
    ca.1705; died probably in Leipzig, after 1750. 1723-1727,
    studied in Jena; probably a pupil of J. Nikolaus Bach; 1727-
    1731, Praeceptor and director of music, Langenburg; 1731,
    appointed director of music and organist, Nördlingen; 1743,
    taught at the Latin School, Nördlingen; 1750, perhaps went to
    Leipzig.
    Vierzehn leichte Praeludien und Fugen, Walter, ed. , Schott
        3877.
SIMONDS, BRUCE. born Bridgeport, Conn. , July 5, 1895. 1917,
    A. B. , 1918, Mus. B. , 1938, A. M. , Yale University; 1919-
    1921, attended Schola Cantorum; 1920-1921, attended Matthay
    School, London; 1921, teacher, 1938, professor of piano,
    1941-1954, dean, School of Music, Yale.
    Dorian Prelude on Dies Irae, Oxford, 1930.
    Prelude on Iam sol recedit igneus, Oxford, 1930.
SINZHEIMER, MAX. born Frankfurt-am-Main, Germany, June 20,
    1894. 1921, Ph. D. , University of Heidelberg; 1913-1914,
    studied at the University of Munich; pupil of Carl Breiden-
    stein, Phillip Wolfrum (organ), Bernhard Sekles, and Walter
    Braunfels (composition); 1921-1924, organist, Christuskirche,
    Mannheim; 1940-1944, organist, Anshe Emet Synagogue,
    Chicago; 1945-1953, organist, Temple Sholom, Chicago; 1957-
    1959, Lakeview Lutheran Church, Chicago; since 1959, or-
    ganist, St. Andrew's Lutheran Church, Chicago; since 1947,
    professor, American Conservatory of Music.
    Sinfonia by Salomone Rossi (transcription), Trans-continental
        Music Publications, 1968.
    Twelve Hymn Prelude and Improvisations, Concordia 97-
        4769, 1967.
SIRET, NICOLAS. French. born ?; died, 1754.
    compositions (3) in Les Maîtres français de l'orgue.
SJÖGREN, JOHANN GUSTAV EMIL. born Stockholm, June 16,
    1853; died Stockholm, Mar. 1, 1918. Studied composition at
    the Conservatory, Stockholm; studied in Berlin and Vienna;
    1891, appointed organist, St. John's Church, Stockholm.
    Fantasie, in The International Organist, p. 60.
    Fantasie, Op. 15, No. 1, in Organ Music of the Netherlands
        and Scandinavia, p. 3.
    Legender, Op. 46, 2 vols. , Hansen.
    Preludium och fuga a-moll, Op. 49, Hansen 14329.
    Preludium och fuga C-dur, Nordiska.
    Preludium och fuga g-moll, Op. 4, Huss & Beer (Stock-
        holm).
ŠKROUP, DOMINIK JOSEF. born Včelákov, Czechoslovakia,
    Aug. 2, 1766; died Osice, Aug. 10, 1830. Studied in
    Pardubice; land registrar, later teacher, Rosice; 1787-

1797, lived in Libišany; until 1800, lived in Bejšt; lived in
Osice.

Orgelkonzert, Bärenreiter CHF 5064.

SLATER, GORDON ARCHBOLD. born Harrowgate, England, 1896.
Studied at York Minster; Mus. D., Durham University;
Fellow, Royal College of Organists; 1927-1930, organist,
Leicester Cathedral; 1931-1966, conductor, Lincoln Symphony
Orchestra; 1931-1966, organist-master of the choristers,
Lincoln Cathedral.

(An) Easter Alleluya on Lässt uns erfreuen, Oxford.

Introitus on Herzliebster Jesu, Novello.

Prelude, Intermezzo and Epilogue, Novello.

Prelude on Cheshire, in Hymn Tune Voluntaries, Oxford.

Prelude on St. Fulbert, in Festal Voluntaries (Easter),

Prelude on St. Botolph, Oxford.

hymn-preludes (2) in Festal Voluntaries (Lent, Easter).
    Novello.

SLAVENSKI, JOSIP. born Cakovec, Yugoslavia, May 11, 1896;
died Belgrade, Nov. 30, 1955. Pupil of Kodály; 1924,
appointed professor, Music Academy, Zagreb; later professor of theory, Conservatory, Belgrade.

Sonata religiosa, Op. 7, organ and violin, Schott, 1966.

SLAVICKÝ, KLEMENT. born Tovačov, Czechoslovakia, Aug. 22,
1910. Composition pupil of Karel Jirák and Josef Sul.

Frescoes.

Invocation, in Nuove Composizioni per Organo 2.

SMART, HENRY THOMAS. born London, Oct. 26, 1813; died
London, July 6, 1879. Left law for the study of music;
pupil of W. H. Kearns; 1831-1836, organist, parish church,
Blackburn, Lancashire; 1836, appointed organist, St. Philip's
Church, London; 1844-1864, organist, St. Luke's, Old Street,
London; composer of part songs and operas.

Original Compositions, Novello.

Variations on London New, Vincent Music Co.

SODERINI(SODERINO), AGOSTINO. Italian. Sixteenth-seventeenth
century. Organist, S. Maria della Rosa, Milan.

Canzone on La Scaramuccia, in Classici Italiani dell'
    Organo, p. 75.

canzoni (2) in L'Arte Musicale in Italia, Vol. III, p. 185.

SÖDERHOLM, VALDEMAR. born Mo, Sweden, Nov. 18, 1909.
1940-1946, organist-choirmaster, Eksjö; since 1946, choirmaster, Hedvig Eleonora Church, Stockholm; 1956, became
teacher, Conservatory, Stockholm.

Ave Crux (1968), Eriks.

Dig vare lov och pris, o Krist (Koralpartita) (1958),
    Nordiska.

Fughetta F-dur, in Orgelmusik vid högmässans avslutning,
    Albert Runbäck, ed., Nordiska.

Gläd dig, du Kristi brud, in Postludier för kyrkoårets
    samtliga sön- och helgdagar, Albert Runbäck and
    Waldemar Ahlén, eds., Nordiska, Vol. 3.

Improvisationer över "O du saligra", Nordiska.

Jesus är min hägnad (Orgelpartita) (1952), Norbergs.

Koralbearbetningar, Op. 21, Norbergs.
Orgelkompositioner (3), Norbergs.
Praeambel och fughetta (1948), Nordiska.
Preludium D-dur, in Orgelmusik vid vigsel, Albert Run-
    bäck, ed. , Nordiska.
Små orgelkompositioner (4), Norbergs.
Sonatin nr. 1 (1949), Nordiska.
Sonatin nr. 2, Nordiska.
Sonatin nr. 3 (1960), Verbum.
Sonatin nr. 4, Norbergs.
Sänd ditt ljus och din sanning (1960), Verbum.
Toccata i C-dur, Verbum.
Toccata i a-moll, Carl Gehrmans.
Toccata (Improvisation över koralen "Gud later sina trogna
    här") (1946), in Orgelmusik vid högmässans avslutning,
    Albert Runbäck, ed. , Nordiska.
Toccata, interludium och fuga över Trettondagens introitus
    (1961), Eriks.
Triptyk, in Musica Organi, Vol. III, p. 143.
chorale preludes (2) in Introituspreludier för orgel, Albert
    Runbäck and Waldemar Ahlén, eds. , Nordiska.
preludes (fiss-moll, h-moll) (2) in Orgelmusik vid jord-
    fästning, Albert Runbäck, ed. , Nordiska.
SÖRENSON, TORSTEN. born Grebbestad, Bohuslän, Sweden,
    Apr. 25, 1908. Since 1946, organist, Oskar Frederiks Kirke,
    Göteborg, Sweden.
Adorazione (1963), Eriks.
Breviarium musicum (1954), Carl Gehrmans.
Lova vill jag Herran (koralvoriationer) (1939), Nordiska.
Mäss-satser (3) (1961-1963), Verbum.
Svit nr. 3 (1952), Nordiska.
Toccata, Op. 12 (1944), in Musica Organi, Vol. III, p. 156.
Toccata (1958), Eriks.
chorale preludes in Introituspreludier för orgel, Albert
    Runbäck and Waldemar Ahlén, eds. , Vol. 1 (2) and
    Vol. 2 (2).
chorale preludes (2) in Koralförspel, Reinhold Andersson
    and Rudolf Norrman, eds. , Vol. 2.
SOKOLA, MILOŠ. born Bučovice, Czechoslovakia, Apr. 18, 1913.
    Composition pupil of Vilém Petrželka, Vítězslav Novák, and
    Jaroslav Křička.
Passacaglia quasi toccata na téma B-A-C-H, in Nuove
    Composizioni per Organo 2.
SOLA, ANDRÉS DE. born Tudela, Navarre, Spain, 1634; died
    Saragossa, Apr. 21, 1696. Nephew of José Jiménez; 1654,
    appointed assistant organist, Cathedral, Saragossa; 1672,
    succeeded his uncle at Cathedral, Saragossa.
tientos (3) in Six Tientos, Orgue et Liturgie, Vol. 74,
    p. 9.
SOLER, (FRAY) ANTONIO. born Olot de Porrera, Spain, Dec. 3,
    1729; died El Escorial, Dec. 20, 1783. Pupil of José Elías;
    choirmaster, Cathedral, Lérida; 1753-1783, organist-choir-
    master, Hieronymite Cloister, El Escorial; 1752-1757, pupil

of D. Scarlatti in Madrid.

Concerto No. 3, E. Power Biggs, ed., Associated Music Publishers, 1956.

Final de la Sonatina, in Les Anciens Maîtres Espagnols, p. 38.

Prelude in C Minor, in A Treasury of Shorter Organ Classics, p. 18.

Seis Conciertos para dos Organos, Samuel Rubio, ed., Union Musical Española, 1933.

Six Concertos, de la Riba, ed., Union Musica Española.

Zwei bei Zwei Sonaten, M. Kastner, ed., Schott 4637.

compositions (4) in Antologia de Organistas Clásicos Españoles, Vol. II, pp. 138-173.

SOMMA, BONAVENTURA. born Chianciano, Italy, July 30, 1893; died Rome, Oct. 23, 1960. Pupil of Respighi; 1911, became director, Santuario di Valle di Pompei; 1926-1960, choir-master, San Luigi dei Francesi; 1939, named teacher, Conservatory, Rome.

Toccata, Edizioni Musicali Casimiri-Capra, Rome, 1954.

SORGE, GEORG ANDREAS. born Mellenbach, Germany, Mar. 21, 1703; died Lobenstein, Apr. 4, 1778. 1721-1778, organist, city and court, Lobenstein; teacher, scholar of temperature and organ building, writer.

Komm, heiliger Geist, Herre Gott, in Anthologie, Concordia; also in Palme, Op. 50, Hesse.

Nun sich der Tag, in Orgel Archiv, W. W. Volckmar, ed., Litolff.

Toccata per ogni Modi, in Spielbuch für die Kleinorgel, Vol. II, p. 62.

chorale preludes (2) in Herings Sammlung, Rieter-Biedermann.

SOTO, FRANCISCO DE. born Palencia, Spain ?, ca. 1500; died Palencia, between Aug. 20 and Sept. 25, 1563. Spanish organist, clavichordist, composer, represented in the printed anthology Libro de Cifra Nueva collected by L. Venegas de Henestrosa (Juan de Brocar, Alcala de Henares, 1557); 1528, appointed chamber musician for Charles V; associated with Cabezón; 1529, musician in chapel of Queen Isabella; later served Philip II until 1550.

Tiento de Sexto Tono, in Early Spanish Organ Music, p. 3.

tientos (2) in H. Anglès, La Musica en la Corte de Carlos V, Instituto Español de Musicologia, Barcelona, Nr. 49 and 50, 1944.

SOTO, (PEDRO DE?). Spanish. Sixteenth century.

Versillos (2) de sexto tono, in Antologia de Organistas Clásicos Españoles, pp. 60-63.

SOWANDE, FELA. born Oyo, Nigeria, May 29, 1905. Studied in Lagos, Nigeria, London University, and Trinity College of Music; pupil of George Oldroyd, Edmund Rubbra, and G. D. Cunningham; 1957, 1961, traveled in the United States; faculty member, University College, Ibadan, Nigeria; 1953, appointed musical director, Nigerian Broadcasting Company;

1953, named honorary organist, Cathedral Church of Christ,
Lagos; Fellow of Royal College of Organists and Trinity
College of London.
  Go Down, Moses, Chappell & Co.
  Oyigiyigi (Introduction, Theme and Variations on a Yoruba
        Folk Theme), Ricordi (New York).
  Prayer, Ricordi (New York).
SOWERBUTTS, JOHN ALBERT.   English.   born 1892.
  Postlude on Hampton (S. S. Wesley), Stainer and Bell,
        1932.
  Six Preludes on Hymn Tunes, Stainer and Bell.
  Toccata on St. Magnus, Stainer and Bell.
SOWERBY, LEO. born Grand Rapids, Mich. , May 1, 1895; died
    Port Clinton, Ohio, July 7, 1968. Pupil of Arthur Olaf
    Andersen, Chicago; organist, First Methodist Church,
    Evanston, Ill. ; 1921-1924, studied at the American Academy,
    Rome, first American to win the Rome prize; 1925-1962,
    teacher of composition, American Conservatory, Chicago;
    1927-1962, organist-choirmaster, St. James' Cathedral,
    Chicago; 1945, won Pulitzer Prize for Canticle of the Sun;
    1962-1968, director, College of Church Musicians, National
    Cathedral, Washington, D. C.
  Advent to Whitsuntide (six chorale preludes) (1961),
        Hinrichsen, 1963.
  Arioso (1942), Gray (St. Cecilia Series 687, 1942.
  Ballade, English horn and organ (with alternate parts for
        violin, viola, and clarinet) (1949), Gray, 1950.
  Behold, O God Our Defender (1964), Gray, 1964.
  Bright, Blithe and Brisk, Gray.
  Canon, Chacony and Fugue (1949), Gray, 1951.
  Carillon (1917), Gray (St. Cecilia Series 244), 1920.
  Chorale Prelude on a Calvinist Hymn (1915), Boston Music
        Company, 1925.
  Chorale Prelude on a melodic fragment from a motet
        by Palestrina (1914), Gray, 1919.
  Chorale Prelude on Palisades (1949), Gray (St. Cecilia
        Series 754), 1950.
  Church Sonata (1956).
  City of God (1964), Gray, 1965.
  Classic Concerto, organ and string orchestra (or piano)
        (1944), Gray, 1946.
  Comes Autumn Time (1916), Boston Music Co. , 1927.
  Concerto in G Major, organ and orchestra (or piano)
        (1936/1937), manuscript.
  Concertpiece, organ and orchestra (1951), Gray, 1954.
  Dialog, organ and piano, Gray.
  Fanfare (1937), Gray (St. Cecilia Series 646), 1938.
  Fantasy, trumpet and organ (1962), Gray, 1964.
  Festival Musick, organ, two trumpets, two trombones,
        kettledrums (1953), Gray, 1955.
  For We Are Laborers Together with God (1965), Gray,
        1965.
  Holiday Trumpets (1958), in Colours of the Organ,

Novello, 1960.

Interlude (from Forsaken of Man) (1949), Gray (St. Cecilia
Series 758), 1950.

(A) Joyous March, Gray (St. Cecilia Series 254).

Jubilee (1959), Gray, 1959.

Madrigal (1915), Gray (St. Cecilia Series 138), 1920.

Mediaeval Poem, organ and orchestra (or piano) (1926),
Gray, 1927.

Meditations on Communion Hymns (1940) (Picardy; Luise;
Pange lingua; Meditation; St. Vincent; Sacra-
mentum unitatis), Gray, 1942.

Pageant (1931), Gray (St. Cecilia Series 555-556), 1931.

Pageant of Autumn (1937), Gray, 1938.

Poem, viola (or violin) and organ (or orchestra) (1942),
Gray, 1947.

Postludium super Benedictus es, Domine, Gray (St. Cecilia
Series 929-930).

Praeludium super Benedictes sit Deus Pater, Gray (St.
Cecilia Series 927-928).

Prelude, actually a Fugue, Interlude and Toccata (1959),
Hinrichsen 600D, 1960.

Prelude on Benediction--Ite Missa est (1916), Boston
Music Co. , 1925.

Prelude on Malabar, in The Modern Anthology, p. 162;
also Gray.

Prelude on Non Nobis, Domine, Gray.

Prelude on Rejoice, Ye Pure in Heart (1913), Gray, 1920.

Prelude on The King's Majesty (1944), Gray, 1945.

Prelude on St. Patrick (1954), Gray, 1956.

Preludes on Deus tuorum militum, Sine nomine, Land of
Rest, Charterhouse, Ad perennis vitae fontem (1955),
Gray, 1956.

Preludes on St. Dunstan's, Capel, Song 46, Were You
There? (1953), Gray, 1956.

Psalm 136 (1964), Gray 1965.

Requiescat in Pace (1920), Gray, 1926.

Rhapsody, in The Modern Anthology, p. 168.

Sinfonia Brevis (1965), Gray, 1966.

(The) Snow Lay on the Ground, Gray (St. Cecilia Series
919).

Sonatina (1944), Gray, 1944.

Suite (Chorale and Fugue; Fantasy for Flute Stops; Air
with Variations; March) (1933-1934), Gray, 1935.

Symphony in G Major (1930), Oxford, 1932.

Toccata (1940), Gray (Contemporary Organ Series 1), 1941.

Two Chorale Preludes (Marion, and Theme from a Palestrina Motet), Gray.

Two Sketches (1963), Gray, 1964.

Wedding Processional (1950), Gray (St. Cecilia Series 781).

Whimsical Variations (1950), Gray (Contemporary Organ
Series 25), 1952.

SPERINDIO (SPERANDIO), BERTOLDO. born Modena, Italy,
ca. 1530; died Padua, Aug. 13, 1570. 1552-1570, organist,

Cathedral, Padua.
> ricercari (2) in L'Arte Musicale in Italia, Vol. III, p. 55.

SPETH, JOHANN (JOHANNES). born Speinshart, Germany, Nov. 9,
1664; died Augsburg, probably after 1719.   Pupil of Abt
Lieblein; 1692, appointed organist, Cathedral, Augsburg;
taught Fugger children; friend of J. K. F. Fischer; 1693,
wrote Ars Magna consoni et dissoni.
> Ach Gott vom Himmel, in Anthologie, Concordia.
> Magnificat, Gregor Klaus, ed. , Willy Müller 23.
> Magnificat Octavi Toni, in Harold Gleason, Method of
>   Organ Playing, p. 63.
> composition in Liber Organi, Vol. 9.

SPEUY, HENDERICK JOOSTSZOON. born Den Briel, The Netherlands, ca. 1575; died Dordrecht, Oct. 1, 1625.   1595-1625,
organist, Grote Kerk and Augustijnen Kerk, Dordrecht.
> Duo on Psalm 24, in Hollandse Koraalkunst, Nederlandse
>   Orgelmuziek.
> Psalm Preludes, F. Noske, ed. , Heuwekemeijer 211, 1963.

STADLMAIR, HANS. born Neuhofen an der Krems, Austria, May 3,
1929.   Composition pupil of Alfred Uhl and J. N. David;
violinist and violist in the Opera and Symphoniekern, Vienna;
since 1956, director, Chamber Orchestra, Munich.
> Zwei Choralvorspiele (1961), Breitkopf & Härtel 6339,
>   1962.

STANFORD, (SIR) CHARLES VILLIERS. born Dublin, Ireland,
Sept. 30, 1852; died London, Mar. 29, 1924.   1870, entered
Queen's College, Cambridge; 1873-1892, organist, Trinity
College; 1875-1876, pupil of Reinecke in Leipzig; 1877,
M. A. , Cambridge University; 1883, honorary Mus. Doc. ,
Oxford University; 1883, appointed professor of composition,
Royal College of Music; 1888, honorary Mus. Doc. , Cam-
bridge University; 1887-1924, professor of music, Cambridge
University.
> Chorale Preludes (8), Stainer & Bell.
> Chorale Preludes, Op. 182, Stainer & Bell.
> Fantasia and Toccata, Op. 57 (1894, revised 1917),
>   Stainer & Bell.
> Fantasie on Intercessor, Op. 187, Stainer & Bell.
> Four Intermezzi, Novello.
> Idyl and Fantasia, Op. 121, G. Schirmer.
> Intermezzo on Londonderry Air, Op. 189, Novello.
> Prelude and Fugue in E Minor, Novello.
> Quasi una Fantasia, Augener, 1921.
> Six Occasional Preludes, 2 books, Stainer & Bell.
> Six Preludes, Op. 88, Breitkopf & Härtel.
> Six Short Preludes and Postludes, Op. 101, 2 sets,
>   Stainer & Bell.
> Six Short Preludes and Postludes, Op. 105, Stainer & Bell.
> Sonata No. 1, Op. 149, Augener, 1917.
> Sonata No. 2, Op. 151 (Eroica), Stainer & Bell, 1917.
> Sonata No. 3, Op. 152 (Britanica), Stainer & Bell, 1918.
> Sonata No. 4, Op. 153 (Celtica), Stainer & Bell, 1920.
> Sonata No. 5, Op. 159 (Quasi una fantasia), Augener, 1921.

Te Deum laudamus Fantasy, G. Schirmer.
Three Preludes and Fugues, Op. 193, Novello, 1923.
Toccata and Fugue in D Minor, Stainer & Bell, 1907.

STANLEY, JOHN.   born London, England, Jan. 17, 1713; died
London, May 19, 1786. Pupil of Reading and Greene; 1724,
named organist, All Hallows; 1726, appointed director of
music, St. Andreas Church, Holborn; 1729, Mus. B. , Oxford
University; 1734, named organist, Temple Church, London;
1779, appointed Master of the King's Band of Musicians;
1782, became organist, Chapel Royal.

Adagio and Fugue (A Minor), Cramer.
Adagio and Trumpet Tune, Cramer.
Allegro, in Anthologia pro Organo, Vol. 4, p. 62.
Concerto for organ and string orchestra in A Major,
   Op. 10, No. 5, Peter le Huray, ed. , Oxford, 1968.
Concerto in C Minor, Peter le Huray, ed. , Oxford.
Concerto No. 1 (D Major), organ and strings, Boosey and
   Hawkes.
Concerto No. 2 (B Minor), organ and strings, Boosey and
   Hawkes.
Concerto No. 3 (G Major), organ and strings, Boosey and
   Hawkes.
Concerto No. 4 (D Minor), organ and strings, Boosey and
   Hawkes.
Concerto No. 5 (A Major), organ and strings, Boosey and
   Hawkes.
Concerto No. 6 (B-flat Major), organ and strings, Boosey
   and Hawkes.
(A) Fancy, Cramer.
Fugue (G Major), Op. 6, No. 7, Cramer.
Gavotta and Variations, Cramer.
Introduction and Allegro, Cramer.
Largo and Allegro, Cramer.
Largo and Fugue (G), Cramer.
Praeludium, in Alte Orgelmusik aus England und Frank-
   reich, p. 15.
Prelude (A Minor), in 18th Century Preludes, 2nd Set,
   Cramer.
Prelude, in Three Old English Voluntaries, Cramer.
Siciliana and Borey, Cramer.
Siciliana, Cramer.
Thirty Voluntaries, Op. 5, 6, and 7, 3 vols. , Hinrichsen
   1033-1035.
Three 18th Century Preludes, Cramer.
Three Voluntaries from Opera Quinta (D Minor, D Major,
   G Minor), Hinrichsen 1713D.
Trio (D Minor), in Three 18th Century Preludes, Cramer.
Toccata for the Flutes, Cramer.
Trumpet tune, in Anthologia pro Organo, Vol. II, p. 69.
Tune for the Flutes (Voluntary in D), Cramer.
Twelve Diapason Movements, in Tallis to Wesley, Vol. 34,
   Hinrichsen 1037.
Voluntaries for Organ (facsimile edition of three sets,

ten voluntaries in each: Op. 5, 6, and 7 (1742),
Oxford, 1957).
Voluntary VIII (A Minor), in English Organ Music of the
Eighteenth Century, Hinrichsen 180, 1951.
Voluntary (A Minor), H. Diack Johnstone, ed. , Novello
EOM 9, 1959.
Voluntary (D Minor), Cramer.
Voluntary (E Minor), Cramer.
Voluntary (G Minor), Cramer.
Voluntary (G Minor), H. Diack Johnstone, ed. , Novello
EOM 8, 1959.
compositions in Masterpieces of Organ Music, Folios 10,
46, and 60.
voluntaries (2) (E Minor, G Major) in Liber Organi,
Vol. 10.
STATHAM, HEATHCOTE DICKEN. English. born Dec. 7, 1889.
Mus. Doc. , Cambridge University; Commander of the British
Empire; Fellow of the Royal College of Organists; 1927-
1967, organist and master of the music, Norwich Cathedral.
Four Diversions, Novello.
Lament, Novello, 1963.
Rhapsody, Cramer, 1927.
Rhapsody on a Ground, Novello, 1944.
Six Chorale Preludes, Novello.
Two hymn-preludes, in Festal Voluntaries (Advent,
Harvest), Novello.
STEEL, CHRISTOPHER CHARLES. born London, 1939. Licentiate,
Royal Academy of Music; 1966, appointed assistant director,
1968, director, Bradfield College.
Fantasy on a Theme of Purcell, Novello.
STEIGLEDER, ADAM. German. died 1633. Pupil of the Nether-
lands organist, S. Lohet; 1580-1583, was in Rome; 1592,
appointed organist, St. Michael, Schwäbisch-Hall; 1625,
went to Stuttgart.
Toccata primi toni, in Spielbuch für die Kleinorgel, Vol. I,
p. 14.
STEIGLEDER, JOHANN ULRICH. born Schwäbisch-Hall, Germany,
Mar. 21, 1593; died Stuttgart, Oct. 10, 1635. 1613-1616,
organist, St. Stephan, Lindau; 1617, appointed organist,
Stiftskirche, Stuttgart, and court musician, Württemberg;
1627, named organist, Heilbronn; taught J. J. Froberger.
Forty Variations on Vater unser, in Ritter Sammlung,
Ries & Erler.
Ricercar (G Major), Siegele, ed. , Schultheiss, 1951;
also Peters D 625.
Vater unser, in Orgelchoräle des siebzehnten und achtzehn-
ten Jahrhunderts, p. 42; also in Notre Père, Orgue
et Liturgie, Vol. 24, p. 3; also in Masterpieces of
Organ Music, Folio 17.
Vier Ricercare, Emsheimer-Keller, ed. , Breitkopf &
Härtel.
STEIN, MAX MARTIN. born Jena, Germany, July 27, 1911. 1931-
1934, studied at the Church Music Institute and University,

Leipzig; studied in Berlin; since 1936, toured as concert
pianist; 1939-1944, taught at the Landesmusikschule, Breslau;
since 1947, director of master classes, R. Schumann Conservatory, Düsseldorf.
> Toccata und Fuge (D Minor), Op. 1, Breitkopf & Härtel
> 5607.

STELLHORN, MARTIN. American. born 1914. Organist-director
of music, Bethel Lutheran Church, University City, Mo.
> Prelude on Italian Hymn, in The Parish Organist, Vol. 1-4.
> Prelude-Toccata on Fang dein Werk, Concordia.

STELZER, THEODORE G. American. born 1892; died 1956.
Professor of education and music, Concordia Teachers College,
Seward, Neb.
> Prelude on Missionary Hymn, in The Parish Organist,
> Vol. 1-4.

STENIUS, TORSTEN. Finnish. born 1918. Organist-director of
music, Swedish Olaus Petri Church, Helsingfors.
> Toccata över den medeltida hymnen Urbs beata Jerusalem,
> in Musica Organi, Vol. III, p. 88.

STOCKMEIER, WOLFGANG. born Essen, Germany, Dec. 13, 1931.
1951-1957, studied at Musikhochschule and University, Cologne;
1957, Ph.D., University of Cologne; 1960, appointed to
faculty, 1962, professor, Musikhochschule, Cologne; 1961,
named Lector, University of Cologne; since 1941, organist
in various churches in the Rhein valley.
> Choralvorspiele und Begleitsätze, Concordia 97-4920.
> Drei Hymnen (1953).
> Drei Inventionen, in Die Orgel, (Concordia 97-4772).
> Meditation (1961).
> Partita über Jauchzt, alle Lande, Gott zu ehren, organ and
> unison choir, Concordia 97-4909.
> Pastoral-Suite für Orgel nach Klavier-stücken von Antonio
> Soler, Concordia 97-4908.
> Sonate (1961), Möseler-Verlag.
> Tokkata I, Concordia 97-4837.
> Variationen über den Bach-choral, Herrscher über Tod und
> Leven, Concordia 97-4907.
> Variationen über ein thema von Johann Kuhnau, in Die
> Orgel, Concordia 97-4771, 1961.
> Zwei Orgelstücke, Concordia 97-4806.

STÖGBAUER, ISIDOR. born Kuschwarda, Germany, 1883. Resides
in Linz, Austria.
> Choralefantasie on Terribilis est locus iste, Op. 4,
> Coppenrath.
> Fantasie und Fuge, Op. 135, in Die Orgel, Series I,
> Vol. 16 (Concordia 97-4888).
> Fantasie und Fuge über ein thema von Anton Bruckner,
> Op. 95, in Die Orgel, Series I, Vol. 15, (Concordia
> 97-4890).
> Four Short Pieces on Chorales and Original Themes,
> Op. 6, Coppenrath.
> Introduction and Fugue on Veni Sancte Spiritus, Op. 7,
> Coppenrath.

Seven Organ Pieces on Chorales, Op. 9, Coppenrath.
STORACE, BERNARDO. born Naples, last half of the seventeenth
    century. Assistant choirmaster, Senate, Messine.
    compositions (23) in Corpus of Early Keyboard Music,
        No. 7.
STOUT, ALAN. born Baltimore, Md., Nov. 26, 1932. 1954,
    B. S., Johns Hopkins University and Peabody Institute; 1959,
    M. A., University of Washington; 1954-1955, won Danish
    Government scholarship to study at the University of Copen-
    hagen; composition pupil of Vagn Holmboe and Wallingford
    Riegger; conducting pupil of Erik Tuxen; Music Librarian,
    Enoch Pratt Library, Baltimore, and later at the Public
    Library, Seattle, Wash.; 1963, became Instructor in theory
    and composition, Northwestern University, Evanston, Ill.
        Eight Organ Chorale, Augsburg 11-9159.
        Serenity, 'cello (bassoon) and organ, Peters 6886.
        Three Organ Chorales, Augsburg.
STRATEGIER, HERMANN. born Arnhem, The Netherlands,
    Aug. 10, 1912. Pupil of his father; studied at the Nether-
    lands Institute for Catholic Church Music, Utrecht; pupil of
    Hendrik Andriessen; organist, Nijmegen; 1935, appointed
    organist, St. Walburgiskerk, Arnhem; 1948, named organist,
    Cathedral, Utrecht; teacher at the National University,
    Utrecht, the Netherlands Institute for Catholic Church Music,
    and the Conservatory, Utrecht.
        Chaconne (1955), in Cantantibus Organis, Vol. I, p. 36.
        Deuxième Passacaglia (1946), Van Rossum.
        Drei kleine Trios.
        Preludium, Intermezzo, en Thema met variaties (1939),
            Van Rossum R. 217.
        Ritornello Capriccioso (1944), Van Rossum R. 396.
        Thirty Short Inventions, McLaughlin and Reilly M-2421;
            also World Library of Sacred Music 106.
        Toccatina (1951), Van Rossum R. 395.
        Tweede Passacaglia, Van Rossum R. 268.
STRAUSS, RICHARD. born Munich, Germany, June 11, 1864; died
    Garmisch-Partenkrichen, Sept. 8, 1949. Great German com-
    poser of tone poems for orchestra and opera.
        Festival Procession (arranged by Reger), (Peters R30).
STROGERS, NICHOLAS. English. Sixteenth and seventeenth cen-
    tury. Compositions found in the Fitzwilliam Virginal Book.
        In nomine, in Altenglische Orgelmusik, p. 11.
STROZZI, GREGORIO. born San Severino, Italy, ca. 1615;
    died ?. Pupil of Sabino; studied law at the University of
    Naples; 1634, became organist, Sant'Annunziata, Naples;
    1645, appointed chaplain at the principal church in Amalfi.
        Capricci da sonare cembali et organi (twenty-nine
            compositions), in Corpus of Early Keyboard Music,
            No. 11.
STRUNGK, DELPHIN. born probably in Braunschweig, Germany,
    1601; died Braunschweig, Oct. 12, 1694. 1631, became
    organist, Hauptkirche Beatae Mariae Virginis, Wolfenbüttel;
    1634, appointed court organist, Celle; 1637, became

organist, St. Marien, Braunschweig; friend of H. Schütz; 1649, named organist, St. Petri; 1650, associated with Martinskirche; 1667, organist, St. Magnus, Braunschweig.

    Herzlich thut mich verlangen, in The First Four Centuries of Organ Music, Vol. II, p. 227; also in The Church Organist's Golden Treasury, Vol. II, p. 73.

    Lass mich, in Alte Meister, p. 98.

    Meine Seele, in Choralvorspiel alter Meister, p. 127.

    choral fantasies (2) in Die Orgel, Series II, Vol. 12, (Concordia 97-4519).

    chorale preludes (2) in Orgel Choräle Sammlung, Metzler.

    composition in Masterpieces of Organ Music, Folio 64.

STRUNGK, NICOLAUS ADAM. baptized in Braunschweig, Germany, Nov. 15, 1640; died Dresden, Sept. 23, 1700. Pupil of his father, Delphin; 1660, appointed first violinist for the Duke of Wolfenbüttel; 1660, entered service of Duke Christian Ludwig, Celle; 1661-1662, went to Vienna to play for Leopold I; 1665, began service to Duke Johann Friedrich, Hannover; 1674, became canon, Beatae Mariae Virginis, Einbeck; produced and wrote operas; 1679, became Music Director, Cathedral, Hamburg; 1682, appointed court composer, Hannover; 1685-1686, traveled to Venice and Rome; 1686, stayed in Vienna; 1688, appointed Vicekapellmeister, Dresden; 1693, organized Leipzig Opera Company.

    Capriccio, in A Brief Compendium of Early Organ Music, p. 26; also Kistner & Siegel.

    composition in Masterpieces of Organ Music, Folio 64.

    double fugues (2) in Organum, Series IV, Vol. 18, Kistner & Siegel, 1962 (Concordia 97-4350).

STUDER, HANS. born Muri near Berne, Switzerland, Apr. 20, 1911. Pupil of Willy Burkhard; 1934-1936, studied at the University and Conservatory, Berne; appointed to the staff of Seminar Neue Mädchenschule, Berne; choir director.

    Choralfantasie: Christ lag in Todesbanden (1963).

    Konzert, organ, wind instruments, and percussion.

    Petite fantaisie pastorale, flute and organ, Bärenreiter 3222.

    Toccata, Aria und Fuge (1960).

    chorale preludes (6) in 21 Orgelchoräler Schweizerischer Komponisten, Krompholz.

STÜRMER, BRUNO. born Freiburg-im-Breisgau, Sept. 9, 1892; died Bad Homburg, Germany, May 19, 1958. Studied at the conservatories of Karlsruhe, Heidelberg, and Munich; 1927, founded music school, Hamburg; until 1945, choral conductor, Kassel; after 1945, lived in Darmstadt and Frankfurt.

    Festive Concerto, organ, three trumpets, three timpani, strings, Bärenreiter 2487.

SULYOK, IMRE. Hungarian. born 1912. Pupil of Kodály; organist, Protestant church, Budapest-Obuda.

    Praeludium, Adagio und Fuge, in Musica Organi, Vol. II, p. 80.

    Sonata, Kultura (Boosey and Hawkes).

    chorale preludes (2) in Musica Organi, Vol. 2.

SUMSION, HERBERT WHITTEN. born Gloucester, Jan. 19, 1899.
Faculty member, Moreley College, London; 1922-1926,
organist-choirmaster, Christ Church, Lancaster Gate, London;
1926-1928, professor of harmony and counterpoint, Curtis
Institute of Music, Philadelphia; 1928, appointed organist-
choirmaster, Gloucester Cathedral.
Air, Berceuse and Procession, Novello.
Allegretto, Oxford.
Canzona, Hinrichsen 333E.
Cradle Song, Oxford.
Elegy, Cramer.
Four Preludes on Well-known Carols (Adeste fideles;
Coventry Carol; Holly and the Ivy; Unto Us a Child Is
Born), Hinrichsen 333A-D.
Intermezzo, Oxford.
Pastoral, in Simple Organ Voluntaries, Oxford.
Quiet Postlude, in Preludes, Interludes, Postludes,
Hinrichsen 600C.
SURZYŃSKI, MIECZYSLAW. Polish. born 1866; died 1924.
Studied in Berlin and Leipzig; organ instructor, Conservatory,
Warsaw.
Annus in cantibus ecclesiae, Op. 42, 5 vols., Gebethner
& Wolff (Warsaw).
Chant de Noël (Koleda), in Noel, p. 29.
Improvisation on Polish Church Song, in Orgel Komposi-
tionen aus alter und neuer Zeit, Gauss, ed., Coppen-
rath.
Preludes (55), Op. 20, Gebethner & Wolff (Warsaw).
Preludes (20), Op. 41, Gebethner & Wolff (Warsaw).
Preludes (55), Op. 55, Gebethner & Wolff (Warsaw).
SWEELINCK, JAN PIETERSZOON. born Deventer, The Netherlands,
May 1562; died Amsterdam, Oct. 16, 1621. Pupil of his
father; 1580-1621, organist, Oudekerk, Amsterdam; taught
H. Scheidemann, Jakob Praetorius, and Samuel Scheidt;
known as deutscher Organistenmacher (maker of German
organists).
Allein Gott in der Höh sei Ehr, in Orgelspiel im Kirchen-
jahr, Vol. 2, Rohr, ed., Schott.
Ausgewählte Werke, 2 vols., Diethard Hellmann, ed.,
Peters 4645 a/b.
Capriccio, in The First Four Centuries of Organ Music,
Vol. I, p. 140.
Choralbearbeitungen, Bärenreiter 2817.
Da pacem Domine, Kalmus.
Fantasie chromatica, in Geschichte der Musik in Beispielen,
p. 163; also Alsbach.
Fantasie über Mein junges Leben, in Alte Meister des
Orgelspiels, Vol. II; also Peters 4301C.
Fantasy in Echo Style (A Minor), in Historical Anthology
of Music, Vol. I, p. 209.
Fantasy in Echo Style, in Historical Organ Recitals,
Vol. I, p. 19; also Alsbach.
Liedvariationen, Doflein, ed., Schott 2482.

O lux beata trinitas, in Organ Preludes Ancient and
 Modern, Vol. 12, W. Sumner, ed. , Hinrichsen.
Opera Omnia: The Instrumental Works, Vol. 1, printed
 for the Vereniging voor Nederlandse Muziekges-
 chiedenis, Amsterdam, 1968: Fascicle I: Fantasias
 and Toccatas, Gustav Leonhardt, ed. ; Fascicle II:
 Keyboard Works, Settings of Sacred Melodies, Alfons
 Annegarn, ed. ; Fascicle III: Settings of Secular
 Melodies and Dances, Works for Lute, Frits Noske,
 ed.
Opera organis concinenda, 2 vols. , Van Rossum M. 700-
 701.
Organ Chorales, Bärenreiter 2817.
Sämtliche Werke, Seiffert, ed. , 4 vols. , Breitkopf &
 Härtel VNM and VNM 47.
Three Chorale Variations, Flor Peeters, ed. , Peters
 6055.
Toccata in A Minor, in Treasury of Early Organ Music,
 p. 38.
Variaties over Est-ce Mars?, Alsbach.
Variationen über Ich fuhr mich über Rhein, in Spielbuch
 für die Kleinorgel, Vol. I, p. 17; also Alsbach.
Variations on My Young Life Hath an End, Peters 4301C.
Variations on Psalm 140, in Hollandsche Koraalkunst,
 Nederlandsche Orgelmuziek.
Variations on O Mensch, bewein, Schott.
Werken voor Orgel en Clavecimbel, Max Seiffert, ed. ,
 Alsbach 12, supplement, Alsbach 12A, 1943.
chorales (3) in Orgelchoräle des siebzehnten und achtzehnten Jahrhunderts.
chorale preludes (24) in Sechs-und-Vierzig Choräle für
 Orgel.
composition in Archives des maîtres d'orgue des seizième-
 dix-huitième siècles, Vol. 10.
compositions in Free Organ Compositions from Lüneburg
 Tablature, John Shannon, ed. , 2 vols. , Numbers 32-
 37 possibly by Sweelinck.
compositions in Masterpieces of Organ Music, Folios 10
 and 32.
compositions in Orgelmeister des siebzehnten und achtzehnten Jahrhunderts.
compositions in Oudnederlandse Meesters, Vol. I (5),
 Vol. II (3), Vol. III (2)
toccata in Anthologia pro Organo, Vol. I, p. 29.
variation on Wo Gott, in Anthologia pro Organo, Vol. III.
SZÖNYI, ERZSÉBET. Hungarian. born 1924. Studied at the
 Academy of Music, Budapest, and Conservatory, Paris; 1948,
 appointed professor, Academy of Music, Budapest; 1959, won
 Erkel Prize.
 Introduzione, Passacaglia e Fuga, in Magyar Orgonazene,
  Sebestyén Pécsi, ed. , Editio Musica Budapest,
  Zenemükiadó Vállat, Budapest, 1966, Vol. I, p. 7.

TACHEZI, HERBERT. born Vienna-Neustadt, Austria, Feb. 12,
   1930. Organ pupil of Alois Forer; composition pupil of Uhl
   and Schiske; since 1959, teacher of harmony and organ,
   Hochschule für Musik, Vienna.
   Partita über Veni sancte spiritus, Doblinger, 1966.
TAGLIAVINI, LUIGI FERDINANDO. born Bologna, Italy, Oct. 7,
   1929. Studied at the Conservatory, Bologna; pupil of Ireneo
   Fuser; municipal music librarian, Bologna; teacher, Con-
   servatory, Bolzano; teacher, Conservatory, Parma; 1965,
   became professor, University of Fribourg, Switzerland;
   faculty member, Summer Academy for Organists, Haarlem,
   The Netherlands.
   Passacaglia on a Theme of Hindemith, Zanibon.
TALLIS, THOMAS. English. born ?, ca. 1505; died Greenwich,
   London, Nov. 23, 1585. 1532, "joculator organorum", Dover
   Priory; 1537, St. Mary-at-Hill, Benedictine Cloister, Billings-
   gate, London; soon afterwards went to Holy Cross, Waltham,
   Essex, and Augustinian Abbey until its dissolution in 1540;
   1540-1542, chorister, Canterbury Cathedral; Gentleman of
   Chapel under Henry VIII, Edward VI, Queen Mary and Queen
   Elizabeth I; taught William Byrd.
   Complete Keyboard Works, Denis Stevens, ed. , Hinrichsen
      1585, 1953.
   Four Pieces from Mulliner Book, Hinrichsen 1585b.
   Iste confessor; Gloria tibi Trinitas, in Treasury of Early
      Organ Music, pp. 10-12.
   Jam lucis, in Hymnes et Antiennes, Orgue et Liturgie,
      Vol. 8, p. 7; also in Alte Orgelmusik aus England
      und Frankreich, p. 18.
   Organ Hymn Verses (3) and Antiphons (4), Hinrichsen
      1585A.
   Pieces (4) from the Mulliner Book, Hinrichsen 1585b.
   (A) Poyncte, in Harold Gleason, Method of Organ Playing,
      p. 80.
   compositions (14) in Early English Organ Music.
   compositions (12) in Mulliner Book.
TANSMAN, ALEXANDER. born Lodz, Poland, June 12, 1897.
   Studied in Warsaw; 1919, moved to Paris; 1927-1928, toured
   United States; 1940, moved to Hollywood, Calif. , to write
   film music; 1946, returned to Paris.
   Deux pièces hébraïques, Eschig.
   Fugue, World Library.
TARTINI, GIUSEPPE. born Pirano, Istria, Italy, Apr. 8, 1692;
   died Padua, Feb. 26, 1770. Studied music and fencing; fled
   to Assisi; pupil of Czernohorsky; 1721, conductor, solo
   violinist, St. Antonio, Padua; 1723-1725, chamber musician
   to Court Kinsky, Prague; founded violin school in Padua.
   Concerto, violoncello solo, orchestra, and organ, Zanibon
      3166.
   transcription in Anthologia Antiqua, Vol. 2.

TAVERNER, JOHN. born Tattershall, Lincolnshire, England, ca. 1490;
died Boston, Lincolnshire, Oct. 25, 1545. 1526-1530, organist
and master of the choristers, Cardinals' College (Christ Church),
Oxford; 1514, became member of Brotherhood of St. Nicholas.
In nomine, in Altenglische Orgelmusik, p. 12.
In nomine, in Mulliner Book, p. 30.
compositions (2) in Early English Organ Music.

TELEMANN, GEORG PHILIPP. born Magdeburg, Germany,
Mar. 14, 1681; died Hamburg, June 25, 1767. Law student,
University of Leipzig; opera composer; 1704, became organist and director of music, Neukirche, Leipzig; director,
Collegium Musicum, Leipzig; 1704-1708, Kapellmeister to
Count Promnitz, Sorau; director, Leipzig Opera House;
court Konzertmeister, Eisenach; 1712, director of music,
choirmaster, Barfüsskirche, Frankfurt; 1721, municipal
director of music in five principal churches in Hamburg;
1722, director, Hamburg Opera; 1722, declined invitation to
become Cantor, Thomaskirche, Leipzig (J. S. Bach accepted
the position.).
Acht Nun komm, in Alte Weihnachtsmusik.
Allein Gott in der Höh, in Choralvorspiele zum Kirchenlied,
Vol. 3, Christophorus.
Christ lag in Todesbanden, Peters.
Christen singt mit frohem Herzen, in Gaide, Op. 50,
Brattfisch.
Concerto in C Major, J. G. Walther, arr. , Hinrichsen 549.
Concerto per la Chiesa, Philip A. Prince, ed. , Novello
EOM 17, 1961.
Easy Chorale Preludes, Kalmus 4005.
Es ist gewisslich, in Orgel Choräle Sammlung, Metzler.
Five Fantasies, Jos. van Amelsvoort, ed. , (Peters D 924).
Forty-eight Chorale Preludes, Alan Thaler, ed. , A-R
Editions, 53 Livingston St. , New Haven, Conn.
Herzlich thut, in The Church Organist's Golden Treasury,
Vol. II, p. 75; also in Anthologie, Concordia;
also in Palme, Op. 50, Hesse.
Komm, heiliger Geist, in The Parish Organist, Vol. 1-4,
p. 85.
Neun variirte Choräle (all manualiter), Kalmus 4004.
Nun freut euch, in Hering's Orgel Musik, Rieter-Bieder-
mann.
Nun komm, in Viens, Sauveur, Orgue et Liturgie, Vol. 19,
p. 19.
Orgelwerke, 2 vols. , Traugott Fedtke, ed. , Vol. I:
Choralvorspiele, Bärenreiter 3581, 1964; Vol. 2:
Twenty little fugues, free organ pieces, Bärenreiter
3582, 1964.
Soul, Adorn Thyself with Gladness in Organ Music for the
Communion Service, p. 22.
Twelve Easy Chorale Preludes, Hermann Keller, ed. ,
Peters 4239.
Twelve Methodical Sonatas, violin and continuo, Vol. 1
(1-6); flute and continuo, Vol. 2 (7-12), Peters.

Twenty Little Fugues, Bärenreiter NMA 13.
Vater unser, Peters.
Vier-und-Zwanzig Variirte Choräle, in L'Organiste litur-
    gique, Vols. 28, 32, and 36.
Wie schön leuchtet, in A la Sainte Vierge, L'Organiste
    liturgique, Vol. 2, p. 15.
Zwanzig kleine Fugen, Upmeyer, ed. , Bärenreiter NMA 13.
compositions in Masterpieces of Organ Music, Folios 5,
    11, 30, and 59.
THALBEN-BALL, GEORGE THOMAS. born Sydney, Australia,
    1896. Fellow of the Royal College of Music, the Royal
    College of Organists, and the Royal School of Church Music;
    1919, appointed professor, Royal College of Music; 1923,
    became organist, Temple Church, London; organist, Royal
    Albert Hall; 1949, named organist, University and City of
    Birmingham; Commander of the British Empire; 1948-1950,
    president, Royal College of Organists.
    Tune in E Major, Bosworth.
    Variations on a Theme by Paganini (pedal solo), Novello.
THATE, ALBERT. German. born 1903. Organist, Düsseldorf;
    instructor, Church Music School, Wuppertal-Elberfeld.
    Es sungen drei Engel, in Choralvorspiel zum Kirchenlied,
        Vol. 7, Christophorus.
    Tut mir auf, in Orgelbuch zum Evangelischen Kirchen-
        gesangbuch, O. Brodde, ed. , Bärenreiter.
    chorale preludes (2) in The Parish Organist, Vols. 5 and
        6.
THIMAN, ERIC HARDING. born Ashford, Kent, England, Sept. 12,
    1900; died 1959. Studied at the Royal Academy of Music;
    pupil of Harold Darke; 1921, became Fellow of the Royal
    College of Organists; 1927, Doc. Mus. , University of London;
    organist-choirmaster, Park Chapel Congregational Church,
    London; 1930, appointed professor of harmony, Royal Acad-
    emy of Music.
    By Verdant Pastures, Gray (St. Cecilia Series 918).
    Canzona, in The Modern Anthology, p. 186.
    Christmas Chime, G. Schirmer.
    Christmas Meditation, G. Schirmer.
    Eight Interludes, 3 sets, Novello.
    Finale in D Minor, in An Easy Album, Oxford.
    Four Chorale Improvisations, Novello, 1933.
    Four Improvisations, Curwen.
    Four Miniatures, G. Schirmer.
    Four Occasional Pieces, G. Schirmer.
    Four Quiet Voluntaries, 2 sets, Novello.
    Improvisation on Crimond, Novello.
    Interludes (2 sets of eight), Novello.
    March for a Pageant, Novello.
    Meditation on a Traditional Hymn Tune, G. Schirmer,
        1968.
    Meditation on A Virgin Most Pure, in Christmas Album,
        Oxford.
    Pastorale in E, Hinrichsen 98, 1938.

Postlude on Adeste fideles, Novello.
Postlude on Harwood's Thornbury, Novello, 1966.
(A) Sequence in Miniature, Gray.
Six Pieces, G. Schirmer.
Three Meditations, G. Schirmer, 1961.
Three Pieces (Meditation on Slane; Pavane; Postlude
   alla marcia), Novello.
Three Preludes on Themes by Orlando Gibbons, Oxford.
Times and Seasons, Novello, 1954.
(A) Tune for the Tuba, Novello, 1947.
Varied Harmonizations of Favorite Hymn Tunes, Novello.
hymn-preludes (2) in Festal Voluntaries (Christmas, Lent),
   Novello.
THOMAS, KURT.   born Tönning, Schleswig-Holstein, Germany,
   May 25, 1904.   Studied at the Conservatory, Leipzig; pupil
   of Grabner and Straube;   1925-1934, teacher of theory, Con-
   servatory, Leipzig;   1934-1939, professor, Hochschule für
   Musik, Berlin;   1939-1945, lived in Frankfurt;   1947-1955,
   professor, Academy of Music, Detmold;   1956, appointed
   Cantor, Thomaskirche, Leipzig.
      Festliche Musick, Op. 35, Breitkopf & Härtel 5539.
      Jerusalem du hochgebaute Stadt, in Das Organistenamt,
         G. Ramin, ed. , Breitkopf & Härtel.
      Variationen über Es ist ein Schnitter, Op. 19, Breitkopf &
         Härtel 5533.
THOMELIN, JACQUES-DENIS.   French.   born ca. 1640;   died
   1693.   Organist, St. André-des-Arts;   one of the organists,
   Chapelle Royale;   1667, named organist, St. Germain-des-
   Prés;   1669, appointed organist, St. Jacques-la-Boucherie.
      Allemande, in Pré-Classiques Français, L'Organiste
         liturgique, Vol. 18, p. 3.
THOMPSON, RANDALL.   born New York City, Apr. 21, 1899.
   1920, B. A. , 1922, M. A. , Harvard University;   pupil of
   Ernest Bloch;   1922-1925, Fellow of the American Academy,
   Rome;   1927-1929, 1936-1937, assistant professor of music,
   Wellesley College;   1929, 1930, won two Guggenheim Fellow-
   ships;   1933, honorary Mus. Doc. , University of Rochester;
   1937-1939, professor of music, University of California,
   Berkeley;   1939-1941, director, Curtis Institute of Music,
   Philadelphia;   1941-1946, head, music division, University of
   Virginia;   1946-1948, professor of music, Princeton Univer-
   sity;   1948, appointed to faculty, Harvard.
      Twenty Chorale-preludes, Four Inventions and a Fugue,
         E. C. Schirmer, Organ Library 1460, 1970.
THOMSEN, PETER.   born in the United States, Sept. 25, 1893.
   Pupil of E. Bangert and Th. Laub;   1918, appointed organist,
   Simeonskirke, Copenhagen;   since 1950, organist, St. Johannes-
   kirke, Copenhagen.
      Forspil til Salmemelodier i kirkestil, Hansen.
      Harpens Kraft, Dan Fog.
THOMSON, VIRGIL.   born Kansas City, Mo. , Nov. 25, 1896.
   Studied in Kansas City, at Harvard University (A. B. , 1922),
   in Boston, Paris, and New York City;   pupil of Wallace

Goodrich and Nadia Boulanger; 1923-1924, organist, King's Chapel, Boston; 1940-1954, music critic, New York Herald Tribune; since 1954, devotes himself to composition and conducting.

Fanfare, Gray (St. Cecilia Series 718).

Fantasia (1921).

Pange lingua (1962), G. Schirmer, 1962.

Passacaglia (1922).

Pastorale on a Christmas Plainsong, Gray (Contemporary Organ Series 14), 1942.

Variations on Sunday School Tunes (1926/1927), Gray, 1954/1955.

Wedding Music.

THORNE, JOHN. English. born ?; died Dec. 7, 1573 in York ?. Vicar-organist, St. Mary-at-Hill; 1560-1573, organist, York Minster.

Exsultabunt sancti, in Altenglische Orgelmusik, p. 36.

THYBO, LEIF. born Hostelbro, Denmark, June 12, 1922. Studied at the Royal Conservatory, Copenhagen; 1952, appointed teacher of theory, Conservatory, Copenhagen.

Concerto I (St. James) (1954).

Concerto II (St. Andrew) (1957).

O hjertekåre Jesus Krist, in Slagt skal Følge slagters, Bitsch & Petersen, eds., Hansen.

Orgelkoraler (4) (1953).

Praeludium (1950).

Preludio, Pastorale e Fugato, Op. 11, Hansen 26780.

chorale preludes (4) in 47 Orgelkorale, B. Johnson, ed., Hansen.

THYRESTAM, GUNNAR OLOF. born Gävle, Sweden, Oct. 11, 1900. 1925-1930, studied at the Royal Conservatory, Stockholm; also studied at the Conservatory, Potsdam; 1955, became organist, Hellig Trefoldighedskirken, Gävle.

Dig skall min själ sitt offer bära (koralpartita), Nordiska.

Cantus Dalecarlia, Norbergs.

Fantasiae sacrae (1956), Norbergs.

Jesus är min vån den bäste (1958), in Annorlunda Koral- förspel, Verbum.

Ludium organicum, Norbergs.

Preludium och fuga i E, Norbergs.

Preludium och fuge e-moll (1947), in Musica Organi, Vol. III, p. 138.

Preludium och fuga nr. 3 i B, Norbergs.

Psalmus verpertinus, Nordiska.

Toccata och fuga, Nordiska.

Tripartita in C (1954), Eriks.

chorale preludes (4) in Koralförspel, Reinhold Andersson and Rudolf Norrman, eds., Nordiska.

TIESSEN, HEINZ. born Königsberg, Germany, Apr. 10, 1887. Studied in Berlin; 1912-1917, music critic; theatre conductor; 1924-1932, conductor of workers' children's choir; 1925, appointed to faculty, Hochschule für Musik, Berlin; 1946-1949, director, Municipal Conservatory, Berlin; 1949,

returned to Hochschule, Berlin.
Music for Viola and Organ, Op. 59, (Peters R E 33).
Passacaglia und Fuge (Concordia 97-1359).
TINEL, PIERRE-JOSEPH-EDGAR. born Sinay, Belgium, Mar. 27,
1854; died Brussels, Oct. 28, 1912. Studied at the Conser-
vatory, Brussels, with Mailly; 1881, appointed director,
Instituut Lemmens; 1882, became director, Institute for
Sacred Music, Malines; 1896, professor of counterpoint and
fugue, 1909, director, Royal Conservatory, Brussels.
Sonata in G Minor, Op. 29, Breitkopf & Härtel.
TIPPETT, MICHAEL. born London, Jan. 2, 1905. Studied at
the Royal College of Music with Morris, Boult, and Sargent.
Preludio al Vespro di Monteverdi, Schott.
TISSOT, (CANON) LÉON-HENRI-ALFRED. born Sorans-lès-
Breurey (Haute-Saône), France, Apr. 10, 1877; died Besançon
(Doubs), Feb. 28, 1964. Pupil of Albert Alain and Maurice
Emmanuel; vicar-organist, 1942, canon, Basilica of Saint-
Ferjeux, Besançon.
Suite eucharistique, Hérelle, 1935.
Seconde suite, in L'Organiste (Nantes), 1941.
TITCOMB, EVERETT. born Amesbury, Mass., June 30, 1884;
died Boston, Dec. 31, 1968. Director of Music, Church of
St. John the Evangelist (Church of the Cowley fathers); pro-
fessor, New England Conservatory of Music, Boston Univer-
sity College of Music; Dean, School for Church Music,
Wellesley; associated with Convent of St. Margaret, Boston.
Aspiration, Gray (St. Cecilia Series 869).
Benedicta Tu, Gray (St. Cecilia Series 794).
Elegy, Gray (St. Cecilia Series 837).
Festive Flutes, in Colours of the Organ, Novello; also
Gray (St. Cecilia Series 847).
Four Improvisations (Puer natus est, Concordia 97-3829;
Alleluia Pascha nostra, Concordia 97-3828; Gaudea-
mus, Concordia; Cibavit eos, Concordia).
Improvisation on Eighth Psalm Tone, Novello; also Gray
(St. Cecilia Series 867).
Improvisation on Oriel, Carl Fischer, 1963.
Improvisation-Toccata on Tonus peregrinus, Flammer.
Pastorale, Gray (St. Cecilia Series 881).
Pentecost, B. F. Wood.
Prelude, B. F. Wood.
Prelude on Terry, McLaughlin & Reilly.
Requiem, in The Modern Anthology, p. 190.
Rhapsody on Gregorian Motifs, Gray (St. Cecilia Series
840).
Suite in E Major, Gray.
Three Pieces, B. F. Wood.
Three Short Organ Pieces on Familiar Gregorian Melodies
(Regina coeli; Credo in unum Deum; Vexilla regis),
B. F. Wood, 1940.
Toccata on Salve regina, Gray (St. Cecilia Series 790).
Two Communions (Adoro te devote; Ave verum), B. F.
Wood, 1943.

Two Compositions (Prelude; Scherzo), B. F. Wood, 1942.
Voluntary on Crimond, Gray (St. Cecilia Series 936).
Wedding Day: Improvisation on O Perfect Love, Gray (St.
    Cecilia Series 880), 1961.
TITELOUZE, JEAN. born St. Omer, France, 1563; died Rouen,
    Oct. 25, 1633. 1585, appointed organist, St. Jean, Rouen;
    1588-1633, organist, Cathedral, Rouen.
    A solis ortus cardine, in Organ Music for Christmas,
        Vol. I, Oxford.
    Ave maris stella, in Anthologia pro Organo, Vol. III,
        p. 50; also in European Organ Music of the 16th
        and 17th Centuries, p. 42.
    Ave maris stella, in Historical Organ Recitals, Vol. I,
        p. 30.
    Complete Works, in Archives des maîtres d'orgue des
        seizième-dix-huitième siècles; also Schott 1869.
    Creator alme siderum, in Les Maîtres français de l'orgue,
        Vol. II, p. 4; also in Little Organ Book, F.
        Peeters, ed. , McLaughlin and Reilly.
    De posuit potentes, in Harold Gleason, Method of Organ
        Playing, p. 174.
    Hymnes de l'église pour toucher sur l'orgue, Norbert
        Dufourcq, ed. , Bornemann, 1965.
    Magnificat, in The First Four Centuries of Organ Music,
        Vol. I, p. 156.
    Magnificat quarti toni, in Liber Organi, Vol. I, p. 4.
    Magnificat tertii toni, in European Organ Music of the 16th
        and 17th Centuries, p. 51.
    Pange lingua, in Alte Meister des Orgelspiels, Vol. II,
        p. 84; also in Historical Anthology of Music, Vol. I,
        p. 208; also in Cantantibus Organis, Vol. II, p. 5.
    Pange lingua, in Anthologia pro Organo, Vol. I, p. 40.
    Pange lingua gloriosi, Peters 4301E.
    Veni creator, in Anthology of Early French Organ Music,
        p. 9.
    Veni creator, in Liber Organi, Vol. II, p. 4.
    compositions in Masterpieces of Organ Music, Folio 23.
    compositions in The Parish Organist, Vol. 8.
    hymns (2) in Cantantibus Organis, Vols. 8 and 12, F.
        Pustet.
    hymns (2) in Orgelspiel im Kirchenjahr, Vol. 2, Schott.
    Magnificats (3) in Alte Orgelmusik aus England und Frank-
        reich.
TOEBOSCH, LOUIS. born Maastricht, The Netherlands, Mar. 28,
    1916. Studied at the School of Church Music, Utrecht, the
    Musieklyceum, Maastricht, and the Conservatoire Royal,
    Liège; 1940-1965, organist-choirmaster, Church of the Holy
    Sacrament, Breda; 1951, won improvisation prize, Interna-
    tional Organ Improvisation Competition, Haarlem; 1965, ap-
    pointed director, Brabant Conservatory.
    Allegro, organ and orchestra, Op. 20, miniature score,
        Donemus 181.
    Fantasy and Fugue, Op. 57 (1956), Van Rossum R. 418.

Postludia (2) (1964), Donemus.
Praeludium et Fuga super Te Deum laudamus, Op. 50,
     (1954), Bergmans.
Three hitherto unpublished Voluntaries, Hinrichsen 1572C.
Tryptique, Op. 15 (1939), Donemus.
TOMBLINGS, PHILIP BENJAMIN. born London, 1902. Fellow of
    the Royal College of Organists; Associate of the Royal Col-
    lege of Music; studied at Exeter Cathedral Choir School;
    1946, appointed director of music, Merchant Taylors' School;
    1948, named Examiner, Associated Board of Royal Schools of
    Music; 1919-1921, organist-choirmaster, Ide (Devon) Church;
    1921-1923, organist-choirmaster, St. Matthew's Exeter; 1923-
    1925, organist-choirmaster, St. Mary's, Berkeley Square,
    London; 1925-1929, assistant music master, Tonbridge School;
    1929-1931, organist-music master, Bloxham School; 1931-
    1946, director of music, St. Lawrence College, Ramsgate.
    Intermezzo, Oxford.
TOMKINS, THOMAS. born St. David's, England, 1572; died Martin
    Hussingtree, near Worcester, June 7 or 8, 1656. Pupil of
    Byrd; ca. 1596-1646, organist and master of the choristers,
    Worcester Cathedral; 1607, Mus. B., Oxford; 1621, one of
    the organists, Chapel Royal.
    Nine Organ Pieces, in Musica Britanica, Vol. V, Stainer
        and Bell, 1955.
    (A) Short Verse, in Liber Organi, Vol. 10, p. 6.
    Three Voluntaries, in Tallis to Wesley, Vol. 17, Denis
        Stevens, ed. , Hinrichsen, 1959.
TORRELLI, GIUSEPPE. born Verona, Italy, Apr. 22, 1658; died
    Bologna, Feb. 8, 1709. Studied in Bologna; 1686-1695,
    viola player, San Petronio; 1695, made concert tour in Ger-
    many; 1697-1699, Kapellmeister to Margrave of Brandenburg,
    Ansbach; 1699, lived in Vienna; 1701, returned to Bologna.
    Concerto in D Major, International Music Co.
TORRIJOS, (FRAY) DIEGO DE. born Toledo, Spain, 1640; died
    El Escorial, Dec. 30, 1691. Hieronymite monk, El Escorial;
    organist-choirmaster, El Escorial.
    Tres Versillos de Primer Tono, in Early Spanish Organ
        Music, p. 31.
TOULEMONDE, A. Belgian. Nineteenth and twentieth century.
    Teacher, Glongowes-Wood College, Sallins, County Kildare,
    Ireland.
    Pastorale, Philippo.
TOURNEMIRE, CHARLES ARNOULD. born Bordeaux, France,
    Jan. 22, 1870; died Arcachon, Nov. 3, 1939. Studied at
    the conservatories of Bordeaux and Paris; pupil of Franck,
    d'Indy, and Widor; organist, St. Nicolas-du-Chardonnet;
    1898-1945, organist, Ste. Clotilde (succeeded Gabriel Pierné);
    1919, appointed professor, Ensemble Music, Conservatory,
    Paris; taught Bonnal, Bonnet, Duruflé, Langlais, and Lesur.
    Andantino, Op. 2, Leduc, 1894; also in The French
        Organist, Vol. I, p. 91.
    Choral Symphony, Op. 69, Schott Frères 6.
    Cinq Improvisations, Maurice Duruflé, ed. , Durand, 1958.

Cinq Noëls originaux, in Noel, C. Fischer.
Deux Fresques symphoniques sacrées, Op. 75 and 76,
      Eschig, 1943.
Fantaisie Symphonique, Op. 61, Gross, 1933.
Offertoire, Op. 10, Gounin, 1896.
(L') Orgue Mystique, Op. 55, 56, 57 (1928-1936), 255
      compositions based on gregorian themes for 51 litur-
      gical services containing the following five pieces for
      each service: prélude à l'introit, offertoire, éléva-
      tion, communion, pièce terminale, Heugel; selections
      from L'Orgue Mystique published in 3 vols. , World
      Library of Sacred Music.
Paraphrase-Carillon (in Assumtione Bienheureuse Vierge
      Marie).
Pastorale, Edition Musicus.
Petites fleurs musicales (40 compositions) (harmonium or
      organ), Op. 66, Procure Générale, 1935/1936.
Pièce symphonique, Op. 16, Schola Cantorum, 1899; also
      in Historical Organ Recitals, Vol. V, p. 98.
Postludes libres (64 compositions for harmonium or organ),
      Op. 68, Eschig, 1935/1936.
Quarante pièces (harmonium), Variae preces, Op. 21,
      Janin (Lyon), 1904.
Scherzetto, in The International Organist, Vol. II, p. 60.
Sei Fioretti, Op. 60, Hérelle, 1932.
Sept Chorale-Poèmes pour les Sept Paroles du Christ,
      Op. 67, Eschig, 1937.
Sortie (Ita missa est), Op. 3, Leduc, 1894; also in The
      French Organist, Vol. II, p. 14.
Suite de morceaux, Op. 19-24, Noël, 1894, 1901.
Suite évocatrice, Op. 74 (Grave; Tierce en taille et récit
      de chromhorne; Flûte d'écho jeu doux et voix hu-
      maine; Caprice), Bornemann, 1938, 1943.
Symphonie Sacrée, Op. 71, Schola Cantorum, 1960; also
      Kalmus 4012.
Symphonie-Choral, Op. 69, Eschig; also Schott, 1939.
Symphonietta (organ part).
Toccata sur un Choral.
Triple Choral, Op. 41, Janin (Lyon), 1912; also Schola
      Cantorum; also in Orgue et Liturgie, Vol. 54; also
      Kalmus 4011.
Trois Poèmes, Op. 59, Lemoine, 1932/1933.
Various Pieces, Op. 21, Delrieu.
TRABACI, GIOVANNI MARIA. born Montepeloso (now Irsina),
      Italy, ca. 1575; died Naples, Dec. 31, 1647. ca. 1595, be-
      came organist, Oratorio dei Filippini; 1601, appointed or-
      ganist, Royal Chapel, Naples; 1614, named maestro di
      cappella, royal chapel, Naples (succeeded Jean de Macque);
      1625-1630, organist, Oratorio dei Filippini again.
      Canzona francese, in Historical Anthology of Music,
            Vol. II, p. 16.
      Ricercate, 2 vols. , in L'Organiste liturgique, Vols. 54
            and 57.

compositions (2) in <u>Anthologia Organistica Italiana</u>.
compositions (9) in <u>L'Arte Musicale in Italia</u>, Vol. III,
  p. 365.
compositions (3) in <u>Classici Italiani dell'Organo</u>.
TRAVERS, JOHN. born England, ca.1703; died London, June
  1758. Singer, St. George's Chapel, Windsor; pupil of Greene
  and Pepusch; 1725, named organist, St. Paul's, Covent Garden, London; later organist, Fulham Parish Church; 1737,
  became organist, Chapel Royal.
    <u>Prelude and Fugue in C Minor</u>, in <u>Tallis to Wesley</u>,
      Vol. 22, p. 1.
    <u>Voluntary in D Major</u>, Novello, 1906.
    composition in <u>Masterpieces of Organ Music</u>, Folio 16.
TREXLER, GEORG. born Pirna, Germany, Feb. 9, 1903. Studied
  at the Conservatory, Leipzig; organ pupil of Straube; 1930,
  appointed organist, 1947, director of music, Propsteikirche,
  Leipzig; since 1935, teacher, 1948, professor, Conservatory,
  Leipzig.
    <u>Gregorian Organ Works</u>, Bärenreiter 5192, also 3 vols.,
      Willy Müller, Vols. 10, 11, and 25.
    <u>Introduktion und Passacaglia über Thema der 8. Symphony</u>
      Bruckner (1949), VEB Breitkopf & Härtel (Leipzig)
      5799.
    <u>Partita über ein eigenes Thema,</u> Breitkopf und Härtel.
    <u>Toccata über Thema, e-moll Messe Bruckner</u> (1949), VEB
      Breitkopf & Härtel (Leipzig) 5775.
TRIQUE, MICHEL. born Congrier (Mayenne), France, Sept. 25,
  1934. 1956-1958, studied at the Ecole Normale de Musique,
  Paris; 1958-1962, studied at the Schola Cantorum; pupil of
  Jean-Jacques Grünenwald, Jean Langlais, and Daniel-Lesur;
    <u>Fugue</u>, in <u>Orgue et Liturgie</u>, Vol. 60, p. 20.
TUNDER, FRANZ. born Burg auf Fehmarn, Germany, 1614; died
  Lübeck, Nov. 5, 1667. 1632-1641, organist, court chapel,
  Gottorp; 1641, appointed organist, Marienkirche, Lübeck;
  father-in-law of Buxtehude.
    <u>Chorale Preludes</u>, Walter, ed., Schott 4783.
    <u>Jesus Christus, unser Heiland</u>, in <u>Choralvorspiel alter</u>
      <u>Meister</u>, p. 130.
    <u>Praeludium</u>, in <u>The First Four Centuries of Organ Music</u>,
      Vol. I, p. 231.
    <u>Sämtliche Choralbearbeitungen</u>, Walter, ed., Schott 2482,
      1959.
    <u>Vier Praeludien</u> (G Minor, F Major, G Minor, G Minor),
      in <u>Organum</u>, Series IV, Vol. 6, (Concordia 97-4338).
    chorale prelude in <u>Alte Meister des Orgelspiels</u>, Vol. II,
      p. 94.
    chorale preludes (2) in <u>Corpus of Early Keyboard Music</u>,
      No. 10, Vol. 2.
    compositions in <u>Masterpieces of Organ Music</u>, Folios 45
      and 63.
TYE, CHRISTOPHER. English. born 1497; died Doddington,
  Cambridge, 1572. 1527-1535, lay clerk, King's College;
  1537, B. Mus., 1545, Doc. Mus., Cambridge and Oxford;

1541-1561, Master of Choristers, Ely Cathedral; Gentleman,
Chapel Royal; 1560, took holy orders.
    compositions (4) in Early English Organ Music.
TÝNSKÝ, RICHARD. born Lvov, Poland (now in Russia) Sept. 29,
1909. Composition pupil of Václav Kaprál; organ pupil of
František Michálek; conductor.
    Phrygian Toccata (1940), Novello; also in Musica Boemica
        per Organo, Jiri Reinberger, ed. , Vol. III, p. 27,
        Státní nakladatelství krásné literatury, hudby a umění,
        Prague, 1958.

UNKEL, ROLF. German. born 1912. Director of music, Radio
    Stuttgart.
    chorale preludes (3) in The Parish Organist, Vol. 1-4.

VALEN, FARTEIN OLAF. born Stavanger, Norway, Aug. 25, 1887;
    died Haugesund, Dec. 14, 1952. Pupil of Max Bruch in Ber-
    lin; 1924, invented an atonal polyphony.
    Pastoral, Op. 34, Edition Lyche 150.
    Prelude and Fugue, Op. 33, Edition Lyche 149.
VALENTE, ANTONIO. Italian. born ca. 1520; died ca. 1580.
    1565-1580, blind organist, Church of Sant'Angelo a Nilo,
    Naples; wrote Intavolatura de Cimbalo (G. Cacchio dell'
    Aquila, Naples, 1576).
    Cinque Verse spirituali, in Classici Italiani dell'Organo,
        pp. 59-63.
    (La) Romanesca con cinque mutanze, in Silva Iberica, p. 4.
    Versi, in L'Arte Musicale in Italia, Vol. III, p. 45.
    Versi Spirituali (43), I. Fuser, ed. , Zanibon 4175.
VAN DEN SIGTENHORST-MEYER, BERNHARD. born Amsterdam,
    June 17, 1888; died The Hague, July 17, 1953. Studied at
    the conservatories of Amsterdam, Vienna, and Paris.
    Fantasie, Op. 41, Alsbach.
    Passacaglia en Fuga, Op. 36, Alsbach.
VAN DESSEL, LODE. Belgian. born Feb. 5, 1909. Studied at
    the Lemmens Instituut, Malines; M. A. , Wayne State Univer-
    sity, Detroit; Fellow of the American Guild of Organists;
    organ pupil of Flor Peeters; composition pupil of Marinus
    De Jong; 1929-1948, organ teacher, Academy of Music,
    Turnhout, Belgium; 1948-1949, organist, St. Thomas' Church,
    Ann Arbor, Mich.; since 1949, organist, St. Aloysius,
    Detroit.
    Choral and Fughetta, Op. 12, Nos. 1 and 2 (First Suite),
        Heuwekemeijer, 1946.
    Fantasia with Choral (Cyclical Suite), Gray, 1960.
    Pre-, Inter-, Postludia on Gregorian Themes of the
        Blessed Virgin, Gregorian Institute of America, 1950.

Recto Tono, Modal Improvisations, World Library of
    Sacred Music, 1966.
Short Modal Improvisations on Chants of the Kyriale,
    Gregorian Institute of America, 1961.
Wedding Music on Gregorian Themes of the Nuptial Mass,
    Gregorian Institute of America, 1950.

VAN HULSE, CAMIL. born St. Nicolas, Belgium, Aug. 1, 1897.
Pupil of Mortelmans and DeGreef; 1923, came to the United
States; organist and director of music, Church of SS. Peter
and Paul, Tucson, Arizona.

Biblical Sketches, Novello.
Christmas Fantasy on St. Magnus, FitzSimons.
Christmas Rhapsody, Novello.
Church Modes, 2 vols., Concordia 97-1431, 97-1432.
Eleven Improvisations on Hymn Tunes, FitzSimons.
Fantasia Contrapunctus on O Filii et Filiae, Witmark.
Festival Postlude on Veni Creator Spiritus, Witmark.
Five Christmas Fantasies, Op. 76, FitzSimons.
Four Short Pieces, Novello.
Meditations on Well-known Hymns, C. Fischer.
Messe Basse No. 1, McLaughlin and Reilly M-1815.
Messe Basse No. 2 on Marian Themes, McLaughlin and
    Reilly, M-1985.
Messe Basse No. 3 for Christmastide, McLaughlin and
    Reilly, M-2129.
Messe Basse No. 4 for Eastertide, McLaughlin and Reilly,
    M-2144.
Nun danket alle Gott, in Ten Pieces for Service Use,
    J. Fischer.
Prelude on Ich freue mich, in Gloria Deo, McLaughlin and
    Reilly.
Seven Preludes and Fugues, Novello.
Seven Preludes for Lent, Concordia 97-1362.
Seven Preludes on Advent Hymns, Concordia 97-1363.
Seven Preludes on Christmas Hymns, Concordia 97-1364.
Seven Preludes on Easter Hymns, Concordia 97-1390.
Seven Preludes on Hymns for Holy Week, Concordia
    97-1365.
Seven Preludes on Plainsong Hymns, Concordia.
Ten Preludes on Hymn Tunes in Free Style, Op. 85,
    C. Fischer, 1957.
Ten Preludes on Well Known Hymns, J. Fischer.
Ten Service Pieces Based on Hymn Tunes, Op. 122,
    FitzSimons, 1962.
Three Chorale Preludes, FitzSimons.
Three Chorale Preludes for Solo Organ, Shawnee.
Toccata, Op. 39, J. Fischer 8231, 1946.
chorale preludes (10) in Little Cycle through the Christian
    Year, Mills.
chorale preludes (2) in The Parish Organist, Vol. 1-4.

VAN MEERT, C. F. born ?; died 1735.
Fugato, in Oudnederlandse Meesters, Vol. III, p. 108.

VANHAL (WANHAL), JAN KŘTITEL (JOHANN BAPTIST). born

Nechanicz, Czechoslovakia, May 12, 1739; died Vienna,
Aug. 26, 1813. Pupil of Dittersdorf; studied in Vienna and
Venice; composed many symphonies, string quartets, piano
pieces, church and chamber works.
> Fugue in C Major, in A Century of Czech Music, Vol. II,
> p. 25.

VAUGHAN WILLIAMS, RALPH (family name is Williams). born
Down Ampney, Gloucestershire, England, Oct. 12, 1872; died
London, Aug. 26, 1958. 1887-1890, attended Charterhouse
School, London; 1890-1892, 1895-1896, attended Royal College
of Music, London; pupil of Parratt, Parry and Stanford;
1894, B. Mus., 1895, B.A., Trinity College, Cambridge
University; 1897-1898, pupil of Max Bruch in Berlin; organist, South Lambert Church, London; 1901, Mus. Doc.,
Cambridge; 1905, appointed editor, The English Hymnal;
1909, pupil of Ravel in France; during World War I served
in artillery in Macedonia and France; 1918, became professor of composition, Royal College of Music; 1920-1928,
conductor, London Bach Choir; 1935, received Order of
Merit.
> Greensleeves, Roper, arr., Oxford, 1947.
> Hymn Prelude on Song 13, Oxford.
> Prelude and Fugue in C Minor (1921), Oxford, 1930.
> Three Preludes founded on Welsh Hymn-tunes (Bryn
> > Calfaria; Rhosymedre; Hyfrydol), Stainer & Bell,
> > 1920.
> Two Hymn Tune Preludes, Oxford.
> Two Preludes on Welsh Hymn-tunes, Oxford, 1964.
> Variations on Aberystwyth, Oxford.
> (A) Vaughan Williams Organ Album, Oxford, 1964.

VENEGAS DE HENESTROSA, LUYS. Spanish. Sixteenth century.
Published the first Spanish book of organ music.
> Libro de Cifra Nueva, Higini Anglés, ed., in La música
> > en la corte de Carlos V, Vol. 2 of Monumentos de
> > la música española, Barcelona, 1944.

VERSCHRAEGEN, GABRIEL. born Eksaarde near Lokeren, Belgium, 1919. Organist, St. Baaf's Cathedral, Ghent; pupil
of Flor Peeters; teacher, Conservatory, Ghent.
> Partita octavi toni super Veni creator, in Cantantibus
> > Organis, Vol. II, p. 40.
> Preludium en Interludium op Puer natus est, in Cantantibus
> > Organis, Vol. I, p. 44.

VETTER, ANDREAS NICOLAUS. born probably at Herschdorf bei
Königsee, Germany, 1666; died Rudolstadt, June 13, 1734.
Pupil of J. Pachelbel in Erfurt; 1690, became organist,
Predigerkirche, Erfurt (succeeded Pachelbel); 1691-1734,
court organist, Rudolstadt.
> Allein Gott, in Laudamus Dominum, p. 6; also in Pro
> > Organo, Harald Lyche.
> Komm, heiliger Geist, in Chorale Preludes by Masters of
> > the Seventeenth and Eighteenth Centuries, p. 69.
> Nun komm, in Viens, Sauveur, Orgue et Liturgie, Vol. 10,
> > p. 7; also in The First Four Centuries of Organ

Music, Vol. II, p. 419; also in Orgel Choräle
Sammlung, Metzler.
chorale prelude in Elf Orgelchoräle des siebzehnten Jahr-
hunderts.
chorale preludes (2) in Eighty Chorale Preludes: German
Masters of the Seventeenth and Eighteenth Centuries.
chorale preludes (4) in Orgelchoräle um J. S. Bach,
G. Frotscher, ed., Litolff.
chorale preludes (2) in Ritter's Sammlung, Ries & Erler.
composition in Das Erbe deutschen Musik, Series I, Vol. 9.
VETTER, HAROLD R.   born Milwaukee, Wis., 1931.   Pastor,
St. Paul Evangelical Lutheran Church, Ellicottville, N. Y.
Wer nur, in The Parish Organist, Vol. 9, p. 35.
VIDERØ, FINN.   born Fuglebjerg, Denmark, Aug. 15, 1906.   1928,
began serving as organist in Copenhagen; 1947, became or-
ganist, Trinitaskirke, Copenhagen; 1935-1945, teacher of
organ, theory, University of Copenhagen; 1959-1960, visiting
professor of organ, Yale University.
Kirketonearterne, Hansen 24091a.
Koralpraeludier og orgelkoraler i sv. koralboken, Engstrom
& Sødring.
Orgelkoraler og salmeforspil, 2 vols., Engstrom & Sødring
7 and 8.
Passacaglia in D Minor, Hansen.
Ten Chorale Preludes and Ten Organ Chorales, Engstrom
& Sødring 6.
Three Chorale Partitas, Engstrom & Sødring.
Twenty-one Hymn Intonations, Concordia 97-5004.
chorale preludes (10) in 50 Koralbearbejdelser, Hansen.
chorale preludes (6) in Forspil till Salmemelodier i kirke-
stil, Hansen.
chorale preludes (5) in Orgelchoraler til Kirkeaaret,
Hansen.
chorale preludes (11) in Seventeen Preludes for the Church
Service, Hamburger & Viderø, eds., Hansen.
VIERNE, LOUIS-VICTOR-JULES.   born Poitiers, France, Oct. 8,
1870; died Paris, June 2, 1937.   Pupil of Franck, Widor,
and Marty; 1892, became assistant to Widor at St. Sulpice;
assistant to both Widor and Guilmant at the Conservatory,
Paris; 1900-1937, organist, Cathedral of Notre Dame, Paris;
from 1912, taught organ, Schola Cantorum; taught Boulanger,
Dupré, and Bonnet.
Allegretto in B Minor, Op. 1, Leduc, 1894; also Kalmus
4041.
Allegro vivace (Symphonie I), in The French Organist,
Vol. I, p. 76.
Communion, Procure Générale.
Elévation; Communion (Messe Basse), in The French
Organist, Vol. II, p. 42.
Marche triomphale pour le centenaire de Napoléon, organ,
brass, and timpani, Salabert, 1921.
Menuet, in Historical Organ Recitals, Vol. 5, p. 88.
Messe Basse, Op. 30, Schola Cantorum, 1913; Lemoine.

Messe basse pour les defunts, Op. 62, Lemoine, 1936.
Pièces de fantaisie, 4 vols., Lemoine, 1926/1927, 1e
    Suite, Op. 51: Prelude; Andantino; Caprice; Inter-
    mezzo; Requiem aeternam; Marche nuptiale; 2e Suite,
    Op. 53: Lamento; Sicilienne; Hymne au Soleil; Deux
    follets; Clair de lune; Toccata; 3e Suite, Op. 54:
    Dédicace; Impromptu: Etoile du Soir; Fantômes; Sur
    le Rhin; Carillon de Westminster; 4e Suite, Op. 55:
    Aubade; Résignation; Cathédrales; Naïades; Gargouilles
    et Chimères; Les cloches de Hinckley.
Prélude in F-sharp Minor, Sénart, 1914.
Prélude funèbre, Leduc, 1896.
Sortie (Messe Basse), in The French Organist, Vol. I,
    p. 61.
Symphonie I, Op. 14, Hamelle, 1899; also Kalmus 4023.
Symphonie II, Op. 20, Hamelle, 1903; Kalmus 4024.
Symphonie III, Op. 28, Durand, 1912.
Symphonie IV, Op. 32, G. Schirmer, 1914.
Symphonie V, Op. 47, Durand, 1925.
Symphonie VI, Op. 59, Lemoine, 1931.
Triptyque, Op. 58, Lemoine, 1936.
Trois Improvisations (Matines; Communion; Stèle pour un
    enfant défunt) (reconstituted by M. Duruflé), Durand.
Vingt-quatre pièces en style libre, 2 vols., Durand, 1914.
compositions (3) in French Masterworks for Organ,
    Alexander Schreiner, ed., J. Fischer 9431, Glen
    Rock, N.J., 1958.
VIERNE, RENÉ. born Lille, France, Mar. 11, 1878; died in
    World War I, Mar. 29, 1918. Brother and pupil of Louis
    Vierne; pupil of Guilmant at the Conservatory, Paris; or-
    ganist, Notre-Dame-des-Champs, Paris.
    Dix pièces de différents styles pour orgue, Bureau d'édition
        de la Schola, 1908; also Kalmus 4040.
    Messe basse, Schola Cantorum, 1914.
    Prayer, in French Masterworks for Organ, Alexander
        Schreiner, ed., J. Fischer, p. 52.
    Prélude grave.
    Trois offertoires, Schola Cantorum, 1914.
    preludes on two gregorian hymns in Interludes, La Schola
        Paroissiale.
VILA, PEDRO ALBERTO. Spanish. born Vich, Spain, 1517; died
    Barcelona, Nov. 16, 1582. Represented in the anthology
    Libro de Cifra Nueva, 1557; 1538-1582, organist, and later
    canon, Cathedral, Barcelona.
    Tiento, in Early Spanish Organ Music, p. 12.
    Tiento, in Anthologia de Organistas Clásicos Españoles,
        Vol. I, p. 37.
VILLARD, JEAN-ALBERT. born Poitiers (Vienne), France,
    Dec. 9, 1920. 1945-1950, studied at the Ecole César-Franck,
    Paris; organ pupil of Edouard Souberbielle, Léonce de Saint-
    Martin, and Maurice Duruflé; composition pupil de Guy de
    Lioncourt; since 1950, organist, Cathedral, Poitiers.
    Appelons Nau sur Noël Poitevin, in Christmas Music by

Various French Composers, p. 3, Kalmus; also in
Orgue et Liturgie, Vol. 40, p. 3.
Elévation, Offertoire, Prélude et Fugue, Edition Carrara
(Bergamo, Italy).
VIOLA, ANSELM. Spanish. born 1739; died 1798.
Sonatina en Fa Menor, in Early Spanish Organ Music, p.
74.
VISÉE, ROBERT DE. French. born ca. 1650; died ca. 1725.
Theorbist and guitarist; ca. 1686-1721, court musician.
Tombeau de DuBut, in Cérémonies funèbres, L'Organiste
liturgique, Vol. 15, p. 8.
VIVIANI, GIOVANNI BONAVENTURA. Italian. Seventeenth century.
Florentine musician; 1672-1676 (1678?), composer, Imperial
court, Innsbruck; ca. 1688, maestro da cappella, Pistoia
Cathedral; composer of opera and oratorio.
Two Sonatas for Trumpet, Musica Rara (London).
VOGEL, WILLEM. Dutch. born 1920.
Es ist ein Ros', Ars Nova.
Fantasie on Song 62, Ars Nova.
Gezang 77 en 22.
Heilige Geist, Ars Nova.
Kleine Partita op Herzliebster Jesu.
Organ Chorale on Song 49, Ars Nova.
Partita on Christus resurrexit, Ars Nova.
Partita on Psalm 121 and Prelude on Psalm 122, Ars Nova.
Partita on Te Deum laudamus.
Partita on Wij loven u, o God and Postlude on Christus
is opgestanden, Ars Nova.
Psalm 43, Ars Nova.
Psalm 43 and Song 3, Ars Nova.
Psalm 77, Ars Nova.
Psalmmuziek, Ars Nova.
Sixteen Chorale Preludes, 3 series, Ars Nova.
Trio Sonate (1947).
Toccata on Psalm 150, Ars Nova.
Valerius Suite.
Variaties op Psalm 92, in Nederlandsche Orgelmuziek,
Zaandam.
chorale preludes (2) in Lent and Easter, Ars Nova.
chorale preludes (3) in Liturgical Suite I, Ars Nova.
chorale preludes (4) in Liturgical Suite II, Ars Nova.
VOGLER, ERNST. Swiss. born Mar. 8, 1929. Organ pupil of
Luigi Favini; composition pupil of Paul Müller; since 1962,
organist, Sargans, Switzerland.
Toccata I (1962), Breitkopf & Härtel, 1963.
Toccata II (1962), Breitkopf & Härtel, 1963.
VOGLER, (ABBÉ) GEORG JOSEPH. born Pleichach bei Würzburg,
Germany, June 15, 1749; died Darmstadt, May 6, 1814.
1763, matriculated, Würzburg University; studied law and
theology; pupil of Martini in Italy; 1773, took holy orders;
traveled a great deal; 1776, founded Mannheimer Tonschule;
1786, became royal Kapellmeister to Gustav III of Sweden;
founded national music school for orchestra musicians; 1792,

made study-trip to Portugal, North Africa, and Greece; 1897, appointed court choirmaster to Ludwig I; taught von Weber and Meyerbeer at the Tonschule, Darmstadt.

Gott der Vater, wohn uns bei, in Reinbrecht's Preludien-
buch, Viewig.

Gott sei gelobet, in Zorn's Preludien, Heinrichshofen.

Hier ist mein Herz, o Seel', in Hering's Orgel Musik,
Rieter-Biedermann.

VOGLER, JOHANN CASPAR. born Hausen bei Arnstadt, Germany,
May 23, 1696; buried Weimar, June 3, 1763. Pupil of J. S.
Bach in Arnstadt and Vetter in Rudolstadt; 1715-1721, or-
ganist, Stadtilm; 1721, appointed organist for the court,
Weimar.

Jesu Leiden, Pein und Tod, in Choralvorspiel alter Meister,
p. 136.

VOLCKMAR, TOBIAS. born Reichenstein, Germany, Mar. 18,
1678; died Hirschberg, Apr. 2 (not 22), 1756. Pupil of
J. Krieger; became organist-cantor, Reichenstein; named
organist, Geibsdorf bei Lauban; 1709, appointed music director, organist, Gnadenkirche, Hirschberg; 1724, made cantor
and music director.

Ach Gott, erhör mein Seufsen, in Seasonal Chorale Preludes, Book I, C. H. Trevor, ed. , Oxford.

Kyrie, Gott, Vater, in Chorale Preludes by Masters of
the Seventeenth and Eighteenth Centuries, p. 73.

chorale preludes (2) in Orgelchoräle um J. S. Bach,
G. Frotscher, ed. , Litolff.

chorale preludes in The Parish Organist, Vol. 8.

composition in Das Erbe deutschen Musik, Series I,
Vol. 9.

compositions in Masterpieces of Organ Music, Folio 19.

VON SALEM, BERNHARD. German. Sixteenth century. Represented by music in Sicher's Tabulaturbuch.

Resonet in Laudibus, in Frühmeister der deutschen Orgelkunst, p. 4.

VOSS, FRIEDRICH. born Halberstadt, Germany, Dec. 12, 1930.
1949-1954, studied at the Musikhochschule, Berlin; composition pupil of Reinhard Schwarz-Schilling; since 1954, devoted
himself to composition.

Partita cromatica (1968), Breitkopf & Härtel, AV 1968.

Toccata (1965), Breitkopf & Härtel 6491.

VRANKEN, JAAP. born Utrecht, The Netherlands, Apr. 16, 1897;
died The Hague, Apr. 20, 1956. Studied in the United States;
1920, returned to Holland; organist, St. Anthony's Church,
The Hague.

Koraal-improvisatie over Quasimodo, in Cantantibus
Organis, Vol. I, p. 15.

Koraalvariaties en Tripelfuga, Van Rossum R. 419.

Preludium en Fuga, Annie Bank.

Toccata en fuga over Veni Sancte Spiritus, Van Rossum
R. 234.

WAGENAAR, BERNARD. born Arnhem, The Netherlands, July 18, 1894; died York, Maine, May 19, 1971. 1914-1920, conductor-teacher in the Netherlands; 1920, came to the United States; 1921-1923, violinist in the New York Philharmonic Orchestra; 1925, began teaching at the Institute of Musical Art; 1927, appointed to the orchestration and composition faculty, Juilliard School of Music, New York City; taught Ellis B. Kohs, Norman dello Joio, and Ned Rorem.

    Ecologue, Gray (Contemporary Organ Series 5).

    Inleiding en fuga op een Russisch thema.

    Introduction and Fugue.

    O Haupt, voll Blut und Wunden.

WALCHA, HELMUT. born Leipzig, Germany, Oct. 27, 1907. Blind pupil of Ramin; 1929, became organist, Friedenskirche, Frankfurt; 1938, appointed professor, Musikhochschule, Frankfurt; since 1946, organist, Dreikönigskirche, Frankfurt-am-Main.

    Choralvorspiele, 3 vols. , Vol. I (1945), Peters 4850, 1954;
        Vol. II (1963), Peters 4871, 1963; Vol. III (1966),
        Peters 5999, 1966.

    Christ ist erstanden, in Cantantibus Organis, Vol. II,
        p. 19.

    Handel concerti, Helmut Walcha, ed. , Schott.

WALMISLEY, THOMAS ATTWOOD. born Westminster, London, Jan. 21, 1814; died Hastings, Jan. 17, 1856. Pupil of his father, Thomas Forbes Walmisley, and godfather, Thomas Attwood; 1830, became organist, Croydon Parish Church; 1833, appointed organist, Trinity and St. John's Colleges, Cambridge University; 1836, professor of music, 1838, B. A. , 1841, M. A. , 1847, Mus. , Doc. , Cambridge.

    Fugue in E Minor, Novello, 1839.

    Larghetto in F Minor, Novello, 1933.

    Organ Pieces, in Tallis to Wesley, Vol. 36, Hinrichsen
        1039.

    Prelude and Fugue in E Minor, Novello.

WALOND, WILLIAM. English. born 1725; died Oxford, 1770. 1757, Mus. B.

    Diapason movement in D Minor, in Twelve Short Pieces
        by Old English Composers, p. 28.

    Introduction and Toccata, Cramer.

    Introduction and Toccata, in Treasury of Early Organ
        Music, p. 18.

    Siciliana, in Three 18th Century Preludes, Cramer.

    Three Cornet Voluntaries for Organ or Harpsichord,
        Gordon Phillips, ed. , in Tallis to Wesley, Vol. 20,
        Hinrichsen 1770A, 1961.

    Three Voluntaries, in Tallis to Wesley, Vol. 32, Hinrichsen 1770B.

    Voluntary I, in Tallis to Wesley, Vol. I, p. 11, Hinrichsen 1713.

compositions in <u>English Organ Music of the Eighteenth</u>
<u>Century</u>, Vol. 2.
WALTHER, JOHANN GOTTFRIED.   born Erfurt, Germany, Sept. 18,
1684;   died Weimar, Mar. 23, 1748.   Pupil of J. Bernhard
Bach in Erfurt;   1702, appointed organist, Thomaskirche,
Erfurt;   1707, became organist, Stadtkirche, and (1720) court
musician, Weimar;   cousin and friend of J. S. Bach;   wrote
first musical encyclopedia, <u>Musicalisches Lexicon</u>, 1732.
<u>Alcuni variationi sopr'un basso continuo del Sig'r Corelli</u>,
in <u>European Organ Music of the 16th and 17th Cen-</u>
<u>turies</u>, p. 143.
<u>Ausgewählte Orgelwerke</u>, Heinz Lohmann, ed. , 3 vols. ,
Breitkopf & Härtel 6508a/c.
<u>Christus der uns selig macht</u>, in <u>Orgel Vorspiele zu den</u>
<u>Melodien des Choralbuchs</u>, Leuckart.
<u>Ciacona über O Jesu, du edle Gabe</u>, in <u>Chacones et Passa-</u>
<u>cailles</u>, <u>Orgue et Liturgie</u>, Vol. 22, p. 27.
<u>(A) Collection of Chorale Preludes</u>, Concordia 97-1462.
<u>Complete Organ Works</u>, Hugo Leichtentritt, ed. , in
<u>Denkmäler deutscher Tonkunst</u>, Vols. 26 and 27,
Breitkopf & Härtel, 1906.
<u>Concerto</u>, in <u>A Brief Compendium of Early Organ Music</u>,
p. 48.
<u>Concerto in A</u>, in <u>Die Orgel</u>, Series II, Vol. 23,
(Concordia 97-4949).
<u>Ein' feste Burg</u>, in <u>The First Four Centuries of Organ</u>
<u>Music</u>, Vol. II, p. 461.
<u>Fünf ausgewählte Orgelstücke</u>, in <u>Organum</u>, Series IV,
Vol. 15, (Concordia 97-4347).
<u>Fuga</u>, in <u>Ricercare, Canzonen und Fugen des 17. und 18.</u>
<u>Jahrhunderts</u>, p. 34.
<u>Fuga</u>, in <u>Spielbuch für die Kleinorgel</u>, Vol. II, p. 56.
<u>Gelobet seist du</u>, in <u>Noël</u>, <u>Orgue et Liturgie</u>, Vol. 4, p. 18.
<u>I Come to Thee, O Blessed Lord</u>, in <u>Organ Music for the</u>
<u>Communion Service</u>, p. 56.
<u>Lobe den Herren</u>, in <u>Anthologia pro Organo</u>, Vol. IV,
p. 48.
<u>Lobt Gott ihr</u>, in <u>Seasonal Chorale Preludes</u> (with pedals),
C. H. Trevor, ed. , Book I, Oxford.
<u>Nun komm</u>, in <u>Viens, Sauveur</u>, <u>Orgue et Liturgie</u>, Vol. 19,
p. 20.
<u>Orgelchoräle</u> (48), Poppen, ed. , Bärenreiter 379.
<u>Orgelkonzerte nach verschiedenen Meistern</u>, Bärenreiter
1920.
<u>Pastorella</u>, in <u>Musica Organi</u>, Vol. I, p. 92.
<u>Praise God the Lord, Ye Sons of Men</u> (Partita), Concordia
97-3860.
<u>Prelude and Fugue in D Minor</u>, Concordia 97-3864.
<u>Prelude and Fugue in A</u>, Concordia 97-3863.
<u>Six Chorale Preludes</u>, Walter Emery, ed. , Novello O. C.
(New) 211.
<u>Three Chorale Preludes</u>, Walter Emery, ed. , Novello
O. C. (New) 196.

Toccata and Fuge, in La Fugue au XVIIIe siècle, Orgue et
   Liturgie, Vol. 15, p. 12.
Variationen über Meinen Jesum, in Alte Meister, p. 100;
   also Peters 4301P.
Wachet auf, in The Lutheran Organist, Concordia.
Warum betrübst, in Anthologia pro Organo, Vol. II, p. 59.
Wie soll ich dich, in Passion, L'Organiste liturgique,
   Vol. I, p. 3; also in Geschichte der Musik in
   Beispielen, p. 431.
chorale preludes (7) in Alte Weihnachtsmusik.
chorale preludes (5) in Choralvorspiel alter Meister.
chorale preludes (5) in Choralvorspiele zum Kirchenlied,
   Vol. 3, Christophorus.
chorale preludes (9) in Chorale Preludes by Masters of
   the Seventeenth and Eighteenth Centuries.
chorale preludes (114) in Denkmäler deutscher Tonkunst,
   Vols. 26 and 27, Breitkopf & Härtel.
chorale preludes in Eighty Chorale Preludes: German
   Masters of the Seventeenth and Eighteenth Centuries.
chorale preludes in The Church Organist's Golden Treasury,
   Vol. I (8), Vol. II (24), Vol. III (15).
chorale preludes (3) in Harold Gleason, Method of Organ
   Playing.
chorale preludes (4) in Laudamus Dominum.
chorale preludes (11) in Orgel Choräle Sammlung, Metzler.
chorale preludes (2) in Orgelchoräle des siebzehnten und
   achtzehnten Jahrhunderts.
chorale preludes in Orgelspiel im Kirchenjahr, Rohr, ed.,
   Vol. I (15) and Vol. 2 (9), Schott.
chorale preludes in The Parish Organist, Vols. 1-4, 5, 6,
   7, 8, and 10.
chorale preludes (5) in Ritter Sammlung, Ries & Erler.
chorale preludes in Seasonal Chorale Preludes (manuals
   alone), C. H. Trevor, ed., Book I (1) and Book II
   (2), Oxford.
compositions in Masterpieces of Organ Music, Commemora-
   tion Folio and Folios 3, 5, 18, 19, 39, and 54.
trios (2) in Schule des klassischen Triospiels.
WALTON, KENNETH. born Tulse Hill, London, Feb. 17, 1904.
   American citizen.
   Christmas Rhapsody, Leeds.
   Cradle Song, Boosey and Hawkes.
   Easter Fantasia, Sprague-Coleman.
   Fantasia on Four Christmas Carols, Broadcast.
   Fantasie on Come, Holy Ghost, Sprague-Coleman.
   Fantasia on Mercy, Boston Music Co.
   Lo, He Comes with Clouds Descending, Leeds, 1943.
   O Come, Emmanuel, Leeds, 1943.
   Prelude on Coventry Carol, Sprague-Coleman.
   Prelude on O Saving Victim, Sprague-Coleman.
WALTON, (SIR) WILLIAM TURNER. born Oldham, Lancashire,
   England, Mar. 29, 1902. Studied at Christ Church College;
   pupil of Hugh Allen; honorary Mus. Doc., Durham University;

1937, Fellow of the Royal College of Music; an outstanding
twentieth-century English orchestral and choral composer.
    Three Pieces (March; Elegy; Scherzetto), Oxford, 1963.
WARNER, RICHARD L. American. born 1908. Faculty member,
Kent State University.
    Dialogue on a Noël, Gray (St. Cecilia Series 787).
    Draw Nigh and Take the Body of the Lord, in Organ Music
       for the Communion Service, p. 30.
    Let All Mortal Flesh, in Organ Music for the Communion
       Service, p. 9.
    Prelude on Quem pastores, Gray (St. Cecilia Series 802).
    Ten Short Preludes on Hymns and Carols, C. Fischer.
WARTECKI, MARCIN. Polish?. Sixteenth century. 1564-1565,
employed at the Polish court.
    compositions (3) in Keyboard Music from Polish Manuscripts,
       in Corpus of Early Keyboard Music, No. 10, Vol. 4.
WATERS, CHARLES FREDERICK. born Epsom, Surrey, England,
1895. 1928-1948, organist, Epsom Parish Church; 1948-
1957, organist, St. James, Malden; since 1966, organist-
choirmaster, All Saints & St. Barnabas, Lambeth, London;
Mus. D. , University of London; Fellow, Royal College of
Organists; Commander of the British Empire.
    Basso Staccato (Alla marcia), Cramer.
    Canon Gavotte, Cramer.
    Fantasy Fugue, Cramer.
    Gloria in Excelsis, Cramer.
    Introit, Cramer.
    Litany, in Preludes, Interludes, Postludes, Hinrichsen
       600C.
    Liturgical Meditations (3), Hinrichsen 588.
    Meditation, Cramer.
    (An) Organ Mass, Hinrichsen 587.
    Pavan, Cramer.
    Pavan, Leonard, Gould & Bottler, 1968.
    Postlude, Cramer.
    Postlude on Nun danket alle Gott, Cramer.
    Prelude on Bourgeois' Psalm 118 (Introit), Cramer.
    Prelude on Tallis' Ordinal, Cramer.
    Reverie, Cramer.
    Romance, Oxford.
    Verset, Cramer.
WEAVER, JOHN. American. Twentieth century. Organist,
Holy Trinity Lutheran, New York City; 1970, appointed
organist-choirmaster, Madison Avenue Presbyterian, New
York City.
    Toccata, Boosey & Hawkes, 1968.
WEAVER, POWELL. born Clearfield, Penn. , June 19, 1890;
died Kansas City, Mo. , Dec. 22, 1951. Pupil of Pietro
Yon and Respighi; piano accompanist.
    Copper County Sketches, Gray.
    (The) Squirrel, J. Fischer, 1926.
    Still Waters, Gray (St. Cecilia Series 777).
WEBBER, WILLIAM SOUTHCOMBE LLOYD. born Chelsea,

England, 1914. 1921-1932, organist-choirmaster, Christ
Church, Newgate Street, London; 1931-1937, studied at the
Royal College of Music (F. R. C. M.); Fellow of the Royal
College of Organists; 1933-1939, organist-choirmaster, St.
Cyprian's, Clarence Gate, London; 1938, D. Mus. , University of London; 1939-1948, organist-choirmaster, All Saints,
Margaret Street, London; since 1945, examiner and professor
in theory and composition, Royal College of Music; 1945-
1964, examiner to the Associated Board of the Royal Schools
of Music; since 1964, director, London College of Music.

> Chorale, Cantilena and Finale, Novello.
> Chorale Prelude on Sacerdos et pontifex, Junfermann.
> Five Versets, Novello, 1964.
> Six Interludes on Christmas Carols, Novello.
> Six Interludes on Passion Hymns, Novello.
> Suite in B-flat Major, Bosworth, 1951.
> Three Improvisations, Novello, 1965.
> hymn preludes (2) in Festal Voluntaries (Advent, Harvest),
> Novello.

WECK, JOHANN (HANS). German. flourished ca. 1510. Organist,
Freiburg-im-Breisgau.

> Spanyöler Tancz, in Historical Anthology of Music, Vol. I,
> p. 104; also in Willi Apel, Masters of the Keyboard,
> p. 44.

WECKMANN, MATTHIAS. born Niederdorla (Mühlhausen), Germany, 1619; died Hamburg, Feb. 24, 1674. Pupil of Heinrich Schütz, Scheidemann, and Jacob Praetorius; 1641, became court organist, Dresden; 1642, appointed to court
position, Copenhagen; friend of Froberger; 1655, became
organist, Jacobikirche and Katrinenkirche, Hamburg.

> Ach, wir, in Choralvorspiel alter Meister, p. 161.
> Gelobet seist du, Jesu Christ, in Elf Orgelchoräle des
> siebzehnten Jahrhunderts.
> Nun freut euch, in The Church Organist's Golden Treasury,
> Vol. III, p. 9; also in Eighty Chorale Preludes:
> German Masters of the Seventeenth and Eighteenth
> Centuries, p. 96; also in Chorale Preludes of the
> Seventeenth and Eighteenth Centuries, Concordia;
> also in Orgel Choräle Sammlung, Metzler.
> Nun freut euch, in The First Four Centuries of Organ
> Music, Vol. II, p. 252.
> Sarabande; Allemande, in Spielbuch für die Kleinorgel,
> Vol. I, p. 44.
> chorale preludes (2) in Orgelchoräle des siebzehnten und
> achtzehnten Jahrhunderts.
> chorale preludes in The Parish Organist, Vol. 8.
> composition in Free Organ Compositions from Lüneburg
> Tablature, Vol. I, p. 45, possibly by Weckmann.
> compositions (14) in Organum, Series IV, Vol. 3,
> (Concordia 97-4335).
> composition in Masterpieces of Organ Music, Folio 35.

WEINBERG, JACOB. born Odessa, Russia, July 5, 1879; died
New York City, Nov. 2, 1956. Studied at the Moscow

Conservatory with Ippolitov-Ivanov and Leschetisky; 1915-
1921, member of the piano faculty, Conservatory, Odessa;
1921-1926, lived in Palestine; 1926, faculty member, Hunter
College and New York College of Music, New York City.
Two Ceremonial Marches, Mercury Music Press.
WEINBERGER, JAROMIR. born Prague, Jan. 8, 1896; died in
Florida, Aug. 9, 1967. 1910-1915, studied at the Conserva-
tory, Prague; pupil of Reger in Leipzig; 1922, came to the
United States; 1922-1923, taught composition, Ithaca College;
1923, returned to Czechoslovakia; lived in Baden (Vienna),
Prague, and Paris; 1939, returned to the United States.
  Bible Poems, Gray, 1939.
  Dedications, Gray.
  Meditations, Gray.
  Six Religious Preludes, Gray, 1946.
  Sonata, Gray.
WEISMANN, WILHELM. born Altdorf, Wittenberg, Germany, 1900.
Professor, Staatliche Hochschule für Musik, Leipzig.
  O Traurigkeit, in The Parish Organist, Vol. 7.
WEISS, EWALD. born Wolhynien, Poland, 1906. Church Music
Director, Bayreuth, Germany; writes in a new tonal idiom.
  Introduktion und Chaconne (1964), Breitkopf & Härtel 6476.
  Zehn Orgelchoräle (1967), Breitkopf & Härtel 6535.
  chorale preludes (2) in Orgelvorspiele, Poppen, Reich &
    Strube, eds., Merseburger.
  chorale preludes (2) in The Parish Organist, Vols. 11 and
    12.
WEITZ, GUY. born Verviers, Belgium, Sept. 5, 1883; died Lon-
don, Mar. 23, 1970. Studied at the Conservatory, Liège, and
Schola Cantorum, Paris; pupil of d'Indy, Guilmant, and Widor;
1914, honorary organist, Westminster Cathedral, London;
1917-1967, organist, Jesuit Church, London.
  Byzantine Suite.
  Christmas Rhapsody.
  De profundis clamavi, in The Modern Anthology, p. 194.
  Fanfare and Gothic March.
  In Paradisum.
  Missa de Angelis.
  Mortify Us by Thy Grace.
  Paraphrase on Regina coeli laetare, Hinrichsen 1046B.
  Prière on Salve regina in Fifth Mode, Hinrichsen 1046D,
    1966.
  Sicilienne.
  Symphony (I), Chester 3038, 1932.
  Symphony II, Chester, 1936.
  Two Pieces on Plainchant, Hinrichsen 1046A.
WELIN, KARL-ERIK. Swedish. born 1934. Associated with
Swedish radio system.
  Introduktion och fuga (1956), Eriks.
WELLESZ, EGON. born Vienna, Oct. 21, 1885. Pupil of Guido
Adler and Schoenberg; 1908, Ph.D., Vienna; 1911-1915,
taught, Neues Conservatorium, Vienna; 1913, appointed lec-
turer, 1930-1938, professor, University of Vienna; 1932,

honorary Mus. Doc., 1943, became lecturer, Oxford University, 1948, University Reader in Byzantine Music; 1946, appointed member of the editorial board, New Oxford History of Music; 1956-1957, lecturer in the United States.

Partita in honorem J. S. Bach, Doblinger.

WERNER, GREGOR JOSEPH. Austrian. born 1695; died Eisenstadt, Mar. 3, 1766. 1728-1766, Kapellmeister to Prince Esterházy (Haydn was Vice-Kapellmeister).

Christmas Pastorella, organ and strings, Bärenreiter 953.

Pastorella in D Major, organ and strings, Bärenreiter 1557.

WESLEY, CHARLES. born Bristol, England, Dec. 11, 1757; died London, May 23, 1834. Son of Charles Wesley, the Methodist preacher and hymn-writer; pupil of Boyce in London; played for King George III; organist, South Street Chapel, Welbeck Chapel, Chelsea Hospital; 1820-1834, organist, Marlybone Parish Church.

Concerto IV, Hinrichsen 290A.

No. 4, from Six Concertos, Op. 2a, 1780, Finzi, ed., Hinrichsen, 1961.

Prelude and Fugue in A Minor, in Tallis to Wesley, Vol. 5, p. 3, Hinrichsen 1757A.

Prelude and Fugue in G Minor, in Tallis to Wesley. Vol. 24, p. 1, Hinrichsen 1757B.

WESLEY, SAMUEL. born Bristol, England, Feb. 24, 1766; died London, Oct. 11, 1837. Son of Charles Wesley, the Methodist preacher and hymn-writer; child prodigy; 1777, played in a Bach-Abel concert; taught privately; 1784-1809, music teacher in a girls' school, Marlybone; encouraged the study of Bach and organized concerts of Bach's works; 1811, appointed director-organist, Birmingham Festival; 1824-1830, organist, Camden Chapel; his last composition was Fugue in B Minor "composed expressly for Dr. Mendelssohn."

Air and Gavotte, Hinrichsen 1766D.

Allegro Fugato (F), Cramer.

Duet for Organ, Walter Emery, ed., Novello EOM 19, 1964.

Fugue in B Minor, in Tallis to Wesley, Vol. 14, p. 9, Hinrichsen 1744B.

Full Voluntary (Prelude and Fugue), in Tallis to Wesley, Vol. 5, p. 7, Hinrichsen 1757A.

Holsworthy Church Bells, Cramer.

(An) Old English Melody, Hinrichsen 1766.

Prelude and Fugue (C Minor), in Tallis to Wesley, Vol. 24, Hinrichsen 1757B.

Prelude and Fugue (D Major), in Liber Organi, Vol. 10, p. 31.

Three Short Pieces, John E. West, ed., Novello.

Trumpet Duet, Cramer.

Twelve Short Pieces, Hinrichsen 1766A.

Two Short Pieces, Basil Ramsey, ed., Novello EOM 3, 1961.

Two Short Pieces in A Minor, Basil Ramsey, ed., Novello EOM 10, 1961.

Voluntary (D Major), Hinrichsen 229.
compositions (2) in Twelve Short Pieces by Old English
    Composers.

WESLEY, SAMUEL SEBASTIAN. born London, Aug. 14, 1810;
    died Gloucester, Apr. 19, 1876. Son of Samuel Wesley;
    choirboy in Chapel Royal; 1826-1832, organist, various Lon-
    don churches; 1832, named organist, Hereford Cathedral;
    1835, became organist, Exeter Cathedral; concertized; 1841-
    1844, held chair of music, Edinburgh University; taught at
    the Royal Academy of Music; 1839, Mus. Doc., Oxford
    University.
        Andante in E Minor, in Tallis to Wesley, Vol. 13,
            Hinrichsen 541B.
        Andante in E-flat Major, in Tallis to Wesley, Vol. 24,
            p. 13, Hinrichsen 1757B.
        Andante in G Major, Hinrichsen 541A.
        Choral Song, in Tallis to Wesley, Vol. 5, p. 16,
            Hinrichsen 1757A.
        Choral Song and Fugue in C, Walter Emery, ed., Novello.
        Fourteen Organ Pieces by S. Wesley and S. S. Wesley,
            Marchant, ed., Wickins, (London) 1909.
        Larghetto in F-sharp Minor, H. A. Chambers, ed.,
            Novello.
        National Anthem with Variations, Novello.
        Selection of Psalm Tunes with Pedal Obligato, John E.
            West, ed., Novello.

WEST, JOHN EBENEZER. born London, Dec. 7, 1863; died
    London, Feb. 28, 1929. Pupil of uncle, Ebenezer Prout, at
    the Royal Academy of Music; organist and choirmaster,
    London churches; 1884, joined editorial staff of Novello
    Company.
        Chorale Fantasie on Bristol, Gray (St. Cecilia Series 92).
        Chorale Preludes (3), Novello.
        Fantasy on two well-known Christmas Carols, Novello.
        Festal Commemoration.
        Grand Chorus, Edition Musicus.
        Improvisation on We Plough, in Harvest Festival Music,
            Novello.
        Pastoral Melody and Lament.
        Postlude in B-flat.
        Prelude on Fatherland, Novello.
        Sonata (D Minor), Novello.
        Three Choral Preludes, Novello.
        Three Preludes, 2 sets.
        Three Short Pieces.
        Variations on an Old Easter Melody, Novello.

WEYRAUCH, JOHANNES WILHELM ROBERT. born Leipzig,
    Feb. 20, 1897. Studied at the Conservatory, Leipzig; pupil
    of Karg-Elert, Riemann, and Schering; 1922-1923, staff
    member, Litolff publishing house; 1924-1936, private music
    teacher, Leipzig; 1936-1961, Kantor and organist of various
    churches, Leipzig; 1946, appointed instructor, 1953-1962,
    professor, theory and composition, Hochschule für Musik,

Leipzig.
Herzliebster Jesu, was hast du verbrochen (Sonata), viola
and organ, (Peters H E 13.3) Sirius.
Präludium, Aria e Fuga (1935), Breitkopf & Härtel 5705.
Sieben Partiten auf das Kirchenjahr; Choralpartita über Nun
bitten wir (1939), Breitkopf & Härtel 5732; Choralpartita über Unüberwindlich starker Held, St. Michael
(1940), Breitkopf & Härtel 5734; Choralpartita über
Heut' triumphieret Gottes Sohn (1939), Breitkopf und
Härtel; Choralpartita über Ich weiss ein lieblich
Engelspiel (1939), Breitkopf und Härtel; Choralpartita
über Singet frisch und wohlgemut (1938), Breitkopf
und Härtel.
Sonate (1954), Peters 1955.
chorale preludes (5) in Einfache Orgelvorspiele, Weber,
ed. , C. Kaiser.
chorale preludes (7) in 73 leichte Choralvorspiele alter
und neuer Meister, H. Fleischer, ed. , Leuckart.
WHETTAM, GRAHAM DUDLEY. born Swindon, Wiltshire, England,
1927.
Fantasia, in Modern Organ Music, p. 24.
Partita, Op. 49, Ascherberg, 1964.
Triptych, Ascherberg, 1966.
WHITE, LOUIE L. born Spartanburg, So. Car. , Aug. 1, 1921.
1946, Mus. B. , Converse College; 1948, Mus. M. , Syracuse
University; composition pupil of Ernest Bacon, Edwin Ger-
sitefski, Pedro San Juan, and Nathaniel Hyatt; 1953-1969,
head, music department, Brearly School, New York City;
since 1964, lecturer in composition, Union Theological Semi-
nary, New York City; since 1970, faculty member, Rutgers
University.
Sonata, Gray.
WHITE, ROBERT. born in England, ca. 1530; died London,
November 1574. 1560, Mus. Bac. , Cambridge University;
1561-1565, choirmaster, Ely Cathedral; 1570, choirmaster,
Westminster Abbey.
Upon ut re mi fa sol la, in Altenglische Orgelmusik, p. 15.
WHITING, GEORGE ELBRIDGE. born Holliston, Mass. , Sept. 14,
1840; died Cambridge, Mass. , Oct. 14, 1923. Organist,
North Congregational Church, Hartford; 1863, pupil of
William Best in Liverpool, England; organist, St. Joseph's
Church, Albany, N. Y. ; organist, King's Chapel, Boston;
1874, went to study in Berlin; 1880-1883, taught at the Cin-
cinnati College of Music; 1883-1897, taught organ, New
England Conservatory, Boston.
Improvisation on a Bach Theme, in Early American Com-
positions for Organ, p. 17.
Six Postludes on Church Melodies, Theodore Presser.
(The) Son of God Goes Forth to War, Theodore Presser.
Twenty Preludes and Postludes, A. P. Schmidt.
WHITLOCK, PERCY WILLIAM. born Chatham, England, June 1,
1903; died Bournemouth, May 1, 1946. Studied at Kings
School and the Royal College of Music; 1912-1930, assistant

organist, Rochester Cathedral; 1924-1928, organist-choir-
master, Chatham Parish Church; 1929-1930, organist,
Borstal Church, Rochester; 1930-1935, director of music,
St. Stephen's, Bournemouth; 1932-1946, borough organist,
Municipal Pavilion, Bournemouth.

> Five Short Pieces (Allegretto; Folk Tune; Andante tran-
> quillo; Scherzo; Paean), Oxford, 1930.
> Four Extemporisations (Carol; Divertimento; Fidelis;
> Fanfare), Oxford.
> Plymouth Suite (Allegro risoluto; Lantana; Chanty; Salix;
> Toccata), Oxford.
> Reflections (After an Old French Air; Pazienza; Dolcezza),
> Oxford.
> Seven Sketches on Verses from the Psalms, Oxford:
> Book 1: Pastorale; Duetto; Plaint; Exultemus;
> Book 2: Préambule; Intermezzo; Sortie.
> Six Hymn-Preludes (2 sets), Oxford, 1945.
> Sonata in C Minor, Oxford.
> Symphony, organ and orchestra.
> Two Fantasy-Chorals (D-flat Major, F-sharp Minor),
> Oxford.

WHITNEY, MAURICE C. born Glen Falls, N.Y., Mar. 25, 1909.
B.S., Ithaca College; M.A., New York University; studied
at Teachers College, Columbia University, Westminster Choir
College, and New England Conservatory; 1935, became
organist-choirmaster, Christ Church, Glen Falls, N.Y.;
1932-1944, school music educator, Hudson Falls, N.Y.;
since 1944, school music teacher, Glen Falls, N.Y.

> Aberystwyth, in The International Organist, Vol. I, p. 80.
> Improvisation on God of Grace, Gray (St. Cecilia Series
> 920).
> Improvisation on Miles Lane, Gray (St. Cecilia Series 811).
> Improvisation on St. Agnes, Gray (St. Cecilia Series 812).
> Joy to the World, Gray (St. Cecilia Series 776).
> (A) Mountain Spiritual, Gray (St. Cecilia Series 769).
> Postlude on Come, Thou Almighty King, Gray (St. Cecilia
> Series 712), 1945.
> Prelude on Nun danket alle Gott, Gray (St. Cecilia Series
> 702).

WIDOR, CHARLES-MARIE-JEAN-ALBERT. born Lyon, France,
Feb. 21, 1844; died Paris, Mar. 12, 1937. Pupil of Lemmens and Fétis; 1860, appointed organist, St. François,
Lyon; 1869-1937, organist, St. Sulpice, Paris (64 years);
1890, appointed professor of organ, Conservatory, Paris
(succeeded Franck); 1896, became professor of composition,
(succeeded Dubois), later director, Conservatory, Paris.

> Adagio (Symphonie VI), in The French Organist, Vol. II,
> p. 38.
> Andante sostenuto (Symphonie Gothique), in French Master-
> works for Organ, J. Fischer, p. 8.
> Chorale and Variations, harp and organ.
> Conte d'Avril, Heugel.
> Domine salvum fac populum, organ and brass, Mercury.

Symphonie I, Hamelle, 1901; Kalmus 4029.
Symphonie II, Hamelle, 1901; Marks, 1936; Kalmus 4030.
Symphonie III, Hamelle, 1901; Kalmus 4031.
Symphonie IV, Marks, 1936; Kalmus 4032.
Symphonie V, Marks, 1936; Kalmus 4033.
Symphonie VI, Hamelle; Marks, 1941; Kalmus 4034.
Symphonie VII, Hamelle, 1901; Marks, 1947; Kalmus 4035.
Symphonie VIII, Marks; also Kalmus 4036.
Symphonie Gothique, Op. 70, Schott 1895.
Symphonie Romane, Hamelle, 1900.
Marche Nuptiale, Heugel.
Pastorale (Symphonie II), in The French Organist, Vol. I, p. 23.
Sinfonia Sacra, organ and orchestra, Op. 81, Hamelle.
Suite latine, Durand, 1927.
Trois nouvelles pièces, Durand, 1934.
Troisième Symphonie, Op. 69, organ and orchestra, Schott.

WIEDERMANN, BEDŘICH ANTONÍN. Czech. born 1883; died 1951. Organ teacher, Conservatory, Prague (succeeded Klička), and at the Composers' College; toured as concert organist in Europe and America.
Drei Stücke, (Bärenreiter AP 1147).
Pastorale Dorico, in Musica Boemica per Organo, Vol. I, p. 68.
Prelude on Passion Chorale, United Music Publishers.
Three Chorale Preludes, Hudebni Matice (Bärenreiter A P 1146).

WIEMER, WOLFGANG. German. born Feb. 16, 1934. Organ pupil of Helmut Walcha; composition pupil of Kurt Hessenberg; 1960, appointed organist, Dornbuschkirche, Frankfurt-am Main; teacher, Laubach.
Choralfantasie über Erhalt uns, Herr (1961), Breitkopf & Härtel 6430, 1964.
Choralvorspiele II (1969), Breitkopf & Härtel 6558, 1970.
Evocation I (1965), Breitkopf & Härtel 6523, 1967.
Evocation II, Breitkopf & Härtel 6557, 1969.
Partita über Jesus Christus, unser Heiland, Breitkopf & Härtel 6407, 1962.
Präludium, Trio und Fuge (1963), Breitkopf & Härtel 6467, 1965.
Sechs Choralvorspiele (1961), Breitkopf & Härtel 6408, 1962.

WIENHORST, RICHARD. born Seymour, Ind., Apr. 21, 1920. 1942, A. B., Valparaiso University, Valparaiso, Ind.; 1948, M. Mus., American Conservatory, Chicago; 1962, Ph. D., Eastman School of Music; composition pupil of Leo Sowerby, Bernard Rogers, Howard Hanson, and Nadia Boulanger; 1947, appointed to faculty, Valparaiso University.
Lord Jesus Christ, Thou Hast Prepared, in Organ Music for the Communion Service, p. 25.
Take Thou My Hands and Lead Me, in Wedding Music, Concordia.

chorale preludes (3) in The Parish Organist, Vols. 1-4, 11, and 12.

WIKANDER, DAVID. born Säfnäs, Sweden, July 21, 1884; died 1955. Studied at the Conservatory, Stockholm; 1914-1934, teacher of singing in folk schools, Stockholm; 1920-1952, organist, Storkyrka.

Jesus från Nasaret, in Himmelriket är nära, Nordiska.

Julmusik över En jungfru födde ett barn idag, Nordiska.

Kyrie eleison, in Orgelmusik vid jordfästning, Albert Runbäck, ed. , Nordiska.

Litet Preludium och Passacaglia över Jesu från Nasaret, Nordiska.

Meditation, Nordiska.

Passacaglia över Jag ville lova och prisa, Nordiska; also in Musica Organi, Vol. III, p. 124.

Preludier till den svenska koralbokens, Verbum.

Sonata över Hit, o Jesu, samloms vi, Nordiska.

Tre Pingstmelodier (1950), Nordiska.

Variationer över två sommarkoraler, Nordiska.

chorale preludes in Introituspreludier för orgel, Albert Runbäck and Waldemar Åhlén, eds. , Vol. I (1), Vol. II (3).

chorale preludes in Postludier för kyrkoårets samtliga sön- och helgdagar, Albert Runbäck and Waldemar Åhlén, eds. , Nordiska, Vol. I (1), Vol. III (2).

WILDBERGER, JACQUES. born Basel, Switzerland, Mar. 1, 1922. Pupil of W. Vogel; teacher, Municipal Academy, Basel.

Fünf Stücke, Gerig.

WILLAERT, ADRIAAN. born Bruges, Belgium, ca. 1490; died Venice, Dec. 8, 1562. Studied in Paris and in Italy; 1527, appointed choirmaster, San Marco, Venice; taught Zarlino, de Rore, and A. Gabrieli; founded Venetian school of composition.

Ricercar, in Geschichte der Musik in Beispielen, p. 102.

ricercars in Oudnederlandse Meesters, Vol. I (3), Vol. II (1), p. 36, Vol. III (1), p. 36.

WILLAN, JAMES HEALEY. born Balham, Surrey, England, Oct. 12, 1880; died Toronto, Canada, Feb. 16, 1968. Organist, London; 1913, went to Canada; taught, Royal Conservatory, Toronto; 1920-1936, vice-principal, Royal Conservatory, Toronto; 1914, appointed teacher, 1932-1964, university organist, 1937-1950, professor, University of Toronto; organist-choirmaster, St. Paul's Church, Toronto; 1921-1928, organist-director of music, St. Mary Magdalene; honorary president, Canadian College of Organists.

Adoro te devote, in Organ Music for the Communion Service, p. 5.

Andante, Fugue and Chorale, Peters 6858, 1965.

Chorale Prelude on Puer nobis nascitur, Oxford.

Elegy, in The Modern Anthology, p. 200.

Ephithalame (Sortie), Berandol.

Epilogue on St. Theodulph, Novello.

Evensong, Peters 6359.

Five Pieces, in Organ Music of Canada, Vol. I, p. 7.
Five Preludes on Plainchant Melodies, Oxford, 1951.
(A) Fugal Trilogy (Chorale and Fugue; Aria and Fugue; Elegy and Fugue), Oxford.
Interlude for a Festival (Coronation Suite), Berandol.
Introduction, Passacaglia and Fugue, Oxford.
Lord of All Hopefulness, Peters.
Matins, Peters 6358.
Passacaglia and Fugue No. 2 (E Minor), Peters 6145.
Postlude in D Major, in An Album of Praise, p. 18.
Postlude in E Minor, in Preludes, Interludes, Postludes, Hinrichsen 600A.
Prelude and Fugue in B Minor, Novello, 1909.
Prelude on Ad coenam agni, Novello.
Prelude on Andernach, Oxford.
Prelude on Slane, Peters 66034.
Prelude on Te lucis ante terminum, Oxford.
Preludes on St. Theodulph and Ascension, in Festal Voluntaries (Lent, Ascension), Novello.
Rondino, Elegy and Chaconne, Novello.
Six Chorale Preludes, 2 sets of six each, Concordia 97-3903 and 97-3905.
Thirty Hymn-preludes, 3 vols., Peters 6100-6013.
Thirty-six Short Preludes or Postludes on Well-known Hymn-Tunes, 3 vols., Peters 6161-6163.
hymn-preludes in The Parish Organist, Vols. 1-4, 7, 8, 11, and 12.

WILLIAMS, DAVID HENRY. born Caerphilly, Wales, Nov. 21, 1919. Organist-choirmaster at the following churches: St. John's Episcopal, Flushing, N.Y., Ft. Washington Collegiate Church, New York City; Saugatuck Congregational Church, Westport, Conn., First Congregational Church, Woodstock, Vt., and St. Andrew's Presbyterian Church, Tucson, Ariz.

Carol Prelude on Bring a Torch, Gray (St. Cecilia Series 864), 1959.
Carol Prelude on God Rest Ye Merry, Gray (St. Cecilia Series 873).
Meditation on Pange lingua, Gray (St. Cecilia Series 857).
Prelude on Veni Emmanuel, J. Fischer.

WILLIAMSON, MALCOLM. born Sydney, Australia, Nov. 21, 1931. Pupil of Eugene Goosens at the Conservatory, Sydney; studied composition in London; organist in England; 1970-1971, composer-in-residence, Westminster Choir College, Princeton, N.J.

Elegy-J. F. K., Weinberger, 1964.
Epitaphs for Edith Sitwell, Weinberger, 1968.
Fons Amoris, Novello, 1965.
Organ Symphony, Novello.
Peace Pieces (1971), Weinberger.
Resurgence du Feu, Chappell.
Vision of Christ Phoenix, Chappell.

WILLS, ARTHUR WILLIAM. born Coventry, England, 1926. Since 1949, organist and master of the choristers, Ely Cathedral;

Doc. Mus.
  Alla Marcia, Novello, 1962.
  Christmas Meditations, Novello.
  Concerto, organ, strings, and timpani, Boosey & Hawkes.
  Deo Gracias, Novello.
  Elegy, Novello.
  Eucharistic Suite, Novello.
  Five Pieces (Procession; Arioso; Intermezzo; Requiem
       aeternam; Finale), Novello, 1963.
  Introduction and Allegro, Novello.
  Postlude, Novello.
  Prelude and Fugue, Novello, 1965.
  Sonata, Boosey & Hawkes.
  Variations on a Carol: I Sing the Birth, Novello, 1967.
WINDSPERGER, LOTHAR. born Ampfing, Germany, Oct. 22, 1885;
  died Wiesbaden, May 29, 1935. 1913, became artistic ad-
  viser, B. Schotts Söhne, Mainz.
     Sonata in E Major, Op. 11, No. 2, organ and cello,
        Schott 1999.
     Sonata in F-sharp Minor, Op. 11, No. 1, organ and
        violin, Schott 1967.
     Three Small Pieces, Schott.
WISHART, PETER CHARLES ARTHUR. born Crowborough, Sussex,
  England, 1921. Studied at Birmingham University; pupil of
  Nadia Boulanger; teacher, Birmingham University; 1961,
  appointed professor, Guildhall School of Music, London.
     Pastorale and Fughetta, Hinrichsen 1040A.
     Trio Sonata in B-flat Major, Oxford.
WITTE, CHRISTIAN FRIEDRICH. born Altenburg, Germany, 1660;
  died Altenburg, Apr. 13, 1716.
     Herr Christ der einig, in Orgelchoräle um J. S. Bach,
        G. Frotscher, ed. , Litolff.
     compositions in Das Erbe deutschen Musik, Series I,
        Vol. 9.
WOLFF, FÉLICIEN. born St. Aubin-les-Elbeuf (Seine-Maritime),
  France, July 21, 1913. Studied at the Conservatory, Paris;
  pupil of Dupré (organ), Noël Gallon, and Paul Dukas (com-
  position); professor of organ and improvisation, Conservatory,
  Grenoble.
     Peinture sur bois, in Liturgie et concert, Orgue et
        Liturgie, Vol. 70, p. 24.
WOLFF, STANLEY DRUMMOND. born London, Feb. 4, 1916.
  Choral scholar, Hereford Cathedral; 1934-1938, Kent Exhibi-
  tioner, Royal College of Music; organ pupil of Walter Alcock;
  pupil of C. H. Kitson, Ernest Bullock, and Percy Buck;
  1933-1935, organist and choirmaster, St. James Church,
  Bethnal Green; 1935-1936, assistant organist, St. Martin-in-
  the-Fields, London; 1937, organist and master of music,
  Kidbrooke Parish Church; 1937, Associate of the Royal College of Music; 1938, B. Mus. , London University; 1938-
  1946, organist and director of music, St. Martin-in-the-
  Fields; 1944, Fellow of the Royal College of Organists;
  1946-1952, organist and director of music, Metropolitan

United Church, Toronto; 1946-1952, teacher of organ and
theory, examiner, Royal Conservatory, Toronto; 1952, appointed Lecturer in church music, Diocesan Theological College, McGill University; organist and master of choristers,
Christ Church Cathedral, Montreal; Mus. Doc.
> Baroque Composers of the Chapels Royal, Concordia 97-
> 4884.
> Baroque Suite, Concordia 97-4859
> Fantasy on Greensleeves, Gordon V. Thompson
> Festival Fanfare, BMI--Canada, Ltd.
> Flourish for an Occasion, Gray (St. Cecilia Series 801).

WOLSTENHOLME, WILLIAM. born Blackburn, Lancashire,
England, Feb. 24, 1865; died London, July 23, 1931. 1887,
Mus. B., Oxford University; 1902, organist, London churches;
although blind, toured United States as recitalist.
> Romanza and Allegretto in E-flat, Novello, 1900.
> Seven Short Postludes, Boosey and Hawkes.
> Seven Short Preludes, Boosey and Hawkes.

WOLTZ, JOHANN. German. Sixteenth/seventeenth century. Organist, Haylbron (Heilbronn) for forty years; compiled Nova
Musices organicae tabulatura (J. J. Genath, Basel, 1617)
which contained organ arrangements of motets, canzonets,
fugues by German and Italian masters.

WOOD, CHARLES. born Armagh, Ireland, June 15, 1866; died
Cambridge, England, July 12, 1926. Studied at the Royal
College of Music; M.A., Mus. Doc., Cambridge; 1924, ap-
pointed professor of music, Cambridge (succeeded Stanford).
> Prelude on Carey's, Stainer & Bell.
> Sixteen Preludes founded on Melodies from English and
> Scottish Psalters, 2 vols., Stainer and Bell, 1912.

WRIGHT, M. SEARLE. born Susquehanna, Penn., Apr. 4, 1918.
Pupil of William Gomph, Joseph Bonnet, and T. Tertius
Noble; studied at Columbia University, New York City;
organist-choirmaster, Chapel of the Incarnation, New York
City; 1952-1971, director of chapel music, St. Paul's Chapel,
Columbia University; faculty member, Union Theological
Seminary; 1969-1971, president, American Guild of Organists;
Fellow of the American Guild of Organists and of Trinity
College of London; 1971, became organist-choirmaster,
Christ Church, Cincinnati, Ohio. 1971, became teacher,
College-Conservatory of Music, University of Cincinnati.
> Carol Prelude on Greensleeves, Gray (St. Cecilia Series
> 798), 1954.
> Fantasy on Wareham, timpani, cymbals, optional chorus,
> trumpets, and tenor trombone, Gray.
> Introduction, Passacaglia and Fugue, Gray, 1962.
> Lyric Rhapsody, Gray.
> Prelude on Brother James' Air, Oxford, 1958.

WYTON, ALEC. born London, Aug. 3, 1921. Studied at the
Royal College of Music and at Oxford University; 1943-1946,
sub-organist, Christ Church Cathedral, Oxford; 1946-1950,
organist-choirmaster, St. Matthew's, Northampton; 1950-
1954, organist-choirmaster, Christ Church Cathedral, St.

Louis, Mo.; 1954, appointed organist and master of choris-
ters, Cathedral Church of St. John the Divine, New York City;
faculty member, Union Theological Seminary; 1964-1969,
president, American Guild of Organists.
  Christ in the Wilderness, Gray.
  Dialogue (Praise Him in The Sound of the Trumpet)
      (Ps. 150), Presser.
  Dithyramb, Gray, 1960.
  Elegy, organ and solo instrument (trumpet, clarinet, oboe,
      soprano vocalise), World Library.
  Fanfare, Gray (St. Cecilia Series 831), 1956.
  Flourish, Presser.
  In Praise of Merbecke, Gray, 1957.
  Land of Rest, in Mixture IV, Flammer.
  (A) Little Christian Year, Carl Fischer, 1964.
  Nativity Suite, Flammer.
  Paean on Hyfrydol, in Angelus, Flammer.
  Preludes, Fanfares and a March, Flammer.

XIMENES (SEE JIMÉNEZ), JOSEP.

YEPES.   Portuguese or Spanish.   Sixteenth century.
     Cancão, in Silva Iberica, p. 8.
YON, PIETRO ALESSANDRO.   born Settimo-Vittone, Italy, Aug. 8,
    1886; died Huntington, L. I., N. Y., Nov. 22, 1943.   Studied
    at the Royal Conservatory, Milan, the Conservatory, Turin,
    and the Academy of St. Cecilia, Rome; 1905-1907, organist,
    Basilica of St. Peter, Vatican City; 1907-1919, 1921-1926,
    organist, St. Francis Xavier, New York City.
  Advent, McLaughlin and Reilly M-1365.
  Christmas in Sicily, G. Schirmer 23909, 1912.
  Concerto gregoriano (E Minor), organ and piano reduction
      of orchestral part, J. Fischer.
  Christo trionfante, J. Fischer.
  Gesu Bambino, J. Fischer, 1917.
  Humoresque (L'Organo Primitivo), J. Fischer, 1946.
  Hymn of Glory, J. Fischer.
  Pastorale (Fourth Sonata), in The Modern Anthology,
      p. 205.
  Second Concert Study, G. Schirmer 25585, 1915.
  Sonata No. 1, G. Schirmer.
  Sonata No. 2 (Cromatica, in E Minor), J. Fischer, 1917.
  Sonata No. 3 (Romantic, in D Minor), J. Fischer, 1922.
  Toccata (D Major), G. Schirmer.
  Toccata on Creator alme siderum, McLaughlin and Reilly.
  Twelve Divertimenti, J. Fischer.
YOUNG, GORDON.   born McPherson, Kansas, Oct. 15, 1919.

B. Mus. , Southwestern College, Winfield, Kansas; 1944-
1946, studied at Curtis Institute of Music, Philadelphia; organ
pupil of Powell Weaver, Alexander McCurdy, and Joseph Bonnet; honorary Sac. Mus. Doc. , Southwestern College; organist, First Methodist Church, Tulsa, Okla. ; organist,
First Presbyterian Church, Lancaster, Penn. ; taught at
Texas Christian University; since 1952, organist and choirmaster, First Presbyterian Church, Detroit.

Air Gracieux, Mills, 1962.
Arabesque, in Mixture IV, Flammer.
Baroque Suite, Flammer, 1963.
Carillon, Flammer, 1959.
Chant Heroique, Galaxy, 1959.
Chorale in E, in Mixture IV, Flammer.
Chorale Prelude on St. Edith, Galaxy, 1959.
Chorale Preludes on Seven Hymn Tunes, Flammer, 1960.
(A) Christmas Prelude, Abingdon Press, 1963.
(A) Christmas Suite, Hope, 1970.
Collage, Flammer, 1969.
Eight Compositions for Organ, Abingdon, 1964.
Eight Voluntaries on Hymn Tunes, Presser, 1961.
Eleven Pieces, Flammer, 1962.
Five Toccatas, Flammer, 1965.
Fourteen Pieces, Sacred Music, 1969.
Gordon Young Organ Music, Broadman, 1970.
Gordon Young Preludes, Hope, 1968.
Gordon Young's Music for Worship, Sacred Songs, 1969.
Holiday for the Pedals, Flammer, 1961.
Hymn Preludes, Flammer, 1964.
Jubilate, Broadman.
Liturgical Suite, Sacred Songs, 1968.
Meditation on St. Anne, Shawnee, 1962.
Nine Pieces, Oxford, 1970.
Nine Pieces, Sacred Music, 1966.
Noel Joyeux, Flammer, 1965.
Noel Preludes, Flammer, 1966.
Organ Solos, Shawnee, 1964.
Perspectives, Flammer, 1970.
Prelude and Fugato on Crusaders' Hymn, Flammer, 1960.
Prelude on Aberystwyth, Seelenbrautigam, Wondrous Love,
     C. Fischer, 1960, 1963, 1963.
Prelude on a Franck Motif, Shawnee, 1962.
Prelude on a Praetorius Motif, C. Fischer, 1964.
Prelude on Shall We Gather, C. Fischer, 1963.
Seven Hymn Voluntaries, Presser, 1965.
Seven Tone Poems, J. Fischer, 1963.
Six Pieces for 11 o'clock Worship, Word.
Soliloquy, Galaxy, 1963.
Ten Christmas Organ Voluntaries, Presser, 1970.
Three Liturgical Preludes, Abingdon, 1962.
Three Service Pieces, J. Fischer, 1962.
Triptych, Oxford, 1969.
Variations on An American Hymn Tune, J. Fischer, 1961.

ZACH, JOHANN (JAN). born Celakovice, Czechoslovakia, Nov. 13,
1699; died Bruchsal, Baden, Germany, 1773. Pupil of
Czernohorsky; 1725, organist, St. Gallus; organist, St.
Martin; before 1737, organist and violinist, Prague, and
organist, Simon and Juda Church; 1745-1756, court Kapell-
meister, Mainz, Germany.
  Four Preludes and Two Fugues.
  Prelude in D and Fuga d'imitazione, Quoika, ed. , Breitkopf
    und Härtel.
  compositions in Ausgewählte Orgelwerke altböhmische
    Meister, Quoika, ed. , Vol. I, Breitkopf & Härtel,
    1948.
ZACHAU (ZACHOW), FRIEDRICH WILHELM. born Leipzig, Ger-
many, Nov. 19, 1663; died Halle, Aug. 14, 1712. Taught
Handel; 1684-1712, organist, Liebfrauenkirche, Halle.
  Choralvorspiele, Breitkopf & Härtel.
  Gesammelte Werke für Tasteninstrumente, Heinz Lohmann,
    ed. , Breitkopf & Härtel.
  In dulci jubilo, in The First Four Centuries of Organ
    Music, Vol. II, p. 403.
  Komm, heiliger Geist, in Choralvorspiel alter Meister,
    p. 168; also in 18 Chorale Preludes of the Seven-
    teenth and Eighteenth Centuries, Pierre Pidoux, ed. ,
    Foetisch.
  Präludium in C-dur, Merseburger 830A.
  Prelude and Fugue in G Major, in La Fugue au XVIIIe
    siècle, Orgue et Liturgie, Vol. 15, p. 18.
  Versets on Nun komm, in Viens, Sauveur, Orgue et
    Liturgie, Vol. 19, p. 8.
  Wir glauben, in The Parish Organist, Vol. 8, p. 46.
  chorale preludes (2) in Alte deutsche Weihnachtsmusik.
  chorale preludes (3) in Alte Weihnachtsmusik.
  chorale preludes in The Church Organist's Golden Treasury,
    Vol. I (1), Vol. II (3), Vol. III (1).
  chorale preludes (2) in Laudamus Dominum.
  chorale preludes (3) in Chorale Preludes by Seventeenth
    and Eighteenth Century Masters, Concordia.
  chorale preludes (3) in Choralvorspiele, Nagels Musik
    Archives.
  chorale preludes (8) in Eighty Chorale Preludes: German
    Masters of the Seventeenth and Eighteenth Centuries.
  chorale preludes (2) in Orgelchoräle des siebzehnten und
    achtzehnten Jahrhunderts.
  chorale preludes (5) in Orgel Choräle Sammlung, Metzler.
  chorale preludes in Orgelspiel im Kirchenjahr, Vol. 1 (5)
    and Vol. 2 (6), Schott.
  chorale preludes in Seasonal Chorale Preludes (manuals
    alone), C. H. Trevor, ed. , Book I (1) and Book II
    (2), Oxford.
  chorale preludes (2) in Seasonal Chorale Preludes (with

pedals), C. H. Trevor, ed. , Book I, Oxford.
chorale preludes (2) in <u>Twenty-five Chorale Preludes of</u>
<u>the Seventeenth and Eighteenth Centuries</u>, P. Pidoux,
ed. , Foetisch.
compositions in <u>Masterpieces of Organ Music</u>, Folio 8.
compositions in <u>The Parish Organist</u>, Vols. 1-4, 5, and 7.
fugues (3) in <u>Organum</u>, Series IV, Vol. 16 (Concordia
97-4348).

ZAGWIJN, HENRI. born Nieuwer-Amstel, The Netherlands, July 17,
1878; died The Hague, Oct. 25, 1954. 1916, appointed teacher, Rotterdam Academy of Music.
<u>Andante</u>, flute and organ, Donemus 131.
<u>Fantasia e Fuga</u> (1952), Donemus.
<u>Paraphrase on Netherlands</u>, Donemus.

ŻELECHOWSKI, PIOTR. Polish. Seventeenth century. (Might
have been related to Marcin Żelechowski, organist of the
Dominican Monastery in Czerwińsk, ca. 1660.)
<u>Fantasie sopra primo tono</u>, in <u>Keyboard Music from Polish</u>
<u>Manuscripts</u>, <u>Corpus of Early Keyboard Music</u>,
No. 10, Vol. 4, p. 70.

ZIMMER, JÁN. born Ružomberok, Slovakia, May 16, 1926.
Studied at the Conservatory, Pressburg, and at the Franz
Liszt Music Academy, Budapest; 1945-1947, staff member,
Rundfunk; 1948-1952, taught music theory and piano, Con-
servatory, Pressburg; pupil of E. Suchoň.
<u>Konzert</u>, organ, strings, and percussion, Op. 27 (1957),
Bärenreiter CHF 5133.

ZIMMERMANN, HEINZ WERNER. born Freiburg, Germany, 1930.
Received diploma from State Music Academy, Freiburg; composition pupil of Julius Weismann and Wolfgang Fortner; 1954-
1963, taught composition and music theory, Protestant School
of Church Music, Heidelberg; since 1963, director, Kirchenmusikschule, Berlin-Spandau; 1967, honorary Doc. Mus. ,
Wittenberg University, Springfield, Ohio.
<u>Orgelpsalmen</u> (4), Merseburger 822.
<u>Wie soll ich dich empfangen</u>, in <u>Neue Orgelvorspiele</u>,
Haag & Hennig, eds. , Merseburger.

ZIPOLI, DOMENICO. born Prato, Italy, Oct. 16, 1688; died
Córdoba, Argentina, Jan. 2, 1726. Pupil of Casini and
Pasquini; 1715, became organist, Jesuit Church, Rome;
1717, became Jesuit missionary to Argentina; organist,
Gesù, Córdoba, Argentina.
<u>Elevazione</u>, in <u>Alte italienische Meister</u>, p. 34.
<u>Keyboard Works</u>, Luigi Tagliavini, ed. , Bärenreiter 5191.
<u>Pastorale</u>, in <u>European Organ Music of the 16th and 17th</u>
<u>Centuries</u>, p. 90; also in <u>The First Four Centuries</u>
<u>of Organ Music</u>, Vol. II, p. 440.
<u>Pezzi scelti</u>, Ruf, ed. , Ricordi Sy 587.
<u>Sarabanda and Giga</u>, Cramer.
<u>Sonate d'intavolatura</u> (1716), 2 vols. , L. F. Tagliavini,
ed. , Müller 19 and 20.
canzonas (2) in <u>Anthologia Organistica Italiana</u>.
compositions (5) in <u>Classici Italiani dell'Organo</u>.

compositions (3) in <u>Liber Organi</u>, Vol. 4.
compositions in <u>Masterpieces of Organ Music</u>, Folio 25.
compositions (13) in <u>L'Arte Musicale in Italia</u>, Vol. III,
    p. 373.
ZIPP, FRIEDRICH OTTO GOTTFRIED. born Frankfurt, Germany,
    June 20, 1914. Studied in Berlin and at the Hoch Conserva-
    tory, Frankfurt; pupil of Armin Knab (composition); since
    1938, taught in Frankfurt.
    <u>Fantasie</u>, Op. 14, Peters 5843.
    <u>Free Organ Pieces</u> (14), 2 vols., Merseburger 851/852.
    <u>Zehn Choralbearbeitungen</u>, Merseburger 882.
    <u>Zwölf kleine Choralvorspiele</u>, Merseburger 824.
    chorale preludes (3) in <u>Orgelbuch zum Evangelischen</u>
        <u>Kirchengesangbuch</u>, O. Brodde, ed., Books 12, 18,
        and 20, Bärenreiter.
    chorale preludes (37) in <u>Orgelvorspiele</u>, Poppen, Reich &
        Strube, eds., Merseburger.
    composition in <u>The Parish Organist</u>, Vol. 12.
ZWART, JAN. born Rotterdam, The Netherlands, Aug. 20, 1877;
    died Zaandam, July 13, 1937. Pupil of Van Eyk, Van Krie-
    ken, and Hendrik de Vries; 1893, became organist in Rotter-
    dam; 1896, organist in Capelle/Ijssel; 1898-1937, organist,
    Evangelical Lutheran Church, Amsterdam; radio organ re-
    citalist; writer on Dutch music.
    <u>Drie Orgelliederen</u>, Zaandam.
    <u>Drie Oud-Hollandse Liederen</u>, Zaandam.
    <u>Enige Gezangen</u>, Zaandam.
    <u>Fantasie op Een veste Burg</u>, Seyffart; also Zaandam.
    <u>Fantasie op her Wilhelmus en Psalm 134</u>, Zaandam.
    <u>God, enkel Licht</u>, in <u>Hollandsche Koraalkunst</u>, Zaandam.
    <u>Musyck over de voysen der Psalmen Davids</u>, Zaandam
    <u>Netherlands</u>, Edition Le Grand Orgue.
    <u>Passie en Paschen</u>, Zaandam.
    <u>Psalm 33 en 51</u>, Zaandam.
    <u>Psalmbewerkingen</u>, Zaandam.
    <u>Suite Kerstfeest No. 1</u>, Zaandam.
    <u>Suite Kerstfeest No. 2</u>, Zaandam.
    <u>Twintig Korte Koraalvoorspelen</u>, Zaandam.
    <u>Vier Geestelijke Liederen</u>, Zaandam.
    <u>Vijf Orgelkoralen</u>, Zaandam.

APPENDIX: ORGAN WORKS OF BACH

Containing a table of the pagination in standard editions
(with cross-references to BWV numbers and chronologies of
Wolfgang Schmieder and Hermann Keller)

Works Cited

Bach-Gesellschaft. Johann Sebastian Bachs Werke, 47 vols.
  Leipzig: Breitkopf und Härtel, 1851-1926. Reprint, Ann
  Arbor, Mich.: J. W. Edwards, 1947.
Bower, John Dykes, and Walter Emery, Sir Frederick
  Bridge, James Higgs, Sir Ivor Atkins, et al., eds.
  The Organ Works of J. S. Bach, 19 vols. London:
  Novello and Co., n. d.
Dupré, Marcel, ed. Oeuvres Complètes pour Orgue de
  J. S. Bach, 12 vols. Paris: S. Bornemann, Editeur,
  1938-1941.
Griepenkerl, Friedrich Conrad, and Ferdinand Roitzsch, eds.
  Johann Sebastian Bachs Kompositionen für die Orgel, 9 vols.
  Frankfurt: C. F. Peters Corp., n. d. Johann Sebastian Bach
  Orgelwerke, 9 vols., Copenhagen: Wilhelm Hansen Forlag,
  n. d., is the same edition. This same edition is also pub-
  lished as Johann Sebastian Bach Complete Organ Works, 9
  vols. New York: Edwin F. Kalmus, 1947. A later edition
  of one volume is Vol. IX, Neue Ausgabe, Hermann Keller,
  ed., New York: C. F. Peters Corp., 1950. The Orgelbüchlein in Bach's original, autograph order is published by
  C. F. Peters Corp. as a separate volume.
J. S. Bach: The Complete Organ Works, from the "Bach-
  Gesellschaft" edition. New York: Lea Pocket Scores,
  n. d.
Johann-Sebastian-Bach-Institut Göttingen and vom Bach-Archiv
  Leipzig. Neue Ausgabe Sämtlicher Werke, to be published in 75 vols. Kassel, Germany: Bärenreiter Verlag, 1954 [in progress]. Organ music is found in the
  three following volumes: Die Orgelchoräle aus der
  Leipziger Originalhandschrift, Hans Klotz, ed., BA 5009,
  1958; Die Einzeln überlieferten Orgelchoräle, Hans
  Klotz, ed., BA 5017, 1961; Präludien, Toccaten, Fantasien und Fugen II, Frühfassungen und Variaten zu I
  und II, Deitrich Kilan, ed., BA 5025, 1964.

Lohmann, Heinz, ed. : Sämtliche Orgelwerke, 10 vols. ,
   Wiesbaden: Breitkopf & Härtel.
Riemenschneider, Albert, ed.   Eighteen Large Chorales for
   the Organ by Johann Sebastian Bach, Bryn Mawr, Pa. :
   Oliver Ditson Co. (Theodore Presser Co. , Distributors),
   1952.
Riemenschneider, Albert, ed.   The Liturgical Year (Orgel-
   büchlein) by Johann Sebastian Bach, Philadelphia: Oliver
   Ditson Co. (Theodore Presser Co. , Distributors), 1933.
Riemenschneider, Albert, ed.   Six Organ Chorals (Schübler)
   by Johann Sebastian Bach, Philadelphia: Oliver Ditson
   Co. (Theodore Presser Co. , Distributors), 1942.
Widor, Charles-Marie, and Albert Schweitzer, eds.   Johann
   Sebastian Bach: Complete Organ Works, vols. 1-5, New
   York: G. Schirmer, Inc. , 1912; reprint, 1940-1941.
   The remaining volumes are published as: Johann Sebas-
   tian Bach; Complete Organ Works, Vols. 6-8, Edouard
   Nies-Berger and Albert Schweitzer, eds.   New York:
   G. Schirmer, Inc. , 1954-1967.

SCHMIEDER INDEX* TABLE OF BACH ORGAN WORKS

Order of Groups Within the Index

Index Numbers	Composition Groups or Titles
525-530	Six trio sonatas
531-552	Larger preludes and fugues
553-560	Eight "Little" Preludes and Fugues
561-566	Fantasias, toccatas, and fugues
567-582	Single preludes, fantasias, fugues, Passacaglia
583-591	Trios, Aria, Canzona, Allabreve, Pastorale, Harmonic Labyrinth
592-598	Six concerti, Pedal Exercitum
599-644	Orgelbüchlein
645-650	Six Chorales (Schübler)
651-668	Great Eighteen Chorales
669-689	Clavierübung, Part III
690-713a	Kirnberger's collection of chorales
714-740	Miscellaneous chorale settings
741-765	Youthful chorales and chorales of questionable authenticity
766-771	Chorale Partitas

[Note to table following: editions are indicated at heads of columns by symbols of publishers' names--see Key following. Blank spaces in table indicate that the edition is in process. A colon separates volume number from page number--25:17 signifies vol. 25, page 17.]

Key to Publishers' Symbols

Bach G	Bach Gesellschaft
Lea	Lea
P/K/H	Peters/Kalmus/Hansen
P. Or	Peters Orgelbüchlein
Schir	G. Schirmer
Born	Bornemann
Novel	Novello
Br. H.	Breitkopf und Härtel
Bären	Bärenreiter
Dit	Ditson
Schm. C	Schmeider chronology
Kel. C	Keller chronology

Abbreviations Used

arr.	arranged	incompl.	incomplete
attrib.	attributed to	mvt	movement
ca.	circa	no.	number
chor.	chorale or chorales	Orgelbüchl.	Orgelbüchlein
Clavierüb.	Clavierübung	pt	part
coll.	collection	transcrip.	transcription
comp.	composed by	unfin.	unfinished
d. a.	doubtful authenticity	variat.	variations
dbl	double	w/	with

*Wolfgang Schmieder, Thematisch-Systematisches Verzeichnis der Musikalischen Werke von Johann Sebastian Bach, Leipzig: Breitkopf & Härtel, 1950. The title of this catalog is often abbreviated BWV (Bach-Werke-Verzeichnis) or S. (Schmieder).

BWV no.	Chorale Collection & No. w/ in Coll.	Title	Bach G	Lea
649	6 'Schübler' Chor. 5	Ach bleib bei uns	25:71	6:13
692	Kirnberger coll. 3	Ach Gott und Herr (J. G. Walther)	40:4	3:4
693	Kirnberger coll. 4	Ach Gott und Herr (J. G. Walther)	40:5	3:5
714		Ach Gott und Herr (canon)	40:43	3:43
741		Ach Gott vom Himmel sieh darein (attrib. J. C. Bach)	40:167	
742		Ach Herr, mich armen Sünder (d. a.)	40:	
743		Ach, was ist doch (d. a.)		
770	partita	Ach, was soll ich	40:189	
644	Orgelbüchl. 46	Ach wie nichtig	25:60	2:60
589		Allabreve (D Major)	38:131	7:57
643	Orgelbüchl. 45	Alle Menschen	25:59	2:59
711	Kirnberger coll. 22	Allein Gott (bicinium) (attrib. Bernhard Bach)	40:34	3:34
717		Allein Gott (12/8)	40:47	3:47
675	Clavierüb. Pt III 7	Allein Gott (F Major)	3:197	1:31
676	Clavierüb. Pt III 8	Allein Gott (6/8)	3:199	1:33
664	18 Chor. 14	Allein Gott (A Major)	25:130	6:72
663	18 Chor. 13	Allein Gott (3/2)	25:125	6:67
662	18 Chor. 12	Allein Gott (coloratura)	25:122	6:64
677	Clavierüb. Pt III 9	Allein Gott (manualiter fughetta)	3:205	1:205
716		Allein Gott (fugue)	40:45	3:45
715		Allein Gott (chor. w/interludes)	40:44	3:44
771		Allein Gott (d. a.) (variat.)	40:195	
653b		An Wasserflüssen Babylon (5-pt dbl pedal)	40:49	6:32
653	18 Chor. 3	An Wasserflüssen Babylon	25:92	6:34
587		Aria in F Major (after François Couperin)	38:22	
744		Auf meinen lieben Gott (d. a.)	40:170	
745		Aus der Tiefe rufe (attrib. to Johann Christoff Bach)	40:171	
686	Clavierüb. Pt III 18	Aus tiefer Not (6-pt dbl pedal)	3:229	1:63
687	Clavierüb. Pt III 19	Aus tiefer Not (4-pt manualiter) Canonic Variations (see Vom Himmel hoch, BWV 769)	3:232	1:66
588		Canzona in D Minor	38:126	7:52
766	partita	Christ, der du bist	40:107	2:61
670	Clavierüb. Pt III 2	Christe, aller Welt (manualiter)	3:186	1:20
673	Clavierüb. Pt III 5	Christe, aller Welt (manualiter)	3:194	1:28
619	Orgelbüchl. 21	Christe, du Lamm	25:30	2:30
627	Orgelbüchl. 29	Christ ist erstanden	25:40	2:40
746		Christ ist erstanden (comp. J. K. F. Fischer)	40:173	
718		Christ lag (Fantasia)	40:52	3:52
625	Orgelbüchl. 27	Christ lag	25:38	2:38
695	Kirnberger coll. 6	Christ lag (3/8 manualiter)	40:10	3:10
611	Orgelbüchl. 13	Christum wir sollen	25:15	2:15
696	Kirnberger coll. 7	Christum wir sollen (Fughetta)	40:13	3:13
684	Clavierüb. Pt III 16	Christ, unser Herr, zum Jordan (C Minor pedaliter)	3:224	1:58
685	Clavierüb. Pt III 17	Christ, unser Herr, zum Jordan (manualiter)	3:228	1:62
620	Orgelbüchl. 22	Christus, der uns selig macht	25:30	2:30
747		Christus, der uns selig macht	40:177	
592		Concerto in G Major (after J. Ernst)	38:149	7:73
593		Concerto in A Minor (after Vivaldi)	38:158	7:82
594		Concerto in C Major (after Vivaldi)	38:171	7:95
595		Concerto in C Major (1 mvt) (after Johann Ernst)	38:196	7:120

P&K/H	P. Or	Schir	Born	Novel	Br. H	Bären	Dit	Schm. C.	Kel. C.
6:4		8:9	10:12	16:10	8:114		70	ca1746	1746/47
		6:18	11:1	18:1	-	3:			
6:3		6:19	11:2	18:2	-	3:			
9:41		6:20	11:3	18:3	9:1	3:3		?	n. d.
K/H9:48									
9:42		6:109	12:50		9:2	3:4			
K/H9:67					-	3:			
P --					10:2			1703/07	
K/H9:68									
9:68		8:114	10:71		10:4			1700/02	n. d.
5:2	55	7:60	7:66	15:123	7:66	1:	137	1717	1717
8:72		1:18	6:60	2:26	4:86			ca1709	1708/17
5:2	54	7:59	7:65	15:121	7:65	1:	134	1717	1717
6:6		6:23	11:9	18:5	9:5	3:11			
6:8		6:27	11:12	18:11	9:11	3:8			n. d.
6:10		7:72	8:28	16:39	8:26	4:		1739	1739
6:12		7:74	8:31	16:40	8:28	4:		1739	1739
6:17		8:64	9:63	17:66	7:143	2:79,179	78	1746/50	1750
6:22		8:60	9:58	17:60	7:136	2:72,172	72	1746/50	1750
6:26		8:56	9:54	17:56	7:131	2:67,168	67	1746/50	1750
6:29		7:79	8:38	16:41	8:34	4:		1739	1739
6:30		6:21	11:6	18:7	9:9	3:			Weimar
9:45		6:1	11:4	18:4	9:8	3:14		1703/07	1703/07
		8:122	10:82		10:60	3:		ca1705	
6:32		6:29	11:15	18:13	7:171				1720
6:34		8:27	9:17	17:18	7:87	2:22,130,133	20	1746/50	1750
9:16			6:55	12:112	6:107			1723/30	1723/29
K/H9:44									
9:46		6:109	12:53		9:13				
K/H9:48									
9:47		6:110	12:54		10:14				
K/H9:63									
6:36		7:100	8:70	16:68	8:64	4:		1739	1739
6:38		7:103	8:74	16:72	8:68	4:		1739	1739
						1:			
4:58		2:71	6:64	2:34	4:81			ca1709	1708/17
5:60		8:78		19:36	10:18	1:		ca1700	n. d.
7:20		7:63	8:14	16:30	8:14	4:		1739	1739
7:27		7:70	8:24	16:37	8:23	4:		1739	1739
5:3	27	7:30	7:34	15:61	7:32	1:	65	1717	1717
5:4	36	7:40	7:45	15:83	7:44	1:	90	1717	1717
		6:110	12:57		-				
K/H6:40		6:31	11:19	18:19	9:18	3:16		bef. 1703	n. d.
5:7	34	7:38	7:43	15:79	7:42	1:	84	1717	1717
6:43		6:34	11:24	18:16	9:15	3:20		1708/17	n. d.
5:8	17	7:15	7:18	15:33	7:18	1:	36	1717	1717
5:9		6:36	11:27	18:23	9:22	3:23		1708/17	Weimar?
6:46		7:96	8:64	16:62	8:58	4:		1739	1739
6:49		7:99	8:69	16:67	8:62	4:		1739	1739
5:10	28	7:30	7:35	15:64	7:33	1:	67	1717	1717
K/H9:74					9:23			1708/17	
8:2		5:2	6:1	11:1	5:40	8:		1716/17	1708/17
8:10		5:12	6:10	11:10	5:49	8:		1716/17	1708/17
8:22		5:26	6:22	11:24	5:62	8:		1716/17	1708/17
8:44		5:52	6:43	11:49	5:84	8:		1716/17	1708/17

BWV no.	Chorale Collection & No. w/in Coll.	Title	Bach G	Lea
596		Concerto in D Minor (after Vivaldi)		
597		Concerto in E-flat Major		
621	Orgelbüchl. 23	Da Jesus an dem Kreuze	25:32	2:32
614	Orgelbüchl. 16	Das alte Jahr	25:19	2:19
702	Kirnberger coll. 13	Das Jesulein soll (d. a.)	40:20	3:20
605	Orgelbüchl. 7	Der Tag, der ist so	25:8	2:8
719		Der Tag, der ist so (d. a.)	40:55	3:55
635	Orgelbüchl. 37	Dies sind die heil'gen	25:50	2:50
678	Clavierüb. Pt III 10	Dies sind die heil'gen (pedaliter)	3:206	1:40
679	Clavierüb. Pt III 11	Dies sind die heil'gen (manualiter fughetta)	3:210	1:44
705	Kirnberger coll.	Durch Adams Fall (d. a.)	40:23	3:23
637	Orgelbüchl. 39	Durch Adams Fall	25:53	2:53
		Eight Little Preludes and Fugues(see Preludes and Fugues, Eight Little		
720		Ein' feste Burg	40:57	3:57
721		Erbarm' dich mein (d. a.)	40:60	3:60
629	Orgelbüchl. 31	Erschienen ist	25:45	2:45
628	Orgelbüchl. 30	Erstanden ist	25:44	2:44
638	Orgelbüchl. 40	Es ist das Heil	25:54	2:54
571		Fantasia in G Major (Concerto, 4/4)	38:67	8:67
572		Fantasia in G Major (12/8)	38:75	8:75
570		Fantasia in C Major	38:62	8:62
563		Fantasia in B Minor con imitazione	38:59	8:59
562		Fantasia in C Minor (fugue unfin.)	38:64	8:64
573		Fantasia in C Major (unfin.)	38:209	
561		Fantasia and Fugue in A Minor	38:48	8:48
537		Fantasia and Fugue in C Minor	15:129	5:129
542		Fantasia and Fugue in G Minor (Great)	15:177	5:177
-		Fugue in C Major	36:159	
946		Fugue in C Major		
Anh. 90		Fugue in C Major (pedal flügel)	38:213	
574		Fugue in C Minor (Legrenzi)	38:94	8:94
575		Fugue in C Minor	38:101	8:101
562		Fugue in C Minor (incompl.)		
580		Fugue in D Major	38:215	
576		Fugue in G Major (4/4)	38:106	8:106
577		Fugue in G Major (12/8) ('Gigue')	38:111)	8:111
581		Fugue in G Major	not listed	
579		Fugue in B Minor (Corelli)	38:121	8:121
578		Fugue in G Minor ('Little')	38:116	8:116
		Fugue in G Minor (Cantata 131)	38:217	
722		Gelobet seist du (chor. w/interludes)	40:62	3:62
697	Kirnberger coll. 8	Gelobet seist du (fughetta)	40:14	3:14
604	Orgelbüchl. 6	Gelobet seist du	25:7	2:7
723		Gelobet seist du	40:63	3:63
748		Gott der Vater, wohn (J. C. Bach or J. G. Walther)	40:177	
703	Kirnberger coll. 14	Gottes Sohn ist kommen	40:21	3:21
600	Orgelbüchl. 2	Gottes Sohn ist kommen	25:4	2:4
724		Gottes Sohn ist kommen	40:65	3:65
613	Orgelbüchl. 15	Helft mir Gott's Güte	25:18	2:18
698	Kirnberger coll. 9	Herr Christ, der ein'ge (fughetta)	40:15	3:15
601	Orgelbüchl. 3	Herr Christ, der ein'ge	25:5	2:5
725		Herr Gott, dich loben (5 pt)	40:66	3:66
617	Orgelbüchl. 19	Herr Gott, nun schleuss	25:26	2:26
726		Herr Jesu Christ, dich (chor. w/interludes)	40:72	3:72

P&K/H	P. Or	Schir	Born	Novel	Br. H	Bären	Dit	Schm. C.	Kel. C.
P. E. 3002						8:		1716/17	1708/17
K/H9:30					6:100				
5:11	29	7:32	7:37	15:67	7:35	1:	71	1717	1717
5:12	20	7:19	7:24	15:43	7:22	1:	45	1717	1717
9:49		6:37	11:28	18:24	9:26	3:		1703/07	Weimar?
K/H--									
5:13	11	7:8	7:9	15:18	7:8	1:	16	1717	1717
		6:38	11:30	18:26	9:28			?	Weimar?
5:14	46	7:50	7:56	15:105	7:56	1:	112	1717	1717
6:50		7:80	8:40	16:42	8:35	4:		1739	1739
6:54		7:84	8:46	16:47	8:42	4:		1739	1739
6:56		6:39	11:32	18:28	9:30	3:			?
5:15	48	7:53	7:59	15:109	7:59	1:	119	1717	1717
6:58		6:41	11:34	18:30	9:32	3:24		1709	1709
		6:44	11:38	18:35	9:36	3:28		bef. 1703	n. d.
5:17	40	7:45	7:50	15:91	7:49	1:	98	1717	1717
5:16	39	7:44	7:49	15:89	7:48	1:	96	1717	1717
5:18	49	7:54	7:60	15:111	7:60	1:	122	1717	1717
9:11		1:34	5:84	12:75	-			1705/06	1700/05
K/H9:25									
4:62		1:46	5:76	9:168	5:16			1705/06	1708/17
8:78		1:2	5:71	12:92	5:2	6:16		ca1709	1700/05
9:1		1:110	5:91	12:71	5:24	6:68		ca1710	1700/05
4:70		3:29	5:73	3:57	5:4			1712/16	1700/23?
			6:75		-	6:18		1722	1717/23?
9:19		1:86	3:18	12:60	2:76			ca. 1710	
K/H9:3									
3:55		3:20	3:1	3:76	2:68			ca. 1716	
2:20		4:40	3:8	8:127	2:56			1708/09	1717/23
8:80					-			ca1720	fugue:1720
				12:100	-				
			5:34		-				
4:40		1:10	5:41	10:230	4:51	6:19,82		1708/09	1700/05
4:54			5:37	12:95	4:58	6:26		1703/04	1700/05
			6:76		-				
K/H9:22									
9:28		1:56	5:50	12:86	4:62			?	1700/05
K/H9:12									
9:4		1:62	6:66	12:55	4:67			1705/06	1700/05
K/H9:18									
					-				
4:50		1:114	5:67	3:60	4:76	6:71		ca. 1709	1708/17
4:46		2:104	5:63	3:84	4:72	6:55		ca. 1709	1708/17
8:85			5:60	2:41	-			?	1708/17
5:102		6:3	11:40	18:37	9:39	3:30, 31		1703/07	1703/07
5:20		6:46	11:44	18:38	9:38	3:32		1708/17	Weimar?
5:19	10	7:7	7:8	15:15	7:7	1:	14	1717	1717
6:61		6:47	11:42	18:39	9:40			?	?
6:62		6:112	12:61		-				
5:22		6:49	11:45	18:41	9:43	3:34		1708/17	Weimar?
5:20	6	7:3	7:3	15:5	7:2	1:	5	1717	1717
6:64		6:50	11:46	18:42	9:42	3:33		?	?
5:23	19	7:18	7:22	15:39	7:21	1:	42	1717	1717
5:25		6:51	11:48	18:43	9:44	3:35		1708/17	Weimar?
5:24	7	7:4	7:5	15:9	7:4	1:	8	1717	1717
6:65		6:4	11:49	18:44	9:47	3:36		?	1703/07
5:26	24	7:26	7:30	15:53	7:27	1:	57	1717	1717
P 9:50		6:9	11:59	18:52	9:56	3:45		?	1703/07
K/H--									

BWV no.	Chorale Collection & No. w/in Coll.	Title	Bach G	Lea
749		Herr Jesu Christ, dich		
632	Orgelbüchl. 34	Herr Jesu Christ, dich	25:48	2:48
709	Kirnberger coll. 20	Herr Jesu Christ, dich (coloratura)	40:30	3:30
655	18 Chor. 5	Herr Jesu Christ, dich (trio in G Major)	25:98	6:40
750		Herr Jesu Christ, mein's Lebens Licht		
727		Herzlich tut mich verlangen	40:73	3:73
630	Orgelbüchl. 32	Heut triumphiret	25:46	2:46
624	Orgelbüchl. 26	Hilf Gott, dass mir's	25:36	2:36
707	Kirnberger coll. 18	Ich hab mein Sach (d. a.)	40:26	3:26
708	Kirnberger coll. 19	Ich hab mein Sach (d. a.)		
639	Orgelbüchl. 41	Ich ruf' zu dir	25:55	2:55
640	Orgelbüchl. 42	In dich hab ich	25:56	2:56
712	Kirnberger coll. 23	In dich hab ich (major melody)	40:36	3:36
615	Orgelbüchl. 17	In dir ist Freude	25:20	2:20
751		In dulci jubilo (trio in G Major, d. a.)		
729		In dulci jubilo (A Major)	40:74	3:74
608	Orgelbüchl. 10	In dulci jubilo (canon)	25:12	2:12
752		Jesu, der du meine Seele (per canonem) (d. a.)		
610	Orgelbüchl. 12	Jesu, meine Freude	25:14	2:14
753		Jesu, meine Freude (incompl.)	40:163	
713	Kirnberger coll. 24	Jesu, meine Freude (fantasia)	40:38	3:38
626	Orgelbüchl. 28	Jesus Christus, unser Heiland	25:39	2:39
688	Clavierüb. Pt III 20	Jesus Christus, unser Heiland, der von uns (cantus firmus in pedal)	3:234	1:68
689	Clavierüb. Pt III 21	Jesus Christus, unser Heiland, der von uns(manualiter fugue in F Minor)	3:239	1:73
665	18 Chor. 15	Jesus Christus, unser Heiland, der von uns (pedaliter, in E Minor)	25:136	6:78
666	18 Chor. 16	Jesus Christus, unser Heiland, der von uns (manualiter, in E Minor)	25:140	6:82
728		Jesus, meine Zuversicht	40:74	3:74
		Kleines harmonisches Labyrinth (see Little harmonic labyrinth)		
631	Orgelbüchl. 33	Komm, Gott, Schöpfer	25:47	2:47
667	18 Chor. 17	Komm, Gott, Schöpfer	25:142	6:84
651	18 Chor. 1	Komm, heiliger Geist (fantasia)	25:79	6:21
652	18 Chor. 2	Komm, heiliger Geist (G Major)	25:86	6:28
650	6 'Schübler' Chor. 6	Kommst du nun	25:74	6:16
671	Clavierüb. Pt III 3	Kyrie, Gott, heiligen Geist	3:190	1:24
674	Clavierüb. Pt III 6	Kyrie, Gott, heiliger Geist	3:196	1:30
669	Clavierüb. Pt III 1	Kyrie, Gott Vater	3:184	1:18
672	Clavierüb. Pt III 4	Kyrie, Gott Vater (manualiter)	3:194	1:28
633	Orgelbüchl. 35	Liebster Jesu, wir sind hier	25:49	2:49
634	Orgelbüchl. 36	Liebster Jesu, wir sind hier		
706	Kirnberger coll. 17	Liebster Jesu, wir	40:25	3:25
730		Liebster Jesu, wir sind(GMajor, d.a)	40:76	3:76
731		Liebster Jesu, wir sind(coloratura, d. a.)	40:77	3:77
754		Liebster Jesu (d. a.)		
591		Little harmonic labyrinth	38:225	
		Lobe den Herren(see Kommst du nun)		
704	Kirnberger coll. 15	Lob sei dem allmächtigen Gott	40:22	3:22
602	Orgelbüchl. 4	Lob sei dem allmächtigen Gott	25:13	2:13
732		Lobt Gott, ihr Christen (E Major)	40:78	3:78
609	Orgelbüchl. 11	Lobt Gott, ihr Christen	25:13	2:13
733		Magnificat, Fugue on	40:79	3:79
648	6 'Schübler' Chor. 4	Meine Seele erhebt	25:70	6:12
616	Orgelbüchl. 18	Mit Fried und Freud	25:24	2:24

P&K/H	P. Or	Schir	Born	Novel	Br. H	Bären	Dit	Schm. C.	Kel. C.
					-				1696/99
5:28	44	7:48	7:54	15:99	7:53	1:	107	1717	1717
5:28		6:52	11:60	18:50	9:54	3:43		1708/17	early
6:70		8:34	9:24	17:26	7:96	2:31,140	30	1746/50	1750
					-			1695/03	1696/99
5:30		6:54	11:62	18:53	9:57	3:46		?	Weimar
5:30	40	7:46	7:51	15:94	7:50	1:	101	1717	1717
5:32	32	7:36	7:41	15:76	7:40	1:	80	1717	1717
6:74		6:55	11:64	18:55	9:59	3:			?
		6:10	11:70	18:58	9:64				
5:33	50	7:55	7:61	15:113	7:61	1:	124	1717	1717
5:35	41	7:56	7:62	15:115	7:62	1:	127	1717	1717
6:94		6:65	11:75	18:59	9:65	3:48		1708/17	early
5:36	21	7:20	7:25	15:45	7:23	1:	48	1717	1717
P 9:50		6:59			9:69			1695/03	?
K/H9:65									
5:103		6:12	11:71	18:61	9:67	3:50,52		1703/07	1703/07
5:38	14	7:12	7:14	15:26	7:14	1:	25,27	1717	1717
					-				
5:34	16	7:14	7:17	15:31	7:17	1:	33	1717	1717
5:112		6:64	12:78		-				
6:78		6:61	11:78	18:64	9:71	3:54		1708/17	1723
5:34	35	7:39	7:44	15:81	7:43	1:	87	1717	1717
6:82		7:105	8:77	16:74	8:72	4:		1739	1739
6:92		7:110	8:82	16:80	8:78	4:		1739	1739
6:87		8:69	9:71	17:74	7:151	2:87,187	86	1746/50	1750
6:90		8:72	9:76	17:79	7:155	2:91,191		1746/50	1750
5:103		6:64	11:83	18:69	9:75	3:58		1722	?
7:86	42	7:47	7:53	15:97	7:57	1:	105	1717	1717
7:2		8:74	9:79	17:82	7:159	2:94,194	96	1746/50	1750
7:4		8:15	9:1	17:1	7:68	2:3,117	2	1746/50	1750
7:10		8:21	9:10	17:10	7:77	2:13,121	12	1746/50	1750
7:16		8:12	10:14	16:14	8:118		87	ca1746	1746/47
7:23		7:66	8:18	16:33	8:18	4:		1739	1739
7:28		7:71	8:26	16:38	8:24	4:		1739	1739
7:18		7:61	8:11	16:28	8:12	4:		1739	1739
7:28		7:69	8:23	16:36	8:22	4:		1739	1739
5:40	45	7:49	7:55	15:102	7:55	1:	110	1717	1717
		7:50		15:101	7:54		111		
5:39		6:14	12:1	18:72	9:76	3:59		1708/17	Weimar
5:105		6:67	12:2	18:70	9:77	3:60			1703/07
5:105		6:68	12:3	18:71	9:78	3:61			
K/H9:50					9:79				
P 9:34			6:58		-				
K/H9:16									
5:41		6:69	12:5	18:73	9:81	3:62		1708/17	Weimar?
5:40	8	7:5	7:6	15:11	7:5	1:	10	1717	1717
5:106		6:15	12:4	18:74	9:82	3:63,64		1703/07	1703/07
5:42	15	7:13	7:16	15:29	7:16	1:	31	1717	1717
7:29		6:70	12:6	18:75	9:83	3:65		?	Weimar
7:33		8:8	10:10	16:8	8:112		57	ca1746	1746/47
5:42	23	7:24	7:28	15:50	7:25	1:	54	1717	1717

BACH ORGAN WORKS

BWV no.	Chorale Collection & No. w/ in Coll.	Title	Bach G	Lea	
657	18 Chor. 7	Nun danket alle Gott	25:108	6:50	
755		Nun freut euch (fughetta, d. a.)			
734		Nun freut euch (Es ist gewisslich) trio, cantus firmus in pedal)	40:84	3:84	
699	Kirnberger coll. 10	Nun komm der Heiden Heiland (fughetta)	40:16	3:16	
599	Orgelbüchl. 1	Nun komm der Heiden Heiland	25:3	2:3	
659	18 Chor. 9	Nun komm der Heiden Heiland (coloratura)	25:114	6:56	
660	18 Chor. 10	Nun komm der Heiden Heiland (trio)	25:116	6:58	
661	18 Chor. 11	Nun komm der Heiden Heiland (cantus firmus in pedal)	25:118	6:60	
756		Nun ruhen alle Wälder			
767	partita	O Gott, du frommer	40:114	2:68	
757		O Herre Gott, dein (d. a.)			
		O Lamm Gottes unschuldig(manualiter)			
618	Orgelbüchl. 20	O Lamm Gottes unschuldig	25:28	2:28	
656	18 Chor. 6	O Lamm Gottes unschuldig	25:102	6:44	
622	Orgelbüchl. 24	O Mensch, bewein	25:33	2:33	
758		O Vater, allmächtiger Gott (3 verses, d. a.)	40:179		
582		Passacaglia and Fugue in C Minor	15:289	7:39	
590		Pastorale in F Major	38:135	7:61	
598		Pedal Exercise (Exercitium)	38:210	8:126	
943		Prelude in C Major (manualiter)	36:134		
567		Prelude in C Major (3/4)	38:84	8:84	
568		Prelude in G Major	38:85	8:85	
569		Prelude in A Minor (3/4)	38:89	8:89	
531		Prelude and Fugue in C Major ('Fanfare')	15:81	4:81	
545		Prelude and Fugue in C Major	15:121	5:212	
547		Prelude and Fugue in C Major (9/8)	15:228	5:228	
549		Prelude and Fugue in C Minor	38:3	8:3	
546		Prelude and Fugue in C Minor('Great')	15:218	5:218	
532		Prelude and Fugue in D Major	15:88	4:88	
539		Prelude and Fugue in D Minor ('Fiddle Fugue')	15:148	5:148	
552	Clavierüb. Pt III	Prelude and Fugue in E-flat Major	3:173	P 1:7 F 1:88	
548		Prelude and Fugue in E Minor('Wedge')	15:236	5:236	
533		Prelude and Fugue in E Minor ('Cathedral')	15:100	4:100	
534		Prelude and Fugue in F Minor	15:104	4:104	
550		Prelude and Fugue in G Major (3/2)	38:9	8:9	
541		Prelude and Fugue in G Major('Great')	15:169	5:169	
535		Prelude and Fugue in G Minor	15:112	4:112	
536		Prelude and Fugue in A Major	15:120	4:120	
543		Prelude and Fugue in A Minor('Great')	15:189	5:189	
944		Prelude and Fugue in A Minor			
551		Prelude and Fugue in A Minor	38:17	8:17	
544		Prelude and Fugue in B Minor('Great')	15:199	5:199	
553-560		Preludes and Fugues, Eight Little	38:23	8:23	
603	Orgelbüchl. 5	Puer natus	25:6	2:6	
654	18 Chor. 4	Schmücke dich	25:95	6:37	
759		Schmücke dich (attrib. J. C. Bach or G. A. Homilius)	40:181		

P&K/H	P. Or	Schir	Born	Novel	Br. H	Bären	Dit	Schm. C.	Kel. C.
7:34		8:44	9:36	17:40	7:111	2:46	45	1746/50	1750
P 9:52		6:77			-			1695/03	n. d.
K/H9:70									
7:36		6:75	12:12	18:80	9:91	3:70		1703/07	n. d.
5:45		6:79	12:15	18:83	9:94	3:73		1708/17	Weimar?
5:44	5	7:2	7:2	15:3	7:1	1:	3	1717	1717
7:38		8:48	9:43	17:46	7:118	2:55,157	54	1746/50	1750
7:40		8:50	9:46	17:49	7:122	2:59,160	58	1746/50	1750
7:42		8:52	9:49	17:52	7:126	2:62,164	62	1746/50	1750
					-			1695/03	1696/99
5:68		8:84	10:26	19:44	10:26	1:		ca1700	n. d.
P --					-				
K/H9:66									
						3:74			
5:46	26	7:28	7:32	15:58	7:30	1:	61	1717	1717
7:45		8:38	9:30	17:32	7:103	2:38,146	36	1746/50	1750
5:48	30	7:33	7:38	15:69	7:36	1:	74	1717	1717
		6:113	12:64		9:98				
1:76		4:91	2:65	10:214	6:2			1716/17	1717/23
1:88		2:96	6:68	12:102	5:28			1703/07	1708/17
P 9:40			6:78					1700/03	1700/05
K/H--									
8:76				12:94				?	
8:77		2:56	5:26	12:91	4:41			1709	
8:82		1:42	5:27	2:30	4:42	6:51		1708	1700/05
4:72		1:104	5:30	10:238	4:46	6:59		ca1709	1700/05
4:2		2:48	1:1	7:74	4:2			ca1709	1700/05
2:2		3:2	1:9	3:70	1:2	6:77(var)		P ca1730	1723/29
								F 1716/17	
2:46		3:8	1:15	9:156	1:19			ca1744	1730/40
4:36		1:4	1:36	2:48	4:10	6:101(var)		ca1703/04	1700/05
2:36		3:34	1:25	7:64	1:8			P ca1730	1730/40
								F ca1716	
4:16		2:57	1:41	6:10	2:18	6:95		ca1709	1706/08
						(Fugue var)			
3:42		2:76	1:52	9:150	2:			1724/25	1717/23
3:2		3:61	P 8:1	P 16:19	2:2			1739	1739
			F 8:85	F 16:83					
			(both 6:28)						
2:64		3:84	1:63	8:98	1:41			1727/36	1730/40
3:88		3:80	1:59	2:44	3:76	6:106(var)		ca1709	1706/08
2:29		4:20	2:1	6:24	2:38			ca1716	1708/17
4:9		1:68	2:17	7:80	3:67			ca1709	1708/17
2:7		4:30	2:9	8:112	1:			1724/25	1723/29
3:48		1:76	2:24	8:120	2:46	6:109(var)		ca1709	1708/17
2:14		4:54	2:31	3:64	1:	6:114(var)		ca1716	1708/17
2:54		4:62	2:38	7:42	1:30	6:121(var)		ca1709	1717/23
					-				
3:84		1:98	2:48	10:208	3:80	6:63		bef. 1706	1700/06
2:78		4:76	2:53	7:52	1:58			1727/36	1730/40
P 8:48-71		2:2-31	5:1-25	1:	4:16ff.			bef. 1710 attrib. Krebs	
5:50	9	7:6	7:7	15:13	7:6	1:	12	1717	1717
7:50		8:30	9:20	17:22	7:91	2:26,136	25	1746/50	1750
		6:114	12:68		-				

BWV no.	Chorale Collection & No. w/in Coll.	Title	Bach G	Lea
768	partita	Sei gegrüsset	40:122	2:76
529		Sonata in C Major	15:50	4:50
526		Sonata in C Minor	15:13	4:13
527		Sonata in D Minor	15:26	4:26
525		Sonata in E-flat Major	15:3	4:3
528		Sonata in E Minor	15:40	4:40
530		Sonata in G Major	15:66	4:66
566		Toccata in E Major (also in C Major)	15:276	7:26
565		Toccata and Fugue in D Minor	15:267	7:17
564		Toccata, Adagio and Fugue	15:253	7:3
540		Toccata and Fugue in F Major	15:154	5:154
538		Toccata and Fugue in D Minor ('Dorian')	15:136	5:136
586		Trio in G Major (Telemann) transcription		
584		Trio in G Minor	33:110	
585		Trio in C Minor	38:219	
583		Trio in D Minor	38:143	7:69
1027a		Trio in G Major (transcrip.)		
735		Valet will ich (B-flat Major)(fantasia)	40:86	3:86
736		Valet will ich (D Major) (cantus firmus in pedal)	40:90	3:90
762		Vater unser (d. a. , coloratura)		
760		Vater unser (attrib. J. C. Bach)	40:183	
636	Orgelbüchl. 38	Vater unser	25:52	2:52
761		Vater unser (attrib. J. C. Bach or Georg Böhm)	40:184	
737		Vater unser (4/2)	40:96	3:96
682	Clavierüb. Pt III 14	Vater unser (E Minor) (5 pt)	3:217	1:51
683	Clavierüb. Pt III 15	Vater unser (manualiter)	3:223	1:57
738		Vom Himmel hoch (D Major) (12/8)	40:97	3:97
701	Kirnberger coll. 12	Vom Himmel hoch (fughetta)	40:19	3:19
606	Orgelbüchl. 8	Vom Himmel hoch	25:9	2:9
700	Kirnberger coll. 11	Vom Himmel hoch (cantus firmus in pedal)	40:17	3:17
769		Vom Himmel hoch (Canonic variat.)	40:137	2:91
607	Orgelbüchl. 9	Vom Himmel kam	25:10	2:10
658	18 Chor. 8	Von Gott will ich	25:112	6:54
668	18 Chor. 18	Vor deinen Thron	25:145	6:87
645	6 'Schübler' Chor. 1	Wachet auf	25:63	6:5
696		Was fürchst du (see Christum, wir sollen)		
641	Orgelbüchl. 43	Wenn wir in höchsten Nöthen sein Wenn wir (see Vor deinen Thron)	25:57	2:57
642	Orgelbüchl. 44	Wer nur den lieben Gott	25:58	2:58
690	Kirnberger coll. 1	Wer nur den lieben Gott (3/4, manualiter)	40:3	3:3
691	Kirnberger coll. 2	Wer nur den lieben Gott (coloratura)	40:4	3:4
647	6 'Schübler' Chor. 3	Wer nur den lieben Gott (C Minor)	25:68	6:10
764		Wie schön leuchtet (fragment)		
739		Wie schön leuchtet (d. a.)	40:99	3:99
763		Wie schön leuchtet (d. a.)		
710	Kirnberger coll. 21	Wir Christenleut (trio, attrib. J. L. Krebs)	40:32	3:32
612	Orgelbüchl. 14	Wir Christenleut	25:16	2:16

P&K/H	P. Or	Schir	Born	Novel	Br. H	Bären	Dit	Schm. C.	Kel. C.
5:76		8:92	10:37	19:55	10:38	1:		ca1700 and 1707/17	n. d.
1:46		5:111	4:44	5:134	6:48			after 1727	1723/28
1:11		5:70	4:10	4:97	6:11			after 1727	1723/28
1:24		5:84	4:22	4:110	6:24			after 1727	1723/28
1:2		5:58	4:1	4:88	6:2			after 1727	1723/28
1:36		5:98	4:34	5:124	6:38			after 1727/	1723/28
1:63		5:130	4:61	5:151	6:65			after 1727	1723/28
3:94 (3:62)		1:22	3:63	8:88	3:20	6:40		ca1707	1706/08
4:27		2:84	3:43	6:2	3:58	6:31		ca1709	1706/08
3:72		2:32	3:29	9:137	3:45	6:3		ca1709	1708/17
3:16		4:2	3:73	9:176	3:2			ca1716	1717/23
3:30		3:47	3:51	10:196	3:32			P 1727/36 F 1716/17?	1717/23
P -- K/H9:42					6:90			1723/30	1723/29
					-			1723/25	
P 9:36 K/H9:38			6:48	12:108	6:84				
4:76		5:143	6:52	2:54	6:78			1717/23	1723/28
P 9:8 K/H9:35					6:94			1723/30	1723/29
7:53		6:80	12:16	19:2	9:102	3:77,81		1703/07	1703/07
7:56		6:84	12:20	19:7	9:106	3:84		?	n. d.
P -- K/H9:72		6:90			9:112				
		6:116	12:70		-				
5:52	47	7:53	7:58	15:107	7:58	1:	116	1717	1717
P 9:54 K/H--		6:117	12:72		-				
7:66		6:88	12:26	19:12	9:111	3:90		?	n. d.
7:60		7:90	8:55	16:53	8:49	4:		1739	1739
5:51		7:95	8:62	16:61	8:56	4:		1739	1739
5:106		6:17	12:28	19:19	9:118	3:94		1703/07	1703/07
7:67		6:92	12:32	19:14	9:116	3:96		1708/17	Leipzig?
5:52	12	7:10	1:11	15:21	7:10	1:	19	1717	1717
7:68		6:94	12:30	19:16	9:114	3:92		1708/17	early
5:92		8:106	10:58	19:73	8:142	2:98,197		1746/47	1746
5:54	12	7:10	7:12	15:23	7:12	1:	22	1717	1717
7:70		8:46	9:40	17:43	7:114	2:51,154	50	1746/50	1750
7:74		8:76	9:82	17:85	7:163	2:113,212	100	1746/50	1750
7:72		8:2	10:2	16:1	8:100 9:22		11	ca1746	1746/47
5:55	52	7:57	7:63	15:117	7:63	1:	128	1717	1717
5:57	53	7:58	7:64	15:119	7:64	1:	131	1717	1717
5:56		6:18 6:96	12:34	19:21	9:120	3:98		1708/17	?
5:56		6:97	12:35	19:22	9:122	3:98		1725	?
7:76		8:6 6:102	10:8 12:79	16:6	8:108 -		41	ca1746	1746/47
P 9:56 K/H--		6:98	12:36	19:23	9:123			1703/07	1703/07
P -- K/H9:49					-				
P 9:60 K/H--		6:103	12:42	19:28	9:128	3:100			
5:58	18	7:16	7:20	15:36	7:20	1:	39	1717	1717

BWV no.	Chorale Collection & No. w/in Coll.	Title	Bach G	Lea
623	Orgelbüchl. 25	Wir danken dir	25:35	2:35
		Wir danken dir (Sinfonia arr. Dupré from Cantata 29)		
765		Wir glauben all (4/2, d. a.)	40:187	
680	Clavierüb. Pt III 12	Wir glauben all (fugue)	3:212	1:46
681	Clavierüb. Pt III 13	Wir glauben all (manualiter)	3:216	1:50
740		Wir glauben all	40:103	
		Wir müssen durch (Sinfonia arr. Dupré from Cantata 146)		
646	6 'Schübler' Chor. 2	Wo soll ich fliehen	25:66	6:8
694	Kirnberger coll. 5	Wo soll ich fliehen (G Minor) (cantus firmus in pedal)	40:6	3:6

P&K/H	P. Or	Schir	Born	Novel	Br. H	Bären	Dit	Schm. C.	Kel. C.
5:59	32	7:35	7:40	15:73	7:39	1:	78	1717	1717
			12:81						
P 9:62		6:120	12:75		9:131				
K/H9:51									
7:78		7:86	8:49	2:38,16:49	8:44	4:		1739	1739
7:82		7:89	8:54	16:52	8:48	4:		1739	1739
7:82		6:121	12:44	19:30	9:133			?	n. d.
					-				
7:84		8:4	10:5	16:4	8:104		27	ca1746	1746/47
P 9:64		6:105	12:46	19:32	9:135	3:103		1708/17	early
K/H9:57									

BIBLIOGRAPHY

Adlung, Jakob. Musica mechanica organoedi. Berlin: F. W.
  Burnstiel, 1768. Facsimile ed. , Christhard Mahrenholz,
  ed. Kassel, Germany: Bärenreiter-Verlag, 1931.
Alain, Marie-Claire. "The Organ Works of Jehan Alain,"
  English translation by Irene Feddern, Diapason, part 1
  (Jan. 1970), p. 20-21; part 2 (Feb. 1970), p. 22-25;
  part 3 (Mar. 1970), p. 6-8.
Aldrich, Putnam. "On the Interpretation of Bach's Trills,"
  Musical Quarterly, vol. XLIX (1963), p. 289-310.
_____. Ornamentation in J. S. Bach's Organ Works.
  New York: Coleman-Ross, 1950.
Altman, Ludwig, ed. Beethoven Organ Works. London:
  Hinrichsen Edition Ltd. , 1962.
Amacker, Marianne. "The Chorale Preludes of Leo Sowerby,"
  Diapason (Aug. 1970), p. 20-21.
Andersen, Poul-Gerhard. Organ Building and Design. Eng-
  lish translation by Joanne Curnutt. New York: Oxford
  University Press, 1969.
Antegnati, Constanzo. L'Arte organica. Brescia, 1608.
  Reprint, Mainz, Germany: Rheingold-Verlag, 1941.
Apel, Willi. "Du nouveau sur la musique française pour
  orgue au XVIe siècle," Revue musicale, vol. XVIII
  (1937), p. 96-108.
_____. "The Early Development of the Organ Ricercare,"
  Musica Disciplina, vol. III (1949), p. 139-150.
_____. "Early German Keyboard Music," Musical Quar-
  terly, vol. XXIII (1937), p. 210-237.
_____. "The Early History of the Organ," Speculum,
  vol. XXIII (1948), p. 191-216.
_____. "Early Spanish Music for Lute and Keyboard
  Instruments," Musical Quarterly, vol. XX (1934),
  p. 289-301.
_____. Geschichte der Orgel- und Klaviermusik bis 1700.
  Kassel, Germany: Bärenreiter-Verlag, 1967.
_____. Harvard Dictionary of Music. Cambridge, Mass. :
  Harvard University Press, 1944. 2nd ed. , 1969.
_____. Masters of the Keyboard. Cambridge, Mass. :
  Harvard University Press, 1947.

_____. "Neapolitan Links between Cabezón and Fresco-
baldi," Musical Quarterly, vol. XXIV (1938), p. 419-
437.

_____. "Spanish Organ Music of the Early 17th Century,"
Journal of the American Musicological Society, vol. XV
(1962), p. 174-181.

_____, Friedrich Wilhelm Riedel, and Thomas M. Laquer.
"Orgelmusik," Die Musik in Geschichte und Gegenwart,
Friedrich Blume, ed. Kassel, Germany: Bärenreiter-
Verlag, 1949-1968, vol. X, p. 331-385.

Armstrong, Thomas. "The Wesleys, Evangelists and Musicians," Organ and Choral Aspects and Prospects. London: Hinrichsen Edition Ltd. , 1958, p. 99.

Armstrong, William H. Organs for America: The Life and
Work of David Tannenberg. Philadelphia: University
Pennsylvania Press, 1967.

Arnold, Frank T. The Art of Accompaniment from a
Thorough-Bass. London: Novello and Co. , 1931.

Arnold, J. H. Plainsong Accompaniment. London: Oxford
University Press, 1927.

The ASCAP Biographical Dictionary of Composers, Authors
and Publishers. Compiled and edited by the Lynn Far-
nol Group, Inc. New York: American Society of Composers, Authors and Publishers, 1966.

Audsley, George Ashdown. The Art of Organ Building, 2
vols. New York: Dodd, Mead and Co. , 1905. Reprint,
New York: Dover Pub. Inc. , 1965.

_____. The Organ of the Twentieth Century. New York:
Dodd, Mead and Co. , 1919.

_____. Organ Stops and Their Artistic Registration.
New York: H. W. Gray Co. , Inc. , 1921.

Bach, C. P. E. Essay on the True Art of Playing Keyboard
Instruments. English translation by W. J. Mitchell.
New York: W. W. Norton and Co. , Inc. , 1949.

Bacon, Allan. "The Chorale Preludes of Max Reger,"
Diapason (Feb. 1962), p. 30-31.

Baker's Biographical Dictionary of Musicians, 5th ed. , re-
vised by Nicolas Slonimsky. New York: G. Schirmer,
1958; Supplement, Nicolas Slonimsky, ed. , 1965.

Bakken, Howard. "Liszt and the Organ," Diapason (May
1969), p. 27-29.

Banchieri, Adriana. Conclusioni nel suono dell'organo.
Bologna, 1608. Facsimile, Minal: Bollettino Biblio-
grafico Musicale, 1934.

Barker, John Wesley. "Reger's Organ Music," Musical

Times, no. 1496, vol. 108 (Oct. 1967), p. 939: no.
1498, vol. 108 (Dec. 1967), p. 1142: no. 1500, vol.
109 (Feb. 1968), p. 170.

Barnes, William Harrison. The Contemporary American
Organ: Its Evolution, Design and Construction. 8th ed.
Glen Rock, N. J. : J. Fischer and Bro. , 1964.

Bedbrook, Gerald Stares. "The Buxheim Keyboard Manuscript," Music Review, vol. XIV (1953), p. 288-294.

_____. Keyboard Music from the Middle Ages to the
Beginnings of the Baroque. London: Macmillan Co. ,
1949.

Bédos de Celles, (Dom) F. L'Art du facteur d'orgues. 3
vols. , 1766-1778. Facsimile reprint, Kassel, Germany:
Bärenreiter-Verlag, 1934-1936.

Beechey, Gwilym. "Parry and His Organ Music," Musical
Times, no. 1508, vol. 109 (Oct. 1967), p. 939; no.
1498, vol. 108 (Dec. 1967), p. 1142: no. 1500, vol.
109 (Feb. 1968), p. 1057.

Benedictines of Solesmes, eds. Liber Usualis. Tournai,
Belgium: Desclée et Cie. , 1950.

Biba, Otto. "The Unknown Organ Music of Austria," Diapason (Jan. 1971), p. 10.

Bichsel, M. Alfred. "The Attaingnant Organ Books," The
Musical Heritage of the Lutheran Church. St. Louis:
Concordia Pub. House, 1959, vol. V, p. 156.

Bitterman, Helen Robbins. "The Organ in the Early Middle
Ages," Speculum, vol. IV (1929), p. 290-410.

Blanton, Joseph. "The Oldest Playable Organ," Diapason
(Apr. 1956), p. 8.

_____. The Organ in Church Design. Albany, Texas:
Venture Press, 1956.

Bodky, Erwin. The Interpretation of Bach's Keyboard Works.
Cambridge, Mass. : Harvard University Press, 1960.

Bolitho, Albert George. "The Organ Sonatas of Paul Hindemith," unpublished dissertation, Michigan State University, 1968.

Bornefeld, Helmut. Orgelbau und neue Orgelkunst. Kassel,
Germany: Bärenreiter-Verlag, 1952.

Boumann, M. A. Orgels in Nederland. Amsterdam:
DeLange, 1949.

Bouvet, Charles. Une dynastie de musiciens français: Les
Couperin, organistes de l'église Saint-Gervais. Paris:
Bossuet, 1919.

Bowles, Edmund A. "A Performance History of the Organ
in the Middle Ages," Diapason (Jan. 1970), p. 13-14.

Bradshaw, Murray C. "Pre-Bach Organ Toccatas: Form,
Style, and Registration," Diapason (Mar. 1972),

p. 26-28.

Brinkmann, Reinhold. "Einige Bermerkungen zu Schönbergs Orgelvariationen," Musik und Kirche, vol. 29, no. 2 (Mar.-Apr. 1969), p. 67.

Brunold, Paul. François Couperin. English translation by J. B. Hanson. Monaco: L'Oiseau Lyre, 1949.

Bukofzer, Manfred F. Music in the Baroque Era. New York: W. W. Norton and Co., Inc., 1947.

Bull, Storm. Index to Biographies of Contemporary Composers. New York: Scarecrow Press, 1964.

Buszin, Walter E. "Buxtehude: On the Tercentenary of His Birth," Musical Quarterly, vol. XXIII (1937), p. 465-490.

_____. "Johann Pachelbel's Contribution to Pre-Bach Organ Literature," The Musical Heritage of the Lutheran Church. St. Louis: Concordia Pub. House, 1959, vol. V, p. 140.

_____. "The Life and Work of Samuel Scheidt," The Musical Heritage of the Lutheran Church. St. Louis: Concordia Pub. House, 1959, vol. V, p. 43.

The Canadian Who's Who, Vol. XI, 1967-1969. Toronto: Who's Who Canadian Publications, 1969.

Carapetyan, Armen. "The Codex Faenza, Biblioteca Communale, 117," Musica Disciplina, vol. XIII (1959), vol. XIV (1960), and vol. XV (1961).

Carlson, Richard A. "Walther's Life; Walther's Works," Organ Institute Quarterly, vol. V, no. 4 (Autumn 1955), p. 29-39.

Cavaillé-Coll, Cécile, and Emmanuel Cavaillé-Coll. Aristide Cavaillé-Coll: Ses origines, sa vie, ses oeuvres. Paris: Librairie Fischbacher, 1929.

Citron, Pierre. Couperin. Bourges: Editions du Seuil, 1956.

Clough, F. F., and G. F. Cuming. "Bach's Organ Works in BWV Numbering," Eighth Music Book. London: Hinrichsen Edition Ltd., 1956, p. 193-206.

Clutton, Cecil, and Austin Niland. The British Organ. London: B. T. Batsford Ltd., 1963.

Cohalan, Aileen. "Messiaen: Reflections on Livre d'Orgue," Music/The A. G. O. and R. C. C. O. Magazine, vol. II (July 1968), p. 26; (Nov. 1968), p. 28; (Dec. 1968), p. 28.

Commer, Franz, ed. Kompositionen für Orgel aus dem 16., 17., und 18. Jahrhunderts, 6 vols. Leipzig: F. E. C. Leuckart, n. d.

Couperin, François. L'Art de toucher le clavecin. English

translation by Mervanwy Roberts. Wiesbaden, Germany: Breitkopf & Härtel, 1933.

Cowell, Henry, and Sidney Cowell. Charles Ives and His Music. New York: Oxford University Press, 1955.

Dannreuther, Edward. Musical Ornamentation. London, 1893-1895. Reprint, New York: Edwin F. Kalmus, n. d.

Dart, Thurston. "Cavazzoni and Cabezón," Music and Letters, vol. XXXVI (1955), p. 2-6.

_____. The Interpretation of Music. London: Hutchison University Library, 1954.

_____. "A New Source of English Organ Music," Music and Letters, vol. XXXV (1954), p. 201-205.

David, Hans T. , and Arthur Mendel. The Bach Reader. New York: W. W. Norton and Co. , 1945.

Davies, Laurence. César Franck and His Circle. Boston: Houghton Mifflin Co. , 1970.

Davison, Archibald T. Protestant Church Music in America. Boston: E. C. Schirmer, 1933.

_____, and Willi Apel. Historical Anthology of Music, 2 vols. Cambridge, Mass. : Harvard Universtiy Press, 1946 and 1950.

Dawes, Frank. "Philip Hart," Musical Times, no. 1469, vol. 106 (July 1965), p. 510.

_____. "The Music of Philip Hart (c. 1676-1749)," Proceedings of the Royal Musical Association, vol. 94 (1967-1968).

Delestre, R. L'Oeuvre de Marcel Dupré. Paris: Procure Générale du Clergé, 1952.

Demuth, Norman. César Franck. New York: Philosophical Library, 1949.

de Wall, Marilou. "Interpretation of French Organ Music of the 17th and 18th Centuries," Diapason (Apr. 1964), p. 42.

_____. "The Tonal Organization of the Seventeenth Century French Organ," American Guild of Organists Quarterly, vol. VIII, no. 1 (Jan. 1963), p. 12; vol. VIII, no. 2 (Apr. 1963), p. 43; vol. VIII, no. 3 (July 1963), p. 89.

Dickinson, A. E. The Art of J. S. Bach. London: Hinrichsen Edition Ltd. , 1950.

_____. Bach's Fugal Works. London: Isaac Pitman and Sons, 1956.

Dictionnaire de la Musique. Marc Honegger, ed. 2 vols. Paris: Bordas, 1970.

Dietrich, Fritz. Geschichte des deutschen Orgelchorals im siebzehnten Jahrhundert, 2 vols. Kassel, Germany: Bärenreiter-Verlag, 1932.

Dolmetsch, Arnold. The Interpretation of the Music of the 17th and 18th Centuries. London: Novello and Co., Ltd., 1915.

Donington, Robert. The Interpretation of Early Music. London: Faber and Faber, 1963.

_____. "Ornamentation," Grove's Dictionary of Music and Musicians, 5th ed., Eric Blom, ed. New York: St. Martin's Press, 1954, vol. VI, p. 365-384.

_____. Tempo and Rhythm in Bach's Organ Music. London: Hinrichsen Edition Ltd., 1961.

Dorsey, Charlene Polivka. "The Fantasie and Ricercari of Girolamo Frescobaldi," American Guild of Organists Quarterly, vol. XII, no. 3 (July 1967), p. 101.

Douglas, C. Winfred. Church Music in History and Practice. New York: Chas. Scribner's Sons, 1937.

Douglass, Fenner. The Language of the Classical French Organ: A Musical Tradition Before 1800. New Haven, Conn.: Yale University Press, 1969.

Doyen, Henri. Mes leçons d'orgue avec Louis Vierne: Souvenirs et Témoignages. Paris: Editions Musique Sacrée, 1966.

Dreisoerner, Charles. "The Themes of Langlais' Incantation," Music/The A.G.O.-R.C.C.O. Magazine, vol. 6, no. 4 (Apr. 1972), p. 41-44.

Dufourcq, Norbert. César Franck. Paris: Editions du Vieux Colombier, 1949.

_____. Esquisse d'une histoire d'orgue en France du XIIIe à la fin du XVIIIe siècle. Paris: Droz et Larousse, 1935.

_____. Le grand orgue et les organistes de Saint-Merry de Paris. Paris: Librairie Floury, 1947.

_____. Les grandes formes de la musique d'orgue. Paris: E. Droz, 1937.

_____. La musique d'orgue française au XXe siècle. Paris: Librairie Floury, 1939.

_____. La musique d'orgue française de Jehan Titelouze à Jehan Alain. Paris: Librairie Floury, 1949.

_____. Nicolas LeBègue (1631-1702). Paris: Librairie Floury, 1954.

_____. "Panorama de la musique d'orgue française au XXe siècle," Revue Musicale, vol. XIX, no. 184 (June 1938), p. 369-376; vol. XIX, no. 185 (July 1938), p. 35-44; vol. XIX, no. 186 (Sept. 1938), p. 120-125; vol. XX, no. 189 (Mar. 1939), p. 103-115.

Dupré, Marcel, ed. G. F. Haendel: Seize Concertos, vol. 1.
    Paris: S. Bornemann, 1937.
_____. Trois Oeuvres pour Orgue de Franz Liszt. Paris:
    S. Bornemann, 1941.

Edson, Jean Slater. Organ-Preludes: An Index to Composi-
    tions on Hymn Tunes, Chorales, Plainsong Melodies,
    Gregorian Tunes and Carols, 2 vols. Metuchen, N. J. :
    Scarecrow Press, 1970.
Eitner, Robert. Quellen-Lexicon. 11 vols. Graz, Austria:
    Akademische Druck-U. Verlagsanstalt, 1959.
Ellinwood, Leonard. The History of American Church Music.
    New York: Morehouse-Gorham, 1953.
Emery, Walter. Bach's Ornaments. London: Novello and
    Co. , Ltd. , 1953.
_____, ed. J. G. Oley: Four Chorale Preludes. London:
    Novello and Co. , Ltd. , 1958.
Encyclopédie de la Musique, Albert Lavignac, ed. Paris:
    C. Delagrave, 1926.
Encyclopédie de la Musique, François Michel, ed. 3 vols.
    Paris: Fasquelle Editeurs, 1958-1961.

Fellerer, Karl Gustav. Beitrage zur Choralbegleitung und
    Choralverarbeitung in der Orgelmusik des ausgehenden
    18. und beginnenden 19. Jahrhunderts. Strassburg:
    Heitz and Co. , 1931.
_____. Orgel und Orgelmusik: Ihre Geschichte. Augsburg:
    Benno Filser, 1929.
Fesperman, John. The Organ as Musical Medium. New
    York: Coleman-Ross, 1962.
_____. "Rhythmic Alterations in 18th Century French
    Organ Music," Organ Institute Quarterly, vol. IX,
    no. 1 (Spring 1961), p. 4-10; vol. IX, no. 2 (Summer
    1961), p. 13-22.
Flade, Ernest. "The Organ Builder, Gottfried Silbermann,"
    Organ Institute Quarterly, vol. III, nos. 3 and 4 (1953);
    vol. IV, nos. 1, 2, 3, 4 (1954).
Flentrop, D. A. "The Schnitger Organ in the Grote Kerk at
    Zwolle," English translation by John Fesperman, Organ
    Institute Quarterly (Summer 1957).
Fosse, Richard C. "Nicolaus Bruhns," The Musical Heritage
    of the Lutheran Church. St. Louis: Concordia Pub.
    House, 1959, vol. V, p. 92.
Frotscher, Gotthold. Geschichte des Orgelspiels und der
    Orgelkomposition, 2 vols. Berlin: Merseberger Verlag,
    1959.

Gallo, William K.   "Dudley Buch--the Organist," <u>Diapason</u>
(Nov. 1971), p. 22-24.
Gastoué, Amédée.   "A Great French Organist, A. Boëly and
His Works," <u>Musical Quarterly</u>, vol. XXX, no. 3 (July
1944), p. 336-344.
_____, and Norbert Dufourcq, eds.   <u>A. P. F. Boëly:</u>
<u>Oeuvres complètes pour orgue</u>, 2 vols.   Paris: Editions
musicales de la Schola Cantorum, 1958.
Gavoty, Bernard.   <u>Louis Vierne, la vie et l'oeuvre</u>.   Paris:
Albin Michel, 1943.
Gay, Harry W.   "Notes upon Jean Titelouze (1563-1633),"
<u>American Organist</u>, vol. 42, no. 9 (Sept. 1959), p. 299-
307.
_____.   "Saint Quentin, Its Collegiate Church and Pierre
du Mage," <u>Diapason</u> (May 1958), p. 8.
_____.   "Study of Brahms' Works Expanded by Vivid De-
tail," <u>Diapason</u> (Mar. 1959), p. 38.
_____.   "To Know Nicolas de Grigny, Perform His Many
Pieces," <u>Diapason</u> (Sept. 1957), p. 18.
Geer, E. Harold.   <u>Organ Registration in Theory and Practice</u>.
Glen Rock, N. J.: J. Fischer and Bro., 1957.
Geiringer, Karl.   <u>Johann Sebastian Bach--the Culmination of</u>
<u>an Era</u>.   New York: Oxford University Press, 1966.
Gibbs, Alan.   "Carl Nielsen's 'Commotio,'" <u>Musical Times</u>,
no. 1441, vol. 104 (Mar. 1963), p. 208.
Gibson, David.   "Franz Liszt's Christmas Tree," <u>Diapason</u>
(Dec. 1970), p. 28.
Gibson, Emily Cooper.   "A Study of the Major Organ Works
of Paul Hindemith," <u>Diapason</u> (Feb. 1971), p. 22-24.
Gillespie, John.   <u>Five Centuries of Keyboard Music</u>.   Bel-
mont, Calif.: Wadsworth Pub. Co., 1965.
Gleason, Harold.   <u>Method of Organ Playing</u>, 5th ed.   New
York: Appleton-Century-Crofts, 1962.
Glyn, Margaret Henrietta.   <u>Early English Organ Music</u>.
London: Plainsong and Medieval Music Society, 1939.
Goléa, Antoine.   <u>Rencontres avec Olivier Messiaen</u>.   Paris:
René Julliard, 1960.
Goode, Jack C.   <u>Pipe Organ Registration</u>.   New York:
Abingdon Press, 1964.
Goodrich, Wallace.   <u>The Organ in France</u>.   Boston: Boston
Music Co., 1917.
Gotwals, Vernon.   "Brahms and the Organ," <u>Music/The</u>
<u>A. G. O. -R. C. C. O. Magazine</u>, vol. 4, no. 4 (Apr. 1970),
p. 38-55.
Grace, Harvey.   <u>French Organ Music, Past and Present</u>.

New York: H. W. Gray Co., 1919.

_____. The Organ Works of Bach. London: Novello and
Co., Inc., 1922.

_____. The Organ Works of César Franck. London:
Novello and Co., Ltd., 1948.

_____. The Organ Works of Rheinberger. London:
Novello and Co., Ltd., 1925.

Grame, Theodore C. "Neglected Organ Music," American
Guild of Organists Quarterly, vol VIII, no. 1 (Jan.
1963), p. 3: vol. VIII, no. 2 (Apr. 1963), p. 53.

Grout, Donald Jay. A History of Western Music. New
York: W. W. Norton and Co., Inc., 1960.

Grove's Dictionary of Music and Musicians, 5th ed., 9 vols.,
Eric Blom, ed. New York: St. Martin's Press, 1954.

Guilmant, Alexandre. "La musique d'orgue," Encyclopédie
de la musique, Albert Lavignac, ed. Part II, vol. II,
p. 1125-1180. Paris: Librairie Delagrave, 1926.

Hardouin, Pierre. "François Roberday (1624-1680)," Revue
de Musicologie, vol. XLV (1960), p. 44-62.

_____. Le Grand-Orgue de St. Gervais de Paris. Paris:
Imprimerie du Campagnonnage, 1949; also L'Orgue,
(1949), p. 91.

Harmon, Thomas. "The Performance of Mozart's Church
Sonatas," Music & Letters, vol. 51, no. 1 (Jan. 1970),
p. 51.

Harrison, G. Donald. "Organ," Harvard Dictionary of
Music, Cambridge, Mass.: Harvard University Press,
1944. p. 523-532.

Harverson, Alan. "Britten's Prelude and Fugue," Musical
Times, no. 1417, vol. 102 (Mar. 1961), p. 175.

Hassman, Carroll. "Messiaen: An Introduction to his Compositional Techniques and an Analysis of 'La Nativité,"
Diapason, (Dec. 1971), p. 22-23; (Jan. 1972), p. 26-
27.

Hathaway, J. W. G. Analysis of Mendelssohn's Organ Works:
A Study of the Structural Features. London: Reeves,
1898.

Heiller, Anton. "Chorales of the Clavierübung, Part 3,"
Diapason (Oct. 1962), p. 8.

Hesford, Bryan. "Dupré's 'Stations of the Cross'," Musical
Times, no. 1425, vol. 102 (Nov. 1961), p. 723-724.

_____. "The Organ Music of Hans-Friedrich Micheelsen,"
Musical Opinion, no. 1138, vol. 95 (July 1972), p. 537-
539.

Heyer, Anna Harriet, compiler. Historical Sets, Collected

Editions and Monuments of Music: A Guide to Their
Contents. Chicago: American Library Association, 1957;
2nd ed. , 1969.

Hinrichsen, Max, ed. Eighth Music Book. London: Hinrichsen Edition Ltd. , 1956.

Howard, John Tasker. Our American Music. New York:
Thomas Y. Crowell, 1946.

Howell, Almonte C. "Cabezón: An Essay in Structural
Analysis," Musical Quarterly, vol. L (1964), p. 18-30.

_____. "French Baroque Organ Music and the Eight
Church Tones," Journal of the American Musicological
Society, vol. XI (1952), p. 106-108.

_____. "The French Organ Mass in the Sixteenth and
Seventeenth Centuries," unpublished dissertation, University of North Carolina, 1953.

Hutchings, Arthur. "The English Concerto with or for Organ," Musical Quarterly, vol. XLVII (Apr. 1961),
p. 195-206.

d'Indy, Vincent. César Franck. English translation by Rosa
Newman. New York: Dover Pub. , Inc. , 1965.

The International Cyclopedia of Music and Musicians, 9th ed. ,
Robert Sabin, ed. New York: Dodd, Mead and Co. , 1964.

Irwin, Stevens. Dictionary of Pipe Organ Stops. New York:
G. Schirmer, Inc. , 1962.

Jeppesen, Knud. Die italienische Orgelmusik am Anfang des
Cinquecento, 2 vols. Copenhagen: Munksgaard, 1943;
2nd ed. , 1960.

Kasling, Kim R. "Some Editorial, Formal and Symbolic
Aspects of J. S. Bach's Canonic Variations on 'Vom
Himmel hoch da komm ich her'," Diapason (May 1971),
p. 18; (June 1971), p. 16-17; (July 1971), p. 20-21;
(Aug. 1971), p. 20-21.

Kasouf, Richard J. "Louis Vierne and His Six Organ
Symphonies," American Organist (Nov. 1970), p. 20-26.

Keller, Hermann. Die Orgelwerke Bachs: Ein Beitrag zu
ihrer Geschichte, Form, Deutung und Wiedergabe.
Leipzig: C. F. Peters, 1948; English translation by
Helen Hewitt, New York: C. F. Peters Corp. , 1967.

Kendall, Raymond. "Notes on Arnold Schlick," Acta Musicologia, vol. XI (1939), p. 136-143.

Kinkeldey, Otto. Orgel und Klavier in der Musik des 16.

Jahrhunderts. Leipzig: Breitkopf & Härtel, 1910.

Kinsky, Georg. "Kurze Oktaven auf besaitenen tasteninstrumente," Zeitschrift für Musikwissenschaft, vol. II (1919-1920), p. 65-82.

Kirby, Frank E. A Short History of Keyboard Music. New York: Free Press, 1966.

Kirkpatrick, Ralph, ed. Johann Sebastian Bach: Goldberg Variations. New York: G. Schirmer, Inc., 1938.

Klinda, Ferdinand. "Die Orgelwerke von Olivier Messiaen," Musik und Kirche, vol. 39 (Jan.-Feb. 1969), p. 10.

Klotz, Hans. "Bachs Orgeln und seine Orgelmusik," Die Musikforschung, vol. II (1950), p. 189-203.

_____. Das Buch von der Orgel: Ueber Wesen und Aufbau des Orgelwerkes, Orgelpflege und Orgelspiel, 6th ed. Kassel, Germany: Bärenreiter-Verlag, 1960. English translation by Gerhard Krapf, The Organ Handbook. St. Louis: Concordia Pub. House, 1969.

_____. "Gedanken zur Orgelmusik Max Regers," Mitteilungen des Max-Reger-Instituts, vol. VII (1958).

_____. Ueber die Orgelkunst der Gotik, der Renaissance und des Barocks: Die alten Registrierungs- und Dispositions-Grundlagen. Kassel, Germany: Bärenreiter-Verlag, 1931-1934.

Koch, Caspar. The Organ Student's Gradus ad Parnassum. New York: J. Fischer and Bro., 1945.

Kratzenstein, Marilou. "A Survey of Organ Literature and Editions," Diapason, Spain and Portugal (Oct. 1971), p. 22-24; Italy (Feb. 1972), p. 22-24; South Germany (Mar. 1972), p. 18-21; North and Middle Germany (July 1972), p. 4-5, and (Aug. 1972), p. 4-6.

Lade, John. "The Organ Music of Flor Peeters," Musical Times, no. 1505, vol. 109 (July 1968), p. 667.

Lang, Paul Henry. Music in Western Civilization. New York: W. W. Norton and Co., Inc., 1941.

Larousse de la Musique, Norbert Dufourcq, Félix Raugel, and Armand Machebey, eds. Paris: Librairie Larousse, 1957.

Lawry, Eleanor. "Symbolism as Shown in Chorale Preludes of Bach Is Studied," Diapason (Aug. 1949), p. 6.

Löffler, Hans. "Die Schüler Joh. Seb. Bachs," Bach-Jahrbuch in Auftrage der neuen Bachgesellschaft, Alfred Dürr and Werner Neumann, eds. Berlin: Evangelische Verlaganstalt, 1953, vol. XL, p. 5.

Long, Page C. "Vierne and His Six Organ Symphonies," Diapason (June 1970), p. 23; (July 1970), p. 7;

(Aug. 1970), p. 8.

Lord, Robert Sutherland. "Organ Music of Jean Langlais: Comments on Performance Style," American Organist (Jan. 1968), p. 27-32.

_____. "Sources of Past Serve Langlais in Organ Works," Diapason (Jan. 1959), p. 24; (Feb. 1959), p. 24.

Lowinsky, Edward E. "English Organ Music of the Renaissance," Musical Quarterly, vol. XXXIX (1953), p. 373-395, 528-553.

Lukas, Viktor. Orgelmusikführer. Stuttgart: Philipp Reclam Jun., 1963.

Lunelli, Renato. L'arte organaria del rinascimento in Roma e gli organi di S. Pietro in Vaticano dalle origini a tutto il periodo Frescobaldiana, Historiae musicae cultores biblioteca, vol. X. Florence, Italy: 1958.

_____. Der Orgelbau in Italien in seinen Meisterwerken vom 14. Jahrhundert bis zur Gegenwart. Mainz, Germany: Rheingold, 1956.

McLean, Hugh. Henry Purcell: The Organ Works. London: Novello and Co., Inc., 1957.

Mahrenholz, Christhard. Die Orgelregister: Ihre Geschichte und ihr Bau. Kassel, Germany: Bärenreiter-Verlag, 1931-1934.

Mansfield, Orlando A. "Mozart's Organ Sonatas," Musical Quarterly, vol. VII (1922), p. 566-594.

_____. "Some Characteristics of Mendelssohn's Organ Sonatas," Musical Quarterly, vol. III (1917), p. 562-576.

Marrocco, W. Thomas, and Robert Huestis. "Some Speculations Concerning the Instrumental Music of the Faenza Codex 117," Diapason (May 1972), p. 3.

Mellers, Wilfrid. François Couperin and the French Classical Tradition. London: Denis Dobson, 1950; Reprint, New York: Dover Publications, Inc., 1968.

_____. "John Bull and English Keyboard Music," Musical Quarterly, vol. XL (1954), p. 364-383, 548-571.

Messiaen, Olivier. Technique de mon langage musical. Paris: Leduc, 1944; English translation by John Satterfield, The Technique of My Musical Language. Paris: Leduc, 1956.

Miller, Hugh W. "John Bull's Organ Works," Music & Letters, vol. XXVIII (1947), p. 25-35.

_____. "Sixteenth Century English Faburden Compositions for Keyboard," Musical Quarterly, vol. XXVI (1940), p. 50.

Milner, Arthur. "The Organ Sonata of Herbert Howells," Musical Times, no. 1462, vol. 105 (Dec. 1964), p. 924.

Moeser, James. "French Baroque Registration," American Organist (June 1967), p. 17.

_____. "Symbolism in J. S. Bach's Orgelbüchlein," American Organist, vol. 47, no. 11 (Nov. 1964), p. 14-20; vol. 47, no. 12 (Dec. 1964), p. 14-22; vol. 48, no. 1 (Jan. 1965), p. 12-16; vol. 48, no. 2 (Feb. 1965), p. 22-25; vol. 48, no. 3 (Mar. 1965), p. 16-22; vol. 48, no. 4 (Apr. 1965), p. 14-21; vol. 48, no. 5 (May 1965), p. 11-14; vol. 48, no. 6 (June 1965), p. 12-17; vol. 48, no. 7 (July 1965), p. 11-13.

Mulbury, David. "Bach's Favorite Pupil: Johann Ludwig Krebs," Music/The A. G. O. Magazine, vol. II, no. 2 (Feb. 1968), p. 24.

Die Musik in Geschichte und Gegenwart, 14 vols., Friedrich Blume, ed. Kassel, Germany: Bärenreiter-Verlag, 1949-1968.

Musikkens Hvem Hvad Hvor. Ludvig Ernst Bramsen, Jr., ed., 2 vols. Copenhagen: Politikens Forlad, 1961.

Noehren, Robert. "The Relation of Organ Design to Organ Playing," Diapason (Dec. 1962), p. 8; (Jan. 1963), p. 8.

_____. "Schnitger, Cliquot, and Cavaillé-Coll," Diapason (Nov. 1966), p. 40-41; (Dec. 1966), p. 28; (Jan. 1967), p. 48-49; (Feb. 1967), p. 44-45.

Nolte, Ewald. "The Magnificat Fugues of Johann Pachelbel: Alternation or Intonation," Journal of the American Musicological Society, vol. IX (1956), p. 19-24.

Oldman, C. B. "Thomas Attwood, 1765-1838," Musical Times, no. 1473, vol. 106 (Nov. 1965), p. 844.

Osborne, William. "Five New England Gentlemen," Music/The A. G. O.-R. C. C. O. Magazine, vol. III, no. 8 (Aug. 1969), p. 27-29.

Owen, Barbara. "American Organ Music and Playing, from 1700," Organ Institute Quarterly, vol. 10, no. 3 (Autumn 1963), p. 12.

_____. "Organ: History," Harvard Dictionary of Music, 2nd. ed. Cambridge, Mass.: Harvard University Press, 1969, p. 615-619.

Paukert, Karel, ed. A Century of Czech Music, 2 vols.
    Chicago: H. T. FitzSimons Co. , Inc. , 1964.
Pauly, H. J. Die Fuge in den Orgelwerken Dietrich Buxte-
    hudes. Regensburg, Germany: G. Bosse, 1964.
Peeters, Flor. "The Belgian Organ School," Sixth Music
    Book. London: Hinrichsen Edition Ltd. , 1950, p. 270-
    274.
Perrot, Jean. L'orgue de ses origines hellénistiques à la
    fin du XIIIe siècle. Paris: Edition A. et J. Picard et
    Cie. , 1965. English translation by Norma Deane,
    The Organ from Its Invention to the End of the Thir-
    teenth Century. New York: Oxford University Press,
    1971.
Pfatteicher, Carl. John Redford, Organist and Almoner of
    St. Paul's Cathedral in the Time of Henry VIII: With
    Especial Reference to His Organ Composition. Leip-
    zig: C. G. Röder, 1934.
Phelps, Lawrence I. "A Short History of the Organ Revival,"
    reprint from Church Music 67.1. St. Louis: Concordia
    Pub. Hous, 1967.
Phillips, Gordon, ed. Handel: Six Fugues or Voluntaries.
    London: Hinrichsen Edition Ltd. , 1960.
_____. "Purcell's Organs and Organ Music," Organ and
    Choral Aspects and Prospects. London: Hinrichsen
    Edition Ltd. , 1958, p. 133-135.
_____. Samuel Wesley and Dr. Mendelssohn, in Tallis
    to Wesley series, no. 14. London: Hinrichsen Edition
    Ltd. , 1962.
_____. The Wesleys, in Tallis to Wesley series, no. 5.
    London: Hinrichsen Edition Ltd. , 1960.
Pidoux, Pierre, ed. Girolamo Frescobaldi Orgel- und
    Klavier Werke. Kassel, Germany: Bärenreiter-Verlag,
    1959, vol. V.
Pirro, André. "L'Art des Organistes," Encyclopédie de
    la Musique, Albert Lavignac, ed. Part II, vol. II,
    p. 1181-1374.
_____. L'orgue de J. S. Bach. Paris: Librairie Fisch-
    bacher, 1897.
Powell, Kenneth G. "An Analysis of the North German Organ
    Toccatas," Diapason (Apr. 1971), p. 27-29.
Praetorius, Michael. Phantasy on the Chorale A Mighty
    Fortress Is Our God, Heinrich Fleischer, ed. St.
    Louis: Concordia Pub. House, 1954.
_____. De Organographia (Part II of Syntagma Musicum).
    Wolfenbüttel, 1619. Facsimile, Kassel, Germany:
    Bärenreiter-Verlag, 1929.
Pruitt, William. "Charles Tournemire and the Style of

Franck's Major Organ Works," Diapason (Oct. 1970), p. 17.

_____. "Charles Tournemire 1870-1949," American Organist (Aug. 1970), p. 20-25.

Raugel, Félix. "The Ancient French Organ School," Musical Quarterly, vol. XI (1925), p. 560-571.

_____. Les grandes orgues des églises de Paris. Paris: Librairie Fischbacher, 1927.

_____. Les organistes. Paris: H. Laurens, 1923.

Redlich, Hans Ferdinand. "Girolamo Frescobaldi," Music Review, vol. XIV (1953), p. 262-274.

_____. "Samuel Wesley and the Bach Revival in England," Seventh Year Book. London: Hinrichsen Edition Ltd., 1952.

Reese, Gustave. Music in the Renaissance. New York: W. W. Norton and Co., Inc., 1959.

Reinburg, Peggy Kelley. "Affektenlehre of the Baroque Era and Their Application in the Works of Johann Sebastian Bach (specifically in the Schübler Chorales)," American Organist (June 1968), p. 15.

Richards, Ruthann. "The Orgelbüchlein--Its History and Cantus Firmus Treatment," Diapason (Oct. 1969), p. 24-25.

Riedel, Johannes. The Lutheran Chorale: Its Basic Traditions. Minneapolis: Augsburg Pub. House, 1967.

Riemann Musik Lexikon, 3 vols., Wilibald Gurlitt, ed. Mainz, Germany: B. Schott's Söhne, 1959.

Ritter, August Gottfried. Zur Geschichte des Orgelspiels, 2 vols. Leipzig: Max Hesse, 1884.

Rockholt, Preston. "...Since 1940--," Music/The A. G. O. Magazine, vol. II, no. 1 (Jan. 1968), p. 26.

Rokseth, Yvonne. La musique d'orgue au XVe siècle et au debut du XVIe, Paris: E. Droz, 1930.

Routh, Francis. "Handel's Organ Works," Handel's Four Voluntaries for Organ or Harpsichord, in Tallis to Wesley series, no. 19. London: Hinrichsen Edition Ltd., 1961.

Rudd, Michael. "Stylistic Features and Compositional Activities in Organ Literature Since World War II," Diapason (June 1968), p. 12; (July 1968), p. 13; (Aug. 1968), p. 14.

Russell, Carlton T. "Manual Music: A Critical Survey," American Organist, vol. LI (Dec. 1968), p. 16; vol. LII (Jan. 1969), p. 16.

Samuel, Claude. Entretiens avec Olivier Messiaen. Paris:
    Editions Pierre Belfond, 1967.
Sceats, Godfrey. The Organ Works of Karg-Elert. London:
    Orphington, 1940; revised ed. , London: Hinrichsen
    Edition Ltd. , 1950.
Schering, Arnold. "Zur Alternatim-Orgelmesse," Zeitschrift
    für Musikwissenschaft, vol. XVII (1935), p. 19-32.
Schlick, Arnolt. Tabulaturen etlicher Lobgesang und Lidlein
    uff die Orgeln und Lauten. 1512, reprint, Klecken,
    Germany: Gottlieb Harms, 1924.
_____. Spiegel der Orgelmacher und Organisten. Mainz,
    1511; facsimile, Kassel, Germany: Bärenreiter-Verlag,
    1959.
Schmieder, Wolfgang. Thematisch-systematisches Verzeichnis
    der musikalischen Werke von Johann Sebastian Bach.
    Leipzig: Breitkopf & Härtel, 1950.
Schnoor, Hans. "Das Buxheimer Orgelbuch," Zeitschrift für
    Musikwissenschaft, vol. IV (1921-1922), p. 1-10.
Scholes, Percy A. , ed. The Oxford Companion to Music,
    9th ed. London: Oxford University Press, 1956.
Schrade, Leo. "Ein Beitrag zur Geschichte der Tokkate,"
    Zeitschrift für Musikwissenschaft, vol. VIII (1925-1926),
    p. 610-635.
_____. "The Organ in the Mass of the 15th Century,"
    Musical Quarterly, vol. XXVIII (1942), p. 329-336,
    467-487.
Schuneman, Robert A. "The Organ Chorales of Georg Böhm,"
    Diapason (Mar. 1970), p. 12-14.
Schweitzer, Albert. J. S. Bach, le musicien-poète. Leip-
    zig, 1905. English translation by Ernest Newman,
    J. S. Bach, 2 vols. London: Breitkopf & Härtel, 1911;
    reprint, London: Adam and Charles Black, 1947.
Shannon, John R. , ed. Free Organ Compositions from the
    Lüneburg Tablatures, 2 vols. St. Louis: Concordia
    Pub. House, 1958.
_____. "North-German Organ Music," Music/The A. G. O. -
    R. C. C. O. Magazine, vol. 3, no. 9 (Sept. 1969), p. 22.
_____. "A Short Summary of the Free Organ Forms in
    Italy, 1450-1650," American Guild of Organists Quar-
    terly, vol. VI, no. 3 (July 1961), p. 75.
Sharp, G. B. "Antonio de Cabezón," Musical Times, no.
    1485, vol. 107 (Nov. 1966), p. 955; no. 1486, vol.
    107 (Dec. 1966), p. 1053.
_____. "Franz Tunder: 1614-1667," Musical Times,
    no. 1497, vol. 108 (Nov. 1967), p. 997.
_____. "J. J. Froberger: 1614-1667, a Link Between the
    Renaissance and the Baroque," Musical Times, no. 1498,

vol. 108 (Dec. 1967), p. 1093.

_____. "Nicolaus Bruhns," Musical Times, no. 1482,
vol. 107 (Aug. 1966), p. 677.

_____. "Nicolas de Grigny, 1672-1703," Musical Times,
no. 1553, vol. 113 (July 1972), p. 705-707.

Siebert, Frederick Mark. "Mass Sections in the Buxheim
Organ Book: A Few Points," Musical Quarterly, vol. L
(1964), p. 353-366.

_____. "Performance Problems in Fifteenth-Century
Organ Music," Organ Institute Quarterly, vol. X,
no. 2 (1963), p. 5.

Smith, Rollin. "Camille Saint-Saëns," Music/The A. G. O. -
R. C. C. O. Magazine, vol. 5, no. 12 (Dec. 1971),
p. 24-26.

Speer, Klaus. "The Organ Verso in Iberian Music up to
1700," Journal of the American Musicological Society,
vol. XI (1958), p. 189-199.

Spelman, Leslie P. "20th Century Netherland Organ Music,"
Music/The A. G. O. -R. C. C. O. Magazine, vol. 4, no. 9
(Sept. 1970), p. 35.

Spiess, Lincoln B. "Michael Praetorius Creuzburgensis:
Church Musician and Scholar," The Musical Heritage
of the Lutheran Church. St. Louis: Concordia Pub.
House, 1959, vol. V, p. 68-71.

Spitta, Philipp. Johann Sebastian Bach, 2 vols. Leipzig,
1873-1880. English translation by Clara Bell and John
Alexander Fuller-Maitland, Johann Sebastian Bach: His
Work and Influence on the Music of Germany, 3 vols.
London: Novello and Co., 1899; reprint, New York:
Dover Publications, Inc., 2 vols., 1951.

Stevens, Denis. The Mulliner Book: A Commentary. London:
Stainer and Bell, 1952.

_____. "Organ Mass," Grove's Dictionary of Music and
Musicians, Eric Blom, ed. New York: St. Martin's
Press, vol. VI, p. 339-344.

_____. "Organists and Organ Music of Tudor Times,"
American Guild of Organists Quarterly, vol. V, no. 2
(Apr. 1960), p. 43-47.

_____. "Pre-Reformation Organ Music in England,"
Proceedings of the Royal Musical Association, vol.
LXXVII (1952), p. 1-10.

_____. "Thomas Preston's Organ Mass," Music & Letters,
vol. XXXIX (1958), p. 29-34.

_____, ed. Thomas Roseingrave: Compositions for Organ
and Harpsichord. University Park, Penn.: Pennsylvania
State University Press, 1964.

_____. Thomas Tomkins. New York: St. Martin's Press,
1957.

_____. Thomas Tomkins: Three hitherto unpublished
Voluntaries (Francies, Verses), in Tallis to Wesley
series, no. 17. London: Hinrichsen Edition Ltd. , 1959.
_____. Tudor Church Music. New York: Merlin Press,
1955.
_____. "A Unique Tudor Organ Mass," Musica Disciplina,
vol. VI (1952), p. 167-175.
Stevenson, Robert Murrell. Juan Bermudo. The Hague:
Nijhoff, 1960.
Stevlingson, Norma. "Performance Styles of French Organ
Music in the 17th and 18th Centuries," Music/The
A. G. O. - R. C. C. O. Magazine, vol. III, no. 2 (Feb.
1969), p. 26.
Sumner, William Leslie. "Arp Schnitger," Organ Institute
Quarterly, vol. V, nos. 2, 3, 4 (1955).
_____. Bach's Organ-Registration. London: Hinrichsen
Edition Ltd. , 1961.
_____. "Beethoven and the Organ," Musical Opinion,
no. 1110, vol. 93 (Mar. 1970), p. 323-325.
_____. "The French Organ School," Sixth Music Book.
London: Hinrichsen Edition Ltd. , 1950, p. 281-294.
_____. The Organ: Its Evolution, Principles of Construc-
tion, and Use. London: Macdonald and Co. , 1952;
3rd. ed. , 1962.
_____. "Organ Music Until the Time of Bach," Eighth
Music Book. London: Hinrichsen Edition Ltd. , 1956,
p. 18-30.
_____. The Organs of Bach. London: Hinrichsen Edition
Ltd. , 1954.
Sutherland, Gordon. "The Ricercari of Jacques Buus,"
Musical Quarterly, vol. XXXI (1945), p. 448-463.

Tagliavini, Luigi Ferdinando. "The Old Italian Organ and Its
Music," Diapason (Feb. 1966), p. 14-16.
Tangeman, Robert. "Mozart's Seventeen Epistle Sonatas,"
Musical Quarterly, vol. XXXII (Oct. 1946), p. 588-601.
Taylor, Stainton de B. The Chorale Preludes of J. S. Bach.
London: Oxford University Press, 1942.
Terry, Charles Sanford. Bach: A Biography. London: Ox-
ford University Press, 1928.
_____. Bach's Chorals, 3 vols. Cambridge, England:
The University Press, 1915-1921.
_____. The Music of Bach: An Introduction. London:
Oxford University Press, 1933: reprint, New York:
Dover Publications, Inc. , 1963.
Tessier, André. Couperin. Paris: Librairie Renouard, 1926.

_____. "Les messes d'orgue de Fr. Couperin," Revue Musicale, vol. VI, no. 1.

Thomerson, Kathleen. "Errors in the Published Organ Compositions of Jean Langlais," American Guild of Organists Quarterly, vol. X, no. 2 (Apr. 1965), p. 47-54.

Tournemire, Charles Arnould. César Franck. Paris: C. Delagrave, 1931.

Trevor, C. H. "The Organ Music of Max Reger and Its Performance," Organ and Choral Aspects and Prospects. London: Hinrichsen Edition Ltd., 1958, p. 78.

Tusler, Robert L. The Organ Music of Jan Pieterszoon Sweelinck, 2 vols. No. 1 of Utrechtse Bijdragen tot de Muziekwetenschap. Bilthoven, the Netherlands: Creyghton, 1958.

_____. "Style Differences in the Organ and Clavicembalo Works of Jan Pieterszoon Sweelinck," Tydschrift voor Musikwetenshap, vol. XVII (1959), p. 149-166.

_____. The Style of Bach's Chorale-Preludes, New York: Da Capo Press, 1968.

Vennum, Thomas, Jr. "The Registration of Frescobaldi's Organ Music," Organ Institute Quarterly, vol. II, no. 2 (Summer 1964).

Vente, Maarten A. Die Brabanter Orgel. Amsterdam: H. J. Paris, 1958.

Walker, John. "Schoenberg's Opus 40," Music/The A. G. O. - R. C. C. O. Magazine, vol. IV, no. 10 (Oct. 1970), p. 33.

Walsh, Stephen. "Schumann and the Organ," Musical Times, no. 1529, vol. 111 (July 1970), p. 741-743.

Waters, Charles F. The Growth of Organ Music. London: Musical Opinion, 1931; 2nd. ed., 1957.

Weigl, Bruno. Handbuch der Orgelliteratur. Leipzig: F. E. C. Leuckart, 1931.

Wer ist wer? Walter Habel, ed. Berlin: Arani, 1970.

West, John Ebenezer. "Old English Organ Music," Proceedings of the Musical Association, vol. XXXVII (1911), p. 1-16.

Westerby, Herbert. The Complete Organ Recitalist. London: Musical Opinion, 1927.

White, John R. "The Tablature of Johannes de Lublin," Musica Disciplina, vol. XVI (1963), p. 137-162.

Who's Who in Music and Musicians' International Directory, 5th ed., W. J. Potterton, ed. London: Burke's

Peerage Ltd. , 1969.

Wickline, Homer. "Flor Peeters' Organ Works Are Intended
to Serve Noble Art," Diapason (Sept. 1947), p. 22.

Williams, Charles Francis Abdy. The Story of Organ Music.
London: Walter Scott Pub. Co. , Ltd. , 1905.

Williams, Peter F. The European Organ 1450-1850. London: B. T. Batsford, 1966.

_____. "J. S. Bach and English Organ Music," Music &
Letters, vol. XLIV (1963), p. 140-151.

_____, ed. Three Voluntaries of the Later 18th Century,
in Tallis to Wesley series, no. 22. London: Hinrichsen
Edition Ltd. , 1961.

_____, ed. The Wesleys, Set Two. London: Hinrichsen
Edition Ltd. , 1961.

Wyly, James. "The Pre-Romantic Spanish Organ: Its Structure, Literature, and Use in Performance," unpublished
dissertation, University of Missouri, 1964.

Young, Clyde William. "Keyboard Music to 1600," Musica
Disciplina, vol. XVI (1962), p. 115-150; vol. XVII
(1963), p. 163-193.

_____. "The Keyboard Tablatures of Bernhard Schmid,
Father and Son," unpublished dissertation, University
of Illinois, 1957.

Young, Percy. "A Survey of Contemporary Organ Music:
England," Church Music 67. 2, p. 25.

INDEX

Foss, 267, 276, 385
France, William, 231
Franck, 173, 188, 190, 191-
    194, 385-386
Frank, P. , 386
Franke, 202, 386
Freixanet, 153, 155, 386
Frescobaldi, 23, 24, 28, 30,
    31, 32, 36, 73, 75, 79,
    100, 120, 121, 386-388
Fricker, Herbert, 388
Fricker, Peter R. , 227,
    230, 388
Friedell, 266, 271, 388
Frigyes, 210
Froberger, 75, 79, 80, 83,
    93, 120, 388-389
Froidebise, 238, 389
frottole, 25
Frottole intabulate... , 25
Fryklöf, 246, 389
Fuenllana, 389
fuga see fugue
fugue, 47, 73, 80, 85, 93,
    140, 153, 156, 165, 174,
    176, 177, 178, 186, 207,
    208, 210, 218, 247, 271
Fumet, 390
fundamentum, 17
Fundamentum organisandi, 8,
    11, 12, 17
Fux, 390

Gabrieli, A. , 22, 24, 26,
    27, 29, 30, 80, 290-291
Gabrieli, G. , 22, 24, 30,
    391
Gade, 242, 243, 244, 391
Gagnebin, 249, 250, 391
gaitilla, 153
Gal, 392
galliard, 16, 153
Gardner, 392
Gaul, 260, 265, 392-393
Gautier, 393

Gay, M. , 393
Gebhard, 203, 393
Gehring, 268, 393
Gehrke, 393
Geiser, Walther, 247, 250,
    393
Genzmer, 203, 393-394
Geoffroy, 122, 394
George, Graham, 232, 394
Gerber, 165, 394
Gerlach, 205, 394
Germani, 252, 274, 394
Ghein, 394-395
Ghent altar piece, 2, 5
Gibbons, C. , 395
Gibbons, O. , 42, 45, 142,
    395
Gibbs, 228, 395
Gigault, 122, 123, 127,
    395-396
Gigout, 188, 190, 195, 396-
    397
gigue, 76, 157
Gilbert, 226, 229, 397
Gilchrist, 259
Gilles, 397
Ginastera, 397
Girod, 217, 397
Giroud, 397
Giustiniani, 158
Glazounow, 397-398
Gleason, 259
Gloria tibi trinitas, 41
glosas see intabulations
Goedicke, 398
Görlitzer Tabulatur-Buch,
    70
Goller, 398
Gonet, 15
Goode, 267, 274, 398
Goodman, 398
Gore, 398
Gorlier, S. , 14
Grabner, 202, 398-399
Grace, 399
Grandjany, 399
Graun, 399